MEMOIRS BY HARRY S. TRUMAN

MEMOIRS BY

Harry S. Truman

YEARS OF TRIAL AND HOPE

SMITHMARK

This edition published in 1996 by SMITHMARK Publishers,
a division of U.S. Media Holdings, Inc., 16 East 32nd Street,
New York, NY 10016.

SMITHMARK books are available for bulk purchase for sales
promotion and premium use. For details write or call the
manager of special sales, SMITHMARK Publishers, Inc.,
16 East 32nd Street, New York, NY 10016; (212) 532-6600.

This edition published by arrangement with Doubleday,
a division of Bantam Doubleday Dell Publishing Group, Inc.
and W.S. Konecky Associates, Inc.

ISBN: 0-8317-7319-7

Printed in the United States of America

10 9 8 7 6 5 4 3 2 1

TO THE PEOPLE OF ALL NATIONS

ACKNOWLEDGMENTS

In the writing of my memoirs and the story of a very trying period of history, I have received invaluable aid and suggestions from many people. A vast amount of research of my personal papers and documents was necessary in my efforts to achieve a true and accurate picture.

I owe a great debt of gratitude to Mrs. Truman, on whose counsel and judgment I frequently called.

I wish to express my special thanks to many members of my administration who took time to go over with me various phases of the past in which they had a part: Dean Acheson, General of the Army George C. Marshall, Samuel I. Rosenman, John W. Snyder, Rear Admiral Sidney Souers, Rear Admiral Robert L. Dennison, W. Averell Harriman, General of the Army Omar Bradley, Charles F. Brannan, Charles Sawyer, Philip B. Perlman, Thomas E. Murray, Stanley Woodward, John Steelman, Charles Murphy, Major General Robert B. Landry; as well as Oscar Chapman, Gordon Dean, J. Howard McGrath, Clark Clifford, Edwin W. Pauley, and Judge Caskie Collet.

To Dean Acheson and Samuel I. Rosenman, who painstakingly read and criticized my manuscript, I wish to convey my special gratitude.

During the past two years David M. Noyes and William Hillman were constantly at my side, helping me to assemble and edit this work. With their collaboration this book has been made possible. To Dave and to Bill I can only say a thousand times, thank you.

To Professor Francis E. Heller of Kansas University I wish to express my sincere appreciation for the invaluable service he rendered. Among those who also helped with historical research during some periods was Professor Morton Royse.

A very heavy burden fell on my personal staff during the writing and rewriting of these memoirs, and I wish to acknowledge with thanks the devoted work of Mr. Eugene Bailey, Miss Rose Conway, and Miss Frances Myers.

I have used some passages from *Mr. President* by William Hillman (Farrar, Straus & Young) for inclusion in my memoirs as part of the historical record.

H. S. T.

PREFACE

I have often thought in reading the history of our country how much is lost to us because so few of our Presidents have told their own stories. It would have been helpful for us to know more of what was in their minds and what impelled them to do what they did.

The presidency of the United States carries with it a responsibility so personal as to be without parallel.

Very few are ever authorized to speak for the President. No one can make decisions for him. No one can know all the processes and stages of his thinking in making important decisions. Even those closest to him, even members of his immediate family, never know all the reasons why he does certain things and why he comes to certain conclusions. To be President of the United States is to be lonely, very lonely at times of great decisions.

Unfortunately some of our Presidents were prevented from telling all the facts of their administrations because they died in office. Some were physically spent on leaving the White House and could not have undertaken to write even if they had wanted to. Some were embittered by the experience and did not care about living it again in telling about it.

As for myself, I should like to record, before it is too late, as much of the story of my occupancy of the White House as I am able to tell. The events, as I saw them and as I put them down here, I hope may prove helpful in informing some people and in setting others straight on the facts.

No one who has lived through more than seven and a half years as

President of the United States in the midst of one world crisis after another can possibly remember every detail of all that happened. For the last two and a half years I have checked my memory against my personal papers, memoranda, and letters and with some of the persons who were present when certain decisions were made, seeking to recapture and record accurately the significant events of my administration.

I have tried to refrain from hindsight and afterthoughts. Any schoolboy's afterthought is worth more than the forethought of the greatest statesman. What I have written here is based upon the circumstances and the facts and my thinking at the time I made the decisions, and not what they might have been as a result of later developments.

That part of the manuscript which could not be physically included in the two volumes of the memoirs, I shall turn over to the Library in Independence, Missouri, where it will be made available to scholars and students of history.

For reasons of national security and out of consideration for some people still alive, I have omitted certain material. Some of this material cannot be made available for many years, perhaps for many generations.

In spite of the turmoil and pressure of critical events during the years I was President, the one purpose that dominated me in everything I thought and did was to prevent a third world war. One of the events that has cast a shadow over our lives and the lives of peoples everywhere has been termed, inaccurately, the "cold war."

What we have been living through is, in fact, a period of nationalistic, social, and economic tensions. These tensions were in part brought about by shattered nations trying to recover from the war and by peoples in many places awakening to their right to freedom. More than half of the world's population was subject for centuries to foreign domination and economic slavery. The repercussions of the American and French revolutions are just now being felt all around the world.

This was a natural development of events, and the United States did all it could to help and encourage nations and peoples to recovery and to independence.

Unhappily, one imperialistic nation, Soviet Russia, sought to take advantage of this world situation. It was for this reason, only, that we had to make sure of our military strength. We are not a militaristic nation, but we had to meet the world situation with which we were faced.

We knew that there could be no lasting peace so long as there were large populations in the world living under primitive conditions and suffering from starvation, disease, and denial of the advantages of modern science and industry.

There is enough in the world for everyone to have plenty to live on happily and to be at peace with his neighbors.

I believe, as I said on January 15, 1953, in my last address to the American people before leaving the White House: "We have averted World War III up to now, and we may have already succeeded in establishing conditions which can keep that war from happening as far ahead as man can see."

H. S. T.

Independence, Missouri

MEMOIRS BY HARRY S. TRUMAN

VOLUME TWO

CHAPTER 1

Within the first few months I discovered that being a President is like riding a tiger. A man has to keep on riding or be swallowed. The fantastically crowded nine months of 1945 taught me that a President either is constantly on top of events or, if he hesitates, events will soon be on top of him. I never felt that I could let up for a single moment.

No one who has not had the responsibility can really understand what it is like to be President, not even his closest aides or members of his immediate family. There is no end to the chain of responsibility that binds him, and he is never allowed to forget that he is President. What kept me going in 1945 was my belief that there is far more good than evil in men and that it is the business of government to make the good prevail.

By nature not given to making snap judgments or easy decisions, I required all available facts and information before coming to a decision. But once a decision was made, I did not worry about it afterward. I had trained myself to look back into history for precedents, because instinctively I sought perspective in the span of history for the decisions I had to make. That is why I read and re-read history. Most of the problems a President has to face have their roots in the past.

Two cruel wars were behind us in which we had seen totalitarian aggressors beaten into unconditional surrender. We had sponsored and helped establish the United Nations Organization, hoping to prevent again the too often recurring plague of humanity—war. I had met with

Churchill and Attlee and Stalin at Potsdam, trying to achieve closer co-operation between the three leading powers.

But in spite of these efforts relations with Russia had become strained. Victory had turned a difficult ally in war into an even more troublesome peacetime partner. Russia seemed bent upon taking advantage of war-shattered neighbors for imperialistic ends. The whole balance of power in the Far East had shifted. Most of the countries in Europe were bankrupt, millions of people were homeless and starving, and we were the only nation that could come to their help. We had already taken emergency relief measures, and we were preparing to do everything we could to avert a great human disaster.

The economic and financial burdens confronting us were staggering. But the adjustments from war to peace were being accomplished in a vigilant and orderly manner, and our economy kept going in high gear with full peacetime employment at a time when we were demobilizing millions of men. We were witnessing the transformation of the United States into a nation of unprecedented power and growing capacity.

But one event occurred in 1945 of such magnitude that it was to revolutionize our relations with the world and usher in a new era for humanity, the fruits and goals and problems of which we cannot even now fully grasp. It was the atomic bomb. With it came the secret of how to harness nuclear energy. I now had a responsibility without precedent in history. The decisions I had to make and the policies I would recommend to Congress on the use and control of atomic energy could well influence the future course of civilization. This was to be the beginning of the period of hope and many trials.

A bill for the control of atomic energy was before the Congress. This bill was the May-Johnson bill, which had been drawn up in the early days after V-J Day, and its approach was military. Its aim was to set up a kind of permanent "Manhattan District" under military control.

In the message I had sent to Congress on October 3 I strongly emphasized the peacetime uses of atomic energy, and for that reason I felt that it should not be controlled by the military. During the fall months of 1945 legislative action had been delayed by a wrangle among Senate committees as to which should properly handle bills affecting atomic power. Behind this dispute was the basic disagreement on whether the new force was primarily a military weapon or a potential source for peaceful civilian development.

The legislative dispute was finally resolved when the Senate set up a Special Committee on Atomic Energy. The chairman of this committee was Senator Brien McMahon of Connecticut, a devoted and talented public servant who deserves a great deal of credit for his legislative leadership in the shaping of the atomic program.

On November 30 I sent a memorandum to certain officials on the handling of the atomic program, stating that I thought the May-Johnson bill should be amended to provide for civilian supremacy, and at the same time raised with Senator McMahon the necessity for establishing civilian control. The senator agreed to seek amendment of the bill. Within a few days, however, he requested an appointment, suggesting that the Secretaries of War and of the Navy also be present. The military services felt very strongly that the control of atomic development should be under their auspices, if not under their immediate jurisdiction, and they were making strong representations to that effect to the Congress.

The meeting took place in my office on December 4. In addition to Patterson, Forrestal, and Senator McMahon, General Groves was present, along with Dr. Edward U. Condon, Director of the Bureau of Standards, and James R. Newman, counsel of the Atomic Energy Committee.

I asked each member of the group to state his position. Then I stated mine, that the entire program and operation should be under civilian control and that the government should have a monopoly of materials, facilities, and processes.

On December 20 Senator McMahon introduced S. 1717, which, in substance, contained this approach to the subject. On December 27 Secretary Patterson submitted a memorandum giving his views and those of some of his advisers in opposition to the McMahon bill. After the most careful study I replied to the Secretaries of War and of the Navy on January 23 with this memorandum, in which I insisted upon civilian control:

I have read the Secretary of War's memorandum of December 27th, giving his view, together with those of certain members of the Interim Committee, on my proposals for specific amendments to the May-Johnson bill.

After careful consideration, it is my judgment that the recommendations contained in my memorandum of November 30th should be adhered to without modification.

I direct your attention to the following items of particular importance:

(1) A commission established by the Congress for the control of atomic energy should be exclusively composed of civilians. This is in accord with established American tradition and has found its way into statutory provisions which expressly prohibit members of the Armed Forces on active status from serving in other Governmental posts. These provisions the May-Johnson bill seeks to modify. In my judgment, the problem of atomic energy does not justify the departure.

I agree that in times of national emergency it may be desirable to call upon members of the Armed Forces to serve in administrative posts for which their experience peculiarly fits them. In such event, the Congress may, as it has in the past, pass specific enabling legislation. But I believe this to be an unusual step, to be invoked by the Congress only when the national interest or safety demands it.

(2) An absolute Government monopoly of ownership, production and processing of all fissionable materials appears to me imperative. *Fissionable* materials are, of course, to be distinguished from *source* materials from which fissionable materials may be derived. By fissionable materials, I mean such as U235, or Plutonium or any substance enriched in these beyond its natural state.

I recognize that administering close controls of fissionable materials may in some respects prove difficult. But the difficulty is small compared to the advantages of government monopoly in dealing with international problems—or compared to the danger of permitting anyone other than the Government to own or produce these crucial substances, the use of which affects the safety of the entire Nation. The benefits of atomic energy are the heritage of the people; they should be distributed as widely as possible. Government monopoly alone will assure both the material safety and the maximum utilization of atomic energy for the public welfare.

(3) Consistent with these principles I believe it essential that atomic energy devices be made fully available for private patents, and regulation of royalty fees to insure their reasonableness. These provisions will assure widespread distribution of the benefits of atomic energy while preserving the royalty incentive to maintain the interest of private enterprise.

While I have covered only three of the major points in my memorandum of November 30th, I deem adherence to all the recommendations in that memorandum to be essential.

The Chairman of the Military Affairs Committee of the House and the leaders in the House should be advised that the Administration desires recommitment of the May-Johnson bill for purposes of amendment or, failing this, that no steps be taken to alter the present status of the bill in the House.

It is my wish, furthermore, that in appearing before Congressional committees or in discussions with Members of Congress relative to atomic energy legislation officials of the Administration present views not inconsistent with the points given in my memorandum of November 30th and reaffirmed herein.

H. S. T.

Civilian control of atomic energy faced many obstacles. Proponents of military control had many friends in the Congress, and Senator McMahon had a difficult time gathering support for his measure. On February 1 he spent nearly two hours with me at the White House discussing his difficulties.

In order to support the McMahon bill publicly, I gave the senator this letter and had it released for publication:

February 1, 1946

My dear Senator McMahon:

You have requested my views on S. 1717, a bill for the domestic development and control of atomic energy. I wish to give you my thoughts at this time because I consider the subject of paramount importance and urgency, both from the standpoint of our welfare at home and that of achieving a durable peace throughout the world.

I appreciate the thorough and impartial manner in which atomic energy hearings have been held before your Committee. I believe that the hearings, in keeping with democratic tradition, have aided the people in obtaining a clearer insight into the problems which such legislation must meet.

You will recall that I sent a special message to the Congress on October 3, 1945, calling for legislation to fix a policy for the domestic control of atomic energy. Since then I have given considerable time to the further study of this most difficult subject. I have had the advantage of additional technical information and expressions of public opinion developed at the hearings. With this background I feel prepared to recommend in greater detail than before what I believe to be the essential elements of sound atomic energy legislation: [The letter then set forth in the same order the three points made in the foregoing memorandum to the Secretaries of War and Navy, in approximately the same language. It then continued:]

4. In my message of October 3rd, I wrote:

"Our science and industry owe their strength to the spirit of free inquiry and the spirit of free enterprise that characterize our country. . . . [This] is our best guaranty of maintaining the preeminence in science and industry upon which our national well-being depends."

Legislation in this field must assure genuine freedom to conduct independent research and must guarantee that controls over the dissemination of information will not stifle scientific progress.

Atomic energy legislation should also insure coordination between research activities of the Commission and those of the proposed National Science Foundation, now under consideration by the Congress.

5. Each of the foregoing provisions for domestic control of atomic energy will contribute materially to the achievement of a safe, effective international arrangement making possible the ultimate use of atomic energy for exclusively peaceful and humanitarian ends. The Commission should be in a position to carry out at once any international agreements relating to inspection, control of the production of fissionable materials, dissemination of information, and similar areas of international action.

I feel that it is a matter of urgency that sound domestic legislation on atomic energy be enacted with utmost speed. Domestic and international issues of the first importance wait upon this action.

To your Committee, pioneers in legislation of vast promise for our people and all people, there beckons a place of honor in history.

Sincerely,
Harry S. Truman

The formulation of a plan for the international control of atomic energy had in the meantime been referred to a special governmental committee which Secretary Byrnes had appointed.

The State of the Union message of January 14 repeated our desire to develop effective control through the United Nations. The delegation which I had sent to the first formal session of the General Assembly of the United Nations in London in January was under instructions to work for the establishment of a United Nations Commission on Atomic Energy. This was in keeping with the agreements reached at Moscow the preceding month.

The plan for such a commission was put before the General Assembly by the British as the host country, was fully supported by our delegation, and was adopted on January 24. It was agreed that the first meeting of the new Commission should be held in New York on June 14, 1946.

While the United Nations deliberated on the establishment of an agency for the discussion of atomic energy controls, a committee appointed by the Secretary of State worked out a plan for such controls which might be placed before the U. N. Commission when it convened.

This committee consisted of five members. The Under Secretary of State, Dean Acheson, was designated as chairman, and with him served John J. McCloy, former Assistant Secretary of War, and three men most directly connected with the development of the bomb, Dr. Vannevar Bush, Dr. James B. Conant, and Major General Leslie R. Groves.

Working with and for the committee was a board of consultants whose job it was to analyze and appraise all facts pertinent to the problem of international control and to formulate proposals. David E. Lilienthal, chairman of the Tennessee Valley Authority, was the chairman of this group. The members were Chester I. Barnard, president of the New Jersey Telephone Company; Dr. J. Robert Oppenheimer; Dr. Charles Allen Thomas, vice-president and technical director of the Monsanto Chemical Company; and Harry A. Winne, vice-president of the General Electric Company.

This board did an outstanding job. It examined every aspect of the problem thoroughly and conscientiously. Its report was unanimously endorsed by the parent committee. It is usually referred to as the Acheson-Lilienthal Report and is a great state paper.

I received the report from Secretary Byrnes on March 21. By that time a number of other developments had taken place that had a bearing on the problem of atomic energy control.

On March 8 Senator McMahon had come to the White House to report that new difficulties were in the offing for the atomic energy bill that he had introduced. Senator Vandenberg was sponsoring an amendment to the bill that would set up a Military Liaison Board which, in effect, would duplicate the proposed Atomic Energy Commission. It would have access to all matters before the Commission, would have the right to insist on consultation with the Commission whenever it desired, and would have the right to appeal to the President any action of the Commission which it believed would "affect the National Defense."

On March 12 the Senate Atomic Energy Committee had approved this amendment, McMahon being the only senator to vote against it. The following day a slightly changed version was adopted by the same margin, again McMahon casting the sole negative vote.

This amendment would have had the effect of defeating the principle of civilian supremacy, and under it the Commission's work would have been subject to the veto of the military. The argument for this military veto was based on the premise that the preservation of the national security is primarily the responsibility of the armed forces. But this is a wrong assumption. The preservation of the nation's safety and defense is an organic and sweeping responsibility that extends to all branches and departments of the government; and only one of its many phases is assigned to the military departments.

I put it in these words to a press conference on March 14:

"I don't think there is a clear understanding by the public, or even in Congress, on what is meant by civilian control of that board. I have tried to make that perfectly clear in my letter of February 2nd. The idea is that the military, of course, has an important part to play and should be consulted, but it is a mistake to believe that only the military can guard the national security. The full responsibility for a balanced and forceful development of atomic energy, looking toward the national economic good, national security, and a firm, clear position toward other nations and world peace, should rest with the civilian group directly responsible to the President. Now the President is the Commander in Chief of the Armed Forces of the United States in the first place; and the civilian board under him would in no way hamper the military in their proper function."

On March 16 I conferred with Secretary of State Byrnes on the possibility that Congress might pass an atomic energy law that would undercut our efforts to bring about international co-operation in the field of atomic power. We had to be in a position where we could put our plan for international control before the United Nations without being handicapped by a domestic law that would have made it impossible for us to participate.

Byrnes advised me that the committee was ready to report any day. He suggested that we appoint a spokesman who would command respect both at home and abroad. Bernard M. Baruch seemed to me to be the logical man, and for several reasons. Not the least important of these was that Baruch enjoyed considerable esteem in the Senate. His association with the administration's plan for the control of atomic energy might help remove some of the opposition to the McMahon bill in Congress. Baruch had also succeeded, over the years, in forming many friendships abroad, including that of Winston Churchill, and during a long life he had acquired the prestige of an "elder statesman." I called on him in the expectation that he would also add weight to the proposal we were about to put before the world.

The Baruch appointment was announced on March 18 and was received very favorably by the press. On the same day my regular weekly conference with the "Big Four" leaders of Congress was devoted exclusively to the McMahon bill. I explained the reasons for the bill as originally drafted and said that I would not accept a law without civilian control.

When Byrnes brought me a final draft of the Acheson-Lilienthal Report, I sat down at once to study it. By some unauthorized means, however, this report fell into the hands of the press. This upset Baruch, and he asked to see me. When he came, he handed me a letter:

March 26, 1946

My dear Mr. President:

I was, of course, very much gratified that you should have expressed such great confidence in me as to appoint me the United States representative on the United Nations Atomic Energy Commission. I do not underestimate either the honor or the responsibility but, as I have become more familiar with the situation, there are certain elements of it which are causing me concern, and which I, therefore, want to discuss with you. As I understand my duties and authority, they consist presently solely of the obligation of representing United States policy on atomic energy, as communicated to me by you directly or through the Secretary of State, before the United Nations Organization. I see nowhere any duty or responsibility on me to participate in the formation of that policy.

This situation has been brought very forcibly to my attention by the press announcements of the report rendered by Mr. Acheson's Committee. I do not underestimate the effect of this publication in the United States or in the world at large, and while I have not had an opportunity to examine the report with care and cannot state my own definite views with respect to it, the letter from Secretary Byrnes to me transmitting the report states that it was unanimously recommended by a Committee headed by the Under Secretary of State. This brings the report pretty close to the category of the United States Government policy.

I have no doubt that the public feels that I am going to have an important relation to the determination of our atomic energy policy. There is no legal basis for this view and now that the Under Secretary of State's Committee Report has been published, the determination of policy will be greatly affected by the contents of this report. Even the superficial and incomplete examination of the subject that I have been able to make in the last few days convinces me that this report is likely to be the subject of considerable and rather violent differences of opinion. Its publication, which I understand to have been unauthorized, does not render the situation any less difficult.

These are the things that have been bothering me, and I wanted to talk them over with you before coming to a final conclusion myself as to whether, in the circumstances, I can be useful to you. I will need a little more time to reflect. As it presently stands, I think that embarrassment all around would be avoided if you would ask Chairman Connally of the Foreign Relations Committee to postpone any action on confirmation of my appointment until I have had a little more time to think things over.

Respectfully yours,
Bernard M. Baruch

I explained to Mr. Baruch that, in the first place, the Acheson-Lilienthal Report was very plainly marked as a working paper and not as an approved policy document. I also informed him that whatever policy he would be asked to represent before the United Nations would have to be a policy approved by me. I pointed out that, under the law, all representatives of the United States at the United Nations were under the supervision of the Secretary of State. Of course, I told him, the Secretary of State would probably request his aid in the preparation of a policy proposal for my approval, but I had no intention of placing him in a role different from other delegates to the United Nations.

Mr. Baruch then went to see Secretary Byrnes, and Byrnes later informed me that he had given Baruch a letter outlining his duties:

April 19, 1946

Dear B. M.:
Summarizing for the record our discussion of April 18 in which Mr. Hancock and Mr. Searle participated, I have asked you to give me the benefit of your advice when, with the President, I attempt to determine the policy of the United States which is to guide you in your representation of the United States on the United Nations Atomic Energy Commission.

You have pointed out that under the statute you are not called upon to determine policy. The fact is that under the law the President determines the policy and transmits such policy through me to the United States representative on the Commission. However, as a practical matter, I know that the President will ask for my views in determining this policy and I, in turn, will ask for your views. That is why I had asked you to be good enough to fully explore the subject.

I have advised you that I am favorably impressed by the report which has come to be called the State Department report and which was prepared under the direction of Mr. Acheson. I have, however, advised you that I am not of the opinion that it is the last word on the subject and, on the contrary, that I shall give careful consideration to any views that may be presented by you after you consider the problem.

I have suggested that submission of your advice should be informal. I hope that you will give me the benefit of your advice from time to time as your study progresses. I suggest this because from time to time I may be called upon to discuss the matter with the President. I would want to give to him, or have you join me in giving to him, any views we thought might be helpful to him in his consideration of the subject.

There is to be no formal report. The decision as to policy is the President's. You and I will advise him just as I advise him on many other matters. While it is the duty of the President to determine policy, it is my thought that when determined it should not be made public by him but should be transmitted to you and you, as representative of the United States, should announce at the meeting of the Commission what is the policy of this Government. However, this will be for the President to decide.

Once the Commission is in operation, there must be close cooperation between you and the Secretary of State. Matters will arise which cannot be foreseen and you must be given discretion to exercise your judgment as to all such matters, only avoiding positions that would be in conflict with the President's policy.

I do not believe that you will have any difficulty about these matters. You will be acting toward me just as I act toward the President. I know what his basic policies are. Knowing that, I do not hesitate to take positions as to matters which could not be anticipated. If they are matters of great importance I try to communicate with him. We have never had any difference in views that was not quickly reconciled. I am sure that will be your experience.

If you need any help from the State Department I am sure it will be granted without question. Should there ever be a question this letter is your authority to call upon the officials of the Department of State for assistance.

I expect to leave Washington Tuesday morning. Good luck to you!

Sincerely yours,
James F. Byrnes

Baruch, who is usually referred to as an "adviser to Presidents," had, of course, full knowledge of the President's responsibility for national policy. His concern, in my opinion, was really whether he would receive public recognition. He had always seen to it that his suggestions and recommendations, not always requested by the President, would be given publicity. Most Presidents have received more advice than they can possibly use. But Baruch is the only man to my knowledge who has built a reputation on a self-assumed unofficial status as "adviser."

I had asked him to help his government in a capacity of my choosing. I had no intention of having him tell me what his job should be. I made that clear to him, in a very polite way, and so did Byrnes, as his letter indicates.

Mr. Baruch's principal contribution to the atomic energy program was that he transformed the Acheson-Lilienthal Report from a working paper into a formal, systematic proposal and that he added a section that called for sanctions against any nation violating the rules. The American plan was put before the United Nations Commission by Baruch on June 14. Within a matter of hours it became evident that the U.S.S.R. had a proposal of its own, and one that was sharply in conflict with the American suggestion.

In the month that followed, Baruch and his associates, notably John Hancock, Ferdinand Eberstadt, and Dr. Richard C. Tolman, presented details of the American proposals to the several committees set up by the U. N. Commission. Russian and Polish opposition was evident. In substance, what the Russians wanted was a plan that would provide for an agreement not to use atomic weapons, for the cessation of bomb production, and for the destruction of all stockpiles. This amounted to a demand that we destroy our atomic bombs and, if we agreed to all this, then the Russians would be willing to discuss arrangements for the exchange of scientific information and the formation of international controls.

Our plan provided for the setting up of immediate controls over raw materials out of which fissionable materials could be made. Only when such controls were established would we consider disposing of our stockpile of bombs.

If we accepted the Russian position, we would be deprived of everything except their promise to agree to controls. Then, if the Russians should launch an atomic armament race, our present advantage and security gained by our discovery and initiative would be wiped out. As I wrote to Baruch on July 10, "We should not under any circumstances throw away our gun until we are sure the rest of the world can't arm against us."

The United Nations Commission eventually adopted, over the objections of Poland and Russia, what was substantially the American plan. The Commission's report was sent to the Security Council. There, backed by the use of the veto, Russia was able to block all further action.

The possibility that Russia would not co-operate in an international control scheme had been anticipated by us. We were prepared, in any event, to safeguard our own national interest.

At the time the British expressed concern over the McMahon bill. They said that this bill would deprive them of the opportunity to share our knowledge and "know-how" and the advantages derived from the years of wartime collaboration with us on the bomb project. Our ambassador to London, Averell Harriman, reported to me that Prime Minister Attlee felt that if the McMahon bill passed, Britain would be forced to undertake the development of atomic energy production on her own. Attlee said he feared the McMahon bill would prohibit the disclosure or sharing of atomic secrets with any foreign power, including the British. The British government took the position that, until such a time as U.N. control might become effective, the British should either have atomic weapons made available to them or at least be supplied with the data necessary to start their own production.

The Combined Policy Committee, which was the British-American body that handled such questions, came to a complete deadlock on April 15, and on the following day Attlee sent me a long message in which he sought to justify the British stand.

The agreed declaration of November 15, 1945, he said, stated that it was our desire that there should be "full and effective cooperation in the field of atomic energy between the United States, the United Kingdom and Canada." This, he thought, could not mean less than full interchange of information and a fair division of the material. The declaration, Attlee said, contained nothing about the sharing of information among ourselves and the clear indication was that this was already provided for. The wartime arrangements under which the major share of the development work and the construction and operation of full-scale plants were carried out in the United States had naturally meant that technological and engineering information had accumulated in our hands. Now, if there was to be full and effective co-operation between us, Attlee declared, it was essential that this information be shared. The British Prime Minister proposed that the Combined Policy Committee should make a further study of the question.

I replied to Attlee on April 20:

"The Secretary of State has informed me of the discussion in the Combined Policy Committee with reference to the request of the representatives of the United Kingdom that they be furnished with full information as to the construction and operation of the atomic energy plants in this country in order that they may proceed to construct a plant somewhere in the United Kingdom.

"The Secretary advises me that the request is based upon the construction placed upon the memorandum dated November 16, 1945, signed by Harry S. Truman, C. R. Attlee and Mackenzie King. That memorandum reads as follows:

"QUOTE 1. We desire that there should be full and effective cooperation in the field of atomic energy between the United States, the United Kingdom and Canada.

"QUOTE 2. We agree that the Combined Policy Committee and the Combined Development Trust should be continued in a suitable form.

"QUOTE 3. We request the Combined Policy Committee to consider and recommend to us appropriate arrangements for this purpose. END QUOTE.

"I would regret it very much if there should be any misunderstanding by us as to this memorandum.

"I think it is agreed by all of us that during the war under the Quebec Agreement the United States was not obligated to furnish to the United Kingdom in the postwar period the designs and assistance in construction and operation of plants necessary to the building of a plant. Therefore, the question is whether this situation was changed and such an obligation assumed by the United States under the language of the memorandum above quoted.

"The language 'full and effective cooperation' is very general. We must consider what was the intention of those who signed the memorandum. I must say that no one at any time informed me that the memorandum was proposed with the intention of having the United States obligate itself to furnish the engineering and operation assistance necessary for the construction of another atomic energy plant. Had that been done I would not have signed the memorandum.

"That such a change in our obligation was not intended at the time is indicated by the working paper prepared by Sir John Anderson and General Groves, a few hours after the signing of a memorandum by you and me. I admit that I was not aware of the existence of this paper, but it shows conclusively that even in the minds of those gentlemen who prepared the agreement we signed, the words 'full and effective cooperation' applied only to the field of basic scientific information and were not intended to require the giving of information as to construction and operation of plants whenever it was requested.

"Paragraph five of that memorandum of intention reads as follows:

"QUOTE. There shall be full and effective cooperation in the field of basic scientific research among the three countries. In the field of development, design, construction, and operation of plants such cooperation, recognized as desirable in principle, shall be regulated by such *ad hoc* arrangements as may be approved from time to time by the Combined Policy Committee as mutually advantageous. END QUOTE.

"As to our entering at this time into an arrangement to assist the United Kingdom in building an atomic energy plant, I think it would be exceedingly unwise from the standpoint of the United Kingdom as well as the United States.

"On November 15, the day prior to the signing of the memorandum first above referred to, the United Kingdom, Canada and the United States issued jointly a declaration of our intention to request the United Nations to establish a commission to control the production of atomic energy so as to prevent its use for military purposes. Our action led to the adoption later by the General Assembly of a resolution creating a commission for that purpose. I would not want to have it said that on the morning following the issuance of our declaration to bring about international control we entered into a new agreement, the purpose of which was to have the United States furnish the information as to construction and operation of plants which would enable the United Kingdom to construct another atomic energy plant. No such purpose was suggested by you or thought of by me.

"We were inspired to issue our declaration by the demands of people the world over that there should be some international control of atomic energy. Ever since, we have been working toward that goal. . . ."

The British Prime Minister did not answer until June 7, when he cabled that he had delayed his reply in order to discuss the matter with the Canadian Prime Minister, Mackenzie King. It was a long summary of the effort of British scientists who, in 1940 and 1941, had been among the first, Attlee said, to explore the military possibilities of atomic energy. In October 1941, President Roosevelt had proposed to Churchill that efforts be co-ordinated. The British had agreed to assist the enterprise in the United States "in the confident belief that the experience and knowledge gained in America would be made freely available," the British Prime Minister said, enabling the British to concentrate on radar and jet propulsion.

Attlee claimed that at Quebec it had been agreed there should be a complete exchange of ideas and information, and because of this the interchange of information in the field of design and construction of large-scale plants was not ruled out. It had been left to the President of the United States, he said, to specify the terms on which any post-war advantages of an industrial or a commercial character should be dealt with as between the United States and Great Britain. Attlee said that British scientists continued their contribution until the atomic bomb was dropped, and at that point the British had considered development of atomic energy at home, expecting to be able to "make use of the experience which had been gained up to that point in the joint enterprise." When war came to an end, the British were told that until new arrangements were concluded the supply of information from the United States must stop, and for that reason, the Prime Minister said, he had gone to Washington to see that the wartime co-operation be continued.

"I was very much reassured," he said in his message, "when you agreed that this should be so and that the Combined Policy Committee should be asked to recommend arrangements to that end."

Attlee contended that he could find no support in the document drawn up by that policy committee that there was no obligation to exchange information about the construction of large-scale plants. He referred to a draft agreement drawn up by a subcommittee of the Combined Policy Committee providing continuance of full and effective co-operation in the exchange of information. "We made it clear in the discussions that our own program would include the construction of large-scale plants," he added. But when the subcommittee report had been submitted to the Combined Policy Committee, it came as a surprise to him, Attlee went on to say, "to find that your government was not prepared to enter into any agreement, not to proceed on the basis of the agreements previously reached between us, nor yet to agree that cooperation should, in fact, continue by administrative action."

Attlee declared he could not agree with the argument that to continue such co-operation would be inconsistent with the public declaration on the control of atomic energy "which you and Mackenzie King and I issued in November. That our three governments stand on a special relationship to one another in this field is a matter of record and was in fact the reason why we took the initiative in issuing the declaration. It is surely not inconsistent with its purpose that the cooperation begun during the war should continue during the peace unless and until it can be replaced by a wider system." The Prime Minister said that in the one important field of joint control of raw materials co-operation was still continuing, adding, "Why then should we abandon all further pooling of information?

"I can see nothing in the Washington declaration," Attlee said, "or in the assembly resolution, which requires us to dissolve our partnership either in the exchange of information or in the control of raw materials, until it can be merged in a wider partnership. I should be sorry to think that you did not agree with this view." He closed his long cable by urging that the continuing co-operation over raw materials be balanced by exchange of information which "will give us, with all proper precautions in regard to security, that full information to which we believe that we are entitled, both by the documents and by the history of our common efforts in the past."

In view of developments in Congress I was unable to send an immediate reply to Attlee's message. There was no certainty that the McMahon bill would gain final approval or whether some version of the original May-Johnson proposal would pass. It was not possible for me to make any statement on policy to Great Britain until the Congress had acted. But, in any case, it was already apparent that, whatever bill the Congress passed, it would seriously hamper and restrict our co-operation with the British in the atomic field. Congress finally passed the McMahon bill in amended form, and I signed it on August 1, 1946. The Atomic Energy Commission, which was established by this bill, took up its duties on January 1, 1947. As its first chairman I selected David E. Lilienthal, who had done such an outstanding job as chairman of the Tennessee Valley Authority. Lilienthal had already acquired knowledge of the problems of atomic energy through his work as chairman of the board of consultants to the Acheson Committee.

The United States was now ready to embark on a program of planned development of atomic energy, for the security of the nation until international control became fact, and for the general benefit of all mankind.

CHAPTER 2

I have never been able to understand all the fuss some
people make about government wanting to do something
to improve and protect the health of the people. I usually find that
those who are loudest in protesting against medical help by the federal
government are those who do not need help. But the fact is that a large
portion of our population cannot afford to pay for proper medical and
hospital care.

As early as I can remember I have been troubled by seeing so many
sick people unable to get the care they need because they and the community lack the means, not only the sick who are so poor that they must
depend upon charity, but the average American family that cannot afford
to pay for the high cost of modern medical care. I saw something of this
problem in my first experience in government as a member of the county
administration. I saw people turned away from hospitals to die because
they had no money for treatment. A little later, as head of the county
government in Jackson County, Missouri, I helped build a hospital to
take care of people who could not get into existing health centers. We
know that there has been considerable progress in many cities and towns
in taking care of the sick and injured, but even in those communities the
patient must prove ability to pay or qualify as a charity patient.

When I became United States senator I supported measures that
provided funds for community hospitals to help correct this. And as
President I was determined to do something more about it.

I have often been asked what business it is of the federal government to concern itself with the medical and hospital care of the people.
Should not this rather be the responsibility of local communities? The

answer is simple. Too many local communities have not met this responsibility and cannot meet it without help.

For one thing, diseases and epidemics are no respecters of city and state boundaries. Our experience in the handling of polio and other threats to national health has proved that no one community can take care of itself. But the most compelling reason for the need of assistance from the federal government was dramatically revealed in the unfitness of millions of our young men and women for military service. World War II had shown that the health of this nation was far from what it should be, and I decided that the time had come for the federal government to do something about it.

I was shocked by the statistics showing the number of our young people who were physically unfit. By April 1, 1945, nearly five million draft registrants between the ages of eighteen and thirty-seven had been examined, and thirty per cent were rejected on grounds of poor health. In addition, about a million and a half men had to be discharged from the Army and Navy for physical or mental disabilities, exclusive of wounds. An equal number had to be treated, while in the armed forces, for diseases that had existed before induction. In fact, thirty-four per cent were unfit. This is a blot and a disgrace for the greatest republic in the history of the world; first in everything but the basic responsibility of making healthful individuals—mentally and physically.

More than one third of the young women who applied for admission to the Women's Army Corps were rejected for physical or mental reasons.

Altogether, nearly eight and a half million young people who should have been in the prime of health were found to be unfit for military service.

This is a terrible indictment. I believed that the United States should be the healthiest country in the world and lead in finding and developing new ways to improve the health of every citizen. As soon as I could direct my attention to the most pressing domestic matters, I proposed a national health program. President Roosevelt had set the stage for a health program in his "economic bill of rights," which included "the right to adequate medical care and the opportunity to achieve and enjoy good health."

On May 24, 1945, a social security plan had been introduced in the Senate by Senators Robert F. Wagner of New York and James E. Murray of Montana and in the House of Representatives by John Dingell of Michigan. This measure proposed for the first time in our history that every man, woman, and child be included in a health-insurance plan and was in the form of an amendment to the Hill-Burton Act for hospital construction.

Although I favored the principle of the Wagner-Murray-Dingell bill, I did not have much hope for its success in getting through Congress. It was too cumbersome, and it aimed in too many directions. For that reason, in my twenty-one-point message to Congress on September 6, 1945, I stated that I would soon submit a national health program.

On November 19, 1945, I sent Congress a message recommending national compulsory health insurance through payroll and other deductions. Under the plan, all citizens would be able to get medical and hospital service regardless of ability to pay. The message suggested that this nationwide system of medical care should be decentralized and completely under local jurisdiction. Local administrative units would be set up to provide for local services to meet local needs and conditions.

It was made clear that under such a program people would remain free to choose their own physicians and hospitals and that by removing the financial barriers between patient and doctor there would be greater freedom of choice by the patient in selecting his physician. The doctors would also be free to work through organizations of their own choosing and to decide whether to carry on in an individual practice or to join with other doctors in group practice in hospitals or in clinics. The physician would remain free to accept or reject patients and to conduct his practice as he always has.

The basic points of my proposal called for:

1. Prepayment of medical costs through compulsory insurance premiums and the general revenues.

2. Protection against loss of wages from sickness and disability.

3. Expansion of public health, maternal, and child health services.

4. Federal aid to medical schools and for research purposes.

5. Stepped-up construction of hospitals, clinics, and medical institutions under local administration.

I cautioned the Congress against being frightened away from health insurance by the scare words "socialized medicine" which some people were bandying about. I wanted no part of socialized medicine, and I knew the American people did not. Under socialized medicine all doctors would work as employees of the government. I was proposing no such system. I reminded the Congress that, although we were a rich nation and could afford many things, we could not afford ill-health. Our belief in insurance against unnecessary loss had become an American tradition, and what was now offered was a workable plan for insurance against loss of one of our most priceless possessions—health.

Many, but not all, of the essential points outlined in my health-insurance plan were in the Wagner-Murray-Dingell bill, on which congressional discussion was centered. This bill also covered a number of other subjects and was therefore needlessly complicated. The long hearings on this bill in 1946 gave the opposition time to organize a well-financed campaign not only against this bill but against the whole idea of federal action to improve the nation's health. The Wagner-Murray-Dingell bill proposed a three-per-cent payroll tax on salaries up to thirty-six hundred dollars to be shared equally by employees and employer and contained many of the points outlined in my health-insurance plan, but not all. At the same time, this bill broadened the areas of social security coverage and unemployment insurance. Partly as a result of this, when the Wagner-Murray-Dingell bill was referred to the Senate Committee on Education and Labor, it became highly controversial and unnecessarily confused the main issue. As the hearings progressed, opposition mounted. This opposition came primarily from the traditional foes of progressive government and from the hierarchy of organized medicine in the United States.

I believed, and still do, that the majority of practicing physicians—the rank and file of the medical profession—understand and approve the desire of the public for health security; and I felt that the views of the medical profession of the country were not expressed fairly by a small group of men who professed to speak for them and who promoted lobbying by medical organizations to further their own interests.

The leaders of the American Medical Association have always insisted that they could provide a satisfactory solution to the nation's problems in medicine and health. The fact is that at no time during my administration did the American Medical Association ever offer anything workable as a substitute for the proposal of compulsory health insurance. This opposition from the American Medical Association was not new. The A.M.A. had fought against public health departments, against proposals for county and community hospitals, and against the Hill-Burton Act for constructing hospitals and clinics throughout the country.

The Wagner-Murray-Dingell bill was killed in the second session of the Seventy-ninth Congress. I renewed the fight for national health legislation in a special message on May 19, 1947, repeating the recommendations of November 19, 1945, and citing once again the urgent need:

"The total health program which I have proposed is crucial to our national welfare. The heart of that program is national health insurance. Until it is a part of our national fabric, we shall be wasting our most precious national resource and shall be perpetuating unnecessary misery and human suffering."

In January 1948 the Federal Security Administrator was asked to undertake a comprehensive study of the possibilities for raising the level of the nation's health and to report to me on feasible goals that might be realized in the next ten years. The study, completed in September of the same year, made it plain that unless federal actions were taken, serious shortages of doctors, dentists, nurses, hospitals, and other medical facilities would continue to grow. With these facts in hand, I transmitted to the Congress in April 1949 four recommendations, asking for (1) legislation providing for national health insurance, (2) legislation to help medical schools expand, (3) increased aid for the construction of hospitals and other medical facilities, and (4) an increase in the amount of federal grants to aid local governments in preventing and controlling disease, to promote maternal and child-care services, services for crippled children, and general public health activities. The final recommendation included a request for additional funds for medical research in the form of fellowships and grants to both private and non-profit agencies.

This program, the message said, would save a great deal more than it would cost. Already four per cent of the national income was being spent for health care. An infinitesimal portion of this expenditure was for the prevention of disease. A national health program, I stressed, would save untold millions in productive working hours alone, although its real value could never be estimated in dollars and cents.

This was essentially the same program I had proposed in 1945. The opposition was still the same—political opponents of my administration, reactionaries, and leaders of "organized medicine." The same false charge of "socialized medicine" was used to discredit the program and to confuse and mislead the people.

In a move to offset the propaganda of the opposition an Executive Order was issued on December 29, 1951, creating the President's Commission on the Health Needs of the Nation, with the intention of setting up a completely non-political and unbiased commission of doctors, labor leaders, farm leaders, educators, and industrialists who would be able to investigate all aspects of the national health situation and to make recommendations based on facts.

I chose Dr. Paul B. Magnuson, former medical director of the Veterans Administration, to head up the Commission. He selected fourteen representatives from all parts of the country to serve on the Commission, and the critical study of the country's total health requirements began.

In a statement published on January 3, 1952, I made clear the reason for the work of the Commission on the Health Needs of the Nation, as follows:

"The purpose of the Commission is to study the facts and to give us the recommendations of high-caliber professional and lay persons. Their findings will help the public to get rid of the confusion that has grown up as a result of the bitter attacks upon any constructive measures I have supported to bring adequate health care to all our people. The fact that we lost over 500 million man-days of work due to illness in the last fiscal year is evidence enough that we must keep fighting the drain on our strength due to sickness and disease."

After twelve months of painstaking research, public hearings, panel discussions of experts held in all parts of the country, interviews and meetings, the Commission presented the findings and recommendations to me on December 18, 1952, in the form of a report entitled "Building America's Health."

The Commission reported that the present system of financing personal health services through voluntary prepayment plans was inadequate to the needs of the people. It ascertained the fact that a serious shortage of doctors existed and predicted that by 1960 the United States would need from twenty-two thousand to forty-five thousand more doctors. It found a shocking deficit in total expenditures for medical research, observing that more money was spent during the preceding year for tombstones and monuments than for research. It discovered that hospitals were shamefully overcrowded and many of them obsolete. At least 230,000 new general-hospital beds were needed, the report stated, plus 330,000 more for mental cases.

The Commission made positive recommendations regarding the financing of personal health services, the creation of more doctors and medical personnel, provisions for increased facilities and research, organization of health services, and perpetuation of the work of the Commission itself. The principal recommendations of the report were:

1. A broad extension of prepayment plans, to operate through large use of group practice and through community health-hospital centers.

2. Federal grants-in-aid, which would be matched by the states, to bolster prepayment insurance plans.

3. Creation of a post of Health and Security in the Cabinet.

4. Creation by Congress of a twelve- to eighteen-member permanent Federal Health Commission to make a continuing study of the nation's health status, with an annual report to the President and Congress.

5. Federal grants for aid to medical education, medical research,

local health services, for hospital construction, and for pilot studies in organizing medical services on a regional basis.

What the Commission was recommending basically represented a compromise between the compulsory national health insurance program, requested in 1945 and throughout my administration, and the current system of private payment to the doctor for each separate service rendered. It suggested that efforts be made to extend voluntary insurance to millions of people not covered, and that the federal and state governments pay the premiums for those who could not afford to pay them. The cost of the program would be an estimated one billion dollars a year in addition to the one billion which the government was already spending for health.

While the insurance program was not the same as the one I had proposed earlier, I felt that the Commission on the Health Needs of the Nation had accomplished a monumental task and that a workable outline for raising our national health standards was now available. It was a thoroughly sound and democratic approach to an urgent domestic problem.

A statement released simultaneously with the publishing of the report urged the continuation of the fight toward maintaining and improving our people's health.

"I, of course, cannot say what the next administration will do in carrying on the work we have undertaken in the health field. It is my hope that careful consideration will be given to the Commission's findings and recommendations. This report deserves the attention of every American. It would be most unfortunate if the same emotionalism which has prevented open-minded study of major health proposals advanced during the past few years were to hinder the proper evaluation which this report merits. . . ."

I have had some stormy times as President and have engaged in some vigorous controversies. Democracy thrives on debate and political differences. But I had no patience with the reactionary selfish people and politicians who fought year after year every proposal we made to improve the people's health. I have had some bitter disappointments as President, but the one that has troubled me most, in a personal way, has been the failure to defeat the organized opposition to a national compulsory health-insurance program. But this opposition has only delayed and cannot stop the adoption of an indispensable federal health-insurance plan.

In the nation's capital, as was shown in the case of the compulsory health-insurance proposal, a small well-organized group can succeed in making itself heard and heeded. The vast majority of the people have no such organized voice speaking for them. It is only the President who is responsible to all the people. He alone has no sectional, no occupational, no economic ties. If anyone is to speak for the people, it has to be the President.

In 1946 I signed a legislative reorganization act, which, among other things, provided that lobbyists had to register and disclose the sources of their income and their expenditures. Although this provision was helpful, the real problem of pressures and influences in the legislature cannot be altogether solved in this way.

My service in the Senate has taught me that in some instances the representatives of special-interest groups can be useful around Capitol Hill. At times they provide congressional committees with facts and figures that otherwise might be hard to get. The experienced legislator knows how to use the "good" lobbyist and how to avoid the "bad" ones.

Lobbyists played an important role in hampering our efforts to keep prices from skyrocketing during the period of reconversion. Their pressure on Congress made our work very difficult. In spite of my repeated requests and the veto of an earlier bill, the price-control law which Congress had passed in July 1946 did not protect the interests of the consumer. In commodities where there was no control, prices began to climb. The price-control bill which Congress passed contained a provision for the dropping of price controls on meat and stipulating that controls could not be restored before August 20. In the first day of free trade at the Chicago stockyards prime beef, which had been under an OPA ceiling of $18 per hundredweight, jumped to $22, and hogs moved from the controlled price of $14.85 to $18.50. During July and August prices of the relatively short supply of livestock went to unprecedented heights and resulted in a crisis in the fall of 1946 which was called a meat shortage. The fact was that the scarcity of meat during September and October was due in large part to the extraordinarily large slaughter in July and August to take advantage of uncontrolled high prices. The large killings of meat animals were gobbled up immediately by the meat-hungry people and created more shortage.

On August 20 the Price Decontrol Board, set up by the law, restored controls on meat after a hearing showing the necessity for price ceilings. But almost two months had gone by in which meat had remained free from all price regulation. During this period unfattened cattle had been rushed to the slaughterhouses in order to make high profits. If, as I recommended, price control had not been allowed to lapse by Congress, this wasteful slaughter of unfattened cattle would not have taken place.

The real blame lay at the door of a reckless group of selfish men—

some of them inside the Congress, some outside—who were encouraging sellers to gamble on the destruction of price control.

The meat situation became so acute that I addressed the American people in a nationwide radio talk on October 14, pointing out that a brief price-control holiday had been considered but that in the long run it would be bad for the country because a famine in meat would surely follow the temporary feast. Another proposed remedy was to order a further price increase on livestock, but that this would be ineffective because the livestock would still be held back in the expectation of the lifting of controls and even higher prices.

Many people had suggested that the government seize the packing houses, but this was no real solution because the seizing of empty packing houses would avail us nothing without the livestock. Some had even suggested that the government adopt the drastic measure of going out on the farms and ranges and seizing the cattle for slaughter, but I rejected this use of extreme wartime emergency power of government. Importation of meat was not the answer because of the unavailability of foreign meat in the amounts that would supply our needs. Besides, the people of other countries were depending upon exportable dressed meat for their own survival.

I announced, therefore, that there was nothing else to be done but to lift controls on meat and that I was directing the Secretary of Agriculture and the Price Administrator to remove all price controls on livestock and livestock products.

Controls had already been lifted on thousands of smaller items where that could be done without great risk. I warned that restraint and common sense would have to be exercised, not only in the meat industry but in all others, if inflation was to be avoided and adequate production achieved. Black marketeering, hoarding, unlawful strikes, and other such selfish tactics would be an invitation to disaster, I said, and could be avoided only if labor, industry, government, and the people used the same kind of teamwork that had always carried us through all our problems. Emil Schram, president of the New York Stock Exchange wrote congratulating me on my speech and expressing the opinion that the release of all controls just as soon as possible was the only solution to the problem of increased production. I replied:

October 18, 1946

Dear Emil:

It is my opinion that we can't possibly release controls hurriedly—the meat situation was a special one, brought about by the inability of the Congress to make up its mind on price control in time.

From the looks of things, the meat situation is going to be a very difficult one to solve next year—they are now rushing half fat cattle to market again because of the outrageous prices that are now prevailing. That, of course, will require a whole year's growth to catch up with normal supply and demand. The price people will have to pay for this meat on the east and west coasts is going to be outrageous, and nobody is going to be happy with it.

It would have been much better if Congress had extended the Price Control Act, as requested nine months before its expiration, and have allowed us to gradually decontrol items as the supply caught up with the demand.

It would not surprise me at all if there are not other inventory strikes in such necessities as clothing and building materials. Should the lid come off building materials and rents, we would be in for a boom that would make the Florida boom look like a Sunday school picnic.

Greed seems to be the keynote nowadays, and I suppose we will just have to face it for what it is worth.

I am not going to be in any hurry releasing these controls if we will get a Congress that will go along and use a little judgment.

With the speeding up of price decontrol on basic commodities during the fall of 1946, it soon became apparent that the time had come when it could serve no useful purpose to continue the remaining controls. I never believed in controls for their own sake and felt that the general control of both prices and wages was justifiable only so long as it was an effective instrument against inflation.

On November 9, 1946, I removed by Executive Order all controls on wages and prices and stated that the larger problem was now the withholding of goods from the market. This was becoming so serious as to threaten key segments of the economy with paralysis, and the blame lay largely on the unworkable price-control law which the Congress had passed.

An important organizational change was made on December 12 with the creation of the Office of Temporary Controls for the purpose of consolidating agencies which had been carrying on the work of reconversion. Centralized in this one administrative body were the Office of War Mobilization and Reconversion, the OPA, the Civilian Production Administration, and the Office of Economic Stabilization. At the same time John R. Steelman was appointed assistant to the President to help me in co-ordinating federal agency programs and policies.

A statement issued in connection with the Executive Order setting up this Office of Temporary Controls said that it would be responsible for carrying out the continuing responsibilities of the OPA and the CPA, plus certain activities of the OWMR. The decontrol of prices and wages and the elimination of rationing from most items had largely ended the functions of the Office of Economic Stabilization.

A Republican-controlled Congress, the Eightieth, had been elected in November. The State of the Union message to the new Congress on

January 6, 1947 forecast recommendations for the repeal of some of the emergency statutes and warned of existing dangers to the economy and the ever-present possibility of rising prices. I also called upon industry to hold the line on prices, and upon labor to refrain from pressing for unjustified wage increases that would force a rise in the price level.

On January 31 I asked the Congress to extend once more the Second War Powers Act beyond March 31, when it was due to expire, pointing out that manpower and wage controls and most price ceilings had been removed by November 1946 and that only a few controls coming under the Second War Powers Act would be needed. One of these was in connection with foods still in critically short supply throughout the world. The principal powers still needed were contained in Title III of the act, which related to priorities and allocation powers.

Another message to the Congress on February 19 recommended the repeal of certain temporary statutes still in effect by virtue of emergencies proclaimed by President Roosevelt in 1939 and 1941 and the repeal of some twenty-four statutes or portions of laws and others which should be temporarily extended or should remain in force. This was proposed as an additional step toward freeing the economy of wartime controls.

The result of this was what was known as the "First Decontrol Act of 1947," which the Congress sent up for my signature on March 31. This legislation effectively ended all emergency controls and war powers but extended for three months certain limited authority essential to maintain some materials controls in order to prevent harm to our own economy and to give concrete support to our foreign policy.

After all agencies of the executive branch had re-examined their needs, a second extension of the Decontrol Act in limited form was requested in order to retain control over the export and import of commodities which had a direct bearing on our foreign relations. This Second Decontrol Act of 1947 was approved on July 15 with the statement that I wished it had not been necessary to request a continuation of the controls contained in the bill but that the world shortages had not been dispelled and the threat of inflation still had not been dissipated. It was made plain that our purpose was the removal of interference with world trade and that the government would use these controls sparingly and dispense with them as soon as conditions permitted.

The relaxing of controls in an orderly and cautious manner was effectuated further by a congressional resolution repealing many of the temporary emergency and war statutes, which I approved on July 25. In a statement accompanying this action, I said that this was part of a sound and systematic program for removing all emergency powers. I explained, however, that the emergencies declared by President Roosevelt on September 8, 1939, and May 27, 1941, and the state of war continued to exist, and it was not possible at that time to provide for the termination of all war and emergency powers.

Unfortunately, Congress did not act on other recommendations for legislation relating to the control powers and for the prevention of inflation. So it was necessary to convene a special session of the Congress on November 17, 1947. The message on the opening day of the session pointed out how prices had been rising and called attention to the effects on the economy resulting from price inflation.

I urged specific legislation to prevent excessive speculation on the commodity exchanges; to authorize the allocation of scarce commodities and extend authority to allocate transportation services; continuation and strengthening of export controls; and authority to impose price ceilings on vital commodities in short supply that basically affected the cost of living. I also recommended extension and strengthening of rent control. The joint resolution of Congress, approved December 28, 1946, was supposed to embody these recommendations. In fact, it failed to include the key measures essential to an effective anti-inflation program, and I said on signing it that it would not reduce the high cost of living and would not keep prices from going even higher.

The issue between the Congress and the President was now completely clear, and on July 15, 1948, in accepting the nomination for President at the Democratic convention in Philadelphia, I strongly criticized this Eightieth Congress for its failure to enact the program recommended to the special session in November 1947, particularly its failure to provide stand-by controls. The Republican convention, held before the Democratic convention, had adopted a platform calling for some of the measures asked of the Eightieth Congress. So in calling the "Turnip Day Special Session" for July 26th,[1] I suggested that they show good faith and implement their platform! I told the Congress that the people were demanding legislative action by their government to check inflation and the rising cost of living and to help in meeting the acute housing shortage. I said that it would be reckless folly if we failed to act against inflation.

This was followed by a public statement on August 5 once more challenging the Eightieth Congress to take further action, as it had

---

[1] July 26 is considered the proper day to sow turnips in Missouri:
On the twenty-sixth of July
Sow turnips, wet or dry.

failed so far to discharge the tasks for which it had been called into special session. Again the only response was a feeble measure which was a far cry from the strong, positive action needed to relieve the country from the hardships of exorbitant prices. The Eightieth Congress, instead of occupying itself with consideration of active measures for coping with the situation, contented itself with following a course which served the ends of special privilege rather than the welfare of the whole nation.

On labor legislation, also, there was a wide gap between the Congress and the President. When the Case bill, designed to strip labor of its rights, reached my desk in 1946, I vetoed that repressive measure. But anti-labor sentiment, inflamed by John L. Lewis's defiance of the government in the fall of 1946, was gaining new strength, and labor legislation became a prime issue in 1947.

On January 6, 1947, in the State of the Union message, I had urged legislation to deal with the basic causes of labor-management difficulties. Specifically warning against punitive legislation under the stress of emotions created by the recent strife in which not only labor and management but the government and the public had been embroiled, I proposed a four-point program:

1. The early enactment of legislation to prevent certain unjustifiable practices, such as jurisdictional strikes, secondary boycotts, and the use of economic forces by either labor or management to decide issues arising out of existing contracts.

2. The extension of the facilities within the Department of Labor for assisting collective bargaining—integration of governmental machinery to provide the successive steps of mediation, voluntary arbitration, and ascertainment of the facts.

3. A broadening of the program of social legislation to alleviate the causes of workers' security—extension of social security, better housing, a national health program, and provision for a fair minimum wage.

4. The appointment of a Temporary Joint Commission to inquire into the field of labor-management relations.

This program offered a sound approach to the nation's industrial problems. But the Eightieth Congress began to hammer out the wrong kind of legislation.

Representative Fred Hartley, Jr., of New Jersey, chairman of the House Labor Committee, introduced a bill which was passed by the House in April. This drastic strike-curb bill, while it contained some good points, was an extremist measure which would abolish the National Labor Relations Board and substitute a Labor-Management Relations Board, make illegal industry-wide strikes, the closed shop, jurisdictional and sympathy strikes, mass picketing, all strikes by government workers, deprive violating unions of their bargaining rights for one year, deprive unlawful strikers of their right to get their jobs back, make unions suable, require unions to make financial reports, and empower the President to obtain injunctions against strikes in interstate transportation, communications, or public utilities.

A similar bill was being formulated in the Senate by the Labor Committee headed by Senator Robert Taft of Ohio. In May a ten-man Senate-House conference committee began combining the Taft bill with the Hartley bill.

The amended Labor-Management Relations Act of 1947, better known as the Taft-Hartley Act, was sent to the White House for my signature on June 18. Two days later I vetoed the act. The veto message listed the objections to it: The bill was completely contrary to our national policy of economic freedom because it would result in more or less government intervention into the collective-bargaining process. Because of its legal complexities the act would become a source of time-consuming litigation which would encourage distrust and bitterness between labor and management. The bill was neither workable nor fair. The Taft-Hartley bill would go far toward weakening our trade-union movement by injecting political considerations into normal economic decisions. I reminded the members of the Congress of the recommendation for a step-by-step approach to the subject of labor legislation in my message on the state of the Union and had suggested the specific problems which we should treat immediately. What had been laid before me was a bill proposing drastic changes in our national labor policy first, before making a careful, non-partisan investigation of the entire field of labor-management relations.

The recommendations I had submitted in January still constituted an adequate basis for legislation which would be moderate in spirit and which related to known abuses, and I urged that appropriate action be taken in that direction.

On the evening following the veto message I spoke over the radio about what this type of legislation would do to the progress made through the years in the area of labor relations, saying that this bill did not resemble the labor legislation recommended to the Congress by the administration, and warning that if it became the law it would create conflicts and discord without correcting the abuses or furthering advances in labor-management relations.

The Senate overruled my veto on June 23, and the Labor-Management Relations Act of 1947 became the law of the land. I had done all within my power to prevent an injustice against the laboring men and women of the United States.

CHAPTER 3

The federal budget is one of the most talked-about activities
of government and one of the least understood. Naturally,
the budget deals with the money needed to meet the obligations of
government. But the obligations of the federal government have become
so enormous in volume and so complex in scope that the budget has
become difficult to grasp except for those who work on it from day to day.

Every household has to work with some kind of budget which sets the
normal limit of expenses against the expected income. Very often expenses run beyond expectation because of emergencies such as an illness,
or income is reduced by business conditions, or extraordinary expenditures such as the purchase of a house or a car. In that case the house-
holder must cut expenses or borrow and pay out of future income, hoping
to achieve a balanced budget at some future date.

Multiplied many million times, this oversimplified illustration is how
the federal government makes out a budget for itself. But the budget
of the federal government involves many special considerations beyond
the requirements of our own people. They arise out of our new position
and responsibilities in the world. The United States, during several years
of my administration, after the war had achieved a balanced budget. In
fact, in three of these years—fiscal 1947, 1948, and 1951— a net surplus
resulted. The international crisis, gravely aggravated by the invasion of
South Korea, prevented a further reduction of the national debt. The
improved budgetary position was due to careful fiscal planning, with
the help of the Treasury and the Bureau of the Budget assisting me
capably to achieve our aims.

The Bureau of the Budget was set up under the law of 1921. The

Director of the Budget Bureau is appointed by the President and is directly responsible to him. In general the function of the Director of the Budget is to "assemble, correlate, revise, reduce or increase the estimates of the several dpartments and establishments," and to make detailed studies to determine any changes for purposes of economy and increased efficiency. The completed budget and its recommendations are transmitted by the President to the Congress at the convening of the regular January session each year.

Of course it cannot be expected that a President can personally do more than take part in the final stages of preparing the budget and then concern himself with only the major items. But I have always taken an intense personal interest in all stages of the preparation of the budget and devoted considerable time to its study and details.

My interest in public finance goes back to 1923, when I first served on the Jackson County Court. This administrative body supervised all the business operations of the county, and here I gained much valuable experience in handling receipts, supervising expenditures, levying taxes, and assessing real and personal property for tax purposes. And in performing these tasks I soon learned that everybody always wants the other fellow to pay for the support of the government.

When I became presiding judge of the county court, I had direct charge of making out the budget and of enforcing its operation. Before I left the court on December 31, 1934, all the county's old indebtedness had been refinanced at more favorable rates, and Jackson County's finances were in excellent condition.

As a United States senator, I served for ten years on the Senate Appropriations Committee. Here I became familiar with the complex financial structure of the federal government and learned what the figures in the national budget meant. I helped to make out ten budgets while on the committee, and I studied in detail every appropriation recommended by President Roosevelt or introduced in the Congress during those years.

Because of that experience I devoted considerable time and effort as President in making out the budget and preparing the budget messages to present to the first session of the Congress each year. The Director of the Bureau of the Budget, who serves in the Executive Office of the President, and the Secretary of the Treasury worked closely with me on the preparation of the budget. I always had firsthand knowledge of all the items that went into the budget. The law requires that the Chief Executive submit annually a recommended budget to the Congress. The United States Government operates, however, on a legislative—and not an executive—budget. The executive budget amounts to a sort of blueprint from which the Congress builds the final and actual budget. The Con-

gress then votes on this budget as it does on any other legislative proposal. Because we have a legislative budget, the President's proposed
appropriations for various purposes may be reduced, increased, or not
passed at all. This is constitutional; the Constitution says that taxes and
appropriations shall be in the control of Congress.

The budget which is produced on the basis of the President's recommendations to Congress each year is always presented a year and a half
in advance of its final operations—that is, it is presented to the Congress
in January for the fiscal year which begins on July 1 and ends on June 30
of the following calendar year. For example, when I took office in April
1945, the 1946 budget had already been approved by the Congress, and
this covered expenditures from July 1, 1945, to June 30, 1946. Consequently, the first budget which I was in a position to submit was not
sent to Congress until January 20, 1946, and was for the fiscal year
beginning July 1, 1946, and ending June 30, 1947.

President Roosevelt had removed the budget operation from the
Treasury Department during his administration and had moved it into
the Executive Office of the President, under the supervision of a Director
of the Bureau of the Budget. Before I began to work on my first budget,
however, I decided to make a change, and with this in mind I called in
Budget Director Harold Smith.

"I want this to be a tripod," I told him, "with the Secretary of the
Treasury assisting you and me in building up the budget."

And that is the way it was done in all eight budgets I made out as
President.

Harold Smith, for reasons of failing health, resigned within the first
year of my presidency, and I appointed James E. Webb to succeed him.
Thereafter I would periodically meet with Director Webb and with
Secretary Snyder, and together we would go over the broad concept of
the budget plan. Furthermore, I followed the same practice with Webb's
successors, Frank Pace and Frederick J. Lawton.

The Budget Director called on Cabinet members and heads of government agencies and discussed with them their requirements. The Defense
Department, which was the biggest spender, was the first department on
which the Director called. Then came the State Department with its
foreign-aid program, and so on down the line. I then built up, after
consultations with Secretary Snyder, a composite picture of what the
gross income would be to meet the requirements of the expenditure
program submitted to the Director by the departments and agencies.

The Budget Director would come to my office at least twice every
week during the formative period. I gave instructions that he was to
have free access to me at all times. I put in twice as much time on the

preparation of the budget as any former President ever did, constantly seeking the proper relation between the long-range integrity of our debt management, the basic and pressing economic and social needs of the people of the United States, and the needs of our allies. In all this there was comparatively little friction between departments, because they all felt that they were having a fair hearing in the consideration of their requirements. Now and again all-day sessions in my office made it possible to get at the real needs, after these discussions I gave positive directives to the departments—directives which I expected them to carry out. I did what I conscientiously thought was right, and then stuck to it.

It was inevitable many pressures were brought to get me to approve larger appropriations. This was particularly true of the military. The military frequently brought pressure to force me to alter the budget which had been carefully worked out to achieve balance with the other needs of the government and our economy as a whole.

If, for example, the three departments of the military establishment were allocated a total of nine billion dollars, the Army, the Air Force, and the Navy would usually ask for an equal three billion no matter what their actual needs might be. Such an arbitrary distribution obviously did not make sense. I therefore insisted that each service justify its demands and prove why it was entitled to an equal division. The services were unable to do this and soon began to break away from the old practice that everything had to be divided into three equal parts. I compelled the three branches to be specific and exact about the requirements they considered essential. Every single item in the military budget had to be justified to me and to the Secretary of the Treasury.

All of them made excessive demands, but the Navy was the worst offender. At one time the Navy had built up a regular hoard in copper and steel plate. We had to put a stop to that, and ultimately each branch of the service was required to state specifically what was needed for each fiscal year. In that way we began to get realism into the military budget. It must be remembered that in addition to immediate needs there had to be included in the military budget such items as the payment for past emergencies and soldiers' pension funds.

Soon after I became President I began to consider the problem of budgeting for the postwar period. V-E Day had been swiftly followed by V-J Day. Both confronted us with the task of financing the government in a conversion from a wartime to a peacetime economy while seeking to maintain a high level of production, consumption, and employment in the country.

We had been forced to build up a tremendous war economy—as near to an all-out war production as had ever been attempted in our history

—only to be suddenly faced with the tremendous task of converting our great production plant to civilian needs and, at the same time, of maintaining a high demand for labor, goods, and services.

Twelve million men and women were in the armed forces and were distributed around the world. Millions more had been drawn from civilian jobs into war production. Many billions of dollars in war contracts were outstanding to enable American industry to schedule the production required to win the war.

The 1946 budget called for enormous expenditures for arms, munitions, Lend-Lease, and other operations of war, but the sudden collapse of Germany and the imminent defeat of Japan made it necessary for me to order drastic reorganizations in the budget. Beginning in the early part of May, I ordered a review of all estimates. I also had all contractual obligations checked to see where cancellations could be made without interfering with the war effort.

I was able to inform the Congress that some sixty billion dollars in war contracts could be canceled. This was a huge sum, but it still left us with a large volume of war expenditures for the battle of Japan.

As the year 1945 proceeded, another and final war loan—the Victory Loan—was completed to provide the funds needed for concluding war operations and financing the demobilization.

The great difficulty that most people have in understanding the federal fiscal program seems to be in confusing the *authorized* budget with the *cash* budget. The authorized budget comes out of the Congress as much as eighteen months before the money is actually spent. The cash budget represents the month-by-month spending by the government of moneys previously appropriated or approved in the authorized budget. The authorized budget can be accepted by the public as a fair estimate of future spending needs, but the cash budget frequently comes in for bitter criticism because it is tied to the actual cash balance of the government.

Whenever there are complaints and dissatisfaction over government spending, it is almost invariably based on the amount of money that has gone out through the cash budget. This, I think, is due partly to human nature and partly to a lack of information or discernment. The public very often acts like the housewife who is pleased with the year's budget which her husband makes out in January but who does not think it looks so good after she sees the money going out for the agreed purchases payday after payday. It is the difference between saying you are going to spend it and actually spending it.

During my administration there was a continuing audit on the part of the Budget Director in all departments. I had people checking all programs to see how they were shaping up within the framework that had been established. Wherever there were unexpected balances I insisted that they be transferred to other programs or to the Treasury, to be applied against the national debt. Department heads had to explain to me their reasons for holding onto unused appropriations where they occurred. The Budget Bureau was continually surveying to see that appropriations, as made and budgeted, were carried out in accordance with the projected plan and, where there were changes, to get a reasonable explanation for them.

The attitude of some congressmen and senators was sometimes a problem. They were interested only in local and sectional problems and projects. I had to watch them all the time. They would make legislative amendments that had the effect of padding appropriations bills, and often these legislators had little understanding of the over-all budgetary requirements of the nation. They were simply after political support from their own areas or were seeking headlines.

It was my feeling that not only the Chief Executive needed to understand the technicalities of the budget but also that everyone who had anything to do with it should have a clear understanding of it. I was especially anxious for the newspaper reporters to have simple, straightforward explanations of the operations of the budget so that they would be qualified to write on the subject with accuracy and understanding, thus conveying a clear picture to the people all over the country.

For that reason it was my practice to hold special press conferences, known as "budget seminars," once a year in the White House. These were conducted for the sole purpose of going over the entire budget in detail to answer clearly any questions the newsmen might have. Each correspondent was provided with a complete copy of the document, and when they had assembled I went over it page by page with them, very much like a teacher in a classroom. The Secretary of the Treasury and the Budget Director drew up special charts and graphs for use at these meetings, and we called into the seminars any government officials who were in a position to assist me in explaining to the press whatever they wanted to know about the budget or whatever I thought they ought to understand more clearly. The Secretary of the Treasury and the Budget Director were invaluable at these meetings, which were by far the longest of the press conferences. They sometimes lasted between two and three hours, and of all the 324 press and radio conferences that were held during my years in the White House, these seminars pleased me most.

The federal budget was one of my more serious hobbies, but it was also much more than that. In fact, I regarded it as one of the most serious of the responsibilities of the President—a responsibility that never failed to prove thoroughly fascinating.

The management of the public debt during my administration can be summarized in three time periods:

1. From April 12, 1945, to June 30, 1946, we were completing the financing of World War II and, at the same time, grappling with the tremendous problems of reconversion.

During the fiscal year from July 1, 1945, to June 30, 1946, there was a budget deficit of $20,700,000,000, reflecting the carry-over of wartime spending. The public debt rose from $234,100,000,000 on April 12, 1945, to a peak of $279,200,000,000 in February of 1946. Thereafter the debt declined to $269,400,000,000 on June 30, 1946.

2. The second period, from a financial point of view, extended from July 1, 1946, until the Korean conflict in 1950. Readjustment was being made without upsetting the economy. During these four fiscal years we were in a period of generally high employment and rising national income. We had completed our reconversion, the wartime armed forces had been largely demobilized, and most of the war contracts had been liquidated. Toward the close of this period, however, the danger of new aggression recurred, and rearmament once again became an expenditure factor with which we had to reckon.

The net budget surplus for these four years amounted to $4,300,-000,000. By applying this surplus and some of the wartime cash balance to debt reduction, the public debt was reduced substantially, reaching a low point of $251,200,000,000 in June 1949, although it was up again to $257,400,000,000 by June 30, 1950.

This was a good record, although it should have been better. I recommended frequently during this period that our surpluses be larger and our debt reduction greater, but the untimely and unfair tax reduction of 1948, passed by the Eightieth Congress over my veto, prevented this.

3. Beginning with the fiscal year 1951, we entered the period that followed the Communist aggression in Korea. Our defense expenditures were sharply increased, and the Congress increased taxes markedly, but not as much as I recommended. During the first two fiscal years following the invasion of Korea we came very close to following the pay-as-you-go policy I recommended. For the two fiscal years 1951 and 1952 we had a net budget deficit of about one half billion dollars, and the public debt rose less than two billion dollars.

From June 30, 1946, to June 30, 1952, we had a net income for the government of three billions over expenditures. That is what I would consider good financing.

After June 1952, as defense expenditures continued to rise, we began to depart seriously from the pay-as-you-go policy. An estimated deficit of $5,900,000,000 was anticipated for the fiscal year of 1953 and $9,900,000,000 for that of 1954, unless changes were made in the tax laws. I cautioned against departing from my policies of paying for defense expenditures as we went along, particularly during a time of high employment and rising national income.

I had reduced the public debt by $28,000,000,000 from the postwar peak. My goal was to bring the total down to $200,000,000,000, but the Congress did not want the political risk of levying sufficient taxes to accomplish this.

In the fiscal year 1947 I had a balanced budget, and this after a devastating world war and a war economy. We had a surplus in the Treasury in 1947, and we had a surplus in 1948 and again in the fiscal year 1951. For the whole six years from July 1, 1946, to June 30, 1952, we took in more money than we paid out. There was no deficit financing while I was President until after June 30, 1952, and there would not have been any then if the Congress had approved my tax program.

Thus, the policy followed during the first two years was aimed at reducing the public debt while still carrying out other programs to maintain a high level of production and consumption. Tax reductions, therefore, seemed unjustifiable during that period. For the middle four years of my administration I worked for a balanced budget and a surplus to reduce the national debt, and accomplished both. Tax increases were reasonable during that prosperous period. The program for the last two years was on a pay-as-you-go basis to offset as far as practicable the expenses of war, foreign aid, and the terrible national debt which still remained on our hands from World War II.

Toward the end of the administration I was faced with two courses to follow in the few months in office remaining after the 1952 election. One was a policy which would drain the Treasury's cash position to rock bottom. We could apply the balance toward a reduction of the debt and leave a lot better picture as to the size of the debt when we went out of office. Or we could do what was best for the country by leaving a comfortable balance in the Treasury and arranging it so that there would be no necessity for the new administration to do any new financing for at least six months, which would give it a chance to get on its feet.

Of course we could have walked out in January and let the new administration shift for itself. That would have been the cold political approach. But the public interest, and not political considerations, was paramount in my mind, and I therefore instructed all departments to work out a briefing program so that the financing and management of the entire government would move along smoothly.

"Go ahead and do the right thing," I told Secretary Snyder.

"You mean by the right thing that you want the incoming administration to have a smooth transition?" Snyder asked.

"That's exactly what I mean," I replied.

We invited the successors to come in in advance, and we gave them office space in the Treasury so there would be no interruption in the management of the monetary program of the government.

In spite of the opportunity we had to reduce the national debt by five billion dollars, which would have looked good for the record of the Democratic administration, I thought that this sum should be made available to the new administration so as to get it off to a good start.

The Republican Eightieth Congress had passed a bill providing that three billion dollars of that year's budget surplus be applied to the budget of the next year. They were thinking that the next President would be a Republican, and in that manner they would be able to take credit for the three billion dollars which had been saved during the Democratic administration. This bookkeeping transaction was not in the province of Congress, and I paid no attention to it.

This Congress also tried to set aside government trust funds. This was like saying, "I am going to publish a financial statement, but I won't show the bills to be paid because they don't have to be paid until next year."

Those trust funds, which were made up of moneys of Social Security, old-age pensions, workmen's compensation, and railroad retirement are held in the Treasury and invested in government bonds. They thus form part of the liability of the government, and the record should make that clear.

I think it would be a good thing if all the assets of government were shown. I often thought that if the government were to make an inventory of its assets—assets such as TVA, Grand Coulee, Hoover, and Bonneville dams, harbors, buildings, and public lands—the total would exceed by far the entire national debt. This, as everyone knows, is the kind of balance sheet a business firm keeps, and in the case of the government such a balance sheet would show it well "in the black." And, in addition to this, I have always thought that so long as the income of the people runs from one and a half times to twice as much as the national debt there is not much need to worry about our ability to support that debt or about the soundness of the country's financial position.

The national debt can represent either investment by the government for the welfare of the people or it may be war expenditures forced upon us, which is a total human and economic waste. The first is a justifiable obligation which should be borne by the government. It stands for something tangible in terms of high living standards, good health, military security, national progress and prosperity. War expenditures, on the other hand, destroy and exhaust and consume the resources of manpower and materials which make up the wealth of the nation. In the eight budgets I made out as President I have felt that the only real waste ever recorded was that for war expenditures thrust upon us.

I think that the virtues of a "balanced budget" can at times be exaggerated. Andrew Jackson paid off the national debt entirely, and the budget was balanced when the unprecedented Panic of 1837 struck. Even the depression following the crash of 1929 overtook a government which was operating in the black.

Government must act quickly in emergencies, such as the depression of the 1930's or the Communist aggression in Korea in 1950. And quick action usually calls for emergency appropriations, like the WPA appropriations of the 1930's, which may well have averted a bloody rebellion in this country. And it is the responsibility of the federal government to undertake these expenditures for the public welfare and security when such action is needed.

Government is an instrument of the people, and unless the people want to support measures, and controls necessary for effective and efficient government, representative government will not mean much.

The way the federal bookkeeping system is set up is a matter of fundamental importance in government. In fact, I believe it is at the root of the basic differences between the philosophies of the Republican and Democratic parties. The Republicans have a materialistic approach to government and to the budget—a hard-down, income-against-outgo sort of attitude, even if it sometimes means the ruining of a whole segment of the population.

I have always felt that the Democratic party stands for a government that encourages a fairer distribution of the nation's prosperity so that every segment of the population will have some access to the good things of life. I was interested always in balancing the figures of the budget, as the record indicates; but I was even more concerned over the balancing of the human budget in this country.

Here is the basic thinking that guided me in my tax and financing program. My objectives were to bring the budget down as soon as possible to around thirty-five billion dollars and, at the same time, keep our taxes at a level that would enable us to reduce the national debt while conditions of prosperity existed.

The Roosevelt administration, in order to meet the cost of reconstruction and the needs for World War II, had to seek revenues wherever they could be found. As a result, the tax structure which I inherited was a bulky, patchwork affair. It was my hope that the Congress would co-operate with me in working out a tax system that would yield us adequate revenues and yet be free of inequities.

As county judge, senator, and President, I consistently kept in mind the same sort of tax philosophy. It was a pay-as-you-go program, except in emergency conditions involving the welfare of the people, at which times I considered it the responsibility of government to act quickly in raising funds for the necessary relief. There is nothing sacred about the pay-as-you-go idea so far as I am concerned, except that it represents the soundest principle of financing that I know.

Taxation, in my opinion, should be used for revenue purposes only. While I fought for a more equal distribution of the nation's prosperity among all its citizens, I never advocated taxing the rich to pay the poor. The rate of taxation, to be fair, must be based upon ability to pay. Every social reform which I sponsored was presented in the form of specific legislation, and never in the guise of taxation.

On tax matters, the Treasury Department usually supplied the framework. But the Ways and Means Committee of the House was very jealous of its authority in this field, and I had to work closely with both groups and keep serious conflicts in policy from disturbing the over-all tax structure.

My chief obstacle was getting the Congress to vote for tax levies to finance the total government program on a pay-as-you-go basis. I do not believe there is any safer way to finance private or public affairs than to make provision for keeping receipts even with expenditures. The Congress would vote in favor of a certain appropriation but then would sometimes refuse to pass legislation that would pay for the new expenditures through additional tax revenues. I had no patience with such practices by Congress, because if a measure deserves an appropriation it is obviously worth the levy to pay for it.

Too many congressmen during my administration heeded the traditional slogan of cynical politics: "Never vote against an appropriation, and never vote for a tax increase." It might be one way to get re-elected, but it is also a sure way of getting the country into financial difficulties.

If it had not been for the Republican Eightieth Congress, my program for ironing out the inequities in the tax system could have gone through without any impediment. However, eager to please the special interests which its majority represented, the Eightieth Congress voted across-the-board tax cuts which were entirely unjustified at that time of high-level incomes and almost full employment. Just half of that amount of tax cut would have permitted my administration to eliminate many of the inequities of the tax structure.

As we got the tax program better in hand, we could have realized practically every goal set up in our original fiscal plan if Korea had not erupted at the time it did. The exemptions could have been raised and broader incentives offered while still keeping the level of production and consumption on an unprecedentedly high plane.

In the pay-as-you-go program there was always the idea that it must be tempered by realities for the purpose of maintaining the economy on a high level. Such a policy is essential to the economic and human well-being of the nation. Of course we did take calculated risks in certain situations which we anticipated much earlier than we were ever given credit for. We saw, for example, that the growth of our population of two and a half million people a year was the same as adding each year a whole new state as large as Florida or Iowa or Louisiana, with all that means to the growth of our market. A growing population is a challenge to a nation's economy, and when the two keep pace with one another stagnation is impossible.

We encouraged a continued high-level economy because we knew we could absorb it with the new population. But a sudden grandstand play to tighten up financially, simply to show that we can balance the budget, can put our whole economy in reverse gear, resulting in tight money and unemployment. There is a political conception that has always seemed to discourage a President from going before the Congress to ask for revenues until he can show that the money has already been spent. It was good politics—I knew. But I also knew it was good financing—and that was my job.

There are more misinformation and plain demagoguery that go into the Congressional Record on taxes and the budget than on all other subjects put together. Most senators and representatives actually know very little about taxes or the budget. On the Appropriations Committee and on the Ways and Means Committee of the House and the Finance Committee of the Senate there have always been some able and conscientious men who have understood government finances. But there have also always been able and conscientious men in both Houses of Congress who spend their time appealing to special interests both on taxes and appropriations.

The Treasury is the business end of the government. Every dime spent in the government has to flow through the Treasury. There is not a thing that happens in the government that does not affect the Treasury, and there must be a stable, sound credit base or else the rest of the government would crack up. The Treasury and the budget are the mechanisms that enable the government to operate; they represent the practical operation of the government.

The Treasury Department of the United States is one of the largest organizations in the executive branch of the government, and the need for tight controls and for efficient operation on a day-to-day basis is crucial to the total operations of government. I was particularly fortunate in having a Secretary of the Treasury who understood the problems of national and international finance thoroughly and who administered the affairs of the Treasury for more than six years with rare skill and wisdom.

John W. Snyder was actually my third Secretary of the Treasury, but he served during the major portion of my administration. Secretary Morgenthau's resignation occurred within three months after I became President, and because I appointed Vinson to the Supreme Court, his secretaryship was of short duration. My selection of Snyder in June 1946 as chief fiscal officer of the government was based on a long association which had existed between us. I had known him when I was presiding judge of the Jackson County Court and he was a bank official in St. Louis, and we had been together in military reserve training. I knew him as a banker who understood the relation of good banking practice to the community, and during my years in the Senate our mutual confidence and friendship had continued to grow.

With Snyder in the Treasury, I was able to bring about some long-needed reforms in the Treasury Department. One of the big accomplishments was a complete revision of the government accounting system. Working with a team made up of the Budget Bureau, the Treasury, and the Government Accounting Office, we were able to set up a uniform accounting procedure throughout the whole government. Where it formerly took from three to six months to get a composite financial statement, it now requires from three to six weeks only.

The most sweeping reorganization was that of the Bureau of Internal Revenue, which was planned and initiated in January 1952. This was part of a long investigation and study to insure proper conduct and greater efficiency in the public service and to protect the government from insidious influence peddlers and favor seekers. Some persons in the Bureau of Internal Revenue had betrayed the public trust, and as soon as the facts were ascertained they were prosecuted.

The following major changes were made in this reorganization of the Bureau of Internal Revenue: (1) The offices of the sixty-four collectors of Internal Revenue were abolished. (2) The Commissioner of Internal Revenue was the only officer to be appointed by the President, with the consent of the Senate. All other positions were to be filled thereafter through Civil Service. (3) The complex system under which more than two hundred separate field officers handled the tax matters in various federal districts was ended, and substituted for them were not more than twenty-five district commissioners who were alone responsible to the Commissioner in Washington. (4) A strong, independent inspection service was established to keep the system under scrutiny at all times. (5) The operations of the Bureau headquarters in Washington were simplified. (6) The salaries to be paid to officials in the Bureau of Internal Revenue were raised in order to obtain the services of the best-qualified people in this highly intricate and technical field of government.

The new, streamlined Revenue Service resulted in clear, direct channels of responsibility and supervision from the lowest field office to the Commissioner. It was organized for thorough inspection and control from top to bottom to assure integrity and fidelity in its operations.

Although it was recommended by the Hoover Commission that the Reconstruction Finance Corporation be placed in the Treasury Department, Snyder and I both felt that the Treasury should not be in the banking and loan business. We believed that the RFC should be preserved as an agency on a skeleton basis so as to be able to expand in times of need. With the tremendous, dynamic economy such as we have in the United States, the threat of a recession or a depression could be materially lessened if the RFC were kept available for immediate credit expansion in an emergency and for its immediate contraction when the emergency no longer existed.

One of the problems that arose in the monetary field at the outset of the Korean action involved the Federal Reserve Board. It was my position that until we could determine the extent of the defense requirements that might result we should maintain a stable position in reference to money rates that affected the management of the public debt.

Under the statutes, the fixing of money rates (discount and interest) is handled by the Federal Reserve Board, which is not part of any of the departments of the government. Therefore, the Treasury could not directly control the money rates that would apply to its debt obligations. It did not seem appropriate to me that we should enter into a period of deficit financing on a rising money-rate pattern. I also felt strongly that in the moment of impending crisis we should not take deliberate steps that could possibly disturb public confidence in the nation's financing.

As the head of the government I felt I had a duty as well as a right to use every available resource to make sure of the success of the defense program. For that reason I invited the members of the Federal Reserve Board to visit with me. At this conference I asked them to give the Treasury their full support for its financing program, just as they had done during World War II.

The Treasury, of course, did not have to have Federal Reserve approval of its security issues, but the practice was to have full consultation with and to expect full co-operation by the Board.

I was given assurance at this meeting that the Federal Reserve Board would support the Treasury's plans for the financing of the action in Korea. This assurance was given entirely voluntarily. At no time during the conference did I attempt to dictate to the Board or tell them what specific steps they ought to take. I explained to them the problems that faced me as Chief Executive, and when they left I firmly believed that I had their agreement to co-operate in our financing program. I was taken by surprise when subsequently they failed to support the program.

Eventually an agreement was reached, but not until the differences of opinion between the Treasury and the Board had caused considerable worry to the President and much added expense to the taxpayers. These problems of discount rates and bond issues are not matters that are likely to make the headlines (except, of course, in the financial publications), yet on their settlement can depend the financial soundness of the government and the prosperity of countless individuals. My approach to all these financial questions always was that it was my duty to keep the financial capital of the United States in Washington. This is where it belongs—but to keep it there is not always an easy task.

CHAPTER 4

One of the strongest convictions which I brought to the office of President was that the antiquated defense setup of the United States had to be reorganized quickly as a step toward insuring our future safety and preserving world peace. From the beginning of my administration I began to push hard for unification of the military establishment into a single department of the armed forces.

The idea of unifying and integrating the Army and Navy into a single department of national defense evolved slowly and against powerful opposition. I had been vitally interested in our military organization since World War I and had studied every plan that had been suggested through the years for its improvement.

In my younger days, having been something of a student of military history, I decided to join the "militia" referred to in Washington's message of 1790. The militia had become the National Guard of the United States.

The experience I had in the National Guard and as a colonel in the Reserve Corps after the war gave me some very definite ideas on what the military department of a republic like ours should be. My experience in the volunteer forces and later on in the Senate was very helpful when I became Commander in Chief.

It had been evident to me, from the record of the Pearl Harbor hearings, that the tragedy was as much the result of the inadequate military system which provided for no unified command, either in the field or in Washington, as it was any personal failure of Army or Navy commanders.

I had not fully realized the extent of the waste and inefficiency existing as a result of the operation of two separate and un-co-ordinated military departments until I became chairman of the special Senate committee created in 1941 to check up on the national defense program. I had long believed that a co-ordinated defense organization was an absolute necessity. The duplications of time, material, and manpower resulting from independent Army and Navy operations which were paraded before my committee intensified this conviction.

As a member of the Appropriations and Military Affairs Committees of the Senate and as chairman of the Special Committee to Investigate the National Defense Program, I was certain that unless something could be done to co-ordinate the activities of the Army and the Navy we would finally end up with two departments of defense and eventually three when the Air Force succeeded in obtaining its special committee in the House and Senate.

The chairmen of the Military and Naval Affairs Committees, especially in the House, where appropriations originate, tended to become Secretaries of War and Navy. There were a couple of House members, chairmen of the Military Appropriations Subcommittee and Naval Affairs Committee, who had to have seventeen-gun salutes, parades, etc., as often as they could find excuses to visit Army posts and naval bases. These gentlemen were the principal stumbling blocks to unification. This was particularly true of the Naval Affairs chairman in the House.

In my various investigations I ran into numerous unnecessary duplications by the Army and the Navy. For example, I found immense air installations located side by side at various points in this country and Panama where the Navy could not land on the Army's airfield, and vice versa. A silly procedure, if I ever saw one. At Pearl Harbor the air bases were as far apart as if they had been on different continents—yet they were practically side by side. Then the Navy had its own "little army that talks Navy" and is known as the Marine Corps. It also had an air force of its own, and the Army, in turn, had its own little navy, both freshwater and salt.

It was my opinion that the Commander in Chief ought to have a co-ordinated and co-operative defense department that would work in peace and in war. Most field commanders who had experience in World War II, whether in the Army or the Navy, were for a unified defense department, and less than a year before I assumed the presidency an article of mine openly advocating the consolidation of the Army and Navy was published in a magazine. Listing examples of appalling waste which had been uncovered by the Truman Committee, I urged a new defense organization in which every element of the nation's defense would be unified in one department under one authoritative head.

In the plan I outlined, procurement of personnel and supplies would be centralized, and the land, sea, and air forces would plan and operate together as one team instead of three. Direct control would be by a *General* Staff, and not a *Joint* Chiefs of Staff such as had existed on an improvised, non-statutory basis during World War II to co-ordinate strategy and operations.

My first opportunity to begin work, as President, on the reorganization of the military structure came in the summer of 1945 when Secretary of the Navy Forrestal suggested legislation increasing the permanent strength of the regular Navy and Marine Corps. The time had come to put an end to piecemeal legislation and separate planning for the services. I wrote Admiral Leahy on August 21 requesting that the Joint Chiefs of Staff review the Navy's proposed legislation from the standpoint of the combined requirements of the armed forces. I suggested that this review should consider our international commitments for the postwar world, the development of new weapons, and the relative position of the services in connection with these factors. As a result of this action, the Joint Chiefs undertook a study of the postwar manpower requirements of the Army and Navy. The Army was directed to produce estimates of its own postwar needs, and the War Department appointed a committee, headed by Brigadier General W. W. Bessell, to make this study.

The Bessell Committee reported in September that because of the absence of high-level guidance on political considerations, and pending a decision on Army-Navy co-ordination, it was impossible to estimate manpower needs accurately. It recommended approval by the Joint Chiefs of the report of its special committee, which had recommended, by a vote of three to one, unification of the Army and Navy in a single department. Agreement could not be reached by the Joint Chiefs, however, and on October 16 the report was sent to me, together with the views of General Marshall, General Arnold, Admiral King, and Admiral Leahy.

In brief, the two generals supported unification, and the two admirals opposed it. Thus I was faced with a direct split of opinion between the Army and Navy Chiefs of Staff on the fundamental principle of a unified military establishment.

In the meantime, the Navy had been preparing its own plan for postwar national security. This program, which was submitted to me on October 18, continued to oppose unification with the Army but suggested that the admittedly serious defects in co-ordination be cured by more effective joint committees. The principal thesis of the Navy's proposal was that military policy must be tied in with national policy through the establishment of high-level agencies. I endorsed fully the Navy's emphasis on the need for some means of more effectively meshing military planning with our foreign policy and agreed also that we needed to provide long-range plans for industrial mobilization consistent with the civilian economy. In other words, it was clear to me that a national defense program involved not just reorganization of the armed forces but actual co-ordination of the entire military, economic, and political aspects of security and defense.

In the meantime, two unification bills had been introduced in the Congress—one by Senator Lister Hill of Alabama and another by Senator Edwin C. Johnson of Colorado. Hearings were opened by the Senate Committee on Military Affairs on October 17, and these dragged along until December 17 without any agreement being reached between Army and Navy representatives.

Seeing the need for presidential intervention, I sent to the Congress on December 19, 1945, a message recommending a reorganization of the armed services into a single department along the following broad lines:

1. There should be a single Department of National Defense charged with the full responsibility for armed national security.

2. The head of this department should be a civilian, a member of the President's Cabinet, to be designated as the Secretary of National Defense. Under him there should be a civilian Under Secretary and several civilian Assistant Secretaries.

3. There should be three co-ordinated branches of the Department of National Defense: one for the land forces, one for the naval forces, and one for the air forces, each under an Assistant Secretary. The Navy should retain its own carrier- or water-based aviation, and the Marine Corps should be continued as an integral part of the Navy.

4. The President and the Secretary should be provided with authority to establish central co-ordinating and service organizations, both military and civilian, where these were found to be necessary.

5. There should be a Chief of Staff of the Department of National Defense, and a commander for each of the three component branches—Army, Navy, and Air.

6. The Chief of Staff and the commanders of the three branches should constitute an advisory body to the Secretary and to the President.

In addition to these points, I also cautioned that the key staff positions in the new department should be filled with officers drawn from all the services, and the post of Chief Staff should be rotated among the several services in order that the thinking of the department would not be dominated by any one or two of the services.

I stated that the unification plan which I offered would provide for: an integrated military program and budget; greater economies through unified control of supply and service functions; improved co-ordination between the military and the rest of the government; the strongest means for civilian control of the military; creation of a parity for air power; systematic allocation of the limited resources for scientific research and development; and consistent and equitable personnel policies.

The Senate Military Affairs Committee appointed a subcommittee late in December to carry on the effort to obtain a unification bill acceptable to both the Army and the Navy. After eight drafts had been rejected, the Thomas-Hill-Austin bill was introduced in the Seventy-ninth Congress on April 8, 1946. The subcommittee had worked hard to achieve a workable bill and still meet the requirements of my message to the Congress, but the final product was unanimously opposed by all Navy witnesses at the subsequent hearings on the bill.

On May 13, 1946, I called Secretary of War Patterson and Secretary of the Navy Forrestal to a conference at the White House. At this conference I urged the necessity of the Army and Navy getting together on the problem of unification. I knew it would work out better if I did not order the two branches of the service to reach an agreement, and I therefore suggested that they sit down together and work out their points of agreement and disagreement and submit the list to me.

On May 31 the two Secretaries submitted a joint letter outlining areas of agreement and disagreement. They were not able to agree on four vital points: a single military establishment; setting up of three co-ordinate branches of the service; control of aviation; and administration of the Marine Corps.

These four points were the basic issues which had always been the cause of conflict between the Army and the Navy. I was deeply disappointed that no substantial progress had been made toward resolving this traditional conflict, and I decided then that the only way in which unification could move forward was for me to settle personally each of the four points of difference between the services. On June 15, after long and deliberate study, I made the decision in a letter to the Secretaries and to the heads of the congressional committees dealing with naval and military matters.

In this decision I supported the War Department's view that a single Department of National Defense was necessary to effective unification. I also supported the War Department's opinion that a separate Air Force should be established, and that the Air Force should take over all land-based aviation, including naval reconnaissance, anti-submarine patrol, and protection of shipping. It seemed to me that no one could give a valid reason for continuing the expensive duplication of land-based air services then existing.

I took the Navy's view that the function of the Marine Corps should continue undisturbed. I felt that if a Marine Corps were necessary, efforts to draw a hard and fast line as to the extent of its participation in amphibious operations and land fighting would be futile. I saw much justification in the Navy's position that the Marine Corps should be permitted to do those things essential to the success of a particular naval campaign.

In addition to the foregoing decisions, I approved the establishment of a Council of Common Defense, a National Security Resources Board, a Central Intelligence Agency, a Procurement and Supply Agency, a Research Agency, a Military Education and Training Agency, and the statutory establishment of the Joint Chiefs of Staff. I urged passage of legislation which would make possible a unification of the services at the earliest possible date, and continued my efforts to get the Army and Navy to agree on the form of such legislation.

Despite the Navy's distaste for some of the basic features of my unification decision, Secretary Forrestal worked hard to attempt to iron out the existing differences. On January 16, 1947, he and Secretary Patterson advised me by a joint letter that a compromise unification plan had been worked out which they both could support.

I was extremely gratified, as it represented a step in the right direction. Unification depended as much upon individual co-operation as upon legislation.

On receiving the news of the agreement I issued a public statement in which a proposed Executive Order set forth in full the responsibilities of each branch of the service under the desired legislation and, on the following day, informed the Congress that a unification bill was being drafted for its consideration.

This development marked the culmination of the long, hard battle to bring the services together. All that remained was to work out the details of the bill. I had appealed to the Eightieth Congress, in my State of the Union message, to give wise and careful consideration to the forthcoming legislation as the one certain way by which we could cut costs and at the same time enhance our national security.

On February 26, 1947, I was able to transmit to the Speaker of the House and Senator Vandenberg a bill which, upon amendment and passage, was to become the National Security Act of 1947. The bill, as finally passed on July 25, was not as strong as the original proposal sent to Congress, since it included concessions on both sides for the sake of bringing together the Army and the Navy. But it put an end to the long and costly arguments over the principle of unification, and for the first time in the history of the nation an over-all military establishment was created.

The new "National Military Establishment" consisted of a Secretary of Defense, to be assisted by three civilian special assistants. His authority over other civilian personnel was restricted to those in his own department, and he had no authority over civilian personnel of the Army, Navy, and Air Force.

The act established executive departments of the Army, Navy, and Air Force, with Secretaries provided for each. For the first time the existence of the Joint Chiefs of Staff was recognized by law.

Within the Military Establishment the act created a Munitions Board to co-ordinate procurement, production, and distribution plans of the services and to plan the military aspects of industrial mobilization; and a Research and Development Board to co-ordinate scientific research relating to the whole national security.

The act also provided for a National Security Council composed of the President and the heads of State, Defense, Army, Navy, Air, Munitions Board, Research and Development Board, and National Security Resources Board. The Council was charged with appraising the national security of the United States and dealing with national security problems of common interest to all segments of the government.

The other valuable agencies created by the act were a Central Intelligence Agency under the Security Council, to correlate and evaluate intelligence activities and data, and a National Security Resources Board to co-ordinate military, civilian, and industrial agencies.

I appointed James V. Forrestal as our first Secretary of Defense, and on September 17, 1947, he was sworn in.

Getting the idea of unification legally approved was only part of the fight for a consolidated military program. Making it work efficiently during the early months occupied a good deal of my time and attention. Secretary Forrestal labored unceasingly to overcome the long-standing rivalries that could not be swept away by an act of Congress. His chief problem was that of defining specific roles and missions of each branch of the service and in determining budgetary allocations to carry out those functions. After a series of conferences within the Defense Department he submitted a new definition of functions to me and recommended that the new statement be substituted for the Executive Order which I had issued at the time the law was enacted. After studying his recommendations, I rescinded my original order and approved on March 27, 1948, the promulgation of the new statement of functions with minor modifications.

During the first year of operation of the National Military Establishment it became apparent to me that the Secretary of Defense needed additional authority to meet his responsibilities. It was clear that the act should be amended to define and strengthen the authority of the Secretary; to authorize an Under Secretary of Defense; to provide the Joint Chiefs of Staff with a chairman; to remove the service Secretaries from the National Security Council, leaving the Secretary of Defense the sole representative of the military; and to correct numerous administrative inefficiencies that a year's experience had revealed.

I sent a message to the Congress on March 5, 1949, proposing these revisions in the National Security Act. On the whole, the recommendations I made progressed smoothly through the processes of legislation, but in the weeks that followed a wide-open battle developed in the press between elements of the Navy and the Air Force.

The conflict resulted from an action by the new Secretary of Defense, Louis A. Johnson, who had succeeded Secretary Forrestal in March. Secretary Johnson canceled the construction of the Navy's new super-carrier. Dispute also arose over anonymous charges alleging irregularities in the Air Force's procurement of the B-36 and the questioning of its combat effectiveness. Some newspapers and the radio were used to level insinuations of improper conduct against almost everyone who favored unification policies that in any way restricted the Navy.

The battle took on the aspects of a revolt of the entire Navy. Secretary John L. Sullivan of the Navy resigned in protest of Johnson's cancellation of the carrier contract, and it finally became necessary for me to replace Admiral Louis E. Denfeld as Chief of Naval Operations in a move to restore discipline. Finally agreement was reached on the necessary revisions, and on August 10, 1949, I signed into law the National Security Act Amendments of 1949, thus moving a step nearer true unification of the armed forces. To me, the passage of the National Security Act and its strengthening amendments represented one of the outstanding achievements of my administration.

To my regret, Congress did not take the other basic step in the field of military legislation which I have always considered of paramount importance to our security. And that was legislation aimed at providing a fair and adequate universal training program. I had asked for this first in the fall of 1945, but no action was forthcoming.

In December 1946, however, I appointed an Advisory Commission on Universal Military Training to study the basic needs as well as the various plans for universal training in relation to over-all planning for national security. I asked the committee[1] to meet with me on December

---

[1] The committee consisted of the following members: Dr. Karl T. Compton,

20, and I took occasion at that time to tell them what my thoughts were on the subject.

"I don't like to think of it," I said, "as a universal military training program. I want it to be a universal training program, giving our young people a background in the disciplinary approach of getting along with one another, informing them of their physical make-up, and what it means to take care of this temple which God gave us. If we get that instilled into them, and then instill into them a responsibility which begins in the township, in the city ward, the first thing you know we will have sold our Republic to the coming generations as Madison and Hamilton and Jefferson sold it in the first place."

After nearly six months of intensive study and a series of hearings in which more than two hundred witnesses were interviewed, the Commission reported its findings to me in June 1947. The members, as a result of their investigations, had arrived at the unanimous conclusion that universal training was an essential element in an integrated program of national security designed to safeguard the United States and to enable it to fulfill its responsibilities to the cause of world peace and the success of the United Nations.

The 445-page report listed three reasons for this conclusion:

1. One of the deterrents to the effectiveness of the United Nations was the belief of other nations that the United States was stripping itself of the strength necessary to support its moral leadership and was thus encouraging other powers to plan campaigns of aggression.

2. Universal training offered the only method through which we could insure a sufficient number and dispersal of trained military manpower without overburdening the country's economy through the maintenance of a huge standing Army, Navy, Air Force, and Marine Corps.

3. By making war universal, devastating, and immediate in its impact, the atomic bomb and new developments in warfare had created a need for trained men in every city and town who would be available at once in an emergency.

The Commission recommended the adoption of universal training for every qualified male citizen for a period of not less than six months.

---

president of the Massachusetts Institute of Technology, chairman; Dr. Harold W. Dodds, president of Princeton University; Joseph E. Davies, former Ambassador to Russia; Truman K. Gibson, Jr., former civilian aide to the Secretary of War; Dr. Daniel Poling, editor of the *Christian Herald*; Mrs. Anna Rosenberg, public and industrial relations consultant; Samuel I. Rosenman, former special counsel to the President; the Reverend Edmund A. Walsh, vice-president of Georgetown University; and Charles E. Wilson, president of the General Electric Corporation.

Every feature of the program was carefully detailed as to the military, educational, physical, moral, and spiritual training needed.

The plan submitted by the Commission in its report was a thoroughly studied elaboration of the views which I had expressed to my Cabinet almost two years before. I had hoped that publication of this report by a group of distinguished and representative Americans would move Congress to action, but again I was to be disappointed.

Three years after the Commission submitted its report I was still trying to get Congress to pass universal training legislation. One of the compelling reasons that kept me urging a training program was the need to do something about the thirty-four per cent of our young men who had been rejected as draftees and volunteers on the grounds of physical defects. I was sure that a large number of that thirty-four per cent could be made physically fit and self-supporting citizens if they had the right sort of treatment.

I am morally certain that if Congress had enacted this program in 1945, when I first recommended it, we would have had a pool of basically trained men, which would have caused the Soviets to hesitate and perhaps not bring on the Berlin crisis or the Korean aggression.

Time was when the United States could be content with a small force of professional soldiers. Unfortunately that day is past. Military strength is now a vital factor in political policy, and both diplomatic and strategic considerations must be blended with care if the nation's policy is to be effective in maintaining the peace.

A President has to know what is going on all around the world in order to be ready to act when action is needed. The President must have all the facts that may affect the foreign policy or the military policy of the United States. Of course he must know what is going on at home, because the attitude of the people of the United States, who, in the final analysis, are the government, must be favorable to any action he takes.

Before 1946 such information as the President needed was being collected in several different places in the government. The War Department had an Intelligence Division—G-2—and the Navy had an intelligence setup of its own—the ONI. The Department of State, on the one hand, got its information through diplomatic channels, while the Treasury and the Departments of Commerce and Agriculture each had channels for gathering information from different parts of the world—on monetary, economic, and agricultural matters.

During World War II the Federal Bureau of Investigation had some operations abroad, and in addition the Office of Strategic Services, which was set up by President Roosevelt during the war and placed under the direction of General William J. Donovan, operated abroad to gather information.

This scattered method of getting information for the various departments of the government first struck me as being badly organized when I was in the Senate. Our Senate committees, hearing witnesses from the executive departments, were often struck by the fact that different agencies of the government came up with different and conflicting facts on similar subjects. It was not at first apparent that this was due to the un-co-ordinated methods of obtaining information. Since then, however, I have often thought that if there had been something like co-ordination of information in the government it would have been more difficult, if not impossible, for the Japanese to succeed in the sneak attack at Pearl Harbor. In those days the military did not know everything the State Department knew, and the diplomats did not have access to all the Army and Navy knew. The Army and the Navy, in fact, had only a very informal arrangement to keep each other informed as to their plans.

In other words, there had never been much attention paid to any centralized intelligence organization in our government. Apparently the United States saw no need for a really comprehensive system of foreign intelligence until World War II placed American fighting men on the continents of Europe, Asia, and Africa and on the islands of the Atlantic and the Pacific.

The war taught us this lesson—that we had to collect intelligence in a manner that would make the information available where it was needed and when it was wanted, in an intelligent and understandable form. If it is not intelligent and understandable, it is useless.

On becoming President, I found that the needed intelligence information was not co-ordinated at any one place. Reports came across my desk on the same subject at different times from the various departments, and these reports often conflicted. Consequently I asked Admiral Leahy if anything was being done to improve the system. Leahy told me that in 1944, at President Roosevelt's direction, he had referred to the Joint Chiefs of Staff a plan for centralized intelligence work prepared by General Donovan. This plan, so Leahy told me, provided for an organization directly under the President and responsible only to him. The Navy, however, had worked out a counterproposal under which there would be a central agency to serve as an over-all intelligence organization, but with each of the departments responsible for national security having a stake in it. Much of the original work on this project was done by Rear Admiral Sidney W. Souers, Deputy Chief of Naval Intelligence.

Sometime later I asked Secretary of State Byrnes to submit his recommendations for a way to co-ordinate intelligence services among the departments, explaining that I had already asked Leahy to look into the subject but that I wanted the State Department's recommendations since the State Department would need to play an important role in the operation.

Secretary Byrnes took the position that such an organization should be responsible to the Secretary of State and advised me that he should be in control of all intelligence. The Army and the Navy, on the other hand, strongly objected. They maintained that every department required its own intelligence but that there was a great need for a central organization to gather together all information that had to do with over-all national policy. Under such an organization there would be a pool of information, and each agency would contribute to it. This pool would make it possible for those who were responsible for establishing policies in foreign political and military fields to draw on authoritative intelligence for their guidance.

In January 1946 I held a series of meetings in my office to examine the various plans suggested for a centralized intelligence authority. My inclination was to favor the plan worked out by the Army and the Navy, with the aid of Admiral Souers, and I was ready to put it into effect. Harold Smith, Director of the Budget, however, urged postponement so that the people in his Bureau could make a thorough analysis of it.

"Do you mean from a budgetary standpoint?" asked Judge Rosenman, who was present at the meeting.

"No," Smith replied. "The intelligence aspects."

"Harold," I said, turning to Smith, "I know you have expert intelligence men in your office, but I like this plan. If your people can make it better, that's all right. But I have been waiting to do this for a long time. So you appoint your men and meet in Admiral Leahy's office with Admiral Souers, get the people from the Department of Justice, and let's get it done."

It was only natural that there were some minor disagreements. The Justice Department, for instance, raised certain objections on behalf of Director J. Edgar Hoover of the FBI, but there were no major differences of opinion, and substantial agreement was soon reached.

On January 20, 1946, I issued an Executive Order setting up the Central Intelligence Group. I placed it under the supervision of a National Intelligence Authority, which was made up of the Secretaries of State, War, and the Navy and my personal representative, Admiral Leahy. I also appointed a Director of Central Intelligence, naming Rear Admiral Souers.

Before issuing the Executive Order setting up the new agency, I ordered the Office of Strategic Services dissolved. Part of their staff and work was taken over by the State Department and part by the War Department.

Admiral Souers had been waiting to return to private life, and I assured him that as soon as the Army, Navy, and State Departments would agree upon a candidate acceptable to me I would release him. About six months later General Hoyt Vandenberg was unanimously recommended, and I appointed him to be the first permanent director. I was glad, however, that Admiral Souers agreed to stay on as consultant to Vandenberg.

Under the new intelligence arrangement I now began to receive a daily digest and summary of the information obtained abroad. I also was given all information sent abroad by the State Department to our ambassadors, as well as that sent by the Navy and War Departments to their forces, whenever these messages might have influence on our foreign policy. Here, at last, a co-ordinated method had been worked out, and a practical way had been found for keeping the President informed as to what was known and what was going on.

The Director of the Central Intelligence Agency, as the Central Intelligence Group was renamed in 1947, became, usually, my first caller of the day. As long as Admiral Leahy continued to be the Chief of Staff to the Commander in Chief, he would join the Director in the conference with me, and upon Leahy's retirement I brought Admiral Souers to the White House in the new capacity of Special Assistant to the President for Intelligence. Thus he, too, sat in with me every morning when the Director of Central Intelligence came in with the daily digest.

At Potsdam I had been impressed with the co-operation between our State, Army, and Navy Departments. Through a co-ordinating committee they had worked out a way of tackling common problems without the usual jurisdictional conflicts. When I assigned a problem, I received prompt and clear-cut answers combining their best judgments. This proved very helpful, and before leaving Potsdam I informed the three departments that I liked this system and requested them to continue to co-operate on all common problems through this committee.

I had the success of this method in mind when, as plans were being drawn up for the unification of the military services, I insisted that policy unification be provided at the same time. I wanted one top-level permanent setup in the government to concern itself with advising the President on high policy decisions concerning the security of the nation. And such a setup was provided by the National Security Act of 1947, which created the National Security Council and also renamed the Central Intelligence Group the Central Intelligence Agency, placing it under the supervision of the NSC.

The creation of the National Security Council added a badly needed new facility to the government. This was now the place in the government where military, diplomatic, and resources problems could be studied and continually appraised. This new organization gave us a running balance and a perpetual inventory of where we stood and where we were going on all strategic questions affecting the national security.

The National Security Council originally was set up with seven members. Besides the President, there were the Secretary of State, the Secretary of Defense, the Secretary of the Army, the Secretary of the Navy, the Secretary of the Air Force, and the chairman of the National Securities Resources Board. The original members of the Council, in addition to myself, were Secretary of State George C. Marshall, Secretary of Defense James V. Forrestal, Secretary of the Air Force W. Stuart Symington, Secretary of the Army Kenneth C. Royall, Secretary of the Navy John L. Sullivan, and the chairman of the National Security Resources Board, Arthur M. Hill.

In 1949 I asked the Congress to make a change in the membership of the Council, and it has since been composed of the President, the Vice-President (added to the list by the Senate), the Secretaries of State and Defense, the chairman of the NSRB, and the President has now statutory authority to add such other heads of executive departments as he may want there.

There was a tendency at first for the members to bring along a needlessly large number of advisers and assistants. It became necessary for me to order in July 1950 that the number of persons in attendance should be held down to those designated by law and only such others as were approved by me or necessary for a particular discussion.

I was gratified that Congress acted on my recommendation to provide a central place in the Executive Department for the study of policy problems. I used the National Security Council only as a place for recommendations to be worked out. Like the Cabinet, the Council does not make decisions. The policy itself has to come down from the President, as all final decisions have to be made by him.

A "vote" in the National Security Council is merely a procedural step. It never decides policy. That can be done only with the President's approval and expression of approval to make it an official policy of the United States. Even when the President sits as chairman in a meeting of the National Security Council and indicates agreement, nothing is final until the Council formally submits a document to the President. The document states that the Council met and recommended such-and-such an action, "which met with your approval." When the President signs this document, the recommendation then becomes a part of the policy of the government.

The National Security Council built a small but highly competent permanent staff which was selected for its objectivity and lack of political ties. It was our plan that the staff should serve as a continuing organization regardless of what administration was in power, for it is vitally important to the national security program that the staff working on the program should be continuous.

Tied in with the National Security Council staff, as an adjunct, is the Central Intelligence Agency, which operates in this way: Each time the Council is about to consider a certain policy—let us say a policy having to do with Southeast Asia—it immediately calls upon the CIA to present an estimate of the effects such a policy is likely to have. The Director of the CIA sits with the staff of the National Security Council and continually informs as they go along. The estimates he submits represents the judgment of the CIA and a cross section of the judgments of all the advisory councils of the CIA. These are G-2, A-2, the ONI, the State Department, the FBI, and the Director of Intelligence of the AEC. The Secretary of State then makes the final recommendation of policy, and the President makes the final decision.

There were times during the early days of the National Security Council when one or two of its members tried to change it into an operating super-cabinet on the British model. Secretary Forrestal and Secretary Johnson, for instance, would at times put pressure on the Executive Secretary. What they wanted him to do was to assume the authority of supervising other agencies of the government and see that the approved decisions of the Council were carried out. The Executive Secretary very properly declined to do this, stating that if it had been the intention of the Congress for him to have that power it would have been specified in the act. As a matter of fact, the draft of the law had called for a "director," and to preclude any misunderstanding, that title had been changed to "executive secretary" by Congress.

Secretary of Defense Forrestal for some time had been advocating our using the British Cabinet system as a model in the operation of the government. There is much to this idea—in some ways a Cabinet government is more efficient—but under the British system there is a group responsibility of the Cabinet. Under our system the responsibility rests on one man—the President. To change it, we would have to change the Constitution, and I think we have been doing very well under our Constitution. We will do well to stay with it.

CHAPTER 5

Americans have always had friendly feelings toward the Chinese. American missionaries, American doctors, and American teachers have spent many years in China, and their Christian and humanitarian efforts were long supported with real fervor by the people at home. Furthermore, within the memory of many Americans, China had shaken off the yoke of monarchy and had begun to wrest herself free from the medieval institutions that were so deeply rooted in that ancient land. This struggle, however had not yet attained success when in 1931 the Japanese began their long program of aggression which, as the years went by, brought ever more extensive areas of the once great kingdom under Japanese control.

The fall of 1945 had brought the United States face to face with the serious complications which had been building up in China over the years. Few realized the depth of the split within China, the tenuous hold of the National Government over outlying areas, and the lack of popular participation in the country's government.

We in America always think of China as a nation. But the truth is that in 1945 China was only a geographical expression. Not since the Manchu Empire broke up in 1911 had there been in China a central government with authority over all the land. This was the state of China when V-J Day came. Chiang Kai-shek's authority was confined to the southwest corner, with the rest of South China and East China occupied by the Japanese. North China was controlled by the Communists and Manchuria by the Russians. There had been no roots of any kind of central Chinese government north of the Yangtze River.

The task of creating a new nation was colossal. President Roosevelt had built up the idea that China was a great power because he looked to the future and wanted to encourage the Chinese people. In reality it would be only with the greatest difficulty that Chiang Kai-shek could even reoccupy South China. To get to North China he would need an agreement with the Communists, and he could never move into Manchuria without an agreement with the Communists and the Russians. It was impossible for Chiang to occupy Northeast China and South Central China with the Communists in between the rail lines. It was perfectly clear to us that if we told the Japanese to lay down their arms immediately and march to the seaboard the entire country would be taken over by the Communists. We therefore had to take the step of using the enemy as a garrison until we could airlift Chinese National troops to South China and send marines to guard the seaports. So the Japanese were instructed to hold their places and maintain order. In due course Chinese troops under Chiang Kai-shek would appear, the Japanese would surrender to them, march to the seaports, and we would send them back to Japan. This operation of using the Japanese to hold off the Communists was a joint decision of the State and Defense Departments which I approved.

Just before Ambassador Hurley returned to Washington in the fall of 1945, he sent a message which included a summary of our wartime approach to China.

"On his return from China in the summer of 1944," Ambassador Hurley wrote, "Vice President Wallace advised President Roosevelt that in his opinion the National Government of the Republic of China would soon collapse. Subsequently, two United States Senators [Brewster and Chandler] predicted that nothing short of a miracle could prevent collapse of the government of China. These opinions were quite generally held by American and Chinese civil and military officials. It was with a full realization of this situation that President Roosevelt sent me to China as his personal representative. President Roosevelt's directives to me were principally as follows:

"1. Prevent the collapse of the National Government of China.

"2. Keep the Chinese armies in the war.

"3. Harmonize the relations between the Chinese and American military establishment.

"4. Unify the anti-Japanese forces of China. . . .

"It may be broadly stated . . . that during the war the objectives of the American policy in China were military. Even economic directives had military objectives. . . ."

Hurley and General Wedemeyer, as chief of staff to Chiang Kai-shek, had done much to give effect to the first three points. The critical one, however, was the fourth one.

The problem of Communism in China differed considerably from political problems elsewhere. Chiang Kai-shek was not confronted by a militant political minority scattered throughout the population but by a rival government that controlled a definite portion of the territory, with about one fourth of the total population.

Our position in China offered us little choice. We could not simply wash our hands of the situation. There were still nearly three million Japanese in China, over one million of them military. Unless we made certain that this force was eliminated, the Japanese, even in defeat, might gain control of China simply by their ability to tip the scales in the contest for power.

The other alternative was equally impracticable. That would have been to throw into China unlimited resources and large armies of American soldiers to defeat the Communists, remove the Japanese from the mainland, and compel Russian withdrawal from Manchuria by force. The American people would never stand for such an undertaking.

We decided, therefore, that the only course of action open to us was to assist in every way in the preservation of peace in China, to support the Generalissimo politically, economically, and, within limits, militarily. But we could not become involved in a fratricidal war in China.

General Wedemeyer described the situation in the final days of the war against the Japanese in these words:

"Unquestionably the Chinese people have many grievances concerning their treatment by warlords and unscrupulous, incompetent officials. However, a satisfactory solution to the China problem or world order will never be accomplished by civil war in this area.

"Based on limited knowledge, neither the Chinese Communist Party nor the Kuomintang is democratic in spirit, or intentions. China is not prepared for a democratic form of government with 95 per cent of her people illiterate and for many other cogent reasons. The inarticulate masses of China desire peace and are not particularly interested in or aware of the various ideologies represented. An opportunity to work, to obtain food and clothing for their families and a happy peaceful environment are their primary concern.

"Conditions here could best be handled by a benevolent despot or a military dictator, whether such dictator be a Communist or a Kuomintang matters very little. From my observation practically all Chinese officials are interested in their selfish aggrandizement. I retain the impression that the Generalissimo's leadership offers best opportunity at

this time for stabilization in the area, political and economic." (Italics added.)

Throughout the war the United States had demonstrated her friendship for China in more than one way. Appropriations for military and economic aid, for example, had exceeded one and a half billion dollars. We had given strong diplomatic support to China while T. V. Soong negotiated with Stalin in Moscow. Out of these talks came the Treaty of Friendship between China and the Soviet Union.

Ambassador Hurley was engaged in an effort to get the Chinese Communists and the government of Chiang Kai-shek to sit down together and solve their differences peacefully. The Ambassador had sent me a series of long cables in which he gave me his views on the situation. He had gone to China at first not as our diplomatic representative but as President Roosevelt's personal representative. He was critical of the State Department, and in many of the cables and reports that I received from him he questioned the judgment and ability of the career diplomats. He felt very strongly, as I did, that America ought to be the champion of anti-imperialism in Asia. Hurley complained that the State Department did not give his reports and recommendations the priority he thought they deserved.

Finally, on September 10, 1945, he restated once again, as he had done on several previous occasions, what he understood to have been President Roosevelt's long-range aims in Asia. He recited what he had done to further these aims and quoted instances of decisions made in Washington which he thought differed in their aims from what he thought the wisest course. Then he asked for permission to return to Washington. "I would like," he cabled to the Secretary of State, "to have an opportunity to discuss the American Asiatic policy with you, sir, and the President."

After he had come back, Hurley called at the White House with Secretary Byrnes, and a week later both Hurley and Wedemeyer came in for a more extended discussion. I made it clear to them that it would be our policy to support Chiang Kai-shek but that we would not be driven into fighting Chiang's battles for him.

General Hurley reported to me that, in spite of all weaknesses which he and Wedemeyer recognized, the prospects for peaceful development in China were favorable. Economically, China's potential was not substantially different from the situation just before 1937. The main problem ahead seemed to be not production but distribution. Financially, our continued aid had placed China in a better position than she had known in years, and politically, General Hurley had just succeeded in bringing the Communist leader, Mao Tse-tung, to Chungking for direct discussion with the National Government leaders. Out of these discussions there came an agreement between the Chinese leaders which was published on October 11, just two days before Hurley first called at the White House. At that moment there was reason to hope that China's problems might be solved.

Hurley had witnessed the preliminary signing of this agreement, and he told me that it promised to lead to true peace in China. The agreement called for a constitutional convention, a national assembly that would write a new constitution, and included provisions that would enable all political parties to take part. Chiang Kai-shek, apparently, would have the strongest voice in this convention since more of his followers would be seated than Communists.

An interim council of forty, appointed by Chiang Kai-shek but with not more than half from his party, would run affairs until the new constitution could come into force. Chiang Kai-shek would have a veto over any of the council's decisions, although three fifths of the council could override such vetoes.

This was a good agreement, and I congratulated Hurley on the fine work that had made it possible. However, the agreement never bore results.

Chiang Kai-shek's forces were moving into areas held by the Japanese, with a large part of his troops being ferried north by our Air Force transports. We had also landed fifty thousand of our marines at several important ports so that, through these ports, the removal of the Japanese could be carried on. The Communists wanted the National Government to stop these troop movements, for they believed that Chiang was taking advantage of the situation to strengthen his positions against them. Nor were they passive about it. They cut the rail lines wherever they could, and the Chungking government soon began receiving reports that the Chinese Communists, contrary to the agreement, were moving into Manchuria. Resentment was rising on both sides as the charges and countercharges increased.

On November 4 our embassy in Chungking reported that civil war seemed to be threatening, and the Political Consultative Conference, which was scheduled to convene November 20, failed to meet. On November 25 Chou En-lai, the principal representative of the Communists in Chungking, left for Yenan, and the next day his first deputy followed him. By now there were reports of armed clashes. I discussed the seriousness of the situation with Hurley at the White House on November 27, and we agreed that it would be best if he returned to Chungking without delay. He assured me that he would only wind up a few personal matters and then return to China.

This conversation took place about 11:30 A.M., but less than two hours later, while the members of the Cabinet were with me for the weekly Cabinet luncheon, I was called to the telephone. One of the White House correspondents called from the National Press Club and, to my astonishment, told me that Ambassador Hurley, in a talk with newspapermen, had attacked the administration, the State Department, our foreign policy, and me personally.

To me, this was an utterly inexplicable about-face, and what had caused it I cannot imagine even yet. I realized, however, that Hurley would have to go, and the Cabinet concurred. The same day I learned to my surprise that a "letter of resignation" from Hurley was given by him to the press; but he would have been out, with or without that letter.

Hurley was an impetuous sort of person. A few weeks later—in January 1946—he made a special effort to see my press secretary, Charlie Ross. He explained to Ross that he was anxious to serve me anywhere and at any time, and he wanted Ross to tell me that nothing he had said at the time of his resignation had been intended as a personal criticism of me.

"He begged me to believe," Ross reported to me, "that he was 'in your corner.'"

Hurley went on to say to Ross, "Byrnes is a smart enough man . . . but he hasn't been given sufficient information by the 'flagpole sitters' in the State Department. . . . There is no reason for Byrnes's agitation over Chinese-Russian relations because they are all spelled out in the agreement by the Chinese and the Russians signed last July or August. . . ." The reason Byrnes had no need to worry was that, according to Hurley, "Stalin keeps his word."

China appeared now to be headed for more trouble. We could not send in the kind of military force that could assure that Chiang Kai-shek would prevail. The only thing we could do was to exert whatever influence we might have to prevent civil war. The man for this job would have to possess unique qualifications and rare skill. At the Cabinet luncheon on the day of Hurley's Press Club speech the name of General Marshall was brought up. He had just turned over his duties as Chief of Staff of the Army to General Eisenhower. No man probably had more fully deserved an honorable and restful retirement than Marshall. Yet I could think of no one who would be better qualified for a difficult mission to China.

I went to the telephone in the Red Room of the White House and called the general at his home in Leesburg. Without any preparation I told him: "General, I want you to go to China for me." Marshall said only, "Yes, Mr. President," and hung up abruptly.

When General Marshall came to the White House two days later to discuss his mission with Byrnes and me, I asked him why he had hung up on me without asking an questions. The reason, he explained to me, was that Mrs. Marshall and he had just driven up to the house, and he had been in the process of unloading some of their belongings when the phone rang. He had not wanted Mrs. Marshall, who was concerned about his health, to know how short-lived their retirement would be, and so he had hung up before she might hear any part of the conversation. He expected to break the news to her gradually, but when he turned on the radio a few minutes later, the very first thing she heard was the news flash announcing the general's mission.

"There was the devil to pay," he confessed.

I went over the Chinese situation with Marshall and Byrnes at great length that afternoon. At Marshall's request, I told him to go ahead and work out with the State Department a set of instructions based on our discussions that would constitute my directive to him on his mission.

These instructions were drafted between Marshall and the State Department, and on December 11 I reviewed them in detail in another conference with Byrnes and Marshall. The final document was handed to Marshall by me, in the presence of Under Secretary of State Dean Acheson, and here are the exact instructions that document contained:

Washington, December 15, 1945

My dear General Marshall:

On the eve of your departure for China I want to repeat to you my appreciation of your willingness to undertake this difficult mission.

I have the utmost confidence in your ability to handle the task before you but, to guide you in so far as you may find it helpful, I will give you some of the thoughts, ideas and objectives which Secretary Byrnes and I have in mind with regard to your mission.

I attach several documents which I desire should be considered as part of this letter. One is a statement of U.S. policy toward China which was, I understand, prepared after consultation with you and with officials of the Department. The second is a memorandum from the Secretary of State to the War Department in regard to China. And the third is a copy of my press release on policy in China. I understand that these documents have been shown to you and received your approval.

The fact that I have asked you to go to China is the clearest evidence of my very real concern with regard to the situation there. Secretary Byrnes and I are both anxious that the unification of China by peaceful, democratic methods be achieved as soon as possible. It is my desire that you, as my Special Representative, bring to bear in an appropriate and practicable manner the influence of the United States to this end.

Specifically, I desire that you endeavor to persuade the Chinese Government to call a national conference of representatives of the major political elements to bring about the unification of China and, concurrently, to effect a cessation of hostilities, particularly in North China.

It is my understanding that there is now in session in Chungking a People's Consultative Council made up of representatives of the various political elements, including the Chinese Communists. The meeting of this Council should furnish you with a convenient opportunity for discussions with the various political leaders.

Upon the success of your efforts, as outlined above, will depend largely, of course, the success of our plans for evacuating Japanese troops from China, particularly North China, and for the subsequent withdrawal of our own armed forces from China. I am particularly desirous that both be accomplished as soon as possible.

In your conversations with Chiang Kai-shek and other Chinese leaders you are authorized to speak with the utmost frankness. Particularly, you may state, in connection with the Chinese desire for credits, technical assistance in the economic field, and military assistance (I have in mind the proposed U.S. military advisory group which I have approved in principle), that a China disunited and torn by civil strife could not be considered realistically as a proper place for American assistance along the lines enumerated.

I am anxious that you keep Secretary Byrnes and me currently informed of the progress of your negotiations and of obstacles you may encounter. You will have our full support and we shall endeavor at all times to be as helpful to you as possible.

The first of the documents attached was entitled "U.S. Policy Toward China."

"The Government of the U.S.," it read, "holds that peace and prosperity of the world in this new unexplored era ahead depend upon the ability of the sovereign nations to combine for collective security in the United Nations organization.

"It is the firm belief of this Government that a strong, united and democratic China is of the utmost importance to the success of this United Nations organization and for world peace. A China disorganized and divided either by foreign aggression, such as that undertaken by the Japanese, or by violent internal strife, is an undermining influence to world stability and peace, now and in the future. The U. S. Government has long subscribed to the principle that the management of internal affairs is the responsibility of the peoples of the sovereign nations. Events in this country, however, would indicate that a breach of peace anywhere in the world threatens the peace of the entire world. It is thus in the most vital interest of the United States and all the United Nations that the people of China overlook no opportunity to adjust their internal differences promptly by means of peaceful negotiations.

"The Government of the U.S. believes it essential:

"(1) That a cessation of hostilities be arranged between the armies of the National Government and the Chinese Communists and other dissident Chinese armed forces for the purpose of completing the return of all China to effective Chinese control, including the immediate evacuation of the Japanese forces. The U.S. is prepared, if so requested by the National Government of China, to assist in arranging for necessary pledges and to request the Governments of the U.K. and the U.S.S.R. to join in this effort.

"(2) That a national conference of representatives of major political elements be arranged to develop an early solution to the present internal strife—a solution which will bring about the unification of China.

"The U.S. and the other United Nations have recognized the present National Government of the Republic of China as the only legal government in China. It is the proper instrument to achieve the objective of a unified China.

"The U.S. and the U.K. in the Cairo Declaration in 1943 and the U.S.S.R., by adhering to the Potsdam Declaration of last July and by the Sino-Soviet Treaty and Agreements of August 1945, are all committed to the liberation of China, including the return of Manchuria to Chinese control. These agreements were made with the National Government of the Republic of China.

"In continuation of the constant and close collaboration with the National Government of the Republic of China in the prosecution of this war, in consonance with the Potsdam Declaration, and to remove possibility of Japanese influence remaining in China, the U.S. has assumed a definite obligation in the disarmament and evacuation of Japanese troops. Accordingly, the U.S. has been assisting and will continue to assist the National Government of the Republic of China in effecting the disarmament and evacuation of Japanese troops in the liberated areas. The U. S. Marines are in North China for that purpose. For the same reason, the U.S. will continue to furnish military supplies and to assist the Chinese National Government in the further transportation of Chinese troops so that it can re-establish control over the liberated areas of China, including Manchuria.

"To facilitate arrangement for cessation of hostilities and pending provisional agreement in the proposed national conference, National Government troops will not be transported by the U.S. into areas, such as north China, when their introduction would prejudice the objectives of the military truce and the political negotiations.

"The U.S. recognizes and will continue to recognize the National Government of China and cooperate with it in international affairs and specifically in eliminating Japanese influence from China. The U.S. is convinced that a prompt arrangement for the cessation of hostilities is essential to the effective achievement of this end. Incidental effects of U.S. assistance upon any dissident Chinese elements will be avoided in so far as possible. Beyond these incidental effects U.S. support will not extend to U.S. military intervention to influence the course of any Chinese internal strife.

"The U.S. is cognizant that the present National Government of China is a 'one-party government' and believes that peace, unity and democratic reform in China will be furthered if the basis of this Government is broaded to include other political elements in the country. Hence, the U.S. strongly advocates that the national conference of representatives of major political elements in the country agree upon arrangements which would give those elements a fair and effective representation in the Chinese National Government. It is recognized that this would require modification of the one-party 'political tutelage' established as an interim arrangement in the progress of the nation toward democracy by the father of the Chinese Republic, Doctor Sun Yat-sen.

"The existence of autonomous armies such as that of the Communist army is inconsistent with, and actually makes impossible, political unity in China. With the institution of a broadly representative government, autonomous armies should be eliminated as such and all armed forces in China integrated effectively into the Chinese National Army.

"In line with its often expressed views regarding self-determination, the U. S. Government considers that the detailed steps necessary to the achievement of political unity in China must be worked out by the Chinese themselves and that intervention by any foreign government in these matters would be inappropriate. The U. S. Government feels, however, that China has a clear responsibility to the other United Nations to eliminate armed conflict within its territory as constituting a threat to world stability and peace—a responsibility which is shared by the National Government and all Chinese political and military groups. It is to assist the Chinese in the discharge of its responsibility that the U. S. Government is willing to participate and to request U.K. and U.S.S.R. participation in arranging the necessary pledges to assure the prompt cessation of such armed conflict.

"As China moves toward peace and unity along the lines described above, the U.S. would be prepared to assist the National Government in every reasonable way to rehabilitate the country, improve the agrarian and industrial economy and establish a military organization capable of discharging Chinese national and international responsibilities for the maintenance of peace and order. Specifically, the U.S. would be prepared to grant a Chinese request for an American military advisory group in China, to dispatch such other advisers in the economic and financial fields as the Chinese Government might require and which this Government can supply, and to give favorable consideration to Chinese requests for credits and loans under reasonable conditions for projects which contribute towards the development of a healthy economy in China and healthy trade relations between China and the U.S.

"It must be clearly recognized that the attainment of the objectives herein stated will call for an expenditure of resources by the U.S. and the maintenance for the time being of United States military and naval forces in China. These expenditures, however, will be minute in comparison to those which this nation has already been compelled to make in the restoration of the peace which was broken by German and Japanese aggression. They will be infinitesimal by comparison to a recurrence of global warfare in which the new and terrible weapons that now exist would certainly be employed. The purpose for which the United States made a tremendous sacrifice of treasure and life must not be jeopardized."

The second document attached was a memorandum for the War Department which read as follows:

"The President and the Secretary of State are both anxious that the unification of China by peaceful democratic methods be achieved as soon as possible.

"At a public hearing before the Foreign Relations Committee of the Senate on December 7, the Secretary of State said:

" 'During the war the immediate goal of the United States in China was to promote a military union of the several factions in order to bring their combined power to bear upon our common enemy, Japan. Our longer-range goal, then as now, and a goal of at least equal importance, is the development of a strong, united and democratic China.

" 'To achieve this longer-range goal, it is essential that the Central Government of China as well as the various dissident elements approach the settlement of their differences with a genuine willingness to compromise. We believe, as we have long believed and consistently demonstrated, that the government of Generalissimo Chiang Kai-shek affords the most satisfactory base for a developing democracy. But we also believe that it must be broadened to include the representatives of those large and well-organized groups who are now without any voice in the government of China.

" 'This problem is not an easy one. It requires tact and discretion, patience and restraint. It will not be solved by the Chinese leaders themselves. To the extent that our influence is a factor, success will depend upon our capacity to exercise that influence in the light of shifting conditions in such a way as to encourage concessions by the Central Government, by the so-called communists, and by the other factions.'

"The President has asked General Marshall to go to China as his Special Representative for the purpose of bringing to bear in an appropriate and practicable manner the influence of the United States for the achievement of the ends set forth above. Specifically, General Marshall will endeavor to influence the Chinese Government to call a national conference of representatives of the major political elements to bring about the unification of China and, concurrently, effect a cessation of hostilities, particularly in North China.

"In response to General Wedemeyer's recent messages, the State Department requests the War Department to arrange for directions to him stipulating that:

"(1) He may put into effect the arrangements to assist the Chinese National Government in transporting troops to Manchurian ports, including the logistical support for such troops;

"(2) He may also proceed to put into effect the stepped-up arrangements for the evacuation of Japanese troops from the China theater;

"(3) Pending the outcome of General Marshall's discussions with Chinese leaders in Chungking for the purpose of arranging a national conference of representatives of the major political elements and for a cessation of hostilities, further transportation of Chinese troops to North China, except as North China ports may be necessary for the movement of troops and supplies into Manchuria, will be held in abeyance;

"(4) Arrangements for transportation of Chinese troops into North China ports may be immediately perfected, but not communicated to the Chinese government. Such arrangements will be executed when General Marshall determines either (a) that the movement of Chinese troops to North China can be carried out consistently with his negotiations, or (b) that the negotiations between the Chinese groups have failed or show no prospect of success and that the circumstances are such as to make the movement necessary to effectuate the surrender terms and to secure the long-term interests of the United States in the maintenance of international peace."

The third enclosure to the letter of instructions was a copy of the press release, which was essentially the same as the statement of policy in Enclosure 1.

Marshall left Washington the next day, December 15, by air. He arrived in China on December 20 and began at once to study the situation. His messages, sent to me through War Department facilities, unfolded a story that, although told in simple words, had all the elements of the historic drama of Chinese history.

General Marshall began his work in China with caution. He spent several days merely listening to people. He talked at length to Chiang Kai-shek, who had little to say about the Communists but showed much concern over the continued presence of the Russians in Manchuria. Marshall also interviewed party leaders of all shadings, including Communists, spoke to numerous officials of Chiang Kai-shek's government, our own embassy people, correspondents, and other Americans on the spot.

He found everyone favoring a united China but no one with practical answers as to how this ideal might be attained. Marshall pointed out this was precisely the problem on which work needed to be done, and he was able to instigate indirectly a meeting between Kuomintang and Communist leaders.

At this meeting the Communists came forward with a proposal for the cessation of hostilities. The Central Government's reaction to this proposal was entirely uncompromising at first but, following a suggestion from General Marshall, a counterproposal was made. This called for immediate cessation of hostilities, the appointment of representatives to consult with Marshall about methods of enforcing the armistice, and the selection of a commission by the Political Consultative Council to make recommendations regarding disputed areas.

Marshall had already made plans for machinery to enforce the cease-fire. He planned to organize teams consisting of government and Communist representatives, each with an American observer, to give an impartial authority to such field action as might be necessary.

By January 8, 1946, negotiations between representatives of the National Government and the Communist party had progressed to the point where an agreement was almost reached. However, the National Government insisted that they should be permitted to continue their troops movements into the provinces of Jehol and Chahar to occupy places vacated or to be vacated by Soviet troops. The Communists, on the other hand, claimed that the key points had already been taken over by them.

The cease-fire order was scheduled to be read at the opening of the Political Consultative Council at ten o'clock on the morning of January 10. The preceding evening Marshall had been able to persuade Chiang Kai-shek to issue an order without reference to Jehol and Chahar, although the final agreement was not reached until the morning of the tenth, a matter of minutes before the time set for the announcement.

As soon as the cease-fire order was issued, Marshall set into motion the plans for the so-called executive headquarters, which was to be located in Peiping. Some delay was encountered, however, because the Communists found it difficult to bring enough officers to Peiping from their scattered units. However, the machinery proved workable when called into action during these initial days.

Marshall now began to work on the next step, the consolidation of the armed forces in China. Again a tripartite committee setup was agreed on, with Marshall in the role of the adviser.

Throughout these events Marshall did everything he could to avoid any semblance of pressure or dictation. He always waited for the Chinese (of both sides) to ask him to join their talks; otherwise, he talked to them only as one individual to another. This, of course, was a drawn-out process, full of frustrations.

Chiang Kai-shek, for instance, requested Marshall to persuade the Communists to accept the proposals of the Central Government in the Political Consultative Council. Marshall countered this by telling the Generalissimo that he could not see that either side had produced any definite programs or proposed actions. He offered Chiang Kai-shek a draft of a bill which would convert the Central Government from an agency of the Kuomintang (which it then legally was), to a coalition, basing its existence on the national sovereignty of all China. This draft also contained a brief bill of rights.

Marshall decided wisely at this point to remain aloof from the political discussions even though he might officially be asked by both sides to act as mediator. His correct view of his mission was that he was to bring the fighting to an end, if possible. He took pains to avoid matters that were wholly political in nature.

In the military field, however, he took a most active part. He acted as chairman of the Committee of Three to supervise the cease-fire, and he acted as adviser to the committee working on the reorganization of the armies in China.

In the early stages the Communist representatives appeared more tractable to Marshall than the leaders of the Central Government, and it was his impression that the Communists felt that they could win their battle on political grounds more easily than on tactical fighting grounds because they had a more tightly held organization, whereas on the Nationalist side there were many contentious elements. And it was also his impression that the Communists were more ready to take their chances in a struggle conducted in the political arena than were the Nationalists. The Nationalists, so it seemed to Marshall, appeared to be determined to pursue a policy of force which he believed would be their undoing.

On February 4 Marshall could report to me that "affairs are progressing rather favorably." The Political Consultative Council appeared on the way to adopting a path toward democratic reform, and agreement on the reorganization of these armies appeared imminent.

At least once a week and sometimes two and three times a week Marshall would send me a long cable report. He had left instructions that these were to be transmitted to me without delay, and I had charged Dean Acheson, the Under Secretary of State, with the specific responsibility of seeing that every communication from the general to the Department of State was acknowledged or answered within twenty-four hours.

The Marshall messages from China enabled me to follow every step as the story unfolded. The general wrote coldly factual reports that included every detail. I could not have asked for a closer view without being a participant myself.

CHAPTER 6

Early in February 1946, Russia began to make trouble in Manchuria. It was apparent, according to reports reaching me, that the Russians intended to use their promised withdrawal from Manchuria as a lever to gain sweeping privileges in that strategic area.

The treaty of mutual defense concluded between Russia and China in August 1945 had recognized that Manchuria was properly part of China, with the reservation of some rights, such as rail transit, to the Russians. All of Manchuria had been occupied by Russian forces after Russia's entry into the war against Japan. The Russians, in a later agreement with the Chinese government, had promised to withdraw their troops, setting February 1, 1946, as the latest date of withdrawal.

On February 9, 1946, Marshall wrote me that Manchuria was a "festering situation," and he went on to report that he told the Chinese Foreign Minister, "China must proceed with her projected unification at the fastest possible pace so as to eliminate her present vulnerability to Soviet undercover attack, which exists so long as there remains a separate Communist government and a separate Communist army in China.

"Secondly," Marshall wrote me, "I told him that I believed he should make no commitment, formal or informal, with the Soviet which would recognize her claims that war booty consisted of the kind of economic concessions she is demanding. . . .

"I told Wang it was my belief that time was running against the Soviet, since the longer her troops remain in Manchuria the more clearly she becomes a deliberate treaty violator in the eyes of the world. . . ."

Marshall told me that he was reporting to me in great detail "because

I feel that it not only involved me in matters beyond my mission but is perhaps more dangerous to world accord than any other present issue. . . .

"I believe that our Government must shortly do more for China in this matter than give advice. . . .

"We must clear our hands out here as quickly as possible in order to avoid the inevitable Russian recriminations similar to those today regarding the British troops in Greece. I mean by this, we must terminate the 'China Theater of Operations' and in its place quickly develop the military advisory group. (Wedemeyer on my urging is actually but unofficially organizing this group in Nanking.) Also, in this connection, we must move all of the Marines out of China but some reconnaissance and transportation and some housekeeping and local guard units. The timing of this last move requires a critical decision. . . . I am not prepared to advise this action now, but I hope I will be ready to do so in another month. Meanwhile I have agreed to considerable reductions in Marine strength. China should announce her intention to send troops into Japan. . . .

"China would then be ready to carry the Manchuria issue to the Far Eastern Commission, with definite evidence of unification, with the embarrassment of the presence of American combat troops removed, and with her status dignified by the fact of her troops having joined the Allied Occupation Forces in Japan. . . ."

On February 12 I answered Marshall:

My dear General Marshall:
    . . . I approve the tentative course of action you outline.
    With regard to a military advisory group for China, a revised J.C.S. paper on the subject is expected soon and their recommendations will be sent to you for comment.
    I am much interested in your suggestion with respect to deactivation of the China theater and should be glad to have your views as to the timing of such deactivation. General Wedemeyer's recent reports indicate that under his present plans movement of Chinese armies to Manchuria will not be completed until September 1, 1946, and that logistical support for these Chinese forces will not be discontinued until October 31, 1946.
    Inasmuch as the movement of Chinese forces into north China is dependent on the development of your mission, I realize that no information on possible timing of this phase of theater activity is yet available and am hopeful that the success of your mission will render this activity unnecessary.
    I shall await with interest your further recommendations with regard to the withdrawal of the Marines from north China.
    Current developments in connection with the presence of British troops in Indonesia and Greece, to which you refer, increase my anxiety to get American armed forces out of China just as soon as they are no longer essential to implement our policy in China.

With regard to your references to the Far Eastern Commission in relation to the Manchurian issue, I believe that the only practicable consideration that the Commission could give to the situation in Manchuria would be in connection with reparations; that is, disposition of Japanese external assets in Manchuria. I assume that you have the same idea. It is our idea that the Far Eastern Commission shall limit itself to consideration of problems and policies directly connected with the surrender, disarmament and control of Japan and that its scope of activity should not be extended to consideration of Far Eastern problems of a more general character.

With renewed assurance of my confidence and high regard.

I had hoped, as did Marshall, that the tripartite committees he set up would quickly put an end to the civil war in China. These committees were cease-fire teams and were each made of one Nationalist officer, one Communist officer, and one American officer from General Marshall's executive headquarters.

To lend the strength of his influence to the cease-fire agreement between the two Chinese armies, Marshall undertook a three-thousand-mile flight through northern China all the way to the borders of Inner Mongolia. He talked to all the principal commanders in the field and reported to me that he had been able to promote a general understanding throughout the region of the purposes of the cease-fire and of the machinery that had been set up to enforce it. While in Yenan he talked with Mao Tse-tung.

Difficulties had been numerous, and many still existed. Nevertheless, Marshall now felt that the first stage of his work had been completed. The two Chinese parties had been brought to a cease-fire agreement, and there was a slight lessening of mutual suspicion in the atmosphere. Marshall now asked to return to Washington for personal consultation with me and to work out a program of help to China with the various departments of government. I was anxious to see him and approved his suggestion.

In advance of his return he had sent me a detailed report on the the situation as he saw it and after his arrival in Washington on March 15 I had several long talks with him.

He told me that, just before he left China, Chiang Kai-shek had at last consented to the entry of cease-fire teams into Manchuria, which he had previously opposed. In fact, it was this event that had led Marshall to believe he could be spared in China in order to take up in Washington several matters which he believed would be of assistance in solving the problems of China. After Marshall's departure from China, however, Chiang Kai-shek had put such severe restrictions on the powers of the cease-fire teams that were to go into Manchuria that they were unable to function. As a result, fighting had broken out again in several areas of Manchuria and had spread from there.

On April 6, for instance, General Gillem, Marshall's deputy, reported that the government authorities were detaining Communist cease-fire team members at Mukden and had arrested others in Peiping. Furthermore, Chinese air force planes had "buzzed" the Communist center of Yenan. The Chinese Communists, on the other hand, occupied key localities in Manchuria just as the Russians departed. In some instances, where Central Government forces were already on the ground, Communist forces attacked them and forced them out.

General Marshall devoted his brief stay in Washington to talks with government officials regarding loans for China and aid in the form of shipping and surplus property. He was able to reach agreements to facilitate the transfer of surplus-property stocks then in China and to assure China of some small coastwise and river shipping. I instructed the Treasury Department to co-operate with him in every way, and an agreement was reached for an immediate loan to China of $500,000,000. Unfortunately, when nothing but the Chinese signature was lacking on this document, Chiang Kai-shek's representative, the Chinese Ambassador in Washington, insisted on changes before he would sign. And to complicate the matter further, the Generalissimo on that same day made a speech in China that was in effect a call to arms. It is no wonder that the Treasury experts felt that it would not be in line with our policy to make a loan if political settlement was not forthcoming in China. They were correct.

General Marshall returned to China on April 18, and almost as soon as he arrived he was confronted with a Communist charge that American planes had strafed their units in Szepingkai. Marshall's headquarters was able to prove that the plane involved, though of American make, belonged to the National Government.

I kept receiving reports of Communist successes in Manchuria during April and May. They captured Changchun, the capital city, after tense fighting, and occupied Harbin, an industrial center of northern Manchuria, without opposition from the government garrison. Chiang Kai-shek rejected an offer of the Communists for a truce in Manchuria in spite of the fact that he was obviously unable to contain them. Hostilities spread into China proper, around Hankow and in the vicinity of Nanking.

Marshall's truce teams were rushed out into areas of conflagration to stem the tide, and cease-fire orders were put into effect in some important provinces. In fact, the situation improved until Marshall found it possible to cable me in the latter part of May that there were signs that the promise of peace in China could be revived. Chiang Kai-shek seemed to accept Communist occupation of most of Manchuria at this stage. He was no longer insisting on the recapture of the cities that had been lost, and he seemed to consider, as a possible compromise, the idea of letting Changchun be managed by a tripartite team from Marshall's executive headquarters. The Communists, of course, were reluctant to give up that key city, even to a neutral agency.

This apparent change in policy was only momentary, however; after Chiang Kai-shek consulted his generals in Mukden and other key locations, he returned to his earlier formula. He wanted the Communists to show their good faith first by restoring communications in North China, which they had cut in many places. He also raised the question of whether Marshall, as an individual, was prepared to guarantee the good faith of the Communists.

For the first time Marshall sounded a discouraging note.

"I am working against time," he cabled, "otherwise I would be quite hopeful. As it is, success depends on the developments in the field more than on the problems of negotiation."

It was only through Marshall's insistence that some basis for peaceful settlement had to be found that at last a temporary cease-fire was arranged for Manchuria. On June 7 both parties consented to a fifteen-day truce, and a small team, headed by Marshall's chief of staff, General Byroade, went to Changchun to supervise the cessation of hostilities.

Marshall had written me that it was his hope that, during the temporary truce, agreement might be reached on a more permanent settlement. But both sides seemed most unwilling to commit themselves. The government commander in Manchuria announced repeatedly that he was ready to resume his advance on the Communist position as soon as the fifteen days had ended. The Communists, on the other hand, rejected the government plans as entirely too demanding. Unfortunately one of Chiang's proposals was that the American members of truce teams should be given the deciding voice whenever the two Chinese were unable to agree. The Communists, of course, saw in this move merely a corroboration of their charge that America was taking the Kuomintang's side, and they would not hear of the plan.

The Communists also objected to the government's demand that, in addition to Manchuria, the Communists should withdraw from certain areas in North China. When the government announced that it was sending two new armies into those areas, Marshall concluded that "at the present moment we have reached an impasse."

There were then a number of Central Government leaders who felt confident that the Communists could be defeated in battle, an estimate that Marshall, from his observations on the ground, considered highly erroneous. He believed that not only would it be impossible for the Generalissimo's forces to win a quick victory but also that, failing such immediate success, they would find themselves confronted by a Communist force backed and supported by the Soviets. In the long run, this could mean only defeat for Chiang—or American full-scale intervention.

But Marshall's patient persistence brought Communist acceptance of the government proposal to give the deciding vote on truce teams to the American member, and, with this obstacle out of the way, negotiations once again appeared to take a more promising turn. The temporary truce was extended eight days to allow more time for talks.

At this moment Marshall was seriously handicapped by various proposals that had been introduced in the Congress and appeared slated for passage—proposals that would have extended Lend-Lease and other aid to the government of Chiang Kai-shek without laying down a condition that he work with General Marshall. This was heartbreaking and contributed greatly to General Marshall's troubles. Of course I could not stop this sort of talk in Congress. In other words, as was to happen again and again in later years, the Chinese government sought to gain advantages from our government by applying pressures from other directions.

Every time someone in Washington or elsewhere in this country made a speech calling for "all-out aid" to Chiang, the "die-hards" in China gained new confidence and sabotaged Marshall's efforts to bring about peace. In turn, the Communists, of course, would point to reports of such statements as evidence of American duplicity. Marshall's delicate task was made infinitely more difficult by the uncritical acts of some in this country who claimed to be friends of the Chinese people but who were only helping the "die-hards."

In China, anti-American propaganda, mass meetings, and demonstrations were increasing. They were instigated alike by the Communists and by the extremists in the Kuomintang.

In July I appointed Dr. J. Leighton Stuart, the distinguished American president of Yenching University in Peiping, as American Ambassador to China. Dr. Stuart was born in China and had spent most of his adult life there. Few men possessed a better knowledge of China, and few Westerners commanded more respect among the Chinese. I knew he would be of considerable help to Marshall. His fluency in the Chinese language, of course, made discussions with the various leaders much easier.

But July also brought the outbreak of intense and widespread fighting. As Marshall reported it, "The Nationalists blamed the Communists for starting fighting in the Kiangsu and Tatung regions, while the Communists blamed the Nationalists in Kiangsu, Shantung and Hupeh." At the same time, the Central Government began a sharp drive against liberal elements of the population. The secret police put many of them under close surveillance, and in Kunming two professors who were members of the Democratic League were assassinated.

The Generalissimo's reaction was one of counseling patience. He told Marshall, in effect, that all would end well. The Communists, however, were unwilling to resume talks as long as fighting continued. Their own control over their troops was apparently being relaxed, and on July 29 a group of armed Communists attacked a small element of American marines, killing three and wounding several others.

The turn of events in China troubled me. The anti-American demonstrations by the Nationalist student groups in such places as Nanking, the new policy of harshness against the liberals, Chiang Kai-shek's insistence on freedom of action in the military field—all these seemed to indicate that the Central Government was turning its back on my effort to preserve the peace in China.

As I interpreted Marshall's reports, there were elements on both sides, among the Kuomintang and among the Communists, who were willing to work together on a peaceful solution. But on each side there were also extremists who wanted no part of negotiations and were determined to settle the fate of their country by force. The Generalissimo himself seemed to take a position between these two groups. In the spring, the influence of the moderates around him must have prevailed, and he agreed to concessions, although with a show of reluctance. Now, however, it appeared that the extreme military cliques had won out and that he was no longer willing to listen to Marshall's counsel.

I decided, with Marshall's approval, to appeal to Chiang Kai-shek in person. On August 10 I asked the Chinese Ambassador to transmit the following message to Chiang:

"Since I sent General Marshall to you as my special envoy, I have followed closely the situation in China. It is with deep regret that I am forced to the conclusion that his efforts have apparently proved unavailing.

"I am certain that General Marshall, in his discussions with you, has reflected accurately the overall attitude and policy of the American Government and of *informed* American public opinion.

"During recent months the rapidly deteriorating political situation in China has been a cause of grave concern to the American people. While it is the continued hope of the United States that a strong and democratic China can yet be achieved under your leadership, I would be less than honest if I did not point out that recent developments have forced me to the conclusion that the selfish interests of extremist elements, equally in the Kuomintang as in the Communist Party, are hindering the aspirations of the Chinese people.

"The Agreements reached by the Political Consultative Conference on January 31st were greeted in the United States as a far-sighted step toward the achievement of national unity and democracy. American disappointment over failure to implement these agreements by concrete measure is becoming an important factor in our outlook with regard to China.

"There exists in the United States an increasing body of opinion which holds that our entire policy toward China must be reexamined in the light of spreading strife, and especially by evidence of the increasing tendency to oppress freedom of the press as well as the expression of liberal views among intellectuals. The recent assassinations of distinguished Chinese liberals at Kunming have not gone unnoticed. Regardless of where responsibility for these cruel murders may lie, the end result has been to focus American attention on the situation in China, and there is a growing conviction that an attempt is being made to settle major social issues by resort to force, military or secret police, rather than by democratic processes.

"Our faith in the peaceful and democratic aspirations of the people of China has been shaken by recent events, but not destroyed. It is still the firm desire of this Government and of the people of the United States to assist China to achieve lasting peace and a stable economy under a truly democratic government. There is a growing feeling, however, that the aspirations of the Chinese people are being thwarted by militarists and a small group of reactionaries, who, failing to comprehend the liberal trend of the times, are obstructing the advancement of the general good of the nation. Such a state of affairs is violently repugnant to the American people.

"Unless convincing proof is shortly forthcoming that genuine progress is made toward a peaceful settlement of China's internal problems, it must be expected that American opinion will not continue in its generous attitude towards your nation. It will, furthermore, be necessary for me to redefine and explain the position of the United States to the American people.

"It is my earnest hope that I may in the near future receive some encouraging word from you which will facilitate the accomplishment of our mutually declared objectives."

When Chiang received this message, he asked Marshall to join him at his summer residence. There, without mentioning my letter, he told the general that he was convinced that the Communists had decided to embark upon a policy of violence. He denied that there had been anything in the conduct of the government that would suggest that its policy was one of force, even before the change in the Communists' attitude.

Marshall reported that "at the present moment the Generalissimo seems clearly inclined to a policy of force as the only acceptable solution." He also said that he had again urged on the Generalissimo the importance of stopping the fighting to clear the air for political negotiations. Only the Communists, Marshall pointed out, would gain if a general conflagration were allowed to develop.

Chiang Kai-shek's reply to my letter placed all blame squarely on the Communists:

"I wish to thank you cordially for your message of August 10th, expressing your genuine concern for the welfare of my country.

"Since General George Marshall's arrival in China, he has labored most unsparingly to achieve our common objective, namely, peace and democracy in China. I, too, have done my utmost despite all obstacles to cooperate with him in his endeavor.

"But the desire for peace has to be mutual, and for the Communists, it must mean that they give up their policy to use armed force to seize political power, to overthrow the Government and to install a totalitarian regime such as those which are now spreading over Eastern Europe. The abandonment of such a policy is the minimum requirement for the preservation of peace in our country. After the conclusion of the January Agreement, the Communists attacked and captured Changchun in Manchuria and attacked and captured Tehchow in Shantung. During the cease fire period in June, they attacked Hsuchow in Northern Kiangsu and Tatung and Taiyuan in Shansi. In the last few days, they have opened a wide offensive on the Lunghai Railway with Hsuchow and Kaifeng as their objectives.

"Of course, mistakes have also been made by some subordinates on the Government side, but they are minor in scale compared to the flagrant violations on the part of the Communists. Whenever any mistake occurs on our Government side, we deal sternly with the offender.

"On August 14th in my V-J Day message, I announced the firm policy of the Government to broaden speedily the basis of the Government by the inclusion of all parties and non-partisans, amounting to putting into effect the programme of peaceful reconstruction as adopted by the Political Consultation Conference on January 30th. I sincerely hope that the Chinese Communist Party will accept our views. The Government on its part will do the utmost to make peace and democracy a reality in this country in the shortest possible time.

"In implementing that policy which has as its aim our mutually declared objective, I am cooperating with General Marshall with all my power. Our success must depend upon the sincerity of the Communists in responding to our appeals. I am counting on your continued support in the attainment of our objective."

In my acknowledgment of Chiang Kai-shek's message I welcomed the indications of further efforts toward the settlement of China's problems and expressed the hope that armed strife would soon cease and that we would then be able to assist China in its tasks of reconstruction and rehabilitation.

Chiang Kai-shek did, in fact, consent to another effort at political settlement. However, contrary to Marshall's judgment, he wanted to see a political agreement concluded before he would agree to a termination of the fighting. The Communists, in the meanwhile, had issued a manifesto for the mobilizing of all available manpower in their areas. According to the Communists, this was a defense measure. According to Chiang, it was clear evidence of the Communists' aggressive intentions.

The stalemate seemed complete. Each side accused the other of having started the fighting, and neither would agree to a cessation until the other had given up any and all advantages gained in the interim.

Marshall now asked the two sides to sit down with Dr. Stuart in an attempt to break the stalemate. The aim was to bring about the creation of the State Council of forty members, which would be the next step forward on the road to political integration.

The Generalissimo set a number of conditions which, he said, the Communists would have to meet before he would agree to a cessation of hostilities, and, in Marshall's opinion, the government forces were in a position to score some immediate successes that might impel the Communists to accept these demands. Marshall believed that the Communists realized this and therefore were trying to get whatever advantages they could gain from local successes.

"There are leading military participants on both sides," he reported to me on August 30, "who confidentially take a somewhat Chinese view that several months of fighting will be a necessary procedure looking to an acceptable adjustment. What happens in the meantime to the hundreds of millions of oppressed people is ignored. Also what happens in the way of Soviet intervention overt or covert is also ignored or not mentioned."

Chiang Kai-shek himself seemed to expect the fighting to continue into the fall. He made it a condition of any cease-fire that the Communists should name their slate of delegates for the National Assembly, which was to convene in November, telling Marshall that he wanted to announce the names at the first formal meeting of the State Council, which he expected would be held on October 10. In other words, he was prepared to have the fighting continue at least until that date.

The Communists, on the other hand, would not proceed with the planning for the State Council unless they were given assurances that the cessation of hostilities would also be taken up. While Chiang Kai-shek had asked Marshall in May if he could guarantee the good faith of the Communists, now in August Chou En-lai wanted Marshall and Stuart to guarantee the good faith of Chiang and his government.

On September 13 Marshall reported that "Dr. Stuart and I are stymied." Their only hope seemed to be that Chou En-lai and the Communists might decide that the fighting was running against them and that they might therefore best yield to the demands of the Generalissimo.

On October 2 Marshall sent three messages, the substance of which was that he considered his mission at a complete impasse. He had in vain pleaded with Chou En-lai to return from his self-imposed exile in Shanghai. He had no success in getting any concessions from Chiang Kai-shek, who had now openly announced that he would seek to occupy the city of Kalgan. The Communists responded with a declaration that an attack on Kalgan would be taken as a symbol of the government's intention to launch unrestricted civil war. Kalgan had been one of the sites which the government had in June agreed to leave in Communist hands.

Marshall reported to me that he had found it necessary to submit a plain-spoken memorandum to the Generalissimo. In this he had stated clearly that he was in disagreement with both the Communists and the Nationalists. Furthermore, he enumerated the points on which he disagreed with each and had then concluded by advising the Generalissimo that, unless some basis for agreement on the termination of hostilities could be reached without delay, he would request that his mission in China be ended. Earlier, Marshall had informed the Communists with equal bluntness that he would withdraw from the task of mediation unless they ceased the personal attacks on him in their press and in their propaganda.

At this stage I was prepared to ask Marshall to come home.

Chiang Kai-shek was persuaded to make a proposal to the Communists, although it was not what we hoped it might be. Indeed, it was rather plain that Chiang Kai-shek was willing to take this step merely in an effort to prevent Marshall from openly proclaiming the collapse of the mediation efforts. The Communists, however, would not hear of any of the Generalissimo's plans until they received assurances that the advance on Kalgan would be called off, and they also wanted assurances that the relative military position would be restored as it had existed at the time of the original cease-fire agreement in January. This, of course, would have meant the giving up by the Nationalists of all advantages they had gained in the interval, a condition the Generalissimo would not accept.

Marshall now wrote me that he had concluded that the Government of the United States could not be involved in a controversy in which the parties were dealing with each other at the point of a gun, and he insisted again that no talks could promise success unless there was first an end to the fighting. On October 5 he reported that in his view his usefulness in China had ceased and that his recall was therefore appropriate.

When the Generalissimo learned that Marshall had recommended the end of the mediation mission, he came forward with the suggestion of a ten-day truce in the operations against Kalgan while discussions on the political and military problems were brought under way. Marshall, always anxious to pass up no opportunity that might lead to a cessation of hostilities, agreed to pass this proposal on to the Communists.

The Communists' reply was that they would agree to a truce, provided it had no time limit, and that they would agree to a conference, provided there was no prior limitation of the subjects to be discussed—a position that Marshall was unable to shake, for the Communist negotiators criticized American policy as partial to the Nationalists and implied that Marshall himself was partial.

On October 9 Marshall traveled to Shanghai to appeal to Chou En-lai in person, but the Communist leader was completely adamant. He was clearly unwilling to concede anything, was suspicious of anything that came from Chiang Kai-shek, and at last told Marshall that he considered American assistance to the Chinese government improper and that he thought Marshall's timing of a public release on the latest proposal was such as to distort the picture to the disadvantage of the Communists. This charge brought from Marshall the reply that since he was no longer respected as impartial he would at once withdraw from any negotiations.

The events in China now moved into a new phase in which General Marshall was only an interested observer. Ambassador Stuart had held a number of interviews with representatives of the small groups that formed the middle ground between the Kuomintang and the Communists, some of which, like the Democratic League, were in alliance with the Communists, while others, such as the Chinese Youth Party, were striving to be independent. These minority parties now entered into the picture as a temporary focus for the efforts at mediation. Marshall and Dr. Stuart kept themselves aloof from these negotiations. The Third Parties' group, however, did report to them what progress was being made.

Chou En-lai, at the persuasion of the mediators, came to Nanking, but this visit unfortunately coincided with a long-planned trip of the Generalissimo to Formosa, a move which the Communists interpreted as an intentional dodge. The Central Government's operations against Antung, in Manchuria, and against Chefoo, in the province of Shantung, heightened the suspicions of the Communists and served as well to discourage the Third Parties' group. Furthermore, Chiang Kai-shek, when he returned from Formosa, reiterated his previous demands, while the Communists repeated their previous rejections.

At the same time, the Generalissimo responded to the urging of the Third Parties and granted a three-day postponement of the convening date of the National Assembly. This body did, in the end, assemble on November 15, but with only a few non-Kuomintang members present.

The Communists considered this the final breach. It was their view that the agreements concluded in January in the Political Consultative Conference made it necessary that, before the National Assembly could be convened, the State Council should be organized and the powers of government transferred to it. The determination of the Central Government to go ahead with the National Assembly consequently was taken by the Communists as the final destruction of the January agreements.

Chou En-lai returned to Yenan, leaving only a rump delegation behind, but before he left, he told General Marshall that he expected the Chiang government to initiate shortly a major military campaign to capture Yenan. This, Chou En-lai said to Marshall, would mean the end of all hope for peace by negotiation.

The Communists had thus turned their backs on the negotiations. Chiang Kai-shek seemed confident that his forces could subdue them. In this Marshall disagreed, and he did not hesitate to point out to the Generalissimo that the Communists could fight a war of attrition, cutting the Nationalist supply lines and communications at will while Chiang's forces sought to maintain the occupation of cities.

Marshall reminded the Generalissimo that, if Russian aid were given to the Communists, their supply line would be much shorter than his own and much more immune from attack. By every means at his command he sought to convince Chiang Kai-shek that in a purely military conflict, however much the odds appeared in his favor at the moment, he would not be able to secure lasting control of the country.

Despite this warning, the Generalissimo remained unconvinced. He was certain that the Communists had never had any intention of cooperating and that only their military defeat would settle the issue. Nor did he take other important matters into consideration. For example, he dismissed Marshall's references to China's precarious economic condition by saying, in effect, that China was accustomed to that.

In spite of these open disagreements over the prospects in view, the Generalissimo asked General Marshall to remain in China as adviser to the government, an offer Marshall declined because he thought the strong anti-American sentiment whipped up by the extremists in the Kuomintang and their predominant position in the government would make the position of any American adviser difficult.

On December 28 General Marshall suggested to me that, if a next effort at negotiations which was then being planned failed, he should be recalled to Washington. It was plain from his reports, too, that this effort was doomed to failure even before it was ever undertaken. I decided not to await this event. On January 3 I instructed the Secretary of State to recall Marshall for consultation on China and "other matters."

The "other matters" were to consist of no less than the entire scope of State Department activities. For while Marshall was still on his way across the Pacific, I announced that he would become Secretary of State.

I had sent General Marshall to China to try to end the fighting and to help put into effect the agreement between the Nationalists and the Communists to form a coalition government. He set up an executive headquarters, and the fighting stopped, temporarily. The Chinese began these endless, oriental negotiations between themselves, and only an expert chess player can follow them. This is the way it goes. Someone makes a proposal which is accepted by the other side, with three qualifications. They are then accepted by the other side with three qualifications to each of the first three qualifications. It was an old Chinese way to be sure nothing would happen. Well, fighting broke out again in 1946, and Chiang Kai-shek then decided he was going to occupy North China and Manchuria. General Marshall argued against it, and General Wedemeyer argued against it, but he went ahead. We furnished him equipment, money, and a water-lift to Manchuria, and he sent the best divisions he had, well trained and well armed, to Mukden. They stayed there until finally the whole thing disintegrated, and they surrendered. They would make a series of extended movements into the country in North China and take up a position in a walled city. Chiang's commanders were very poor. They had a walled-city complex. They thought the open country was dangerous. Open country was the one place in which they should have been. But they thought a walled city was fine; they could see people coming. Of course no one came, and they stayed in the city. The Communists cut their communication lines and broke up their single-track railroad so it was no good to them. At the beginning of 1947 General Marshall threw in the towel. He said that both parties were unwilling to carry out their agreements. Chiang Kai-shek would not heed the advice of one of the greatest military strategists in history and lost to the Communists.

There is no question that Marshall's mission failed to yield the results he and I had hoped for. Fighting soon enveloped all of China, and it did not end until the Communists were masters of the land and Chiang Kai-shek, with the remnants of his army, sought refuge on Formosa.

The Marshall mission had been unable to produce results because the government of Chiang Kai-shek did not command the respect and support of the Chinese people. The Generalissimo's attitude and actions were those of an old-fashioned warlord, and, as with the warlords, there was no love for him among the people. There is no doubt in my mind that if Chiang Kai-shek had been only a little more conciliatory an understanding could have been reached. I am not one to believe in the value of hindsight. Whether or not I was right in sending General Marshall to China does not depend on what some think they know today. It depends only on what we were able to know in 1945. At that time the belief was general that the various elements in China could be persuaded to unify the country. Of course the struggle for power would continue, but there was no reason why the National Government could not be successful in this struggle, as non-Communist governments had been in Europe, if it attended to the fundamental needs of the people and the country. It seemed then that it was the only practicable course. Hurley and Wedemeyer led me to think that they believed so, and so did our military and diplomatic experts. Some of these experts believed, however, that America could force unity on China—that, in effect, we could "ram it down their throats." Those who took this attitude, of course, would have been the wrong men for the job. Marshall, in my belief, was the right man because he was deeply steeped in democracy and sincerely believed in letting the people determine their own fate. He was a firm believer in the principle of civilian supremacy over the military as a principle that not only applied in the United States but was essential to the welfare of any nation.

I knew General Marshall very well. In the days of the Senate Committee to Investigate the National Defense Program we had regular weekly conferences, and out of these continuous contacts grew my high regard for him as a man and as a soldier. He understood clearly what I hoped to accomplish in China, and he acted entirely in accord with the policy I outlined to him on the eve of his departure.

Neither Marshall nor I was ever taken in by the talk about the Chinese Communists being just "agrarian reformers." The general knew he was dealing with Communists, and he knew what their aims were. When he was back in Washington in March, he told me that their chief negotiator, Chou En-lai, had very frankly declared that, as a Communist, he believed firmly in the teachings of Marx and Lenin and the eventual victory of the proletariat. Marshall's messages from China show, also, that he fully assumed that the Chinese Communists would, in the end, be able to count on Russian support.

Neither had I been taken in by Stalin's declaration at Potsdam that the Chinese Communists were not really "proper" Communists, nor by his later statement to Harriman that he thought the civil war in China would be foolish. I realized that the Communists had been engaged in a struggle for the power in China for nearly twenty years. What I hoped to achieve was to see China made into a country in which Communism would lose its appeal to the masses because the needs of the people and the voice of the people would have been answered.

I knew that peace in the world would not be achieved by fighting more wars. Most of all, I was always aware that there were two enormous land masses that no western army of modern times had ever been able to conquer: Russia and China. It would have been folly, and it would be folly today, to attempt to impose our way of life on these huge areas by force!

In 1945 and 1946, of all years, such thoughts would have been rejected by the American people before they were even expressed. That was the time when congressmen in Washington joined in the call to "get the boys back home," and our influence throughout the world, as well as China, waned as the millions of American soldiers were processed through the discharge centers.

Our only hope was that we might be given an opportunity to bring to China the kind of economic aid that might restore that country's health and that, in doing so, we would be able to weaken the Communists' appeal. But such aid could not be sent until tranquillity had been restored in the nation, nor would it be effective until the government commanded enough respect to be able to make certain that none of this aid would be diverted into the pockets of warlords and profiteers.

In the end, of course, Chiang was defeated by loss of support among his own people and by American arms, as many of his own generals took their armies, equipped through our aid, into the enemy camp. It was when that sort of surrender began to occur on a large scale that I decided to cut off further shipments to China.

Yet while Marshall was in China it was the Central Government and not the Communists who scored important military gains, although Marshall analyzed them as spurious gains and accurately forecast the eventual failure of the Generalissimo's military campaign. But that failure, in my opinion, and the defeat of the National Government of China were due primarily to their refusal to heed Marshall's advice.

It is important to repeat that Marshall was advising, not dictating. I had sent him to China not to intervene in the affairs of that country but to render whatever aid we could to the cause of peace there. He was not sent to do Chiang Kai-shek's job for him. If General Marshall returned from his mission without results, it was because neither of the parties really wanted to live up to the agreement to form a coalition government to unite China.

The solution I tried to reach through Marshall was the only one by way of which Chiang Kai-shek might have saved himself without full-scale military intervention by the United States. To achieve a proper and fair appraisal of Marshall's mission, it is important to bear in mind that even before he left for China there already existed a formal agreement in writing between the Central Government and the Communists to work toward national unity. This is the agreement that was brought about previously with the assistance of Ambassador Hurley when he headed our diplomatic mission to China, and had this not already been in existence I would not have sent Marshall to China. My sole purpose in sending him was to help carry out a program willingly subscribed to by the Chinese leaders. In no sense was it our intention to impose our will upon the Chinese people.

CHAPTER 7

In early 1946 Russian activities in Iran threatened the peace of the world.

Russia and Britain had concluded an agreement with Iran in 1942 which allowed Russian and British troops to be stationed on Iranian soil for a period ending six months after the termination of hostilities. At the London Conference of Foreign Ministers in September 1945, Bevin and Molotov had agreed that this meant that all foreign troops would be withdrawn from Iran not later than March 2, 1946.

However, during the month of November the State Department received reliable reports that instead of preparing for withdrawal the Russians were adding to their forces. It was also reported that the Russians were interfering with efforts by the government in Teheran to suppress rebellious elements in the northern part of the country, and especially in the province of Azerbaijan.

On November 23 I had Secretary Byrnes bring up the matter before the Cabinet. Byrnes suggested at that time that we speed up the departure of American troops in Iran. We had used Iran as a supply route to Russia by arrangement with the British, the Russians, and the Teheran government. This meant that we maintained a few thousand service troops in the country. While this involved only a relatively small force, we intended to set the example of withdrawal and then ask the Russians to agree that all foreign troops would be out of that country by January 1.

The approach to Russia was made on this basis, but on December 3 the Russians rejected the proposal. A few days later the Moscow radio informed the world that a revolutionary government had been set up in Azerbaijan. The Iranian government at once charged that this rebel government owed its existence to the Russians and was supported by Russian military forces.

When Byrnes was in Moscow for the conference of Foreign Ministers later in December, the Russians refused even to discuss the question of withdrawal of foreign troops from Iran.

On January 19 Iran formally charged Russia before the Security Council of the United Nations with interference in her internal affairs. But the Security Council was unable to act because Russia contended that the dispute was not a matter which that body was competent to handle. The Russians simply announced that they would ignore any questions they might be asked about Iran. The Security Council then agreed to let Russia and Iran settle the matter by direct negotiation. It was, of course, unlikely that Iran would be able to resist Russian demands while Soviet troops were still occupying her territory. Under such conditions there could hardly be any equality at the bargaining table.

March 2, the day on which the Russians had agreed with Britain and Iran that they would withdraw their troops, came and passed, but the Russians did not leave Iran. On the contrary, Moscow announced that "some troops" would remain in Iran for an unspecified time.

This was a gross violation of the agreements made. It also meant that Iran would be required to negotiate with Russia while a gun was at her head. I decided that the Russian government ought to be informed on how we felt about this kind of conduct in international relations. I asked Secretary Byrnes to bring with him, to his weekly conference with me, all available documents on the Iranian situation.

At this conference, on March 4, we discussed all aspects of the problem and reviewed its many dangerous implications. As a result, Byrnes sent a note to Moscow that would, while still being diplomatically polite, make it very plain that we did not like the way Russia was behaving in Iran and, specifically, that Russian troops were still there in spite of the solemn promises repeatedly made by the Kremlin that they would be out of Iran not later than March 2.

The note which George F. Kennan, our Chargé d'Affaires, delivered at the Kremlin on March 6 said in part, ". . . The decision of the Soviet Government to retain Soviet troops in Iran beyond the period stipulated by the Tripartite Treaty has created a situation with regard to which the Government of the United States, as a member of the United Nations and as a Party to the Declaration Regarding Iran dated December 1, 1943, can not remain indifferent. . . . The Government of the United States, in the spirit of friendly association which developed between the United States and the Soviet Union in the successful effort against the common enemy and as a fellow member of the United Nations, expresses the earnest hope that the Government of the Soviet Union will do its part, by withdrawing immediately all Soviet forces from the territory of Iran, to promote the international confidence which is necessary for peaceful progress among the peoples of all nations. . . ."

There was no official reply to this note. Russian press reports, however, said that the State Department was "mistaken," that there were no Russian troop movements in Iran. Then the Kremlin shifted tactics and began hammering away at Winston Churchill for his Fulton, Missouri, speech and at me for sponsoring the speech. It was at Westminster College in Fulton that Churchill first referred to the "iron curtain" publicly. The Russians had resorted to the old game of kicking up the dust when you do not want the other fellow to see too well.

But our intelligence continued to report the presence of Russian troops in Iran. The Iranians, moving into areas from which the Russians had said they had pulled out, found the roads blocked by Russian troop units. Three major Russian columns were reported on the march, one toward the capital city of Teheran, another swinging toward the Turko-Iranian border. The signs were plain that Russia was determined to have her way and that she intended to ignore the U.S. and the U.N. alike.

As I saw it, three things were involved. One was the security of Turkey. Russia had been pressing Turkey for special privileges and for territorial concessions for several months. The Turks had resisted all these demands, but their position would be infinitely more difficult if Russia, or a Russian puppet state, were able to outflank her in the east.

The second problem was the control of Iran's oil reserves. That Russia had an eye on these vast deposits seemed beyond question. If the Russians were to control Iran's oil, either directly or indirectly, the raw-material balance of the world would undergo a serious change, and it would be a serious loss for the economy of the Western world.

What perturbed me most, however, was Russia's callous disregard of the rights of a small nation and of her own solemn promises. International co-operation was impossible if national obligations could be ignored and the U.N. bypassed as if it did not exist.

I talked over all these points with Secretary Byrnes and Admiral Leahy. Then I told Byrnes to send a blunt message to Premier Stalin. On March 24 Moscow announced that all Russian troops would be withdrawn from Iran at once. The threat to Turkey had been removed, although it had not vanished and continued to demand our attention. Iran could negotiate with Russia without feeling threatened; indeed, its parliament rejected later the accord entered into by its government, a clear sign that fear had been removed from the land.

The world was now able to look more hopefully toward the United Nations. But Russia's ambitions would not be halted by friendly reminders of promises made. The Russians would press wherever weakness showed—and we would have to meet that pressure wherever it occurred, in a manner that Russia and the world would understand. When Communist pressure began to endanger Greece and Turkey, I moved to make this policy clear and firm.

It was not long before the same issue was presented to us again in the same part of the world. Turkey and Greece had become subjected to heavy pressures from the Russian bloc. Each of them had valiantly sought to repel these pressures, but now their strength was waning and they were in need of aid.

Turkey was, of course, an age-old objective of Russian ambitions. The Communists were only continuing what the Czars had practiced when they tried to gain control of the area that blocked Russian exit into the Mediterranean Sea. Stalin had brought up the subject of the Dardanelles at the Potsdam conference. But Attlee and I had stuck firmly by the principle that had been laid down in the Montreux Convention, that the straits should be open to the commercial shipping of all nations. For that reason nothing more was done about this subject at Potsdam, except to agree that each of the powers might discuss the subject directly with Turkey. This was entirely appropriate since the agreement, by its terms, was up for review in 1946.

Our ideas on the revision of these terms were transmitted to the Turkish government in a note on November 2, 1945. We informed the Turks that we would wish any revision to conform to three principles: (1) The straits to be open to the merchant vessels of all nations at all times; (2) the straits to be open to the transit of warships of the Black Sea powers at all times; (3) save for an agreed limited tonnage in time of peace, passage through the straits to be denied to the warships of non-Black Sea powers at all times, except with the specific consent of the Black Sea powers or except when acting under the authority of the United Nations. Copies of this note were sent to the Soviets—who made no reply—and to the British, who followed with a similar statement to the Turkish government.

Meanwhile, however, the Russians, in addition to their efforts to outflank Turkey through Iran, were beginning to exert pressure on Turkey for territorial concessions. In July 1946, Moscow sent a note to Ankara proposing a new regime for the Dardanelles that would have excluded all nations except the Black Sea powers. In other words, both we and the British would have been eliminated from any future agreement, and Turkey would have been faced by a combination of three Communist states: Russia, Rumania, and Bulgaria. The second and far more ominous part of the Soviet proposal was that the straits should be put under joint Turkish-Russian defense.

This was indeed an open bid to obtain control of Turkey. If Russian troops entered Turkey with the ostensible purpose of enforcing joint control of the straits, it would only be a short time before these troops would be used for the control of all of Turkey. We had learned from the experience of the past two years that Soviet intervention inevitably meant Soviet occupation and control. To allow Russia to set up bases in the Dardanelles or to bring troops into Turkey, ostensibly for the defense of the straits, would, in the natural course of events, result in Greece and the whole Near and Middle East falling under Soviet control.

The Turkish government sought our advice, and Acting Secretary of State Acheson placed the matter before me. I directed the State, War, and Navy Departments to make a careful study of the situation. The Secretaries of the three departments, with the Chiefs of Staff, moved with speed and brought me a unanimous recommendation that we take a strong position. I met with the Secretaries and the Chiefs of Staff and discussed the development thoroughly around a map on my desk to evaluate the situation in the Middle East. I approved the recommendations submitted. We co-ordinated our views with those of our allies, taking a strong position, which was at once communicated to the Turkish government. At the same time, the Turkish government received similar views and support from the British and French.

In addition, I told the Acting Secretary to have our Ambassador in Ankara tell the Turkish leaders orally that, in the language of diplomats, "the reply was formulated only after full consideration had been given to the matter at the highest levels." Without making specific commitments, our envoy was also instructed to suggest that we felt the Turkish reply to Moscow should be "reasonable, but firm."

The note to Russia made it plain that, if the straits should become the object of Russian aggression, the "resulting situation would constitute a threat to international security and would clearly be a matter for action on the part of the Security Council."

The Turkish government, encouraged by the American attitude, rejected the Soviet demands and showed admirable determination to resist if Russia should resort to open violence. But Turkey's Army, though sizable, was poorly equipped and would have been no match for the battle-tested divisions of the Kremlin.

More serious still was the drain which this continued exertion made on the nation's economy. Toward the close of 1946 our Ambassador reported from Ankara that "Turkey will not be able to maintain indefinitely a defensive posture against the Soviet Union. The burden is too great for the nation's economy to carry much longer."

This appraisal was confirmed by General Bedell Smith, our Ambassador to Russia. In his report of January 9, 1947, Ambassador Smith said that he had no doubt that the Kremlin would resume its efforts to encroach upon Turkish sovereignty, and he expressed the belief that, unless long-term aid was forthcoming from the United States and England, Turkey had no hope of surviving.

While Turkey's plight was entirely due to Russia's postwar intransigence, the condition of Greece had its beginning in the World War II occupation of that nation.

Greece had suffered tragically in World War II. Her people had offered heroic resistance to Mussolini's army, but at last the combined might of Germany and Italy had broken the Greek armies.

Resistance continued, however, throughout the country, and soon it had come to crystallize around two principal groups. One of these, the so-called EAM, was under Communist domination; the other remained loyal to the King and his government in exile. Between the vicious practices of the German forces of occupation and the constant fighting between the resistance groups, normal life in Greece virtually ceased. Fields and factories were idle. People starved, and disease took untold numbers.

In September 1944 the Germans withdrew. British forces landed in Greece, and the government in exile returned. But neither peace nor prosperity came to the strife-torn country. Cabinet succeeded cabinet, none of them able to offer a solution to the country's ills. The EAM withdrew to the hill areas of the north, refused to surrender its weapons, and was soon openly defying the government. The government, in turn, seemed to encourage irresponsible rightist groups. Violence flared up in numerous sections, and economic recovery made little, if any, headway.

The Communists, of course, thrived on the continuing conditions of misery, starvation, and economic ruin. Moscow and the Balkan satellite countries were now rendering open support to the EAM. Intelligence reports which I received stated that many of the insurgents had been trained, indoctrinated, armed, and equipped at various camps beyond the Greek borders. Under Soviet direction, the reports said, Greece's northern neighbors—Yugoslavia, Bulgaria, and Albania—were conducting a drive to establish a Communist Greece.

What little stability and order could be found in Greece was due primarily to the presence there of forty thousand British troops and to the counsel and support given to the Greek government by the British.

But as early as the fall of 1945 the British had suggested to us that they would like our assistance in Greece, especially financial help to the Greek government.

I had authorized the State Department to enter into discussions with the British on terms of economic aid to Greece, but we were also anxious to assure that conditions in Greece would justify any loans which might be granted. For that reason I approved the sending of a note to Greece in January 1946 which urged the government of that country to apply itself to a program of economic stabilization. We offered to aid in such a program with both advisers and funds.

Little progress was made, however, as the cleavage between the extremes of Right and Left in Greece seemed to become wider and wider. The return of the King only added fuel to the flames. At last, in December 1946, the Greek government complained to the Security Council of the United Nations that outside assistance was being received by the insurgent groups. A United Nations mission was dispatched to Greece to investigate the situation. At about the same time, the Greek government accepted our long-standing offer of technical advice on their economic problems, and I sent Paul Porter, former Administrator for the OPA, as the head of an economic mission.

However, before Porter was in a position to draw any conclusion from his inspections on the spot, events forced a decision that made Porter's mission—and our earlier approach to the problems of Greece—outdated.

On February 3 a cable to the State Department from Ambassador MacVeagh in Athens reported rumors that the British would withdraw their troops from Greece, or at least a sizable part of them. On February 12 Secretary of State Marshall brought me a dispatch from MacVeagh urging that we give immediate consideration to supplying aid to Greece. The British, the Ambassador reported, were not able to keep up even the little they were doing.

On February 18 Mark Ethridge of the U. S. Investigating Commission cabled that all the signs pointed to an impending move by the Communists to seize the country. On February 20 our embassy in London reported that the British Treasury was opposing any further aid to Greece because of the precarious financial condition in which Britain found herself.

But the crisis came sooner than we expected. In the late afternoon on Friday, February 21, the British Ambassador asked to see General Marshall. However, he was out of town, attending the bicentennial celebration of Princeton University. An appointment was made for Monday, and the State Department obtained from the British Embassy a copy of the official note which the Ambassador would deliver to the Secretary.

The note informed us that Britain would have to pull out of Greece no later than April 1. Acheson telephoned me immediately about the contents of the note, and I asked him to go to work on a study of the situation with which we were faced. Acheson alerted the State-War-Navy Coordinating Committee, and over the weekend they prepared a memorandum of recommendations of what ought to be done.

On Monday, February 24, Secretary Marshall brought me the official copy of the note which he had received formally that morning from the British Ambassador. This note set forth the difficulties confronting the United Kingdom in the fulfillment of her overseas commitments and advised us that as of March 30, 1947, it would be necessary for the United Kingdom to withdraw all support to Greece.

General Marshall and I discussed the impending crisis with Secretaries Forrestal and Patterson, and the three departments pressed their study of all aspects of the situation. In his talk with the British Ambassador, Secretary Marshall learned that the British were planning to take their troops out of Greece as soon as this could be conveniently done.

The urgency of the situation was emphasized by dispatches from our representatives in Athens and Moscow. General Smith recorded his belief that only the presence of British troops had so far saved Greece from being swallowed into the Soviet orbit. From Athens, Ambassador MacVeagh sent a picture of deep depression and even resignation among Greek leaders; their feeling seemed to be that only aid given at once would be of use. Time, MacVeagh urged, was of the essence.

At three o'clock on Wednesday, February 26, Marshall and Acheson brought me the result of the studies of our experts. The State-War-Navy Coordinating Committee had met that morning in an extended session and had agreed on a general policy recommendation. General Eisenhower furnished a memorandum from the Joint Chiefs of Staff supporting the conclusion reached from a military point of view.

Under Secretary Acheson made the presentation of the study, and I listened to it with great care. The diplomatic and military experts had drawn the picture in greater detail, but essentially their conclusions were the same as those to which I had come in the weeks just passed as the messages and reports went across my desk.

Greece needed aid, and needed it quickly and in substantial amounts. The alternative was the loss of Greece and the extension of the iron curtain across the eastern Mediterranean. If Greece was lost, Turkey would become an untenable outpost in a sea of Communism. Similarly, if Turkey yielded to Soviet demands, the position of Greece would be extremely endangered.

But the situation had even wider implications. Poland, Rumania, and the other satellite nations of eastern Europe had been turned into Communist camps because, in the course of the war, they had been occupied by the Russian Army. We had tried, vainly, to persuade the Soviets to permit political freedom in these countries, but we had no means to compel them to relinquish their control, unless we were prepared to wage war.

Greece and Turkey were still free countries being challenged by Communist threats both from within and without. These free peoples were now engaged in a valiant struggle to preserve their liberties and their independence.

America could not, and should not, let these free countries stand unaided. To do so would carry the clearest implications in the Middle East and in Italy, Germany, and France. The ideals and the traditions of our nation demanded that we come to the aid of Greece and Turkey and that we put the world on notice that it would be our policy to support the cause of freedom wherever it was threatened.

The risks which such a course might entail were risks which a great nation had to take if it cherished freedom at all. The studies which Marshall and Acheson brought to me and which we examined together made it plain that serious risks would be involved. But the alternative would be disastrous to our security and to the security of free nations everywhere.

What course the free world should take in the face of the threat of Russian totalitarianism was a subject I had discussed with my foreign policy advisers on many occasions in the year just passed. To foster our thinking in long-range terms I had approved the establishment in the State Department of a Policy Planning Staff. George F. Kennan, one of our foremost experts on Russia, was to head this group.

A President has little enough time to meditate, but whenever such moments occurred I was more than likely to turn my thoughts toward this key problem that confronted our nation.

We had fought a long and costly war to crush the totalitarianism of Hitler, the insolence of Mussolini, and the arrogance of the warlords of Japan. Yet the new menace facing us seemed every bit as grave as Nazi Germany and her allies had been.

I could never quite forget the strong hold which isolationism had gained over our country after World War I. Throughout my years in the Senate I listened each year as one of the senators would read Washington's Farewell Address. It served little purpose to point out to the isolationists that Washington had advised a method suitable under the conditions of *his* day to achieve the great end of preserving the nation, and that although conditions and our international position had changed, the objectives of our policy—peace and security—were still the same. For the isolationists this address was like a biblical text. The America First organization of 1940–41, the Ku Klux Klan, Pelley and his Silver Shirts—they all quoted the first President in support of their assorted aims.

I had a very good picture of what a revival of American isolationism would mean for the world. After World War II it was clear that without American participation there was no power capable of meeting Russia as an equal. If we were to turn our back on the world, areas such as Greece, weakened and divided as a result of the war, would fall into the Soviet orbit without much effort on the part of the Russians. The success of Russia in such areas and our avowed lack of interest would lead to the growth of domestic Communist parties in such European countries as France and Italy, where they were already significant threats. Inaction, withdrawal, "Fortress America" notions could only result in handing to the Russians vast areas of the globe now denied to them.

This was the time to align the United States of America clearly on the side, and the head, of the free world. I knew that George Washington's spirit would be invoked against me, and Henry Clay's, and all the other patron saints of the isolationists. But I was convinced that the policy I was about to proclaim was indeed as much required by the conditions of my day as was Washington's by the situation in his era and Monroe's doctrine by the circumstances which he then faced.

There are a great many men who labor diligently behind the scenes before a policy statement can be announced. The President, of course, can neither speak nor listen to each and every one of them. But their work ends where the President's work begins, for then he has to make the decision. And where they have spent days, perhaps months, in the study of just one situation, the President faces a multitude of decisions every day. To illustrate, this is what was happening. At the time that I was weighing the problem of aid to Greece and Turkey, Ernest Bevin had just made a public statement about our Palestine policy that cast a dark shadow over our relations with Britain; the economy bloc in the new Eightieth Congress was threatening to cut some vital government programs out of the budget, including our overseas information services; Secretary Marshall was getting ready to attend his first Foreign Ministers' conference; there were events in Argentina, in Indonesia, in China that called for decisions; Senator McKellar was blocking the atomic energy program by his stubborn opposition to the confirmation of David Lilienthal as chairman of the Atomic Energy Commission; the bill for the unification of the services was at last ready for Congress; the press wanted me to announce my plans for 1948. Amidst all these demands on his time, the President must be ready to perform the necessary functions of a head of state, whether they be ceremonial or informal, and he can, of course, never close his doors to the public and, even less so, to the press.

Yet decisions like these cannot be made in a hurry, and I never did make momentous decisions without hard preparatory work, study, and much thought. I always made it a point to listen to as many people as I could. And after that first sad experience with the Lend-Lease termination, I never put my initials of approval on a piece of paper without reading it with care.

The vital decision that I was about to make was complicated by the fact that Congress was no longer controlled by the Democratic party. While expecting the help of such fine supporters of the idea of bipartisanship in foreign affairs as Senator Vandenberg and Congressman Eaton of New Jersey, I realized the situation was more precarious than it would have been with a preponderantly Democratic Congress. It seemed desirable, therefore, to advise the congressional leadership as soon as possible of the gravity of the situation and of the nature of the decision which I had to make. I asked Secretary Marshall and Acheson to return the following day at ten, when I would have the congressional leaders present. At ten o'clock on the morning of February 27 Senators Bridges, Vandenberg, Barkley, and Connally, Speaker Martin, and Representatives Eaton, Bloom, and Rayburn took their seats in my office. Congressman Taber had been invited but was not able to be present. He called later in the day, and I discussed the situation with him.

I explained to them the position in which the British note on Greece had placed us. The decision of the British Cabinet to withdraw from Greece had not yet been made public, and none of the legislators knew, therefore, how serious a crisis we were suddenly facing. I told the group that I had decided to extend aid to Greece and Turkey and that I hoped Congress would provide the means to make this aid timely and sufficient.

General Marshall then reviewed the diplomatic exchanges and the details of the situation. He made it quite plain that our choice was either to act or to lose by default, and I expressed my emphatic agreement to this. I answered congressional questions and finally explained to them what course we had to take.

The congressional leaders appeared deeply impressed. Some in the group were men who would have preferred to avoid spending funds on any aid program abroad. Some had, not so long ago, been outspoken isolationists. But at this meeting in my office there was no voice of dissent when I stated the position which I was convinced our country had to take.

During the days that followed, State Department experts busied themselves with different aspects of the situation. The economic offices sought to estimate how much aid the Greek economy would need and could effectively use. The political officers were engaging in consultations with British, Greek, and Turkish representatives. The legal officers were preparing drafts of the necessary legislation. Other departments, too, were giving top-level attention to the Greek problem. Secretary of the Navy Forrestal, in particular, participated actively and had several lengthy conversations with Dean Acheson. It was the latter, however, as Under Secretary of State, who co-ordinated the planning being done. General Marshall was due to leave for Moscow shortly and was concentrating on plans for the Foreign Ministers' conference there.

I had to absent myself from Washington for several days on a state visit—the first one ever undertaken by an American President—to our neighboring republic of Mexico.

On my return to the capital in the late hours of March 6 I received a full report of all developments, including those affecting the Greek situation. The Greek government had formally asked for American aid. Both our embassy and the Porter mission asked for urgent consideration of the request.

I had planned to spend a few days in Key West to get away from the daily round of callers and get some work done without interruption, but decided to remain in Washington and go before Congress at the earliest moment to ask for the aid which Greece—and Turkey—so desperately needed.

There was much to be done and little time to do it. One of the first things was to place the matter before the Cabinet. A meeting was scheduled for March 7, and the greater part of it I devoted to a review of the Greek situation. I told the Cabinet of the decision to send aid to Greece and asked their advice on the best way to do it. Acheson outlined the problem that confronted us. He reviewed the role the British had played and what their withdrawal would mean. He informed the Cabinet, however, that the British had agreed to continue some support of the Greek government for another three months.

I explained the proposed request to Congress for the sum of $250,000,000 for Greece and $150,000,000 for Turkey but that I realized that this would be only the beginning.

There was general agreement. Secretary of Labor Schwellenbach had some misgivings of a political nature: He suspected that anti-British elements at home might charge that we were "again" pulling British chestnuts out of the fire. Several members of the Cabinet stressed the need for governmental reform in Greece. There was considerable discussion on the best method to apprise the American people of the issues involved.

On this last point I asked Secretary of the Treasury Snyder to head a committee to make recommendations to me. This group, with Acheson, Forrestal, Harriman, Patterson, Clinton Anderson, Schwellenbach, and John Steelman as members, met the next day. The committee recommended that, in order to emphasize the gravity of the situation, I appear in person before a joint session of the Congress.

I had already invited a group of congressional leaders to meet in my office on March 10. This group was larger than the one which had met with me on February 27. It included Senators Barkley, Connally, Taft, Vandenberg, and White, Speaker Martin, and Representatives Bloom, Cannon, Eaton, Halleck, McCormack, Rayburn, Short, and Taber. Dean Acheson was also present, and for two hours he and I discussed the Greek situation with the lawmakers. Vandenberg expressed his complete agreement with me. I answered questions by the congressmen similar to those asked at the first meeting. There was no opposition to what had to be done.

The drafting of the actual message which I would deliver to the Congress had meanwhile been started in the State Department. The first version was not at all to my liking. The writers had filled the speech with all sorts of background data and statistical figures about Greece and made the whole thing sound like an investment prospectus. I returned this draft to Acheson with a note asking for more emphasis on a declaration of general policy. The department's draftsmen then rewrote the speech to include a general policy statement, but it seemed to me half-hearted. The key sentence, for instance, read, "I believe that it should be the policy of the United States . . ." I took my pencil, scratched out "should" and wrote in "must." In several other places I did the same thing. I wanted no hedging in this speech. This was America's answer to the surge of expansion of Communist tyranny. It had to be clear and free of hesitation or double talk.

On Wednesday, March 12, 1947, at one o'clock in the afternoon, I stepped to the rostrum in the hall of the House of Representatives and addressed a joint session of the Congress. I had asked the senators and representatives to meet together so that I might place before them what I believed was an extremely critical situation.

To cope with this situation, I recommended immediate action by the Congress. But I also wished to state, for all the world to know, what the position of the United States was in the face of the new totalitarian challenge. This declaration of policy soon began to be referred to as the "Truman Doctrine." This was, I believe, the turning point in America's foreign policy, which now declared that wherever aggression, direct or indirect, threatened the peace, the security of the United States was involved.

"I believe," I said to the Congress and to a nationwide radio audience, "that it must be the policy of the United States to support free peoples who are resisting attempted subjugation by armed minorities or by outside pressures.

"I believe that we must assist free peoples to work out their own destinies in their own way.

"I believe that our help should be primarily through economic and financial aid which is essential to economic stability and orderly political processes."

After I delivered the speech, the world reaction to it proved that this approach had been the right one. All over the world, voices of approval made themselves heard, while Communists and their fellow travelers struck out at me savagely. The line had been drawn sharply. In my address I had said that every nation was now faced with a choice between alternative ways of life.

"One way of life," I said, "is based upon the will of the majority, and is distinguished by free institutions, representative government, free elections, guarantees of individual liberty, freedom of speech and religion and freedom from political oppression.

"The second way of life is based upon the will of a minority forcibly imposed upon the majority. It relies upon terror and oppression, a controlled press and radio, fixed elections, and the suppression of personal freedoms. . . .

"The seeds of totalitarian regimes," I said in closing, "are nurtured by misery and want. They spread and grow in the evil soil of poverty and strife. They reach their full growth when the hope of a people for a better life has died.

"We must keep that hope alive.

"The free peoples of the world look to us for support in maintaining their freedoms.

"If we falter in our leadership, we may endanger the peace of the world—and we shall surely endanger the welfare of our own nation."

When I ended my address, the congressmen rose as one man and applauded. Vito Marcantonio, the American Labor party representative from New York, was the only person in the hall who remained seated. Congress began the following day to work on legislation to put the program into effect. Meanwhile, members of my official family were busy rushing such aid and encouragement to Greece as I could provide without special congressional approval. Secretary Forrestal, on my instructions, dispatched the aircraft carrier *Leyte* and nine other vessels on a visit to Greece as a token of our intention, hoping to persuade the British to stay on, at least until our aid to Greece became effective.

Ambassador to Greece MacVeagh, the Ambassador to Turkey, Edwin C. Wilson, and Paul Porter were called back to Washington to give the benefit of their on-the-spot observations and their advice.

On April 5, on the occasion of the annual Jefferson Day Dinner, I added further emphasis to the ideas I had expressed in the address to Congress.

"We know," I said, "that as long as we remain free, the spirit of Thomas Jefferson lives in America. His spirit is the spirit of freedom. We are heartened by the knowledge that the light he kindled a century and a half ago shines today in the United States. It shines even more strongly and steadily than in his time. What was then an untried faith is now a living reality.

"But we know that no class, no party, no nation, has a monopoly on Jefferson's principles. Out of the silence of oppressed peoples, out of the despair of those who have lost freedom, there comes to us an expression of longing. Repeated again and again, in many tongues, from many directions, it is a plea of men, women and children for the freedom that Thomas Jefferson proclaimed as an inalienable right.

"When we hear the cry of freedom arising from the shores beyond our own, we can take heart from the words of Thomas Jefferson. In his letter to President Monroe, urging the adoption of what we now know as the Monroe Doctrine, he wrote:

" 'Nor is the occasion to be slighted which this proposition offers of declaring our protest against the atrocious violations of the rights of nations by the interference of any one in the internal affairs of another.'

"We, like Jefferson, have witnessed atrocious violations of the rights of nations.

"We, too, have regarded them as occasions not to be slighted.

"We, too, have declared our protest.

"We must make that protest effective by aiding those peoples whose freedoms are endangered by foreign pressures.

"We must take a positive stand. It is no longer enough merely to say, 'We don't want war.' We must act in time—ahead of time—to stamp out the smoldering beginnings of any conflict that may threaten to spread over the world. . . .

"The world today looks to us for leadership.

"The force of events makes it necessary that we assume that role.

"This is a critical period of our national life. The process of adapting ourselves to the new concept of our world responsibility is naturally a difficult and painful one. The cost is necessarily great.

"But it is not our nature to shirk our obligations. We have a heritage that constitutes the greatest resource of this nation. I call it the spirit and character of the American people.

"We are the people who gave to the world George Washington, Thomas Jefferson, Andrew Jackson, Abraham Lincoln, Woodrow Wilson, and Franklin D. Roosevelt.

"We are a people who not only cherish freedom and defend it, if need be with our lives, but we also recognize the right of other men and other nations to share it.

"While the struggle for the rights of man goes forward in other parts of the world, the free people of America cannot look on with easy detachment, with indifference to the outcome.

"In our effort to make permanent the peace of the world, we have much to preserve—much to improve—and much to pioneer. . . ."

Meanwhile, Congress debated the aid-to-Greece bill thoroughly and conscientiously. My hope that it would be passed before March 31 was not realized, but the Senate approved the legislation on April 22, and the House voted for it, 287 to 107, on May 9. On May 22, 1947, I signed the bill. With this enactment by Congress of aid to Greece and Turkey, America had served notice that the march of Communism would not be allowed to succeed by default.

The Communist rebels in Greece and their accomplices north of the border realized, of course, that the arrival of American aid would prove their undoing. They made every effort, therefore, to secure a victory before our aid might become effective. There was no doubt that the rebels were masterminded from the satellite countries. On May 23, 1947, the United Nations Balkan Investigating Commission had formally concluded that Yugoslavia, Bulgaria, and Albania were supporting the uprising against the Greek government. The vote in the Commission was 8 to 2; Russia and Poland, of course, were the "nays"; France abstained. Early in June the situation in northern Greece turned increasingly worse for the government forces. On June 9 our embassy reported "marked deterioration"; on the sixteenth the Greek government appealed for speed in the shipment of aid; it also asked that a larger proportion of the aid to be given be devoted to military equipment.

On July 9 the British Foreign Office told our Ambassador in London that their experts were extremely concerned over the Greek situation and thought that all prospects were gloomy. On July 16 General Marshall sent me a memorandum on the situation in Greece that began with the words, "The Greek situation has taken a serious turn in the last three days." Sizable guerrilla units had crossed the frontier from Albania. It appeared that they were aiming at the occupation of some larger communities that could serve as centers for a "people's republic."

I called the Secretary of the Navy and asked him how large a part of our Mediterranean fleet he might be able to move to Greek ports. Secretary Forrestal informed me that it would be entirely practicable to have a large part of the Mediterranean squadron shifted on short order. He expressed a belief that such a visit would have some deterrent effect on the activities of the Communist guerrillas but was unwilling to estimate how the American public might react.

Meanwhile, Dwight P. Griswold, former governor of Nebraska, whom I had named to be the administrator of our aid program in Greece, had arrived there. He was vigorously starting to build up a staff and to make arrangements for the reception and distribution of aid supplies. The Greek government, however, continued to show itself mostly concerned with military matters. The Greeks wanted equipment, advisers, money to expend its army, and would have given all our aid to the military if we had let them do it. Both Ambassador MacVeagh and Griswold worked steadily to induce the government to broaden its base and to seek the widest possible popular support.

Thus, even as we undertook to bolster the economy of Greece to help her combat Communist agitation, we were faced with her desire to use our aid to further partisan political, rather than national, aims. The overriding task that seemed to confront American policy in Europe was to provide an incentive for the Europeans to look at the situation in the broadest possible terms rather than in narrowly nationalistic, or even partisan, focus. Indeed, by the time this problem came to beset us in Greece, General Marshall had already made his famous Harvard speech, out of which grew the Marshall Plan.

CHAPTER 8

Never before in history has one nation faced so vast an undertaking as that confronting the United States of repairing and salvaging the victors as well as the vanquished. The complete surrender of the Axis powers did not bring any relaxation or rest for our people. They had to face and were ready to make whatever new sacrifices were necessary to insure the peace. This was the most destructive of all wars. There were no battle fronts, and civilian populations were, unhappily, military targets as much as were the armed forces, because they were part of the industrial and economic centers involved in a total war.

Attacks on industrial communities, the bombing of transportation, utilities, and other facilities strained to the breaking point the economic life already drained by the voracious needs of the armed forces.

Nations, if not continents, had to be raised from the wreckage. Unless the economic life of these nations could be restored, peace in the world could not be re-established.

In the first two years that followed V-J Day the United States provided more than *fifteen billion dollars* in loans and grants for the relief of the victims of war. We did everything humanly possible to prevent starvation, disease, and suffering. We provided substantial aid to help restore transportation and communications, and we helped rebuild wrecked economic systems in one major country after another.

For the first time in the history of the world a victor was willing to restore the vanquished as well as to help its allies. This was the attitude of the United States. But one of our allies took the conqueror's approach to victory.

The Russians wanted twenty billion dollars in reparations, and I told them at Potsdam that we did not intend to pay the reparations bill as we had so largely done after World War I. That was the only way they could collect these reparations now, because the vanquished were prostrate. We would rather make grants for rehabilitation to our allies and even to former enemies. In contrast, the Russians, wherever they could, stripped the countries they occupied, whether friends or enemies, of everything that could be carried off. Poland, Rumania, and Czechoslovakia are shining examples of the rewards that come for helping the ungrateful Russians.

The assistance we gave, which averted stark tragedy and started progress toward recovery in many areas of the world, was in keeping both with the American character and with America's new historic responsibility. To help peoples in distress was not only a tradition of our country but was also essential to our security. By rebuilding Europe and Asia, we would help to establish that healthy economic balance which is essential to the peace of the world.

By 1947, however, after two years of substantial, though piecemeal, emergency assistance, it was apparent that an even larger and more comprehensive program was needed to achieve the rebuilding of the economy of Europe. Speed was essential, because the West now faced the increasing pressure of Communist imperialism. And at the same time I felt that no amount of American aid would lead Europe to lasting recovery unless the nations of Europe themselves could also help cure some of their own chronic economic ills. With this thought in mind, I was looking for some method that would encourage the peoples of Europe to embark upon some joint undertaking that would eventually lead to effective self-help.

In the fall of 1946 the State-War-Navy Coordinating Committee was asked to join in this study and to submit recommendations for action. It seemed to me now that our experience with the Greek-Turkish aid program gave us a basis for an approach to a plan of economic assistance to our ailing allies.

On March 12, 1947, I made a policy speech in which I sought to outline the position the United States would take wherever there were active threats to the independence and stability of free nations.

A few days earlier, at Baylor University in Waco, Texas, I had expressed my belief that free world trade was an inseparable part of the peaceful world.

I said, "Our foreign relations, political and economic, are indivisible. We cannot say that we are willing to cooperate in the one field and are unwilling to cooperate in the other." I cited the economic war of the 'thirties, when nations strangled normal trade, depositors lost their savings, and farmers lost their lands. The lesson in history, I said, was plain: Freedom of international trade would provide the atmosphere necessary to the preservation of peace. My advisers were already at work seeking further practical ways to strengthen international co-operation in economic matters.

We had sent food to Europe, but millions there still did not have enough to eat. We had made loans to the countries of Europe, but the war had so disrupted the patterns of trade and industry there that the amounts we loaned were far less effective than we had hoped. I was disturbed because the loan to Britain had failed to accomplish what we thought it would.

Detailed reports came to my office daily from our government agencies about conditions abroad. A steady stream of appeals poured in from representative leaders of many foreign nations, virtually all of whom expressed the gravest concern over the economic situation and over the gains which Communism might score if there were no improvement. On April 26, when Secretary Marshall returned from the Moscow conference of Foreign Ministers, he arrived in a pessimistic mood. He had gone to Moscow with the hope that he could persuade the Russians that the United States was working for peace. The Russians, however, were interested only in their own plans and were coldly determined to exploit the helpless condition of Europe to further Communism rather than co-operate with the rest of the world.

Marshall's report confirmed my conviction that there was no time to lose in finding a method for the revival of Europe. General Marshall is one of the most astute and profound men I have ever known. Whenever any problem was brought before him, he seemed to be able to put his finger at once on the very basic approach that later would usually be proposed by the staff as the best solution. He talked very little but listened carefully to everything that was said. Sometimes he would sit for an hour with little or no expression on his face, but when he had heard enough, he would come up with a statement of his own that invariably cut to the very bone of the matter under discussion.

As Secretary of State, Marshall had to listen to more staff talk than when he was Chief of Staff. He would listen for a long time without comment, but when the debates between members of his staff seemed destined to go on interminably and he could stand it no longer, he would say, "Gentlemen, don't fight the problem; decide it." Dean Acheson told me a characteristic story about Marshall when he first took over as Secretary of State. Marshall had asked Dean Acheson to stay on as Under Secretary and said, "I want the most complete and blunt truths from you, particularly about myself." Dean Acheson replied, "Do you, General?" "Yes," Marshall said. "I have no feelings except a few which I reserve for Mrs. Marshall."

What Marshall perceived in the plans which his State Department staff laid before him was the importance of the economic unity of Europe. If the nations of Europe could be induced to develop their own solution of Europe's economic problems, viewed as a whole and tackled co-operatively rather than as separate national problems, United States aid would be more effective and the strength of a recovered Europe would be better sustained.

This was precisely the approach I had in mind. Marshall and I were in perfect agreement. It was my feeling that, beyond economic considerations, the idea of co-operation would stimulate new hope and confidence among the nations of Europe and thus provide a realistic argument against the Communists' counsel of despair.

This idea, as an approach to the European problem, was first expressed in public at Cleveland, Mississippi, on May 8, 1947, when Under Secretary of State Dean Acheson delivered what might be called the prologue to the Marshall Plan. Originally, it had been planned for me to speak at this meeting, but I had other commitments and asked Dean Acheson to fill the engagement. The Acheson speech contained the basic elements of the proposal which was given full development and expression a month later by Marshall.

The key point of the Acheson speech was his emphasis that the reconstruction of Europe would have to be dealt with as *one* problem. He stressed the interrelation of food and freedom. "The war," he said, "will not be over until the people of the world can again feed and clothe themselves and face the future with some degree of confidence." He then went on to offer a balance sheet of our past relief efforts and pointed out that further, more comprehensive financing would be necessary. Such use of our economic and financial resources would help preserve our own freedoms and democratic institutions because it would contribute to the security of our nation to widen the economic margins on which human dignity and free institutions abroad were struggling to survive.

Acheson's speech did not receive the attention it deserved at the time, although it contained the beginning of the proposal later made at Harvard by Secretary Marshall. On June 5, 1947, the Secretary of State outlined to a commencement audience a course of action for the United States in dealing with the European crisis.

This was a speech that was typical of the man. It was matter-of-fact and without oratorical flourishes, compact and to the point, and the

Secretary began it with a brief review of the economic condition of Europe.

Then he went on to set out a course of action: "It is logical," he said, "that the United States should do whatever it is able to do to assist in the return of normal economic health in the world, without which there can be no political stability and no assured peace. Our policy is directed not against any country or doctrine but against hunger, poverty, desperation and chaos. Its purpose should be the revival of a working economy in the world so as to permit the emergence of political and social conditions in which free institutions can exist. Such assistance must not be on a piecemeal basis as various crises develop. Any assistance that this government may render in the future should provide a cure rather than a mere palliative. Any government that is willing to assist in the task of recovery will find full cooperation . . . on the part of the United States Government. Any government which maneuvers to block the recovery of other countries cannot expect help from us. Furthermore, governments, political parties or groups which seek to perpetuate human misery in order to profit therefrom politically or otherwise will encounter the opposition of the United States."

Then came the key section of the plan: "It is already evident that, before the United States Government can proceed much further in its efforts to alleviate the situation and help start the European world on its way to recovery, there must be some agreement among the countries of Europe as to the requirement of the situation and the part those countries themselves will take in order to give proper effect to whatever action might be undertaken by the government. It would be neither fitting nor efficacious for this government to undertake to draw up unilaterally a program designed to place Europe on its feet economically. This is the business of the Europeans. The initiative, I think, must come from Europe. The role of this country should consist of friendly aid in the drafting of a European program and of later support of such a program so far as it may be practical for us to do so."

This was our proposal, that the countries of Europe agree on a cooperative plan in order to utilize the full productive resources of the continent, supported by whatever material assistance we could render to make the plan successful.

I had referred to the idea as the "Marshall Plan" when it was discussed in staff meetings, because I wanted General Marshall to get full credit for his brilliant contributions to the measure which he helped formulate. And it was Marshall who had envisioned the full scope of this approach. He had perceived the inspirational as well as the economic value of the proposal. History, rightly, will always associate his name with this program, which helped save Europe from economic disaster and lifted it from the shadow of enslavement by Russian Communism. Almost immediately following his enunciation of the idea in his Harvard speech, the term "Marshall Plan" became commonplace in the press and radio of the United States and other countries around the world, and I was glad to see his name identified with the plan. I believe the fact that a man of Marshall's world standing made the proposal of this policy helped greatly in its eventual adoption. He was one of the very few men in the government who had stayed in intimate contact with the day-by-day developments of this country's wartime operations in both hemispheres. Both as military strategist and diplomat, he was known and respected abroad as few men have been in the history of the United States. And at home he enjoyed the confidence and esteem of the average citizen regardless of political preferences, as well as the admiration of congressional leaders. Marshall's entire personality inspired confidence. I recall the worried months of early 1944, just before the Normandy invasion. There were many men in the Congress who harbored doubts and misgivings about the cross-Channel attack that was then generally expected, but General Marshall came to Capitol Hill and spoke to about four hundred and fifty of us members of Congress, and his quiet, determined manner, his complete command of all the facts of the situation quieted whatever fears anyone may have had. Most notably, too, everyone present respected the secrecy which the general asked us to observe. This was typical of the manner in which the man affected those who knew him. It is not surprising that all his recent detractors are men who never knew the measure of responsibility that was Marshall's, nor the manner in which he discharged that responsibility.

His many years in wartime Washington had endowed Marshall with a thorough knowledge and appreciation of the role of Congress. As head of the vast Army of World War II, he had dealt with administrative problems of unprecedented magnitude. These experiences proved invaluable when he addressed himself to the practical implementation of the plan which his Harvard University speech had set in motion.

The response to Marshall's speech was immediate, electrifying the free world. Ernest Bevin, Great Britain's Foreign Secretary, assuming the lead and quickly followed by French Foreign Minister Georges Bidault, informed Secretary Marshall that they were ready to take the kind of initiative he had suggested. Invitations went out from London and Paris to every European nation except Spain for a conference to attempt to draw up a comprehensive recovery program.

Russia's reaction was also immediate. For a short while it appeared as if Marshall's proposal might not only result in economic reconstruction but also in a lifting of the iron curtain. A little surprisingly, Mr. Molotov agreed to come to a preliminary meeting at which Bevin and Bidault proposed to lay out the agenda and procedure for the plenary meeting of the conference. However, Ambassador Bedell Smith correctly advised us from Moscow that Molotov had no intention of taking part in any constructive undertaking. What he was trying to do was to exploit the situation for Russia's own propaganda purposes. He sought to have Bevin and Bidault ask the United States for a dollar-and-cents figure of the total aid that Europe might expect. Of course the State Department would have been compelled to reply that we could not make a commitment in such a form, and the Soviets could have proclaimed to the world that we were hedging on our proposal.

As a French diplomatic observer put it, "The Soviets want to put the United States in a position where it must either shell out dollars before there is a real plan or refuse outright to advance any credits." French Foreign Minister Bidault told our Ambassador that "Molotov clearly does not wish this business to succeed, but on the other hand his hungry satellites are smacking their lips in expectation of getting some of your money. He is obviously embarrassed."

Indeed, Czechoslovakia accepted the invitation to the conference and Poland was also evidently eager to participate. In a dramatic move, however, the Kremlin ordered them to withdraw their acceptances, and Molotov departed from Paris with a blast against capitalism and the United States.

Sixteen nations were represented in Paris for the opening of this conference on July 12, 1947: Austria, Belgium, Denmark, France, Greece, Iceland, Ireland, Italy, Luxembourg, the Netherlands, Norway, Portugal, Sweden, Switzerland, Turkey, and the United Kingdom. And although Western Germany was not formally represented, its requirements as well as its ability to contribute to any general plan were considered by the conference.

The report of this conference was transmitted to Secretary Marshall on September 22, and two days later the Secretary placed it, and a number of related papers, on my desk for study. The report described the economic situation of Europe and the extent to which the participating countries thought they could solve their problems by individual or joint efforts. After taking into account these recovery efforts, the report then estimated the extent to which the sixteen countries would be able to pay for the imports they had to have.

I now made public a report of the studies by three separate committees which I had named to investigate the state of our own natural resources, as well as the impact on our economy of aid to other countries, and the character and quantities of resources available for aid to foreign countries. I also asked a number of congressional and administration leaders to meet in my office on Monday, September 29, to discuss plans for determining what action we should now take. Those invited to attend were the Secretary and the Under Secretary of State (Robert A. Lovett had succeeded Dean Acheson on July 1), the Secretaries of Agriculture and Commerce, and the following members of Congress: from the Senate, Bridges, Connally, Lucas, Vandenberg, and White; from the House, Arends, Bloom, Eaton, Halleck, Rayburn, and Wolcott.

I informed the congressmen of the details of the report and told them that it appeared that it would require $580,000,000 to take care of immediate European needs until March 31 of the following year, the earliest date on which the proposed plan could be made effective. I asked the chairman of the Senate and House committees on Foreign Relations and Foreign Affairs and on Appropriations to give earnest consideration to the need for speedy aid to western Europe, and we also discussed the possibility of calling Congress back into session to cope with the problem.

On October 1 letters went to the appropriate committee chairmen asking them to consider this a most urgent matter, especially in the light of the steady deterioration of the situation in France and Italy. A special session of Congress was called to meet on November 17. On October 23 I met with the congressional leaders and told them that I had taken this action partly so that Congress might take steps to halt the rising price spiral within our own nation but mostly to meet the crisis in western Europe.

On the following night I delivered a radio talk from the White House. I said that while we were considering a long-range program to aid European recovery, we would have to help some nations through an immediate crisis. "The most imminent danger exists in France and in Italy. If the economies of these countries collapse and the people succumb to totalitarian pressures, there will be no opportunity for them or for us to look forward to their recovery so essential to world peace."

Speaking in a similar vein when the special session of the Congress convened, I stressed that stopgap aid could be no substitute for a comprehensive long-range plan but that we needed to extend this immediate aid if we did not wish to see the very basis of our program destroyed before it could be put in operation.

On December 19, 1947, I sent a message to Congress setting forth the part the United States should play in a comprehensive plan for the recovery of Europe.

"In developing this program, certain basic considerations have been kept in mind:

"First, the program is designed to make genuine recovery possible within a definite period of time, and not merely to continue relief indefinitely.

"Second, the program is designed to insure that the funds and goods which we furnish will be used most effectively for European recovery.

"Third, the program is designed to minimize the financial cost to the United States, but at the same time to avoid imposing on the European countries crushing financial burdens which they could not carry in the long run.

"Fourth, the program is designed with due regard for conserving the physical resources of the United States and minimizing the impact on our economy of furnishing aid to Europe.

"Fifth, the program is designed to be consistent with other international relationships and responsibilities of the United States.

"Sixth, the administration of the program is designed to carry out wisely and efficiently this great enterprise of our foreign policy."

This whole thing was to be done, I advised the Congress, in the expectation that European recovery could be substantially completed in about four years. The total cost over the four years had been calculated at $17,000,000,000. I asked the Congress to authorize the appropriation of this amount and to provide $6,800,000,000 of this amount by April 1, 1948, to cover the initial—and most critical—period of fifteen months, to June 30, 1949.

Seventeen billion dollars sounded like a huge sum, and of course it was. But compared to the financial cost alone of World War II, it seemed small. The money to be invested in the rebuilding of decent standards of living in Europe would amount to only five per cent of the sums we had expended to defeat the Axis. It would represent less than three per cent of our total national income during the time that the program would be in effect. The estimates of the experts showed that it was well within the capacity of the American people to undertake.

I had not lost sight of the United Nations and our obligation to it. "Our support of European recovery," I said in my message to Congress, "is in full accord with our support of the United Nations. The success of the United Nations depends upon the independent strength of its members and their determination and ability to adhere to the ideals and principles embodied in the Charter. The purposes of the European recovery program are in complete harmony with the purposes of the Charter—to insure a peaceful world through the joint efforts of free nations. Attempts by any nation to prevent or sabotage European recovery for selfish ends are clearly contrary to these purposes.

"It is not feasible to carry out the recovery program exclusively through the United Nations. Five of the participating countries are not yet members of the United Nations. Furthermore, some European members are not participating in the program. United States support of the European recovery program will enable the free nations of Europe to devote their great energies to the reconstruction of their economies. On this depend the restoration of a decent standard of living for their peoples, the development of a sound world economy and continued support for the ideals of individual liberty and justice. . . .

"This joint undertaking of the United States and a group of European nations, in devotion to the principles of the United Nations, is proof that free men can effectively join together to defend their free institutions against totalitarian pressures, and to promote better standards of life for all their peoples."

Congress acted on my request as quickly as it was possible for it to act. The lawmakers did not accept the full amount proposed. Three and one half months later, on April 3, 1948, I signed the European Recovery Act passed by Congress. Two days later I announced the appointment of Paul G. Hoffman as Economic Cooperation Administrator with Cabinet rank.

Credit is due to Republican Senator Arthur H. Vandenberg and to Republican Representative Charles A. Eaton, the chairmen, respectively, of the Senate Committee on Foreign Relations and the Committee on Foreign Affairs of the House of Representatives. In a Congress dedicated to tax reduction and the pruning of governmental expenditures, they championed this program in a truly bi-partisan manner. A subsequent Congress changed the administrative structure of the plan and merged it with military assistance programs into a Mutual Security Administration.

The job of economic rehabilitation was successfully accomplished at far less cost than had been anticipated. I had told the congressional leaders that I thought seventeen billions of dollars over a four-year period would do the job of economic rehabilitation successfully. Thirteen billions did it.

The Marshall Plan will go down in history as one of America's greatest contributions to the peace of the world. I think the world now realizes that without the Marshall Plan it would have been difficult for western Europe to remain free from the tyranny of Communism.

CHAPTER 9

Russia was caught off guard by the Marshall Plan. Moscow quickly realized that when the Marshall Plan began to function, the opportunity to communize western Europe by exploiting her economic miseries would be lost. Failing to prevent Allied co-operation for European recovery, Russia sought to retaliate by two moves. The first move was to set up a counterpart of a Marshall Plan under Russian auspices for her satellites. This was designed to cut off whatever flow of trade and commerce had been resumed between eastern and western Europe. This would also retard the restoration of the normal, prewar flow of commerce so essential to these countries in Europe.

The second and even more provocative move was to risk a military incident in Berlin designated to test our firmness and our patience. The British, French, and American forces were in close quarters with the Russians in Berlin. Each occupied separate zones in the former capital, which was surrounded entirely by German territory held by the Russians, and all movement of American, British, and French personnel and supplies to our areas in Berlin was through a narrow corridor controlled by the Russians. Under the provisions of the agreement between Roosevelt, Churchill, and Stalin, the military government to rule Germany was to be jointly directed from Berlin.

There has been a lot of discussion over the origin of the East-West division of Germany. Our military experts had been fully aware of the fact that Russia's power would enable her, once our invading forces had drawn German strength from the Eastern Front, to drive deep into Germany. Therefore, boundaries that were agreed on long before the fighting came to an end reflected the expectations of the Allied military planners as to where their troops might find themselves at the war's end.

For the first year after the war the British and Americans made every effort to make a joint control succeed. The Russians, however, with a good assist from the French, defeated these efforts. The French were fearful of Germany. Of course three German invasions in seventy years had given them ample grounds to fear the Germans. But their desire to see Germany dismembered led them to obstruct a number of joint-control measures at a time when such co-operation might still have been possible.

The Russians, on their part, seemed determined to treat their zone of Germany virtually as if it were Soviet conquered territory. They sealed off all contacts between their part of Germany and the areas occupied by us, the British, and the French, and this left little choice to the officials of the three governments in the western part of Germany. Arrangements had to be made for some restoration of normal economic activity, and in order to facilitate it, "bi-zonal" machinery was set up to cover both the British and American zones. Later the French joined in the arrangements.

Of the many reports I received on conditions in Germany, one of the summaries was given me by W. Averell Harriman, who was Secretary of Commerce at the time. Late in the summer of 1947, after a visit to Germany, Harriman said, "We are putting in too little too late. As a result, we have lost a considerable part of the expenditures made so far. The German economy has been living on its reserves, both human and material, and it is still on the decline. We will have to increase our current expenditures in order to reduce the total cost over the years. . . . Material reserves are being rapidly consumed. There is inadequate fertilization for agriculture. Industry is using up its spare parts and stocks. Transportation has cannibalized bad-order locomotives and freight cars to keep others running. We shall face one crisis after another unless steps are taken promptly to turn the downward trend upward. . . . We cannot attain our basic objectives unless we are ready to move rapidly to reconstruct German life from its present pitiful and chaotic condition. The recovery of Germany in feeding and in industrial production has lagged far behind western Europe. We cannot revive a self-supporting western European economy without a healthy Germany playing its part as a producing and consuming unit."

This was the lowest point in German postwar conditions. Increased appropriations soon became available, West German needs were included in Marshall Plan estimates, and the bi-zonal organization helped to restore some measure of industrial activity.

The Russians, meanwhile, became less and less tractable, and on

March 20, 1948, their representative finally walked out of the Allied Control Council. For most of Germany, this act merely formalized what had been an obvious fact for some time; namely, that the four-power control machinery had become unworkable. For the city of Berlin, however, this was the curtain-raiser for a major crisis.

On March 31 the deputy military governor of the Soviet Union, General Dratvin, notified our military government in Berlin that in two days, beginning April 1, the Russians would check all U.S. personnel passing through their zone for identification and would inspect all freight shipments and all except personal baggage.

Our military government authorities rejected these conditions. They pointed out that we had been assured free access to Berlin at the time our troops withdrew from Saxony and Thuringia into their own zones. The Russians claimed that no such agreement had been made. They declared that they had the full right to control all traffic in their zone. They began to stop our trains at the zonal border and turn them back when the train commanders under orders, refused to submit to inspection. Between April 1 and July 1 Russian orders sealed off all highway, rail, and river traffic into and out of Berlin. "Technical difficulties" was given as the reason by the Russians.

The nature of these "difficulties" soon became apparent. On June 18 the British, French, and Americans announced that the three western zones would immediately set up a new type of currency. The Russians had plates of the currency in use at the beginning of the occupation and had been able to flood the western zone with money printed in the east zone, thus deliberately adding to the inflation which threatened to block Germany's effort at recovery. In due course we changed the plates, but Russia continued to manipulate the east mark. Our currency reform was designed to give Germany a sound mark to use in the west. And of course the good western currency was preferred by all Germans. The Russians opposed our currency reform because it exposed the basic unsoundness of their own currency. And it became one of the major points of contention during the discussions on the Berlin blockade. The importance the Russians attached to our move was soon obvious: They offered to reopen the approaches to the city of Berlin if the Western powers would call off the currency change-over.

What the Russians were trying to do was to get us out of Berlin. At first they took the position that we never had a legal right to be in Berlin. Later they said we had had the right but that we had forfeited it.

The entire setup of the four powers in Berlin, involving our withdrawal from areas intended for Russian occupation, had been negotiated as a military matter by the generals in the field. General Lucius

Clay later blamed himself for not having insisted on a confirmation of the agreement in writing. It is my opinion that it would have made very little difference to the Russians whether or not there was an agreement in writing. What was at stake in Berlin was not a contest over legal rights, although our position was entirely sound in international law, but a struggle over Germany and, in a larger sense, over Europe. In the face of our launching of the Marshall Plan, the Kremlin tried to mislead the people of Europe into believing that our interest and support would not extend beyond economic matters and that we would back away from any military risks.

I brought up the situation at the Cabinet meeting of June 25. Secretary of the Army Kenneth Royall maintained constant touch with General Clay in Germany and reported that a serious situation was developing. I asked Royall to inquire from General Clay whether the situation was serious enough to consider the removal of the families of our personnel in Berlin. Clay thought it unwise to do so for the psychological effect the move might have. Clay was forced to make emergency arrangements to have essential supplies flown into the city, since Berlin, by now, was effectively blockaded by the Russians both by land and by water.

On June 26, the day after I discussed the Berlin crisis with the Cabinet, I directed that this improvised "airlift" be put on a full-scale organized basis and that every plane available to our European Command be impressed into service. In this way we hoped that we might be able to feed Berlin until the diplomatic deadlock could be broken.

Negotiations had been transferred to Moscow, where on July 6 the representatives of the three Western powers, with our Ambassador, W. Bedell Smith, acting as spokesman, put their case before the Russians. The Soviet reply, given on July 14, dropped all pretenses of "technical difficulties" and made it abundantly clear that the blockading of Berlin by the Russians was a major political and propaganda move. The Soviets refused, at this time, to talk about Berlin except as part of discussions covering the entire subject of Germany. They rejected our condition that the blockade be lifted before any talks could start.

I issued instructions to have General Clay and his State Department adviser, Robert Murphy, called to Washington to make a report.

The Russians were obviously determined to force us out of Berlin. They had suffered setbacks recently in Italy, in France, and in Finland. Their strongest satellite, Yugoslavia, had suddenly developed a taste for independent action, and the European Recovery Program was beginning to succeed. The blockade of Berlin was international Communism's counterattack. The Kremlin had chosen perhaps the most sensitive objective in Europe—Berlin, the old capital of Germany, which was and is a symbol to the Germans. If we failed to maintain our position there, Communism would gain great strength among the Germans. Our position in Berlin was precarious. If we wished to remain there, we would have to make a show of strength. But there was always the risk that Russian reaction might lead to war. We had to face the possibility that Russia might deliberately choose to make Berlin the pretext for war, but a more immediate danger was the risk that a trigger-happy Russian pilot or hotheaded Communist tank commander might create an incident that could ignite the powder keg.

General Clay came to the White House on July 22, 1948, to attend the meeting that day of the National Security Council, and I asked him to report on the situation in Germany.

Here, in substance, is what he said: The abandonment of Berlin would have a disastrous effect upon our plans for Western Germany. It would also slow down European recovery, the success of which depended upon more production, particularly from Western Germany. The Germans in general were more concerned than the Allies about the possibility of our leaving Berlin. We should be prepared to go to any lengths to find a peaceful solution to the situation, but we had to remain in Berlin.

The attitude of the German people, Clay added, was in some respects unbelievable. The party leaders in Berlin who made up the City Magistrate, with headquarters in the Soviet zone, had absolutely refused to accept Soviet control. The people of Berlin were determined to stand firm even if it required undergoing additional hardships.

He reported that the airlift had been averaging about 2400 to 2500 tons per day, which was more than enough to handle food requirements but was inadequate to include the necessary amounts of coal. The minimum required to sustain Berlin without extreme hardship was estimated to be 4500 tons per day. For the summer 3500 tons per day might suffice, but additional tonnage would be required during the winter.

At the moment, the airlift operation involved fifty-two C-54's and eighty C-47's. Two round trips were made each day, involving more than 250 landings. Seventy-five additional C-47 planes would enable us to bring in 3500 tons daily.

I asked the Air Force Chief of Staff what problems would be involved in making these additional planes available and was told by General Vandenberg that if we put more planes on the Berlin airlift the Military Air Transport Service would become disrupted. We would also find that we would need at least one more major airfield inside Berlin to handle the traffic and at least one major maintenance depot at the other end.

In answer to a question by Secretary Marshall, General Vandenberg said that the maximum airlift would involve using planes which are intended for emergency use, many of which might be destroyed in case of hostilities. This would adversely affect our capabilities to wage strategic warfare. If the majority of our planes were caught and destroyed, this would delay our ability to supply our forces and hold outlying bases. General Vandenberg also pointed out that the air lanes to Berlin belonged to the Russians as well as us and that if we increased our traffic to the point where they could claim that they were forced out, international incidents might result.

I then asked General Clay what risks would be involved if we tried to supply Berlin by means of armed convoys. The general said he thought the initial reaction of the Russians would be to set up road blocks. Our engineers would be able to clear such obstacles, provided there was no Russian interference, but the next step the Russians would take, General Clay thought, would be to meet the convoys with armed force.

Robert Lovett, who was in attendance with Secretary Marshall, asked Clay if he thought the Russians might try to block our airplanes with fighter patrols or by other methods. General Clay said he felt that the Russians would not attack our planes unless they had made the decision to go to war.

I asked General Clay if there were any indications known to him that the Russians would go to war. He said he did not think so. What they seemed to be aiming at was to score a major victory by forcing us out of Berlin, either now or after fall and winter weather forced us to curtail the airlift, without, however, extending the conflict.

We discussed the kind of assistance that we might expect from our allies if the conflict became more intense. I stated it as my judgment that if we moved out of Berlin we would be losing everything we were fighting for. The main question was: How could we remain in Berlin without risking all-out war?

General Vandenberg said again that he felt the concentration of aircraft necessary to provide Berlin with all its supplies by air would mean reducing our air strength elsewhere, both in planes and in personnel. An emergency would find us more exposed than we might be able to afford.

I did not agree with the Air Force Chief of Staff. I asked him if he would prefer to have us attempt to supply Berlin by ground convoy. Then, if the Russians resisted that effort and plunged the world into war, would not the Air Force have to contribute its share to the defense of the nation? I answered my own question: The airlift involved less risks than armed road convoys. Therefore, I directed the Air Force to furnish the fullest support possible to the problem of supplying Berlin.

General Vandenberg interjected that that would not be possible unless additional airfield facilities were constructed in Berlin. General Clay pointed out that he had already selected a site for an additional field and that construction, using German manpower, could begin at once. General Vandenberg then assured me that the Air Force would devote its entire energy to the carrying out of my order.

I was compelled to leave the meeting at this point, but the Council continued to discuss various phases of the problem, such as the number of planes that could be put on the airlift at once and the number of dependents to be retained in Berlin.

We had to be prepared to expand the airlift to a maximum while continuing talks with the Russians to see if the blockade could not be removed by agreement. On July 30 Ambassador Smith and his French and British colleagues handed the Russian Foreign Ministry the Allied reply to the Russian note of July 14. We declared that the Russian reply had offered no constructive suggestion. The situation was full of dangers to world peace, and for that reason the three ambassadors requested a conference with Stalin and Molotov.

This interview with Stalin and Molotov took place on August 2 at nine o'clock in the evening. Stalin, as was so often the case, appeared more open to argument than his subordinates had been, and the meeting resulted in a more relaxed atmosphere. Stalin indicated that he was willing to have the transport restrictions lifted, provided arrangements were made to have both the eastern and western types of German currency circulate in all of Berlin. He no longer insisted that there had to be a conference on all-German problems before the blockade was lifted, but he wished it recorded that it was the "insistent wish" of the Soviet government that the Allies postpone the next steps planned in the integration of the western zones.

However, when Ambassador Smith and his colleagues sat down with Molotov to put this understanding into a formal statement, the Russian position once again turned uncompromising and hard. Four lengthy meetings produced no agreement. Our representatives objected to the inclusion in the Russian draft of a sentence that, in substance, would have had us admit that we were being readmitted to Berlin by sufferance only. Molotov rejected the Western draft because it asserted that we were in Berlin as a matter of established right. The Russian version said that transportation restrictions imposed after the date of the currency reform would be lifted, but since the currency reform did not come into effect until late in June, such an undertaking would not have included a great many of the prior restrictions. What was more important, if we signed this statement, we would have agreed to the Russian contention that the blockade was a "defense" against our currency measure. In addition, the Russian draft would have vested the control of both currencies in use in Berlin in one bank, completely controlled by them, and would have given a Russian-controlled agency supervision over all of Berlin's external trade.

These drafting sessions with Molotov proved so futile that we instructed Smith to ask for another personal conference with Premier Stalin. This meeting took place on August 23, and again Stalin appeared much more interested in reaching a basis for understanding than Molotov had been. On the matter of how far back the lifting of restrictions should extend, Molotov again insisted that the statement should promise only the lifting of those restrictions that had been imposed after June 18. Stalin, however, thought it would be better to have the statement read "the restrictions lately imposed" and to have it understood that if any restrictions had been imposed prior to June 18 they would also be lifted. Stalin also agreed that the Soviet bank that was to control the two Berlin currencies would, in turn, be under four-power control.

But Molotov again proved difficult when the diplomats sat down to draw up a communiqué and a set of instructions for the four military governors in Berlin who, it had been agreed, should work out the details. In the end, in fact, it was impossible to issue even an interim communiqué to inform the public that technical questions had been referred to Berlin, because Molotov refused to agree to any text except in his terms.

The discussions among the four military governors never got out of the stage of frustration. Marshal Sokolovsky, the Russian representative, at once took a position diametrically opposed to the explicit assurances which Stalin had given the ambassadors, declaring that he would not even consider the removal of any of the restrictions imposed before June 18. Indeed, he tried to put new restrictions in, this time on air traffic. He also stated categorically that control by the four powers of the bank issuing the currency certificates was out of the question. The week of technical discussions in Berlin proved even more futile than the month of negotiations in Moscow.

The airlift, meanwhile, steadily expanded. On August 20 Secretary of the Army Royall reported to the National Security Council that the combined British-American lift had averaged 3,300 tons daily and that the maximum for any day's lift had now reached 4,575 tons. Of this tonnage, the British, using everything they had available by way of transport planes, had flown in about one third. The stockpiles in Berlin were slowly growing; there was now a 25-day reserve of coal and a 30-day reserve of food in that city. On September 9 Secretary of the Air Force Symington informed the National Security Council that since early August the daily average lift had been increased to 4,000 tons and that it was likely that 5,000 tons a day could be reached if additional cargo planes were allocated.

At this September 9 meeting of the NSC we discussed at length the implications of the apparent failure of the negotiations with the Russians. Marshall and Lovett reviewed the diplomatic events of the past month and concluded that apparently we would have no alternative but to put the case before the United Nations. Under Secretary Lovett called attention to the fact that the Soviets had announced that they would hold air maneuvers in a general area that included the air lanes used by our airlift. We informed the Russians that we would not halt our air operations.

Secretary Marshall pointed out that time was on the side of the Soviets. We could continue and even step up the airlift, but even though it had been more successful than had been expected, the Russians could try our patience by ever-new methods. Just recently, for instance, there had been Communist-led riots in the western zones of Berlin, and the situation was so dangerous that the slightest element added might be the fuse to spark a general conflagration.

Some voices were raised in America calling for a break with the Russians. These people did not understand that our choice was only between negotiations and war. There was no third way. As long as the Russians were willing to continue talks—however futile—there would be no shooting.

Ambassador Smith was directed to hand Molotov an *aide-mémoire* which listed the specific causes of the failure of the Berlin talks and stated our position in the plainest language possible. Molotov's reply was the same old story. All the blame was on our side, and nothing much could be done until we accepted the Soviet position in its entirety.

The Foreign Ministers of France, Britain, and the United States, who were at that moment conferring in Paris, issued a statement on September 26, 1948, calling the Soviet reply "unsatisfactory" and announcing that the case would now be placed before the United Nations. I was at that time crossing the country on one of my crucial political campaign trips, but I kept in close and constant touch with all developments. Messages and documents were all forwarded to me for approval. Robert Lovett, as Acting Secretary of State, was as meticulous as General Marshall in making sure that the President was constantly advised of developments and his approval obtained before any major step was taken or important statements issued.

The American complaint against Russia was formally submitted to the United Nations in a note which Ambassador Warren Austin handed to Trygve Lie, the Secretary General of the U.N., on September 29. The note drew attention to the "serious situation which has arisen as a result of the unilateral imposition by the Government of the Union of Soviet Socialist Republics of restrictions on transport and communications between the western zones of occupation in Germany and Berlin," and charged that the action was a threat to the peace under Chapter VII of the Charter. The note also made it clear that the United States regarded the Soviet action as a pressure device to secure political objectives.

The Soviet government took the position that there would have been no blockade if the Western powers had acceded to the Russian position. Furthermore, so Mr. Vishinsky argued in the Security Council of the United Nations, there was no blockade in the sense of traditional international law and, therefore, there could be no real threat to peace. The Soviet Union, Vishinsky said, would not take part in any discussion of the blockade before the Security Council.

Our spokesman before the Security Council throughout this dispute was Professor Philip Jessup of Columbia University. Jessup was one of the leading authorities on international law, and he gained the respect of the world for the statesmanlike manner in which he represented the case for the Western powers before the U.N.

The battle of diplomacy was overshadowed, however, by the drama of the aerial convoys that day after day winged their way into Berlin. By mid-October General Clay could state as a proven conclusion that the airlift was no longer an experiment. Even adverse weather could not keep our supply planes from making their runs from the western zones into the blockaded former capital of Germany.

General Clay made this report at another meeting of the National Security Council on October 22, 1948, when he placed before us an account not only of the technical achievement of the airlift but also of the effect our action in Berlin had had on the German people. They had closed ranks and applied themselves to the tasks of reconstruction with new vigor. It had turned them sharply against Communism. Germany, which had been waiting passively to see where it should cast its lot for the future, was veering toward the cause of the Western nations.

The Soviet leaders made further attempts toward the end of the year to induce the Berliners to weaken in their determination to stick with the West. On November 30, Soviet intrigues led to the splitting up of the Berlin city council, and the city was thus, for all practical purposes, split in two. The Russians also introduced a new identification system that made contacts between the eastern and western portions of the city almost impossible, and they changed the system of distribution for electric power, virtually disrupting the transport setup.

Meanwhile, the Security Council of the United Nations had a technical committee working on recommendations for a solution of the currency deadlock. Our reaction to these proposals was that our experience with the Russians impelled us to reject any plan that provided for a four-power operation. We had learned that the Russians would usually agree in principle but would rarely perform in practice. We wanted a settlement, but we could not accept a settlement that would put the people of Berlin at the mercy of the Soviets and their German Communist hirelings.

This is where things stood as 1948 ended and 1949 began. We had fought off the Russian attempt to force us out of Berlin. The longer the blockade continued, the more the technical efficiency of the airlift improved, and the more the people of Germany looked toward the West to strengthen them in their determination to remain free. Berlin had become a symbol of America's—and the West's—dedication to the cause of freedom.

The Kremlin began to see that its effort to force us out was doomed. Russia's toughness and truculence in the Berlin matter had led many Europeans to realize the need for closer military assistance ties among the Western nations, and this led to discussions which eventually resulted in the establishment of NATO. Berlin had been a lesson to all.

Late in January 1949 the Kremlin released a series of answers given by Premier Stalin to questions submitted by an American correspondent. Stalin had used this device—and correspondents—on other occasions to indicate changes in attitude or policy. At this time he answered a question with regard to the Berlin blockade, saying that there would be no obstacle to the lifting of the traffic restrictions if restrictions imposed by the three Western powers and by the Russians were lifted at the same time.

Dean Acheson, whom I had appointed Secretary of State after my election in 1948, made his regular call at the White House after this Stalin interview was published. We went over the answers of the Russian Premier with great care. We noticed that for the first time since June 1948 the Berlin blockade was not tied to the currency matter in the Russian statement. Acheson suggested, and I approved, that we instruct Jessup to find out from the Russian delegation at the U.N. if this had been intentional.

On February 15, 1949, Dr. Jessup found an informal opportunity to pass a few words with Mr. Malik, the Soviet representative at the U.N., while the delegates were in their lounge. Jessup observed to Malik that

Stalin's answer made no reference to the currency problem in the Berlin matter. Was this omission of any significance? Mr. Malik said he did not know but that he would ask. Exactly one month later he had an answer: The omission was "not accidental." This is an example of how difficult it was to do business with the Russians on a straightforward basis.

The Russians were still insistent that we call off our actions to create a West German government. But they were no longer insistent that this had to be done first before they would call off the blockade. They were now willing to agree that all restrictions on traffic in and out of Berlin imposed by either side after March 1, 1948, would be lifted, and that then the Council of Foreign Ministers should be convened to discuss "matters arising out of the situation in Berlin, and matters affecting Germany as a whole." Thus the Russians were ready to retreat. On May 4 a communiqué announced that the four governments concerned— the United States, Great Britain, France, and the U.S.S.R.—had agreed: The blockade of Berlin would end on May 12.

More than fourteen months had passed since the first restrictions had been imposed by the Russians. A little over a year had elapsed during which Berlin had been supplied by means of the airlift.

This achievement by the Air Force deserves much praise. Technically, it was an extremely difficult job—so difficult that even the Air Force chiefs themselves at first had serious doubts that it could be done. It proved a beacon light of hope for the peoples of Europe.

When we refused to be forced out of the city of Berlin, we demonstrated to the people of Europe that with their co-operation we would act, and act resolutely, when their freedom was threatened. Politically it brought the peoples of western Europe more closely to us.

The Berlin blockade was a move to test our capacity and will to resist. This action and the previous attempts to take over Greece and Turkey were part of a Russian plan to probe for soft spots in the Western Allies' positions all around their own perimeter.

CHAPTER 10

The fate of the Jewish victims of Hitlerism was a matter of deep personal concern to me. I have always been disturbed by the tragedy of people who have been made victims of intolerance and fanaticism because of their race, color, or religion. These things should not be possible in a civilized society. Russia and Poland, in recent history, had been terrible persecutors of the Jews, and east of the Rhine, ghettos were the rule, some of them going back to the Middle Ages. But the organized brutality of the Nazis against the Jews in Germany was one of the most shocking crimes of all times. The plight of the victims who had survived the mad genocide of Hitler's Germany was a challenge to Western civilization, and as President I undertook to do something about it. One of the solutions being proposed was a national Jewish home.

The question of Palestine as a Jewish homeland goes back to the solemn promise that had been made to them by the British in the Balfour Declaration of 1917—a promise which had stirred the hopes and the dreams of these oppressed people. This promise, I felt, should be kept, just as all promises made by responsible, civilized governments should be kept.

My first official contact with the problem took place within a few days of the time I became President, when Secretary Stettinius had sent me a letter offering to "brief" me on Palestine before I might be approached by any interested parties. It was likely, he said, that efforts would soon be made by some of the Zionist leaders to obtain from me some commitments in favor of the Zionist program, which was aimed at unlimited Jewish immigration into Palestine and the establishment there of a Jewish state.

Stettinius said, "There is continual tenseness in the situation in the Near East largely as a result of the Palestine question, and as we have interests in that area which are vital to the United States, we feel that this whole subject is one that should be handled with the greatest care and with a view to the long-range interests of this country."

Two weeks later Joseph C. Grew, who in Stettinius' absence was the Acting Secretary of State, sent me a further memorandum on the subject, informing me that "although President Roosevelt at times gave expression to views sympathetic to certain Zionist aims, he also gave certain assurances to the Arabs which they regard as definite commitments on our part. On a number of occasions within the past few years, he authorized the Department to assure the heads of the different Near Eastern Governments in his behalf that 'in the view of this Government there should be no decision altering the basic situation in Palestine without full consultation with both Arabs and Jews.' In his meeting with King Ibn Saud early in 1945, Mr. Roosevelt promised the King that as regards Palestine he would make no move hostile to the Arab people and would not assist the Jews as against the Arabs.

"I am attaching a copy of a memorandum summarizing the conversation between Ibn Saud and Mr. Roosevelt, of which the original is presumably with Mr. Roosevelt's papers. After the meeting, this memorandum was approved by both the President and the King, so that it may be regarded as completely authentic. On April 5, only a week before his death, the President signed a letter to Ibn Saud in which he repeated the assurances which he had made to the King during the meeting. A copy of this letter is also attached.

"The Arabs, not only in Palestine but throughout the whole Near East, have made no secret of their hostility to Zionism and their Governments say that it would be impossible to restrain them from rallying with arms, in defense of what they consider to be an Arab country. We know that President Roosevelt understood this clearly, for as recently as March 3, after his trip to the Near East, he told an officer of the Department that, in his opinion, a Jewish state in Palestine (the ultimate Zionist aim) could be established and maintained only by military force.

"I should be glad to furnish you with any additional background material. . . ."

I was fully aware of the Arabs' hostility to Jewish settlement in Palestine, but, like many Americans, I was troubled by the plight of the Jewish people in Europe. The Balfour Declaration, promising the Jews the opportunity to re-establish a homeland in Palestine, had always seemed to me to go hand in hand with the noble policies of Woodrow Wilson, especially the principle of self-determination. When I was in the

Senate, I had told my colleagues, Senator Wagner of New York and Senator Taft of Ohio, that I would go along on a resolution putting the Senate on record in favor of the speedy achievement of the Jewish homeland.

But the State Department's concern was mainly with the question of how the Arabs would react and that this was the wrong time to raise the Palestine question. In another memorandum, on June 16, 1945, the Acting Secretary of State said the State Department's view was that Palestine was one of the problems which should come up for settlement after the war through the United Nations Organization, and that in any event no decision regarding it should be taken without full consultation with both the Arabs and Jews. The memorandum closed with this well-intended advice on the subject of the likely call on me by Zionist leaders: "It does not seem, therefore, that you need go any further, unless you care to do so, than to thank the Zionist leaders for any materials which they may give you and to assure them their views will be given your careful consideration."

The Arab states presented their reasons for opposing a Jewish state and increased immigration to Palestine in letters to the State Department. The Egyptian Prime Minister, Nokrashy Pasha, wrote me directly:

". . . It is greatly to be regretted that persecutions of the Jews in certain European countries during the past half century and more, and especially their greatly intensified sufferings since the rise of Nazism, should have been seized upon by certain political elements to advance the politico-racial theories of Zionism and to appeal to the world at large for the support of their program. Unfortunately the brunt of their effort has concentrated on Palestine where the Arabs, who, throughout their history, have shown great tolerance and even hospitality toward the Jews, are the innocent victims of propagandas, pressures and deprivations which they are quite unable to bear. Why, from a perfectly objective point of view, one small nation of 1,000,000 people living in a very small territory should be forced to accept in 25 years immigrants of an alien race up to nearly 50 per cent of their own number is hard to understand. The difficulties of absorbing such large numbers of aliens have been so great that the Arabs are firmly resolved to oppose any further increase in immigration. This principle has already been approved by a British White Paper. But this has not been the most serious aspect. Now, the guests at the Arab's table are declaring that in any case they are going to bring in large numbers of their kinsmen, take over all of his lands, and rule to suit themselves. It is this program of setting up a Jewish State in which the Arabs will be either reduced to the inferior status of a minority or else have to leave their homes that arouses their firm determination to resist at all costs."

This was my reply to the Egyptian Prime Minister:

". . . I wish to assure you that the views set forth in the memorandum have received my careful attention. I am fully aware of the deep interest of the Arab countries in reaching an equitable solution of the Palestine question, and I wish to renew the assurances which your Government has previously received to the effect that in the view of the Government of the United States no decision should be taken regarding the basic situation in Palestine without full consultation with both Arabs and Jews. . . ."

Similar replies were given to the heads of government of other Arab states who wrote in the same vein. It was my position that the principle of self-determination required that Arabs as well as Jews be consulted. To assure the Arabs that they would be consulted was by no means inconsistent with my generally sympathetic attitude toward Jewish aspirations.

It was my belief that world peace would, in the long run, be best served by a solution that would accord justice to the needs and the wants of the Jewish people who had so long been persecuted. The acts of extremists in Palestine, whether Jewish or Arab, I condemned and deplored, but I also felt that it was important that some encouragement be given to the Jews who wanted to further their cause by accepted democratic methods.

I had already decided that Palestine would be one of the subjects I would want to bring up in discussion with Churchill at the Potsdam meeting, and on July 24 I sent the following memorandum to him inviting him to discuss the subject with me:

"There is a great interest in America in the Palestine problem. The drastic restrictions imposed on Jewish immigration by the British White Paper of May, 1939, continue to provoke passionate protest from Americans most interested in Palestine and in the Jewish problem. They fervently urge the lifting of these restrictions which deny to Jews, who have been so cruelly uprooted by ruthless Nazi persecutions, entrance into the land which represents for so many of them their only hope of survival.

"Knowing your deep and sympathetic interest in Jewish settlement in Palestine, I venture to express to you the hope that the British government may find it possible without delay to lift the restrictions of the White Paper on Jewish immigration into Palestine.

"While I realize the difficulties of reaching a definite and satisfactory settlement of the Palestine problem, and that we cannot expect to discuss these difficulties at any length at our present meeting, I have some doubt whether these difficulties will be lessened by prolonged delay. I hope, therefore, that you can arrange at your early convenience to let me have your ideas on the settlement of the Palestine problem, so that we can at a later but not too distant date discuss the problem in concrete terms."

Before Churchill could reply to this note, however, he was succeeded by Clement Attlee as Prime Minister. From Attlee there came, on July 31, a brief note acknowledging my memorandum to Churchill and promising that it would receive attention.

When I returned from Potsdam and held my first press conference, a reporter asked me what position the Government of the United States had taken at Berlin with regard to Palestine. Of course there had been no official discussion of Palestine at the conference, but there were private talks. I stated my position to the press in these words:

"The American view on Palestine is that we want to let as many of the Jews into Palestine as it is possible to let into that country. Then the matter will have to be worked out diplomatically with the British and the Arabs, so that if a state can be set up there they may be able to set it up on a peaceful basis. I have no desire to send 500,000 American soldiers there to make peace in Palestine."

The State Department continued to feel that we should stay out of any activity that might offend the Arabs, and the department's Division of Near Eastern Affairs prepared a memorandum on the subject in September 1945.

The memorandum dealt only with the question of further immigration into Palestine. In 1939 the British had issued a White Paper that sought to strike a medium between the Zionists' desire to have the country opened for Jewish immigrant and the Arab resistance to any addition to the Jewish element of Palestine. The White Paper had promised a stated number of immigration "certificates" to the Jews but had also promised that no more than that number would be issued.

With the end of the fighting in Europe, the demand for certificates increased sharply, and it immediately became clear that the early fall of 1945 would see the limit reached. Unless the Arabs agreed, there would be no further Jewish immigration. Since it was hardly conceivable, the memorandum said, that formal Arab acquiescence could be secured, the British would be faced with a difficult decision: whether to abide by the White Paper policy and thus, in effect, terminate Jewish immigration into Palestine, or to establish a new interim policy whereby Jewish immigration would continue, at least for the time being, until the Palestine mandate was revised and brought under the United Nations. The memorandum added that Zionists were demanding that one million Jews be admitted into Palestine as rapidly as possible.

The memorandum went on to say:

"No government should advocate a policy of mass immigration unless it is prepared to assist in making available the necessary security forces, shipping, housing, unemployment guarantees. . . . In view of the foregoing, the United States should refrain from supporting a policy of large-scale immigration into Palestine during the interim period. The United States could support a Palestine immigration policy during the interim period which would carry restrictions as to numbers and categories, taking into account humanitarian considerations, the economic welfare of Palestine and political conditions therein. The British Government, as the mandatory power, should accept primary responsibility for the policy and be responsible for carrying it out."

As I studied these conclusions, however, it did not seem to me that such an approach would solve the basic human problem. The fate of the thousands of Jews in Europe—really only a fraction of the millions whom Hitler had doomed to death—was a primary concern. Among the millions who had been displaced by the war, they had suffered more and longer than any other group, yet their condition had barely improved since the fighting had ended.

In June 1945 I had sent Earl G. Harrison, the dean of the University of Pennsylvania Law School, on a mission to Europe to investigate the conditions of those displaced persons called "non-repatriables," and his report was submitted in late August. It showed that these people—and a great many of them were Jews—were still housed in camps, still without hope for their future. And it also pointed out that very few among the Jews wished to return to the countries from which they had come originally.

"If there is any genuine sympathy for what these survivors have endured," he wrote, "some reasonable extension or modification of the British White Paper of 1939 ought to be possible without too serious repercussions. For some of the European Jews, there is no acceptable or even decent solution for their future other than Palestine. This is said on a purely humanitarian basis with no reference to ideological or political considerations so far as Palestine is concerned.

"It is my understanding, based upon reliable information, that certificates for immigration to Palestine will be practically exhausted by the end of the current month [August, 1945]. What is the future to be? To anyone who has visited the concentration camps and who has talked with the despairing survivors, it is nothing short of calamitous to contemplate that the gates of Palestine should be soon closed.

"The Jewish Agency of Palestine has submitted to the British Government a petition that one hundred thousand additional immigration certificates be made available. A memorandum accompanying the petition makes a persuasive showing with respect to the immediate absorptive capacity of Palestine and the current, actual man-power shortages there.

"While there may be room for difference of opinion as to the precise number of such certificates which might under the circumstances be considered reasonable, there is no question but that the request thus made would, if granted, contribute much to the sound solution for the future of Jews still in Germany and Austria and even other displaced Jews, who do not wish either to remain there or to return to their countries of nationality.

"No other single matter is, therefore, so important from the viewpoint of Jews in Germany and Austria and those elsewhere who have known the horrors of concentration camps as is the disposition of the Palestine question."

The Harrison report was a moving document. The misery it depicted could not be allowed to continue, and I sent a message to General Eisenhower, asking him to do what he could about improving conditions in the camps. I also wrote on August 31, 1945, the following long letter to Attlee about the Palestine problem:

"Because of the natural interest of this Government in the present condition and future fate of those displaced persons in Germany who may prove to be stateless or non-repatriable, we recently sent Mr. Earl G. Harrison to inquire into the situation.

"Mr. Harrison was formerly the United States Commissioner of Immigration and is now the Representative of this Government on the Inter-governmental Committee on Refugees. The United Kingdom and the United States, as you know, have taken an active interest in the work of this Committee.

"Instructions were given to Mr. Harrison to inquire particularly into the problems and needs of the Jewish refugees among the displaced persons.

"Mr. Harrison visited not only the American zone in Germany, but spent some time also in the British zone where he was extended every courtesy by the 21st Army Group.

"I have now received his report. In view of our conversations at Potsdam I am sure that you will find certain portions of the report interesting. I am, therefore, sending you a copy.

"I should like to call your attention to the conclusions and recommendations appearing on page 8 and the following pages—especially the references to Palestine. It appears that the available certificates for immigration to Palestine will be exhausted in the near future. It is suggested that the granting of an additional one hundred thousand of such certificates would contribute greatly to a sound solution for the future of Jews still in Germany and Austria, and for other Jewish refugees who do not wish to remain where they are or who for understandable reasons do not desire to return to their countries of origin.

"On the basis of this and other information which has come to me I concur in the belief that no other single matter is so important for those who have known the horrors of concentration camps for over a decade as is the future of immigration possibilities into Palestine. The number of such persons who wish immigration to Palestine or who would qualify for admission there is, unfortunately, no longer as large as it was before the Nazis began their extermination program. As I said to you in Potsdam, the American people, as a whole, firmly believe that immigration into Palestine should not be closed and that a reasonable number of Europe's persecuted Jews should, in accordance with their wishes, be permitted to resettle there.

"I know you are in agreement on the proposition that future peace in Europe depends in large measure upon our finding sound solutions of problems confronting the displaced and formerly persecuted groups of people. No claim is more meritorious than that of the groups who for so many years have known persecution and enslavement.

"The main solution appears to lie in the quick evacuation of as many as possible of the non-repatriable Jews, who wish it, to Palestine. If it is to be effective, such action should not be long delayed."

Secretary Byrnes was then leaving to attend the session of the Council of Foreign Ministers in London, and I asked him to take this letter to Attlee.

In his reply the Prime Minister contended that the Jews were not actually using the numbers of certificates which were being made available to them. He also held the view that they were insisting upon the complete repudiation of the White Paper and the immediate granting of one hundred thousand certificates regardless of the effect on the situation in the Middle East which this would have. Furthermore, he denied in a second message that there had been any discrimination against Jews in the displaced persons camps in the British zones, and suggested that if immediate relief was needed, two camps at Philippeville and Felada, in North Africa, could be used.

With respect to Palestine, the Prime Minister said that there had been solemn undertakings given by my predecessor, by myself, and by Mr. Churchill that before a final decision was made there would be consultation with the Arabs, and he considered that any other course would "set aflame the whole Middle East." He assured me, however, that the British government would make every effort to deal with the problem of admittance to Palestine "in the interval," but urged that we attempt nothing further until the United Nations could assume charge of the situation.

The Harrison report was made public later in September, along with a letter that I had sent to General Eisenhower asking him to do whatever he could to improve the conditions of the displaced persons in our zone in Germany.

Meanwhile, the British were enforcing their laws and cracking down hard on efforts to bring unauthorized immigrants into Palestine. People who were still wearing their concentration-camp uniforms were being turned back as they tried to land in Palestine without certificates.

The Zionists, on the other hand, were impatiently making my immediate objective more difficult to obtain. They wanted more than just easier immigration practices. They wanted the American government to support their aim of a Jewish state in Palestine.

It was my attitude that America could not stand by while the victims of Hitler's racial madness were denied the opportunities to build new lives. Neither, however, did I want to see a political structure imposed on the Near East that would result in conflict. My basic approach was that the long-range fate of Palestine was the kind of problem we had the U.N. for. For the immediate future, however, some aid was needed for the Jews in Europe to find a place to live in decency.

The State Department continued to be more concerned about the Arab reaction than the sufferings of the Jews. Early in October, Secretary Byrnes began to suggest to me that we ought to publish the letter President Roosevelt had sent to King Ibn Saud just before his death, thinking that that would make it plain to the American public that we would not endorse the Zionist program. In fact, he prepared a statement for me to make that would reaffirm what Roosevelt had said, and he wanted me to release it from the White House along with Roosevelt's letter of April 5.

I decided that it would be well for the American people to understand that we wished to maintain friendship with the Arabs as well as with the Jews, so I authorized Byrnes to release the letter in question from the State Department. I saw no reason, however, why I, by a public statement, should take a position on a matter which I thought the U.N. ought to settle.

A message from Attlee, which I received on October 2, indicated that serious efforts were being made by the British to come up with an answer to the Palestine problem. The Prime Minister advised me that he and his Cabinet were giving deep thought to means of helping the

Jews in Europe and to the question of Palestine. He also pointed out that the two problems were not necessarily the same and that both were bristling with difficulties. Then, on October 19, the British presented a formal proposal to the Secretary of State for a joint Anglo-American inquiry into the problems of Palestine. This document gave a good insight into the difficulties the British faced and their desire to avoid any immediate decision. The message said that the British government considered it of great importance "that Jews should be enabled to play an active part in building up the life of the countries from which they came, in common with other nationals of these countries." The British proposed that a joint Anglo-American "Committee of Enquiry" should, as a matter of urgency, be set up at once, under a rotating chairmanship, to examine the position of the Jews in British- and American-occupied Europe; to make an estimate of the number of such Jews whom it might prove impossible to resettle in the country from which they originated; to examine the possibility of relieving the position in Europe by immigration into other countries outside Europe; and to consider other available means of meeting the needs of the immediate situation.

The British plan was that the committee should in the first place visit British- and American-occupied Europe in order to inform themselves of the character and magnitude of the problem created by the war. Having done so, it was to turn its attention to countries that might be in a position to accept them. In the light of the committee's investigations it would then make recommendations to the two governments for dealing with the problem in the interim until such time as a permanent solution could be submitted to the United Nations.

The question of Jewish immigration into Palestine would be only one of a number of things to be considered by the committee. The British note went on to say that the terms of the mandate required them to facilitate Jewish immigration and to encourage settlement by Jews on the land, while insuring that the rights and position of other sections of the population were not prejudiced thereby. This dual obligation, to the Jews on the one side and to the Arabs on the other, the note said, had been the main cause of the trouble which had been experienced in Palestine during the past twenty-six years. Every effort, it added, had been made by the British to devise some arrangement that would enable Arabs and Jews to live together in peace and co-operate for the welfare of the country, but all such efforts had been unavailing. Any arrangement acceptable to one party had been rejected as unacceptable to the other.

"The fact has to be faced," the British note read, "that there is no common ground between the Arabs and the Jews. They differ in religion and in language; their cultural and social life, their ways of thought and conduct, are as difficult to reconcile as are their national aspirations. These last are the greatest bar to peace. Both communities lay claim to Palestine; the one on the ground of a millennium of occupation, the other on the ground of historic association and of an undertaking given to it during the first World War. The antithesis is thus complete. . . ."

The British suggested that the committee would, in the course of its investigation, make an examination on the spot of the political, economic, and agricultural conditions which were at that time held to restrict immigration into Palestine. The British expected to deal with the Palestine issue in three stages. First they would consult the Arabs with a view to an arrangement that might insure that for the time being there would be no interruption of Jewish immigration at the then current monthly rate. Then they would explore, with the parties primarily concerned, the possibility of devising other temporary arrangements for dealing with the Palestine problem until a permanent solution of it could be reached. And, third, they would prepare a permanent solution for submission to the United Nations. For the immediate future, however, the British government had decided that the only practicable course was to maintain the present arrangement for immigration. They feared, they said, that "any violent departures decided upon in the face of Arab opposition would not only afford ground for a charge of breach of faith against His Majesty's government but would probably cause serious disturbances throughout the Middle East, involving a large military commitment, and would arouse widespread anxiety in India."

I instructed Secretary Byrnes to prepare a reply which would indicate that we were willing to take part in the proposed committee inquiry but that we wanted to concentrate on speedy results. Furthermore, I suggested that Palestine should be the focus of the inquiry and not just one of many points. I wanted it made plain that I was not going to retreat from the position which I had taken in my letter to Attlee on August 31. I did not want the United States to become a party to any dilatory tactics.

The British were none too happy with our reaction. Bevin wrote to Byrnes, insisting that the inquiry should extend to places other than Palestine as potential settlement areas for European Jews. We held to our point of view, however, lest the inquiry result in drawing things out interminably, and when the proposed meeting was held, this point of view prevailed.

CHAPTER 11

The fact that there had been an exchange of messages between Washington and London in contemplation of an Anglo-American investigation into the problem of homeless Jews in Europe soon became public. On October 30 I received this wire from Zionist spokesmen, which said, in part:

. . . From press reports we now learn that a proposal is under consideration by the governments of Great Britain and of the United States to establish a joint commission which is to study, once more, the situation of Jews in Europe and their emigration needs, and which, in the teeth of the Harrison report, is again to determine how many of them want to go to Palestine and how many can be placed elsewhere. . . .

What is called for is a policy not a further inquiry. Based upon bitter experience over many years, we venture to affirm that the setting up of the proposed commission will bring the solution not one step nearer. It will, on the contrary, further complicate the situation, make for interminable delays and lead to confusion worse confounded.

Within the last seven years, three major intergovernmental conferences and committees, in addition to our own War Refugee Board appointed in 1944 and already dissolved, have sought to deal with the question of Jewish refugees and of Jewish immigration. They comprised the International Conference on Refugees, called by President Roosevelt at Evian in 1937, the Intergovernmental Committee on Refugees, established as a result of that conference, and the Bermuda Conference on Refugees, called in 1943. Each of these efforts ended in dismal failure, stemming from the central assumption that doors of Palestine, unlawfully barred to Jewish immigration by the British government under the terms of its White Paper of 1939, must remain barred. They concentrate their attention on the possibility of immigration to other countries, but none of these countries were in fact willing to admit

Jewish refugees in substantial numbers. On the other hand, had the doors of Palestine been kept open, hundreds of thousands of Jews, now dead, might have been alive today.

We beg of you not to countenance further commissions and inquiries at a continued cost in human life and human misery, which can only ascertain facts already well known.

What is urgently needed, is not another roving expedition or a further time-consuming investigation but immediate concrete measures in conformity with a policy long established and clearly defined by valid international agreements. . . . We therefore respectfully submit that what is called for immediately is:

1. The immediate admission of 100,000 Jews into Palestine, as requested by you, Mr. President. This is an urgent necessity which can and should be met without affecting the "basic situation." . . .

2. The abandonment or revocation forthwith by the British government of the White Paper of 1939. Its promulgation was a unilateral act of the British government in violation of the mandate, in defiance of the express opinion of the Permanent Mandates Commission of the League of Nations, and without the approval of the United States. Its abrogation is a responsibility which rests upon the British government alone.

3. A joint pronouncement by the British and American governments indicating their intention to support and pursue a Palestine policy, consonant with the original purpose and underlying intent of the Balfour Declaration and the Palestine mandate.

4. Following such joint pronouncement, it would be most useful to constitute a joint commission to explore ways and means by which both countries may cooperate in the implementation of the announced policy in the light of their respective interests and responsibilities. We hope, too, that the United States may find it possible to cooperate in such economic projects as would be of benefit not only to the people of Palestine and to the possibilities of Jewish settlement there, but to the peoples of the entire Middle East, whose countries are poverty-ridden and underdeveloped.

In conclusion, we would like to stress as forcibly as we can the dangers of further postponement and evasion of the central, inescapable issue. That issue is the fulfillment of the international pledges given to the Jewish people, based on their historical connection with Palestine, to facilitate their settlement in that country and the re-establishment there of their national home. It is evident that commissions are no substitute for action clearly indicated.

We appeal to our government again to employ all its moral and political influence that justice and humanity may triumph.

We send you, Mr. President, expression of our highest esteem.

> Stephen S. Wise, Abba Hillel Silver,
> Co-Chairmen,
> American Zionist Emergency Council

One of our main problems was that Palestine was not ours to dispose of. It had been legally entrusted to the British by action of the League of Nations—to which we did not belong—and the British were, in fact, in possession of Palestine.

In my own mind, the aims and goals of the Zionists at this stage to set up a Jewish state were secondary to the more immediate problem of finding means to relieve the human misery of the displaced persons.

Since the diplomats were having so much trouble in agreeing on the scope and purpose of the proposed committee of inquiry, the matter was not taken up again until Attlee came to Washington in mid-November. Out of these talks with Attlee there came an understanding with regard to Palestine. The British, finding that I was unwilling to change my earlier position, accepted the scope of inquiry which the State Department had worked out for the Anglo-American Committee. I announced the agreement on November 13 and, at the same time, released the text of my letter to Attlee of August 31, when I had asked him to provide for the entry into Palestine of one hundred thousand Jews.

On December 10 I announced the names of the American members of this joint committee, a group made up of Judge Joseph C. Hutcheson, a highly respected federal judge from Texas, who was designated the American chairman; Dr. Frank Aydelotte, former president of Swarthmore College and then the director of the Institute for Advanced Study at Princeton; Frank W. Buxton, editor of the Boston *Herald*; William Phillips, a veteran of our diplomatic service; James G. McDonald, who had been the League of Nations' High Commissioner for Refugees; and O. Max Gardner, former governor of North Carolina. Mr. Gardner was unable to accept the appointment, and I appointed in his place Bartley C. Crum, a California attorney. The committee began its work with public hearings in Washington on January 4, 1946, and then traveled to Europe and the Near East to study the situation on the spot. Its report was presented to me on April 22, 1946, by the American chairman, Judge Hutcheson. The committee recommended unanimously that one hundred thousand certificates be issued for immigration into Palestine and that actual immigration be pushed forward as rapidly as possible.

As for Palestine, the committee urged that it be made into a land in which neither Jew nor Arab would dominate. They suggested the adoption of these three principles:

"I. That Jew shall not dominate Arab and Arab shall not dominate Jew in Palestine.

"II. That Palestine shall be neither a Jewish state nor an Arab state.

"III. That the form of government ultimately to be established shall, under international guarantees, fully protect and preserve the interests in the Holy Land of Christendom and of the Moslem and Jewish faiths."

The committee concluded, however, that the relations of Jews and Arabs were at the present so strained that any attempt to establish independence or nationhood would only result in civil strife. For that reason they recommended that the mandate be continued, that eventually there should be a trusteeship agreement with the United Nations, and that the terms of the trusteeship agreement should aim at bringing Arabs and Jews closer together.

The recommendations of the committee included the proposal that full Jewish immigration be made possible and the land laws protecting the Arabs without giving equality of protection to the Jews be repealed or changed.

The committee's report was careful and complete. Judge Hutcheson and his colleagues had done a notably conscientious job, and I felt that the committee was pointing in the right direction. On April 30 I issued a statement in which I expressed my agreement with the substance of their proposal. However, it remained now to persuade the British to take action on the report. I studied it further, and having consulted with Dean Acheson and other advisers (Byrnes was in Paris), I sent this message to Attlee:

May 8, 1946

FROM THE PRESIDENT TO PRIME MINISTER ATTLEE:
I have been considering the next steps which should be taken with regard to Palestine and believe that the first thing to be done is to initiate the consultations with Jews and Arabs to which both our governments are committed. I believe the report of the Anglo-American Committee of Inquiry offers a basis for such consultations and I contemplate the adoption of the following procedure, on which I should welcome your comments:

The report will be brought by this government in the immediate future to the attention of the Jewish and Arab organizations specified below as well as the government of Arab states with which this government maintains relations with the request that they transmit their views on it within a certain period, say two weeks. On receipt of their views this government will consult the British government and then proceed to determine its attitude toward the report as a whole and to issue a public statement as to the extent to which it is prepared to accept the report as the basis for its Palestine policy.

I imagine that the British government will wish to take concurrent action and should be glad to know if this assumption is correct. In view of the urgency surrounding the question of admission to Palestine of the 100,000 Jews whose entry is recommended by the Committee, I sincerely hope that it will be possible to initiate and complete the consultations with Arabs and Jews at the earliest possible moment.

The organizations and groups in question would be: American Zionist Emergency Council, American Jewish Committee, American Jewish Conference, American Council for Judaism, American Jewish Congress, Institute for Arab American Affairs, Agudas Israel of America, New Zionist Organization of America, Jewish Agency, League of Arab States, Arab Higher Committee, Governments of Iraq, Syria, Lebanon, Egypt, Trans-Jordan, Saudi Arabia and Yemen.

Attlee replied at once, asking for time to discuss the matter with his Foreign Secretary, Bevin, who, like Byrnes, was in Paris, and two days later there followed a more extensive message from the Prime Minister. The British wanted as many of the foreseeable difficulties as possible ironed out before any policy was announced. In his second message, on May 10, 1946, Attlee said that the British were agreeable that consultations with the Jews and Arabs be initiated as quickly as possible. He pointed out, however, that Britain was at that moment engaged in important and delicate negotiations with Egypt and suggested a postponement until May 20 or later. Attlee said also that a period of two weeks for the Jews and the Arabs to prepare for the conference was too short and that a month would be better. He added that some provision should be made to study the ultimate findings with reference to the financial and military liabilities which would be involved.

Meanwhile, we had heard from the Arab countries. In a body, the diplomatic representatives of the Arab states in Washington called on Acting Secretary of State Acheson to voice their protest against the committee's recommendations.

I could appreciate Attlee's problems, even though I was unwilling to admit the necessity for further delay. I decided, therefore, that I would accede to his wish to delay the communications to the Arabs and Jews until May 20, but then I wanted to see the entire problem pushed forward with dispatch. On May 16 I held a long conference with Dean Acheson about the Palestine matter, following which I sent this message to Attlee:

"I have given careful consideration to your two messages concerning Palestine and am pleased to note that you and your colleagues share our feeling regarding close collaboration between our two governments. We are proceeding with arrangements for consultations with Arabs and Jews so that the communication to them may be made on May 20. I hope that this will be agreeable to you and that your government will take concurrent action. I am still most anxious to have these consultations completed as early as possible but in view of your feeling that two weeks would be too short I am agreeable to extending the period to one month. We are drawing up a covering memorandum to be handed to Arab and Jewish representatives at the time their views on the Committee's report are requested and we will furnish your government with an advance copy of this memorandum. We assume the British government will let us have an advance copy of any covering memorandum it may decide to use.

"As regards question of studies to be made by experts of the two governments with respect to certain matters arising out of the report, we are proceeding to organize an appropriate group from among officials of this government. However, as the British embassy has already been informed by the Department of State, we do not believe it would be advisable to have these discussions between experts of the two governments precede the requests for the views of Arabs and Jews. It is our belief that the latter (i.e. the consultations) might serve to clarify issues involved and narrow the field in which expert discussions would take place. At the same time, however, we believe at least preliminary expert discussions can be initiated as soon as the views have been requested. In this connection it would be of the greatest usefulness if we might have as soon as possible some indication of the subjects which your government thinks should form the basis of these discussions, as well as any further detailed suggestions.

"We have noted your proposal for an eventual conference which would include Jewish and Arab representatives. We believe that this is something which our two governments should have in mind during the consultations with interested parties and that it is at least possible such a conference might be convened at a suitable time if results of consultations with Arabs and Jews indicate that a conference would be helpful. For the moment I do not feel able to give you a more definite reply on this point."

To the heads of the Arab states who had backed up their ministers by personal telegrams to me, there went individual messages similar to this one to the Regent of Iraq:

May 17, 1946

HIS ROYAL HIGHNESS
PRINCE ABDUL ILAH
REGENT OF THE KINGDOM OF IRAQ

I have the honor to acknowledge the receipt of your telegram of May 9, 1946, and have taken careful note of your government's views with respect to the report of the Anglo-American Committee of Inquiry as set forth therein.

You will recall that on a number of occasions the government of the United States has informed the Arab governments that in its view no change should be made in the basic situation in Palestine without prior consultation with both Arab and Jewish leaders.

You may rest assured therefore that no decision regarding the Committee's report will be made without prior consultation with the government of Iraq.

I desire also at this time to send Your Highness my personal greetings and best wishes for the welfare of your people.

Harry S. Truman

The official reaction in England to the report of the Anglo-American Committee was not encouraging. As soon as it was published, Clement Attlee told the House of Commons that, before taking any action on the report, his government would ask the United States to share the additional military and financial responsibilities that he thought would arise.

He also said that large-scale immigration into Palestine would not be resumed until the illegal Jewish armed units were eliminated.

The British press, in the weeks to follow, set a tone that was decidedly unfriendly. Many of the newspapers said or implied what Ernest Bevin, the Foreign Secretary, later said in a speech on June 12—that our interest in helping the Jews enter Palestine was due to our desire not to have them in the United States.

I realized that it would be difficult to get action from the British, but while there was much clamor in the United States that something be done, the country was neither disposed nor prepared to assume risks and obligations that might require us to use military force. Nevertheless, I wanted to have a full appraisal of the military factors involved and asked Dean Acheson to get an opinion from the Joint Chiefs of Staff.

The Joint Chiefs of Staff urged that no U.S. armed forces be involved in carrying out the committee's findings. They recommended that in implementing the report the guiding principle should be that no action should be taken that would cause repercussions in Palestine which would be beyond the capabilities of British troops to control. The Chiefs of Staff also noted that if the question of using any U.S. forces should arise, only very limited forces could be spared from tasks in which we were already engaged. Such forces might be of a size to help pacify the situation *in Palestine,* but they believed that the political shock attending the reappearance of U.S. armed forces in the Middle East would unnecessarily risk serious disturbances throughout the area far out of proportion to any local Palestine difficulties.

The Joint Chiefs of Staff were also of the opinion that carrying out the findings of the report by force would prejudice British and U.S. interests in much of the Middle East. And if this were to happen, they suggested that the U.S.S.R. might replace the United States and Britain in influence and power through the Middle East. To this they added that control of oil in the Middle East was a very serious consideration, and they concluded, therefore, that no action should be taken that would commit U.S. armed forces or turn the peoples of the Middle East away from the Western powers, since we had a vital security interest there.

This report put our military leaders on record. They were primarily concerned about Middle East oil and in long-range terms about the danger that the Arabs, antagonized by Western action in Palestine, would make common cause with Russia. The second argument in particular was one that I had not lost sight of at any time. The pressure against Turkey and the incidents in Iran all pointed only too clearly to the fact that the Russians would be ready to welcome the Arabs into their camp.

The British Prime Minister cabled me on May 27, sending me a catalog of subjects which he thought should be taken up when the experts of our two governments sat down together. Out of the ten recommendations of the committee, the British had built up no less than forty-three "subjects" which they felt needed discussion by the experts. My reaction was that this procedure would only serve to postpone any relief for the hundred thousand homeless Jews we still wanted to see admitted into Palestine. I replied, therefore, that that problem should be taken up without delay, even before the experts might be ready to go into the other subjects listed by the British. I offered the assistance of the United States with transportation and temporary housing for these immigrants, and I repeated that it was my primary concern to relieve suffering by the admission of these hundred thousand to the land they wanted to make their home.

The Prime Minister's reply to my proposal was negative. The British did not want to discuss the matter of the hundred thousand immigrants without talking about all aspects of the Palestine problem. In my answer I told Attlee that I could appreciate his point of view but that I saw no reason why it should not be possible to make all arrangements for the admission of the hundred thousand at once so that there would be no further delay once the experts had reached agreement on the more general questions. Attlee then cabled that on June 14 he had designated a British delegation to discuss with our delegation the findings of the committee.

Meanwhile, I had instructed the Secretaries of State, War, and the Treasury to form a Cabinet committee, with alternates, on Palestine to consult with the British. Henry F. Grady, who had returned from Greece, where he headed the American observers at the national elections, was named chairman of the alternates.

These alternates made a careful study of all points raised by the British in their list of subjects to be discussed. By late June, Attlee wrote that he was ready for the joint talks to get under way.

My efforts to persuade the British to relax immigration restrictions in Palestine might have fallen on more receptive ears if it had not been for the increasing acts of terrorism that were being committed in Palestine. There were armed groups of extremists who were guilty of numerous outrages. On June 16 eight bridges were blown up near the Trans-Jordan border, and two other explosions were set off in Haifa. The following day there was a pitched battle between Jews and British troops in Haifa, after explosions had started a fire and caused great damage in the rail yards there. British officers were kidnaped. Others were shot at from passing automobiles. Explosions took place in ever-increasing numbers, and the British uncovered a plot by one extremist group to kidnap the British commander in chief in Palestine.

The British government then decided to take drastic action, and Attlee advised me of the plans in advance in a personal message on June 28. He said that the High Commissioner had been authorized to take such steps as he thought necessary to break up illegal organizations, including the arrest of any individual against whom there was clear evidence of responsibility for the current campaign of violence. He regretted, he wrote, that such action should have become necessary while we were engaged in discussing the report of the Anglo-American Committee, but his government had been forced to conclude that they "could no longer, without abdication of our responsibility as the Mandatory Government, tolerate such open defiance and that, while discussions regarding the future of Palestine are proceeding, law and order must be maintained."

I replied to Attlee on July 2, 1946:

"Replying to your message of June 28, I join with you in regretting that drastic action is considered necessary by the mandatory government while discussions of the report of the Anglo-American Committee are in progress. I also join with you in a hope that law and order will be maintained by the inhabitants of Palestine while efforts are being made toward a solution of the long term policy."

The British, because of the violence in Palestine, were anxious to get the discussions of the joint committee under way as soon as possible. I accommodated Attlee in this matter by sending Grady and his group over on July 10, a week earlier than had been planned, and by making the presidential plane available to get them there.

During the two weeks that followed, this joint Cabinet committee sat and deliberated in London. Because both Attlee and I knew how sensitive the Jews and Arabs were on the issues involved, it had been agreed to observe strict secrecy until agreement could be announcd. However, leaks apparently developed, and on July 25 the American press published a fairly detailed account of the recommendations of the committee.

In substance, the plan proposed by the committee was the creation in Palestine of something resembling a federal system of two autonomous states but with a very strong central government. Approximately fifteen hundred square miles (of a total of forty-five thousand) were to become a Jewish state. The central government would retain control of the cities of Jerusalem and Bethlehem, as well as of the southernmost section of Palestine, the Negeb. The remainder of Palestine would become an Arab state.

Of most importance, however, the plan provided that the central government would have reserved powers of such extent that the two states to be set up would have very little control over anything except wholly local matters. Included among subjects under central government control would be immigration.

The government of the provinces would consist of elected assemblies, but the speakers of these assemblies would be appointed by the British, and no bill would become law without the assent of these appointed officials. The executive would also be appointed by the British, in the form of a council of ministers.

Neither the Jews nor the Arabs welcomed this plan. It satisfied nobody. The Arabs even objected to the proposal in the report that, in order to help the transition, there should be an outright grant of fifty million dollars from the United States to aid the Palestinian Arabs.

The situation was not improving. Only a few days before, Jewish terrorists had blown up the King David Hotel in Jerusalem with considerable loss of lives. Some solution had to be found, both to the problem of Jews in need of a home and to the rising tide of unrest in the Near East. I studied the proposed plan with care. But I was unable to see that anything could come out of it except more unrest. The plan made the admission of the hundred thousand conditional on its being accepted by the Arabs, so no relief was offered in that direction either. Nor was this the kind of plan that I had hoped would result. It seemed a retreat from the fine recommendations that had been made by the Anglo-American Committee of Inquiry earlier in the year. I therefore felt compelled to inform Attlee that the Government of the United States could not go along.

"After further study of recommendations of American and British groups," my message of August 12 said, "and after detailed discussion in which members of my cabinet and other advisers participated, I have reluctantly come to the conclusion that I can not give formal support to the plan in its present form as a joint Anglo-American plan.

"The opposition in this country to the plan has become so intense that it is now clear it would be impossible to rally in favor of it sufficient public opinion to enable this government to give it effective support.

"In view of the critical situation in Palestine and of the desperate plight of homeless Jews in Europe I believe the search for a solution to this difficult problem should continue. I have therefore instructed our embassy in London to discuss with you or with appropriate members of the British government certain suggestions which have been made to us and which, I understand, are also being made to you.

"Should it be possible to broaden the coming conference sufficiently to consider these suggestions, it is my earnest hope that the conference may make possible a decision by your government upon a course for which we can obtain necessary support in this country and in the Congress so we can give effective financial help and moral support."

Attlee acknowledged my message and then sent a more detailed reply on August 18, observing that it was a great disappointment to him that we were unable to give support to the plan recommended by the expert delegations. He expressed the hope that out of the coming conference with the Arabs and the Jews "some solution will emerge which, even if not fully accepted by either Arabs or Jews, may be possible of implementation without too gravely endangering the peace of Palestine or of the Middle East as a whole."

But by the fall of 1946 the situation looked, as I wrote to a friend, "insoluble." As I said in this letter, "not only are the British highly successful in muddling the situation as completely as it could possibly be muddled, but the Jews themselves are making it almost impossible to do anything for them."

The Jewish Agency for Palestine, the official spokesmen for the Zionists, had just declared that it would not even sit down with the British to discuss their proposals. Meanwhile, the Jewish extremists in Palestine were continuing their terrorist activities. And top Jewish leaders in the United States were putting all sorts of pressure on me to commit American power and forces on behalf of the Jewish aspirations in Palestine.

I understood the position of the British government. They found themselves hard-pressed throughout the empire, unable to muster either the funds or the forces to take care of all their responsibilities, and yet anxious to relinquish as little of their standing as a world power as possible. They had spent many years and millions of pounds cultivating the friendship of the Arab world, both to secure the life line of the empire through the Suez Canal and to gain access to the oil resources of the Middle East. They were, understandably, most reluctant to antagonize the Arabs.

The Arabs were as uncompromising as the Jews. They made an appearance at the round-table talks which the British convened late in January 1947, but they would not yield an inch from their position that Palestine was Arab country and should be kept Arab. The talks collapsed, therefore, on February 4, 1947, and the British then decided to put the whole matter before the United Nations. This decision was announced in London on February 14. There was, of course, a good deal of criticism, especially of Foreign Secretary Bevin's handling of the situation. Certainly he did not help matters when he told a Labor party caucus that American Zionists were to blame and later when he stated in the House of Commons that all would have been well if only

I had not spoiled his plans by sticking to the idea that one hundred thousand Jews should be given a home in Palestine.

He was referring, of course, to a statement I had made on October 4, 1946, which happened to be the Jewish holiday of Yom Kippur. Presidents have often made statements on this holiday, so the timing was nothing unusual, and what I had said was simply a restatement of my position; namely, that I wanted to see one hundred thousand Jews admitted to Palestine. A few days later Governor Dewey said that several hundred thousand should be admitted, and Bevin now told the British House of Commons that I had made my statement to forestall Dewey's —in other words, I had taken my position for political reasons only.

This was a very undiplomatic—almost hostile—statement for the Foreign Secretary of the British government to make about the President of the United States. He knew this had been my position all along.

The President of the United States, of course, cannot spend his time replying to personal attacks and insinuations. If he did, his time would be fully occupied with nothing else. So while I was outraged by Mr. Bevin's unwarranted charge, I had Charlie Ross issue a very moderate, entirely impersonal statement from the White House that pointed out that the matter of getting one hundred thousand Jews into Palestine had been the cornerstone of our Palestine policy since my first letter to Attlee in August 1945.

On April 2, 1947, the United Nations received a formal request from the British for General Assembly consideration of the Palestine problem. The British also suggested that a special session be convened at once in order to authorize a U.N. special committee that might make a preliminary study. Mr. Bevin had told the House of Commons on February 18 that "after two thousand years of conflict, another twelve months will not be considered a long delay." The callousness of this statement and its disregard for human misery had brought forth strong demands in England itself for speedy action.

On May 15 the General Assembly set up a special committee, designated as UNSCOP—the United Nations Special Committee on Palestine. The committee, on which none of the so-called great powers was represented, agreed that the British mandate in Palestine should be brought to an end and that, under U.N. auspices, a form of independence should eventually be worked out in Palestine. The majority of the committee then recommended that independence should take the form of two separate states, one Jewish and one Arab, tied together in an economic union. The city of Jerusalem, however, should be under direct U.N. trusteeship.

The Jews welcomed this report with mixed emotions. Some of them wanted all of Palestine as a Jewish state—but most of them saw this partition plan as their opportunity to realize the dream of a Jewish state in their coveted "homeland."

The Arabs' reaction was quite plain: They did not like it. They made it clear that partition would not be carried out except over their forceful opposition. On October 9 I was informed that the Arab League Council had instructed the governments of its member states to move troops to the Palestine border, ready for later use, and the public statements of the Arab leaders were belligerent and defiant.

I instructed the State Department to support the partition plan.

CHAPTER 12

I was of the opinion that the proposed partition of Palestine could open the way for peaceful collaboration between the Arabs and the Jews. Although it was difficult under the present circumstances to bring the Arabs and the Jews together, I could foresee that under the proposed plan of the United Nations, calling for an economic union of the partitioned areas, the Jews and the Arabs might eventually work side by side as neighbors.

For many years I have been interested in the history of that great region. I knew that it had once been the seat of great world powers and had supported many millions of people. The empires of Nebuchadnezzar and Darius the Great, like the kingdom of Rameses II in the valley of the Nile, had made full use of the riches of the area. But after those great empires had gone their way, there had been divisions and internal warfare and a general decline. Except for a short period, the Arabs had never brought the area back to the position of influence and power it had once had, although certain potentials were still there. I felt that a development program could be worked out so that a great industrial system could be set up under the Jews, and the productive potential of this region could be used to the mutual benefit of the Jews and Arabs. The whole region waits to be developed, and if it were handled the way we developed the Tennessee River basin, it could support from twenty to thirty million people more. To open the door to this kind of future would indeed be a constructive and humanitarian thing to do, and it would also redeem the pledges that were given at the time of World War I.

These were the thoughts I had about the future of the area, and the partition proposal impressed me as the most practicable way to make progress in that direction. It was always my hope that a solution could be worked out without bloodshed. Certainly little could be said for a solution that would destroy a hundred thousand lives so that another hundred thousand could be saved.

My purpose was then and later to help bring about the redemption of the pledge of the Balfour Declaration and the rescue of at least some of the victims of Nazism. I was not committed to any particular formula of statehood in Palestine or to any particular time schedule for its accomplishment. The American policy was designed to bring about, by peaceful means, the establishment of the promised Jewish homeland and easy access to it for the displaced Jews of Europe.

Many Jews, however, chose to believe that our Palestine policy was the same as the Zionist program for the State of Israel. Whenever it failed to conform, they would charge that we had turned pro-Arab. The Arabs, of course, looked at our attitude in an even more partisan and hostile light.

The simple fact is that our policy was an American policy rather than an Arab or Jewish policy. It was American because it aimed at the peaceful solution of a world trouble spot. It was American because it was based on the desire to see promises kept and human misery relieved.

But the issue was embroiled in politics, not only with us but abroad too. The Jews were for partition—but not all the Jews. The Arabs were against partition—but could not agree how completely they were against it. The British, at least, seemed of one mind: They were determined to wash their hands of the whole matter.

It was a discouraging prospect indeed. As I wrote to one of my assistants, "I surely wish God Almighty would give the Children of Israel an Isaiah, the Christians a St. Paul, and the Sons of Ishmael a peep at the Golden Rule."

But the matter had been placed in the hands of the United Nations, and, true to my conviction that the United Nations had to be made to work, I had confidence that a solution would be found there.

This was my reply to all who appealed to me in those days. The General Assembly of the United Nations was debating the matter, and its decision would reflect the will of the nations of the world. I spoke in this vein to Dr. Chaim Weizmann, the venerable leader of the world Zionists, when he called on me on November 19, and a few days later I received a letter from him which reveals some of the problems of the day:

New York, November 27, 1947

Dear Mr. President:

The gracious manner in which you received me on Wednesday, November 19th, emboldens me to address you in this critical hour which is one of suspense and anguish for me. I am disturbed to hear from unimpeachable sources that two unwarranted rumours are afloat which do us injustice and possible damage.

It is freely rumoured in Washington that our people have exerted undue and excessive pressure on certain delegations and have thus "over-played" their hand. I cannot speak for unauthorized persons, but I am in a position to assure you, my dear Mr. President, that there is no substance in this charge as far as our representatives are concerned. They have had a very limited number of contacts with all delegations and have endeavoured to lay the situation squarely before them. At no time have they gone beyond the limits of legitimate and moderate persuasion. With some delegations such as those of Greece and Liberia, we have had no more than one conversation throughout the present Assembly.

Fears are also expressed that our project in Palestine may in some way be used as a channel for the infiltration of Communist ideas in the Middle East. Nothing is further from the truth. Our immigrants from Eastern Europe are precisely those who are leaving the Communist scene with which they do not wish to be integrated. Otherwise, they would not leave at all. Had there been a serious attempt by the Soviets to introduce Communist influences through our immigration, they could easily have done so in previous decades. Every election and all observation in Palestine testifies to the trivial hold which Communism has achieved in our community. An educated peasantry and a skilled industrial class living on high standards, will never accept Communism. The danger lies amongst illiterate and impoverished communities bearing no resemblance to our own.

Unfortunately Dr. Weizmann was correct only to the extent that his immediate associates were concerned. The facts were that not only were there pressure movements around the United Nations unlike anything that had been seen there before but that the White House, too, was subjected to a constant barrage. I do not think I ever had as much pressure and propaganda aimed at the White House as I had in this instance. The persistence of a few of the extreme Zionist leaders— actuated by political motives and engaging in political threats—disturbed and annoyed me. Some were even suggesting that we pressure sovereign nations into favorable votes in the General Assembly. I have never approved of the practice of the strong imposing their will on the weak, whether among men or among nations. We had aided Greece. We had, in fact, fathered the independence of the Philippines. But that did not make satellites of these nations or compel them to vote with us on the partitioning of Palestine or any other matter. No American policy worthy of the name will ever treat any other nation as a satellite. It is basic to the way of life of democratic peoples that they respect the opinion of others—whether they happen to be weak or strong, rich or poor. The kind of "direct approach" some of my correspondents had been making could never gain my approval.

The General Assembly passed the partition plan on November 29, 1947, although it did not actually put partition into effect. Instead, it merely gave its approval to the majority recommendations of the Special Committee (UNSCOP) and asked the Security Council to see that they were carried out. Consequently, a committee was set up to channel the change-over in peaceful ways. The General Assembly, however, did not prescribe a detailed procedure for the carrying out of the recommendations.

I point this out because the impression was spread by many of our newpapers that the General Assembly had approved a specific blueprint, whereas it had merely accepted a principle. The way in which this principle might be translated into action had yet to be found. It was my constant hope that it would be a peaceful way.

The hopes for an adjustment without bloodshed, however, were very slim. The British, who had said all along that they would "accept" the U.N. decision but would enforce it only if both Jews and Arabs agreed, now announced, on December 3, that they would consider their mandate at an end as of May 15, 1948. The Arabs, on the same day, served notice on the world that they would defend their "rights."

Every day now brought reports of new violence in the Holy Land. On January 15, 1948, the Jewish Agency advised the United Nations that an international police force would be required to put partition into effect. But no such police force existed, and to set up one would require more agreement than existed among the powers at the time. The United Nations Commission on Palestine agreed, however, that a police force would be needed, and Trygve Lie, the Secretary General of the United Nations, began laborious discussions to get one started.

The Jews, realizing that there was little chance to get international enforcement, announced that they would establish a Jewish militia force. The British said they would not permit this as long as they were in control. The Arabs, meanwhile, were making plans for a national administration for all of Palestine, and the military forces of the Arab states that adjoin Palestine more and more openly began to enter that country. On February 13 it was reported to me from our diplomatic missions in the area that the Arabs were expected to start full-scale military operations in late March.

I published an appeal to the Arab leaders to preserve the peace and practice moderation. They rejected it flatly, charging that the United States had contributed to the unrest in the Near East by supporting the Zionist cause. That was on February 17, 1948. I gave my approval to a

State Department proposal that the full conciliatory powers of the Security Council be invoked. A serious threat to the world's peace was developing in Palestine, with neither side willing to be swayed. We wanted a peaceful settlement and were trying hopefully to get it.

The Jewish pressure on the White House did not diminish in the days following the partition vote in the U.N. Individuals and groups asked me, usually in rather quarrelsome and emotional ways, to stop the Arabs, to keep the British from supporting the Arabs, to furnish American soldiers, to do this, that, and the other. I think I can say that I kept my faith in the rightness of my policy in spite of some of the Jews. When I say "the Jews," I mean, of course, the extreme Zionists. I know that most Americans of Jewish faith, while they hoped for the restoration of Jewish homeland, are and always have been Americans first and foremost.

As the pressure mounted, I found it necessary to give instructions that I did not want to be approached by any more spokesmen for the extreme Zionist cause. I was even so disturbed that I put off seeing Dr. Chaim Weizmann, who had returned to the United States and had asked for an interview with me. My old friend, Eddie Jacobson, called on me at the White House and urged me to receive Dr. Weizmann at the earliest possible moment. Eddie, who had been with me through the hard days of World War I, had never been a Zionist. In all my years in Washington he had never asked me for anything for himself. He was of the Jewish faith and was deeply moved by the sufferings of the Jewish people abroad. He had spoken to me on occasion, both before and after I became President, about some specific hardship cases that he happened to know about, but he did this rarely. On March 13 he called at the White House.

I was always glad to see him. Not only had we shared so much in the past, but I have always had the warmest feelings toward him. It would be hard to find a truer friend. Eddie said that he wanted to talk about Palestine. I told him that I would rather he did not and that I wanted to let the matter run its course in the United Nations.

I do not believe that in all our thirty years of friendship a sharp word had ever passed between Eddie and me, and I was sorry that Eddie had brought up the subject.

Eddie was becoming self-conscious, but he kept on talking. He asked me to bear in mind that some of the pro-Zionists who had approached me were only individuals and did not speak for any responsible leadership.

I told him that I respected Dr. Weizmann, but if I saw him, it would only result in more wrong interpretations.

Eddie waved toward a small replica of an Andrew Jackson statue that was in my office.

"He's been your hero all your life, hasn't he?" he said. "You have probably read every book there is on Andrew Jackson. I remember when we had the store that you were always reading books and pamphlets, and a lot of them were about Jackson. You put this statue in front of the Jackson County Courthouse in Kansas City when you built it."

I did not know what he was leading up to, but he went on.

"I have never met the man who has been my hero all my life," he continued. "But I have studied his past as you have studied Jackson's. He is the greatest Jew alive, perhaps the greatest Jew who ever lived. You yourself have told me that he is a great statesman and a fine gentleman. I am talking about Dr. Chaim Weizmann. He is an old man and a very sick man. He has traveled thousands of miles to see you, and now you are putting off seeing him. That isn't like you."

When Eddie left I gave instructions to have Dr. Weizmann come to the White House as soon as it could be arranged. However, the visit was to be entirely off the record. Dr. Weizmann, by my specific instructions, was to be brought in through the East Gate. There was to be no press coverage of his visit and no public announcement.

Dr. Weizmann came on March 18, and we talked for almost three quarters of an hour. He talked about the possibilities of development in Palestine, about the scientific work that he and his assistants had done that would someday be translated into industrial activity in the Jewish state that he envisaged. He spoke of the need for land if the future immigrants were to be cared for, and he impressed on me the importance of the Negeb area in the south to any future Jewish state.

Dr. Weizmann was a man of remarkable achievements and personality. His life had been dedicated to two ideals, that of science and that of the Zionist movement. He was past seventy now and in ill-health. He had known many disappointments and had grown patient and wise in them.

I told him, as plainly as I could, why I had at first put off seeing him. He understood. I explained to him what the basis of my interest in the Jewish problem was and that my primary concern was to see justice done without bloodshed. And when he left my office I felt that he had reached a full understanding of my policy and that I knew what it was he wanted.

That this was so was shown the following day. That day our representative in the United Nations, Ambassador Austin, announced to the Security Council that the United States Government would favor a temporary trusteeship for Palestine pending a decision on Palestine's permanent status. Some Zionist spokesmen branded this as a reversal of American policy. Dr. Weizmann, however, was one of the few prominent Zionists who did not choose this opportunity to castigate American policy. He knew, I am sure, what the direction of American policy really was. The following morning Judge Rosenman called to see me on another matter. As he was leaving, I asked him to see Dr. Weizmann and tell him that there was not and would not be any change in the long policy he and I had talked about.

I was always aware of the fact that not all my advisers looked at the Palestine problem in the same manner I did. This was nothing unusual, of course. It is the job of the military planners to consider all matters first and always in the light of military considerations. The diplomat's approach is—or in any case should be—determined by considerations of our relations to other nations. The Secretary of the Treasury thinks in terms of budget and taxes. Except for the members of his personal staff, each presidential adviser has and should have a departmental outlook.

In the Palestine situation the military kept talking about two things: our inability to send troops to Palestine if trouble should break out there and, secondly, the oil resources of the Middle East. Secretary Forrestal spoke to me repeatedly about the danger that hostile Arabs might deny us access to the petroleum treasures of their countries. The Joint Chiefs of Staff, on several occasions, submitted memoranda to show that we could not afford to send more than a token force to the area.

The Department of State's specialists on the Near East were, almost without exception, unfriendly to the idea of a Jewish state. Their thinking went along this line: Great Britain has maintained her position in the area by cultivating the Arabs; now that she seems no longer able to hold this position, the United States must take over, and it must be done by exactly the same formula; if the Arabs are antagonized, they will go over into the Soviet camp.

I was never convinced by these arguments of the diplomats. I want to say, however, that in these differences of opinion between the White House and the State Department on the business of Palestine there was never any question as to who made the decisions and whose policy would be followed. Where some of our diplomats, and especially the gentlemen on the Near Eastern desks, differed was on the speed with which we should progress, not on the direction of the movement.

I had agreed in February that efforts should be made to have the U.N. restore peaceful conditions in Palestine. Accordingly, our delegation at Lake Success proposed on February 25 that conversations be held among the five permanent members of the Security Council to determine how serious a threat to world peace we faced in Palestine.

The British remained aloof from these discussions, but the other four delegations conferred and noted that the day of British withdrawal— May 15—would find Palestine without effective authority and the United Nations unprepared to step into the gap. In effect, it seemed difficult, if not impossible, to find any basis for reconciliation between the parties: The Jews fervently wanted partition; the Arabs opposed it hotly; and the British were determined to free themselves of the entire entanglement.

Under these conditions, and faced with the evidence of mounting violence inside Palestine, the Security Council was to decide whether or not it would accept the General Assembly resolution of November 29, 1947, as the basis for a Palestine solution. That is the reason that our State Department proposed, on March 19, 1948, that unless a peaceful transition to the partitioned status could be found the former British mandate should be placed under the United Nations Trusteeship Council. This was not a rejection of partition but rather an effort to postpone its effective date until proper conditions for the establishment of self-government in the two parts might be established.

My policy with regard to Palestine was not a commitment to any set of dates or circumstances; it was dedication to the twin deal of international obligations and the relieving of human misery. In this sense, the State Department's trusteeship proposal was not contrary to my policy.

On the other hand, anybody in the State Department should have known—and I am sure that some individual officials actually expected— that the Jews would read this proposal as a complete abandonment of the partition plan on which they so heavily counted and that the Arabs would also believe that, like them, we had come to oppose the solution approved by the General Assembly. In this sense, the trusteeship idea was at odds with my attitude and the policy I had laid down.

There were, however, some tactical advantages to a shift of the debate from the Security Council with its veto to the Trusteeship Council, where decisions were made by majority vote. In addition, it was only a matter of weeks before the British would leave Palestine and thus change the entire situation. There was always a chance that the United Nations might find a solution to forestall the inevitable outbreak of violence, so it seemed worth while to allow that proposal to be discussed in the meanwhile.

The suggestion that the mandate be continued as a trusteeship under the U.N. was not a bad idea at the time. However, there were strong suspicions voiced by many that the diplomats thought of it as a way to prevent partition and the establishment of the Jewish homeland.

There were some men in the State Department who held the view that the Balfour Declaration could not be carried out without offense to the Arabs. Like most of the British diplomats, some of our diplomats also thought that the Arabs, on account of their numbers and because of the fact that they controlled such immense oil resources, should be appeased. I am sorry to say that there were some among them who were also inclined to be anti-Semitic.

Secretary Marshall and Under Secretary Lovett saw eye to eye with me, as did Ambassador Austin at the United Nations. Austin had had long experience on the Senate Foreign Relations Committee and believed firmly in the ideal of the United Nations. In the Senate he had been one of the most effective of its leaders. He was not one to talk much for the headlines, but behind the scenes he knew how to make his influence felt and to bring factions to agree. I have always considered myself very fortunate that I could find a man of his high qualifications for appointment to the ticklish U.N. job.

On May 14 I was informed that the Provisional Government of Israel was planning to proclaim a Jewish state at midnight that day, Palestine time, which was when the British mandate came to an end. I had often talked with my advisers about the course of action we would take once partition had come about, and it was always understood that eventually we would recognize any responsible government the Jews might set up. Partition was not taking place in exactly the peaceful manner I had hoped, to be sure, but the fact was that the Jews were controlling the area in which their people lived and that they were ready to administer and to defend it. On the other hand, I was well aware that some of the State Department "experts" would want to block recognition of a Jewish state.

Now that the Jews were ready to proclaim the State of Israel, however, I decided to move at once and give American recognition to the new nation. I instructed a member of my staff to communicate my decision to the State Department and prepare it for transmission to Ambassador Austin at the United Nations in New York. About thirty minutes later, exactly eleven minutes after Israel had been proclaimed a state, Charlie Ross, my press secretary, handed the press the announcement of the *de facto* recognition by the United States of the provisional government of Israel.

I was told that to some of the career men of the State Department this announcement came as a surprise. It should not have been if these men had faithfully supported my policy.

The difficulty with many career officials in the government is that they regard themselves as the men who really make policy and run the government. They look upon the elected officials as just temporary occupants. Every President in our history has been faced with this problem: how to prevent career men from circumventing presidential policy. Too often career men seek to impose their own views instead of carrying out the established policy of the administration. Sometimes they achieve this by influencing the key men appointed by the President to put his policies into operation. It has often happened in the War and Navy Departments that the generals and the admirals, instead of working for and under the Secretaries, succeeded in having the Secretaries act for and under them. And it has happened in the Department of State.

Some Presidents have handled this situation by setting up what amounted to a little State Department of their own. President Roosevelt did this and carried on direct communications with Churchill and Stalin. I did not feel that I wanted to follow this method, because the State Department is set up for the purpose of handling foreign policy operations, and the State Department ought to take care of them. But I wanted to make it plain that the President of the United States, and not the second or third echelon in the State Department, is responsible for making foreign policy, and, furthermore, that no one in any department can sabotage the President's policy. The civil servant, the general or admiral, the foreign service officer has no authority to make policy. They act only as servants of the government, and therefore they must remain in line with the government policy that is established by those who have been chosen by the people to set that policy.

In the Palestine situation, as Secretary Lovett said to me after the announcement of the recognition of Israel, "They almost put it over on you."

The new State of Israel at once began to organize its machinery of government, and on January 25, 1949, held its first democratic elections. Following this, the United States on January 31, 1949, extended *de jure* recognition.

The Arab reaction to the establishment of Israel was violent. The Egyptian government advised the Secretary General of the United Nations formally on May 15 that its troops were crossing the Palestinian border in order "to restore order." This was, of course, no more than the Arab League following through on its threat to prevent by any means the creation of a Jewish state in Palestine, but the United Nations at once took action to prevent the spread of the hostilities. A mediator was dispatched to Palestine and succeeded in getting the Jews and the Arabs to agree to a temporary truce of four weeks, and later to another truce period. This kept the general fighting in check but did not prevent more localized conflict, when some of the younger leaders of the new state of Israel proved themselves to be as belligerent as the heads of the Arab League.

It was my hope that out of the efforts of the United Nations mediator there might come a solution that would give the Jews a homeland in which they might safely build their future. What that homeland was to be was defined, so far as I was concerned, by the partition resolution of November 1947. The platform of the Democratic party for the 1948 campaign contained a statement on Israel that expressed clearly what I had in mind.

"We approve the claims of the State of Israel," this statement read, "to the boundaries set forth in the United Nations resolution of November 29 and consider that modifications thereof should be made only if fully acceptable to the State of Israel. . . . We continue to support, within the framework of the United Nations, the internationalization of Jerusalem and the protection of the holy places in Palestine." This statement had been drawn up with the concurrence of the State Department. It represented my deep conviction that not only the general promise of the Balfour Declaration should be kept but also the specific promise of the U.N. resolution. I had assured Dr. Weizmann that these promises would be kept. The Jewish homeland was not to be just a matter of form; it had to be given the space and the opportunity to prove itself.

The U.N. mediator, the Swedish Count Bernadotte, then proposed in September that there should be a different kind of partition: He would give West Galilee in the north to Israel but let the Negeb in the south go to the Arabs. I did not like this change. It looked to me like a fast reshuffle that gave to the Arabs the Negeb area, which still remained to be fully settled. If, however, one looked only at the map and how the two partition proposals appeared there, the Bernadotte plan may have seemed an improvement; it seemed to reduce the number of friction points along a long frontier between the Jews and the Arabs. In any case, Secretary Marshall informed the United Nations that it seemed to him that it was a fair and sound proposal.

Zionists, who saw a pro-Arab behind every State Department desk, at once claimed that this was another reversal of United States policy. Some even went so far as to claim that the Bernadotte plan had been drawn up originally in our State Department. It was not only the Zionists who objected; the Arabs also opposed the Bernadotte proposal because it would have recognized "a Jewish state called Israel."

I conferred with members of my staff on September 28, after the news of Marshall's comment on this new proposal. We were in Oklahoma City at the time, aboard my special train during the election campaign. I reviewed the situation, and it was discussed at length. It was clear to me that the Bernadotte plan was so different from the original partition plan that it could not be accepted without a change in policy. I told my staff, therefore, that I would issue a statement reaffirming the Israel plank of the Democratic platform, and I told them to go ahead and draft such a statement. I would use it in an early speech, after consultation with Marshall or Lovett.

When Secretary Marshall returned from Paris on October 9 to report to me on the activities of the United Nations, we discussed this matter among other problems. Marshall explained that his comment on the Bernadotte plan had been intended primarily to encourage negotiation between the Arabs and the Jews so as to say, in effect, that the partition plan was not completely rigid. I decided, therefore, that it would not be necessary to issue a statement on Israel at this time. I was satisfied that the Secretary understood my position and, in turn, I had no desire to display publicly any differences about specific points as long as there was agreement on the general policy.

However, several days later the British and the Chinese introduced a joint resolution in the United Nations that was sharply anti-Israel in tone. It was a call for a cease-fire in Palestine, but it placed the blame rather one-sidedly on the Jews, and it called upon both sides to withdraw from the Negeb—which by this time was predominantly in Jewish hands. Marshall, at my request, was visiting Greece and Italy, and in the absence of his personal leadership of our delegation at the United Nations I thought it best to make certain that no unauthorized comments should be made on this new resolution. This was the reason for the following memo which I had Lovett relay to Marshall:

October 17, 1948

FROM: THE PRESIDENT
TO: THE SECRETARY OF STATE
   I request that no statement be made or no action be taken on the subject of Palestine by any member of our delegation in Paris without specific authority from me and clearing the text of any statement.

It had been my desire all along to keep foreign policy out of the campaign of 1948. I wanted the world to know that, however divided the American people might be on political issues at home, they would stand as one in their relations to other nations. In other words, I wished to keep foreign policy bi-partisan by keeping it out of the campaign altogether. However, Governor Dewey, the Republican candidate, chose to make a public statement on our Palestine policy. In this statement he tried to imply that I had gone back on the Democratic platform, and in doing so he had, in effect, attacked my integrity.

This attack I could not permit to go unchallenged. I communicated with Marshall (through Lovett) so that he might understand why it had become necessary for me now to make the statement we had earlier agreed not to make. There was no alternative unless I wanted the political charge to be believed. I was so deeply convinced that the policy toward Palestine had been right and would continue to be right that I had no choice but to reaffirm my position.

I did this on October 28 in a speech in Madison Square Garden in New York. The words I used were almost the same as those that had been drawn up a month earlier after the conference on the train in Oklahoma City.

"The subject of Israel," I said, " . . . must not be resolved as a matter of politics in a political campaign. I have refused consistently to play politics with that question. I have refused, first, because it is my responsibility to see that our policy in Israel fits in with our foreign policy throughout the world; second, it is my desire to help built in Palestine a strong, prosperous, free and independent democratic state. It must be large enough, free enough, and strong enough to make its people self-supporting and secure."

In a personal letter to Dr. Chaim Weizmann, now the President of the State of Israel, I put these thoughts in more specific words. Dr. Weizmann, in a long and warm letter, had congratulated me on my election, and on November 29 I wrote a reply. In many ways it sums up my feelings and my attitude toward the plight of the Jews and the emergence of the new state. This is my letter to Dr. Weizmann:

November 29, 1948

PERSONAL AND CONFIDENTIAL
Dear Mr. President:

Today—the first anniversary of the Partition Resolution—is a most appropriate time for me to answer your last letter, dated November 5th.

As I read your letter, I was struck by the common experience you and I have recently shared. We had both been abandoned by the so-called realistic experts to our supposedly forlorn lost cause. Yet we both kept pressing for what we were sure was right—and we were both proven to be right. My feeling of elation on the morning of November 3rd must have approximated your own feelings one year ago today, and on May 14th and on several occasions since then.

However, it does not take long for bitter and resourceful opponents to regroup their forces after they have been shattered. You in Israel have already been confronted with that situation; and I expect to be all too soon. So I understand very well your concern to prevent the undermining of your well-earned victories.

I remember well our conversations about the Negeb, to which you referred in your letter. I agree fully with your estimate of the importance of the area to Israel, and I deplore any attempt to take it away from Israel. I had thought that my position would have been clear to all the world, particularly in the light of the specific wording of the Democratic Party platform. But there were those who did not take this seriously, regarding it as "just another campaign promise" to be forgotten after the election. I believe they have recently realized their error. I have interpreted my re-election as a mandate from the American people to carry out the Democratic platform—including, of course, the plank on Israel. I intend to do so.

Since your letter was written, we have announced in the General Assembly our firm intention to oppose any territorial changes in the November 29th Resolution which are not acceptable to the State of Israel. I am confident that the General Assembly will support us in this basic position.

We have already expressed our willingness to help develop the new State through financial and economic measures. As you know, the Export-Import Bank is actively considering a substantial long-term loan to Israel on a project basis. I understand that your Government is now in process of preparing the details of such projects for submission to the Bank. Personally, I would like to go even further, by expanding such financial and economic assistance on a large scale to the entire Middle East, contingent upon effective mutual cooperation.

Thank you so much for your warm congratulations and good wishes on my re-election. I was pleased to learn that the first Israeli elections have been scheduled for January 25th. That enables us to set a definite target date for extending de jure recognition.

In closing, I want to tell you how happy and impressed I have been at the remarkable progress made by the new State of Israel. What you have received at the hands of the world has been far less than was your due. But you have more than made the most of what you have received, and I admire you for it. I trust that the present uncertainty, with its terribly burdensome consequences, will soon be eliminated. We will do all we can to help by encouraging direct negotiations between the parties looking toward a prompt peace settlement.

Very sincerely yours,
Harry S. Truman

CHAPTER 13

If I had heeded the desire of my family, I would have made plans to leave the White House at the end of my first term. I took no steps and made no moves at any time to discourage anyone from seeking nomination to succeed me. From a personal standpoint, I had no desire, just as I had none in 1944, to undertake a national political campaign merely for the sake of gratifying private ambitions. I had already been President of the United States for more than three and a half years.

The compelling motive in my decision to run for the presidency in 1948 was the same as it had been in 1944. There was still "unfinished business" confronting the most successful fifteen years of Democratic administration in the history of the country. The hard-earned reforms of the years since 1933 which insured a better life for more people in every walk of American life were taking permanent root in the 1940's. These benefits were still vulnerable to political attack by reactionaries and could be lost if not safeguarded by a vigilant Democratic administration.

I never wanted to fight for myself or to oppose others just for the sake of elevating myself to a higher office. I would have been happy to continue serving my community as a county judge. I would have been even happier as a senator, and would have been content to stay entirely clear of the White House. I had accepted the nomination as Vice-President not with a sense of triumph but with a feeling of regret at having to give up an active role in the Senate.

I have been asked how I could have had a part in a campaign for a fourth term for Franklin D. Roosevelt in 1944 against my conviction that no President should serve more than two terms.

The answer is simple—I knew what would have happened in 1944 if Roosevelt and his ideals were not allowed to continue through those extremely critical times. If the forces of reaction could gain control during the emergency when both domestic and foreign affairs were in a dangerously volatile condition, I knew that within a matter of months the postwar period would witness the repeal or nullification of much of the enlightened social program for which Roosevelt and the Democrats had fought so hard since 1933. Even though the President was physically not as strong, he was a sure winner for the forces of liberalism, and I wanted to do all I could to help.

Again in 1948 there was no doubt as to the course I had to take. The world was undergoing a major readjustment, with revolution stalking most of the "have-not" nations. Communism was making the most of this opportunity, thriving on misery as it always does. The course of freedom was being challenged again—this time from a new and powerful quarter, Soviet Russia.

I had learned from my negotiations with the intransigent Russian diplomats that there was only one way to avoid a third world war, and that was to lead from strength. We had to rearm ourselves and our allies and, at the same time, deal with the Russians in a manner they could never interpret as weakness.

Within our own nation I had seen many well-meaning groups who campaigned for "peace at any price" while apologizing for the aggressive acts of the Russians as merely a reflection of Russian reaction to our own tough policy. Many respectable Americans espoused such ideas without realizing the danger to which they were subjecting our national security and the freedoms for which we had fought so hard.

In 1948 I felt that just as my years in the Senate had prepared me for the presidency, the years I spent serving out the term of Roosevelt prepared me to carry out our proposed program of domestic development and foreign security. I also felt, without undue ego, that this was no time for a new and inexperienced hand to take over the government and risk the interruption of our domestic program and put a dangerous strain on our delicately balanced foreign policy.

I had ample demonstration—in the functioning of the Eightieth Congress—of what could happen to a forward-looking administration program. The destructive and reactionary attitude of the Eightieth Congress convinced me of the urgent need for more liberalism in government rather than less. I felt it my duty to get into the fight and help stem the tide of reaction if I could until the remaining basic aims of the New Deal and the Fair Deal could be adopted, tried, and proved.

During their control of the Eightieth Congress, the Republicans had shown that they did not want—indeed, did not understand—an enlightened program. They did not understand the worker, the farmer, the everyday person. Theirs was an unreasoning, emotional resistance to progress. Any legislative proposal to improve the lot of the general public, in working conditions, health risks, or long-range social security, aroused their opposition. Most of them honestly believed that prosperity actually began at the top and would trickle down in due time to benefit all the people.

In foreign affairs the Republican leadership was still suffering the aftereffects of isolationism. It had apparently learned but little since the wrecking of the League of Nations by the "twelve willful men." Without the inspired self-reversal and the brilliant, intelligent leadership of Senator Arthur Vandenberg and that of Charles A. Eaton, chairman of the House Foreign Affairs Committee, we could never have achieved any bi-partisan policy in the conduct of foreign affairs. Without the leadership of these enlightened Republicans during those two years, the United Nations, the Marshall Plan, NATO, and other projects would have been hampered, if not blocked completely, by the selfish Republican majority.

Thus, many things combined to convince me that I had to make a fight for it—the threat being posed by Russian imperialist Communism; the misguided clamor for appeasement in the name of peace as advocated by the so-called Wallace Progressives; the large bloc of traditional Republican isolationists; and the coalition of southern Democrats and northern Republicans, who hoped to compel the repeal of a great deal of New Deal legislation and a return to the laissez-faire doctrine of pre-depression days. These forces had to be defeated or our country would be thrown back to the hard times of reaction.

I have always found comfort and guidance in the lessons of history, and I realized that my position in 1948 was, historically, nothing new. When Thomas Jefferson campaigned for the presidency in 1800, his decision was based primarily on his conviction that the Federalists were stifling the true democratic concept of the new republic, and he swept them out of office and restored liberalism in government after his election. Again, when Andrew Jackson staged a revolution against the forces of reaction, which once more had entrenched themselves in the federal government, he picked up the broken thread of liberalism which had been all but lost sight of during the administration of John Quincy Adams.

The Jacksonian era of progressive enlightenment, which began in 1829, was cut off in 1840 with the election of William Henry Harrison and John Tyler. Whig-Republican conservatism settled over the land for a lengthy siege, and although Abraham Lincoln had a genuine sympathy and a dedicated heart for the common man, it was not until 1885 that liberal policies in government were once again given an opportunity to work for the people. This opportunity disappeared in the years of the so-called "good old days" of Benjamin Harrison and William McKinley. I believe that William Jennings Bryan had the same vision that Jefferson and Jackson had demonstrated, especially when he led the revolt of the South and the West against the moneyed interests of the conservative East in 1896, but Republican conservatism had grown too strong for him.

One outstanding Republican President, Theodore Roosevelt, contributed to the perpetuation of progressivism in American life. Under his administration the country made great strides, particularly in the conservation of natural resources. After the best policies of Theodore Roosevelt's seven years in office disintegrated during the Taft administration and the federal government was again recaptured by the reactionary, backward-looking Republicans of that day, it was up to Woodrow Wilson to introduce the "New Freedom"—a period of truly liberal Democratic progress.

In 1916 Wilson had to face the decision of staying with the job he had started in the interests of all the people or giving up the gains which had been made since 1913. By accepting the challenge, the Democrats were able to bring about changes which are recognized today as some of the most valuable contributions to our way of life, even though many of them were canceled out from 1921 to 1933, when control of the affairs of the nation was once more in the hands of the special interests.

What happened in 1933 and the years following is recent history. I was privileged to be on the scene during the national rebirth of a system of government under Franklin Roosevelt which was dedicated to making the country's wealth and privileges available to all the people rather than to just a few. I saw him building an international diplomacy which put America in the position of world leadership. With a Democratic Congress, he wove the thread of liberal progressivism back into the fabric of American government and made it stronger than ever before.

Down through the history of the presidency of the United States a succession of strong liberal Presidents had fought the fight for liberalism and for a better life for the common man: Jefferson, Jackson, Lincoln, Theodore Roosevelt, Wilson, Franklin Roosevelt. With such a heritage handed down to me, I could not reject lightly the opportunity and the responsibility which were mine in 1948. I had to make a fight for its continuation. If I could keep the thread unbroken, I thought it my duty to try to by participating in a presidental campaign, I saw no reason for considering any other course of action.

What I wanted to do personally for my own comfort and benefit was not important. What I could do to contribute to the welfare of the country was important. I had to enter the 1948 campaign for the presidency.

It seemed to me that the only possible argument the opposition could advance in asking the voters to turn the Executive Department over to them in 1948 was a desire for a change after fifteen years of control of the government by the Democrats. But the voters' action in 1946 had put a Republican Congress in legislative control, and in my coming campaign to persuade the voters that the time for a change had not yet come, it was obvious that the Eightieth Congress would stick out like a sore thumb. It was my Exhibit A.

Agriculture had been hurt by the Eightieth Congress, for it had denied farmers a flexible system of price supports and rejected my recommendations for programs to assure adequate consumption of farm products and a more stable future for the farmers.

The threat of inflation, which should have been overcome in 1946, had been renewed by the failure of the Republican Eightieth Congress to restore price controls at a special session which I called in November 1947. It chose to think of the few, for whom ever-increasing prices meant ever-increasing profits, rather than of the needs of the many for whom the one tested weapon which would prevent excessive prices without hampering production was price control.

Over my veto, the Eightieth Congress passed a Republican tax bill in the spring of 1948 which gave forty per cent of its tax relief to the less than five per cent of the taxpayers with net incomes of more than five thousand dollars a year. It also advocated the withdrawal of the federal government from the field of inheritance taxation to encourage the creation of tax-free havens, where persons of great wealth could establish fictitious residences in order to escape the just taxation of their estates.

By enacting the Taft-Hartley Act in 1947, the Eightieth Congress attempted to shackle American labor and to give overwhelming power to employers. The Republican majority ripped apart the Department of Labor, crippling the functions of that department and making it extremely difficult for the department to carry out its mission of fostering, promoting, and developing the welfare of the wage earners.

After the United States had offered a home in this country to the United Nations, the Eightieth Congress failed to follow up immediately with enabling legislation. This cast a damper over our relations with other countries throughout the world who were struggling together for peace. It was a typical gesture of isolationism, as was the reluctance— almost the refusal—of the Congress to support the European Recovery Program and cutting down to one year the request to continue the Trade Agreements Program for three years.

The Republican Eightieth Congress, in control of national legislation for the first time in fourteen years, had managed to reverse the sound democratic policies of collective bargaining, social security, rent controls, price controls, and other instruments of government designed to insure equality of privilege for the great majority of people. Instead, the Congress had ignored the repeated recommendations of the President and had yielded to the pressures and lobbies of special privilege in housing, in prices, in taxes, in agriculture, in labor and industrial relations, in foreign trade, and in virtually every other major field of national and international policy.

The Eightieth Congress, in short, had shown that the Republican party had always been, and continued to be, the party of special privilege. That is why I made it clear in every one of my campaign speeches that in reality there was just one issue for the people to vote on—the choice between special interests and the public welfare.

I was sure that the American people would agree with me if they had all the facts. I knew, however, that the Republican-controlled press and radio would be against me, and my only remaining hope of communicating with the people was to get the message to the people in a personal way.

The communications facilities of the country represented another issue in the 1948 campaign. The figures showed that approximately ninety per cent of the press and radio opposed me and supported the other candidates. This was to be expected, as most were owned, operated, or subsidized by the same private interests that always benefited from Republican economic policies. Even the segments of the press and radio which were not directly controlled by anti-administration interests depended to a great extent upon the advertising revenue which came from the wealthy, and often selfish, private groups. The power companies, for instance, purchased millions of dollars' worth of newspaper and magazine space in which to attack the public utility program of the federal government. Other lobbies and pressure groups, like the National Association of Manufacturers and the United States Chamber of Commerce, were constant contributors to press and radio in the guise of advertisers and sponsors.

My chief objection was not to the space and time which were purchased by the Republicans, because the same were for sale to the Democrats. I did resent, however, the commonplace practice of distorted editorials and slanted headlines in the press and of outright misrepresentation in the daily offerings of the columnists and commentators. The worst offense of all was the editing and distorting of the facts in the news.

If the facts were presented in the news columns of the press and in the newscasts over the air, I was satisfied and paid no attention to expressions of opinion or character assassinations by certain columnists and commentators. But the danger which I saw was the confusion of fact with mere speculation, by which readers and listeners were undoubtedly misguided and intentionally deceived. The attempts of the gossip and scandal columnists and commentators were usually obvious and therefore of no consequence, but when the serious analysts and "ivory tower" critics strayed from the facts—as they frequently did— the public was in danger of being misled by those in whom it had placed some degree of credence and confidence. It is common knowledge that the mere fact that a statement appears in print makes it credible to many people.

It was my conviction that the major media of communication had failed in their responsibility to present facts as facts and opinion as opinion. It seemed to me that many owners, publishers, and columnists of the press and radio were deliberately irresponsible during a time of extreme importance to the people of the United States and that they were not living up to the responsibilities attached to the constitutional privileges of freedom of the press and freedom of speech. As far as I was concerned, they had sold out to the special interests, and that is why I referred to them in my campaign speeches as the "kept press and paid radio."

Too many candidates have lived in fear of the press and radio and have courted their good will as if the outcome of the election depended upon it. But I had learned the error of this idea in my own political life. In my own state I always faced the overwhelming majority of press opposition. I overcame it at every turn and never had any respect for the so-called political influence of the press. My opinion has not changed over the years. Any good politician with nerve *and a program that is right* can win in the face of the stiffest opposition.

My familiarity with the history of past presidential campaigns was another factor that kept me from worrying about the press opposition I faced in 1948. Since the election of Jefferson in 1800 there had been thirty-six presidential campaigns in which the press had supposedly played an important part. In eighteen of these campaigns the press had supported the losing candidate, and in the other eighteen it had been behind the winner. This was the clearest proof I needed that I had nothing to fear regarding the influence of the newspapers and the newer medium of radio.

This was the prospect that faced me in the summer of 1948. The opposing party, which had gained strength in the off-year elections, had already expressed its intention—through the Eightieth Congress—of tearing down the structure which the Democrats had built over a period of sixteen years for the purpose of improving the welfare and security of the people. Coupled with this threat was the influence of a hostile press which promoted the policies of the Republican party and did all it could to discredit and sabotage the policies of my administration.

It was not an encouraging situation that confronted me, but I was not brought up to run away from a fight when the fight is for what is right. Supposedly scientific predictions that I could not win did not worry me one bit.

Public-opinion polls had reached their peak as an American institution during the summer of 1948. Several of these, such as those conducted by George Gallup and Elmo Roper, had established reputations for accuracy that were quite impressive, and many politicians, newspapermen, businessmen, and labor leaders began to look to these surveys as a guide to their actions.

Almost unanimously the polls taken before the 1948 Democratic convention showed my popularity with the American people to have hit an all-time low. This was a condition that resulted from the efforts made by the American press to misrepresent me and to make my program, policies, and staff appear in the worst light possible. The charts indicated that I had gone from an approval of somewhere around seventy per cent of the total population immediately after I had succeeded to the presidency to the neighborhood of thirty-six per cent in the spring of 1948.

I never paid any attention to the polls myself, because in my judgment they did not represent a true cross section of American opinion. I did not believe that the major components of our society, such as agriculture, management, and labor, were adequately sampled. I also know that the polls did not represent facts but mere speculation, and I have always placed my faith in the known facts.

Although the polls did not bother me personally, I was aware that some of the Democratic leaders were discouraged by the dismal picture being painted by the forecasters. I saw that the press was giving widespread publicity to the predictions that the voters would repudiate me and my administration in the fall elections, and I had learned from experience that false propaganda can mislead even the most intelligent and well-meaning people.

I knew that I had to do something about this concerted effort of the pollsters and the Republican-controlled press to drug the populace with their statistics and propaganda. Even some of my closest friends and advisers were counseling me to change my mind about going after the nomination in July.

Early in May I had an idea—perhaps the only one that the critics admitted was entirely my own. In order to circumvent the gloom and pessimism being spread by the polls and by false propaganda in the press, I decided that I would go directly to the people in all parts of the country with a personal message from the President. It would mean riding thousands of miles by train and making talks at all hours at stops along the way where crowds could be assembled to hear the facts. But it was the only alternative.

Two Presidents before me had undertaken tours similar to the one I planned. Andrew Johnson had "swung around the circle" between Chicago and Washington seeking support for his reconstruction plan, which was violently opposed by the Congress. Johnson spoke at many points along his route in an effort to explain to the people that his plan for rehabilitating the Southland, based on Lincoln's proposals, was for the welfare of the whole nation, and that the harsh plan sponsored by the Congress would damage the prosperity and expansion of the North as well as the South. He was treated unmercifully by the Radicals and by the partisan press of that day and ended his tour discouraged and defeated. I believe that Johnson would have put his plan through if he had not given up in the face of criticism and had carried his personal campaign into other sections of the country.

Woodrow Wilson's trip across the country to plead the cause of the League of Nations in 1919 was another experience that ended in misfortune. When his health broke, he was unable to continue his appearances, and the train that took him back to Washington was virtually a funeral train.

Like the tours of Johnson and Wilson, the one which I planned in June of 1948 was to inform the people what the President and his administration were doing in the face of the false reports that were being disseminated. I wanted the people in the out-of-the-way places to have a chance to see and hear their President face to face so that they could form their opinions of me and my program on the basis of firsthand acquaintance rather than on the basis of polls and propaganda.

My purpose was to explain the workings of American foreign policy and the status of our domestic problems in a way that the people could understand. I also felt obligated to make clear the obstructionist role which the Eightieth Congress was playing. I was convinced that the average, everyday American did not have the full story of what was going on and that it was necessary for me to get out of Washington long enough to discuss the facts of the situation directly with the people.

I traveled all the way to the West Coast and back, making seventy-six speeches in the cities, towns, and villages along the way. I had never lost the faith, as some of those around me seemed to, and I found renewed encouragement and confidence in the response that came from the crowds that gathered at all the train stops on this first tour. They seemed glad to see me and eager to hear for themselves what I had to tell them.

I tried a method of speaking which I had not used before, except on informal occasions. On the seventy-six speeches which I made on this tour, seventy-one were "off the cuff." I used notes sometimes to adapt my statements to local interests, but these were never more than a few lines and were usually handed to me only a minute or so before I began speaking.

My first formal experience at extemporaneous speaking had come just a few weeks before I opened the whistle-stop tour in June. After reading an address to the American Society of Newspaper Editors in April, I decided to talk "off the cuff" on American relations with Russia. When I finished my remarks about thirty minutes later, I was surprised to get the most enthusiastic applause that I had ever received from a group made up mainly of Republicans.

On May 14 I again tried my hand at speaking without a manuscript when I addressed a rally of the Young Democrats in Washington. A New York newspaper called the speech a "fighting one in the new Truman manner." I decided that if speaking without a prepared copy or getting away from reading a prepared text was more effective in getting my ideas and feelings across, I would use that method on the trainside talks which I planned to make in the future. It was a style which I was to follow in my acceptance speech at the Democratic convention and in most of the speeches which I was to deliver in the campaign from Labor Day up to the November election.

One aspect of the political situation in 1948 which dismayed most of my supporters and advisers was the threat of a split within the Democratic party over the issue of civil rights. The defection by some of the southern states, notably South Carolina, Alabama, and Mississippi, was something I had anticipated, however, since I first took a stand as President on this greatly misunderstood and misrepresented subject. From the early days of my administration I insisted on a workable fair employment practices program and on the enforcement of civil rights as guaranteed by the Constitution.

The beginning of this splinter opposition dated all the way back to December 5, 1946, when I had appointed a committee to investigate and report on the status of civil rights in America. I took this action because of the repeated anti-minority incidents immediately after the war in which homes were invaded, property was destroyed, and a number of innocent lives were taken. I wanted to get the facts behind these incidents of disregard for individual and group rights which were reported in the news with alarming regularity, and to see that the law was strengthened, if necessary, so as to offer adequate protection and fair treatment to all of our citizens.

I directed that the committee's survey should not be confined to the problem of any one minority group but should extend to all areas of racial and religious discrimination. It was a simple approach to one of the oldest problems of a democratic society, yet the leaders of "white supremacy" began at once their campaign of demagoguery to attempt to nullify my efforts to develop federal safeguards against racial discrimination. It was this movement which culminated in the bolt of part of the southern bloc in 1948 under the misleading name of States' Rights Democrats.

The Fair Employment Practices Committee had been established by an Executive Order of President Roosevelt on June 25, 1941, "to encourage full participation in the national defense program by all citizens . . . regardless of race, creed, color or national origin." The committee was continued until June 30, 1946, under the National War Agency Appropriations Act and was terminated at that time against my wishes. The FEPC had shown that, in the majority of wartime cases, discriminatory practices by employers and unions could be reduced or eliminated by simple negotiation when the work of the negotiator was backed by a firm national policy.

Nevertheless, there were many unresolved cases handled by the FEPC which indicated to me that executive authority was not enough to insure compliance in the face of organized opposition. I saw that legislative authority would be required to put an end to such un-American practices. The Committee on Civil Rights was set up to get the facts and to publicize as widely as possible the need for legislation.

In the Executive Order creating the committee, I pointed out that the nation was losing ground in civil rights and that the preservation of the liberties was the duty of every branch of government and every public official—state, federal, and local. The constitutional guarantees of individual liberties and of equal protection under the law clearly place on the federal government the duty to act when state or local authorities abridge or fail to uphold these guarantees. I felt that the federal government was hampered, however, by inadequate civil-rights statutes and that the Department of Justice lacked the tools to enforce such statutes as there were. This was a condition that I wanted to see corrected.

Speaking to the fifteen members of the Committee on Civil Rights at the White House on January 15, 1947, I said: "I want our Bill of Rights implemented in fact. We have been trying to do this for 150 years. We are making progress, but we are not making progress fast enough. This country could very easily be faced with a situation similar to the one with which it was faced in 1922." I was referring, of course, to the revival of terrorism in that year by the Ku Klux Klan.

Six months later I restated the motives of my civil-rights program in an address to the annual convention of the National Association for the Advancement of Colored People on June 29, 1947. "As Americans," I asserted, "we believe that every man should be free to live his life as he wishes. He should be limited only by his responsibility to his fellow countrymen. If this freedom is to be more than a dream, each man must be guaranteed equality of opportunity. The only limit to an American's achievement should be his ability, his industry and his character."

In October of the same year the Civil Rights Committee delivered its report, which showed that a positive need existed for legislation to secure the rights of American minority groups. The report listed ten important recommendations, as follows:

(1) Establishing a permanent Commission on Civil Rights, a joint Congressional Committee on Civil Rights, and a Civil Rights Division in the Department of Justice. (2) Strengthening existing civil-rights statutes. (3) Providing federal protection against lynching. (4) Protecting more adequately the right to vote. (5) Establishing a Fair Employment Practices Commission to prevent unfair discrimination in employment. (6) The modification of the federal naturalization laws to permit the granting of citizenship without regard to the race, color, or national origin of applicants. (7) Providing home rule and suffrage in presidential elections for the residents of the District of Columbia. (8) Providing statehood for Hawaii and Alaska and a greater measure of self-government for our island possessions. (9) Equalizing the opportunities for residents of the United States to become naturalized citizens. (10) Settling the evacuation claims of Japanese Americans.

I asked for specific civil-rights legislation in my message to the Congress on February 2, 1948, to enact these recommendations into law. At the same time I urged the abolition of segregation and discrimination in the use of transportation facilities by both public officers and the employees of private companies throughout the country. And later

I incorporated these recommendations into the 1948 platform of the Democratic party.

The platform of a political party is a promise to the public. Unless a man can run on his party's platform—and try to carry it out, if elected—he is not an honest man. All campaign oratory that is not based on principles and issues represented in a definite platform is sheer demagoguery. When a party has no principles and issues on which to stand, it invariably turns to personalities and to the use of the "big lie" technique, ignoring the only basis upon which a political campaign can be logically conducted.

I was one of those who had helped write the Democratic party platform in my own state during the 1934, 1938, and 1942 campaigns and the national platform in 1936, 1940, and 1944. I believed in the principles these platforms advanced, and when I was elected President, I tried to carry out the platform promises that had been made. The basic principle in all of those platforms was the benefit of the average man who has no pull in Washington. To me, party platforms are contracts with the people, and I always looked upon them as agreements that had to be carried out. That is why I was perfectly willing to risk defeat in 1948 by sticking to the civil-rights plank in my platform.

There were people around me, of course, who were anxious to prevent any sort of split in the Democratic party, and efforts were made to soften the approach to the civil-rights issue. I would not stand for any double talk on this vital principle, however, and insisted on plain language being used. Members of the Cabinet and others warned me that I was riding to a defeat if I stuck to my FEPC orders and if I did not let up on the battle for civil-rights legislation. But I wanted to win the fight by standing on my platform, or lose it the same way.

I was reasonably sure, far in advance of the convention, that there would be a splintering off of the South or at least a portion of it. The attitude which had been taken by Southerners toward the policy of integration in the armed forces was well known. Practically all of the training camps in World War II were located in the South because of climate conditions, and the idea of integration, therefore, encountered strong resistance. The Southerners were especially bothered by integration among construction workers, who were employed without discrimination as to race for the purpose of building the government's training camps, and they were not happy over the orders on fair employment. I expected trouble, and it developed promptly at the 1948 convention.

The military establishment—particularly the Navy—had been strongly opposed to my policy of integration in the armed services, but I had forced it into practice. Then they discovered that no difficulty resulted from integration after all. Integration is the best way to create an effective combat organization in which the men will stand together and fight. Experience on the front has proved that the morale of troops is strengthened where Jim Crow practices are not imposed.

I felt also that any other course would be inconsistent with international commitments and obligations. We could not endorse a color line at home and still expect to influence the immense masses that make up the Asian and African peoples. It was necessary to practice what we preached, and I tried to see that we did it.

Every Democratic platform since 1932 has stressed the devotion of our party to the constitutional ideal of civil rights. But what aroused many Southerners now was that I meant to put this pledge into practice. When the Southerners saw in 1948 that I meant to put it into effect, they bolted the party. When J. Strom Thurmond, the governor of South Carolina, who headed the revolt, made his dramatic departure from the convention floor in Philadelphia with his followers, he was asked by a reporter to clarify his position.

"President Truman is only following the platform that Roosevelt advocated," the reporter pointed out.

"I agree," Thurmond replied, "but Truman really *means* it."

Despite the clarity with which the Civil Rights Committee had expressed its findings and recommendations, and the wide publicity which I had encouraged on the subject, the program which I insisted be included in the platform was shamefully distorted and misrepresented by political demagogues and press propaganda. My appeal for equal economic and political rights for every American citizen had nothing at all to do with the personal or social relationships of individuals or the right of every person to choose his own associates. The basic constitutional privilege which I advocated was deliberately misconstrued to include or imply racial miscegenation and intermarriage. My only goal was equal opportunity and security under the law for all classes of Americans.

The States' Rights Democrats claimed that this was not a bolt from the Democratic party. They said they represented the true Democrats of the Southland. It was a bolt. It also was a manifestation of prejudice. I had seen at first hand a similar reaction in 1928, when Al Smith ran for the Presidency on the Democratic ticket. I was very active in Jackson County politics at that time and did everything I could to carry the county for him. Still, because of anti-Catholic prejudice, our traditionally Democratic county voted Smith down by thirty thousand votes. Because of the success of that prejudice the belief was then stated that no Catholic, Jew, or Negro could ever hold high public office again. That was twenty-five years ago, and the prejudice has now become much less apparent, although it has yet to be overcome. Hitler's persecution of the Jews did much to awaken Americans to the dangerous extremes to which prejudice can be carried if allowed to control government actions.

I never did believe that the great mass of Southerners had the same viewpoint as the minority Dixiecrat contingent. I was raised amidst some violently prejudiced Southerners myself, and I believe the vast majority of good Southerners understand that the blind prejudices of past generations cannot continue in a free republic. Much progress in civil rights has been made voluntarily by the South itself, and it was to help and to speed this progress that my program was designed. It was because they understood this that the reasoning people of the eleven states that had once formed the Confederacy did not withdraw from the Democratic convention and join with the splinter party.

I did not discount the handicap which the loss of a "Solid South" presented as far as my chances of winning the election were concerned. I knew that it might mean the difference between victory and defeat in November. I knew, too, that if I deserted the civil-liberties plank of the Democratic party platform I could heal the breach, but I have never traded principles for votes, and I did not intend to start the practice in 1948 regardless of how it might affect the election.

I was confident that the voters would see that the Dixiecrats were trying in vain to build a platform on an issue that was not a reality but a fiction. With this confidence—which few of those around me seemed to share—I was willing to take the risk imposed on my chances of being elected President in my own right.

Although many candidates for the presidency have had to cope with splits within their parties, the situation which I faced in 1948 was without a comparable precedent in the history of American politics. I was confronted not with one major defection in the Democratic party but with two bolts of sizable proportions. In addition to the faction which was preparing to withdraw its support from me and to pick an alternate candidate on the platform of States' Rights Democrats, there were the so-called Progressives under the leadership of another Democrat, Henry Wallace.

Under President Roosevelt, Wallace had served as one of the best Secretaries of Agriculture this country ever had, and he enjoyed considerable personal prestige as Vice-President during Roosevelt's third term. He was not an opponent to be discounted, and it was predicted that he would get a large vote.

After I became President I found it necessary to part with Henry Wallace when I found him interfering with my conduct of foreign policy.

I felt then that he cherished an idealistic notion that he would be able to stir up a following in the country that could elect him President. The creation of the Progressive party in 1948 was an attempt on the part of Wallace and his supporters to materialize that aspiration.

Some honest and well-meaning agitators for peace with Russia at any price found in Wallace a spokesman for their point of view. He had consistently maintained that I was too rough in dealing with the Soviets and that peace could be obtained if we were more conciliatory in our approach. He had made many trips for Roosevelt—to China, South America, and Russia, including Siberia—and these activities had given him a world prominence and contributed to the development of a considerable and enthusiastic following for him.

There was, however, a sinister aspect to the Wallace movement. It provided a front for the Communists to infiltrate the political life of the nation and spread confusion. Without the conscious knowledge of many members of the new Progressive party, the Reds were working swiftly and skillfully to gain control of the nominating convention and to dominate party committees and the platform.

Wallace himself, who seemed to have been transformed into a mystic with a zeal that verged on fanaticism, was apparently unaware of the purposes to which the Communists were putting his "progressive" movement. I always felt that he was an honest man and a faithful public servant but that he simply did not understand what was happening.

I knew from personal experience with the Russians that Wallace's dream of appeasement was futile and that, if allowed to materialize, it would be tragic. I had learned that the Russians understood only force. Wallace did not think this was true, but he did not have the experience with the Soviets that had been mine.

I realized that the Progressives would cost me votes, but, like the Dixiecrats, they stood for principles which I knew I must reject.

My nomination for the presidency by the Democratic party in 1948 was also challenged by a third movement within the ranks. This threatened to develop at any time during the spring into a full-fledged boom for General Dwight D. Eisenhower.

Among the chief agitators who claimed that I was not perpetuating the New Deal policies of President Roosevelt were the late President's sons, James and Elliott, former Cabinet members James F. Byrnes and Harold Ickes, and Senator Claude Pepper of Florida. There were many others who felt that because the press and the polls made it appear that my chances of success in the campaign were falling away to almost nothing someone else should get the Democratic party nomination.

General Eisenhower, who was at the peak of his popularity after his brilliant military accomplishments of World War II, seemed to be the logical choice for those who sought a dark-horse candidate to oppose me for the nomination. The professional liberals who were attempting to promote him as the Democratic nominee showed, however, that they were not familiar with the history and procedure of political conventions. When the President is sitting in the White House, the National Convention of his party has never gone against his recommendations in the choice of a candidate or in the formation of a platform on which that convention is to operate.

The President is traditionally the leader of his party. He has great influence with the National Committee, and usually the party will nominate a chairman of the convention who is friendly to the President and who meets the approval of the Chief Executive. And no matter how many detractors there may be, the chairman controls the organization of the convention. The convention will operate in the manner in which the chairman and the President want it to.

Even Theodore Roosevelt, with his tremendous popularity, could not take the nomination in 1912 from the incumbent President Taft, who had more than half of his own party against him. Consequently, all Teddy Roosevelt could do was to bolt the Republican party and run on the unsuccessful "Bull Moose" ticket. In 1908, though, when Theodore Roosevelt was in the White House, he could pick the party candidate just as Taft could reserve the nomination for himself in 1912. The same was true of Wilson in 1916.

In 1948 I was in a position to control the nomination. When I had made up my mind to run, those in the party who turned against me could do nothing to prevent it. For this reason, Thurmond and Wallace had to bolt the Democratic party and stir up their own following. If Eisenhower had gone after the Democratic nomination, there would have been a four-way split in the party, but otherwise the situation would have remained unchanged. Presidential control of the convention is a political principle which has not been violated in political history.

The boom for Eisenhower never developed in 1948 because the general resisted the efforts of those who tried to change his mind. Actually, it would be difficult to speculate on what would have been the outcome if Eisenhower had declared in 1948. The Eisenhower boom failed to get the support of any of the other splinter groups. The Progressives, after all, were critical of the military leadership and policy of the United States, and the Dixiecrats were not supporting anybody or anything in particular—they were simply protesting against a civil-rights program.

The rumor that Eisenhower would run probably had its origin in the White House. In one of his calls on me as Chief of Staff, the general and

I had a discussion of politics and military heroes. I asked him if he intended to run for President. He told me that he had no intention of running for the office and cited a letter which he had written to a friend in which he had given reasons for his decision not to run. In that letter, which had been released in January of that year, Eisenhower wrote: "The necessary and wise subordination of the military to civil power will be best sustained when life-long professional soldiers abstain from seeking high political office."

Eisenhower showed me this letter, and I told him that I thought he was using good judgment. I said that I did not think he could add anything to his splendid career, and that the only thing he would accomplish by getting into politics would be to detract from his reputation, just as General Grant did when he was inveigled into running. A political position, I told Eisenhower, is far different from a military one. The head of a military organization is not subject to attack by his underlings, but a President has no underlings and must expect attacks from every source.

I personally felt that, regardless of Eisenhower's chances as an independent in 1948, the statement which most effectively summed up that situation was the one by House Minority Leader Sam Rayburn, who did not go along with the move by the professional liberals to run the general for the presidency. Rayburn put it this way: "No, won't do. Good man, but wrong business."

I realized, of course, that the boom for Eisenhower and the defections of the Progressives and the States' Righters would cut into my voting strength on Election Day. But I knew that it was my duty to carry forward the program that had taken the nation from the depths of the depression to prosperity and world leadership, and I was convinced that the American people would want to have it carried forward—if only they were given the facts. And these I was determined to give them.

CHAPTER 14

From the time I returned to the White House on June 18 from my western tour to the opening day of the Democratic National Convention on July 12, I had little time to devote to active politics. The administration of the national government was my first business. My personal affairs and my political duties had to be fitted into the schedule wherever they could be made to fit.

For the first time, however, it was possible for the President to view the proceedings of the convention on television in the White House, and I was able to witness the major events in Philadelphia without leaving my work. Other lines of communication direct to Democratic National Headquarters kept me constantly informed on the proceedings, so that nothing that was taking place there escaped my attention.

It was arranged that after the preliminaries of the convention were disposed of Governor Donnelly of Missouri would nominate me at the final session. I made my plans to appear at the convention on July 14 to accept the nomination in person.

The work of a national political convention has always been a fascinating operation to me. For the party in power, much of the mechanics of the process is worked out in advance by the President, the chairman, and the party leaders.

After the convention is called to order by the chairman of the National Committee, officers are elected. The three key positions are the permanent chairman, the secretary of the convention, and the parliamentarian, whose rulings enable the convention to run in an orderly manner. The next step is the appointment of committees—on credentials, rules, platform and resolutions, and permanent organization. The committee procedure is the same as that practiced in the House of Representatives.

After the committees are appointed, the business then proceeds, permitting speechmaking and the general build-up of enthusiasm among the delegates for their candidates. As soon as the credentials committee has reported and the rules committee has reported on the procedure by which the convention will be governed, the next important task is the adoption of a platform. This takes place whenever the resolutions committee, which writes the platform, is ready to make its report to the convention.

If the resolutions committee disagrees on some paragraphs of the platform, a minority report will bring the issue to the convention for decision. It was the civil-rights paragraph, of course, which precipitated the biggest fight for the 1948 Democratic convention and which on the third day prompted thirty-five delegates from the southern states to walk out to organize the States' Rights Democratic movement.

When the platform is adopted, the nominations for President are in order. These are always accompanied by much flourish and speechmaking, many parades and great outbursts of enthusiasm. After each state and territory has been given an opportunity to make nominations, the roll call begins for the voting. If no nominee has a majority, of course another ballot is taken, and the balloting continues until one candidate has a majority. The simple majority was introduced in 1936, at which time the old two-thirds rule, long required for nomination in Democratic conventions, was abolished.

As soon as the President is nominated, the convention proceeds to the nomination of a Vice-President. With that, the convention adjourns, and the party is ready to go out and fight for election.

There was some question as to who the vice-presidential candidate would be at the 1948 Democratic National Convention. J. Howard McGrath, chairman of the National Committee, called me from Philadelphia and advised me that the key members of the convention could not decide on a candidate, though he said that most of them wanted Supreme Court Justice William O. Douglas. McGrath asked me to try to persuade Douglas to accept the nomination.

I had tried once before to interest Douglas in politics when I had asked him in February 1946 to take the place of Secretary of the Interior Ickes. Douglas said then that if I insisted he would accept, but that he had decided to make the Supreme Court his career. He said, "When President Roosevelt appointed me to the Court I was at first not too happy, but after a year I had gotten to like it and it seemed to fit me and my temperament, and I had decided to make it my career for life." Douglas told me he wanted to discuss the matter with Chief Justice

Harlan F. Stone. "The Chief Justice said he was concerned that I might take the post," Douglas told me later, "just when we were in the middle term of the Court." That day the Chief Justice came to see me and, speaking in that gentle tone of his, said: "Please quit disturbing my court." I answered just as gently: "You ought to let Bill make that decision." A week later Justice Douglas came to the White House to tell me that after talking it over with the Chief Justice he had decided to remain on the Court.

As he was leaving, Justice Douglas said: "Did you know that you were my candidate to replace Wallace as Vice-President on the ticket with Roosevelt in 1944?" "Did you know who my candidate was?" I asked him. Douglas answered, "Yes, it was Jimmy Brynes. I think my judgment on that was better than yours."

After the message from McGrath, requesting me to name a candidate for Vice-President, I put through a telephone call to Justice Douglas at a camp sixteen miles from Lostine, Oregon, where he was vacationing. I told Douglas I wanted him on the ticket with me as Vice-President. The telephone connection was bad and all I could make out clearly was that he wanted to talk it over with his family and friends and that he would telephone me from Portland, Oregon, the next day. The following day, which was a Saturday, Douglas telephoned me from the Benson Hotel in Portland, Oregon. We talked for about ten minutes, and Douglas asked if he could not give his final answer on Monday. He said, "I would like to do it, though I had made up my mind, as I said two years ago, to remain on the Supreme Court." I told him I would wait until Monday. On Monday, Douglas called me and said: "I am very sorry, but I have decided not to get into politics. I do not think I should use the Court as a steppingstone." I replied: "I am disappointed. That's too bad." Justice Douglas later called on me to say: "Unfair and vicious reports were circulated that I kept you, Mr. President, dangling for an answer. That was not true. I had a devil of a decision to make. All my sentimental intentions were to do it. My only reason for refusing was my desire to stay on the Court, as I had decided at the time when you asked me to join your Cabinet as Secretary of the Interior."

At about the time I received Douglas' refusal to run on the ticket, the Senate minority leader, Senator Barkley, called me from Philadelphia. Leslie Biffle, the Secretary of the Senate, was on the phone with Barkley, but it was the senator from Kentucky himself who asked me if I would object if he tried to be named for Vice-President. Biffle then added that he felt sure Barkley could be nominated if I agreed.

"Why didn't you tell me you wanted to be Vice-President?" I said to Barkley. "It's all right with me." It was after this conversation that the two of them went to work, and when the time came, the convention nominated Barkley.

My approval of Barkley as a running mate was not a matter of sudden impulse. I had long respected him as one of the ablest debaters on the floor of the Senate. He was a hard-working, honest politician and one of the most popular men in the Democratic party. As a thoroughly acceptable candidate to the South, Barkley made an ideal partner to run with me in 1948.

On July 14 I boarded the presidential train with my family and members of the White House staff. Over the radio, while en route to Philadelphia, I heard Governor Donnelly as he nominated me with a magnificent speech, and after arriving in Philadelphia and having dinner on the train, I left with members of my party for Convention Hall.

When I arrived, the convention was locked in last-minute argument, and the voting had not yet begun. Barkley and I were ushered into a special suite on the floor beneath the convention. It was a small group of rooms used as dressing rooms for show performers, and there was a balcony overlooking the city of Philadelphia. Off in the distance lay the Delaware River, but the yards of the Pennsylvania Railroad formed the immediate foreground, with the city spreading everywhere beyond.

It was a hot, clammy night, though it was pleasant on the balcony. And as I sat there, waiting for the final business of the convention to come to a close and for the signal that would call me to appear to accept the nomination, I let my mind run back, as I frequently do, over America's century and a half of political life. I reflected on the experiences of some of the thirty-one men who had preceded me in office and on the conventions and campaigns that had loomed as large in their lives as this one now did in my own. I was forced to wait for four long hours on that balcony and so had time for reflection. Furthermore, the setting was strangely quiet, and I seemed far removed from the turmoil and the hubbub of the convention within the crowded hall. I clearly recall the thoughts that passed through my mind.

I was not impatient, and as I waited for the long-delayed signal that would eventually call me to the great convention hall inside, I was thinking of the early period of our country's history when there were no political parties and no nominating conventions at all. As I sat there on that balcony, I was looking toward Philadelphia's city hall, its tall tower topped by the great statue of William Penn. And that made me think of the historical events which had taken place in this "City of Brotherly Love" which William Penn had founded, and of Independence Hall farther east on Chestnut Street.

George Washington was far ahead of his contemporaries as a leader because of his military contribution during the Revolutionary War. But after the war, and before he became President, he presided over the Constitutional Convention here in Philadelphia and so played an important part in establishing our form of government. Thus in two ways he could be said to be "the father of his country," which may explain why there was practically no partisan feeling toward him, at least during the earlier years of his administration. To the people of his day as well as of ours this great American was in a class by himself. He was not a professional soldier, but a citizen-soldier in the best sense. He worked his way from the bottom to the very top in the volunteer forces.

As my thoughts turned to Washington and the early days of the Republic, I recalled how the people began to experience the workings of the Constitution as an instrument of the people instead of for special privilege. Under the administration of the second President, John Adams, the trend was to interpret the Constitution more and more in favor of those who controlled the land and the banks. But Thomas Jefferson, largely through individual correspondence, aroused a wave of public opinion which resulted in his election in 1800 after a lengthy and involved tie vote with Aaron Burr.

After Jefferson became President, he continued to use his organizational talents and was soon in a position to control the Congress through the committee chairmanships and through the people of greatest influence in both Houses. He was a master politician, and this helped make him a great leader. A President has to be a politician in order to get the majority to go along with him on his program.

When Jefferson retired, James Madison continued his policies. Then Monroe followed with the "era of good feeling," when there were no political parties to speak of, because for a period of about twenty-four years the Democrats—who were then called Republicans because they were for a republic and not for a monarchy—had complete control of the government from top to bottom.

One of the things that was in my mind was that as head of the party I would leave it a going concern, turning over to my successors a strong party that stood for the principles which would be best for the most people.

I recalled the three-way fight of 1824, when the old system of a congressional nominating caucus was discarded for the modern convention method. That movement started in the state of Tennessee, which passed resolutions calling for the end of caucus nominations on the ground that they were unconstitutional and inexpedient. The caucus went ahead and nominated William Crawford for President, but two other candidates had already been nominated by state legislatures—Jackson in Tennessee and Clay in Kentucky. Later John Quincy Adams was nominated in Massachusetts. The confusion brought about by the old caucus system led to the adoption of nomination by convention.

That was an unusual election year in many respects. Each state held its own election day, and more than six weeks passed from the time the voting began until the final results were known. More than that, none of the candidates received a majority of the electoral votes, and the names of the three with the largest number of votes were sent to the House of Representatives, which was to choose the President.

Clay was the man who received the smallest number of votes and who was therefore free to swing his influence to assure the election of any one of the other candidates. He was accused of making a trade with Adams for appointment to the position of Secretary of State in Adams' Cabinet in return for his support, though I never believed that. Andrew Jackson, however, was one of those who believed that Clay had sold out to Adams, and it is true that though Jackson received ninety-nine electoral votes, the largest number cast for any of the candidates, he lost the election to Adams in the House of Representatives. He was strongly partisan, of course, and also suspected John C. Calhoun of influence-peddling during that campaign of 1824. Years later, when Jackson left the White House, he is said to have remarked, when asked if there was anything he thought he had left undone: "I should have hanged Calhoun and shot Henry Clay!"

The real political battle of our early days came in 1828, when the modern political parties shaped up in the form in which we know them today. Jackson was recognized as the "man of the people"—an advocate of the liberal interpretation of democracy as practiced by Jefferson. Adams ran for re-election with the support of the people who controlled the United States Bank and who opposed the settlement of the new West without the supervision of private interests. Adams was also supported by the anti-Masons. He always claimed that Jackson won in 1828 with the support of the Masons. Adams a bitter anti-Mason for the rest of his life.

One thing I always liked about Jackson was that he brought the basic issues into clear focus. People knew what he stood for and what he was against, and "the friends of General Jackson"—as his supporters called themselves—always knew that he represented the interests of the common people of the United States. He carried out his platform pledges after his triumph over Adams in the election. He caused the destruction of the United States Bank and ruined the Federalist party completely. It is said a number of Federalist leaders, including Daniel Webster, were on the bank's payroll.

With Jackson's election in 1828 and again in 1832, the nominating convention was established as a permanent method of selecting presidential candidates. Also, the general election day for all the states had its beginning during that time. There were a great many splinter parties which came into being with the introduction of the mass convention method, such as the Anti-Masons, the Know-Nothings, the Equal Righters, and others. But most important, the Democratic party became completely revitalized under Jackson, and its liberal ideals were put into effect for the benefit of the people.

Meanwhile, the Whig party came to life to oppose what the Democratic party represented. Their candidate in 1836 was William Henry Harrison, but Jackson called on a national convention of Democrats in Baltimore to nominate his choice for the presidency, Martin Van Buren, and the "Little Magician" was nominated and elected largely on the strength of Jackson's influence.

I recalled the election of 1840, which was preceded by one of the strangest campaigns in the history of our country. The Whigs ran Harrison again, and they had no platform at all. It was nothing more than a ballyhoo campaign based on slogans, the principal one of which was "Hard Cider and Log Cabins," even though Harrison had never lived in a log cabin. He was the son of a wealthy family in Virginia and personally took almost no part in the campaign. Van Buren, however, made a poor campaign and was badly beaten by his own performance, as well as by the Whig phrase, "Tippecanoe and Tyler too," and the great depression of 1837.

Tyler, who because of Harrison's untimely death became President within a month after his election to the vice-presidency, was what I would call a Whig-Democrat. He was a man of principle and had resigned from the Senate rather than vote for expunging from the record the censure of President Jackson. But he was unpopular with the Whigs because he would not let Daniel Webster, his Secretary of State, and Henry Clay run the government. Webster tried to make Tyler the "acting President," but Tyler said that he had taken office as President and he was going to *be* President. He organized a new Cabinet and did not let the Cabinet tell him what to do.

I have often been accused of having a stubborn streak. Perhaps it came to me from Tyler, who was a close kinsman of my ancestors. At any rate, I felt exactly the same way he did about the office of President. Regardless of what else might be said about me, I wanted it to be made clear that as long as I was in the White House I ran the executive branch of the government, and no one was ever allowed to act in the capacity of President of the United States except the man who held that office. This accounted for some difficulties that I could otherwise have avoided, but—like Tyler—I had no intention of being an "acting President."

I thought of Tyler's successor, James K. Polk. This was the man who was nominated by the Democratic convention in Baltimore after a long session in which the convention had not been able to agree on candidates. He was the first "dark horse" candidate in our history—a Speaker of the House who had been very active in the support of Jackson. Incidentally, he is one man who has been very much overlooked in the history of this country. He made the statement when he ran that he would not run for a second term. He put his program through in that four-year term and retired to die three months and eleven days later.

The main issues with which Polk had to deal were the annexation of Texas and the settlement of the difficulties with Mexico. He offered to purchase all that part of the United States, including Arizona, New Mexico, and California, for the sum of forty-five million dollars, but he could not get the deal agreed to by Mexico. As a result, the country went to war with Mexico over the border area, though in the settlement with Mexico after the termination of hostilities, Polk saw to it that fifteen million dollars was paid to the Mexicans in exchange for the greatest territorial addition to the continental United States except the Louisiana Purchase.

Polk was a positive man. He campaigned on the Texas and Oregon questions, among other things, and settled every issue before his term of office expired.

The Mexican War produced a military hero who was sent to the White House by the Whigs on the basis of his record as a soldier, but Zachary Taylor knew nothing about politics and had no set approach to governmental affairs. As a result, Henry Clay and Daniel Webster ran the government. Webster was Secretary of State, just as he had been under Harrison and for a time under Tyler, and stayed on through the remainder of Taylor's unexpired term, which was filled by Millard Fillmore, the Vice-President, from the time of Taylor's death just a year and a half after he was elected. Taylor died of eating too much watermelon and drinking cherry bounce at a Fourth of July celebration, so it is said.

Franklin Pierce was a good-looking man from New Hampshire who did not have to work for the presidency in 1852. The Whigs were falling apart over the slavery question, and their two great leaders, Clay and Webster, died in the same year. The Democrats nominated Pierce, who stayed at home during the campaign, while the Whig candidate, General Winfield Scott, traveled through the country making campaign speeches. It was a situation in which Scott's supporters were divided, and Pierce happened to be acceptable to both the North and the South, although he had no platform. Scott was overwhelmingly defeated.

Glamour has often played an active role in the selection of American Presidents. Pierce, like Harding, was chosen partly because "he looked like a President." Pierce had been in the Mexican War as a brigadier general under Scott. Pierce was a volunteer, Scott a regular. Both had been nominated because their military records had made them well known. I have never felt that popularity and glamour are fundamentals on which the Chief Executive of the government should operate. A President has to know where he is going and why, and he must believe in what he is doing.

Throughout history, those who have tried hardest to do the right thing have often been persecuted, misrepresented, or even assassinated, but eventually what they stood for has come to the top and been adopted by the people.

A man who is influenced by the polls or is afraid to make decisions which may make him unpopular is not a man to represent the welfare of the country. If he is right, it makes no difference whether the press and the special interests like what he does, or what they have to say about him. I have always believed that the vast majority of people want to do what is right and that if the President is right and can get through to the people he can always persuade them. In my own case, communication through a press which was ninety per cent hostile was a real problem, so I had to make many long trips in order to get my message through to the people.

A President cannot always be popular. He has to be able to say *yes* and *no,* and more often *no* to most of the propositions that are put up to him by partisan groups and special interests who are always pulling at the White House for one thing or another. If a President is easily influenced and interested in keeping in line with the press and the polls, he is a complete washout. Every great President in our history had a policy of his own, which eventually won the people's support.

James Buchanan, who was a compromise candidate in a time of compromises. Six years earlier the Compromise of 1850 had been offered as an effort to keep the South and the North from going to war over the slavery question, but it was only a postponement of the problem. The Democrats had split up over the Kansas-Nebraska Bill of Senator Stephen A. Douglas. Buchanan, who had been in England during most of the controversy, was the most "available" candidate by 1856 because he was not associated in the minds of the people with either side.

This was the campaign that saw the birth of the Republican party. The Whigs had disbanded and their remnants were revitalized along united anti-slavery lines in the new party, which held its first nominating convention in Philadelphia and chose John C. Frémont as its candidate for President. The campaign which the Republicans put on in the fall of 1856, based on "free soil, free speech, and Frémont," was similar to the circus-like performance of the "Hard Cider and Log Cabin," "Tippecanoe and Tyler Too" campaign of the Whigs in 1840. The new party only narrowly lost the election to the Democrats, but it was gathering strength for the victory of 1860, when Abraham Lincoln was the nominee.

It seemed an odd coincidence to me, as I sat there waiting for the call from the convention, that perhaps the closest parallel to the political situation which confronted me at that moment in 1948, with the Dixiecrats and Progressives in revolt, was the split of the Democratic party in 1860. At that time, however, after fifty-seven ballots, the convention at Charleston, South Carolina, failed to agree on a candidate and adjourned. The southern Democrats withdrew and, at a convention of their own, nominated John C. Breckinridge. The northern and western Democrats reconvened at Baltimore and eventually chose Stephen A. Douglas as their candidate. There was a minor splinter party among the conservatives, called the Constitutional Union party, with John Bell as the nominee, but the Republicans easily rode through the breach, and Lincoln was elected by a large majority of the electoral vote but by a minority of the popular vote.

Thus the two-party system broke down during the latter part of the 1850's. The South seceded, and the Republican party, during and after the Civil War, maintained control of the government from 1860 to 1884. The war years were difficult for Lincoln. If it had not been for victories by the Union armies in 1864, he might very well have lost to the Democratic candidate, General George B. McClellan, who was running on a "stop the war" platform. But Lincoln was re-elected. His running mate, Andrew Johnson, became President when Lincoln was assassinated, a short time after the inauguration in March. Johnson was more of a Democrat than a Republican, but he had run on Lincoln's "National Union" ticket at Lincoln's suggestion as a representative of the border states to offset the President's unpopularity there. Lincoln had dropped Hannibal Hamlin of Maine because he wanted a Union ticket. Lincoln was elected in 1864 on the American Union ticket and not on the Republican ticket.

Johnson was one of the most mistreated of all Presidents. The press attacked him unmercifully for almost everything he did, including the purchase of Alaska for $7,200,000. The newspapers referred to the new territory as "Johnson's Russian fairy land" and "Seward's Ice Box," and between the press and the Radical Republicans, Johnson was given one of the hardest administrations in our history. I could sympathize with him, because I had received a good measure of the same kind of opposition.

If a man does not have a background and experience in politics, he must have something else in his favor if he is to run for the presidency of the United States. Usually the alternative to a political career has been a military career. Washington was the hero of the Revolution; Jackson won the only great victory in the War of 1812, at New Orleans, though he won it after the peace treaty had actually been signed; Taylor was made prominent by the battle of Buena Vista. And the Civil War produced four generals who became Presidents—Grant, Hayes, Garfield, and Benjamin Harrison.

Grant was typical of the soldier-President. Without any understanding of political machinery, he was able to ride into office on the popularity which military victory always brings. People are always grateful and happy when a war ends in victory, and time after time they have bestowed the honor of the highest political office upon their military heroes.

Grant had voted only once in his life—in 1856—and he cast a Democratic vote then. As a matter of fact, he was the logical Democratic candidate in 1868, but his break with President Johnson made him appear to be a Radical Republican. He wavered for a long time, concealed his intentions from both parties, and finally changed his politics to run on the Republican ticket, winning by a very slight popular majority.

Popularity and glamour are only part of the factors involved in winning presidential elections. One of the most important of all is luck. In my own case, luck was always with me, though there was never any intention on my part to make things work my way. If a man starts out to make himself President, he hardly ever arrives. Henry Clay is an outstanding example. He was so sure he would be President that he twice refused the vice-presidency, and in both cases he would have succeeded to the highest office because of the death of the President. James G. Blaine was another such man. And I was convinced, as I sat waiting to be called into the convention, that Thomas E. Dewey was another whose determined efforts to make himself President would never materialize.

A President needs political understanding to *run* the government, but he may be *elected* without it. There are many factors that have entered into the people's selection of their Chief Executive from time to time. In Grant's second election to the presidency, the chief factor was money.

He did no campaigning of any kind, while his lieutenants poured money in every direction that would bring in votes. And he won, despite a bolt by Liberal Republicans, who nominated Horace Greeley, editor of the New York *Tribune,* at their convention in Cincinnati.

Greeley had the support of some Democrats, while the Straight Democrats supported a third candidate, Charles O'Conor. Greeley's defeat was helped along by the cartoons of Thomas Nast, creator of the Republican elephant, and the poor old man died three weeks after the election as the worst-beaten man who ever ran for the presidency. I never did believe that newspapermen belong in politics any more than politicians belong in the newspaper business.

The election of 1876 was one of the most confused of all. Samuel Tilden, the Democratic nominee, was elected, but the electoral votes of three carpetbag states and Oregon were disputed. Tilden needed only one more electoral vote, but Rutherford B. Hayes was the Republican nominee, and when the Congress unconstitutionally appointed an election commission to decide the votes to be received, he was declared elected.

President Grant was so worried about the situation that he had Hayes sworn in on a Saturday afternoon, March 3, the day before inauguration day. The Democrats were threatening "Tilden or blood," but Tilden said he would not urge his people to go to war over an election, because he thought the country would come out all right. Hayes made a good President; he ordered the withdrawal of federal troops from the South.

In the convention of 1880, the Democrats nominated Winfield Scott Hancock, a 250-pound general who had saved the battle of Gettysburg on the first day for the North. The Republican party was badly split that year, with one faction supporting Grant, another Blaine, and another John Sherman. James Garfield had nominated Sherman with the best speech of the convention. The convention was hopelessly deadlocked. Rutherford B. Hayes is said to have gotten in touch with the chairman of the convention and, on the strength of the speech nominating Sherman, suggested Garfield's nomination.

Garfield was elected, with Chester A. Arthur as Vice-President. Arthur, who had been Collector of the Port of New York, had been nominated for reasons of expediency, but that was not true of Garfield, and though he had been a Civil War general, he turned out to be a good Chief Executive. It is my belief that any man who sincerely tries to live up to the responsibilities of the office cannot keep from growing in the presidency. Garfield, however, had little time to grow, for unfortunately he was shot by an assassin in July following his inauguration, and he died in September.

The Democratic party, which by now had been out of power for so many years, closed ranks behind Grover Cleveland in 1884. He was opposed by James G. Blaine, the Republican candidate, known as the "plumed knight from Maine," but Cleveland was elected. The campaign, however, was a bitter one, and the press clearly demonstrated how abusive it could be. Furthermore, the abuse and the criticism continued throughout the four years that followed. Cleveland was renominated in 1888 and in the election of that year actually received more popular votes than Benjamin Harrison, his Republican opponent. Despite this, however, he lost in the electoral college. Harrison, who had made the tariff an issue in the campaign, became President despite his minority vote. Four years later—in 1892—Cleveland, running for the third time, was re-elected to his second term. Cleveland was re-elected on the strength of the "Billion Dollar" Congress, which spent a billion dollars in the two sessions and, it was claimed, brought on the Panic of 1893. Cleveland had a lot of trouble with strikes and riots, but the Democratic party, as usual, was on the liberal side during his second administration. But the President was not. He became an ultra-conservative. His older son became a leading Republican in Baltimore, Maryland.

The campaign of 1896 was the first of which I personally took much notice, and four years later, when I was sixteen, I was a page at the Democratic convention in Kansas City which nominated William Jennings Bryan for a second time.

Bryan had been only thirty-six years old when, at the Chicago convention of 1896, he made his famous "Cross of Gold and Crown of Thorns" speech which won him his first presidential nomination. He was one of my heroes. I remember that there were seventeen thousand people in the old convention hall in Kansas City when Bryan spoke. There were no loudspeakers, and a man had to have a real carrying voice to be heard in that hall. At the convention of 1900 another candidate for the Democratic nomination—Judson Harmon of Ohio—was on the platform and was having a time making himself heard. Bryan came out on the rostrum and everyone stood up and shouted. Bryan said: "Why don't you give the gentleman from Ohio a chance to speak?" Harmon tried again, but the tumult continued and he had to quit. Bryan took charge. But so great was the enthusiasm of the delegates for the great orator that he was nominated at once—by acclamation. His appeal that day was like nothing else I have ever heard. He had a bell-like voice that carried well and he knew how to use it.

Despite Bryan's popularity with the people in 1896, the Republicans and the "gold" Democrats elected their ticket. Four years later McKinley was re-elected and was sworn in in 1901, and assassinated in September of the same year.

McKinley was sometimes described as "the President Mark Hanna made," Hanna being the millionaire senator from Cleveland who virtually bought the election while McKinley stayed at home and spoke only to such delegations as came to his house from time to time. This was the first of the "front porch" campaigns. I do not approve of "front porch" campaigns. I never liked to see any man elected to office who did not go out and meet the people in person and work for their votes.

The first President I ever saw was Teddy Roosevelt—William McKinley's successor. It was in 1904, after Roosevelt had just about served out the remainder of McKinley's second term and wanted to be elected President in his own right. He was in Kansas City on a trip through the Middle West, and I was working in the National Bank of Commerce at that time. I ran down to the corner of Tenth and Main streets just to see what a President looked like. Roosevelt made an excellent speech. I was disappointed to find that he was no giant, but a little man in a long Prince Albert coat to make him look taller. After I became President I often thought back to that time. I found out that the people usually ran to see the President and not the man. A few decades back I had done exactly the same thing—running to see the President—who was then Teddy Roosevelt.

It was Theodore Roosevelt who in 1912 helped bring about the return of the Democrats to the presidency. In 1908 William Howard Taft had been hand-picked by Roosevelt as his successor. Before Taft's term was over, however, Teddy was displeased with the result, and he wanted the nomination for himself. Teddy had been far to the left for a Republican —but still right of center as far as the Democrats were concerned—and had put into effect a lot of liberal ideas such as conservation of natural resources and the checking of "malefactors of great wealth." Taft was an ultra-conservative and partial to the special interests. He was not willing to use the full power of the presidency.

Although Taft had more than half of his party against him, he was the incumbent President and, as such, he controlled the convention of 1912. Not even Roosevelt himself, with his large following, could change that all-important political fact. He bolted the Republican convention and had himself nominated on the "Bull Moose" ticket. This defeated Taft and permitted the Democrats to come back into power with the election of one of our greatest Presidents, Woodrow Wilson.

Wilson brought about significant reforms during his first term, such as the Federal Trade Commission, the Federal Reserve System, the tariff reforms, and a great many others in the public interest. Shortly after his second term began, the country became involved in World War I. He was very much against entry into the European conflict and tried his best to keep out. His race against Charles Evans Hughes in 1916 was based on the slogan, "He Kept Us Out of War," and he won on the strength of that and his "New Freedom" accomplishments.

No President could have kept us out of that war and still maintained the sovereignty of the United States Government under the circumstances that existed at that time. He did succeed in bringing about a cessation of hostilities in 1918 by his Fourteen Point speech setting out a plan for a just peace. After the armistice was signed, Wilson spent the rest of his term in an endeavor to set up the League of Nations to insure the peace of the world. Because of the opposition which he faced in the Senate, he worked himself up to such a point that he had a stroke, which was eventually fatal.

In the campaign of 1920 the people were tired of the war and were intrigued by the promise of Warren G. Harding, the Republican candidate, for a "return to normalcy"—whatever that meant. Harding was a handsome man who had been picked by the forces of conservatism and private wealth to protect the special interests. He was one of the darkest horses ever chosen at a convention, and his nomination was a surprise to him as well as to everyone else. The contest was supposed to be between General Leonard Wood and Governor Frank Lowden of Illinois, but after the balloting had failed to show an edge for either man, the political bosses got together and picked Harding "because he looks like a President." This convention produced the term "smoke-filled room" to suggest that strings had been pulled to manipulate the convention. The "smoke-filled room" was nothing new, but Harding's nomination dramatized the tag and made it stick. Calvin Coolidge, because of his handling of a police strike in Boston while he was governor of Massachusetts, was chosen as Harding's running mate.

The Republicans won by a landslide that year. Running on the Democratic ticket were Governor James Cox of Ohio and Wilson's Assistant Secretary of the Navy, Franklin D. Roosevelt. Governor Cox had been an outstanding congressman and an efficient governor of Ohio. He would have made a good President.

When Coolidge succeeded to the presidency at Harding's death in 1923, he announced that he would be a candidate the following year. "Business as usual" was his motto, although Will Rogers put it another way: "Keep Cool with Coolidge and Do Nothing." In 1924, at one of the most chaotic Democratic conventions in years, the delegates held ballot after ballot trying to decide between William G. McAdoo and Alfred E. Smith, who had been put in nomination by Franklin Roosevelt. On the one hundred and third ballot the convention finally named John W. Davis as a compromise candidate. I remember listening to the whole thing over the radio while I was eastern judge of the county court in Jackson County. There was a tremendous split in the Democratic party, and Coolidge won in another Republican landslide.

I recalled the 1928 Democratic convention in Houston. There were two or three native-son nominations that year, including Jim Reed of Missouri. But Al Smith was given the nomination, and that set off the most vicious anti-Catholic, anti-Jewish, anti-Negro movement that we have ever had during any political campaign. The Ku Klux Klan was near the top of its influence since its revitalization after World War I, and there was more slander and mud-slinging going on than at any time I can remember.

The Republicans held their convention that year in Kansas City, and they had a time meeting their expenses. As presiding judge of the county court, incidentally, I helped take care of the situation, because it brought people into Kansas City and Jackson County. Consequently I had more tickets to the convention than some of the Republican leaders, and I was present when Hoover was nominated. Andrew Mellon was in control of that convention, just as Mark Hanna had been at the nomination of McKinley.

In the election that followed, the South's opposition to Al Smith gave Hoover many southern states, and he won by a comfortable margin. In the general election two years later, however, almost all the people who were running for office in the South and had supported Hoover were defeated. That was the price they had to pay for going "off the reservation" in 1928. And the great depression which began in 1929 marked the end of Republican rule. Franklin Roosevelt and the Democrats were swept into office in 1932.

Roosevelt's plurality in the 1936 election was the greatest ever received in a national election up to that time, and he won all but eight of the electoral votes. Alf Landon of Kansas was the unsuccessful Republican contender. This was the first presidential election I saw from the Washington end. I had begun serving in the United States Senate the year before.

With Hitler overrunning the countries of western Europe, Roosevelt decided to break precedent and run for the third term. Roosevelt chose Henry Wallace as his running mate, although Jesse Jones, Paul McNutt, Jim Farley, and William Bankhead were also nominated. But Wallace was named.

In 1944 Wallace was again a candidate for renomination for the vice-presidency, and the Democrats had quite a time in keeping him from being renominated. Roosevelt had decided upon me for the vice-presidency, although he did not tell me in advance, but he did not want publicly to turn down Wallace. He had the kindliest heart in the world and never liked to hurt anyone. He would do all sorts of maneuvering to get rid of people he did not want without his being the one to fire them.

It was now past midnight in Philadelphia. Messages were being delivered from the floor. Delegates and friends were drifting in and out. I was growing more and more impatient. It hardly seemed possible to me, in the early-morning hours of July 15, 1948, that so much had happened since that 1944 convention at which I was nominated for the vice-presidency and that shortly I was to take my place before the 1948 Democratic National Convention to accept the nomination for President of the United States. Into this situation, as into every major experience which I went through in that high office, I went with a consciousness of the history of American government and politics. The caucuses and conventions of the forty national elections which had preceded that of 1948 were as real to me as the one before which I was about to make my appearance. They were typical of the American way of life and of the wonderful system of self-government that had developed over a period of 160 years. I was both proud and humble to be able to take an active part in that development.

The convention system has its faults, of course, but I do not know of a better method for choosing a presidential nominee. There has been a great deal of talk regarding the need of a presidential primary, but there is not a man in the country who could afford the expenses of both a primary and a campaign. The physical effort alone is no small consideration. In theory, it sounds plausible, but the great population centers of the country would have virtual control of the nomination for President. Yet it has been my experience that the "country boys" sometimes know more about the political needs of the country than the experts from the big city.

Unless the federal government itself were to bear the expense of the nomination and election of the candidates for the presidency, as some of us in the Senate favored, there would be no way for an individual to meet the expense of the necessary campaigns. I had to make a double campaign for the United States Senate in Missouri in 1934 and again in 1940, and the cost was an unconscionable item. The primary nomination for senators is all right, I think, but a practicable approach to a presidential primary has never yet been worked out.

The convention system has one peculiar advantage—if it does not work out successfully, it will not work at all. We have not yet had what we would call a "bad" President produced by this system.

The ideal situation would be for all the candidates—local, state, and national—to be heard on a fair basis by all the people of the country over the communication facilities of the nation, so that there would be no political advantage to anyone for reasons of personal wealth, or because of influence or favoritism on the part of the newspapers, radio, or television. When the people become informed, money alone will never work for political parties. People do not like the idea of a purchased public office, and this applies particularly to the presidency. That is the reason for the limitation on contributions to campaigns.

Actually, there are two big evils which have to be overcome if the operation of our election system is not to be hampered or endangered. The old "boss" system was a vicious arrangement in both parties. Men like Mark Hanna of Cleveland, George Cox of Cincinnati, Bill Thompson of Chicago, Tom Pendergast of Kansas City, Ed Crump of Memphis, and dozens of others, exercised undue influence over the selection of candidates. But none of them was more wonderful than the present-day advertising-press approach to politics.

Experts in the advertising field, especially, are adept at working the "big lie" technique, and the Republican party for a long time has had the support of powerful advertisers, the press, radio, and television. This combination *could* work to defeat the will of the people.

The convention had tried to complete the nomination of President and Vice-President by ten o'clock, but it was after midnight before the balloting began. On the first roll call I was named as the nominee by 947½ votes. Senator Richard Russell of Georgia, a faithful Democrat, was given 263 votes by the Southerners who had refused to bolt the convention with the Dixiecrats. Paul V. McNutt received the other half vote. And Alben Barkley was then nominated for the vice-presidency by acclamation.

At about two o'clock in the morning the signal came. The convention was ready to hear my acceptance of the nomination for President of the United States.

CHAPTER 15

At 2 A.M. I was escorted to the convention floor above and onto the speaker's platform. The huge hall was packed with weary, perspiring delegates who had spent three days and nights in bedlam. They were still capable of making noise, however, and they greeted me with thundering applause.

But it was clear to me that the work of the opposition in propagandizing against my chances of winning—plus the splintering within our own party—had taken its toll. The Democratic party was dispirited and dejected. I meant to give them something to cheer about and something to campaign for. It was not the first time in history that a President had personally appeared at a convention hall to accept the nomination. The first nominee to do so was Franklin D. Roosevelt, when he flew to the convention in 1932. The effect was the same in both cases, I think. It reinvigorated the whole party in 1948, as it had in 1932.

Barkley, who had accompanied me to the platform, made a short acceptance speech first. Then I was introduced. I had studied the acceptance speeches of two or three other Presidents, principally Roosevelt's, and had made up my mind that I would spring my first big surprise of the campaign in that speech.

The acceptance speech is a formal procedure which closes or follows the action of a political convention. When a man is nominated, he must accept formally if he intends to run.

I had been working on my notes for the speech on the train and went over them in the room downstairs just before the escorting committee arrived to usher me to the convention floor. I had my notes in a black notebook, which I placed on the lectern as I waited for the hall to grow quiet enough for me to speak.

It took only a short sentence to bring the delegates to their feet. That was when I said, "Senator Barkley and I will win this election and make these Republicans like it—don't you forget that." I meant just that, and I said it as if I meant it. There could be no mistake. I intended to win.

The Democrats had been waiting to hear somebody say positively that we were going to win, and the effect on them was electric. They saw right then and there that there was going to be a fight for Democratic principles by the man who was the head of the party. That gave them the shot in the arm they so badly needed.

I had learned from my June tour that people wanted the facts before they would fight for or against anything. I felt that the convention would react in the same manner as the crowds at the train had done when they heard the facts straight from the President of the United States. I was not fooling and they knew it.

I made a tough, fighting speech. I recited the benefits that had been won by the Democratic administrations for the people. "Never in the world," I said, "were the farmers of any republic or any kingdom or any other country as prosperous as the farmers of the United States; and if they don't do their duty by the Democratic party, they are the most ungrateful people in the world."

I pointed out that wages and salaries had increased from $29,000,-000,000 in 1933 to more than $128,000,000,000 in 1947. "That's labor," I added, "and labor never had but one friend in politics, and that is the Democratic party and Franklin D. Roosevelt. And I say to labor what I have said to the farmers: They are the most ungrateful people in the world if they pass the Democratic party by this year."

Then I tore into the Eightieth Congress, emphasizing that "the Republican party favors the privileged few and not the common, everyday man. Ever since its inception, that party has been under the control of special privilege, and they concretely proved it in the Eightieth Congress. . . . They proved it by the things they failed to do. . . ."

I listed in detail the failures of the Republican-controlled Congress and I did not pull any punches. Then, toward the end of the speech, I played my trump card. I announced:

"On the twenty-sixth day of July, which out in Missouri we call 'Turnip Day,' I am going to call Congress back and ask them to pass laws to halt rising prices, to meet the housing crisis—which they are saying they are for in their platform.

"At the same time, I shall ask them to act upon other vitally needed measures, such as aid to education, which they say they are for; a national health program; civil rights legislation, which they say they are for; an increase in the minimum wage, which I doubt very much they are for; extension of the Social Security coverage and increased benefits, which they say they are for; funds for projects needed in our program to provide public power and cheap electricity. By indirection, this Eightieth Congress has tried to sabotage the power policies the United States has pursued for fourteen years. That power lobby is as bad as the real estate lobby which is sitting on the housing bill.

"I shall ask for adequate and decent laws for displaced persons in place of this anti-Semitic, anti-Catholic law which this Eightieth Congress passed.

"Now my friends, if there is any reality behind that Republican platform, we ought to get some action from a short session of the Eightieth Congress. They can do this job in fifteen days, if they want to do it. They will still have time to go out and run for office.

"They are going to try to dodge their responsibility. They are going to drag all the red herrings they can across this campaign, but I am here to say that Senator Barkley and I are not going to let them get away with it."

This announcement of a special session of the Congress electrified the convention to a new pitch of confidence and enthusiasm. I was telling the Democrats that we were calling the bluff of the Republican opposition and that we were going to fight them with everything we had.

Of course I knew that the special session would produce no results in the way of legislation. But I felt justified in calling the Congress back to Washington to prove to the people whether the Republican platform really meant anything or not. Every item of legislation which I called essential to the welfare of the country was included in the Republican platform and needed to be acted upon without delay. Yet I knew they would run out on their platform.

Just as I had predicted, the "Turnip Day" session of the Congress came and went without any response to my demands for constructive legislation promised by the Republican party platform. The Republican leaders turned a deaf ear to my warning that the American people would expect some kind of action before the election, and ignored the recommendations which I made in a six-page message on July 27. After two weeks of doing nothing, the special session adjourned.

The stage was now set for the active 1948 presidential campaign. I picked Labor Day, which was on September 6, to sound the starting gun of my bid for the presidency, and most of my opponents did the same. The field, besides Thomas Dewey for the Republicans, Henry Wallace for the Progressives, and J. Strom Thurmond for the States'

Rights Democrats, included a number of minority candidates: Norman Thomas for the Socialists, among others.

While I knew that the southern dissenters and the Wallace-ites would cost some Democratic votes, my opponent was the Republican party. The campaign was built on one issue—the interests of the people, as represented by the Democrats, against the special interests, as represented by the Republicans and the record of the Eightieth Congress. I staked the race for the presidency on that one issue.

The Labor Day speech at Cadillac Square in Detroit set the pace for the campaign speeches that were to follow. "As you know," I told a nationwide audience, "I speak plainly sometimes. In fact, I speak bluntly sometimes. I am going to speak plainly and bluntly today. These are critical times for labor and for all who work. There is great danger ahead. Right now, the whole future of labor is wrapped up in one simple proposition.

"If, in this next election, you get a Congress and an administration friendly to labor, you have much to hope for. If you get an administration and a Congress unfriendly to labor, you have much to fear, and you had better look out. . . .

"If the Congressional elements that made the Taft-Hartley Law are allowed to remain in power, and if these elements are further encouraged by the election of a Republican President, you men of labor can expect to be hit by a steady barrage of body blows. And, if you stay at home, as you did in 1946, and keep these reactionaries in power, you will deserve every blow you get. . . .

"Remember that the reactionary of today is a shrewd man. He is in many ways much shrewder than the reactionaries of the twenties. He is a man with a calculating machine where his heart ought to be. He has learned a great deal about how to get his way by observing demagogues and reactionaries in other countries. And now he has many able allies in the press and in the radio.

"If you place the government of this country under the control of those who hate labor, whom can you blame if measures are thereafter adopted to destroy the powers, prestige, and earning power of labor?

"I tell you that labor must fight now harder than ever before to make sure that its rights are kept intact. . . .

"I know from my own experience with labor leaders and unions that the ability of labor to discipline itself and to cooperate with other groups in the country is steadily growing.

"During the war, when I was surveying American industry as Chairman of the Senate Investigating Committee, I came to know the conditions under which labor works and lives. I came to know and respect the minds and spirit of workers and union leaders. I saw them and talked to them, and visited their homes in scores of communities. I watched them at work in hundreds of plants.

"Labor has always had to fight for its gains. Now you are fighting for the whole future of the labor movement. We are in a hard, tough fight against shrewd and rich opponents. They know they can't count on your vote. Their only hope is that you won't vote at all. They have misjudged you. I know that we are going to win this crusade for the right!"[1]

On September 17, I began an extended tour. I had warned my staff and the reporters who prepared to make the trip with me that I was going out to win the election. "I'm going to fight hard," I told Senator Barkley. "I'm going to give them hell." We would be on the road most of the time for the next six weeks, getting up at all hours to make stops at any place where people wanted to see me.

At first the critics referred to my tour as a "one-man circus" and called it less efficient and less dignified than the campaign being put on by the Republicans. But as the crowds grew larger and larger and more people flocked to my train than showed up around the Dewey train, our opponents began to get worried.

The trip across Ohio from Cincinnati to Cleveland was made in the daytime on the Cincinnati, Hamilton and Dayton Railroad, which goes through a whole string of little towns, and the crowds there were immense. Former Governor Lausche, who was a candidate for the governorship of Ohio, got on the train just south of Columbus, intending to get off again at Columbus. At that little town where Lausche got on there was a crowd of from six to eight thousand people, and at the next one the crowd was even larger. At Columbus the crowd was so big they could not even get into the station.

"Is this the way all the crowds have been?" the governor asked.

"Yes," I said, "but this is smaller than we had in most states."

"Well," he said, "this is the biggest crowd I ever saw in Ohio," and he rode on to Cleveland with us. He gave our ticket his fullest support.

Another interesting trip was from Albany to Buffalo. We started early in the morning in a driving rainstorm from the Albany station, where there was a huge crowd of people. And at every station along the way it was still pouring down rain, but there were overflow crowds everywhere—even in those Republican congressional districts.

It was the same in Pennsylvania as it had been in New York.

I saw that the crowds had turned up in greater numbers in June when

---

[1] There were over one hundred thousand people massed in Cadillac Square, and I was encouraged by their response. It was a good start for my campaign.

I made the western tour to dedicate Grand Coulee Dam in Washington. I felt that if people in such places as Butte, Montana, Grand Coulee, and Sacramento (there were ten thousand people at the Sacramento station at seven o'clock in the morning, and in Los Angeles I was told there were a million people on the streets) were as interested as they appeared to be, they could not be fooled by the press.

It was quite a campaign. I worked my staff almost to death. I believe that at one time or another I put them all to bed, and despite its long hours and hard work I gained weight during the campaign. I worked the reporters very hard too.

The major public-opinion polls, meanwhile, continued, through the press and over the air, up to the very day of the election, to predict my defeat. Only Louis Bean, an economist of the Department of Agriculture, and a few others forecast any chance of a Democratic victory.

The technique I used at the whistle stops was simple and straightforward. There were no special "gimmicks" or oratorical devices. I refused to be "coached." I simply told the people in my own language that they had better wake up to the fact that it was their fight.

If they did not get out and help me win this fight, I emphasized, the Republicans would soon be giving the farmers and the workers the little end of the stick again. I spoke bluntly and sincerely, and warned the people that if they were fools enough to accept the little end again, they deserved it.

I also clarified the issues which the Republicans were trying to make complex for the voters. I talked to them as human beings with real needs and feelings and fears. I talked to them about their jobs, their homes, and the cost of living. I treated them not like crowds of people but like businessmen, tenant farmers, housewives, married veterans, laboring men, teachers—individuals with interests for whom I, as President, had a genuine concern.

One of the things I tried to keep out of the campaign was foreign policy. There should be no break in the bi-partisan foreign policy of the United States at any time—particularly during a national election. I even asked that a teletype machine be set up on the Dewey train so that the Republican candidate personally could be informed on all the foreign developments as they progressed, and I did so, because I did not want to encourage the possibility of a partisan, political approach to foreign policy. I saw to it that Dewey received important messages that came to me on the subject of international affairs.

There were many danger spots in our foreign relations at the time. The Jews, Arabs, Egyptians, and Syrians had been fighting a shooting war, and I was trying to get an agreement among those people to stop the shooting. Also, we were endeavoring in every way we could to get the free countries of Europe in a co-operative mood in order to meet the Soviet threat to take over the free world. We were working for disarmament and for the proper control of nuclear energy for peaceful purposes in the world, and any partisan reversal of policy would have meant turmoil at home and in the rest of the world. I was particularly worried about the effects any such move would have in the rest of the world.

The business of the government went on as usual from aboard the presidential train. As in all of my absences from Washington, long or short, the mail pouches were delivered to me from the White House every day. I always had a regular staff with me so that the White House was wherever the President happened to be. I also held a lot of conversations by telephone over a communications system installed on the train, and I always maintained a complete and close contact with the government.

A President can never get away from the urgent and never-ending duties of his office. A political campaign provides no escape. It increases his burdens, and this was critically true during 1948. The autumn of that year was the worst possible time for me to have to wage a political campaign, for at the same time we were negotiating foreign policy matters with the stubborn and suspicious Russian totalitarian government.

We were rapidly exhausting all traditional avenues of negotiation. The United Nations forum—the organization which had been set up for the exchange of views and the adjustment of differences—was being subverted by the Russians into a propaganda sounding board, and our normal diplomatic channels were being stifled and frustrated by Russian truculence.

A number of special missions of businessmen, industrialists, educators, and top military people yielded nothing toward improving our relations, not even the slightest encouragement that they could be improved. I reviewed in my mind every precedent I could recall in an effort to arrive at some new and more promising approach.

I recalled that in the closing days of World War I there was evidence of considerable strain in British-American relations. For many reasons, mostly trivial, and largely related to our expeditionary forces, a certain coolness toward the British was manifest in several important areas in the United States, notably in Washington, D.C.

Coincident with the development of this mutual cooling off, a distinguished visitor came to the United States and made diplomatic history. He was the Chief Justice of England, Viscount Reading, who, quietly and in a spirit of refreshing candor and directness, managed to melt away most of the tender, sore spots.

Lord Reading arrived unheralded and without the benefit of the usual preliminary publicity build-up. He departed just as quietly, but behind him he left a much-improved feeling between our two countries. Many people felt then that his timely visit, his complete disassociation from the everyday run of diplomacy and politics, and the manner of the man himself accounted for this uniquely successful mission.

What we most urgently needed, I felt, was a totally new approach—along with the right man to make it. The current political contest for the presidency was a serious handicap, for though the State and Defense Departments were kept out of the campaign, they were at the same time part of my administration. Nor could we use anyone from the other political camp for the reason that identification with Dewey was no asset either.

In the meantime, the Wallace Progressives were gathering steam with their shrill campaign of "warmongers" which they directed at both major parties. This was precisely the line of propaganda used by the Communists, and it made for a further irritant in an already bad situation. The Wallace theme of preaching appeasement found emotional response among several minority groups who innocently swallowed the tempting notion of peace at any price. I believe that Wallace himself was a victim of his own naïveté.

It was for these reasons that I found it necessary to interrupt my scheduled activities right at the height of the campaign so as to work out some new approach to the Kremlin in an effort to ease the tensions and to get on with our many unfinished negotiations with the Russians. I thought of sending Chief Justice Fred M. Vinson on a special mission to Moscow for an informal exchange of views and impressions with Stalin.

I telephoned Justice Vinson on Sunday, October 3, and asked him to meet with me on a most urgent matter.

When Vinson came to the White House, I outlined to him what I had in mind. When I finished, he remained silent for a considerable time. When he spoke, he said he fully understood the gravity of the situation, and that he wished he could undertake this crucial mission, but that if the decision were left solely to him he would be compelled to decline.

Vinson held that the justices should confine themselves to their Court duties and stay out of all side activities, especially in a political year, and he added that he, as Chief Justice, could not break his own rule, even on a matter of such overriding importance. I then waited for Vinson to say what I knew he would.

"Mr. President," he said, "as Chief Justice I must decline to undertake this mission to Moscow. But if you make it as a presidential request, I shall have a clear duty to comply."

"I am sorry, Fred, to do this to you," I said to him, "but in the interest of the country and the peace of the world I am compelled to request you to go."

Vinson's response was: "I'll be ready in a few days."

This was the situation as I presented it to Chief Justice Vinson:

The Russians simply did not understand—or *would* not—our peaceful intentions and our genuine desire to co-operate through the United Nations toward the establishment of a climate of peace; that we did not want to force and had no intention of forcing our way of life upon them or anyone else, as we would resist to the utmost any attempt to impose another system upon us; that I wanted to see if we could not understand one another a little better, and we had to do something about our poor communications. Surely our side had tried. The Russians must also try if the future of the world and the very survival of civilization were not to be lost.

I pointed out to Vinson that we had made all manner of approaches to the Russians, from Roosevelt to Hull, Hopkins, Davies, Nelson, Hurley, Harriman, Byrnes, and Marshall. Through some of these efforts we had received some hopeful signs, only to have them fade again into suspicion and intransigence. The Russians had tried our patience. But we had kept our tempers and kept trying to get along with them.

In our dealings with the Russians we had learned that we had to lead from strength and that any show of weakness was fatal. But there was never the suggestion of belligerency in our attitude. We made every effort to talk reason and co-operation with them, and we meant it. But for reasons best known to them they either could not, or would not, believe us.

One of our big international issues of the moment was the organization of a setup by the United Nations for the peaceful handling of atomic energy, and the wrangling about the key point of inspection was now in full swing at the United Nations meeting in Paris. The uncompromising position which the Russian bloc took on this decisive provision left little hope that we would reach a practical and enforceable international agreement on the control of atomic energy with the Communist bloc.

I told Vinson that the Russian spokesmen were acting as if they intended to wreck any sane proposal for the handling of atomic energy by the United Nations. Perhaps we were not making our position and ourselves clear to the Russian High Commmand. I warned Vinson that the Russians would not trust either us or themselves to talk freely and frankly. I hoped that this new approach would provide Stalin an opportunity to open up, and I wanted to try it.

Above all, I hoped that Vinson's mission, as an off-channel approach to Stalin, might expose the Russian dictator to a better understanding of our attitude as a people and of our nation's peaceful aspirations for the whole world. I had a feeling that Stalin might get over some of his inhibitions if he were to talk with our own Chief Justice.

I asked Vinson to point out to Stalin that the folly and tragedy of another war would amount to an act of national suicide and that no sane leader of any major power could ever again even contemplate war except in defense. Surely the next war—an atomic war—could have no victors, and the total annihilation of vast areas was as unthinkable as it was abhorrent.

This was the big challenge to the leaders of the world and this is why we created a United Nations. This is why we kept on with our negotiations, and this is why we were prepared to go to any practical lengths to insure the future survival of the world.

Play it by ear, I said to Vinson. Let Stalin see clearly, from the outset, that this is no probing maneuver in the accepted diplomatic sense. Make it clear that this is on the highest level of frankness—a free, uninhibited expression of attitudes, doubts, fears, suspicions, and perhaps even ambitions.

If we could only get Stalin to unburden himself to someone on our side he felt he could trust fully, I thought that perhaps we could get somewhere. But of course if the Russians were hell-bent for communizing and dominating the world on a rule-or-ruin basis, there was little we could do by the negotiation route. Even then we had to exhaust every conceivable avenue of approach, as I told Vinson, and we had to keep trying. That was why I wanted him to go to Moscow and to see if he could not get Stalin to open up.

Of course I assured the Chief Justice that this mission in no way constituted an action to circumvent the Secretary of State, the United Nations, and most certainly none of our allies.

"I intend," I explained, "to discuss the purpose of this mission and mean to have the full agreement of our allies before you leave for Moscow. I will also tell our own people. But first, everyone who is concerned will be duly informed before any public announcement is made. We must be careful in all respects, or this could misfire and be misunderstood as a unilateral action. I will telephone Marshall in Paris from the Map Room Monday morning before we do anything further. I am sure that he will be for it, as he always is for any constructive move to advance the cause of peace."

Vinson and I had a second visit on this subject that same Sunday evening, and we reached an agreement on the scope of the mission, the timing, the clearances, and the public statement.

Sunday afternoon I instructed Press Secretary Charlie Ross to notify the networks to allocate a half hour for a public statement of major importance. I also alerted the Under Secretary of State, Robert Lovett, to make the necessary preparations for clearances with Stalin to receive Vinson on arrival in Moscow and told him that I was preparing a personal message to Stalin regarding Vinson. I further instructed those involved in the undertaking to maintain the strictest confidence and to take every possible precaution against premature leaks to the press.

But before the complicated international machinery could be coordinated and all clearances obtained, there was an unfortunate leak to an unfriendly newspaper, and a big outcry of "appeasement," "politics," "unilateral action" was picked by other newspapers and press services. The Vinson mission was severely embarrassed before it could even be fully explored with all the powers concerned. Most of the outcry by the press was, as usual, the result of poor information, half-truths, and deliberate distortion of the facts.

Following the premature publication of the proposed Vinson mission to Moscow, a number of complications set in that compelled me to reconsider the advisability of this mission. I had a talk with Secretary Marshall in Paris and found him upset over the misinterpretations by other delegates of the purpose of this mission. It seemed that there had developed a feeling that by this move I was circumventing the United Nations, which would tend to undermine their prestige and their authority. This was precisely what I wanted to avoid and why I insisted that great care be taken to clear with all governments concerned before formally announcing the nature and purpose of the Vinson mission.

But the damage was done. There was no longer any use in going ahead with this project. I thereupon summoned Secretary Marshall to return to Washington for a meeting with me to repair some of the damage and used the occasion to clarify some of the speculations that had risen in the wake of the now much-talked-about mission.

Following my conference with Secretary Marshall, I issued a statement which set forth the facts and helped to clear away many misunderstandings concerning the mission.

"General Marshall has returned to Washington at my request," this statement read, "to report to me on the progress of the work of the various United Nations bodies in Paris. I had a long talk with him this morning, and again this afternoon, he gave me a detailed picture of what has been taking place in Paris, and we discussed questions relating to the future course of this Government in the various matters at issue.

"With regard to the report published in the morning's press concerning a possible journey of Chief Justice Vinson to Moscow, the facts are as follows: On last Tuesday, when I communicated with Secretary Marshall, I told him of my continuing great desire to see peace firmly established in the world, and of my particular concern at this time over the attitude taken by the Soviet representatives regarding the atomic problem. I said that I was wondering whether their attitude did not reflect a misunderstanding in the minds of the Soviet leaders so serious, from the standpoint of world peace in general, that we would be remiss if we left undone anything that might conceivably serve to dispel it. I asked the Secretary whether he felt that a useful purpose would be served by sending to Moscow Chief Justice Vinson, in an effort to make the Soviet leaders understand the seriousness and sincerity of the feelings of the people of the United States about these matters. Secretary Marshall described to me the situation which we faced in Paris, and, in the light of his report and the possibilities of misunderstanding to which any unilateral action, however desirable otherwise, could lead at present, I decided not to take this step.

"My talk with Secretary Marshall has been gratifying to me. I was glad to hear his report of the unity which has prevailed between ourselves and the French and British representatives in Paris in all phases of the handling of the Berlin crisis, and of the earnest efforts being made by the Security Council and the General Assembly of the United Nations to find solutions to many of the other problems which have been troubling people everywhere. I was glad to be able to assure him of the determination with which people in this country are supporting our efforts to find the road to peace."

There was a speech I was scheduled to make before the American Legion Convention in Miami in October. In this I planned to cover the essence of the Vinson mission and I wanted to use the occasion for a major foreign policy speech. I also wanted to use the occasion to overcome any damage the Wallace campaign may have caused in stirring up among some of the minority groups the feeling that this administration was not doing all it could in the interest of peace. They were distorting for political purposes the facts about our efforts for peace and our foreign policy. They were dangerously wrong—and their falsehood in branding the administration as warmongering was harmful. The

Vinson mission would have served also to spike this political maneuver.

In the speech before the American Legion I said:

"Unfortunately—and I say that advisedly—unfortunately, a dark fog of distrust has risen between the Soviet Union and the West, distorting and confusing our relations. It is clear that little progress is likely to be made in settling disputes between the western powers and Soviet Russia, so long as there is so much distrust.

"If that distrust is to be dispelled, there needs to be evidence of long-range peaceful purposes—evidence that will enable the world to shake off the fear of war, reduce the burden of armaments, and concentrate on useful economic activities.

"In recently considering sending a special emissary to Moscow, my purpose was to ask Premier Stalin's cooperation in dispelling the present poisonous atmosphere of distrust which now surrounds the negotiations between the western powers and the Soviet Union. My emissary was to convey the seriousness and sincerity of the people of the United States in their desire for peace.

"This proposal had no relation to existing negotiations within the scope of the United Nations or the Council of Foreign Ministers. Far from cutting across these negotiations, the purpose of this mission was to improve the atmosphere in which they must take place and so help in producing fruitful and peaceful results.

"At this time, I want to make it perfectly clear that I have not departed one step from my determination to utilize every opportunity to work for peace. Whenever an appropriate opportunity arises, I shall act to further the interests of peace within the framework of our relations with our allies and the work of the United Nations.

"I am working for peace, and I shall continue to work for peace.

"Both we and the Soviet Union have a fundamental job to do—the job of raising the living standards of our peoples.

"We must remember that many a serious crisis has in the past been resolved without war. We must remember that the struggle for existence among nations, as among individual men, goes on all the time, and expresses itself in many ways other than war. We must remember that rivalry among nations is an old story. History shows that rival powers can exist peacefully in the world.

"Patience must be our watchword. When the destiny of all mankind is at stake, we need to exercise all the patience we can muster. We should utilize every opportunity to strengthen the United Nations for the great undertakings which lie ahead.

"The people of the world are looking to their leaders to dispel the fog of distrust which now confuses the approach to peace. At the present moment, I would only add that our nation has never failed to meet the great crises of its history with honor and devotion to its ideals."

The reaction of the delegates of the Legion convention was surprisingly warm. The reaction of the country as a whole was equally encouraging. It soon became apparent that a great many people who had been attracted to the Wallace peace offensive had thought the better of it and now began to realize that the prospects for peace were to be best served in the hands of this Democratic administration.

I felt all along that, although the Vinson mission and its high purpose turned out to be a casualty brought about by a hostile press, it still had a practical use. Although I think it would have been better for the mission to have been consummated, still there was a meaning that was implicit in this undertaking that said for all to hear and know that we would do anything that was honorable and practicable to pursue peaceful negotiations without, of course, "going it alone" or attempting to function outside the United Nations.

Even during the height of the campaign I would not allow these basic attitudes on our foreign policy to be suppressed or submerged. And the operations of our government had to be maintained without disruption. There was a complete White House staff on the job in Washington, and the members of the Cabinet went right on with their business, keeping in constant communication with me. Very few members of my Cabinet made any political speeches unless they were asked something specific on a subject relating to their departments.

As the campaign gathered speed, I stepped up my schedule of the whistle stops. In all, I traveled about 31,700 miles and delivered more than three hundred speeches—356, to be exact. I was used to hard work, and my job was cut out for me. I campaigned for thirty-five days and averaged about ten speeches every day. On one single day I delivered sixteen speeches.

Twelve to fifteen million people gathered in big crowds and small groups along the railroad junctions and stops from one end of the country to the other. Sometimes I would bring Mrs. Truman and Margaret, who were making their first tour with me, out on the rear platform to meet the crowds. At other times I would speak for a few minutes alone before the train started off for the next stop.

My one-man crusade took effect. The people responded with increasing enthusiasm as the day of election neared. I never doubted that they would vote for me, although my advisers were still not optimistic and the polls continued to hack away at my chances of getting elected. I believed that when the people learned the facts for themselves they would make the right decisions; that people still prefer to make up their own minds about candidates upon the basis of direct observation, despite all the claims of how society depends today upon newspapers, radio, and other media of communication.

On October 31, 1948, I returned from the bedlam of the longest and hardest political campaign of my career to the restful quiet of my home in Independence. The tumultuous weeks of speechmaking, handshaking, and traveling day and night had culminated in St. Louis the night before in a tremendous rally. I felt that I had given the voters a clearer view of the choice before them and that the response from the grass roots of America was so great that it would carry me back to the White House for four years as an elected President.

The following day, which was the eve of the election, I made two more speeches. The first was a non-political address to members of the Ararat Shrine in the Kansas City Auditorium during the afternoon. That night I spoke from the living room of my home to about seventy million Americans listening over the four major radio networks. I was introduced by vice-presidential candidate Barkley, who spoke from his home in Paducah, Kentucky.

This was my final appeal to the voters to decide between the principles of the party for the people and the party for the special interests. I warned the nation that their vote would not be just for one man or another but would affect every person and his family for years to come.

With this, I was through. There was nothing to do but wait for the results.

At four-thirty in the afternoon on Election Day, Jim Rowley and Henry Nicholson, who were first and second in command of the White House Secret Service detail, drove with me from my home down to the Elms Hotel at Excelsior Springs, Missouri, a resort about thirty miles northeast of Kansas City. We had slipped away from the reporters, who spent the rest of the night trying to find me. They kept telephoning my family at Independence, hoping to get some information. At Excelsior Springs, after taking a Turkish bath, I went upstairs to my room at six-thirty, had a ham sandwich and a glass of milk, turned on the radio to listen to some of the eastern returns, and then went to bed. I was reported some thousands ahead.

I awoke at midnight and again listened to the radio broadcast of Mr. H. V. Kaltenborn. I was about 1,200,000 ahead on the count but, according to this broadcaster, was still undoubtedly beaten.

About four o'clock in the morning Rowley came into my room and advised me to tune in again on Kaltenborn's broadcast. I did so, and learned that at that time I was over 2,000,000 ahead, but the commentator continued to say he couldn't see how I could be elected.

I told Rowley and Nicholson that we had better go back to Kansas City, because it looked very much as if we were in for another four years, and we arrived in Kansas City at about six o'clock Wednesday morning, November 3. At ten-thirty I received a telegram from Governor Dewey congratulating me on my election.

The final figures showed that I had received 24,105,695 votes, carrying twenty-eight states. Dewey had 21,969,170 votes, carrying sixteen states. Wallace and Thurmond polled slightly over 1,000,000 votes each. I lost four of the southern states to the Dixiecrats—South Carolina, Mississippi, Alabama, and Louisiana. But I carried all thirteen of the country's biggest cities and the seven large agricultural states—Missouri, California, Iowa, Illinois, Texas, Minnesota, and Wisconsin. If it had not been for the half million American Labor party votes which went to Wallace in New York State, I would have beaten Dewey in his own state by a majority of about 300,000. As it was, he carried New York by only 61,000 votes.

My majority in the electoral college was greater than my popular majority. I had 304 electoral votes (it was finally 303, because one fell out in Tennessee), despite the loss of 38 votes to Thurmond in: South Carolina 8, Mississippi 9, Alabama 11, and Louisiana 10. The key states in the election had been Ohio and California, which had fluctuated throughout the night until the late counting of votes had put them in the Democratic column to stay. Without Ohio and California, I would have been assured of only 254 electoral votes, twelve less than the required 266.

The 1948 election proved the pollsters and forecasters so wrong and unreliable that to this day their reputations have not been fully restored and their influence is much reduced. It was almost universally predicted, right up to the last minute, that I would lose the election. Then it was predicted that, because no candidate would receive a majority of electoral votes, the election would be thrown into the House of Representatives.

What I tried to do in 1948, as always, was to make a living, going Democratic party that stood and fought for human rights. I wanted to keep it a party that represented the common people, no matter how it was maligned or how many attempts were made to destroy it from within. The effort succeeded in spite of the two splinter groups, and won with almost a majority of the popular vote.

The greatest achievement was winning without the extreme radicals in the party and without the Solid South. It is customary for a politician to say that he wants all the votes he can get, but I was happy and pleased to be elected to the presidency by a Democratic party that did not depend upon either the extreme left-wing or the southern bloc. And of course I did not want the reactionary votes which went for my Republican opponent. The fundamental purpose of the campaign in 1948 was to put the Democratic party on its own feet and to leave it intact. This was achieved.

It was a historic victory for the party. The Democrats recaptured the Republican House by a landslide and obtained control of the Senate. My long campaign against the Eightieth Congress had convinced the voters that a turnover was necessary, and I was given an overwhelmingly Democratic Congress to replace the one which had blocked the administration's domestic progress for two years.

Two days after the election the presidential special train took me to Washington. There was a great demonstration in the Union Station in St. Louis, and when I arrived in the capital city, one of the largest crowds I have ever seen in Washington took part in a "home-coming" celebration.

As the Vice-President-elect and I rode up Pennsylvania Avenue to the plaudits of immense crowds, I saw a sign on the front of the Washington Post Building which said, "Mr. President, we are ready to eat crow whenever you are ready to serve it."

I sent that great newspaper word that I did not want anyone to eat crow, that I was not elated or in a mood myself to crow over anyone. I said I felt the tremendous responsibility that was mine for the next four years, and that I hoped for the support of all the people in carrying out the program which I thought they had entrusted me to accomplish.

On arriving at the White House, I had a Cabinet meeting and a series of conferences to plan immediate repeal of the Taft-Hartley Act, as promised in the campaign. There was much work to be done, and I was eager to get on with it. On the advice of the White House physician, however, I left Washington on November 7 for a two weeks' rest in Key West but continued to hold daily conferences with the new Vice-President-elect and with other party leaders to outline the program to go before the Eighty-first Congress in January 1949.

CHAPTER 16

My thoughts kept going back, as I approached inauguration day, to someone I particularly wanted near me but
who would not be there. I wished that my mother had lived long enough
to see me sworn in as an elected President.

A year and a half ago, on July 25, 1947, serious news reached me
from my mother's home in Grandview, Missouri.

More than five months earlier she had fallen and had broken her right
hip. She was ninety-four at the time, and it was plain that the injury
was serious. Nevertheless, the first reports were good, and we confidently hoped for her recovery. Twice previously—once when she was
eighty-eight and again when she was ninety—she had recovered from
similar but lesser fractures of her left hip. Now, however, recovery
was slow.

I visited her within two days of the accident, and twice again in the
months that followed—once for twelve days when she took a turn for
the worse. And of course I kept constantly in touch with her through my
sister Mary, my brother Vivian, and her physicians. My own physician,
too, Brigadier General Wallace Graham, saw her frequently.

At first the reports were excellent, and it was felt that she would be
out of bed in six weeks or so. In May, however, her condition took a
turn for the worse, and it was then that I spent twelve days with her in
Grandview. By May 30, however, she was better again and all of us
were reassured. In the weeks that followed, her condition improved. She
sat up now and again, and before the end of June, Mary reported that
she was "getting along fine," though the fracture was healing very slowly.
On July 12 she was "feeling much better" after having been kept in bed

for several days, and on the nineteenth Dr. Graham, who had gone to Grandview to see her and to consult with her physician, reported that she was recovering from the setback of the week before and that he would return to Washington.

Now, however, a new and adverse report had come. Dr. Graham, of course, had returned only a few days before and had reported progress. On that account my first thought was to send him back to Grandview again, knowing that he would be quick to let me know whether I should follow. Early on the following morning, however—the morning of July 26—word came from Dr. Joseph W. Greene of Independence that Mother was not expected to live through the day, and I asked to have my plane ready at once.

It was only a little after noon when, with a small party, I boarded the plane. An hour or so later a message was received by the pilot which General Graham handed to me. Mother, it reported, had passed away.

I had had more than an inkling of what I might expect, but no one can really be prepared for the passing of his mother. I read the words, but I could not describe my feelings if I would.

"Well," I remember saying to the general, "now she won't have to suffer any more."

Then I glanced at the message again.

"She must have passed away," I added, "just a little while after we took off."

Two days later she was buried beside my father in Forest Hill Cemetery in Kansas City, and little more than twenty-four hours later I was back in Washington.

When I succeeded Franklin Roosevelt, my mother had so wisely said it was no occasion for her to rejoice. She said that she could only feel grieved that President Roosevelt had died. But now that I had been elected directly by the people as President in my own right, it would have been a great thrill for her to be present as her son took the oath.

The Democratic National Committee had asked my approval for full-scale ceremonies for the inauguration, and I agreed. After a hard-fought campaign victory had been snatched from a predicted disaster, and I thought the party was entitled to have its day of celebration. For several days before inauguration, crowds streamed into Washington and besieged the White House. On January 18 there was a formal dinner for the Vice-President-elect and myself. On the day before the inauguration, January 19, there was a reception at the Shoreham Hotel given by Governor Forrest Smith of my home state, Missouri. From there I hurried back to Blair House for a change into formal evening clothes for the Electors' Dinner at the Mayflower Hotel, finishing the evening at the National Guard Armory, where Mrs. Truman, Margaret, and I were the guests of honor at a gala concert and show staged by the Inaugural Committee. It was late when we returned to Blair House.

Inauguration day, January 20, 1949, started with a breakfast with ninety-seven veterans of Battery D, which I commanded in France in 1918. These friends of World War I crowded around me, shaking my hand and calling me "Mr. President" until I put a stop to it. "We'll have none of that here," I told them, and insisted that they call me "Captain Harry" as they had done in the Argonne thirty years before.

Our former regimental chaplain, Monsignor L. Curtis Tiernan, said grace before that breakfast, and then, with thirty years of memories to recount, we paid far less attention to our orange juice and our country ham, our hominy grits and fried eggs, than to each other. We fought the war again, as veterans always do, and reminded each other of endless happenings that would no doubt have seemed very unimportant to anyone but ourselves. I reminded them of the part they were to play in the inaugural parade. Despite their lack of uniforms, they were to be a kind of "guard of honor" for me and were to march in two long lines beside my car all the way from the Capitol to the reviewing stand before the White House. No one knew better than I that they were not the physical specimens they had been three decades earlier, but "I'm sure," I told them, "that you can still make 120 steps a minute for a mile and a quarter." Before I left, they sang a special song or two that had been composed for the occasion by one of their number—Eugene Donnelly of Kansas City—and then they presented me with a handsome gold-handled ebony cane which I promised faithfully to use every morning on my daily walk.

Even on inauguration day there is work a President must do, and I went from that breakfast to my office at the White House. Then, having returned to Blair House, Mrs. Truman, Margaret, and I, together with Senator Barkley, Chief Justice Vinson, and some of the members of the Cabinet, drove around Lafayette Park to St. John's Episcopal Church, where we attended an impressive ten o'clock service. Afterward we returned once more to Blair House, and then the Joint Committee of Congress arrived to escort me to the Capitol.

The oath-taking ceremony—first that of the Vice-President and after that, as has long been customary, that of the President—was scheduled for noon, but in the rotunda of the Capitol the gathering of diplomats, members of Congress, justices of the Supreme Court, and governmental officials was so great, and so many amenities had to be exchanged, that the signal for the Marine Band to play "Hail to the

Chief" was not actually given until twelve-fourteen. Only then did Chief Justice Vinson and Associate Justice Stanley Reed, both in their official robes, enter the inaugural stand before the Capitol's east front.

More than a hundred thousand people, it was estimated, filled the great open space between the Capitol, the Supreme Court Building, and the Congressional Library as Vice-President Barkley and I made our way to the inaugural stand.

At twelve twenty-three Associate Justice Reed swore Senator Barkley in as Vice-President, and six minutes later I took the oath from Chief Justice Vinson. The words were the same that I had repeated three years and nine months earlier when I had been called so unexpectedly to the White House, but then only a handful of people were with me in the Cabinet Room. I raised my hand; once more I swore faithfully to defend the Constitution of the United States, repeating the short and simple oath, and kissed the Bible. Then I stepped to the rostrum to begin my inaugural address, which is traditionally a part of the ceremony:

"Mr. Vice President, Mr. Chief Justice, and fellow citizens, I accept with humility the honor which the American people have conferred upon me. I accept it with a deep resolve to do all that I can for the welfare of this nation and for the peace of the world.

"In performing the duties of my office, I need the help and the prayers of every one of you. I ask for your encouragment and for your support. The tasks we face are difficult, and we can accomplish them only if we work together.

"Each period of our national history has its special challenges. Those that confront us now are as momentous as any in the past. Today marks the beginning not only of a new Administration, but of a period that will be eventful, perhaps decisive, for us and for the world.

"It may be our lot to experience, and in a large measure to bring about, a major turning point in the long history of the human race. The first half of this century has been marked by unprecedented and brutal attacks on the rights of man, and by the two most frightful wars in history. The supreme need of our time is for men to learn to live together in peace and harmony."

I called attention to the uncertainties that faced the world, and to the faith by which the people of America have always lived, referred to the false philosophy which had made such headway throughout the world, misleading many peoples and adding to their sorrows and their difficulties.

"That false philosophy," I said, "is Communism.

"Communism is based on the belief that man is so weak and inadequate that he is unable to govern himself, and therefore requires the rule of strong masters.

"Democracy is based on the conviction that man has the moral and intellectual capacity, as well as the inalienable right, to govern himself with reason and justice.

"Communism subjects the individual to arrest without lawful cause, punishment without trial, and forced labor as a chattel of the state. It decrees what information he shall receive, what art he shall produce, what leaders he shall follow, and what thoughts he shall think.

"Democracy maintains that government is established for the benefit of the individual, and is charged with the responsibility of protecting the rights of the individual and his freedom in the exercise of those abilities of his."

I then spoke of our hopes for the future—of the possibilities for world improvement that lay within the scope of the United Nations, the European Recovery Program, and other measures aimed at the betterment of life all about the world.

"We must embark on a bold new program," I said, "for making the benefits of our scientific advances and industrial progress available for the improvement and growth of underdeveloped areas."

I proposed four important major courses of action. The first was continued support for the United Nations and its related agencies; second, a continuation of the program for world economic recovery; third, strengthening of the freedom-loving nations against the dangers of aggression.

"More than half the people of the world are living in conditions approaching misery," I said in outlining the fourth point. "Their food is inadequate. They are victims of disease. Their economic life is primitive and stagnant. Their poverty is a handicap and a threat both to them and to more prosperous areas.

"For the first time in history humanity possesses the knowledge and the skill to relieve the suffering of these people.

"The United States is pre-eminent among nations in the development of industrial and scientific techniques. The material resources which we can afford to use for the assistance of other people are limited. But our imponderable resources in technical knowledge are constantly growing and are inexhaustible.

"I believe that we should make available to peace-loving people the benefits of our store of technical knowledge in order to help them realize their aspirations for a better life. And, in cooperation with other nations, we should foster capital investment in areas needing development.

"Our aim should be to help the free peoples of the world, through their own efforts, to produce more food, more clothing, more materials for housing, and more mechanical power to lighten their burdens.

"We invite other countries to pool their technological resources in this undertaking. Their contributions will be warmly welcomed. This should be a cooperative enterprise in which all nations work together through the United Nations and its specialized agencies wherever practicable. It must be a world-wide effort for the achievement of peace, plenty, and freedom.

"With the cooperation of business, private capital, agriculture and labor in this country, this program can greatly increase the industrial activity in other nations and can raise substantially their standards of living.

"Such new economic developments must be devised and controlled to benefit the people of the areas in which they are established. Guaranties to the investor must be balanced by guaranties in the interest of the people whose resources and whose labor go into these developments.

"The old imperialism—exploitation for foreign profit—has no place in the concepts of democratic fair dealing.

"All countries, including our own, will greatly benefit from a constructive program for the better use of the world's human and natural resources. Experience shows that our commerce with other countries expands as they progress industrially and economically.

"Greater production is the key to prosperity and peace. And the key to greater production is a wider and more vigorous application of modern scientific and technical knowledge.

"Only by helping the least fortunate of its members to help themselves can the human family achieve the decent, satisfying life that is the right of all people.

"Democracy alone can supply the vitalizing force to stir the peoples of the world into triumphant action, not only against human oppressors, but also against their ancient enemies—hunger, misery and despair.

"Our allies," I pointed out, "are the millions who hunger and thirst after righteousness.

"In due time, as our stability becomes manifest, as more and more nations come to know the benefits of democracy and to participate in growing abundance, I believe that those countries which now oppose us will abandon their delusions and join with the free nations of the world in a just settlement of internal differences.

"Events have brought our American democracy to new influence and new responsibilities. They will test our courage, our devotion to duty, and our concept of liberty.

"Steadfast in our faith in the Almighty, we will advance toward a world where man's freedom is secure. To that end we will devote our strength, our resources, and our firmness of resolve. With God's help the future of mankind will be assured in a world of justice, harmony, and peace."

At twelve-fifty the ceremony was ended, and with Vice-President Barkley beside me, I entered the leading car in the long parade down Pennsylvania Avenue.

In my inaugural address I wanted to make it clear that lasting freedom and independence cannot be achieved among free nations unless they possess the means to maintain their free institutions and their national integrity against aggressive movements that seek to impose totalitarian regimes upon them. The seeds of such regimes are nurtured by misery and want. They spread and grow in the soil of poverty and discontent. They reach their full growth when the hope of the people for a better life has died.

We could not falter in accepting the responsibilities of leadership which had fallen to us. On March 12, 1947, I had asked the Congress to provide authority for assistance to Greece and Turkey, both threatened by Soviet power. I had also asked the Congress, at the request of those countries, to authorize the detail of American civilian and military personnel to Greece and Turkey to assist in reconstruction and to supervise the use of such materials as would be furnished.

The assistance then asked amounted to little more than one tenth of one percent of the $341,000,000,000 the United States had contributed toward the winning of World War II. It was common sense that we should safeguard this investment.

The American people have always been traditionally altruistic, and the spirit of neighborliness has been a characteristic of our society since the earliest days, even when there was not a great deal to share with each other but hardship and privation.

It is, of course, easy to be generous in the midst of plenty. I knew that Americans would respond to Point Four, as they respond to all realistic calls for help. The program was thoroughly practical because it would open up new opportunities for development and prosperity to all nations.

My request for aid to Greece and Turkey occasioned a three-month debate all around the world. But when the debate was over, the course for the United States was set.

Under the program, American personnel as well as funds were furnished to assist Greece in such fields as industry, agriculture, public finance, foreign trade, public administration, shipping, and labor. Projects for the development, rehabilitation, or construction of Greek roads, bridges, railroads and airfields, housing, land reclamation, mining, steel and textile industries, fisheries, irrigation, reforestation, food processing, and public health were initiated.

The American mission to Greece established a program to provide farmers with information on the operation and care of agricultural machinery and the techniques of weed killing and tree grafting. Other programs included the training of nurses in Greece, the establishment of a tuberculosis-control directorate in the Ministry of Hygiene, and the sending of one Greek physician to the United States and five to Denmark for training in tuberculosis-control techniques.

In Turkey similar programs were carried out. More than 380 Turks were trained as heavy road-equipment operators. In addition, members of the United States Air Mission worked with the Turkish Department of Roads and Bridges to assist in the modernization of its organization and procedures.

Like the Marshall Plan, the Greek-Turkish program accomplished its purpose magnificently. But—like the Marshall Plan—it was an emergency aid program only, and its period of usefulness was limited to the amount of the appropriation granted. These two programs, however, gave notice to the world of America's purpose to lead the free nations in building the strength to preserve their freedoms. They hinted a new concept which was to be enunciated two years later—the idea of a continuing and self-perpetuating program of technical assistance to the underdeveloped nations of the world which would enable them to help themselves to become growing, strong allies of freedom.

This new idea, which was entirely distinct from the Marshall Plan and the Greek-Turkish program, was spelled out for the first time in my inaugural address. "We must embark on a bold new program," I announced, "for making the benefits of our scientific advances and industrial progress available for the improvement and growth of underdeveloped areas."

Thus was launched what came to be universally known, within a matter of months, as the "Point Four program," because it was the fourth of the four important courses of action set forth in the inaugural address.

To call the undertaking a "bold new program" was no exaggeration. It was an adventurous idea such as had never before been proposed by any country in the history of the world. Its announcement on January 20, 1949, created a great deal of interest and excitement, and my answers at a press conference six days later re-emphasized both the novelty and the boldness of the plan:

"Mr. President," I was asked, "can you give us any background on the origin of Point Four?"

"The origin of Point Four has been in my mind," I replied, "and in the minds of the government, for the past two or three years, ever since the Marshall Plan was inaugurated. It originated with the Greece and Turkey proposition. Been studying it ever since. I spend most of my time going over to that globe back there, trying to figure out ways to make peace in the world."

"Can you tell us," I was asked, "how you are going to implement it?"

"It's a policy of the Administration over the next four years," I replied, "and it's something that will have to be implemented generally. I have asked the Secretary of State to get together with the heads of the Departments of the Government, and try to work out preliminary plans for an approach to it. I can't tell you just what is going to take place, where it is going to take place, or how it is going to take place. I know what I want to do."

I knew from my study of American history that this country was developed by the investment of foreign capital by the British, the Dutch, the Germans, and the French. These countries invested immense sums in the development of our railroads, mines, oil lands, and the livestock industry. This included ranches, cattle breeding, and the packing industry. The first packing house west of the Mississippi River was built by a Frenchman, a count in Napoleon's army. After two world wars, in each of which the United States was used as a source of supply for munitions and materials by the European countries, the invested funds in the United States of Britain, Holland, Germany, and France were depleted. Germany's were confiscated.

It seemed to me that if we could encourage stabilized governments in underdeveloped countries in Africa, South America, and Asia, we could encourage the use for the development of those areas some of the capital which had accumulated in the United States. If the investment of capital from the United States could be protected and not confiscated, and if we could persuade the capitalists that they were not working in foreign countries to exploit them but to develop them, it would be to the mutual benefit of everybody concerned.

The Point Four idea, then, originated at about the same time as the Marshall Plan concept. It was never intended, however, to have any connection with the Marshall Plan, which was purely for postwar rehabilitation in the countries of western Europe whose production and economy were ruined by the war. Point Four was conceived as a world-wide, continuing program of helping underdeveloped nations to help themselves through the sharing of technical information already tested and proved in the United States.

I was thinking in terms of a foreign policy for a nation that was the free-world leader. During the administrations of Roosevelt and myself, it had been proved that the way to build a successful economy in which the most people enjoyed high standards of living was to keep the national resources out of the hands of special interests and in the possession of the people themselves. This was our program domestically, and I wanted to make it a permanent part of our foreign policy.

Point Four was aimed at enabling millions of people in underdeveloped areas to raise themselves from the level of colonialism to self-support and ultimate prosperity. All of the reports which I had received from such areas of the world indicated that a great many people were still living in an age almost a thousand years behind the times. In many places this was the result of long exploitation for the benefit of foreign countries, of developments for foreign benefit rather than for the interest of the native peoples. This was the curse of colonialism, and I, for one, have always hoped to see it disappear.

What I hoped Point Four would accomplish was to provide technical assistance so that these peoples themselves, with a very small capital investment from us, would be able to develop their own resources. The principal item of expenditure would be the skill of our technicians teaching these people how to help themselves.

In this country we had both the capital and the technical "know-how." I did not see how we could follow any other course but to put these two great assets to work in the underdeveloped areas in order to help them elevate their own standards of living and thus move in the direction of world-wide prosperity and peace. The alternative, as I saw it, was to continue to allow those vast areas to drift toward poverty, despair, fear, and the other miseries of mankind which breed unending wars.

The Point Four program was a practical expression of our attitude toward the countries threatened by Communist domination. It was consistent with our policies of preventing the expansion of Communism in the free world by helping to insure the proper development of those countries with adequate food, clothing, and living facilities. It was an effort to bring to such people, not the idealism of democracy alone, but the tangible benefits of better living through intelligent co-operation.

Thus the plan was realistic as well as idealistic. Common sense told me that the development of these countries would keep our own industrial plant in business for untold generations. The resources of such areas as Mesopotamia, Iran, India, North Africa, and huge sections of South America have hardly been touched, and their development would be as beneficial to American trade as to the areas themselves. It would enable the peoples of many areas to subsist on trade and not aid.

This, then, was the idea which I broached at the outset of my second term. It was generally recognized and accepted as a good idea. The next problem was to make it work.

I immediately instituted a series of conferences on the subject of how best to implement the Point Four program and ordered the Secretary of State to direct the planning necessary to translate the program into action. The Assistant Secretary of State for Economic Affairs, Willard L. Thorp, was designated to co-ordinate the planning of the program, and interdepartmental consultations were set up through a Committee on Economic Foreign Policy.

In developing the program, I made it clear that all existing private and governmental activities would be utilized. American business enterprises overseas and private non-profit organizations such as the Rockefeller Institute or the Institute of International Education could furnish much valuable information and assistance in making technical services available to underdeveloped countries. Governmental services, in addition to the United Nations specialized agencies, that were utilized included the Interdepartmental Committee on Scientific and Cultural Cooperation, the Institute of Inter-American Affairs, the Economic Cooperation Administration, and the Export-Import Bank.

On June 24, 1949, I sent a special message to Congress recommending an appropriation of not more than forty-five million dollars to inaugurate the program. This included ten million dollars that had been requested in the 1950 budget[1] for similar activities, and the sum recommended was designed to cover United States participation in the program both of international agencies and of direct assistance by this country.

I called for legislation that would authorize an expanded program of technical assistance for the underdeveloped areas of the world and an experimental program to encourage the investment of private funds for the economic development of these areas. Such development would strengthen the United Nations and help toward world peace. The development of these areas had become one of the major elements of our foreign policy.

On September 27 legislation was introduced in the Congress to carry out the program, but no action was taken before adjournment in October. Meanwhile, I utilized every opportunity to point out the possibilities of the plan. Talking informally to a businessmen's dinner forum on October 20, 1949, I said that in the Mesopotamian Valley alone there could be

---

[1] The 1950 budget is presented to Congress in January 1949. Fiscal years begin July 1 of the preceding year.

a revival of the Garden of Eden that would take care of thirty million people and feed all the Near East if it were properly developed. I explained in detail how the Zambezi River Valley in Africa and a similar area in southern Brazil could also be converted into sections comparable to the Tennessee Valley in our own country if the people of those regions only had access to the "know-how" which we possessed.

The State of the Union message on January 4, 1950 urged the Congress to adopt the legislation then before it to provide for an increase in the flow of technical assistance and capital to the underdeveloped regions. It was more essential than ever "if the ideas of freedom and representative government are to prevail in these areas, and particularly in the Far East, that their people experience in their own lives the benefits of scientific and economic advances."

The message pointed out that this program would require the movement of large amounts of capital from the industrial nations, particularly from the United States, to productive uses in the backward areas, that recent world events made prompt action imperative.

"This program," I said, "is in the interest of all peoples—and it has nothing in common with either the old imperialism of the last century or the new imperialism of the Communists."

The plan was laid before the United Nations early that year, and in the first official act taken on the Point Four idea, the United Nations Economic and Social Council endorsed the program on March 4, 1949, and drafted some proposals which were adopted later in the year.

It was not until June 5, 1950, however, that Point Four became a reality. On that date I signed the act to provide foreign economic assistance which was passed by the second session of the Eighty-first Congress. Point Four was embodied in this act as Title IV, the "Act for International Development." The same legislation included also the Economic Cooperation Act of 1950, the China Area Aid Act of 1950, the United Nations Palestine Refugees Aid Act of 1950, and the International Children's Welfare Work Act of 1950.

Among the appropriations authorized for these various purposes was $34,500,000 for the technical assistance program. Specific appropriations were contained in the General Appropriation Act of 1951, approved on September 6, 1950.

The sum appropriated for technical assistance was small in comparison with the need and was ten and a half million dollars less than the minimum requested. But it was a beginning, and already Point Four had become a symbol of hope to those nations which were being fed Communist propaganda that the free nations were incapable of providing a decent standard of living for the millions of people in the underdeveloped areas of the earth. This money, together with the contributions of other countries, would have a cumulative effect in promoting the well-being of such people.

Pursuant to the Act for International Development, an Executive Order was issued on September 8, 1950, delegating to the Secretary of State the responsibility for carrying out the Point Four program and establishing the International Development Advisory Board. This Board was set up for the purpose of considering desirable plans for accomplishing the objectives and policies of the Point Four program. Nelson Rockefeller became the first chairman of the Board.

Soon after the responsibility for the implementation of the program had been delegated to the State Department, the technical staff which was assembled by the Secretary of State became known as the Technical Cooperation Administration. On November 14, 1950, I appointed Dr. Henry Garland Bennett as Administrator of the TCA. A former college president, Dr. Bennett had distinguished himself in three assignments abroad for the federal government. In 1945 he had gone to Quebec as a United States delegate to the first session of the Food and Agriculture Organization of the United Nations. In 1949 he had been in Germany on an agricultural survey mission for the United States Army of Occupation. In April of 1950 he had acted as adviser to the government of Ethiopia on the organization of an agricultural training center along the lines of American land-grant colleges.

Dr. Bennett was the guiding spirit of the actual working out of the Point Four program until his untimely death in an airplane accident in Iran hardly more than a year later. His death was a terrible loss to Point Four. He knew the world situation in every corner of it by actual contact. He had the full concepts of TCA at his fingertips.

Thus, within two years after the inaugural address, the minimum machinery for setting the Point Four program under way was put together and ready to go into operation.

We lost no time. In March 1951, barely six months after the first Point Four budget was approved by the Congress, about 350 technicians were at work on more than a hundred technical co-operation projects in twenty-seven countries. Thirty-five governments in Latin America, Africa, and Asia had asked the United States Government for specific help in solving their problems through the Point Four program.

Also by March of 1951 there were 236 Point Four trainees from thirty-four countries in the United States for advanced study, and plans were under way to bring in many more during the next six months.

By the end of March the United States had concluded Point Four general agreements with twenty-two countries in the less developed areas of the world. Primary emphasis was put on food supply, since food is a key to all productivity. Other projects contributing to food supply, such as prevention of disease, basic and vocational education, transportation, development of fibers and insecticides, were given an important place in the Point Four program.

By the end of 1951 Point Four had been extended to thirty-three countries, and the State of the Union message of January 9, 1952, summarized the progress of the program, pointing out that during the year the United States had made available millions of bushels of wheat to relieve the famine in India. But far more important in the long run, I said, was the work which Americans were doing in India to help the farmers themselves raise more grain.

"This is our Point Four program at work. It is working, not only in India, but in Iran and Paraguay and Liberia—in thirty-three countries around the globe. Our technical missionaries are out there. We need more of them. We need more funds to speed their efforts, because there is nothing of greater importance in all our foreign policy. There is nothing that shows more clearly what we stand for and what we want to achieve."

As the value of the plan became clearer to the Congress, subsequent laws were passed authorizing and providing funds for its operations. For the fiscal year 1952, the budget was expanded from the original appropriation of $34,500,000 to $147,900,000, and for the fiscal year 1953 this amount was increased to $155,600,000.

Changes in personnel and organization were made necessary in 1952, but the program continued to grow in scope and activity. After Dr. Bennett's death, Stanley Andrews, a former official of the Department of Agriculture, became director of the program. Rockefeller resigned at the close of 1951 to devote his attention to private administration of technical assistance and was succeeded in January 1952 by Eric A. Johnston, former Administrator of the Economic Stabilization Agency.

Under the consolidation of current aid programs in 1952, technical and economic assistance in Southeast Asia and the Pacific was placed under the Mutual Security Agency, headed by Averell Harriman, while the Technical Cooperation Administration of the State Department continued to administer economic and technical assistance in the Middle East, South Asia, the American republics, and the independent states of Africa.

At the time I left the presidency in January 1953, the Point Four program had been in operation less than thirty months. During that short period the program had relieved famine measurably in many portions of the world, had reduced the incidence of diseases that keep many areas poverty-stricken, and had set many nations on the path of rising living standards by their own efforts and by the work of their own nationals.

For example, Chimbote, Peru, a pesthole of malaria for generations, was virtually free of it. The incidence of malaria in the Shan States of Burma was cut from fifty per cent to ten per cent. A typhus epidemic in Bukan, Iran, was checked and the disease stamped out. Entire school systems emphasizing vocational and technical training went into operation in various countries of Asia, the Middle East, Africa, and Latin America.

A monetary, fiscal, and banking system was introduced in Saudi Arabia. Schools of medicine, public health, and nursing were set up in several countries. A 75,000-acre irrigation project in the Artibonite Valley of Haiti got under way. A great multi-purpose hydroelectric plant was constructed in the Mexican state of Michoacán. Irrigation projects in Jordan were started to create 120,000 acres of arable land providing homes and six-and-a-quarter-acre tracts for 21,000 families consisting of 105,000 individuals.

Demonstrations of improved seed achieved high yields in Iran, particularly in the Ardebil-Moghan area of Azerbaijan, where the first crop in four years was harvested as a result of an emergency program of planting and culture advice. Egyptian farmers were supplied with tractors to aid in converting three million acres of desert, which had resulted from overgrazing, into arable land. In India fifty-five rural development projects were launched to raise food production, provide potable water, foster irrigation, introduce fertilizer, teach reading and writing, devise better tools, improve village workshops, and better the forms of land-ownership.

Some 2,445 United States technicians in thirty-five countries were putting such programs as these into effect. Thirty-four of those countries sent 2,862 of their most promising young specialists abroad, mostly to this country, as trainees for post-graduate training in their specialties. They, and the technicians they train in turn, release the American technical missionaries for pioneer work in other fields.

We found that even in countries which were anti-American the relations between United States technicians and their local counterparts were excellent. The program in action had the effect of disarming hostile propagandists and in discouraging the advance of both Communism and extreme nationalism.

There were, of course, some great difficulties encountered in the implementation of the program. Chief among these was the attempt, both at home and abroad, by selfish interests to change the character of the program by shifting the emphasis from technical assistance to financial aid. Point Four was not conceived as a lending program or as a giveaway plan. Its basic aim is to spread knowledge that will aid others to improve themselves.

The American taxpayers, who approved the Point Four program, showed their general support of the plan from the beginning. There was little or no opposition in the press to this effort of the government to help other countries to help themselves. The only dangerous threat to the continued success of the plan, as I saw it, was that which might come from the reactionaries and isolationists.

It is a program which requires vision. It has been estimated that an improvement of only two per cent in the living standards of Asia and Africa would keep the industrial plants of the United States, Great Britain, and France going at full tilt for a century just to keep up with the increased demand for goods and services.

Only America could undertake such a unique approach to world affairs. Our population, unlike that of other great nations, is made up of strains from every population around the world, and when we became the most powerful nation in the world, we tried to put into effect the ideals of all races and nationalities which we had written into the Constitution and the Declaration of Independence.

The American approach to world affairs was best demonstrated by the manner in which we treated conquered nations after the first and second world wars. We set up the means to feed and clothe and take care of the physical needs of the people. We rehabilitated the conquered nations instead of attempting to keep them conquered and prostrate. We asked for no reparations.

This was something new in the history of nations. The traditional practice had always been for the conqueror to strip the defeated countries and to make off with whatever spoils were available. Our idea has been to restore the conquered nations of Germany, Italy, and Japan to prosperity in the hope that they would understand the futility of aggression as a means of expansion and progress. We had to refute the historic claim that a nation must use aggression and military means to gain markets.

The satellite countries of Russia are the unhappiest places in the world, so far as we can find out from the information that comes from behind the iron curtain. This is in sharpest contrast with the situation that exists in Cuba, Canada, Mexico, and other nations that lie in the portion of the world of which we are a part. No neighbor of ours is afraid of us, and they like to do business with us because we accept their competition instead of demanding their subjection.

The technical assistance program was not an anti-Communist measure. We would have included Russia in the program if she had been willing. As early as Potsdam, in July and August of 1945, I was prepared to offer the Russians aid for war recovery. Without co-operation, of course, we could not help them to help themselves.

The Point Four program, therefore, was not against Communism or against anything else. It was a positive plan of self-help for any country that wanted it. It recognized the historic fact that colonialism had run its course and could no longer be made to work for a few favored nations.

In its immediate and long-range effects, however, Point Four provided the strongest antidote to Communism that has so far been put into practice. It was created and designed to operate on a continuing basis to point the way to better living for more and more of the world's people—and thus the way to a more lasting peace. Thus it stands as a vitally important development in the search for peace, which lies at the very heart of America's foreign policy.

CHAPTER 17

On April 4, 1949, I stood by Secretary of State Dean
Acheson as he signed his name, on behalf of the United
States, to a treaty which was the first peacetime military alliance concluded by the United States since the adoption of the Constitution.
Earlier in our history (before the Constitution was written), the colonies
had signed a military alliance with France. The document Acheson
signed was the North Atlantic Treaty, and the occasion was the closing
ceremonial event of a historic meeting, held in the auditorium of the
Department of Labor in Washington, D.C.

The North Atlantic Treaty was one more step in the evolution of our
foreign policy, along with the United Nations Charter, the Greek-
Turkish Aid Program, and the Marshall Plan. Because of the Marshall
Plan, the economy of western Europe began, within a short time, to
show evidence of recovery. But the problems of Europe were not only
economic. There was fear of aggression and, therefore, lack of confidence in the future. A large volume of European capital had been
transferred abroad before and during World War II, and this was now
needed in western Europe to rebuild its cities and its industries. Capital,
however, was not likely to flow to countries threatened by Communist
conquest.

In 1947 and 1948 the Communists were pushing hard in Europe.
Even as the Marshall Plan was being launched, they captured the gov-
ernment of Hungary. This was the first seizure of a government by
Communists which was openly supported by Russia since the fighting
had stopped in Europe. The following month the Kremlin ordered
Czechoslovakia and Poland to call off their participation in the Marshall
Plan.

In early 1948 still another series of events jarred the free world. In Czechoslovakia, which had so long been the stronghold of democracy in central Europe, a ruthless Communist leadership, backed by the Russian Army at the border, demanded the full powers of government. President Eduard Beneš, the able successor to the great Masaryk, held out for four days before yielding to the pressure. On February 25, 1948, however, democratic Czechoslovakia, for the second time in less than nine years, fell under the heel of totalitarianism. Two weeks later, Jan Masaryk, son of the founder of the Czech republic and a close friend and associate of many statesmen in the countries of western Europe, died in Prague under mysterious circumstances that suggested foul play. His death was a dramatic symbol of the tragic end of freedom in his nation.

In Poland, where Russian armies had set up a Communist government at the end of the war, the Russians now dropped all pretext of Polish sovereignty. A Russian Red Army marshal was sent to take over the Polish Army. At about the same time, Stalin "invited" little Finland to sign a "pact of friendship" with the Soviet Union. There were threats of what would happen if the "invitation" was not accepted. To the people in Europe, who were just beginning to take courage from the Marshall Plan, these Communist moves looked like the beginning of a Russian "big push."

I had planned to deliver an address on the menace of Communism on March 17, 1948, at a St. Patrick's Day observance in New York. The grave events in Europe were moving so swiftly, however, that I felt it necessary to report to the nation first through Congress. Therefore, I asked Speaker Joseph W. Martin to arrange for me to address a joint session of the Congress, suggesting March 17 as the date.

"Almost three years have elapsed," I told the Congress, "since the end of the greatest of all wars, but peace and stability have not returned to the world. We were well aware that the end of the fighting would not automatically settle the problems arising out of the war. The establishment of peace after the fighting is over has always been a difficult task. And even if all the Allies of World War II were united in their desire to establish a just and honorable peace, there would still be great difficulties in the way of achieving that peace.

"But the situation in the world today is not primarily the result of natural difficulties which follow a great war. It is chiefly due to the fact that one nation has not only refused to cooperate in the establishment of a just and honorable peace, but—even worse—has actively sought to prevent it. . . .

"One nation . . . has persistently obstructed the work of the United Nations by constant abuse of the veto. . . .

"But that is not all. Since the close of the hostilities, the Soviet Union and its agents have destroyed the independence and democratic character of a whole series of nations in Eastern and Central Europe.

"It is this ruthless course of action, and the design to extend it to the remaining free nations of Europe, that have brought about the critical situation in Europe today.

"The tragic death of the Republic of Czechoslovakia has sent a shock throughout the civilized world. Now pressure is being brought to bear on Finland, to the hazard of the entire Scandinavian peninsula. Greece is under direct military attack from rebels actively supported by her Communist dominated neighbors. In Italy, a determined and aggressive effort is being made by a Communist minority to take control of that country. The methods vary, but the pattern is all too clear.

"Faced with this growing menace, there have been encouraging signs that the free nations of Europe are drawing closer together for their economic well-being and for the common defense of their liberties. . . .

"At the very moment I am addressing you, five nations of the European community, in Brussels, are signing a 50-year agreement for economic cooperation and common defense against aggression.

"This action has great significance, for this agreement was not imposed by the decree of a powerful neighbor. It was the free choice of independent governments representing the will of their people, and acting within the terms of the Charter of the United Nations.

"Its significance goes far beyond the actual terms of the agreement itself. It is a notable step in the direction of unity in Europe for protection and preservation of its civilization. This development deserves our full support. I am confident that the United States will, by appropriate means, extend to the free nations the support which the situation requires. I am sure that the determination of the free countries of Europe to protect themselves will be matched by an equal determination on our part to help them to protect themselves."

I then urged the Congress to complete legislative action on the European Recovery Program and to provide for a strengthening of national defense through universal military training and the restoration of Selective Service.

That evening my speech to the Society of the Friendly Sons of St. Patrick in New York struck the same note:

"Free men in every land are asking: 'Where is this leading? When will it end?'

"I can bring you tonight no simple or easy answer.

"But I can express my firm conviction that, at this moment in history, the faith and strength of the United States are mighty forces for the prevention of war and the establishment of peace.

"Our faith and our strength must be made unmistakably clear to the world."

Ernest Bevin, the British Foreign Secretary, had informed Secretary of State Marshall as early as January 13, 1948, that England was planning to approach France and the so-called Benelux countries (Belgium, Netherlands, Luxembourg) with a proposal for a series of bilateral defense agreements. The pattern he had in mind was that of the Dunkirk Treaty, a postwar agreement by which Great Britain and France had agreed to come to each other's defense in case of renewed German aggression.

General Marshall brought Bevin's message to me. I thought it was a good beginning—a step in the right direction. If the countries of western Europe were ready to organize for their joint defense, that would be an important contribution to the peace of the world.

Bevin in his message had asked what our attitude would be toward this new alliance. I authorized Marshall to inform the British Foreign Secretary that we agreed with them on the urgent need for concerted measures by the nations of western Europe. As in the case of the European Recovery Program, we welcomed European initiative and would give their undertaking our wholehearted sympathy; the United States would do anything it properly could to assist the European nations to bring this or a similar project to fulfillment.

With this backing from the United States, Bevin approached the French and the Benelux countries. It was from the three small nations that a counterproposal came for one regional arrangement rather than a series of two-party treaties. M. Spaak, the Belgian Foreign Minister, was largely responsible for this change, and it was in this form that the treaty was made. I think to Spaak goes the credit for lining up the Europeans for the treaty.

But even as the Brussels Pact was signed, it was clear that it would take a far more important political act to dispel the fears and to restore full confidence among the western European nations. The State Department had already made some extensive studies and drawn up lists of possible courses of action. In my own mind there was no doubt that much more would have to be done in order to bolster Europe's will to resist—and to recover.

But I always kept in mind the lesson of Wilson's failure in 1920. I meant to have legislative co-operation. Our European friends apparently remembered the League of Nations too; they were most anxious to have not only a presidential declaration of policy but also a congressional expression confirming it.

Under Secretary of State Lovett and the Republican foreign policy spokesman, Senator Arthur H. Vandenberg, went to work on a congressional declaration of policy which put the Senate on record as favoring regional arrangements "based on continuous and effective self-help and mutual aid."

This was Senate Resolution 239, which Senator Vandenberg skillfully steered through the Senate to overwhelming approval by that body. On the final roll call, on June 11, 1948, only four senators voted against it. Even counting pairs and announced positions of senators absent from the floor, there were seventy-nine for and only six against the resolution.

Senator Vandenberg was thoroughly familiar with the workings of the Senate and knew how to get results. He could take ideas conceived by others—many in this case came from the State Department—and then include an element or two that would add his legislative trademark without changing anything basic. From then on he would fight for the ideas without letting up. When Vandenberg died, nobody in the Republican ranks was able to step into his shoes.

Meanwhile, the State Department was working out the details for our support of Western Union, which was the name given to the Brussels Pact arrangements. The plan was sent to the National Security Council for further study, and at the Council meeting on April 22, 1948, Lovett announced that the plan was being rewritten in order more closely to approach the language used in the Senate resolution that he and Vandenberg were then preparing.

On April 23 Lovett came to see me with a top-secret telegram from the British Foreign Secretary, Ernest Bevin, in which were outlined the possible risks involved in a formal treaty association by the nations of the North Atlantic area. He said that he had discussed these risks in the greatest secrecy with Prime Minister Attlee and a few of his closest colleagues, and they had agreed that the summoning of a conference by the United States Government to discuss defense arrangements for the North Atlantic area would be the best guarantee of peace at the present moment. I instructed the State Department to circulate this message to the members of the National Security Council for their immediate information.

The principal risk involved, Bevin said, was that the Russians might be so provoked by the formation of a defense organization that they would resort to rash measures and plunge the world into war. In this, our experts agreed with the British. On the other hand, if a collective security system could be built up effectively, it was more than likely that the Russians might restudy the situation and become more co-operative.

The British Foreign Secretary also pointed out that an Atlantic security system was probably the only way in which the French could be brought to agree to a rebuilding of Germany. Such a system would give all the free nations of Europe the sense of confidence they needed to build peace and prosperity in the world.

Bevin thought that to be effective the security arrangements must carry real assurance for the nations of free Europe. He reminded us that in 1940 the British government knew that the American Chief Executive held strong sympathies for them, but they had to fight on without knowing positively what help, if any, America would give. He then expressed the opinion that it would be very difficult for the British, or other free nations, to stand up to new acts of aggression unless there was a definitely worked-out arrangement, which included the United States, for collective resistance against aggression.

At the meeting of the National Security Council on May 20, 1948, Under Secretary Lovett explained that the Vandenberg Resolution, if passed by the Senate, would put us in a stronger position to discuss with the countries of western Europe measures to strengthen our national security as well as theirs. He pointed out that there were two basic factors in our planning: First, we wanted to get away from the one-way arrangements in which we did something for foreign countries without receiving anything in return; second, we did not want any automatic, unlimited engagements under our constitutional system. We could not agree upon anything amounting to a guarantee. But we had to give assurances sufficient enough to inspire the confidence and bolster the faith of the countries of Europe who felt themselves under constant and heavy Soviet pressure.

Secretary of State Marshall then informed the NSC that he had that morning received a message from Bevin declaring that evidence was needed that the United States was willing to assume certain obligations, and that Bevin also felt that negotiations should be initiated from Washington.

The military point of view was represented by Secretary of the Army Royall, who reported that the Joint Chiefs of Staff felt we should not commit ourselves to any defense arrangement until we knew what they were. For that reason we should send observers only to the military talks which the Western Union nations were planning to hold in London in July. Royall suggested that any arrangement made should be sufficiently flexible so that Spain, Germany, and Austria could later be added.

Secretary of Defense Forrestal pointed out that the French seemed to think that the first item on any regional security program should be the re-equipping of twenty-five French divisions. Our Chiefs of Staff, however, were of the opinion that our own strength should be bolstered first. They admitted, however, that if that course were followed it would be some time before the French could get what they wanted.

Mr. Lovett observed that it was virtually impossible to get Congress to approve substantial shipments of military equipment to other powers except for an emergency. If Congress believed that we were thinking of a revival of Lend-Lease, he added, there would be drastic cuts in domestic military appropriations.

The National Security Council then recommended to me that the line of action proposed by the State Department should generally be followed, though with proper weight given both to the comments of the Joint Chief of Staff and to any changes that might be made in the Vandenberg Resolution during Senate debate.

On July 2 I approved a policy statement which said that the Vandenberg Resolution should be implemented to the fullest extent possible and that the Department of State should now go ahead with the preliminary conversations which the Brussels Pact powers had suggested.

It was decided also that U.S. military representatives should go to London to take part in the five-power military discussions there, although on a non-membership basis, and that we should seek to convince the Brussels Pact nations to proceed with military talks at once, even though the U.S. commitment was not to be made formal until later. Furthermore, the Department of State was to explore the possibility of including Norway, Denmark, Iceland, Italy, and perhaps Portugal and Sweden in the proposed arrangement and suggest for later adherence of Spain, Germany, and Austria, or the western zones of the last two countries. If Canada was willing to participate, the Department of State was to arrange for Canadian attendance at the London military talks.

If, as a result of the diplomatic talks with the Brussels Pact nations, we became convinced that some further political commitment from us was necessary at this time in order to bolster public morale and confidence in western Europe, then we should undertake to discuss such an association with those countries. This was the cornerstone of the defense program, but no U.S. commitment should be entered into without the fullest bi-partisan clearance here.

At the same time, the National Security Council proposed certain recommendations which I approved and which later became the Mutual Defense Assistance Program.

The two proposals—Mutual Defense Assistance Program and association with the Brussels Pact powers—supplemented each other, and yet they were independent of one another. The Congress had on several occasions authorized the giving of aid in the nature of military supplies and technical advice to certain nations. MDAP was intended to replace this piecemeal approach by a comprehensive program which would permit us to aid in the defense of those countries whose strategic location made them most important to the security of the United States in such amounts and at such times as a broad military and political view of the situation might demand.

The program was a long-range proposition and not a stopgap measure. It should not jeopardize the minimum needs of our own armed forces, as determined by the Joint Chiefs of Staff. It should be tied in with the European Recovery Program in such a way that the total of the two programs would not endanger the stability of our domestic economy. The countries participating in the program should be encouraged to eliminate overlapping production by standardizing weapons and matériel.

This was the summer of 1948. Berlin was blockaded, and it was not yet at all certain that the airlift would succeed. Free men in Europe and in Asia, eager to resist aggression, could not wait for the future delivery of arms, which might come too late. Indeed, the main purpose of this aid proposal was to make sure that we did not have another tragic instance of "too little and too late"—the kind of thing that had helped Hitler subjugate Europe.

The State Department wasted little time getting the talks with the Brussels Pact powers under way. The first session of these talks was held on July 6, with Under Secretary Lovett heading the American delegation, and the ambassadors in Washington of Great Britain, France, the Netherlands, Belgium, and Canada representing their respective countries (the Belgian also attended on behalf of Luxembourg).

These conversations were held in the utmost secrecy. A special security system was applied so that only a bare minimum of documentary material was distributed. Special couriers handled all papers. Telephone discussion of matters covered in the conference was absolutely ruled out, and telegraphic communication was held to a minimum. Only a very restricted number of persons were allowed to handle any of the documents involved.

This system was the same that the Brussels Pact powers had established for their own use in negotiations and was intended to prevent leaks to Soviet agents.

Because of the crucial importance of these meetings I wanted to make sure that I had all the information. Under Secretary of State Lovett called on me regularly, bringing the minutes of each meeting with him. The sessions were marked by a completely frank exchange of views, sometimes to the point of bluntness. Rarely has a group of diplomats, representing six different nations, sat around one table and spoken with such complete frankness.

Next to Lovett, Dr. Van Kleffens, the Netherlands Ambassador, was the outstanding member of the group. He seemed to have a remarkable grasp of the thing that mattered and was always able to supply the right word at the right time. It was he who first expressed the hope that the association which the Vandenberg Resolution had envisaged would take the form of a "North Atlantic Pact."

At last, after numerous sessions of working committees, an agreed statement was prepared, to be submitted to the respective governments. Here are the most important points of that statement:

The first section discussed the situation in Europe as it affected security. Here it was clearly recognized that the Soviet advance was a direct result of the war, which had created a vacuum in central and eastern Europe where German power had once prevailed. The Soviets' actions were described as part of an avowed drive for maximum extension of power and influence. At this stage the Soviet Union was capable of extending her domination over the continent of Europe by force.

The conferees noted that while there was no evidence that the Soviets had a timetable for armed aggression there was a constant danger of incidents developing from the international tension, and it was part of Soviet technique to apply pressure wherever an advantage might be gained. Furthermore, the extension of a minor incident could easily result in war and in the Soviet conquest of the continent of Europe.

This was the key point:

The Marshall Plan had brought some relief, but the constant threat of unpredictable Soviet moves resulted in an atmosphere of insecurity and fear among the peoples of western Europe. Something more needed to be done to counteract the fear of the peoples of Europe that their countries would be overrun by the Soviet Army before effective help could arrive. Only an inclusive security system could dispel these fears.

The next question was what countries should be associated in such a system. It was pointed out that enemy occupation of the territories of Norway, Denmark, Iceland, Ireland, and Portugal (with their dependent territories in the Atlantic area, such as Greenland and the Azores) would represent a threat to the security of western Europe. The conference took note of the fact that all of these nations might not be willing or prepared to assume the commitments of such an association. It was suggested, therefore, that there might be different classes of association, with varying degrees of obligation.

It was agreed that there might be countries which, while not "Atlantic" in geography, might have such significance to Atlantic defense plans that they should be associated with the Atlantic nations. The case of Italy was especially in point, and the agreed statement recorded the fact that the United States delegation had particularly insisted that Italy should, in some manner, be brought into any proposed arrangement.

The problems of Spain and Western Germany, it was decided, would eventually have to be determined, but it was too early to attempt it at this particular moment. An outline of proposed provisions for a North Atlantic security arrangement was attached to the conference report.

The Brussels Pact nations wanted the North Atlantic pact to state that, if a member was attacked, the other members would supply all the military and other aid and assistance in their power. This, of course, implied going to war. Our delegation was instructed to take the position that this was an obligation which, in view of our Constitution, we were not prepared to assume.

Canada proposed a compromise. This provided that in case of attack on a member state the other members should consider this an attack on themselves. But instead of becoming immediately involved in war, the compromise provided that each nation would be expected to lend aid to the victim in accordance with its own constitutional processes. In plain language this means there is an obligation to give all aid possible, but subject to the constitutional procedures of each country.

When the treaty was later given its final form, this compromise became, in substance, Article V—the key provision of the treaty.

On October 13 Canada notified the State Department that she was ready to enter into a treaty along the general lines suggested by the agreed statement of September 9. Two weeks later word was received that the Brussels Pact nations had agreed in principle to the negotiation of such a North Atlantic security pact.

When the negotiators came together again, following these decisions by Canada and the Brussels Pact nations, it took little time to produce a draft treaty. When the National Security Council reviewed the situation in my presence on January 6, 1949, Under Secretary Lovett spoke in highly complimentary terms about the spirit in which the talks had been carried on.

Obviously, each government had its own problems. The French were anxious to have the treaty extended to cover their North African possessions. The British were a little reluctant to include the Italians. As I observed at this NSC meeting, this reluctance was understandable: One had to remember that the British had had some bad experiences with Italy in recent years. But I said that nothing would ever be accomplished if people spent all their time pondering flaws and worrying about difficulties. Making policy means making decisions. We must look forward with faith and confidence.

In working out the North Atlantic Treaty we had made a truly momentous decision. As I described it to the National Security Council, it could be called "an offensive-defensive alliance to maintain the peace in the North Atlantic area but without automatic provision for war."

With the North Atlantic Treaty and the corresponding Western Hemisphere arrangement concluded at Rio de Janeiro, we gave proof of our determination to stand by the free countries to resist armed aggression from any quarter. I considered this so basic to our position in the world that I included the North Atlantic Treaty, along with adherence to the U.N., the Marshall Plan, and the Point Four program, among the foundations of our foreign policy in my inaugural address on January 20, 1949.

By that time the diplomats had nearly completed their work on the treaty text. Dean Acheson, who was now Secretary of State, spent considerable time with key members of the Senate Committee on Foreign Relations in order to familiarize them with the document and the issues behind it.

The formal signing of the treaty took place in Washington on April 4, 1949, and in my remarks on that occasion I said that this treaty was indeed an act of neighborliness, and compared the twelve nations to a group of householders who decide that they have so much in common that it would be to their mutual advantage to associate themselves more formally.

The treaty itself, I observed, was simple and straightforward. We hoped that it would serve to prevent World War III. Surely, if something like it had existed in 1914 and in 1939, the acts of aggression that had pushed the world into two disastrous wars would not have happened.

The treaty was a reaffirmation of our dedication to the cause of peace, to the ideal of peaceful settlement of disputes that was represented by the organization of the United Nations. The pact was a shield against aggression and against the fear of aggression—a bulwark that would permit us to get on with the real business of government and society, the task of achieving a fuller and happier life for all our citizens.

On April 12 I sent the treaty to the Senate with a message asking for its ratification. It was, I told the senators, a long step on the road to peace. We would need to work continuously in the advancement of peace by taking those practical and necessary steps that events would call for. But no better foundation could be found for the future of peace in the world than the step which we had taken by allying ourselves with the nations of the North Atlantic area for our mutual defense.

The Senate gave the North Atlantic Treaty as thorough an examination as only that great deliberative body can give. The critics had the fullest opportunity to be heard, and every conceivable objection was discussed and answered. The debate ended on July 21, when eighty-two senators voted to ratify the treaty, far more than were needed under the constitutional requirements for a two-thirds vote for the ratification of treaties. One senator was not voting; thirteen answered "Nay" when their names were called. Eleven of these thirteen were Republicans.

On July 25 I affixed my signature to the treaty ratification and thus completed American accession to the pact. On August 24, 1949, a sufficient number of ratifications had been deposited to bring the treaty into effect. This, officially, is the day on which NATO became a reality.

We realized, of course, that much still remained to be done if the new arrangement was to prove effective. As soon as the treaty had been ratified, I asked the Congress to provide approximately $1,400,000,000 for a military assistance program, both for the NATO countries and others, such as Greece, Turkey, and the Philippines. There were three different types of assistance planned under this program. First, we wanted to help the nations that were friendly with us to increase their own military production. Second, we would transfer to them some essential items of military equipment. And third, we would send some of our experts abroad to help train and equip their military forces.

I explained the purpose of the military assistance program to the 50th Annual Encampment of the Veterans of Foreign Wars in these terms:

"The purpose of the military assistance program is to prevent aggression. Our European partners in the North Atlantic Treaty are not strong enough today to defend themselves effectively. Since the end of the war they have been concentrating on rebuilding their war-torn economies. We can strengthen them, and ourselves, by transferring some military means to them, and joining with them in a common defense plan. The military assistance program is based on the same principle of self-help and mutual aid that is the cornerstone of the European recovery program and the North Atlantic Treaty.

"We are not arming ourselves and our friends to start a fight with anybody. We are building defenses so that we won't have to fight.

"Our aid will be limited to the material necessary to equip mobile defense forces. These forces will constitute no threat to the independence of other nations. The democratic nations have no desire for aggression; they only want to be able to defend their homes. . . .

"The cost of such a program is considerable, but it represents an investment in security that will be worth many times its cost. It is part of the price of peace. Which is better, to make expenditures to save the peace, or to risk all our resources and assets in another war?"

Administrative machinery under the treaty organization was set up without delay. A North Atlantic Council was formed on September 17, 1949, with the Foreign Ministers of the participating nations as members. The Cabinet officers in charge of defense in the several member nations formed a Defense Committee and under that body a Military Committee of top-ranking generals and admirals from all twelve nations went to work at once.

The first major task was to reach an agreement on how to work out the defense of the NATO area. Up to this time each country had its own defense plans, but now it became necessary to think of the area as one. This did not involve specific national defense positions but, instead, the over-all strategic approach. This plan was worked out without delay, and the NATO Council gave its approval on January 6, 1950.

Secretary Acheson brought the plan to me and I examined it at length, with the assistance of my diplomatic, military, and economic advisers. I thought it was a good plan and one that would serve the interest of the United States well. On January 27, 1950, I formally approved this proposal for the strategy that would control a major part of our defenses and occupy a major share of our defense efforts.

The NATO defense was based on the idea of a "balanced force"— that is, on the use of a NATO defense force to which each country would contribute its share. This was one of the problems. The Dutch, for instance, with their long tradition of seafaring and exploration, did not want to restrict their Navy, yet the plan called for them to concentrate on certain types of ground forces. Almost all the member nations indicated their understanding of the basic principles involved; namely, that by avoiding duplication of effort more could be accomplished. However, there was also the thought present, and sometimes expressed, that they wanted to have a balanced defense of their own in case NATO did not succeed. In other words, it was again a question of confidence, a question of overcoming uncertainty and doubt.

In Congress there were demands for proof that the Europeans would carry an appropriate share of the burden of common defense. In Europe, just as understandably, there was reluctance to extend risks and expenses until America's participation was clearly evident.

In addition, there were Europe's internal tensions that complicated the job. France was unwilling to give up any part of its preoccupation with the defense against Germany. The Benelux countries wanted to make sure that Britain as well as France shared in the actual defense arrangements in their part of Europe. The Scandinavians felt they were out on a flank and dangerously exposed on their end of the strategic arc. England tried to preserve her strength for the preservation of the remnants of her empire. And this is just the beginning of the list.

Through a series of conferences, Secretary Acheson worked with great patience and skill to drive home the point that NATO would have no meaning at all unless a really joint effort was made at common defense and mutual aid, and his arguments won the day. There would have been no NATO without Dean Acheson.

The major problem in these discussions soon proved to be the question of German participation in the defense of Europe. The German people, divided between East and West, were still under occupation following the defeat and destruction of Hitler. But the land they inhabit is the very core of Europe, and the people who live in it have proved over the centuries that they have the will and the ability to defend it. Without Germany, the defense of Europe was a rear-guard action on the shores of the Atlantic Ocean. With Germany, there could be a defense in depth, powerful enough to offer effective resistance to aggression from the East.

The logic behind this situation is very plain. Any map will show it, and a little arithmetic will prove what the addition of German manpower means to the strength of the joint defense of Europe.

To bring the Germans into the defense arrangements of Europe and to spur the Europeans on to great efforts themselves were the two main efforts required in making NATO work. The Germans wanted restoration of their full sovereignty before they assumed their place in the scheme of defense, but the French kept insisting that Germany had to be kept under controls. In conference after conference it seemed impossible to break this deadlock.

When Dean Acheson went to these conferences, he would send me a daily cable with a full summary of the day's events. This was not the same as the report which the delegation secretary would compile for the use of the State Department. It was an entirely personal account, dictated by the Secretary himself and intended for me alone. In this manner I would know from day to day what was going on behind the closed doors of the conference. Acheson always kept me fully informed about every move he intended to make.

One of the most important of this series of NATO conferences was the one held in New York in September 1950.

I had been reviewing the difficulties that had been encountered in Europe and realized we had to take into account the anxiety of our European allies in the face of the developments in the Far East. Many of them were fearful that we would now turn most of our attention to

Korea and that the European defense would become subordinate. It was therefore decided, as evidence of our concern about the defense of Europe, to send over additional United States troops. These American forces would be part of a balanced European defense force which would include the Germans. This force eventually would have a supreme commander.

Acheson took this plan with him when he went to New York to meet French Foreign Minister Schuman and British Foreign Secretary Bevin for preliminary talks on September 12. Both statesmen realized at once that we had moved a very considerable distance to encourage European action, but Schuman's instructions from his government were to oppose any arrangement that would bring about the creation of a German army or of anything that could serve as the framework for such an army. Bevin was immediately taken with the idea of a supreme commander. He thought the appointment of a supreme commander, especially an American, would spur the Europeans to action more than anything else. Our thought on this was to do what had been done in World War II in the molding of the invasion forces: set up a joint staff to work on preliminaries and appoint a supreme commander when there is something for him to command.

Acheson described the situation to me:

September 15, 12:15 A.M.
PERSONAL FOR THE PRESIDENT FROM ACHESON
After two days of conferences which had persistently failed in coming to grips with the central problem of the defense of Europe, I asked for and obtained a private conference attended only by me, Bevin, Schuman and our three High Commissioners for Germany. The purpose of this talk was to get away from minor difficulties of language and really reach the essence of the problem. This purpose was achieved; and, while the results were immediately discouraging, I think that we may be getting somewhere.

I pointed out that you had been able to bring about a complete revolution in American foreign policy, based upon the realities of the international situation. We were prepared to take steps which were absolutely unprecedented in our history, to place substantial forces in Europe, to put these forces into an integrated force for the defense of Europe, to agree to a command structure, to agree to a supreme commander, to join in a program for integrating European production, to take far reaching steps in the financial field, but all based upon the expectation that others would do their part, and that the entire scheme would result in the creation of such power that chances of peace would be immeasurably improved; and, if contrary to our hopes and beliefs war should come, we had a first class chance to win it. I went on to say that this involved a defense in Europe as far to the east as possible, and that such a defense was not possible without facing squarely and deciding wisely the question of German participation. I pointed out that in our discussions the British and French had been prepared to accept what we offered, had been reticent about their own contributions;

and had flatly refused to face in any way the question of German participation. I, therefore, wanted to talk about this question with the gloves off and see exactly where we stood.

The ensuing discussion brought out very clearly two fundamental facts. The first was that Bevin who really agreed with me, had been put under wraps by his government and was not permitted to say anything. This grows out of the current debate in the House of Commons on this very subject, in which the Labor Government has a pathological fear of Churchill and does not dare say anything for fear that it will leak to the American press and be used by Churchill in the debate. I hope that this situation is not permanent and may clear up in the near future.

On the part of Schuman the difficulty was deeper. His attitude was that he was not able or willing, as the spokesman of his government, to take any decision even on principle in regard to German participation until the forces of the Allies had been so strengthened in Europe that the French Government could face the psychological reaction to the creation of German armed force.

When it became clear that neither man had any discretion and that therefore argument could not result in any immediate change of position, I suggested that we examine the positions taken by each of them solely for the purpose of clarifying our minds so that when they had some flexibility returned to them, we would understand how each of us thought about the various points.

I think it is fair to say that the discussion was useful. It completely blew out of the water the practicality of leaving the beginning of the formation of German military units until the Allied forces were completely supplied with equipment. I think it destroyed any logical basis to their fear that the bringing of Germans into the creation of Allied strength in the west increased the possibility of preventive war by the Russians as against the mere creation of Allied strength. I think we showed that it was quite possible to deal with the German Government on the issue, not as supplicants, but merely as agreeing to proposals already made by Adenauer to contribute units to European forces and to force him to accept conditions to our acceptance of his proposal.

All this was useful, but the discussion ended with one situation quite clear: That they were prepared to accept what we offered but they were not prepared to accept what we asked. In this situation I am now taking the attitude, not that we are imposing specific conditions, but that we are unable to proceed with the discussion until their attitude is made more clear. The result is that no agreed papers on the matters on which they are ready to agree will issue from our delegation. We have ended the first part of our tripartite meeting with communique which cannot announce decisions and, therefore, says merely that we are continuing our discussions in the Council and will resume them next week.

In the Council meetings I intend to argue the issues all over again and have already been assured of vigorous support from the smaller European countries. It seems highly unlikely that we can reach satisfactory conclusions by Saturday night, but I feel sure that the British and French will become increasingly uncomfortable on their seats. It may be that we shall have to have further meetings. It may be that I shall have to come back to you for further instructions before the matter goes too far. For the present there is no need for you to worry, although I think you must face the strong possibility of leaks to the press and stories that all is not going well. I feel reasonably sure that we can work this out; that it may be a question of whose nerve lasts longer, but that it just must come out in the right way.

I am dictating this wire to you myself so that you may know my mind fully and instruct me at any point where you think I may be wrong or give me any guidance which you want me to have. I shall keep you fully and intimately informed.

Bevin was instructed by his government to join Acheson in working for a united defense force with German participation. As a result of Acheson's efforts, all member countries except France accepted the idea of a united force, though the countries on the outer rim of the alliance, such as Norway and Portugal, were not as enthusiastic about it as the Benelux countries. But in principle, only French objections remained in the path of erecting an effective defense for western Europe.

The talks with the French and British were continued while the Atlantic Council was recessed. The Defense Ministers of the three countries joined the Foreign Ministers at the conference table. France sent Jules Moch. From London came Emanuel Shinwell. And I sent General George C. Marshall, whom I had just persuaded to return from his well-deserved retirement, to take over the serious job of running the Defense Department in this period of crisis.

In the candid talks to these men it became very plain that the French knew just as well as we or the British that they would need German manpower if Europe was to be successfully defended. They were convinced that the French parliament would never agree to any proposal that would permit Germans to be armed before there was a European defense force actually in being. The French Defense Minister, M. Moch, said quite frankly that he would need the answer to three questions before he could make up his mind about German participation in the united force that was planned:

1. How many German divisions are contemplated?
2. How many U.S. divisions will be sent to Europe?
3. When can the U.S. send them?

I was glad to learn that General Marshall and Mr. Shinwell were able to persuade the French minister that it was possible to agree in principle without having specific answers to these questions. Marshall drew up a list of ten items that could be done by the NATO powers without further delay and without prejudicing a later decision on the questions Moch wanted answered. What was more important, Marshall urged, was to draw up an understanding in principle. The United States, for instance, could state that it would send additional troops to Europe as soon as possible, but, with fighting under way in Korea, it could not specify a date. In the same way, the French could agree that a united force should be built up for the defense of Europe and that German manpower should be included, even though it was not possible at this stage to say how large or how small a part the Germans should play. I thought that this typical, clearheaded approach by Marshall made a lot of sense.

In a later separate meeting, Acheson and Marshall assured Schuman and Moch that we would be willing to discuss with the French the problem of helping them with the financing of their military program. With this assurance, the French were now willing to agree to the general principles of the proposal that Acheson had originally placed before Bevin and Schuman. On September 26 a communiqué from New York announced that the North Atlantic Council had agreed on the establishment of a unified force for the defense of Europe. This left a great many things still to be agreed on. M. Pleven, the French Premier, came out with a plan that would let the Germans participate in the European defense force but only as additions to existing regimental combat teams. This was at least something to work on, even if it did not satisfy everybody.

The main thing, we all thought, was to get the project of a unified force started. It had been understood by all concerned that the supreme commander to be designated would be an American. As a matter of fact, in our planning of the program I had always had General Eisenhower in mind as the logical man for this unique job. As the Allied commander in Europe during World War II, General Eisenhower had shown remarkable ability in leadership in heading up a combined headquarters for the forces of several nations. He was very popular in Europe, and at the head of a European defense headquarters would demonstrate our determination and our desire to make the joint effort a success.

On October 19 I added this handwritten postscript to a letter to Eisenhower: "First time you are in town, I wish you'd come in and see me. If I send for you, we'll start the 'speculators' to work."

General Eisenhower called on me at the White House on October 28. I told him what I had in mind for him to do. He heard me out in silence and then said he would accept the assignment. Eisenhower told me that he would take it because he was a soldier and this was a call to duty. But it was the kind of duty, he told me, that he accepted gladly because it was a job that very badly needed to be done. He believed firmly, he said, in the importance of bringing the nations of Europe together and doing it speedily.

Two days later I received the Defense Ministers and defense chiefs of the NATO countries and was able to tell them in confidence that a top-ranking general would be available for the NATO High Command and that I had already conferred with him about it.

The appointment itself was not made until December 18. The procedure was for the North Atlantic Council to pass a resolution in which they asked me to designate an American officer as Supreme Commander for the Allied Powers in Europe. At the same time, Dean Acheson sent me a message from the Council meeting in Brussels in which he reported that the Council members had unanimously expressed the hope that I would appoint General Eisenhower. I replied at once that General Eisenhower had been so designated.

The new Supreme Commander left for Europe in January 1951 for a quick survey of the situation. He returned then to Washington and made a full report to me, and I suggested that he also report on the European situation to the Congress, and by radio to the nation. I think these reports were effective because they were made with utmost candor and sincerity.

Eisenhower reported to me, and later at a Cabinet meeting, that while he had found general agreement on the principles of a unified defense for Europe, and general agreement also that such a defense could be successfully organized, he found it much tougher trying to reach an understanding with each country as to its contribution. He said that at each stop on his recent survey trip he would ask, "What are you going to do? You have to tell me exactly what you are going to do so that I can report back to the United States Government."

The answers to this question, Eisenhower said, all tripped over one hard, tough fact. This fact was the poverty of western Europe. General Eisenhower said he had found that this poverty meant that no one yardstick could be used to measure the contributions of the various countries. We could not, for example, expect the western Europeans to spend the same percentage of their budget on defense that we were going to spend. They were so desperately poor that some of them could not spend any more than they were already doing.

The main thing, Eisenhower said when he spoke at the Cabinet meeting, was for us to get this "combined spiral of strength going up." "These people," he said, "believe in the cause. Now, they have got to believe in themselves. They have got to have confidence that they can do the job. The way we can give them that confidence is by sending equipment and by sending American units over there to help morale."

General Eisenhower was fully in accord with my policy in Europe. He worked for it diligently and devotedly from the day of his appointment as Supreme Commander until he returned to the United States in 1952 to enter the political arena. Throughout his stay in Europe he frequently wrote to me directly or through Averell Harriman, and he was always assured of my full support in everything he was doing in Europe.

Near the end of his first year in Europe, in early January 1952, Eisenhower wrote me a long, detailed letter reporting on the first year's work. He reviewed the progress that had been made in the direction of a European army and discussed some of the major things that still remained to be done. He took the position that those countries of the alliance on the continent of Europe would have to work toward economic and political consolidation. Britain could not easily be fitted into such a picture, and he agreed with the British that they should be associated with the proposed European Defense Community but not directly take part in it. But there was some hope, in Eisenhower's opinion, that the return of Winston Churchill to the government in England would mean more emphasis on political union. Eisenhower urged me to persuade Churchill, in his forthcoming visit to Washington, to make "a ringing statement that would minimize British non-participation and emphasize British moral, political, and military support for the European Army."

Churchill's visit was a welcome reunion with an old friend, and I was looking forward to it. Though he had been out of the government for six years, we had remained in frequent personal contact. To greet him once again as head of His Majesty's Government was a distinct pleasure for me, even though I knew we would have to resolve many difficult problems between the two of us and our staffs.

During the three days of discussion with Churchill, we covered a great range of topics, and among them was NATO. Churchill commented that he realized very well the great burden that the United States was carrying in the common cause, and said that the United Kingdom would bear all it could. However, he pointed out that they had drawn very heavily on the life and energy of the fifty million people in their island in recent years, and added that great overseas investments had been lost to them. England, he said, had a great many problems that could be traced to the past. The point now was that there was no use in the United Kingdom's pretending that it could bear burdens that it could not bear.

I replied to the Prime Minister that, in the fifty years before World War I, the British and the French and the Germans had invested many billions of dollars in our country. Some of this had been used up, in World War I and World War II, as the British and the French paid for their war supplies. The German investment, of course, had been taken over as enemy property. "Your reserves," I said, "are now in effect a financial surplus here, which we hope to get reinvested abroad under Point Four and in other ways. The rehabilitation of the free world is one of the most important things we have to do. We want to keep the free world a going concern."

I reminded the Prime Minister that we had sent abroad some sixty billion dollars since the end of the war but that it was important to bear in mind that this was an election year and that Congress was rarely inclined to increase foreign spending while an election was in the offing.

Churchill said he certainly understood what effect an election had on a country's position in the world. England had gone through a general election during the past year, and it certainly made it difficult for His Majesty's Government to act with vigor while its political life was at stake. But he thought that they were through now with electioneering in England, "for a few years at any rate."

The approach of the 1952 presidential election caused a great deal of anxiety in friendly capitals. Everywhere the same doubts and fears began to spring up again that had been so dominant before the treaty was signed and General Eisenhower sent over to organize the defense. We found that statesmen of other nations were holding back because they wanted to be sure that the commitments they might make would not be made to an American who voted for an isolationist administration.

They were relieved, therefore, so our diplomats reported, to know that the nominees of both parties were men who believed in the basic need for NATO and European defense. But it is one of the facts of American foreign policy, and one that those in responsibility must bear in mind, that an impending change in administration in Washington makes our friends abroad anxious and our enemies hopeful. They all remember what happened when Harding replaced Wilson, and what calamity it meant for the world.

When the time came for me to turn over the reins of the government to General Eisenhower, NATO was one of the projects that I could pass on to him in the full knowledge that he would understand my motives and share them. He had, after all, played a most important part in it.

The treaties with Germany and the European Defense Community Treaty still awaited completion. We had hoped that these treaties would be ratified toward the end of 1952, but both in France and, to a lesser degree, in Germany resistance to the proposed arrangements had flared up sharply in November, and further delay was likely, though this was delay over matters of timing and emphasis, not over principles.

The structure of western European defense had been built—built largely because we were ready to break with tradition and enter into a peacetime military alliance; because we had been ready to assume not only our share but the leadership in the forging of joint forces; because we had recognized that the peace of the world would best be served by a Europe that was strong and united, and that therefore European unity and European strength were the best guarantees for the prevention of another major war.

CHAPTER 18

I was raised on a farm, and even as a boy I helped my father there. My home state of Missouri is primarily a farm state, and my brother Vivian farms to this day. I know what the farmer's problems are. I learned early, when I worked in a bank, how important the farmers' prosperity is to the welfare of the country.

When the crops failed, two things happened to the bank; the farmers withdrew their deposits, and later many farmers came to borrow money on their land. When the farmers were hurt, merchants and tradesmen suffered. To see this happen was a basic lesson in economics. It was a practical demonstration that prosperous farmers make for a prosperous nation, and when farmers are in trouble the nation is in trouble.

In 1921 the bottom fell out of agricultural prices, and throughout the twenties the farmer was barely able to hang on. Then came 1932 and the victory of the Democrats. Sound policies followed, restoring farm prosperity, for the New Deal knew that farm income had to be stabilized if the national economy as a whole was to be stabilized. Soil conservation, the Triple A, Farm Credit Administration, rural electrification—all these and other measures contributed to the return of farm prosperity. Then World War II gave this trend a strong push as American crops were shipped overseas to help feed our allies and as greatly increased employment at home increased domestic food consumption to an all-time high. Even after the war, relief shipments and Marshall Plan aid continued to demand the products of American farms.

Throughout these years the government had guaranteed the price of farm products at a fixed level, but the continued high demand had kept the government-guaranteed surplus at a minimum. The result was that in 1948 the American farmer had reached an economic position better than he had ever known before.

Cash farm income was up to more than thirty billion dollars a year from less than five billion in 1932, and the farm-mortgage debt had dropped twenty-five per cent since 1941. Bank deposits and savings of farmers were twenty-two billion dollars, the highest in our history.

While this agricultural prosperity was due partly to special factors in the postwar situation, the sound farm legislation which had been adopted since 1932 provided a much better basis for sustained farm prosperity than we had ever had before. In 1932, for example, we had had no soil-conservation program, no price-support program, no school-lunch program, and only a limited agricultural-research program.

But the farmers still had reason to be fearful. A sudden change, such as that of 1921, might cause the bottom to fall out of agricultural prices, and I intended to do everything I could to prevent an agricultural depression from happening. The farmer, I felt, was entitled to real protection against a postwar slump, and the nation as a whole had to be protected against a farm depression. I wanted a program of action to insure that the gains made since 1932 would be held and that we could move forward with the job of building our economy on a foundation provided by the organized, sustained, and realistic prosperity of American agriculture.

I was concerned about the many farm families who were not sharing fairly in the progress of American life. In too many rural communities, as my reports showed, housing, medical services, and educational facilities were still inadequate. Some farms were still isolated by poor roads. Others were still without the benefits of electricity.

It was my conviction that the federal government had a definite responsibility in building for lasting agricultural abundance and in making farm life attractive to future generations of Americans. The sound and far-reaching legislation of the preceding sixteen years constituted an excellent basis for continued progress, but we needed a number of extensions and improvements in our farm program.

Most of all, we needed a permanent system of price supports for agricultural commodities. I believed that the entire nation should be protected against the wide swings in farm prices that in the past had caused economic insecurity that affected all of us. Furthermore, we needed a more vigorous soil-conservation program, and it was important that steps be taken to maintain adequate markets for farm products and to improve the methods of distributing them to consumers.

In order to provide answers to these and other problems, I asked Charles F. Brannan, the Secretary of Agriculture, to make an over-all study of the farm situation and to draw up specific proposals, as Brannan and I had discussed various plans and ideas on three or four different occasions. When the final draft of his report was ready, he came to the White House, and we went over it item by item.

The purpose of the program was to assure the farmer a stable income, and the device by which this was to be accomplished made good sense to me. Each commodity affected would be allowed to seek its level in the market. Then, if this level was below a fair return to the farmer, the government—at the end of a predetermined period—would pay the farmer directly the difference between what he got on the average for his commodity over the particular marketing period and what was calculated by a formula to be a fair price.

There was nothing new about this approach. It had been applied to cotton as the first price mechanism in 1937 and 1938 and was being used for the support of sugar beets, as it still is. Each year every producer of sugar beets and sugar cane in the United States receives a check from the government for the difference if the price at which he sells his crop is less than the price determined by a statutory formula. Similar legislation for wool has been in effect for an equally long period.

Specifically, the plan Brannan asked me to approve would see that perishable commodities like meat, dairy products, poultry, and eggs would be put on the market at prices which consumers could afford. The program was to apply first of all to dairy products, for many marketing studies indicated that milk prices and milk consumption were closely related. As the price of milk goes down, the volume of milk consumed goes up correspondingly. Thus we could almost put our finger on how many more quarts of milk could be sold at a given lower market price, and this approach also provided a reliable index for other commodities.

The basic idea of the plan was to approach the economics of agriculture not from the point of view of agriculture, as had formerly been done, but with an eye to production and abundance. We wanted to make it increasingly worth while for the farmer to produce, and at the same time keep, the consumer price level at a point at which the average man could afford to buy. Without some such policy, the price level of farm products plays its part in a vicious circle: the more the farmer plants, the less he gets, the less he can spend; the less he spends, the fewer non-farm goods are bought; the fewer non-farm goods are sold, the less money is available to pay for the things the farmer wants to sell. And the Brannan Plan, as it soon came to be called, was a blueprint for breaking this circle.

"Price supports," Brannan pointed out, "are the farmer's equivalent of the laboring man's minimum-wage, social-security, and collective-bargaining arrangements." Like labor, the farmer lacks equality at the bargaining table. The prices he pays for products are generally fixed, many times by monopolies or by tacit agreements among producers. But the individual farmer must sell when his crops are ready for the market, and the result is that he must take whatever price he is offered. I remember years when wheat was as low as forty-four cents a bushel, and other times when it went as high as three dollars. I know that corn has fluctuated between twenty-two cents and $2.88—rye between thirty cents and four dollars—cotton between five and forty cents a pound.

The old laissez-faire theorists would tell us that the answer is to cut down on producing units until the fittest survive. But this theory is without humanity, for in human terms it means the breakup of homes, the destruction of families, and the surrender of the family farm to the absentee landlord or the corporate owner. No American government worthy of the name can allow this sort of thing to recur every twenty years or so. The farmers' sense of security is a vital part of the foundation of American life.

What was important about the Brannan Plan was that it shifted the emphasis in price supports from commodity purchases to production payments. Under the law as it then read—and as it still reads today, I regret to say—the price of agricultural products is supported either by government loans at the parity level or by government purchases in the open market. The result is that large surpluses accumulate in the government warehouses whenever prices fall below the guarantee level set by Congress, but the consumer does not get the benefit of the excess supply. This sets in motion a spiral effect: the consumer, because of higher prices, buys less; the farmer, for the same reason, is encouraged to raise even more; and the imbalance tends to become worse.

Under the Brannan Plan, however, if the price of a given product included in the plan should fall below support levels, the government would make a direct payment to the farmer for the difference between the price he received and the support price. The consumer, nevertheless, would have the benefit of the lower price. He would be encouraged to purchase more. This increased demand would tend to bring the price up again. And in this way the support of the farmer would be self-compensating and, in the true sense of the word, would contribute to the general welfare.

There was also another important change in the manner in which we proposed to make price supports available. As I have always seen it, there is only one really sound reason for farm-price supports, and that is to maintain a decent standard of living for ordinary farm families. However, under the commodity-purchase program, large payments were being made (and still are) to corporations operating vast acreages almost as if they were factories in mass production. But these are not the kinds of farm operators who require government support to hold their position. There is probably a place in our economy for this kind of farm operation, but it is not as vital to the life and welfare of the nation as the work of the millions of families who—often literally— "toil in the sweat of their brow."

The Brannan Plan contained a provision that would have excluded from production payments the yields of any one farm over and above a certain limit. This limit was defined as eighteen hundred units of production, and at 1949 prices this would have meant, in practice, about twenty thousand dollars' worth of the affected commodity.

The unit of production was defined as ten bushels of corn or the cash equivalent in other crops. The reason corn was chosen as the basic crop is, of course, evident: our farm economy is essentially a corn economy. Not only do we raise large amounts of corn, but also virtually all our cattle and dairy production depends on corn as the principal feed staple.

No other country in the world runs its whole agricultural economy on corn. This is explained by the fact that the United States produces every year about 3,300,000,000 bushels of corn, and out of this production come all of our poultry, eggs, beef, hogs, and all of our livestock products. There are other feed grains, of course, but all of our farm stock from chickens to the finest cattle depends primarily on corn for production.

By fixing the unit of production in terms of corn, the relationship of all other farm products to be supported would be stabilized in reference to the price of corn. If, for example, eighteen hundred units of production in corn brought a cash return of twenty thousand dollars, then whatever yielded twenty thousand dollars in wheat or rye or potatoes would also be eighteen hundred units of production. And eighteen hundred units was to have been the maximum on which production payments were to be made.

Representatives of associations of small farmers complained that this limit was too high and that it did not channel the proposed benefits to the small operator who needed them most. But it was not the purpose of the plan to redistribute the wealth. I wanted a farm program that would serve the farm, and I wanted it designed in such a way that agricultural corporations would not be able to grow fat on it. The unit limitation as written would have applied to only about two per cent of the farm operators of the United States, but these produced twenty-five per cent of the total dollar volume of all the farm products of the nation.

Secretary Brannan warned me that this recommendation in favor of what we called the family-sized farmer would be attacked as containing political implications. It was a new and unusual proposal for farm economy, he said, and would probably be criticized as too radical or labeled a political gesture. This did not trouble me, however, for I had given the provision most careful study.

"Well, Charlie, I said, "it is right, isn't it?"

Brannan replied that, in his opinion, it was.

"Then it stays in," I told him.

Interestingly enough, the unit limitation was hardly criticized at all, and the reason for this, I believe, was that the critics of the plan saw the irrefutable reasoning on which the limitation policy was based.

As soon as the proposals were made public, a great hue and cry was raised in the press over what many writers called the socialistic and political implications of the Brannan Plan. Secretary Brannan discussed the program at a joint hearing of the House Committee on Agriculture and the Senate Committee on Agriculture and Forestry on April 7, 1949, and from then on there was a great deal of heated discussion on the floor of both the House and the Senate with respect to the plan.

I had expected criticism of this sort. All the ballyhoo that was raised over the Brannan Plan was similar to the furor that was created by the American Medical Association over the health-insurance program. The American Farm Bureau Federation, which represented the special-interest farmers under the leadership of Allan B. Kline, attacked the price-support program on the same grounds that the private utilities companies fought every attempt of the government to make public power available to the people, and as the American Medical Association fought the health program which would benefit all the people.

I paid no attention to the "anti-Brannan Plan" campaign, which cost the Farm Bureau members more than half a million dollars in one year. I knew what the farmers themselves wanted and needed because I had talked with thousands of them personally in 1948 about it. I have never been interested in what the big, expensive lobbies in Washington have to say about farming, real estate, electricity, medicine, or any other subject. They do not represent the views of the man on the job. Instead, they represent selfish special interests who support the lobbies to fight their legislation battles for them.

What I had to overcome was the traditional attitude toward such scare words as "socialization," "socialism," and "subsidization." Industry and business have demanded subsidies from the federal government for generations—in the form of mailing permits, freight rates, tariffs disguised by the word "protective" for special-privilege use, tax privileges for plant construction, and other fields. In our time, agriculture is no less dependent upon such assistance than industry, labor, or business. The parity device is only one effort that has been made in the interest of bringing farming up to the level shared by other segments of the economy.

The Brannan Plan was nothing new. It was consistent with the policy of every Democratic administration that has tried to elevate the standards of living of the American rural population through price supports and through a score of other measures designed to strengthen and stabilize this basic occupation.

The opposition has always tried to convince the farmer that he is being placed under the heel of controls. To make the parity legislation work, the farmers must agree to controls. In every election since Roosevelt the Republicans have tried to coax the farmer to vote down controls, so that parities would then find their own level. If the farmer finally accepts this advice, the bottom will drop out of prices and he will go back to 1921.

My hope was to see the farmer go on to even higher levels of prosperity than he enjoyed throughout the administrations of Roosevelt and myself. This could have been accomplished only through a positive program such as the one worked out with Secretary Brannan. Unfortunately the Congress refused to enact the plan into law.

CHAPTER 19

All my life I have fought against prejudice and intolerance.

As a young man I was disturbed by the attitude of some people toward other races and religions. And as I grew older, I could never understand how people could forget the origins and blessings of their own freedom.

I have little patience with people who take the Bill of Rights for granted. The Bill of Rights, contained in the first ten amendments to the Constitution, is every American's guarantee of freedom.

Equality of opportunity and equal justice under the law are not mere phrases or fine words. These are the living achievements of a people who had rebelled against despotism. Many generations had fled to this country to get away from oppression by their own governments. And it has always troubled me how some who called themselves Americans could themselves become oppressors.

Those old and young fellows who wrote the Constitution knew what they were doing. They had been pounded down by the absolute monarchy of George III. They knew the meaning of oppression and persecution.

Jefferson was one of those who said that he would not support the Constitution if the Bill of Rights was not made part of it.

One of the most important guarantees under the Bill of Rights is the right to claim exemption from self-incrimination. This is a fundamental basis of our liberty and is provided for in the Fifth Amendment.

With the advent of Communism the world has been introduced to the outrage of brain-washing. By this method men and women are forced to confess against themselves, whether they are guilty or not.

In the police state no individual has any immunity from persecution. People condemned to brain-washing can have no hope because they are deprived of all rights.

In this country every person is protected against persecution by the Bill of Rights.

In recent years I have been alarmed by the reckless attempts to undermine some of the guarantees in the Bill of Rights. Men like McCarthy have made it appear that any person claiming his rights under the Fifth Amendment is guilty. McCarthy has even gone so far as to brand as "Fifth Amendment Communists" those persons who sought to invoke their constitutional rights. He has charged these witnesses with abusing the Fifth Amendment.

The fact is that the abuse came not from the people invoking the Fifth Amendment but from those who made it appear that a man claiming his rights under it is automatically guilty without having been proved guilty.

We must understand, of course, that as a matter of government necessity, in the investigation of crime or subversion, it is essential for the investigative authorities to have sources of information which they cannot reveal. But when it comes to an individual being charged with a crime, under our procedure he has a right to be confronted with his accusers.

If the government cannot produce witnesses in court, then it cannot prosecute. And if a man cannot be prosecuted in the courts, then he should not be persecuted by a Senate or House committee. That is my theory. Of course every government does its best to get rid of every disloyal employee. But we should not, and we did not, want to treat the remaining 99.9 per cent of government employees, who are decent and honorable, in a way that would ruin their reputations.

When you have over 2,300,000 people employed in the national government, some are bound to be bad and some weak. Persons in government, like other people, are exposed to associations and temptations that occasionally may break down some of them. But I do not believe in taking hearsay charges against any person, especially against anyone who has the background to qualify as a government servant.

Frequently hearsay evidence is accepted as the truth and is used to smear a government employee in such a way that he cannot defend himself. This is what the Communists do, what McCarthy did, what the so-called Un-American Activities Committee in the House did. It simply cannot be squared with the Bill of Rights.

Any move to abridge the rights of the individual under the Constitution—no matter in what form—is a danger to the freedom of all.

Self-appointed guardians of the country and bigots have even carried on attacks against our schools and colleges and churches. "Little Dies Committees" have sprung up in some state legislatures, and the epidemic of investigations has infected school boards and town councils.

I do not believe schoolteachers should be required to take a special oath.

I think it proper, where a school is publicly supported, that a teacher take the same oath of office as any other public official to support the Constitution of the United States and the government of the state in which the teacher lives.

But it is wrong to tell teachers not to discuss or not to teach subject matter that should be taught in a free educational system. We should have freedom to teach and to learn, and that does not mean that a teacher is disloyal because he teaches everything there is to learn. There is no limit to knowledge. A person learns as long as he lives.

In education we must not limit the opportunities for generating ideas. People must have freedom of mind for research that makes progress, otherwise there is no use in having an educational system. If everyone remained in the same groove and were taught exactly the same thing, we would end up with a nation of mediocrities. Men with ideas can express those ideas only where there is freedom of education.

Whenever we come to the point where we are spying on each other, as was done under Hitler and Mussolini and as is now done in Russia and Spain, we cease to be the republic we were set up to be. If we cannot have confidence in our neighbors and the teachers who are teaching our children, then our country is in trouble.

Everyone has the right to express what he thinks. That, of course, lets the crackpots in. But if you cannot tell a crackpot when you see one, then you ought to be taken in.

I don't think there is any danger that this country will be upset from within.

From 1930 to 1953 we had the greatest social and economic revolution in our history without violence. This was done in an orderly manner under the Constitution by the majority of the people, through the ballot, without curtailing the rights of individuals. Of course this great social change did not please some people, especially those who would like to see in this country a higher class and a lower class of society. But the everyday man today has more of the better things of life, the country is better off, and, anyway, the people will not stand for being divided into classes.

But no matter what social and economic changes are brought about, a real democracy is always careful to protect the minority from the majority.

In the federal, state, county, and city governments, unless the men in control are strongly imbued with the constitutional rights of the people, the first thing you know you will have the Ku Klux Klan, or the Silver Shirts, or something like the German Bunds, organized on the basis of direct action or taking the law into their own hands. Then people will be accused and condemned without any chance of defending themselves.

When the Klan was at its height, homes were invaded and people were tarred and feathered and run out of town. The Klan was anti-Catholic, anti-Jewish, and anti-Negro. I remember some towns in Oklahoma at that time where they had signs, "Negro, don't let the sun set on you here."

Our ideas of freedom came from many people. The greatest government in the history of the world grew out of the inspiration, energy, and ideas which were brought here by the English, the Scotch, the Irish, the Danes, the Swedes, the Dutch, the Germans, the Poles, the Jews, the Italians, and others who came to these shores in search of freedom.

We want to be careful that those freedoms contained in our Bill of Rights are not destroyed by those who incite fear and hysteria and cause injustice.

In times of crisis, involving the security of the nation, the government has to take special measures, of course, to protect itself against sabotage and disloyalty. The operations of the government, with its many defense and diplomatic secrets, must be safeguarded against foreign agents.

But I have always believed that if we are to maintain our republic, in keeping with the Bill of Rights, the government has the paramount responsibility of protecting the rights of the individual against injustice and false accusations.

I recall the periods of mass hysteria in this country which led to witch hunts. Demagogues and unprincipled individuals have always seized upon crises to incite emotional and irrational fears. Racial, religious, and class animosities are stirred up. Charges and accusations are directed against many innocent people in the name of false "patriotism" and hatred of things "foreign."

During such periods of mass excitement, individuals in government are particularly singled out for attack. In recent years, as in other periods, some of the charges have arisen from political rivalry, others from employees seeking to profit at the expense of others, usually their superiors. In such an atmosphere, when one isolated individual employee is found to be disloyal, the incident is used by demagogues to intensify the hysteria, and there is a tendency to condemn *all* employees of the government. There are chronic intolerants among us who are all too ready to condemn a whole race of people, a religious group, a labor union, or a political party when it is discovered that there is one offender among them. This type of wholesale condemnation hurts government morale, and it hurts the country.

I believe that people in positions of responsibility in government should know the historical background of these periods of mass hysteria and the events which have led to them.

For example, during the period when the French Revolution reached its height with the Jacobins in power in France, Jefferson was accused of being a Jacobin, and therefore disloyal. Congress passed the Alien and Sedition Laws in 1798 because it thought that the French revolutionists were trying to gain control of our government.

To enforce the Sedition Laws, the Bill of Rights had to be thrown out the window. When sanity returned, most of the bills which had not expired were repealed.

Later, in 1919, there was the period in which A. Mitchell Palmer, as Attorney General, used the forces of government in raids on many citizens. It was a terrible thing. That was the "Communist hysteria" program of its day.

During other periods of hysteria, attacks on the rights of individuals were made on other pretexts in total disregard of guarantees under the Bill of Rights. But we recovered from all of them. And we will continue to return to sanity after each attack because we have freedom of the press, freedom of religion, a free educational system, and our people vote in free elections giving them control and the right to change their government. When we have these fits of hysteria, we are like the person who has a fit of nerves in public—when he recovers, he is very much ashamed—and so are we as a nation when sanity returns.

This is why I never believed that this government could be subverted or overturned from within by Communists. The security agencies of the government are well able to deal quietly and effectively with any Communists who sneak into the government, without invoking Gestapo methods.

The business of security is a highly specialized operation requiring skilled technicians, experts, and constant vigilance. Security often requires secret action instead of public moves, since open publicity may actually hurt security.

We did not recognize Soviet Russia until 1933. I think that President Roosevelt was right in giving diplomatic recognition to Russia. In doing so he laid down, at that time, certain conditions to be met by the Soviet

Union. One of the most important of these was the Russian commitment to cease all activities inciting revolutionary or Communist propaganda in the United States.

We soon found out that Russia did not keep agreements and that the subversive propaganda did not cease. The Soviet Union used the Third International, or Comintern, as an instrument and a front of revolutionary policy, using the pretext that she had no control over its activities. I have known some politicians in this country who claimed to have no control over their followers if they wanted to break agreements.

During this period the American people were undergoing great economic and social reforms brought on by the economic and financial collapse of the 1930's. Some of our young people and intellectuals seemed attracted to the Russian experiment of setting up a new economy based on Communism. Most of these young people and intellectuals soon learned that they had been duped into believing that Russia was really trying to create a new kind of social and economic order that would abolish depressions, unemployment, hunger, and war. They soon realized that a colossal hoax was being perpetrated by a group of cruel but skillful fanatics who set up a dictatorship with all the trappings of a state religion. What this new system brought to Russia was not Communism or Socialism but simply another type of dictatorship. The individual became the subject of the state in perpetual enslavement, and, as the Russians themselves soon found out, depression, unemployment, hunger, and war were not abolished.

The Soviet Union, getting its power principally from its millions of enslaved labor and vast resources, concentrated on the building of a gigantic military machine. This posed a new kind of threat to the world, because it combined a major military power and a revolutionary force bent upon conquering the world through subversion, revolutionary intrigue, and fifth columns.

Those responsible for the conduct of our government security were fully alert to, and aware of, the new threat of a Communist menace.

In this same period Fascism had begun to develop in Europe. Hitler and Mussolini, using the Communist threat as a means to seize power, began to threaten the peace. As a result of this international tension, Communist and Fascist activity and intrigue were intensified here at home.

It became necessary for the government, in order to keep subversion out of its ranks, to seek special legislation.

Congress passed the Hatch Act on August 2, 1939, under which it was made unlawful for any employee of the government to have membership in a party which advocated the overthrow of the constitutional form of government of the United States. The responsibility of investigation under the Hatch Act was placed in the hands of the Federal Bureau of Investigation.

In this atmosphere of international fear and intrigue it was natural that some demagogues would be tempted to make political capital out of the situation. In 1939, when I was nearing the end of my first term in the Senate, a congressman from Texas, Martin Dies, was sounding off about Communists in government. As chairman of the first House Committee on Un-American Activities he made many wild charges. He conducted hearings in a manner which I charged from the floor of the Senate as being most un-American itself. Witnesses before his committee were too often browbeaten, falsely accused, and given no opportunity to have either the source of charges against them revealed or a chance to disprove the accusations. In fact, people were being tried before a congressional committee instead of a court of law. This was a dangerous misuse of the investigatory powers of Congress, which are solely for the purpose of helping in the preparation of legislation. The methods used by the Dies Committee set a precedent which has plagued the Congress ever since.

I recall Vice-President Garner, that sage from Uvalde, saying to me at that time, "The Dies Committee is going to have more influence on the future of American politics than any other committee of Congress." I did not agree with him. I could not believe that the people would be long misled by the types of charges that were being hurled about or be influenced by such procedures in the handling of so important a matter. I was wrong, and unfortunately Jack Garner's prophecy came true. Something of the quality of American justice and fair play has been sacrificed by the methods of Congressman Dies and his successors in congressional investigations.

In 1939 Europe moved from crisis to crisis. In September, Europe went to war. Although the Fascists and the Communists were supposedly implacable foes, Hitler and Stalin cynically concluded, as a prelude to the war, a non-aggression pact and agreed to divide Poland between themselves. The Western world was shocked.

When Russia invaded Finland, after moving into Poland to the Curzon Line, American public opinion became more outraged with the Communists than at any time since the Communists took over Russia.

Our government, armed with the Hatch Act, now became even more vigilant.

One of the dramatic ironies of history growing out of the Russian-German piratical arrangements over Poland was the German attack on Russia. Without warning, in reckless disregard of everything but conquest, Hitler suddenly turned and struck at the Soviet Union. Once again the balance of the world was changed. And with that came a reversal of our attitude toward Russia.

By necessity and compulsion, Russia was now fighting along with the British and the French against the Nazis. Churchill immediately welcomed Russia as an ally fighting for the same cause, and he was joined in embracing Russia as an ally by all the nations at war with Hitler and Mussolini.

The American people now looked at Russia more sympathetically as the menace of Hitler became more frightening.

Russia soon found that her industrial resources were woefully inadequate against the highly mechanized and rapidly advancing German armies. Stalin appealed desperately to us for assistance, asking for raw material, food, machinery, as well as military and transportation equipment. Our government wanted to help.

It was during this period of America's growing sympathy for Russia that many extremists and pro-Russian supporters began to agitate for all-out support for the Soviet Union. With this surge of sentiment for Russia, it had become the duty of those responsible for our security to take additional precautions to protect the vital interests of this government and nation.

The Russians exploited this sympathy with typical Communist duplicity by subverting sympathizers in many walks of life and duping scores of others.

Some of our most patriotic citizens, including top military and political figures, believed then that Russia could be trusted to help establish a durable peace in the world.

Then came the infamous Japanese attack on Pearl Harbor and the declaration of war against us by Hitler and Mussolini which plunged this nation into World World War II. The Russians now were our active allies and every Russian soldier was fighting our war, just as the Americans woud soon be fighting Russia's war.

In this common battle for survival against most powerful and ruthless foes, we embarked on a gigantic program of supplying the Russian armies with all the material we could spare. We began to send them large quantities of food at a sacrifice to our own needs. We embarked on a vast shipping program and sustained severe losses in an effort to run the blockade of the German submarines.

Although their lives depended upon our help, the Russians showed some signs of strange behavior. They would not exchange information with our military and would not permit our planes to land behind their lines, even if such planes were being delivered to them. They asked that the planes and other supplies be delivered at northern ports or at a Russian base in Iran, south of the Caucasus.

This Russian attitude became even more evident as the tide of victory began to turn and the Russians were in pursuit of the Germans on their front.

But we kept up our help to the Russians, and we made every effort to get along with them. There were several reasons for our doing this. Every enemy engaged by the Russians was one less for us to face. The war in the Pacific was far from being won, and we needed the Russians to help us there. World peace could not be possible without Russian participation.

While we were going along trying to work with the Russians, our professional security people were on the alert. They had a basic rule, and that was to give the benefit of the doubt to no one where there was any suspicion of split allegiance.

From 1940 an organization was set up by a directive of President Roosevelt, made up of the FBI, ONI, and G-2, and charged with all investigatory responsibility in the field of subversion, espionage, and sabotage.

In 1942 President Roosevelt issued a war directive which empowered the Civil Service to bar anyone from employment in government where there was any reasonable doubt as to loyalty.

On February 5, 1943, President Roosevelt issued Executive Order 9300.

Under this order an interdepartmental Committee of Five was appointed to consider and recommend action to all departments of the government, except the War and Navy Departments, on all matters where charges of subversive activity had been made against employees. The War and Navy Departments had their own investigatory machinery, but these departments could also call on this Committee of Five.

This committee was empowered to receive all completed investigation reports made by the Federal Bureau of Investigation on complaints filed with them and advise all departments and agencies on the procedure and action to be taken. In turn the committee had to report to the FBI actions taken by the departments.

The Executive Order specifically provided that nothing should be done by this committee to limit the authority of any department or agency to suspend any employee as provided by law, to bar an immediate arrest, and to transfer to court jurisdiction any case in which the Department of Justice might find such action warranted.

Thus the government had been engaged since 1942 in checking the loyalty of its employees. Changes and improvements were made as defects appeared in the system. Investigations by the Civil Service Commission under the leadership of Arthur S. Flemming had been augmented by the FBI.

In 1946 I directed a sweeping study of the government's loyalty procedures to tighten the security program without violating the Bill of Rights.

On November 25, 1946, I issued Executive Order 9806, creating the President's Temporary Commission on Employee Loyalty. I instructed this Commission, first, to inquire into the standards and procedures for investigation of persons employed by the government or applicants for government jobs; second, to inquire into the removal or disqualification of any disloyal or subversive persons; third, to recommend improvements in existing legislative and administrative procedure in connection with loyalty investigations; fourth, to establish administrative responsibility in loyalty cases and define standards of loyalty so as to protect the government against the employment of disloyal or subversive persons; fifth, to set up standards of procedure to insure fair hearings to persons accused.

I appointed the following to serve on the Commission (as representatives of their respective agencies):

A. Devitt Vanech, Special Assistant to the Attorney General, Department of Justice (chairman);

John E. Peurifoy, Special Assistant to Under Secretary of State for Administration, Department of State;

Edward H. Foley, Jr., Assistant Secretary of the Treasury, Department of the Treasury;

Kenneth C. Royall, Under Secretary of War, Department of War;

John L. Sullivan, Under Secretary of the Navy, Department of the Navy; and

Harry B. Mitchell, President, Civil Service Commission.

The Commission submitted its report to me on March 20, 1947. It pointed out that historically the Civil Service Commission was prohibited from inquiring into an employee's or prospective employee's political or religious opinions or affiliations and that this had been considered essential to a non-partisan public service. It was only with the Hatch Act of 1939 that a category of "pernicious political activity" had been identified that could properly be prohibited and searched out. The Commission's report then traced the development of legislative and executive action since 1939 aimed at the elimination of disloyal persons from the government service.

The Commission concluded, on the basis of a comprehensive survey of government agencies, that there was virtually no uniformity in the administrative handling of the problem. Standards of judgment differed from agency to agency, as did procedures. There was also considerable difference of opinion as to the kind of program that would best accomplish the purpose.

That some sort of program for combating subversion within the government was needed, the Commission was entirely agreed upon. They had heard testimony from the various intelligence and security agencies of the government, who had told them exactly what the international situation was and that attempts to infiltrate our government might be expected. On this last point the Commission reported that while it believed that "the employment of disloyal or subversive persons presents more than a speculative threat to our system of government, it [the Commission] is unable, based on the facts presented to it, to state with any degree of certainty how far-reaching that threat is."

The Commission said that it realized that on this whole subject of employee loyalty hysteria, emotion, and irresponsible thinking could easily play havoc and that an intelligent, realistic, and factual approach was needed. The Commission recommended that each department and agency should set up its own loyalty procedures but that minimum standards should be set up for all government agencies by Executive Order. All persons entering the employ of any department or agency should be investigated for loyalty, in most instances by the Civil Service Commission. All present employees' names should be checked against the FBI files for information that might adversely reflect on their loyalty.

The procedure for the determination of loyalty cases, the Commission recommended, should consist of a loyalty board in each agency and a loyalty review board in the Civil Service Commission. This review board should act as a co-ordinator of agency policies in the field of employee loyalty, as an adviser to the President and to the agencies in these matters, and as an appeal board for cases handled by the agency loyalty boards except where the law gave to the agency the right to make summary dismissals.

The employee charged with being disloyal should be entitled to a written notice of the charges and to an administrative hearing, including the right to be represented by counsel of his own choosing.

The Commission recommended that "the underlying standard for either refusal or employment or removal from employment in loyalty cases shall be that, on all the evidence, reasonable grounds exist for believing that the person involved is disloyal to the government of the United States." A number of factors were then listed that might contribute to such a finding.

I examined the report of the Commission with great care. It seemed to me that, generally, it approached the subject in a sane and sensible manner. In a few instances I felt that its points could be made more specific, and these sections were changed in accordance with my wishes before the Executive Order incorporating the recommendations was published. For instance, the Commission suggested that intentional and unauthorized disclosure of confidential information might serve as one of the criteria of disloyalty; this struck me as open to abuse, and I asked that a phrase be added to the effect that this would apply only where the circumstances indicated disloyalty to the United States. In another section, where the Attorney General was to be directed to compile a list of subversive organizations, I added the requirement that no organization should be placed on this list without prior investigation and formal determination of its subversive nature.

In the Executive Order (No. 9835) which I issued on March 22, 1947, I emphasized two facts that I felt should control the program:

1. That although the loyalty of by far the overwhelming majority of all government employees was beyond question, the presence in the government service of any disloyal or subversive person constituted a threat to our democratic processes, and

2. That maximum protection must be afforded the United States against infiltration of disloyal persons into the ranks of its employees, *and* equal protection from unfounded accusation of disloyalty must be afforded the loyal employees of the government.

By this new Executive Order I felt that we had tightened the precautions against subversive infiltration. But at the same time we had set up machinery to protect the individual against false charges based on rumors or unsubstantiated gossip.

The program as I saw it operate had a lot of flaws in it. It was by no means a perfect instrumentality. By and large, it did give anyone who was accused as fair an opportunity to have his case adjudicated as was possible under the climate of opinion that then existed.

Under the Executive Order of 1947, when a person was accused of belonging to a subversive organization or engaging in any activities that would be called subversive or disloyal, he was given a hearing in the first instance before a loyalty board, and he was allowed to have counsel before that board.

The accused was provided with a résumé of the charges, omitting everything that was considered secret. In many instances the accused was confronted with the accuser or was told who had made the charges, provided the accusers agreed to appear.

The accused first appeared before a departmental loyalty board named by the head of the department.

The report and findings of the board were made to the head of the department. The head of the department could either approve the recommendations of the board or reject them. But, in any case, the accused had the right to appeal to the Loyalty Review Board if he was a permanent civil servant, and to a regional board if he had only temporary status.

Regional boards were set up throughout the country by the Civil Service Commission. If the accused was dissatisfied with the findings of the Regional Board, he had the right of another appeal to the Loyalty Review Board. The Loyalty Review Board was the top organization. Members of this Board were appointed by me.

I selected the twenty-three members of this Review Board on the basis of their known ability and their representation of different walks of life. They came from the top ranks of executives, lawyers, businessmen, and the professions.

Seth Richardson was named to head the Board. He was a prominent conservative Republican and worked in close contact with the Department of Justice.

One of the defects of the loyalty program, which we did not realize at the outset, was that once a person had been cleared by a loyalty board, or finally by the Loyalty Review Board, all of the data about that individual remained in the files. Every time a cleared employee moved from one job to another, his file was reviewed again, so that he was forced to answer the same charges over and over again. In fact, he had to be cleared over and over again. This is not in the tradition of American fair play and justice.

During the latter part of 1947 and 1948, with the Republicans in control of the Eightieth Congress, some House committee chairmen introduced bills in an effort to have Congress join in the administration of the loyalty program. In one instance the House Committee on Expenditures in the executive departments attempted through a rider on an appropriation bill to gain access to the confidential reports of the Civil Service Commission on employees in government.

The confidential reports of the Civil Service Commission, as well as those of the FBI, contain many unsupported, uninvestigated, and unevaluated charges and are never intended for public consumption or distribution. A confidential report on any employee may of necessity contain items based on suspicion, rumor, prejudice, and malice, and therefore, if released, may do great harm to the reputations and careers of many innocent people.

On March 28, 1948, the House Committee on Expenditures in the Executive Departments submitted a joint resolution requiring any department of the government to give up any information in its possession, confidential or otherwise, to a committee of Congress requesting it.

In requesting passage of the resolution, the committee said it wanted such a law because I had instructed the executive departments to preserve the secrecy of the confidential information contained in the loyalty-program files.

In my order to the departments I said:

"This information is necessary in the interest of our national security and welfare to preserve the confidential character and sources of information furnished, and to protect government personnel against the dissemination of unfounded or disproved allegations."

I therefore instructed the departments to refer all congressional requests for such information to the Office of the President, "for such response as the President may determine to be in the public interest in the particular case."

The reason for this order was well illustrated in the action of the House Appropriations Committee in January and February 1948, when it investigated the security procedures of the State Department. The committee undertook this investigation in the course of considering the appropriations requested by the State Department.

The State Department gave full co-operation to the committee investigators to the extent of permitting them to examine and make abstracts of the information in the confidential personnel files. These files included unsubstantiated rumors and suspicion as well as proven facts and indicated in detail the progress which the investigators had made in every case.

In total disregard of their obligation to protect the secrecy of these files, the committee placed into public record the abstract of these files, omitting only the names and substituting symbols. The danger of this kind of procedure is that it may help the real subversives to find out who is being watched and what the government knows about them. It would also tend to injure innocent employees who might be readily identified by other employees through the disclosure of the records.

By this procedure the committee was putting the entire State Department under suspicion, for this was like saying to a group of people gathered in a room, "One of you in this room is a crook," without naming the culprit or backing up the charge with evidence. The result is that everybody in that room is a suspect until cleared. This was the technique used in public statements by demagogues which led so many people to condemn unjustly a whole department in the government. There is good reason why congressional committees, except in extraordinary cases, should be barred from having access to secret unevaluated personnel information.

In 1949 Congress began to include in various appropriation bills riders giving heads of departments the power to discharge employees on security grounds without any right of appeal. This was first applied to the Departments of State and Defense.

This legislation empowered the head of a department to fire an employee in a security case at his own discretion, for any reason, without requiring him to state a reason other than "security." In effect, the Congress was attempting to remove the safeguards of individual right laid down in my 1947 Executive Order, for all that needed to be done was to call a loyalty case a security case and there was no longer any review outside the departments.

The heads of most departments were very careful about the use of this power. But reports were coming to the White House of some arbitrary handling of individual cases where on the flimsiest pretext people were being fired on security grounds.

Some reports showed that people were being fired on false evidence. These reports were distressing to me, as I was very anxious that no injustice be done to any individual and that no individual be deprived of his rights.

On August 8, 1950, I sent a message to Congress recommending legislation to remedy certain defects in the laws concerning employees' loyalty and security. I said in part:

"More than three years ago, the Executive Branch revised and improved its procedures for dealing with questions of employee loyalty and security. These new procedures have proved effective in protecting the Government against disloyal persons and persons whose employment constitutes a security risk. . . .

"Over the last few years, we have successfully prosecuted several hundred cases in the courts under existing internal security laws. In this process we have obtained a great deal of experience in the application of these laws. We have discovered a few defects, some of them minor and others of greater importance, in some of the existing statutes. In view of the situation which confronts us, it is important that these defects be remedied. At this time, therefore, I wish to recommend that the Congress enact certain legislation before the close of the present session."

The first recommendation to the Congress was to remedy certain defects in the present laws concerning espionage, the registration of foreign agents, and the security of national defense installations. This could be done by clarifying and making more definite certain language in the espionage laws, by extending the statute of limitations for peace-time espionage from 3-years by requiring persons who had received instruction from a foreign government or political party in espionage or subversive tactics to register under the Foreign Agents Registration Act, and by giving broader authority than existed for the President to establish security regulations concerning the protection of military bases and other national defense installations.

Second, I recommended that the Congress enact legislation permitting the Attorney General to exercise supervision over aliens subject to deportation and to require them, under the sanction of criminal penalties, to report their whereabouts and activities at regular intervals.

I reminded the Congress what my basic attitude in this matter had always been:

"I am determined that the United States shall be secure. I am equally determined that we shall keep our historic liberties. . . ."

But Congress, in an atmosphere of emotion and excitement, chose to go along with the advocates of extreme measures.

On September 23, 1950, Congress enacted the Internal Security Act. This bill was passed over my veto within twenty-four hours. I had disapproved of this bill because the Department of Justice, the Department of Defense, the Central Intelligence Agency, and the Department of State advised me that the bill would seriously damage the security and the intelligence operations for which they were responsible.

I believed, too, that this bill would give government officials vast powers to harass all of our citizens in the exercise of their right of free speech. Government stifling of the free expression of opinion is a long step toward totalitarianism. There is no more fundamental axiom of American freedom than the familiar statement: In a free country, we punish men for the crimes they commit but never for the opinions they have.

One of the bad results of the act soon came to pass. The Communists now began to scurry underground. Through many devices such as changes of name, of physical appearance, of occupations, and residence they made it more difficult for our agents to keep track of them.

But since this act was now the law of the land, I set up the Subversive Activities Control Board and appointed Seth Richardson as chairman. To take his place as chairman of the Loyalty Review Board, I named another Republican, former Senator Hiram Bingham of Connecticut.

It is one of the tragedies of our time that the security program of the United States has been wickedly used by demagogues and sensational newspapers in an attempt to frighten and mislead the American people.

The McCarthys, the McCarrans, the Jenners, the Parnell Thomases, the Veldes have waged a relentless attack, raising doubts in the minds of people about the loyalty of most employees in government.

If the same methods and standards were applied to private institutions, like banks, for instance, the discovery of one or two dishonest tellers or bookkeepers would be used to condemn all the employees and officers of all banks. This would obviously be grossly unfair, and if all banks were thus attacked, it would surely result in the people losing confidence in our banking system, with serious damage to the system and to the nation.

So when the government expels a few of its undesirable employees, it should not in all decency be used to agitate doubts about all the people in government. Even more reprehensible is unwarranted persecution by demagogues on false charges and gossip about people they dislike. The sacred rights of these individuals, guaranteed by the Bill of Rights, have been sacrificed or placed in continuous jeopardy by the repetition of unsubstantiated charges and accusations.

Our growth as a world power has increased the number of government employees, as it has those of private business, and has made it necessary to extend our operations all over the world. Our government has become the largest employer in the nation.

If the government is to be able to meet its full responsibility to the nation and the people, it must maintain a high morale as much as a high standard of competence.

Demagogic attacks on the loyalty of government employees greatly hamper the task of conducting the government efficiently. Many good people quit government rather than work in an atmosphere of harassment. And these reckless attacks have made it doubly difficult to attract good people to government service.

In such an atmosphere of fear, key government employees tend to become mentally paralyzed. They are afraid to express honest judgments, as it is their duty to do, because later, under a changed atmosphere and different circumstances, they may be charged with disloyalty by those who disagree with them. Our nation cannot afford or permit such a mental blackout.

Early in 1951 I called on Admiral Nimitz to head a commission of leading citizens to make a comprehensive and basic study of the whole loyalty program. I wanted recommendations on what the government needed to provide greater protection to the rights of individuals and at the same time maintain zealous watch over its security.

I chose Admiral Nimitz for this task because in previous discussions I had had with him he expressed himself vigorously about the need of protecting fully every individual right. He was not only our greatest naval strategist in the Pacific and a forthright leader of men but also a devout patriot, always at his country's call, no matter what the task. He understood the problems of security and loyalty as well as anyone in the country.

I appointed the following to serve with Admiral Nimitz on the Commission on Internal Security and Individual Rights:

Most Reverend Emmet M. Walsh, D.D., Coadjutor Bishop of Youngstown, Ohio; Right Reverend Karl Morgan Block, D.D., Bishop of California, San Francisco, California; Miss Anna Lord Strauss of Washington, D.C.; Russell C. Leffingwell of New York; Mr. Charles H. Silver of New York; Honorable John A. Danaher of Washington, D.C.; Mr. Harvey S. Firestone, Jr., of Akron, Ohio; and Mr. William E. Leahy of Washington, D.C.

On January 23, 1951, a public statement announcing the appointment of the Commission declared, in part:

"Today we are particularly concerned by the threat to our government and our national life arising from the activities of the forces of communist imperialism. . . . At the same time we are concerned lest the measures taken to protect us from these dangers infringe the liberties guaranteed by our Constitution and stifle the atmosphere of freedom in which we have so long expressed our thoughts and carried on our daily affairs. . . ."

I wanted to make it clear that I would not tolerate the intrusion of partisan politics: "To keep these problems from falling into the arena of partisanship, I am appointing this Commission of distinguished citizens on a non-partisan basis. I believe the people of this country will receive from them an authoritative judgment on these problems, based on the facts, and formulated in the national interest, with no question of political advantage."

When I met with Admiral Nimitz, I told him that I was troubled by the growing persecution mania being directed against government employees. What I thought was badly needed was a civil-rights program for the people who work in the government. If I had yielded to the clamor by agreeing to a reckless dismissal of the people under fire, I could have silenced many critics—at the cost of ruining the reputations of many innocent people.

When Admiral Nimitz started to staff the Commission he found that there were statutes which imposed serious restrictions on the employment of persons. For example, they would limit any counsel for the Commission in his professional activity for a period of two years after his services with the Commission ceased. They would also curtail the business activity of any of the businessmen I had appointed. Congress had lifted this so-called "conflict-of-interest" restriction in several recent instances, and Admiral Nimitz asked that it be removed in this instance in order that the Commission might recruit a staff equal to its high task.

Congressman Walter introduced a bill for this purpose, and it was favorably reported by the House Committee on the Judiciary and passed the House on March 15, 1951. This measure was then transmitted to the Senate, where it was referred to the Senate Committee on the Judiciary.

Senator McCarran, who was chairman of the Senate Judiciary Committee and whose record for obstruction and bad legislation is matched by that of only a very few reactionaries, blocked the bill in his committee. By this obstruction McCarran succeeded in killing this legislation and kept the Nimitz Commission from making a non-partisan and honest study of the government's loyalty-security program.

This was another move by McCarran calculated to check the administration's program and to encourage the demagogues in the Congress. It left the Nimitz Commission with no choice but to resign as a body.

On October 26, 1951, I wrote Admiral Nimitz:

"Now that the Congress has adjourned without completing action on the legislation which was necessary if the Commission on Internal Security and Individual Rights was to operate effectively, I have concluded reluctantly to accept the resignation of the members of the Commission.

"I had hoped that the Congress would be as anxious as I am to make sure that our procedures for maintaining the security of the government service are working effectively. I had hoped that the Congress would be so anxious as I am to make sure that the Bill of Rights is not undermined in our eagerness to stamp out subversive activities. . . ."

Earlier, on June 6, 1951, Seth Richardson, chairman of the Subversive Activities Control Board, was compelled to resign for reasons of health. In his letter of resignation he said, in part, "I have been advised by my doctors that it is imperative that I be at once hospitalized for immediate, extensive, critical surgical attention. . . .

"The Board is presently carrying on a hearing of vital national importance under great difficulties, and I feel that it would not be in the public interest, or my own, for me to remain indefinitely as an inactive member and chairman. . . .

"I deeply appreciate the faith and the esteem you have shown me—a life long contentious Republican—in affording me opportunities to engage in important non-partisan public services, free from any suggestion of political motives, and so intimately affecting the vital field of national loyalty. . . ."

Replying to Richardson, I said, "Ever since you returned to duty in the government on November 11, 1947, as Chairman of the Loyalty Review Board, you have been guarding our security against subversion and protecting our heritage of Constitutional Government.

"You brought to the Federal Loyalty Program a balanced, mature judgment and a leadership which resulted in the rooting out, from our government, of the guilty while always protecting the innocent. Your magnificent performance on the Loyalty Review Board prompted me last October to appoint you as Chairman and member of the Subversive Activities Control Board.

"I noted with a chuckle your description of yourself as 'a life long contentious Republican.' The job to which I called you demanded integrity, discretion, sound judgment, and ability to view all problems, no matter how complex, with complete detachment and objectivity. Those qualities you possessed in abundance. Best of all, you 'don't panic easy' . . ."

Impatient at the delay of the Senate Judiciary Committee and its failure to take action to enable the Nimitz Commission to go to work, I decided to put the study of the program into the hands of the National Security Council.

On July 14, 1951, I sent the following letter to James S. Lay, Jr., executive secretary of the National Security Council:

Dear Mr. Lay:

I have become seriously concerned by a number of reports I have heard recently concerning the administration of the provisions of existing law which authorize the head of the various departments and agencies to discharge Government employees, or to refuse Government employment to applicants, on the ground that they are poor security risks.

If these provisions of law are to achieve their purpose of protecting the security of the Government without unduly infringing on the rights of individuals, they must be administered with the utmost wisdom and courage. We must never forget that the fundamental purpose of our Government is to protect the rights of individual citizens and one of the highest obligations of the Government is to see that those rights are protected in its own operations.

The present situation does not make for good administration. There are no uniform standards or procedures to be followed in the different departments and agencies concerned. Neither is there any provisions for review at a central point as there is in the case of the Government Employee Loyalty Program. This is a problem that falls within the scope of the work which I have asked to have undertaken by the Commission on Internal Security and Individual Rights. However, the work of that Commission has been delayed because of the failure of the Senate Committee on the Judiciary to report legislation which would exempt the members and staff of the Commission from the conflict-of-interest statutes.

I believe that the present problems involved in the administration of the Government Employee Security Program are so acute that they should be given at least preliminary consideration without waiting further for the Commission on Internal Security and Individual Rights. Consequently, I should like the National Security Council, utilizing its Interdepartmental Committee on Internal Security, and with the participation of the Civil Service Commission, to make an investigation of the way this program is being administered, and to advise me what changes are believed to be required. In particular, I should like consideration given to whether provision should be made for uniform standards and procedures and for central review of the decisions made in the various departments and agencies.

When the Commission on Internal Security and Individual Rights is able to resume its work, it would, of course, have the benefit of the work done pursuant to this request.

I am asking each of the departments and agencies concerned to cooperate fully in this study.

Sincerely yours,
HARRY S. TRUMAN

The National Security Council worked on this study for many months. This work was done by an interdepartmental committee on internal security, composed of officers and technicians in the security field from the various departments and included the head of the FBI, the security officer of the State Department, and a general from the Department of Defense.

The report of this committee came to me on April 29, 1952. It was a comprehensive and detailed study. It made many recommendations to improve procedures and pointed up the need for uniform standards for all security employees. It also recommended that the Civil Service Commission review agency decisions in security-risk cases.

On August 8, 1952, after giving the report considerable thought, I wrote Robert Ramspeck, chairman of the Civil Service Commission, expressing my conclusions. In my letter to Mr. Ramspeck I said, in part:

"The most desirable action at this time would be to merge the loyalty, security and suitability programs, thus eliminating the overlapping, duplication and confusion which apparently now exists. It is my understanding that the status of the incumbent employees' loyalty program is now so advanced that there would be little or no obstacle to accomplishing this. . . .

". . . In the meantime, however, departments and agencies having employee security programs should re-examine their procedures, and should assist them in assuring adequate procedural safeguards for the protection of all personnel who are subject to employee security programs."

In plain words, I wanted to make sure that if an employee was terminated on grounds that he was unsuitable—but not undesirable—he should not be branded as disloyal or as a security risk.

This was an evil twist that the loose critics and demagogues were putting on many of the people who quit or were dismissed for routine reasons by the government.

The government's loyalty program was a vast undertaking that took the time and work of many of the top men in the government. Commissions to help in this program were composed of leading citizens of both political parties. They sat in review of the administration's program and recommended changes.

The issue of world Communism and its inroads is a national and not a partisan issue. I deplore the fact that the work of running down Communists within the country and meeting their threat around the world should have been made a political issue.

There never should have been competition on the anti-Communist issue between Congress and the Executive, and between the Democrats and the Republicans. I never considered it a partisan issue. As a matter of fact, I appointed prominent Republicans to head the loyalty review programs and did my part to keep it from becoming a political matter.

We maintained a constant vigilance against the new technique of infiltration and betrayal by the agents and dupes of the Communists. But those of us who had faith in the institutions of this country never acted out of a sense of panic or fear that these enemies could ever succeed.

The United States was the prime but not the only target of Soviet espionage. Our vigilance had to go beyond our frontiers as we cooperated with our allies and other nations menaced by Communist imperialism.

Our foreign policy was aimed to preserve the peace, and we fought the Communist threat everywhere and in many ways. We were trying to build a free world so that mankind could be given the hope of overcoming the recurring disasters of hunger, disease, exploitation, and imperialist expansion.

Our foreign policy was mistakenly called by some a policy of containment. This is not true. Our purpose was much broader. We were working for a united, free, and prosperous world.

The Communists, however, have other ideas. They are out to dominate the world. By betrayal, infiltration, and subversion they have taken over millions of helpless people. The foreign policy we pursued checked and stopped this trend at the most critical point in our history, and working with our allies, we helped save Western civilization.

The demagogues, crackpots, and professional patriots had a field day pumping fear into the American people. They launched a campaign of poison-pen letters. No man in public life was safe from their invectives and attacks.

Many good people actually believed that we were in imminent danger of being taken over by the Communists and that our government in Washington was Communist-riddled.

So widespread was this campaign that it seemed no one would be safe from attack. This was the tragedy and shame of our time.

I refused to lose confidence in the good sense of the American people. I knew this period of hysteria would eventually run its course, as did all other such unhappy periods in our past.

In times past, situations similar to that through which we were passing had happened. There was Salem, the Alien and Sedition Laws, the Anti-Masons, the Know-Nothings (who were anti-Catholic), the Ku Klux Klan in the late 1860's, "Rum, Romanism and Rebellion" in 1884, the Ku Klux Klan in 1920, 1924, and 1928. In 1928 Al Smith was knocked out by the Ku Klux Klan, which was anti-Catholic, anti-Jewish, anti-Negro.

The country had reason to be proud of and have confidence in our security agencies. They had kept us almost totally free of sabotage and espionage during the war. All the foreign agents who were caught had been run down by the established intelligence agencies of the government. Those suspected of being spies or subversives were under continued surveillance by these agencies.

Ironically enough, some of our secrets got out because certain good citizens did not realize what they were doing.

A number of dangerous leaks affecting national security resulted from news stories by people whose patriotism or loyalty could not be questioned.

For instance, a certain columnist wrote an article for a national weekly publication which gave locations of our atomic installations. Our intelligence would have liked as easy a way to learn the locations of Russian atomic installations from Russian sources. Atomic installations will be the first targets in a possible war. Yet such vital information was made available to the Russians in one of our magazines.

Then a whole series of air photographs of our principal cities—Washington, New York, Detroit, Chicago, and others—was printed as page-one news by one of the newspaper chains.

In an effort to put a stop to some of these defense leaks, Secretary of Defense Forrestal had called in a group of newspaper publishers—about six or eight, as I recall it—to see if they could not be persuaded to work out a voluntary censorship arrangement. The publishers told Forrestal, "It is your responsibility to stop your own people from giving information to the press." Certain publishers seem to forget that the responsibility belongs to them as well as to the government, and the destruction of the country would destroy them also.

In another instance a trade magazine published information about one of our top-secret air developments. I directed the head of the CIA to find out from the editor how he came to publish such information. It was clear from the report I received that the information was given to this editor by a top official in one of the military services. The editor said, "You can't expect us to be more careful than your own people." Further investigation disclosed this leak was committed by this official in order to help get a certain budget through the Congress.

The rivalry for the attention and the support of Congress was, in part, responsible for many news leaks. "Potomac fever," too, creates a great desire on the part of people to see their names in print.

This competition for attention reached a point where some of the services even wanted to boast openly of their top-secret achievements.

I directed that the strictest measures be taken to stop these leaks to the press by anyone in the government.

I found it necessary to issue orders restricting the sources of information by setting up a central clearinghouse to determine what information it was safe to release. The press and radio branded this action a form of censorship and even charged that it was done to cover up wrongdoings, which of course was not true.

Congressional committee hearings were also a fertile source of security information. One of our top military leaders was so upset by leaks, after he had testified on secret matters in executive sessions of congressional committees, that he threatened to refuse to appear before these committees. So swift and deliberate were the leaks that often the secret information he had given the committee in executive session would be on the news tickers even before he could return to his office.

I ordered a study made by our intelligence people to see how much vital information was actually being made available to foreign countries by speeches and statements published in the Congressional Record. The percentage was disturbingly high.

This was not information given out by the fuzzy dupes or Communist sympathizers. None of these could get such information because they had no access to classified material. This information was being given out by gossipy politicians who, because of rivalry, were blinded to what they were doing. In this respect, Washington politicians and newspaper and magazine publishers are in the same class.

One of the ablest top intelligence men in the government said this about our security setup: "I don't think anything more could have been done against subversion, espionage and sabotage. Those functions were being carried out during the war and after the war and are functioning today. With respect to government personnel, some fuzzy situations were permitted to exist that should have been remedied, but we must recognize the difficulties that confronted us in the early period.

"While the professional security people in the government were aware of the problems and were vigilant, some political and less experienced officials could not always distinguish between honest liberals and troublesome radicals. It was not easy always to separate from among the extreme radicals the misguided zealots and those who were disloyal. As a matter of fact, the professional security people had difficulty in proving that among the suspects there were really Communists. It was hard to pin anything on them. I don't think the government could have gotten them out.

"It must be remembered that all the so-called non-security people had difficulty in shifting from their acceptance of the Russians as our allies to the Russians now being our enemies. For example, in security circles there was a feeling that even when General Eisenhower was in charge of Germany, there were some questionable characters on his staff, and we had to send over a task force to clean it up.

"You cannot shift the position of a country doing everything in the world for an ally to veering around to considering him an enemy without some confusion, and that's the field through which we have travelled."

CHAPTER 20

America's security and the security of the free world depend to a large degree on our leadership in the field of nuclear energy.

We owe a great debt of gratitude to a small group of scientists who have made this possible. The peace of the world, in a large measure, was in the hands of a few dedicated men, who in 1945 and 1946 ignored the postwar stampede to private life, men who resisted or turned down tempting offers from industry and universities and stayed on at Los Alamos to continue research on atomic development. They knew that atomic development had just begun, and they wanted to stay with it because other nations would surely do what they could to overcome our lead.

They were certain that unless we continued with research along many lines that had been developed at Los Alamos and in other American laboratories our position and our safety would be threatened.

We were on the threshold of important discoveries, and I was anxious for us to advance our work in nuclear development so that we might produce whatever new weapons were needed to safeguard our military position and thereby strengthen our hand in efforts to secure the peace. I wanted to do everything possible to encourage those scientists to stay with the government and to build our great laboratories—laboratories in which the thermonuclear knowledge was developed which was soon to enable us to produce the super-bomb—the H-bomb.

On midnight on December 31, 1946, a civilian agency—the Atomic Energy Commission—took over top management of atomic research and production in the United States. This Commission consists of five members appointed by the President and confirmed by the Senate. The President designates one of the members as chairman of the Commission and also names a general manager who is subject to Senate confirmation.

The AEC has broad powers and full control over its own operations. It is responsible for the conduct of all research, development, and production in the field of atomic energy. Only the President, however, can authorize the use of an atomic bomb. Only the President can decide the nature of the weapons to be made. Only the President can decide whether a weapon can be detonated for test purposes. Only the President can approve where and when the weapons may be shipped or stored. In fact, the President even sets the annual goal of the number of bombs and the quantity of material to be produced.

But the President is no less concerned with the development and uses of atomic power for peaceful purposes. Through his control of the budget he is able to provide guidance and stimulation to the Commission.

To assist the Commission in the exercise of its powers, the law established the Joint Congressional Committee on Atomic Energy, composed of nine senators and nine representatives, and the Atomic Energy Commission is required to keep the congressional committee fully and currently informed with respect to the Commission's activities.

The law also provides for a Military Liaison Committee, which is appointed by the Secretary of Defense and consists of two representatives from each of the three armed services, plus a chairman, who may be either a military man or a civilian. The Liaison Committee keeps the Atomic Energy Commission "fully informed of all atomic energy activities" of the Defense Department, and the Commission, in turn, must keep the committee informed about all of its activities in the military field. The Military Liaison Committee has "authority to make written recommendations to the Commission on matters relating to military application." In cases where a difference of opinion might arise between the Military Liaison Committee and the Atomic Energy Commission there is a provision in the law whereby the committee may carry the matter through the Secretary of Defense to the President. The President's decision is final.

As a final step, the law provides for a General Advisory Committee of nine members to be appointed by the President "from civilian life." This Advisory Committee supplies scientific and technical advice to the Atomic Energy Commission and also to the Military Liaison Committee.

I had a great many suggestions made to me about the men to be appointed to the Atomic Energy Commission. These are the men I finally selected as the first members of the Commission: David E. Lilienthal, designated as chairman, Robert F. Bacher, Sumner T. Pike, Lewis L. Strauss, and William W. Waymack.

In choosing the members of the Commission I paid no attention to their politics. As a matter of fact, as it turned out, not a single member of the original Atomic Energy Commission was a member of the Democratic party. Lilienthal always called himself an independent in politics. The four others were Republicans. I have always followed the principle that politics and the atom do not mix.

The newly established Commission had a tremendous job ahead of it. It had to convert a gigantic enterprise from a temporary wartime operation to permanent operation of much greater scope. The Manhattan District was a wartime project set up to produce the atomic bomb to shorten the war. This was its only purpose. And up to the time of the establishment of the AEC, the government operated the atomic production facilities behind a veil of total military secrecy. Now, however, the project would come under the scrutiny of Congress, in addition to the authority of the President. Henceforth, the Commission would have to justify its work to congressional committees.

Congress quickly demonstrated its keen interest in embarking upon an extensive debate before confirming the nominees to the Commission. The Senate took three months before taking final vote, in which they confirmed all five. But even while awaiting confirmation, the Commission took full charge of the atomic program. The first thing they did was to analyze and survey the existing situation, and three months later they made a report to me. In this, their first report, I was advised that there were serious weaknesses in the operation from the standpoint of national defense and security. The number of bombs was disappointing, and those we had were not assembled. The highly skilled civilians who had been trained to do the assembling had scattered to better-paying jobs in private employment. The training of military personnel to perform the assembly operations was not yet completed.

While there had been some test explosions at Bikini during 1946 for strategic purposes, the more advanced type of bomb on hand had yet to be tested. Furthermore, there were serious questions about the supply of raw uranium. Most of it at that time came from the Belgian Congo, and the demand exceeded the supply.

The first task, therefore, was to bring the entire production program on an even keel. This meant shutting down some facilities and pushing the work of others.

Of course the reasons for these actions were not only highly technical, they were also reasons which the Russians would have given much to know. Senators and representatives were expressing concern about production, and some of them seemed to think that *any* kind of expansion of the atomic program, especially the weapons program, was worth while. Actually, of course, in order to build a sound program for the future, it was more prudent, as the scientists and the military were advising, not to go all out in any one direction.

The atomic program, furthermore, had to be geared to the needs of our foreign policy as well as of our national defense, and it was my responsibility as President to maintain a balance between these and other factors all the time.

The Joint Committee on Atomic Energy had been set up by the Congress to keep a constant vigil on the activities of the AEC. Senator Brien McMahon and Senator Bourke Hickenlooper, the Democratic and Republican senior members on this body, soon made themselves into specialists and, to a degree, special pleaders.

I spent considerable time with Brien McMahon in late 1945 and 1946 while the work on atomic energy legislation was going on, and I was impressed by his grasp and understanding of the problems of atomic power. Then, when Senator Hickenlooper became chairman of the Joint Committee in January 1947, he and I held a number of constructive meetings in connection with his new duties.

It was not easy for some members of Congress to realize just how complex a thing they were dealing with. On one occasion, for instance, Senator Hickenlooper called the White House and said his committee urgently needed a certain highly classified document. He was quite sure they could not proceed unless they had it.

I invited him to come over to see me, and when he came in I took him to the Cabinet Room, gave him the document, and asked him to read it. The document was a long one, and about an hour and a half later the senator came back into my office. He was visibly shaken.

"I now wish you hadn't given me this thing to read," he said. "I'd rather not have known anything about it."

I said, "Now you see why this should not properly be brought before your committee."

The important point, however, is this: Regardless of who was chairman of the Joint Committee, McMahon or Hickenlooper, I dealt with him in the same open and frank manner. Party politics, so far as I was concerned, had no business in the atomic picture. I was glad to see that the members of the Joint Committee were most careful about observing strict atomic security. Still, there was always the risk that a public row would result in vital secrets getting out.

The Joint Committee was primarily concerned with atomic developments as such, and it was always pushing for more production. Some of its members tended to oversimplify the problem and took the position that all that was necessary to the program was for the military to tell the AEC, "We want so many bombs," and then it would be up to the AEC to deliver. But in addition to the fact that it was unwise to let the military have control in this way, it was impossible to schedule production on a military requisition basis. There was not enough raw material in sight to satisfy our needs.

The bulk of the uranium available to us came then from the Belgian Congo. However, in 1944 we had made an agreement with the British that called for a combined effort to acquire as much uranium (and some other scarce materials) as possible. While the war was on we had no difficulties with the allocation of these materials. The entire nuclear program was then centered in the United States, and, except for negligible amounts, all uranium available to the British-American-Canadian combination was allocated to the United States. But after the war, arrangements had to be changed. The visiting scientists and technicians, who had now returned to their home countries, had set up facilities of their own, and they needed uranium for their experiments.

In the meantime, our own needs had greatly increased. After a period of negotiations with the British we reached a temporary agreement in July 1946 for an approximately equal division of all the uranium produced from the Belgian Congo between ourselves and the United Kingdom. By this division, however, the British were now getting more than they could put to any practical use, while we were left short. In order to correct this difficulty and in order to get a more proportionate distribution of this uranium, we reopened negotiations in late 1947, and the discussions which followed were held in Washington.

On January 7, 1948, the two countries reached a new agreement for a revised, but still temporary, allocation. This *modus vivendi,* as it was always referred to in later negotiations, now provided that all uranium produced in the Belgian Congo during 1948–49 should go to the United States. In addition to this, we were given an option on a portion of the British stockpile.

In exchange for this major concession we agreed to disclose to the British nuclear data in nine specified areas of information, an agreement which was in keeping with the provisions and the spirit of the Atomic Energy Act. Information about atomic weapons was specifically excluded, and both countries promised that they would not pass any information on to any other country. A very minor exception was made for New Zealand because of the work done by New Zealand scientists on British atomic energy installations.

At the end of 1947 a group of unusually qualified experts brought me an appraisal of our atomic progress. This report came from the General Advisory Committee, which included, among others, such outstanding men of science as J. Robert Oppenheimer, James B. Conant, Lee A. DuBridge, Enrico Fermi, and I. I. Rabi.

Here is Dr. Oppenheimer's letter reporting on their first year's work:

GENERAL ADVISORY COMMITTEE
to the
UNITED STATES ATOMIC ENERGY COMMISSION
Washington, D.C.

December 31, 1947

The President
The White House
Washington, D.C.

My dear Mr. President:

A year has passed since you named us to the General Advisory Committee, to advise the Atomic Energy Commission "on scientific and technical matters relating to materials production and research and development." We were prepared to understand the importance of the work of the Commission for the welfare of the United States. Thus we have taken our duties as advisors very earnestly, have devoted to them much time and study, and for at least fifteen days, at intervals throughout the year, have held meetings at which all of us were present. We have had frequent and candid discussions with the Atomic Energy Commission, with its staff, and with the Military Liaison Committee, and have reported such recommendations as we were able to make to the Commission in seven detailed reports, which ncessarily have a very high classification.

Our activity during this year reflects not only the sense of great importance which we attach to successful development of this field; it also reflects the difficulties with which the Commission was faced in assuming its responsibilities, and the unsatisfactory state of its inheritance. We very soon learned that in none of the technical areas vital to the common defense and security, nor in those looking toward the beneficial applications of atomic energy, was the state of development adequate. Important questions of technical policy were undecided, and in many cases unformulated. Giant installations and laboratories were operating with confused purposes and with inadequate understanding of the importance and relevance of the technical problems before them. Our atomic armament was inadequate, both quantitatively and qualitatively, and the tempo of progress was throughout dangerously slow. This state of affairs can in large measure be attributed to the long delays in setting up an atomic energy authority, and to the inevitable confusions of policy and of purpose which followed the termination of the war. The difficulties were increased by the fact that the wartime installations and laboratories, which served so well their primary function of developing atomic weapons for early military use, were in most cases not suited to continue the work as the nature of the technical problems altered, and as the transition from wartime to peacetime operation changed the conditions under which rapid progress might be possible.

It has thus been our function to assist the Commission in formulating technical programs, both for the short and for the somewhat longer term. These programs are aimed in the main at three objectives:

(1) The development, improvement and increase of atomic armament.

(2) The development of reactors for a variety of purposes.

(3) The support of the physical and biological sciences which in one way or another touch on the field of atomic energy.

As to the improvement of our situation with regard to atomic weapons, we are glad to report that the year has seen great progress, and that we anticipate further progress in the near future. From the beginning, we shared with the Commission an understanding of how dangerous complacency could be with regard to our work in this field. We have been much gratified at the establishment of Pacific proving grounds, where the performance of altered and improved weapons can be put to the test of actual proof and measurement. While much yet remains to be done, and while the long term program of atomic armament is only in its earliest beginning, we nevertheless believe that steps already taken to improve our situation, and others which will follow as time makes them appropriate, have gone very far toward establishing this activity on a sound basis.

Atomic reactors have many purposes. They can produce the fissionable materials which can be used in atomic weapons or as fuel for other reactors. They can be useful instruments of research in the physical and biological sciences and in technology. They may, within a decade, be developed to provide sources of power for specialized application, for instance, for the propulsion of a limited number of naval craft. They may, within a time which will probably not be short, and which is difficult to estimate reliably, be developed to provide general industrial power, and so make important contributions to our whole technological and economic life. This variety of purpose, the novelty of the field, and the relatively small number of men trained to work in it, makes substantial progress in the development of atomic reactors difficult to realize. Many steps have been taken by the Commission during the past year to encourage work in this field, to invite the participation of industry, to promote the completion and construction of promising specific designs, and to enlist the participation of qualified experts. Yet, it is the opinion of the Advisory Committee that much yet remains to be done, that new personnel and new talent must come to contribute, and that many years will elapse before our work in this field has the robustness and vigor which its importance justifies. As an aid to the Commission, we have attempted to formulate the prospects, and to give some estimates of the nature of the effort required, for attainment of the various objectives. We believe that a more widespread understanding of the nature of the problems, and of the contributions which engineers can and must make, and of the way in which industry can helpfully participate, are essential for the health of these efforts.

In the support of basic science, we have welcomed the broad interpretation of its responsibilities which the Atomic Energy Commission has maintained. We studied in detail the proposals recently adopted for making certain radioactive isotopes available, primarily for biological and medical research, not only within this country, but abroad. We see in this a prudent but inspiriting example of the extension to others of the benefits resulting from the release of atomic energy, an extension sure to enrich our knowledge and our control over the forces of nature.

During the last year we have frequently come upon a problem, the further consideration of which seems to us essential. We have been forced to recognize, in studying the possible implementation of technical policy, how adverse the effect of secrecy, and of the inevitable misunderstanding and error which accompany it, have been on progress, and thus on the common defense and security. We believe that in the field of basic science, the Commission has inherited from the Manhattan District, and has maintained, an essentially enlightened policy. Even in the fields of technology, in industrial applications, in military problems, the fruits of secrecy are misapprehension, ignorance and apathy. It will be a continuing problem for the Government of the United States to re-evaluate the risks of unwise disclosure, and weigh them against the undoubted dangers of maintaining secrecy at the cost of error and stagnation. Only by such re-evaluation can the development of atomic energy make its maximum contribution to the securing of the peace, and to the perpetuation and growth of the values of our civilization.

We are, my dear Mr. President

Very sincerely yours,

James B. Conant
Lee A. DuBridge
Enrico Fermi
I. I. Rabi
Hartley Rowe
Glenn T. Seaborg
Cyril S. Smith
Hood Worthington
J. R. Oppenheimer,
Chairman

[s] J. R. Oppenheimer
For the Committee

This was a most informative and provocative letter, and it raised, among other interesting points, the question of secrecy. My position on secrecy in connection with the military application of atomic power has always been the same. I have been uncompromisingly opposed to sharing or yielding atomic military secrets to any other government.

The Atomic Energy Commission was meticulous in providing me with information. Some of it was highly technical, so that I had to do considerable studying to come to grips with it. And of course I would never presume to pass judgment on technical opinions. But I always asked for all points of view, even on technical questions, before giving approval to any major decision.

Under the law, I had to fix each year the amount of fissionable materials that should be produced in the following year. To reach a decision, I would have before me a joint recommendation from the Defense Department and the Atomic Energy Commission. This was always highly secret, and exceptional precautions were taken to keep it secret.

For example, in no document in my office, in the AEC, or anywhere in government, could anyone find the exact figure of the number of bombs in stockpile, or the number of bombs to be produced, or the amount of material scheduled for production.

If anyone should happen to run across a document dealing with atomic weapons production, he will find either a cipher or a blank in the space where the actual figure should appear. The figure in question would be recorded on separate and detached pieces of paper safeguarded in a special way and of which only a bare minimum of copies exist.

While there were many problems of adjustment in those days among the several agencies interested in our atomic energy policies, they had no effect upon the continuity and perseverance in the research laboratories. One of the broad areas of research on which the laboratories had been working from the very beginning was the hydrogen atom.

When the atomic program first got under way during World War II, the scientists concentrated their immediate efforts on the "heavy elements"—especially uranium. During 1947 and 1948 we combined our emphasis on uranium and plutonium as sources of atomic power, but research on the "light elements," of which hydrogen is the most important, was carried on at the same time without letup or interruption.

It was in the year 1949 that many developments in the atomic nuclear field demanded our attention and many important decisions had to be made. By early 1949 the Atomic Energy Commission had succeeded in getting most of the "kinks" out of the atomic program, and we were moving forward in the whole area of atomic energy.

To aid me in resolving major questions of fact and policy, I called on a special committee of the National Security Council. This consisted of the Secretary of State, Dean Acheson; the Secretary of Defense, Louis Johnson; and David Lilienthal, chairman of the Atomic Energy Commission.

The first study I assigned to this committee had to do with our atomic energy relations with Great Britain, Canada, and other friendly nations. On February 10, 1949, when I gave the committee this assignment, we faced the problem of continuing co-operation with Great Britain despite the fact that the agreement under which we were operating would expire at the end of 1949.

The Special Committee reported to me on March 2, 1949, with a recommendation that we make a new approach so as to bring as much atomic material and production as possible to the North American continent. This, the committee said, would mean that the three countries —the United States, Great Britain, and Canada—would draw together as closely as they had been joined in their wartime collaboration.

I approved the recommendation that we try to reach such an arrangement, and also expressed to the committee my desire that before we undertook any negotiations with the British and Canadians we fully inform the key members of Congress of both parties about our intentions. To this end I called a private conference at Blair House on the evening of July 14, 1949. In addition to the key members of the Joint Committee on Atomic Energy and Vice-President Alben Barkley, the three members of the Special Committee of the NSC were present. General Eisenhower attended in his capacity as acting chairman of the Joint Chiefs of Staff, and among the congressmen present were Senators McMahon, Hickenlooper, Tydings, and Vandenberg, and Representatives Sam Rayburn, Carl Durham, and Sterling Cole.

I opened the meeting by advising the group that our agreement with Great Britain for the procurement of uranium was about to expire and that the British were asking us to resume our full co-operation in atomic matters, a relationship that had lapsed. I pointed out that we had to have the uranium and the British wanted some of our scientific information, adding that the solidarity of Great Britain and the United States was one of the cornerstones of the world's peace. There was a highly responsible leadership in Britain regardless of which of the two major parties controlled the government.

Britain had many noted scientists, who had made considerable progress toward an atomic bomb and would undoubtedly soon develop their own. I pointed out that a British scientific mission participated extensively in the research and development and later in the production of atomic bombs at Los Alamos. Furthermore, they had participated in the preparation and evaluation of the Bikini tests. Similar scientific missions had participated in the research and development at Oak Ridge in the separation of U-235. In addition, British and Canadian scientists were in consultation with our scientists at the Metallurgical Laboratory in Chicago on the design of the heavy-water reactor built at Chalk River, Canada.

I related how in 1947 Britain, Canada and the United States had adopted a uniform system for handling the information jointly developed. In January 1948 the three governments had agreed upon a *modus vivendi* providing for co-operation involving exchange of scientific and technical information in certain defined areas, as well as collaboration on matters of raw materials. Now, however, this agreement was coming to an end, and I proposed that we conclude a new agreement based on full partnership, subject to the terms of the Atomic Energy Act; this, I thought, could be done by having all available uranium brought to this country for processing and storage. The British and Canadian scientists could then join their American colleagues to work with them. To overcome any complaints the British might have that they were being excluded from the atomic weapons field, we could arrange to have a number of our unassembled bombs placed in the British Isles.

Acheson, Johnson, and Lilienthal spoke in considerable detail in support of this plan. Senator Vandenberg, however, spoke sharply against the proposal. He was of the opinion that the British should accept our dominant position in the atomic field, and gave two reasons for his point of view.

First, he cited the fact of our aid to Great Britain during and since World War II. Second, he expressed himself as believing that any other approach would result in the kind of duplication of effort which the North Atlantic Treaty was supposed to eliminate in the field of common defense.

Senator Hickenlooper also opposed the suggestion. His principal reason for objection was his distrust of British security, and he did not think we should take the risk at this time.

The other legislators present were more sympathetic to the idea, but there was a general feeling among them that a majority of Congress would refuse to go along.

As was my custom, I adjourned the meeting without announcing a decision. I had listened to as many sides as possible, and now I had to draw my own conclusion. It seemed to me more important to maintain bi-partisan support for the atomic program than to insist on a program which was opposed by strong elements in Congress, and I therefore instructed our delegation to the exploratory talks to be held in September to work for an arrangement that would *not* include the sharing of weapons data.

By the spring of 1949 we had think of atomic weapons on a different scale. We now had a stockpile, but I wanted to know whether the weapons we hand on hand and those that were planned were adequate in number and whether we were keeping up with technological progress.

In July I again called in the Special Committee of the National Securing Council, telling them now to assess the rate of progress being made in our atomic program. There were many questions that needed study, and one of these was how we were now to distribute our defense dollar. Both the Special Committee of the National Security Council and the Joint Chiefs of Staff were considering how best to prepare ourselves militarily so as to keep our strength in balance and avoid weakness by overemphasizing one category of defense at the expense of another.

As a result of my request, the Special Committee brought this important conclusion to me: that production of atomic weapons should be stepped up. At the same time, they recommended that the newly developed B-36 bomber be given a priority second only to atomic weapons, for the B-36 was designed as a long-range plane capable of delivering our new-type A-bomb on any target in the world.

Prior to this, on April 20, 1949, General Hoyt Vandenberg, Chief of Staff of the Air Force, had reported to me in detail the plans of the Strategic Air Command. By the use of maps and graphs he showed me exactly what the Strategic Air Command expected to do in case war broke out. It was after I had had this briefing by the Air Force that I sent the following memorandum to the Secretary of Defense:

"Yesterday afternoon I listened with interest to an Air Force presentation of plans for strategic bombing operations, in the event of war, against a potential enemy. I should like to examine an evaluation by the Joint Chiefs of Staff of the chances of successful delivery of bombs as contemplated by this plan, together with a joint evaluation of the results to be expected by such bombing."

Secretary Johnson, in a reply to me, reported that the Joint Chiefs of Staff were already at work on such an evaluation. The men who are responsible for our military planning can never be satisfied with their preparations and conclusions. Their plans are never frozen and fixed. They are forever shifting and improving their ideas in order to keep pace with the current of progress and power in the world. Occasionally some newspaperman gets wind of the existence of certain military plans and reports them as the fixed position of the government. This happened frequently during my administration, and such reports are often as damaging as they are inaccurate.

In government there can never be an end to study, improvement, and the evaluation of new ideas, and no one is more conscious of this than the President, for he can see how the machinery of government operates.

I have been impressed by both the speed and thoroughness of the response of departments when I asked for detailed studies, even on the most difficult problems. As President, I always insisted on as complete a picture as possible before making a decision, and I did not want fuzzy statements that concealed differences of opinions.

I wanted to hear all sides when there was disagreement, but even more important, I wanted to know when disagreements existed among my advisers. I do not believe that the President is well served if he depends upon the agreed recommendations of just a few people around him, boiled down to a brief statement submitted to him for approval.

This may be efficiency in military administration, but not in government at the top level. In the long run the best results come from intensive study of different viewpoints and from arguments pro and con. I have spent many hours, late at night and early in the morning, poring over papers giving all sides. Many times I was fairly convinced in my own mind which course of action would be the right one, but I still wanted to cover every side of the situation before coming to a final decision.

As far as the atomic program was concerned, I talked to the AEC Commissioners both individually and as a group. I talked to scientists and to military advisers. I called in foreign policy experts and heard their views. They were not always in accord, of course, but in my mind I was firmly committed to the proposition that, as long as international agreement for the control of atomic energy could not be reached, our country had to be ahead of any possible competitor. It was my belief that, as long as we had the lead in atomic developments, that great force would help us keep the peace.

In all my dealings with the Atomic Energy Commission I made it a practice to conclude each discussion with the admonition that we must keep ahead. But our monopoly came to an end sooner than the experts had predicted. An atomic explosion took place in Russia in August 1949.

The intelligence experts had different opinions about it, but in general none of them had looked for the Russians to detonate any atomic device before 1952. Fortunately, the Long Range Detection System of the Air Force had become fully developed in early 1949, and it was through this network that we were able to learn, in surprising detail, that an atomic explosion, not under our control, had taken place.

On September 3, 1949, one of the planes operating in the Long Range Detection System collected an air sample that was decidedly radioactive, and the entire detection machinery at once went into high gear. The cloud containing the suspicious matter was tracked by the United States Air Force from the North Pacific to the vicinity of the British Isles, where it was also picked up by the Royal Air Force, and from the first these developments were reported to me by the CIA as rapidly as they became known.

Then the scientists went to work and analyzed the data. The Air Force specialists, the AEC's experts, and consultants called in from universities went over the available information. Then a special committee, composed of Vannevar Bush, J. Robert Oppenheimer, Robert F. Bacher, and W. S. Parsons, reviewed the findings. There was no room for doubt. Between August 26 and 29 an atomic explosion had been set off somewhere on the Asiatic mainland.

General Hoyt Vandenberg, who as Chief of Staff of the Air Force was directly responsible for the long-range detection program, reported these facts to me on September 21. I was surprised, of course, that the Russians had made progress at a more rapid rate than was anticipated.

There has been a great deal of misinformation and deliberate distortion in stories about this period. The nation has not been well served in this connection, and no one has been helped by these unreliable reports. Men of science have been embarrassed by having their candid professional disagreements made to appear like personal feuds. Public officials have found themselves pictured as either villains or heroes, depending upon the columnist or commentator whose opinion you heard or read.

The Government of the United States was not unprepared for the Russian atomic explosion. There was no panic, and there was no need for emergency decisions. This was a situation that we had been expecting to happen sooner or later. To be sure, it came sooner than the experts had estimated, but it did not require us to alter the direction of our program.

The first persons I wanted to be informed about the Russian atomic explosion, even before I made a public statement, were the members of the Congressional Joint Committee on Atomic Energy. I therefore asked Senator McMahon, the chairman, and Senator Hickenlooper, the ranking Republican member, to join me in my office at the White House the following day, September 22. Hickenlooper was out of town, however, and so McMahon came alone.

I showed him the report I had received from the Air Force, together with the evaluations of the scientists. We discussed the meaning of the event, and I informed McMahon that a public announcement would be made the following day.

It was at eleven o'clock in the morning on September 23, just after I had given the news to the regular meeting of the Cabinet, that I issued through Press Secretary Ross the following public statement:

"I believe the American people, to the fullest extent consistent with national security, are entitled to be informed of all developments in the field of atomic energy. That is my reason for making public the following information.

"We have evidence that within recent weeks an atomic explosion occurred in the U.S.S.R.

"Ever since atomic energy was first released by man, the eventual development of this new force by other nations was to be expected. This probability has always been taken into account by us.

"Nearly four years ago I pointed out that 'scientific opinion appears to be practically unanimous that the essential theoretical knowledge upon which the discovery is based is already widely known. There is also substantial agreement that foreign research can come abreast of our present theoretical knowledge in time.' And, in the Three-Nation Declaration of the President of the United States and the Prime Ministers of the United Kingdom and Canada, dated November 15, 1945, it was emphasized that no single nation could in fact have a monopoly of atomic weapons.

"This recent development emphasizes once again, if indeed such emphasis were needed, the necessity for that truly effective enforceable international control of atomic energy which this government and the large majority of the United Nations support."

One of the positive effects of this development was to spur our laboratories and our great scientists to make haste on hydrogen bomb research. By the early fall of 1949, development of the "super"—the thermonuclear or hydrogen—bomb had progressed to the point where we were almost ready to put our theories into practice. I believed that anything that would assure us the lead in the field of atomic energy development for defense had to be tried out, but a most complicated and baffling problem had arisen, and the alternatives were a long way from clear-cut.

The first problem was to decide how much of the AEC's energies and resources should be devoted to an early test that might show us whether or not the H-bomb would work. In order to do this, uranium now going into A-bomb production would have to be diverted. But how far could a program now working so successfully (the uranium-plutonium process) be cut back for tests on a method that might fail?

Everything pertaining to the hydrogen bomb was at this time still in the realm of the uncertain. It was all theory and assumption. Even the scientists and the Commission were divided. And, in addition, the questions with which we were concerned related not only to matters of scientific knowledge but also to our defense strategy and our foreign policy. All of these had to be weighed.

On the AEC, Chairman David Lilienthal, Sumner Pike, and Robert Bacher favored a policy of going slow on the hydrogen bomb. Gordon Dean and Lewis Strauss, however, saw no reason for any delay and wanted to go ahead at once with a test program.

The Commission gave me a full account of its differences of opinion, and individual members expressed their own views in separate letters. I once again sought the advice of the Special Committee of the National Security Council, with Dean Acheson, Louis Johnson, and David Lilienthal as members.

"I have recently received," I wrote this committee on November 10, "a report by the Chairman of the Atomic Energy Commission which raises the question as to whether the United States should proceed with the construction of 'super' atomic weapons. This question involves consideration not only of the factors presented by the Atomic Energy Commission in its report but also political and military factors of concern to the Departments of State and Defense.

"To assist me in reaching a decision with respect to this vital question, I am therefore designating the Secretary of State, the Secretary of Defense and the Chairman of the Atomic Energy Commission as a special committee of the National Security Council to advise me on this problem. I suggest that each member of the committee provide from his agency appropriate staff officers to prepare under your supervision the necessary studies. I desire that the committee analyze all phases of the question including particularly the technical, military and political factors, and make recommendations as to whether and in what manner the United States should undertake the development and possible production of 'super' atomic weapons. Included in these recommendations, I should like to have the advice of the Council as to whether and when any publicity should be given this matter. . . ."

On January 31, 1950, at twelve-thirty, the Special Committee came to the White House with their report. It was a unanimous recommendation signed by all three members—Dean Acheson, Louis Johnson, and David Lilienthal, and the gist of their recommendation was this: that I should direct the AEC to take whatever steps were necessary to determine whether we could make and set off a hydrogen weapon. Concurrently with this, the Special Committee recommended a reexamination of our foreign policy and our strategic plans, both diplomatic and military.

I approved these recommendations and issued a public statement:

"It is part of my responsibility as Commander-in-Chief of the armed forces to see to it that our country is able to defend itself against any possible aggressor.

"Accordingly, I have directed the Atomic Energy Commission to continue its work on all forms of atomic weapons, including the so-called hydrogen or super-bomb.

"Like all other work in the field of atomic weapons, it is being and will be carried forward on a basis consistent with the overall objectives of our program for peace and security.

"This we shall continue to do until a satisfactory plan for international control of atomic energy is achieved. We shall also continue to examine all those factors that affect our program for peace and this country's security."

On February 24, about a month later, the Secretary of Defense and the Joint Chiefs of Staff submitted a recommendation to step up our program sharply by "immediate implementation of all-out development of hydrogen bombs and means for their production and delivery."

The military chiefs were going on the assumption that the test of the H-bomb would be successful and that for this reason they recommended authorization to plan for full-scale production of facilities, equipment, and appropriate carriers.

I referred this proposal for examination to the Special Committee of the National Security Council, which made a thorough study of all phases of the situation and on March 9 brought me a detailed report. In this I was informed that, according to my directive of January 31 (to the Atomic Energy Commission), the scientists at Los Alamos had turned their maximum efforts to a research and development program that would enable us to test a thermonuclear weapon as soon as possible, and that they were now of the opinion that a test of the first step in the process could take place sometime in 1951.

If the first test succeeded, then the entire process might be ready for testing by late 1952. The Special Committee reported that after a careful examination of all the facts it had been concluded that "there are no known additional steps which might be taken for further acceleration of the test program."

With these conclusions reached, it was now necessary to decide whether the AEC should proceed with its plans for the production of materials needed for thermonuclear weapons on the assumption that the tests would be successful.

There were many considerations involved, including the expense. The tests would cost an estimated ninety-five million dollars, and the diversion of parts of the U-235 bomb program would cost considerably more. The plants for the production, the main substance needed for the hydrogen bomb, would take, even on a modest scale, two hundred million dollars as a start. There would also be about one hundred million dollars involved in development programs that were less directly related to the making of the bomb.

It is obvious that a great many facts had to be studied in order to make a decision like this. Still, it is the President's responsibility to draw all ideas and all the obtainable facts together and balance them. He cannot allow himself to be swayed in any one direction. He must balance the military with the foreign policy, and both with the nation's economy.

Studying the report of the Special Committee, I had noted that the production facilities for one of the components could also be used for our current atomic program and in other fields of defense production.

Thus there would not be a total loss even if it turned out that the process failed to work. This, however, was still the big "IF."

Later in 1950 and in early 1951, Dr. Ulam and Dr. Teller, at Los Alamos, made new discoveries that changed the picture. But in March 1950 it was still to be proved that the fusing of a light atom like hydrogen could be achieved.

These were the circumstances at the time. Nevertheless, on March 10 additional emphasis was given to the H-bomb research by my declaring it to be "of the highest urgency," and I directed the Commission to plan at once for quantity production. Then, once we knew that the H-bomb was feasible, production on it should get under way as soon as possible.

As a result of this decision, the huge Savannah River project of the Atomic Energy Commission was started, and other expansions were made in the AEC plant facilities.

Meanwhile, the State Department policy planners and the planners in the Defense Department had been hard at work on the re-evaluation of our objectives which I had asked them to make in the directive of January 31, and I received from the two departments a first draft of their conclusions on April 7.

The report began with an analysis of the world situation. It pointed out that within the past thirty-five years the world had gone through two world wars, had seen two major revolutions, in Russia and in China, had witnessed the passing of five empires and the drastic decline of two major imperial systems, the French and the British. These events had basically altered the historical distribution of power until now there were only two major centers of power remaining, the United States and the Soviet Union.

The United States, the report continued, had its fundamental purpose clearly defined. The Preamble to the Constitution of the United States lists the aims of the American people in simple words that cannot be misunderstood: ". . . to form a more perfect Union, establish Justice, insure domestic Tranquillity, provide for the common defense, promote the general Welfare, and secure the Blessings of Liberty to ourselves and our Posterity."

In short, our fundamental aim was and is to assure the integrity and vitality of the free society we live in, a society that is based upon the dignity and worth of the individual.

The fundamental design of the Soviet Union, on the other hand, is a world dominated by the will of the Kremlin. Whether we like it or not, this makes the United States the principal target of the Kremlin—

the enemy that must be destroyed or subverted before the Soviets can achieve their goal.

The danger spots in the situation were discussed, and close attention was given to the effect of Russian atomic strength, as it was likely to develop over the next few years.

Our foreign policy aimed at building up rapidly the combined political, economic, and military strength of the free world.

The power of the atom is of key importance in a search for a peaceful world. With its vast potentialities for power development, the atom can bring welfare and prosperity to a world at peace. On the other hand, in a world that is close to the brink of war as ours has been for the past few years, the atom's power in the wrong hands can spell disaster. In the right hands, however, it can be used as an overriding influence against aggression and reckless war, and for that reason I have always insisted that, within the resources of a balanced security system and a balanced economy, we stay ahead of all the world in atomic affairs.

The development of the hydrogen bomb was one direction in which we held our commanding lead. But we were also able to adapt the A-bomb to new uses, even to the point where it became possible to build atomic cannons, to put atomic warheads on guided missiles and atomic-powered units into submarines.

As we were putting the atomic principle to new uses, however, we found it difficult to do the necessary testing at such remote places as Bikini and Eniwetok. In the summer of 1952 Gordon Dean, who had succeeded Lilienthal as AEC chairman, came to me with a proposal that we set up a test site in the continental United States. He recommended a location in Nevada, some seventy miles north of Las Vegas, but he also told me that the few top government officials with whom this had been discussed had been most doubtful about the proposal. One of them told him flatly: "The people of the United States will never stand for shooting off A-bombs in this country."

"Gordon," I asked, "if we set up this testing ground, will it really help our weapons program from the standpoint of time?"

Dean assured me that it would.

"Can this be done in such a way that nobody will get hurt?" I asked.

Dean said that every precaution would be taken.

I told him to go ahead. I suggested, however, that it might be well to do it without fanfare, and very quietly to advise the key officials in the area of the plans we had for the testing area.

By the end of 1952 twenty separate atomic detonations had been set off at the Nevada testing grounds on Yucca Flats, and a great number of different devices had been tested. Troops had been brought in to test defensive equipment and tactics, and several battalions of the Army were already equipped with new-type cannon capable of firing atomic shells. Furthermore, another important milestone in the development of the use of atomic power took place on June 14, 1952, when we laid the keel of the U.S.S. *Nautilus,* the first submarine and the first seagoing vessel of any kind to be operated by atomic power.

Meanwhile, the field of atomic energy for peacetime uses received continuous attention. On every occasion when Lilienthal, or later Gordon Dean, conferred with me, I asked for a report on research and industrial development efforts. Atomic energy can and should be turned into a power of vast benefit to humanity—unless, of course, men are foolish enough to let that power be turned to destruction.

Among the peaceful developments of the period was the building of a reactor at Arco, Idaho, that could turn out more fissionable material than was put into it. That this experiment was successful should prove of the greatest importance for the future development of atomic power for peaceful uses. It means that the way had been cleared for uses of atomic power that will be economically feasible; it meant that "atoms for peace" could now be talked about as something real and not merely a hope.

Thermonuclear power developments were moving on, in spite of unavoidable delays by material shortages. A crucial test came off successfully in March 1951 at Eniwetok. This was a tremendously important event, for it proved that the scientific calculations were correct, and with that knowledge in hand it now became possible to make further definite plans. Major progress was made shortly thereafter at a planning conference at Princeton, New Jersey, in June 1951, where the most important idea that was presented had to do with a novel plan for producing the hydrogen bomb in quantity.

On June 12 Gordon Dean brought me a full report of this meeting and of the program that was agreed upon. He said that if I approved this program now, we could expect our first full-scale thermonuclear test by early fall of 1952, and I took Dean's report with me for further study.

A week later he got my approval to go ahead.

One complication with this H-bomb test that we did not anticipate at the time was the combination of weather and American politics. When the fall of 1952 rolled around and preparations seemed near completion, the Atomic Energy Commission called for a weather forecast for the Eniwetok test site so that they could fix the exact date for the test. The weather in that part of the Pacific is such that in the fall only one or two days each month will give ideal conditions, and the best date for the test, it turned out, was November 1, only three days before the election.

Gordon Dean came to me and said that he and some of the other AEC Commissioners felt that it might perhaps not be desirable to set off the first full-scale H-bomb test so near to the election date. They were of the opinion that the explosion would surely not remain a secret and that it might be judged a political maneuver. I asked Gordon Dean if he knew of any other suitable date and what it would cost to postpone the test shot. He told me. I then instructed him to forget politics and hold the test on whatever date weather conditions would be most favorable. I think he knew what my answer was going to be before he came, for more than once he had heard me say that political considerations should never be tolerated in the nation's atomic program.

The first test of a hydrogen bomb, which was set off on November 1, 1952, was a dramatic success. So powerful was the explosion that an entire island was blown away and a huge crater left in the coral. It was an awesome demonstration of the new power, and I felt that it was important that the newly elected President should be fully informed about it. And on the day after the election I requested the Atomic Energy Commission to arrange to brief President-elect Eisenhower on the results of the test as well as on our entire nuclear program.

At the time the new administration took over, the nation had been through nearly seven and a half years of the atomic age. We had invested seven billion dollars in research and development in nuclear energy. By 1953 the nation had a stockpile of atomic bombs, together with the means for delivering these bombs to the target. It also had a growing arsenal of tactical weapons using atomic warheads, a submarine under construction powered by atomic energy, and a successfully tested hydrogen bomb and facilities for its production. By 1953 atomic energy had been applied successfully in the fields of medicine and biology, and research was being pushed still further for economically feasible peacetime uses. Furthermore, we had taken the leadership in proposing United Nations control of atomic power. In the interest of peace, we kept pressing for international control in the face of obstructive resistance of the Russians.

It is to the scientists, the members of the Commission, and the dedicated workers in laboratories and in factories to whom all credit must go. The roster of the membership of the Atomic Energy Commission, its staff and its advisory groups, reads like a list of the best men who have been attracted to public service. Some of them were subjected to harassment and abuse because they spoke their minds and refused to play politics with the program, but these are the men who keep democracy in the lead.

In this list of atomic developments, I have put the peaceful uses and the military uses side by side. It is a matter of practical necessity in the kind of world in which we live today that we gave priority to security, but I have always had the profound hope that atomic energy would one day soon serve its rightful purpose—the benefit of all mankind.

I would have been more than happy if our plan for international control had been carried out and if *all* efforts of the world's scientists could have been bent toward finding ways and means to make the atom serve man's wants and needs. It will always remain my prayer that the world will come to look upon the atom as a source of useful energy and a source of important healing power, and that there will never again be any need to invoke the terrible destructive powers that lie hidden in the elements.

CHAPTER 21

Before World War II there were probably few Americans who knew or thought much about Korea other than that it was a strange land in far-off Asia. Except for a small sprinkling of missionaries, Americans had had little occasion to know the "land of the morning calm" until our occupation forces landed there in the late summer of 1945.

Korea, once a kingdom to some extent dependent on China, had come under the domination of Japan after the Sino-Japanese War of 1894–95. Later—in 1910—the Japanese did away with all pretense and annexed the country, treating it as a conquered province.

At the Cairo conference in November 1943, President Roosevelt, Chiang Kai-shek, and Prime Minister Churchill had agreed that, "mindful of the enslavement of the people of Korea," they were "determined that in due course Korea shall be free and independent."

Later, at Teheran, the future of Korea was discussed in conferences between Roosevelt and Stalin. Stalin said that he had seen the Cairo Declaration and that "it was right that Korea should be independent." He also agreed that the Koreans would need some period of apprenticeship before full independence might be attained, perhaps forty years.

Korea was again discussed when President Roosevelt and Stalin talked privately during the Yalta conference in February 1945. President Roosevelt brought up the question of trusteeships in general and said that for Korea there ought to be a three-power trusteeship with the Soviets, the Chinese, and the United States represented. He cited the Philippines as an example of how long it might take Korea to become prepared for full self-government. The islands had required forty years;

perhaps Korea might be ready in twenty or thirty years. Stalin said that the shorter the period of trusteeship, the better it would be, and he was also of the opinion that the British should be asked to join in the trusteeship arrangement. Furthermore, he confirmed this understanding after I succeeded to the presidency, telling Harry Hopkins on May 28, 1945, that Russia was committed to the policy of a four-power trusteeship for Korea.

Korea was mentioned by Molotov but not discussed at my conferences with the Russian Premier and the British Prime Ministers at Potsdam. However, the Potsdam Declaration clearly implied that Japan would not be allowed to retain Korea. Also, when the military chiefs of our three nations conferred, it was agreed that following Russia's entry into the Pacific war there should be a line of demarcation in the general area of Korea between American and Russian air and sea operations. There was no discussion of any zones for ground operations or for occupation, for it was not expected that either American or Soviet ground troops would enter Korea in the immediate future.

The 38th parallel as a dividing line in Korea was never the subject of international discussions. It was proposed by us as a practicable solution when the sudden collapse of the Japanese war machine created a vacuum in Korea. We had no troops there and no shipping to land forces at more than a few locations in the southern half of the peninsula. The State Department urged that in all Korea the surrender of Japanese forces should be taken by Americans, but there was no way to get our troops into the northern part of the country with the speed required without sacrificing the security of our initial landings in Japan. In view of the fact that Stalin had concurred in the idea of a joint trusteeship, we expected that the division of the country would be solely for the purpose of accepting the Japanese surrender and that joint control would then extend throughout the peninsula.

The Russians, however, began at once to treat the 38th parallel as a permanent dividing line. They would allow no traffic across the line except with their express permission in each case. Since most of Korea's meager industrial plant was north of the parallel and most of its good farming area south of it, the division of the country disrupted the normal economic life of the nation and added to the misery of its people.

Our commander in Korea, Lieutenant General John R. Hodge, tried to open talks with his Russian counterpart, but his efforts were regularly rebuffed. After three months of occupation, General Hodge reported on the situation in Korea to the Joint Chiefs of Staff, expressing the opinion that the dual occupation of Korea, with Russia north and the United States south of the 38th parallel, imposed an impossible condition upon our occupation missions of establishing sound economy and preparing Korea for future independence. In South Korea the United States was being blamed for the partition, and resentment was growing against all Americans in the area. The Koreans, the general reported, knew full well that under the dual occupation any talk of real freedom and independence was purely academic, but they wanted their independence and were beginning to think that the Allied powers were not sincere in their promise. By occidental standards, Hodge wrote, the Koreans were not ready for independence, but it was also growing daily more apparent that their capacity for self-government would not greatly improve as long as the dual occupation continued.

The Allied interim solution of trusteeship was so strongly disliked by the Koreans that, in Hodge's opinion, "if it is imposed now or at any future time, it is believed possible that the Korean people will actually and physically revolt."

General Hodge wrote, in summary, "The U.S. occupation of Korea under present conditions and policies is surely drifting to the edge of a political-economic abyss from which it can never be retrieved with any credit to the United States' prestige in the Far East. Positive action on the international level or the seizure of complete initiative in south Korea by the U.S. in the very near future is absolutely essential to stop this drift. Specifically and urgently needed are:

"(1) Clarification and removal of 38th degree barrier so as to unify Korea. (2) Clear-cut statement of policy regarding status of former Japanese property in Korea and reparations as applied to any such property. (3) Reiteration of allied promise of Korean independence accompanying foregoing acts. (4) Establish complete separation of Korea from Japan in the minds of the press, the public, the State and War Departments and allied nations.

"Under present conditions with no corrective action forthcoming I would go so far as to recommend we give serious consideration to an agreement with Russia that both the U.S. and Russia withdraw forces from Korea simultaneously and leave Korea to its own devices and an inevitable internal upheaval for its self-purification."

It had already been decided to take up the matter on the governmental level. When Secretary Byrnes went to Moscow in December 1945, the question of Korea was one of the items he was to take up with Molotov.

The subject was brought up at the first meeting of the Foreign Ministers under the agreed agenda heading, "the creation of a unified administration for Korea looking toward the establishment of an independent Korean government." Secretary Byrnes introduced copies of a letter which Ambassador Harriman had addressed to Molotov on November 8 asking that the Soviet commander in Korea be given authority to consult with the American commander with a view to working out arrangements for such common problems as communications, commerce, currency, and other outstanding issues in Korea.

Molotov showed at once how difficult it was to deal with him. This letter, he said, dealt with matters other than government administration and therefore had no connection with the topic on the agenda. He wanted the discussion confined to the matters of administration and trusteeship.

The next day Mr. Byrnes brought in a statement of United States policy toward Korea. This statement began with a review of the Cairo Declaration, which, it was stressed, committed us to the establishment of an independent Korea. To attain this end, we proposed immediate action to abolish the separate zones of military administration and the creation of a unified administration as the temporary but necessary preliminary to a four-power trusteeship under the United Nations. We said we expected that independence might then be granted within five years.

Molotov asked for time to study our statement, and it was not until December 20 that he returned to the subject. Then he admitted that the Soviet Union had agreed to the idea of a four-power trusteeship, but, he said, this was a long-term rather than an immediate question. He then proposed on behalf of the Soviet government that a provisional government be set up in Korea to undertake all necessary measures for the development of industry, agriculture, and transportation of Korea and the national culture of the Korean people. A joint commission of representatives of the Soviet and United States commands in Korea should assist in the formation of such a provisional government, consulting with Korean democratic parties and social organizations, and presenting its recommendations to the respective governments for their consideration. The commission should also work out trusteeship proposals for the joint consideration of Great Britain, China, and the United States. Meanwhile, representatives of the United States and Soviet commands in Korea should meet within two weeks to consider urgent questions relating to both zones and to work out measures for the establishment of permanent co-ordination between the two commands in the administrative-economic sphere.

Secretary Byrnes informed Mr. Molotov the following day that, with two minor changes, this proposal would be acceptable to us, and it was incorporated in the communiqué of the Moscow conference.

This was reported to me by Byrnes on his return to the United States.

As had been agreed at Moscow, the American and Russian commanders in Korea met on January 16, 1946, but almost at once it became clear that no results would come from their talks. The Russians insisted that the conference had no authority to discuss anything except minor accommodations between the two zones. Our representatives took the position that the discussions should point toward the eventual joining of the zones. In the end, by February 5, only limited agreements had been reached on such matters as the interchange of mails, the allocation of radio frequencies, and the movement of persons and goods across the parallel. Even these understandings later proved difficult to translate into action, so that the net result of the commanders' talks was limited to occasional exchanges of mail and the exchange of small military liaison teams.

The Joint Commission provided for in the Moscow agreement began its work at Seoul, the ancient capital of Korea, on March 20, 1946. This Commission, which was, of course, the key element in the plan agreed upon at Moscow, was deadlocked almost from the start. We took the position that all Koreans were free to express their opinions and that the Commission should listen to representatives of any Korean political or social group that wished to be heard. The Russians, however, insisted that only those Koreans should be allowed to address the Commission who had given full support to the terms of the Moscow agreement. Virtually all the political parties active in our zone, however, had expressed their disappointment that independence would be postponed and a trusteeship phase instituted first, and by Russian standards that disqualified them from being heard by the Joint Commission. Korean Communists, of course, had refrained from open opposition to the Moscow agreement, and because of this, if the Russians had had their way, no one but the Communists would have been allowed to speak on behalf of the Korean people.

The Joint Commission adjourned *sine die* on May 8 without ever having come to grips with the problems of the nation. General Hodge made several efforts in the next few months to reach a basis for agreement with his Soviet counterpart, but with no results.

Meanwhile, one of the very few Americans who was allowed to visit the Russian zone of Korea submitted his report to me. Edwin W. Pauley, my personal representative in reparations matters, with the rank of Ambassador, visited the Russian-occupied zone of North Korea from May 29 to June 3, 1946, and was taken on an inspection of industrial plants by the Russian authorities there. He also spent considerable time in our zone of Korea. Upon the completion of his visit to Korea he wrote me a letter giving a summary of his observations:

June 22, 1946

Following are some observations, conclusions, and recommendations on the Korean situation based upon a firsthand inspection by myself and my staff in Korea. I have also given consideration to interviews with people in our Occupation Forces in Korea as well as Koreans and members of the Soviet Occupation Forces in Northern Korea.

Frankly, I am greatly concerned with our position in Korea and believe it is not receiving the attention and consideration it should. While Korea is a small country, and in terms of our total military strength is a small responsibility, it is an ideological battleground upon which our entire success in Asia may depend. It is here where a test will be made of whether a democratic competitive system can be adapted to meet the challenge of a defeated feudalism, or whether some other system, i.e. Communism will become stronger.

It is clear from the actions of the Soviets that they have no immediate intention of withdrawing from Korea for the following reasons:

1. They apparently are stalling on taking any joint action with the United States toward setting up a trusteeship, toward forming anything resembling a provisional government, or doing anything that might in any way hamper their entrenching themselves more firmly in Northern Korea.

2. They are propagandizing and promoting a Communist Party and a Soviet type of program which would establish loyalty to Moscow as the highest form of loyalty to Korea. To this end they are riding roughshod over all political factions which might oppose or even question such a philosophy. For example, the streets of Northern Korea are decorated with Soviet propaganda posters. Most of these posters publicize the Soviet Government, and include large pictures of Stalin and Lenin.

Many of the posters read as follows:
"Long live the friendship of the Soviet Union and Korea."
"The Soviet Government is the highest form of Democracy."
"We will raise the honor of the Red Army still higher."
"For the Fatherland, for the party, for Stalin."
"Long live Stalin, the creator of our victories."
"In a strange land a fighter must be more observant and on guard."
"The first teacher of a Red Army soldier is his Sergeant."

From the above it is clear that the Soviet Government does not intend to allow the United States exclusive use of the word "Democracy." "Democracy" means one thing to the Soviets, and quite another to the United States. To us it means, among other things, freedom of speech, assembly, and press. The Soviet interpretation of "Democracy" is expressed in terms of the welfare of the masses.

In considering the effect of Soviet propaganda on the Koreans, it must be remembered that about 70% of the present 27,000,000 people in Korea are small farmers and fishermen. Only a few have ever voted or even have the right to vote. They have little knowledge of national or international economic affairs, and are easily swayed by golden tongues and promises.

3. Communism in Korea could get off to a better start than practically anywhere else in the world. The Japanese owned the railroads, all of the public utilities including power and light, as well as all of the major industries and natural resources. Therefore, if these are suddenly found to be owned by "The People's Committee" (The Communist Party), they will have acquired them without any struggle of any kind or any work in developing them. This is one of the reasons why the United States should not

waive its title or claim to Japanese external assets located in Korea until a democratic (capitalistic) form of government is assured.

4. The Soviets are taking no substantial amount of capital equipment from Korea, although they may be taking certain stocks and products of current production.

5. They are devoting considerable effort to rejuvenate economic activity in Northern Korea probably directed toward replacing the broken economic ties to Japan with new economic ties to the U.S.S.R.

6. The Soviet Army is obviously ensconcing itself for a long stay. Officers' families are already with them. The Army is virtually operating the railroads. Statements by high ranking officers show no indication of any plan of leaving or even a hope of leaving. . . .

That fall the Russians conducted elections in their zone for local "People's Committees." Ninety-three and one third per cent of the voters went to the polls in a great demonstration of "loyalty" to the new regime. In accordance with Soviet practice, the voters did not have the embarrassment of having to choose between candidates. There was only one slate.

In our portion of Korea the keyword was "education, not indoctrination." Our military government allowed fullest freedom of speech, even where Koreans criticized the American occupation. Of course the majority of the Koreans wanted neither American nor Russian soldiers in their country, and the Communists made good use of this anti-foreign sentiment. There were disorders and demonstrations in our zone in the fall of 1946, and in a few instances our troops had to fire into threatening mobs.

The people of Korea had never known democratic government, and our methods were thus often misunderstood. When our military government tried to hear all factions, it was accused of indecision. When it warned against acts of violence, it was charged with partiality. Syngman Rhee, the veteran fighter for Korean independence, actually accused General Hodge and the military government of "trying to build up and foster the Korean Communist Party."

In January 1947 General Hodge reported that Korea might in fact engage in civil war unless American-Russian co-operation brought about some solution to the nation's problems. Economically, the country seemed to be going from bad to worse. Black markets were driving prices sky-high and draining the market of supplies. Floods, strikes, and the general deterioration of facilities as a result of the war brought about an almost complete breakdown of transportation.

On February 24, 1947, General Hodge reported to me in person at the White House. He gave me a full description of the economic distress and the political unrest in Korea. He described what the military government had done to prepare the way for a provisional government for our zone but recommended again that Russia and the United States find a joint solution to Korean problems. Earlier, General MacArthur had endorsed this recommendation when Hodge made it in writing from his headquarters in Seoul, urging that measures be taken immediately to break the U.S.-Russian deadlock in Korea by diplomatic means.

On the basis of these reports from General Hodge and General MacArthur, I approved Secretary Marshall's plan for one more effort to make the Joint Commission work. In April and May 1947 the Secretary of State exchanged letters with Molotov regarding Korea, and it appeared that the Soviet government was willing to modify its position. Arrangements were therefore made for the Joint Commission to resume its work at Seoul on May 21, 1947.

This development met with much opposition among the Koreans, who did not care to have the subject of trusteeship revived. Syngman Rhee was prominent in leading this opposition, and General Hodge was seriously worried that Rhee would use extreme rightist groups to sabotage the work of the Commission.

The Commission, on which Major General Albert E. Brown was the senior American representative, appeared at first to get off to a good start. The Russians were willing to hear any Korean group, regardless of its past position, which was now ready to support the policy of the Moscow agreements. Early in July, however, the Soviet delegation reverted to the position it had taken in the 1946 meetings of the Joint Commission. The Russians insisted again that those parties and individuals who had opposed the trusteeship provisions of the Moscow agreement were ineligible for consultation. Once again the basic issue of freedom of expression was raised, and on this point our representatives could not yield. Our delegation continued, however, to make efforts toward some joint action, but not one of its proposals was favorably considered by the Russians.

On August 26, 1947, we proposed to the Russians that the four powers who were to constitute the trusteeship powers for Korea—Britain, China, the U.S.S.R., and the United States—should meet in Washington on September 8 to find a way to carry out the Moscow agreement. With this invitation we submitted a seven-point proposal:

1. Early elections shall be held to choose provisional legislatures for each of the Russian and American zones. Voting shall be by secret, multi-party ballot on a basis of universal suffrage, and elections shall be held in accordance with the laws adopted by the present Korean legislatures in each zone.

2. These provisional zonal legislatures shall choose representatives in

numbers which reflect the proportion between the populations of the two zones, these representatives to constitute a national provisional legislature. This legislature shall meet at Seoul to establish a provisional government for a united Korea.

3. The resulting provisional government of a united Korea shall meet in Korea with representatives of the four powers adhering to the Moscow agreement on Korea to discuss with them what aid and assistance is needed in order to place Korean independence on a firm economic and political foundation and on what terms this aid and assistance is to be given.

4. During all the above stages the United Nations shall be invited to have observers present. . . .

5. The Korean provisional government and the powers concerned shall agree upon a date by which all occupation forces in Korea will be withdrawn.

6. The provisional legislatures in each zone shall be encouraged to draft provisional constitutions which can later be used as a basis for the adoption by the national provisional legislature of a constitution for all of Korea.

7. Until such time as a united, independent Korea is established, public and private Korean agencies in each zone shall be brought into contact with international agencies established by or under the United Nations. . . .

The Russians flatly rejected the suggestion. The Moscow agreement, they insisted, provided for a joint commission as the first step toward Korean independence, and any other approach to the subject would be in violation of that agreement. Our proposals were "unacceptable."

This left us no alternative but to conclude that direct negotiations with the Russians about Korea would be futile. I therefore instructed Secretary Marshall to place the issue before the General Assembly of the United Nations, which was about to convene at Lake Success, New York. Marshall presented our side of the controversy and asked the United Nations to do what "the inability of two powers to reach agreement" had so far prevented, which was to reunite Korea.

The Russians countered this move with a proposal made in the Joint Commission on September 26, that all occupation troops in Korea be withdrawn at the same time, sometime early in 1948. The American delegation to the Joint Commission replied that they had no power to enter into such an agreement. The Russian suggestion was thereupon repeated in a formal communication to the State Department. Acting Secretary of State Lovett replied that we could not enter into separate agreements while the principal issue was pending before the United Nations.

We had, however, given thought to the question of troop removal. Our armed forces had been drastically reduced from their wartime peaks, and there was strong congressional pressure to reduce military spending even further. Our commitments were many, but our forces were limited. I instructed the State and Defense Departments to weigh our commitments and consider where we might safely withdraw.

The Joint Chiefs of Staff made a careful study of the military aspects of a troop withdrawal from Korea and in September 1947 reported that we had little strategic interest in maintaining our undermanned occupation units in that country. At the time, the membership of the J.C.S., besides Admiral Leahy, consisted of General Eisenhower, Admiral Nimitz, and General Spaatz. Their views were incorporated in the following memorandum which was addressed to the Secretary of State, who brought it to me.

25 September 1947

The Joint Chiefs of Staff consider that, from the standpoint of military security, the United States has little strategic interest in maintaining the present troops and bases in Korea for the reasons hereafter stated.

In the event of hostilities in the Far East, our present forces in Korea would be a military liability and could not be maintained there without substantial reinforcement prior to the initiation of hostilities. Moreover, any offensive operation the United States might wish to conduct on the Asiatic continent most probably would by-pass the Korean peninsula.

If, on the other hand, an enemy were able to establish and maintain strong air and naval bases in the Korean peninsula, he might be able to interfere with United States communications and operations in East China, Manchuria, the Yellow Sea, Sea of Japan and adjacent islands. Such interference would require an enemy to maintain substantial air and naval forces in an area where they would be subject to neutralization by air action. Neutralization by air action would be more feasible and less costly than large-scale ground operations.

In the light of the present severe shortage of military manpower, the corps of two divisions, totaling some 45,000 men, now maintained in south Korea, could well be used elsewhere, the withdrawal of these forces from Korea would not impair the military position of the Far East Command unless, in consequence, the Soviets establish military strength in south Korea capable of mounting an assault on Japan.

At the present time, the occupation of Korea is requiring very large expenditures for the primary purpose of preventing disease and disorder which might endanger our occupation forces with little, if any, lasting benefit to the security of the United States.

Authoritative reports from Korea indicate that continued lack of progress toward a free and independent Korea, unless offset by an elaborate program of economic, political and cultural rehabilitation, in all probability will result in such conditions, including violent disorder, as to make the position of United States occupation forces untenable. A precipitate withdrawal of our forces under such circumstances would low the military prestige of the United States, quite possibly to the extent of adversely affecting cooperation in other areas more vital to the security of the United States.

When the Joint Chiefs made this report, they had available to them the results of a later much-talked-about study trip which Lieutenant General Albert C. Wedemeyer had undertaken at my request. General Wedemeyer had made a firsthand study of the situation in the summer of 1947, and on the question of American troop withdrawal he stated his conclusions in these words:

"So long as Soviet troops remain in occupation of North Korea, the United States must maintain troops in South Korea or admit before the world an 'ideological retreat.' The military standing of the United States would decline accordingly; not only through the Far East, but throughout the world. . . .

"Except as indicated above, and the fact that its occupation denies a potential enemy the use of warm-water ports and the opportunity to establish strong air and naval bases in the peninsula, the United States has little military interest in maintaining troops or bases in Korea. In the event of major hostilities in the Far East, present forces in Korea would most likely be a military liability as they could not be maintained there within our present military capabilities.

"There are three possible courses of action with reference to United States Occupation Forces in Korea:

"They may be withdrawn immediately, which would abandon South Korea to the Soviet Union through pressures which could be exerted by the North Korean People's (Communist) Army and is therefore an unacceptable course from the strategic viewpoint.

"They may remain in occupation indefinitely, which course would be unacceptable to the American public after Soviet withdrawal, and would subject United States to international censure.

"They may be withdrawn concurrently with Soviet occupation forces."

General Wedemeyer then recommended that this third course be followed, preferably on the basis of agreement with the Russians, and that we assist the South Koreans in the building and training of a native defense force before our troops were withdrawn.

To invite some form of agreement with the Russians on Korea, I gave approval to a detailed plan which was placed before the General Assembly of the United Nations. We proposed that elections be held in the two zones before March 31, 1948, under U.N. supervision, as the first step toward the establishment of a national government. This government, we urged, should then be asked to build up its own security forces, organize the machinery of government, and then arrange with the occupying powers for withdrawal of their troops. To supervise the elections and speed the subsequent steps, we suggested the creation of a United Nations Temporary Commission on Korea.

The Russians replied with the charge that we had violated the Moscow agreement by taking the case to the United Nations in the first place. Then they introduced a resolution calling for immediate withdrawal of occupation troops. This resolution was defeated, both in the First Committee and in the plenary session of the General Assembly, whereupon the Soviet representatives announced that if a U.N. commission on Korea were set up the Soviet Union would not be able to take part in its work.

The American spokesman before the General Assembly was Mr. John Foster Dulles, and the General Assembly adopted, with only the Soviet bloc abstaining, the United States proposal for Korea.

The United Nations Temporary Commission on Korea was set up accordingly. This body held its first meeting in Seoul on January 12, 1948, although the Russian commander in North Korea would not allow the Commission to enter the area north of the 38th parallel. He even refused to accept communications addressed to him by the Commission.

The Interim Committee of the General Assembly then instructed the Commission to carry out its work in whatever part of Korea it could reach. The Commission was to supervise free elections, which were held on May 10, 1948, and in spite of organized efforts by the Communists to create disorders and to sabotage the election, four out of five eligible South Koreans registered to vote, and better than ninety per cent of those registered cast their ballots. The election, the first free election in Korean history, was, so the U. N. Commission later reported, "a valid expression of the free will of the electorate in those parts of Korea which were accessible to the Commission and in which the inhabitants constituted approximately two-thirds of the people of all Korea."

The National Assembly elected by the people of the American zone met for the first time on May 31, 1948. It chose Mr. Syngman Rhee as chairman and then proceeded to the writing of a constitution for the Republic of Korea. This task was completed on July 12, the new constitution for Korea being promulgated on July 17. On July 20 Syngman Rhee was elected President of the Republic of Korea by the National Assembly.

The next step in the establishment of the Republic of Korea, in accordance with the General Assembly resolution, was the transfer of governmental authority from the military command and civilian occupation agencies in the southern zone to the newly constituted Republic of Korea. Our military government officers had, in the three years past, built up a complete governmental system, staffed almost completely by Koreans. This made the turnover easy.

I instructed the State Department to put it into effect as soon as possible. The people of Korea wanted a government of their own, and they were entitled to have it. On August 15, 1948, therefore, the Republic of Korea was formally proclaimed, and the American military government came to an end. Arrangements were made for the new government to assume control of the several police and security forces, and a property and financial settlement was concluded on September 11.

The Soviet occupation authorities in North Korea countered the establishment of the Republic of Korea when, on September 9, a "Democratic People's Republic of Korea" was proclaimed in Pyongyang. Then, ten days later, the Soviet Foreign Office advised our embassy in Moscow that all Soviet forces would be withdrawn from Korea by the end of December 1948. It later informed us that this had been done on schedule.

We, of course, were in favor of troop withdrawals. I have always believed that there is nothing that more easily creates antagonisms than the presence of unwanted soldiers, foreign or domestic. That was the way people in the southern states felt during the terrible reconstruction period, and when I was a very small boy I had heard much of southern reactions from my father and mother and from friends of my family. My father was just as unreconstructed as my mother was.

We knew, however, that the Russians had built up a "People's Army" in North Korea. We knew that Communist infiltration into South Korea was considerable. We knew that the new government of Syngman Rhee would find it difficult to resist effectively if it were attacked. However, a careful estimate had been made by our experts of the chances of survival of the new Republic of Korea, and the conclusion had been reached that "its prospects for survival may be considered favorable as long as it can continue to receive large-scale aid from the U.S."

In the spring of 1948 the National Security Council reported to me that we could do one of three things: We could abandon Korea; or we could continue our military and political responsibility for the country; or we could extend to a Korean government aid and assistance for the training and equipping of their own security forces and offer extensive economic help to prevent a breakdown of the infant nation. The Council recommended, however, that we choose the last course, and I gave my approval.

Secretary of the Army Royall said that in his talk with General MacArthur in early February 1949 the general expressed himself in favor of prompt withdrawal of our troops from Korea. Furthermore, when the National Security Council reviewed the situation in Korea on March 22, 1949, it had before it a report from MacArthur, stating that the training and combat readiness of the new security forces of the Korean Republic had reached such a level that complete withdrawal of U.S. troops from Korea was justified and would not adversely affect our position in Korea.

The South Koreans, by that time, had brought together an army of about sixty-five thousand men, and their training had progressed very satisfactorily. They were aided in their tasks by an advisory group of about five hundred officers and men from our Army. Except for that group, the last of our troops left Korea on June 29, 1949.

Shortly before the expiration of the military appropriations for Korea (for fiscal 1949), I sent a message to the Congress asking for economic aid to Korea in the amount of $150,000,000. Unfortunately the Congress took over four months to authorize this sum, and when I asked for another sixty million dollars for the same purpose in the budget for 1950–51, the request was actually defeated in the House of Representatives, with most of the negative votes coming from the Republican members. While it was later passed as part of a combined Korea-China aid bill, it can be said that, generally, Congress was in no hurry to provide the aid which had been requested for Korea by the President.

To bolster Korea's military position, I approved a defense agreement, which was signed on January 26, 1950. We continued, however, to be concerned over the internal and economic situation in South Korea. One of the reasons, though a minor one, why I had approved the policy of troop withdrawal was the danger that we might be unable to escape involvement in the political arguments of the young state. President Syngman Rhee is a man of strong convictions and has little patience with those who differ with him. From the moment of his return to Korea in 1945, he attracted to himself men of extreme right-wing attitudes and disagreed sharply with the political leaders of more moderate views, and the withdrawal of military government removed restraints that had prevented arbitrary actions against his opponents. I did not care for the methods used by Rhee's police to break up political meetings and control political enemies, and I was deeply concerned over the Rhee government's lack of concern about the serious inflation that swept the country. Yet we had no choice but to support Rhee. Korea had been overrun and downtrodden by the Japanese since 1905 and had had no chance to develop other leaders and leadership.

We knew that Rhee's government would be in grave danger if the military units of North Korea were to start a full-scale attack. For that reason we wanted him to make his own area as stable as it could be made, and, in addition, we wanted him to bring a measure of prosperity to the peasants that would make them turn their backs on the Communist agitators.

CHAPTER 22

As I discussed Korean policy with my advisers in the spring of 1948, we knew that this was one of the places where the Soviet-controlled Communist world might choose to attack. But we could say the same thing for every point of contact between East and West, from Norway through Berlin and Trieste to Greece, Turkey, and Iran; from the Kuriles in the North Pacific to Indo-China and Malaya.

Of course each commander believed that his area was in the greatest danger. It is obvious that the final decisions on the allocation of forces and matériel cannot be left to an area commander and must be made by the top-level command.

The intelligence reports from Korea in the spring of 1950 indicated that the North Koreans were steadily continuing their build-up of forces and that they were continuing to send guerrilla groups into South Korea.

There were continuing incidents along the 38th parallel, where armed units faced each other.

Throughout the spring the Central Intelligence reports said that the North Koreans might at any time decide to change from isolated raids to a full-scale attack. The North Koreans were capable of such an attack at any time, according to the intelligence, but there was no information to give any clue as to whether an attack was certain or when it was likely to come. But this did not apply alone to Korea. These same reports also told me repeatedly that there were any number of other spots in the world where the Russians "possessed the capability" to attack.

On Saturday, June 24, 1950, I was in Independence, Missouri, to spend the weekend with my family and to attend to some personal family business.

It was a little after ten in the evening, and we were sitting in the library of our home on North Delaware Street when the telephone rang. It was the Secretary of State calling from his home in Maryland.

"Mr. President," said Dean Acheson, "I have very serious news. The North Koreans have invaded South Korea."

My first reaction was that I must get back to the capital, and I told Acheson so. He explained, however, that details were not yet available and that he thought I need not rush back until he called me again with further information. In the meantime, he suggested to me that we should ask the United Nations Security Council to hold a meeting at once and declare that an act of aggression had been committed against the Republic of Korea. I told him that I agreed and asked him to request immediately a special meeting of the Security Council, and he said he would call me to report again the following morning, or sooner if there was more information on the events in Korea.

Acheson's next call came through around eleven-thirty Sunday morning, just as we were getting ready to sit down to an early Sunday dinner. Acheson reported that the U. N. Security Council had been called into emergency session. Additional reports had been received from Korea, and there was no doubt that an all-out invasion was under way there. The Security Council, Acheson said, would probably call for a cease-fire, but in view of the complete disregard the North Koreans and their big allies had shown for the U.N. in the past, we had to expect that the U.N. order would be ignored. Some decision would have to be made at once as to the degree of aid or encouragement which our government was willing to extend to the Republic of Korea.

I asked Acheson to get together with the Service Secretaries and the Chiefs of Staff and start working on recommendations for me when I got back. Defense Secretary Louis Johnson and Chairman of the Chiefs of Staff General Omar Bradley were on their way back from an inspection tour of the Far East. I informed the Secretary of State that I was returning to Washington at once.

The crew of the presidential plane Independence did a wonderful job. They had the plane ready to fly in less than an hour from the time they were alerted, and my return trip got under way so fast that two of my aides were left behind. They could not be notified in time to reach the airport.

The plane left the Kansas City Municipal Airport at two o'clock, and it took just a little over three hours to make the trip to Washington. I had time to think aboard the plane. In my generation, this was not the first occasion when the strong had attacked the weak. I recalled some earlier instances: Manchuria, Ethiopia, Austria. I remembered how each time that the democracies failed to act it had encouraged the aggressors to keep going ahead. Communism was acting in Korea just as Hitler, Mussolini, and the Japanese had acted ten, fifteen, and twenty years earlier. I felt certain that if South Korea was allowed to fall Communist leaders would be emboldened to override nations closer to our own shores. If the Communists were permitted to force their way into the Republic of Korea without opposition from the free world, no small nation would have the courage to resist threats and aggression by stronger Communist neighbors. If this was allowed to go unchallenged it would mean a third world war, just as similar incidents had brought on the second world war. It was also clear to me that the foundations and the principles of the United Nations were at stake unless this unprovoked attack on Korea could be stopped.

I had the plane's radio operator send a message to Dean Acheson asking him and his immediate advisers and the top defense chiefs to come to Blair House for a dinner conference.

When the Independence landed, Secretary of State Acheson was waiting for me at the airport, as was Secretary of Defense Johnson, who himself had arrived only a short while before. We hurried to Blair House, where we were joined by the other conferees. Present were the three service Secretaries, Secretary of the Army Frank Pace, Secretary of the Navy Francis Matthews, and Secretary of the Air Force Thomas Finletter. There were the Joint Chiefs of Staff, General of the Army Omar N. Bradley, the Army Chief General Collins, the Air Force Chief General Vandenberg, and Admiral Forrest Sherman, Chief of Naval Operations. Dean Acheson was accompanied by Under Secretary Webb, Deputy Under Secretary Dean Rusk and Assistant Under Secretary John Hickerson, and Ambassador-at-Large Philip Jessup.

It was late, and we went at once to the dining room for dinner. I asked that no discussion take place until dinner was served and over and the Blair House staff had withdrawn. I called on Dean Acheson first to give us a detailed picture of the situation. Acheson read us the first report that had been received by the State Department from our Ambassador in Seoul, Korea, at nine twenty-six the preceding evening:

According Korean army reports which partly confirmed by KMAG field advisor reports North Korean forces invaded ROK territory at several points this morning. Action was initiated about 4 A.M. Ongjin blasted by North Korean artillery fire. About 6 A.M. North Korean infantry commenced crossing parallel in Ongjin area, Kaesong area, Chunchon area and amphibious landing was reportedly made south of Kangnung on east coast. Kaesong was reportedly captured at 9 A.M., with some 10 North Korean tanks participating in operation. North Korean forces, spearheaded by tanks, reportedly closing in on Chunchon. Details of fighting in Kangnung are unclear, although it seems North Korean forces have cut highway. Am conferring with KMAG advisors and Korean officials this morning re situation.

It would appear from nature of attack and manner in which it was launched that it constitutes all out offensive against ROK.

Muccio

There were additional messages from Ambassador Muccio, too, giving more details, but all confirmed that a full-fledged attack was under way, and the North Koreans had broadcast a proclamation that, in effect, was a declaration of war.

Earlier that Sunday evening, Acheson reported, the Security Council of the United Nations had, by a vote of 9 to 0, approved a resolution declaring that a breach of the peace had been committeed by the North Korean action and ordering the North Koreans to cease their action and withdraw their forces.

I then called on Acheson to present the recommendations which the State and Defense Departments had prepared. He presented the following recommendations for immediate action:

1. That MacArthur should evacuate the Americans from Korea—including the dependents of the Military Mission—and, in order to do so, should keep open the Kimpo and other airports, repelling all hostile attacks thereon. In doing this, his air forces should stay south of the 38th parallel.

2. That MacArthur should be instructed to get ammunition and supplies to the Korean army by airdrop and otherwise.

3. That the Seventh Fleet should be ordered into the Formosa Strait to prevent the conflict from spreading to that area. The Seventh Fleet should be ordered from Cavite north at once. We should make a statement that the fleet would repel any attack on Formosa and that no attacks should be made from Formosa on the mainland.

At this point I interrupted to say that the Seventh Fleet should be ordered north at once but that I wanted to withhold making any statement until the fleet was in position.

After this report I asked each person in turn to state his agreement or disagreement and any views he might have in addition. Two things stand out in this discussion. One was the complete, almost unspoken acceptance on the part of everyone that whatever had to be done to meet this aggression had to be done. There was no suggestion from anyone that either the United Nations or the United States could back away from it. This was the test of all the talk of the last five years of collective security. The other point which stands out in my mind from the discussion was the difference in view of what might be called for. Vandenberg and Sherman thought that air and naval aid might be enough. Collins said that if the Korean army was really broken, ground forces would be necessary. But no one could tell what the state of the Korean army really was on that Sunday night. Whatever the estimates of the military might be, everyone recognized the situation as serious in the extreme.

I then directed that orders be issued to put the three recommendations into immediate effect.

As we continued our discussion, I stated that I did not expect the North Koreans to pay any attention to the United Nations. This, I said, would mean that the United Nations would have to apply force if it wanted its order obeyed.

General Bradley said we would have to draw the line somewhere. Russia, he thought, was not yet ready for war, but in Korea they were obviously testing us, and the line ought to be drawn now.

I said that most emphatically I thought the line would have to be drawn.

General Collins reported that he had had a teletype conference with General MacArthur. The Far East commander, he told us, was ready to ship ammunition and supplies to Korea as soon as he received the green light.

I expressed the opinion that the Russians were trying to get Korea by default, gambling that we would be afraid of starting a third world war and would offer no resistance. I thought that we were still holding the stronger hand, although how much stronger, it was hard to tell.

I asked the three Chiefs of Staff, Collins, Vandenberg, and Sherman, what information they had on Russian forces in the Far East. Then I asked Admiral Sherman what the location of the Seventh Fleet was. The admiral said the fleet was nearing the Philippines, two days out of Japan, and when I asked how long it would take to bring these ships to the Formosa Strait, he replied that it would take one and a half to two days.

I asked General Collins how many divisions we had in Japan and how long it would take to move two or three of them to Korea. The general gave the information.

Next I asked the Secretary of the Air Force Finletter and General Vandenberg what the present disposition of the Air Force was and how long it would take to reinforce our air units in the Far East.

I instructed the service chiefs to prepare the necessary orders for the eventual use of American units if the United Nations should call for action against North Korea, and meanwhile General MacArthur was directed to send a survey party to Korea to find out what kind of aid would be most effective and how the military forces available to the Far East commander might be used. He was also to furnish such ammunition and equipment to the Republic of Korea as he could spare, and was authorized to use air and naval cover to assure the delivery of these supplies and to protect the American dependents being evacuated from Korea. The Seventh Fleet was placed under MacArthur's command and was to have its base at Sasebo, Japan.

As the meeting adjourned, Acheson showed me a message which had reached him from John Foster Dulles, who had just returned to Tokyo from Korea. For some time Dulles had been at work for the State Department on the preparation of the peace treaty with Japan, and he too seemed to have little doubt about the course of action we had to take.

"It is possible," his message read, "that South Koreans may themselves contain and repulse attack, and, if so, this is best way. If, however, it appears they cannot do so then we believe that US force should be used even though this risks Russian counter moves. To sit by while Korea is overrun by unprovoked armed attack would start disastrous chain of events leading most probably to world war. We suggest that Security Council might call for action on behalf of the organization under Article 106 by the five powers or such of them as are willing to respond."

By Monday the reports from Korea began to sound dark and discouraging, and among the messages that arrived was one from Syngman Rhee asking for help in the telegraphic style of the State Department messages:

"Beginning in early morning 25 June, North Korean Communist Army began armed aggression against South. Your Excellency and Congress of US already aware of fact that our people, anticipating incident such as today's, established strong national defense force in order to secure bulwark of democracy in the east and to render service to world peace. We again thank you for your indispensable aid in liberating us and in establishing our Republic. As we face this national crisis, putting up brave fight, we appeal for your increasing support and ask that you at the same time extend effective and timely aid in order to prevent this act of destruction of world peace."

The Korean Ambassador, who brought me President Rhee's appeal, was downhearted almost to the point of tears. I tried to encourage him by saying that the battle had been going on for only forty-eight hours and other men in other countries had defended their liberties to ultimate victory under much more discouraging circumstances. I told him to hold fast—that help was on the way.

But the Republic of Korea troops were no match for the tanks and heavy weapons of the North Koreans. Seoul, the capital of Syngman Rhee's government, seemed doomed; Communist tanks were reported in the outskirts of the city. Rhee moved his government to Taegu, about one hundred and fifty miles to the south.

Throughout Monday the situation in Korea deteriorated rapidly. I called another meeting at Blair House Monday night. The same persons who attended the first meeting were again present except Secretary of the Navy Matthews, while Assistant Secretary of State Matthews took Rusk's place. MacArthur's latest message was alarming:

". . . Piecemeal entry into action vicinity Seoul by South Korean Third and Fifth Divisions has not succeeded in stopping the penetration recognized as the enemy main effort for the past 2 days with intent to seize the capital city of Seoul. Tanks entering suburbs of Seoul. Govt transferred to south and communication with part of KMAG opened at Taegu. Ambassador and Chief KMAG remaining in the city. FEC mil survey group en route to Korea has been recalled, under this rapidly deteriorating situation.

"South Korean units unable to resist determined Northern offensive. Contributory factor exclusive enemy possession of tanks and fighter planes. South Korean casualties as an index to fighting have not shown adequate resistance capabilities or the will to fight and our estimate is that a complete collapse is imminent."

There was now no doubt! The Republic of Korea needed help at once if it was not to be overrun. More seriously, a Communist success in Korea would put Red troops and planes within easy striking distance of Japan, and Okinawa and Formosa would be open to attack from two sides.

I told my advisers that what was developing in Korea seemed to me like a repetition on a larger scale of what had happened in Berlin. The Reds were probing for weaknesses in our armor; we had to meet their thrust without getting embroiled in a world-wide war.

I directed the Secretary of Defense to call General MacArthur on the scrambler phone and to tell him in person what my instructions were. He was to use air and naval forces to support the Republic of Korea with air and naval elements of his command, but only south of the 38th parallel. He was also instructed to dispatch the Seventh Fleet to the Formosa Strait. The purpose of this move was to prevent attacks by the Communists on Formosa as well as forays by Chiang Kai-shek against the mainland, this last to avoid reprisal actions by the Reds that might enlarge the area of conflict.

I also approved recommendations for the strengthening of our forces in the Philippines and for increased aid to the French in Indo-China.

Meanwhile the Security Council of the United Nations met again and adopted on June 27 the resolution calling on all members of the U.N. to give assistance to South Korea.

That same morning, Tuesday, I asked a group of congressional leaders to meet with me so that I might inform them on the events and the decisions of the past few days. With me that morning, in addition to the "Big Four" (Barkley, McFarland, Rayburn, McCormack), were Senators Connally, Wiley, Alexander Smith, George, Tydings, Bridges, and Thomas of Utah, and Representatives Kee, Eaton, Vinson, and Short. Acheson, Johnson, Pace, Matthews, Finletter, and the Joint Chiefs of Staff were present, with some of their aides.

I asked the Secretary of State to summarize the situation. Then I pointed out that it was the United Nations which had acted in this case and had acted with great speed. I read a statement which had already been prepared for release to the press later that day, and I asked for the views of the congressional leaders.

Senator Wiley asked what forces General MacArthur had dispatched so far. Secretary Johnson assured him that MacArthur had sent his air and naval units as soon as he had received his instructions to do so.

Senator Tydings said that his Armed Services Committee had that morning acted to extend the draft act and to give the President power to call out the National Guard.

Senator Smith commented that in Korea we would act as members of the U.N. rather than as a single nation. I said this was correct but pointed out that, so far as our action concerned Formosa, we were acting on our own and not on behalf of the U.N.

John McCormack wanted to know from Admiral Sherman if the Navy would not have to be enlarged, and Secretary Johnson replied that the Joint Chiefs had already begun to study such expansion of the services as might be needed but that a balanced program would be maintained.

Congressman Kee, Senator Connally, and the Secretary of State made several suggestions regarding the wording of the U.N. resolution, and Dewey Short expressed the hope that other nations would join in supporting the U.N. in this cause.

The congressional leaders approved of my action. On that same day Thomas E. Dewey, Republican leader, pledged his full support.

This is the statement I gave out to the press at the conclusion of this meeting with the congressional leaders:

June 27, 1950

STATEMENT BY THE PRESIDENT

In Korea the Government forces, which were armed to prevent border raids and to preserve internal security, were attacked by invading forces from North Korea. The Security Council of the United Nations called upon the invading troops to cease hostilities and to withdraw to the 38th parallel. This they have not done, but on the contrary have pressed the attack. The Security Council called upon all members of the United Nations to render every assistance to the United Nations in the execution of this resolution. In these circumstances I have ordered United States air and sea forces to give the Korean Government troops cover and support.

The attack upon Korea makes it plain beyond all doubt that Communism has passed beyond the use of subversion to conquer independent nations and will now use armed invasion and war. It has defied the orders of the Security Council of the United Nations issued to preserve international peace and security. In these circumstances the occupation of Formosa by Communist forces would be a direct threat to the security of the Pacific area and to United States forces performing their lawful and necessary functions in that area.

Accordingly I have ordered the Seventh Fleet to prevent any attack upon Formosa. As a corollary of this action I am calling upon the Chinese Government on Formosa to cease all air and sea operations against the mainland. The Seventh Fleet will see that this is done. The determination of the future status of Formosa must await the restoration of security in the Pacific, a peace settlement with Japan, or consideration by the United Nations.

I have also directed that United States Forces in the Philippines be strengthened and that military assistance to the Philippine Government be accelerated.

I have similarly directed acceleration in the furnishing of military assistance to the forces of France and the Associated States in Indo-China and the dispatch of a military mission to provide close working relations with those forces.

I know that all members of the United Nations will consider carefully the consequences of this latest aggression in Korea in defiance of the Charter of the United Nations. A return to the rule of force in international affairs would have far-reaching effects. The United States will continue to uphold the rule of law.

I have instructed Ambassador Austin, as the representative of the United States to the Security Council, to report these steps to the Council.

Our allies and friends abroad were informed through our diplomatic representatives that it was our feeling that it was essential to the maintenance of peace that this armed aggression against a free nation be met firmly. We let it be known that we considered the Korean situation vital as a symbol of the strength and determination of the West. Firmness now would be the only way to deter new actions in other portions of the world. Not only in Asia but in Europe, the Middle East, and elsewhere the confidence of peoples in countries adjacent to Soviet Union would be very adversely affected, in our judgment, if we failed to take action to protect a country established under our auspices and confirmed in its freedom by action of the United Nations. If, however, the threat to

South Korea was met firmly and successfully, it would add to our successes in Iran, Berlin, and Greece a fourth success in opposition to the aggressive moves of the Communists. And each success, we suggested to our allies, was likely to add to the caution of the Soviets in undertaking new efforts of this kind. Thus the safety and prospects for peace of the free world would be increased.

The top-level policy discussions were continued on Wednesday, June 28, when I opened another meeting of the National Security Council with a survey of the most recent developments reported from Korea. I told the departments concerned that I wanted a complete restudy made of all our policies in areas adjoining the U.S.S.R., and Secretaries Johnson and Acheson reported that a study of some of the immediate aspects growing out of the Korean situation had already been begun.

At this point Vice-President Barkley joined the meeting. He had been detained on Capitol Hill, but for a good cause, for he was able to report that the Senate had just voted unanimously to extend the draft.

Secretary Acheson pointed out that the unanimity of support for my policy might not be of lasting duration. What had been done in Korea had had tremendous effect, but the responsibilities that went with it were equally significant, for what had been done in the last three days might ultimately involve us in all-out war.

I replied that the danger involved was obvious but that we should not back out of Korea unless a military situation elsewhere demanded such action.

Averell Harriman, who had just arrived from Europe, observed that the people there had been gravely concerned lest we fail to meet the challenge in Korea. After my decision had been announced, he said, there had been a general feeling of relief, since it had been believed that disaster would otherwise be certain. He added that the Europeans were fully aware of the implications of my decision.

The Vice-President mentioned that he had heard one of the senators doubt the willingness of other NATO countries to help. I said that we had just received a specific offer by the British to furnish naval assistance, and I asked Secretary Johnson to provide the Vice-President with the details so that Barkley might be able to inform the members of the Senate.

The Secretary of the Air Force, Thomas Finletter, brought up the question of mutual understanding between Washington and the Far East Command in Tokyo. He felt that personal contact might help us avoid mistakes and suggested that General Vandenberg be sent over to inform General MacArthur more specifically on the thinking in Washington.

It was my opinion, however, that at the present moment the Chiefs of

Staff were most urgently needed in Washington. Nevertheless, I understood the need for mutual understanding between Washington and Tokyo and expressed my regret that General MacArthur had so consistently declined all invitations to return to the United States for even a short visit. There had been no opportunity for him to meet me as Commander in Chief. I felt that if the Korean conflict was prolonged I would want to see General MacArthur.

Secretary of the Army Pace reported that instructions had been issued to military intelligence to be alert for any evidence of Soviet participation in the Korean fighting, and wanted to know if there were any other special intelligence targets. I replied that our strategic intelligence was watching other areas besides Korea and I thought that Soviet activities in the vicinity of Yugoslavia, in Bulgaria especially, and in the vicinity of northern Europe should be given special attention.

The Army Secretary also reported that arrangements had been made for a system of military briefings to be given on Capitol Hill, whereupon I told the Vice-President that I wanted to be certain that those briefings were bi-partisan and that I wanted him to select those to attend them.

The National Security Council met again Thursday, when Secretary of Defense Johnson introduced a proposed directive to General MacArthur. The final paragraph of this proposed directive, however, permitted an implication that we were planning to go to war against the Soviet Union. I stated categorically that I did not wish to see even the slightest implication of such a plan. I wanted to take every step necessary to push the North Koreans back behind the 38th parallel. But I wanted to be sure that we would not become so deeply committed in Korea that we could not take care of such other situations as might develop.

Secretary Pace expressed the belief that we should be very careful in authorizing operations above the 38th parallel and that we should clearly limit such operations. I agreed, pointing out that operations above the 38th parallel should be designed only to destroy military supplies, for I wanted it clearly understood that our operations in Korea were designed to restore peace there and to restore the border. Secretary Acheson said that the Air Force should not be restricted in its tasks by a rigid application of the 38th parallel as a restraining line, but he wanted to be sure that precautions would be taken to keep the air elements from going beyond the boundaries of Korea. He suggested that the directive to MacArthur include some instructions in the case of Soviet intervention, perhaps to the effect that he defend his positions and our forces, and report at once for further instructions from the President.

I accepted this suggestion, and I told Acheson and Johnson to get together and work out the wording.

The Secretary of State then reviewed the reply received from the Soviets to our appeal to them to help bring the fighting in Korea to an end. Acheson expressed the belief that a statement which had been released in Peiping, taken together with the Russian reply, seemed to indicate that the Soviets would not intervene themselves but might help the Chinese Communists to do so. Acheson suggested, and I approved, the public release of our note to the U.S.S.R. and their reply.

The Secretary of State reported offers of assistance from Australia, Canada, New Zealand, and the Netherlands. I said that it was my hope that the forces assisting South Korea could be made truly representative of the United Nations.

Before closing the meeting I asked the Secretary of Defense to prepare a directive in my name to General MacArthur instructing him to make a full and complete report on the situation in the Far East each day.

A little later that day Secretary Acheson returned to the White House, and among the things we discussed was a communication from the Chinese government offering assistance in Korea. Chiang Kai-shek had instructed his Ambassador to tell us that he was willing to send ground forces numbering up to thirty-three thousand men but that he had neither air nor sea units and that U.S. assistance would be needed to get the ground forces from Formosa to Korea and then to supply them there.

I told Acheson that my first reaction was to accept this offer because I wanted, as I had said to the National Security Council earlier in the day, to see as many of the members of the United Nations as possible take part in the Korean action. Acheson suggested that the situation of Nationalist China was different from that of other U.N. members. Formosa was one of the areas most exposed to attack. That had been the reason we had dispatched the Seventh Fleet, and it would be a little inconsistent to spend American money to protect an island while its natural defenders were somewhere else. He also raised the question whether the troops of the Generalissimo would not require a great deal of re-equipping before they could go into combat under modern conditions.

I asked Acheson to bring up the matter the next day at a meeting with Defense Secretary Louis Johnson and the Joint Chiefs. The following morning I was still inclined to accept the Chinese offer. Frank Pace, the Secretary of the Army, telephoned me at five o'clock in the morning. He said that he had just spoken to General Collins, who had had a long telecon conference with MacArthur. General MacArthur had asked for the conference immediately upon his return from a flying trip to the Korean front line. MacArthur said he was convinced that only American ground units could stop the North Korean advance. He had asked for permission to commit one regimental combat team at once and to build up to two divisions as rapidly as possible.

The Secretary of the Army asked for my instructions.

I told Pace to inform General MacArthur immediately that the use of one regimental combat team was approved.

At seven that morning a staff colonel from the Joint Chiefs' office came over to brief me on the night's reports from Korea. As soon as he had finished, I called Pace and Johnson and told them to be prepared to discuss at a meeting at 8:30 A.M. MacArthur's request for authority to commit the two divisions and the offer of troops by Chiang Kai-shek.

At this meeting I had with me about the same group that met with me at Blair House the evening of my hurried return from Independence. I informed the meeting that I had already granted authority for the use of the one regimental combat team and that I now desired their advice on the additional troops to be employed. I asked if it would not be worth while to accept the Chinese offer, especially since Chiang Kai-shek said he could have his thirty-three thousand men ready for sailing within five days. Time was all-important.

At the same time I asked them to consider carefully places where trouble might break out. What, for instance, would Mao Tse-tung do? What might the Russians do in the Balkans, in Iran, in Germany?

Secretary Acheson suggested that if Chinese troops from Formosa appeared in Korea the Communists in Peiping might decide to enter that conflict in order to inflict damage on the Generalissimo's troops there and thus reduce his ability to defend himself whenever they might decide to try an invasion of Formosa.

The Chiefs of Staff pointed out that the thirty-three thousand men offered, even though the Generalissimo called them his best, would have very little modern equipment and would be as helpless as Syngman Rhee's army against the North Korean tanks.

Furthermore, the transportation they would require would be better used if we assigned it the task of carrying supplies and additional man-power of our own to MacArthur.

I was still concerned about our ability to stand off the enemy with the small forces available to us, but after some further discussion I accepted the position taken by practically everyone else at this meeting; namely, that the Chinese offer ought to be politely declined. I then decided that General MacArthur should be given full authority to use the ground forces under his command.

The first American ground troops sent into the Korean fighting were infantrymen from the 24th Infantry Division. By sea and by air, units of this veteran combat organization were rushed to the front lines to slow down the Communist advance, and the story of their action will always remain a glorious chapter in the history of the American Army. Inspiringly led by that wonderful fighting commander, Major General William F. Dean, the men of the 24th, most of them young recruits without battle experience, put up one of the finest rear-guard actions in military history.

I kept myself posted on the battle-front situation by way of a daily briefing which I was given each morning by General Bradley or by an officer from the Joint Chiefs' office. I also arranged for the National Security Council to meet each week, and at each of these meetings a briefing on the Korean situation was given by General Bradley himself or by an officer of his staff. This began on July 6, 1950, at the first meeting of the National Security Council after American troops had been committed to the ground action. It was then that General Bradley described the difficult position of the 24th Division and reported that the 25th Division, also from Japan, stood ready to move to Korea but that shipping was critical in the Far East and that another week would pass before these reinforcements could reach the front lines.

The Vice-President asked if we knew how many North Koreans were in the operation, and General Bradley told him that our intelligence estimated that there were ninety thousand. Vice-President Barkley then inquired how many troops were now engaged on our side, and Bradley told him that there were now about ten thousand Americans and about twenty-five thousand ROK regulars. Bradley also mentioned a new type of bazooka that was being rushed to Korea to give the troops there a weapon capable of stopping the heavy Russian-made tanks the North Koreans were using.

Navy Secretary Matthews asked about possible additional North Korean forces that might be brought in, and General Bradley said that intelligence from the Far East reported two more enemy divisions in North Korea that had not been committed, in addition to the possibility of elements, Korean or Chinese, that might be brought in from Manchuria.

In reply to a question from Secretary Snyder, Bradley said that North Korean divisions were smaller than ours, running about ten thousand men, but Secretary Pace added that the estimate of the intelligence agencies was that there were two hundred thousand Chinese Communist troops in Manchuria.

Furthermore, he went on to say that all three service Secretaries felt strongly that we should re-examine our entire "military posture" for the days ahead. I agreed, adding that it was my understanding that

Secretary Johnson had already set in motion the machinery for such a re-evaluation in motion.

There is a deceiving simplicity in saying that "the military posture is re-examined." Many of our armchair strategists think of war as if it were simply a map maneuver.

What a nation can do or must do begins with the willingness and the ability of its people to shoulder the burden. In 1945–46 the American people had chosen to scuttle their military might. I was against hasty and excessive demobilization at the time and stated publicly that I was, and General Eisenhower, then Army Chief of Staff, spoke out against it also. The press and the Congress, however, drowned us out.

Then there is the problem of what kind of military force to maintain —within the limits of what Congress and the people are willing to support. Today's military leaders are almost all technical specialists, and it is only natural that each should feel that his particular specialty is the most important aspect of the national defense picture. The same goes for the geographic distribution of national strength. Each area commander feels that it is his duty to have his area interests taken care of first, often without consideration of what goes on elsewhere in the world.

I have always understood this kind of thinking. When I was in command of Battery D in World War I, that was the center of the whole war effort for me, and I could and did argue with the battalion staff for always more and better equipment and attention for my outfit. As senator, my investigations had given me an insight into the constant contest between the war theaters for the lion's share of the war production, and as President, I always tried to listen to all sides before approving what I thought was the most balanced approach.

I did not lose sight of this approach when Korea broke on us. In Korea, the Communists challenged us, but they were capable of challenging us in a similar way in many places and, what was even more serious, they could, if they chose, plunge us and the world into another and far more terrible war. Every decision I made in connection with the Korean conflict had this one aim in mind: to prevent a third world war and the terrible destruction it would bring to the civilized world. This meant that we should not do anything that would provide the excuse to the Soviets and plunge the free nations into full-scale all-out war. I could not agree with the tactics or approach of those who, like Chiang Kai-shek in a speech on July 3, 1950, wanted the U.N. to charge the Russians with the full responsibility for this Korean conflict and to demand that Moscow put an end to it. This kind of bluster is certain to lead into an impossible dilemma. If these suggestions had been followed and the

Soviets had ignored the order, as in all likelihood they would have done, either the United Nations would have stood convicted of weakness or World War III would have been on.

It was our policy to strengthen the weak spots in the defense of the free world. Iran, Greece, Berlin, and NATO all stand as landmarks in the fight against Communism. In the same way, our increased aid to Indo-China and the Philippines and our move for the defense of Formosa by the Seventh Fleet were designed to reinforce areas exposed to Communist pressure. Yet every one of these steps had to be taken without losing sight of the many other places where trouble might break out or of the danger that might befall us if we hazarded too much in any one place.

Clement Attlee and his Cabinet had a similar world-wide view, and we agreed early in July, at Attlee's suggestion, to hold British-American talks in Washington. I designated General Bradley and Ambassador Jessup to speak for us, and the British were represented by their Ambassador, Sir Oliver Franks, and Marshal of the R.A.F. Lord Tedder, chairman of their Joint Services Mission in Washington. In these discussions, all the world's danger spots were reviewed to determine what policies the two countries should pursue in common in case of further Communist aggressions. Our representatives stated that it was our policy to concentrate our attention on the main trend of Soviet intentions. Korea, in the view of the conferees, had greatly increased the risk of total war. This reflected my own view as I had expressed it to Bradley and Jessup and to other leaders of the administration. If a second serious blow were to follow the one in Korea, it might well mean inescapable general war. It was in line with this policy that certain proposed flying photo-reconnaissance missions were not permitted. Some Air Force planners had proposed, on July 6, to fly some very high-level photo missions over Dairen, Port Arthur, Vladivostok, Karafuto, and the Kurile Islands. Fortunately, however, there were those on the Air Force staff who realized that political questions were involved and asked for State Department advice. Dean Acheson brought the matter to me. I told him that I took a most serious view of any such plan. I asked him to get in touch with Secretary of the Air Force Finletter and tell him that I wanted him to make it very plain to the Air Force commanders in the Far East that it was contrary to our policy to engage in activities that might give the Soviet Union a pretext to come into open conflict with us. All it would take would be for some of these photo-reconnaissance planes to be shot down by the Russians. This, of course, would create a new and more serious situation.

It was only natural for the Air Force commanders in the Far East to plan such reconnaissance missions. The information to be gained in this way would have been of help to their local situation. But there were over-all considerations that outweighed these local advantages, and the decision, therefore, had to be against the proposal.

This view was also taken by the agencies that prepared the studies on which I based my decisions.

General MacArthur was naturally preoccupied with Korea. Almost as soon as he was given the mission of aiding the South Koreans against the aggressors, he had worked out a strategic plan and began then to call for the troops necessary to carry out his plan.

His request for additional troops deserved high priority. I gave approval to an immediate alert order for the 2d Infantry Division, in addition to the 1st Marine Division, which was already preparing for the move to Korea, and instructed Secretary Johnson to call on Selective Service to furnish the armed forces with manpower needed to fill up the skeleton units and ships. I then directed that General Collins and General Vandenberg fly to Tokyo to confer with General MacArthur.

A few days earlier I had approved a proposal prepared jointly by the Departments of State and Defense to introduce in the U.N. a resolution creating a unified command in Korea, asking us to name a commander and authorizing the use of the blue U.N. flag in Korea. This resolution was approved by the Security Council on July 7, and on the following day I named General MacArthur to the post of U.N. commander.

On July 12 Lieutenant General Walton Walker arrived in Korea and established headquarters there for his Eighth Army and took over the command of United Nations forces in Korea. Meanwhile, our forces were still fighting a rear-guard action and were withdrawing steadily and doggedly toward the beachhead city of Pusan.

The American press made dramatic news out of this retreat. News stories spoke of entire units being wiped out and exaggerated the rout and confusion. Truth was that a small band of heroic youngsters led by a few remarkable generals was holding off a landslide so that the strength for the counterpunch could be mustered behind their thin curtain of resistance. The fact is that there was more panic among the civilians at home than among the soldiers in Korea.

By this time, however, General MacArthur had already conceived the basic plan for the counterattack. On July 7 the general had advised the Joint Chiefs of Staff that his basic operating plan would be to stop the enemy armies; to exploit fully the control of the sea and of the air; and, by amphibious maneuvers, to strike behind the mass of the enemy ground forces.

These major plans were the topics which General Collins and General Vandenberg discussed with General MacArthur during their visit with him. They had also discussed the problem of meeting the needs of the Far East Command within the over-all requirements of national policy and the use of Allied troop elements in Korea.

General MacArthur agreed to the use of Allied troops within his command, even though he realized that an amalgamation of nationalities would make his job more difficult. He did, however, advise against accepting the offer of thirty-three thousand Chinese Nationalist troops made by Chiang Kai-shek. He offered the opinion that these troops would be of little effect in Korea; they were infantry, without artillery or other support elements, and of unknown quality. They would, he said, require extensive logistical support from us and, in fact, would be an albatross around our necks for months. Furthermore, it was his opinion that the diversion of this force from Formosa to Korea would leave a gap on that island that would invite attack. He suggested that he would himself go to Formosa and explain the situation to Chiang Kai-shek.

As for the plans for the counterattack, it seemed that General Collins had serious misgivings about it. The MacArthur plan was for two divisions to land by sea near Inchon, in the vicinity of Seoul, and for one regimental combat team to be air-dropped in the same area. At the same time, the forces in the Pusan beachhead would break out toward the north. It was a bold plan worthy of a master strategist.

To make this plan possible required, however, a considerable stepping up of the rebuilding of the armed forces, and almost every time he communicated with us the Far East commander asked for increased numbers of troops. The JCS would scrutinize these recommendations and then submit their proposals to the Secretary of Defense. Of course I was not asked to decide on each and every troop movement decision. Nevertheless, basic decisions which the law placed in my responsibility were often necessary. Thus, on July 31, I approved a recommendation that four National Guard divisions be called into active federal service.

Earlier, on July 19, I had asked Congress to remove the limitations on the size of the armed forces and had urged legislation to authorize the establishment of priorities and allocations of materials to prevent hoarding and requisitioning of necessary supplies. I then stated that it would be necessary to raise taxes and to restrict consumer credit, and that an additional ten billion dollars for defense would be needed.

An advance copy of this message was sent to General MacArthur to inform him of the approach that was being taken at home. He thanked me for this in a most courteous telegram.

CHAPTER 23

On July 31 General MacArthur undertook the flying trip to Formosa that he had discussed with General Collins and General Vandenberg when they had visited him in Tokyo.

Our policy toward Formosa had been one of the topics discussed in Washington on July 27 at a meeting of the National Security Council. There was a recommendation from the Joint Chiefs before the Council that we grant all-out aid to the Chinese Nationalists so as to enable them to defend themselves against a possible Communist attack on the island. Many other phases of the situation were discussed. I approved three specific proposals: the granting of extensive military aid to Nationalist China; a military survey by MacArthur's headquarters of the requirements of Chiang Kai-shek's forces; and the plan to carry out reconnaissance flights along the China coast to determine the imminence of attacks against Formosa.

These decisions were communicated to General MacArthur by the Joint Chiefs of Staff on August 3, and on the same day I also informed him that I was sending Averell Harriman to Tokyo at once to discuss the Far Eastern political situation with him. Harriman's report to me on his meetings and conversations follows. (For reasons of brevity and for military security I have omitted portions of the Harriman memorandum.)

General MacArthur met me at Haneda Airport on our arrival at 9:45 A.M., August 6, 1950. He drove me to the guest house at the Embassy. As the window between the driver and his aide, and ourselves, was open, our conversation was general.

He described the satisfactory political development in Japan since my last visit. He spoke of the great quality of the Japanese; his desire to work, the satisfaction of the Japanese in work, his respect for the dignity of work. He compared it unfavorably to the desire in the United States for more luxury and less work.

He considered Communist infiltration into Japanese life was in no sense a threat as Communist ideas did not appeal to the Japanese, but, more importantly, it had the Russian label. The Japanese both feared and hated the Russians.

The reaction among the Japanese to our action in Korea was one of relief, as they interpreted it to mean that we would vigorously defend them against Russian invasion. They were not disturbed by our temporary difficulties, since they understood the military difficulties caused by the surprise attack. Their pride had been aroused by "his" confidence in them, shown by the withdrawal of most of the American troops. He could withdraw them all without any danger of disorder in Japan. . . .

He arranged for me and the officers with me to attend the morning briefing at 10:30 at Headquarters, and that I should call on him at his office at 11:30.

I had a 2½ hour talk with MacArthur in the morning: lunch with him and Mrs. MacArthur for the entire party, and then a further two-hour talk from 5:30 to 7:30 in the afternoon.

On Tuesday morning, after my return from Korea, we had a further four-hour talk before my departure.

The first 2½ hours included a military discussion at which Generals Ridgway and Norstad participated. General Almond also was present.

I will not attempt to divide the conversations chronologically, but largely by subject.

Our first talk on Sunday morning covered the military situation as he saw it.

I explained to him that the President had asked me to tell him that he wanted to know what MacArthur wanted, and was prepared to support him as fully as possible. I asked MacArthur whether he had any doubts about the wisdom of the Korean decision. He replied, "absolutely none." The President's statement was magnificent. It was an historic decision which would save the world from communist domination, and would be so recorded in history. The commitment of our ground forces was essential, and victory must be attained rapidly.

MacArthur described his firm conviction that the North Korean forces must be destroyed as early as possible and could not wait for a slow build-up. He emphasized the political and military dangers of such a course; the discouragement that would come among the United Nations including the United States; the effect on Oriental peoples as well as on the Chinese Communists and the Russians. He feared that Russia and the Chinese Communists would be able to greatly strengthen the North Korean forces and that time was of the essence, or grave difficulties, if not disaster, were ahead. . . .

He did not believe that the Russians had any present intention of intervening directly, or becoming involved in a general war. He believed the same was true of the Chinese Communists. The Russians had organized and equipped the North Koreans, and had supplied some of the trained personnel from racial Koreans of the Soviet Union who had fought in the Red Army forces. The Chinese Communists had cooperated in the transfer of soldiers who had fought with the Chinese Communist forces in Manchuria. These had not come over as units, but had been released in Manchuria, and reorganized into North Korean forces after they had been transported to North Korea. Their leadership was vigorous. A number of Russian officers were acting as observers but undoubtedly giving direction. Their tactics had been skillful, and they were as capable and tough as any army in his military experience.

He described the difference between the attitude towards death of Western-ers and Orientals. We hate to die; only face danger out of a sense of duty and through moral issues; whereas with Orientals, life begins with death. They die quietly, "folding their arms as a dove folding his wings, relaxing, and dying."

MacArthur could not see why we could not quickly recruit experienced combat non-commissioned officers, so badly needed, among the many who had served in the last war. He thought we could get the fast ships and airplanes to transport the needed troops rapidly. To think that we might fail in this, he said, "makes me feel sick in my stomach." (Both of these things he said on Tuesday morning.)

MacArthur wants maximum UN ground forces possible, as many as 30,000 or 40,000. He will take battalions (1,000 men) just as fast as they can come, with only their small arms. Actually, heavier artillery would be welcome, but the need is so great that he would take them with their small arms only. He feels the British should send a brigade from Hong Kong or Malaya; thinks it could be replaced from the United Kingdom. The French could send some forces from Indochina. A brigade from Pakistan and Turkey would be most welcome. Canada should send some troops. . . . Although he recognized the value of Eastern troops, he wasn't sure the Philippines could spare anything just now.

He has no doubts of the political outcome, once there is victory. Victory is a strong magnet in the East, and the Koreans want their freedom. When Syngman Rhee's government is reestablished in Seoul, the UN-supervised elections can be held within two months, and he has no doubt of an over-whelming victory for the non-communist parties. The North Koreans will also vote for a non-communist government when they are sure of no Russian or communist intervention. He said there was no need to change the Consti-tution, which now provides for 100 seats for the North. Korea can become a strong influence in stabilizing the non-communist movement in the East.

MacArthur thinks highly of Ambassador Muccio. He said they worked together fully and effectively.

In my first talk with MacArthur, I told him the President wanted me to tell him he must not permit Chiang to be the cause of starting a war with the Chinese communists on the mainland, the effect of which might drag us into a world war. He answered that he would, as a soldier, obey any orders that he received from the President. He said that he had discussed only military matters with the Generalissimo on his trip to Formosa. He had refused to discuss any political subjects whenever the Generalissimo at-tempted to do so. The Generalissimo had offered him command of the Chinese National troops. MacArthur had replied that that was not appro-priate, but that he would be willing to give military advice if requested by the Generalissimo to do so . . .

For reasons which are rather difficult to explain, I did not feel that we came to a full agreement on the way we believed things should be handled on Formosa and with the Generalissimo. He accepted the President's position and will act accordingly, but without full conviction. He has a strange idea that we should back anybody who will fight communism, even though he could not give an argument why the Generalissimo's fighting communists would be a contribution towards the effective dealing with the communists in China. I pointed out to him the basic conflict of interest between the U.S. and the Generalissimo's position as to the future of Formosa, namely, the preventing of Formosa's falling into hostile hands. Perhaps the best way would be through the medium of the UN to establish an independent government. Chiang, on the other hand, had only the burning ambition to use Formosa as a stepping-stone for his re-entry to the mainland. MacArthur recognized that this ambition could not be fulfilled, and yet thought it might be a good idea to let him land and get rid of him that way. He did not seem to consider the liability that our support of Chiang on such a move would be to us in the East. I explained in great detail why Chiang was a liability, and the great danger of a split in the unity of the United Nations on the Chinese-Communist-Formosa policies; the attitude of the British, Nehru and such countries as Norway, who, although stalwart in their determination to resist Russian aggression, did not want to stir up trouble elsewhere. I pointed out the great importance of maintaining UN unity among the friendly countries, and the complications that might result from any mis-steps in dealing with China and Formosa.

MacArthur would never recognize the Chinese Communists, even to the use of the veto in seating the Communists. He believes it would only strengthen the prestige of Mao Tse-tung's government in China and destroy what he considers should be our objective; the splitting of the present supporters of Mao Tse-tung and the developing of strengthened resistance movements. He does not believe the Chinese want to come under Russian domination. They have historically opposed invasion from the North. We should be more aggressive than we have been so far as creating stronger dissension within China. . . .

I emphasized the importance of getting evidence on the participation of the Chinese Communists in supporting the North Korean attack and present operations. There will be considerable support in seating the Chinese Communists at the next meeting of the Assembly. I explained that if we could obtain real evidence of direct support for the North Koreans, this might be the reason by which we could prevent the seating of the Communists on the moral issue involved.

In all, I cannot say that he recognizes fully the difficulties, both within the world and within the East, of whatever moves we make within China in our position with the Generalissimo in Formosa. He believes that our policies undermine the Generalissimo. He has confidence that he can get the Generalissimo to do whatever he is asked to undertake; is prepared to deal with the political problems, but will conscientiously deal only with the military side, unless he is given further orders from the President. . . .

He is satisfied the Chinese Communists will not attempt an invasion of Formosa at the present time. His intelligence and photographs show no undue concentration of forces, although they are building airstrips. He is convinced that the 7th Fleet plus the air jets from the Philippines and Okinawa, B-29's and other aircraft at his disposal, can destroy any attempt which may be made. He believes that the Chinese National troops can be organized to fight effectively and destroy any Communist troops which might get through. Should the Chinese Communists be so foolhardy as to make such an attempt, it would be the bloodiest victory in Far Eastern history, and would strengthen favorably morale in the East. . . .

He spoke about the problem of the island of Quemoy, close to the mainland. The Generalissimo claims to have 70,000 men there which is important from the standpoint of eventually landing on the mainland, but has no value to the U.S. The Generalissimo considers Formosa part of China. MacArthur didn't see any evidence of a desire for independence so far, even among the Formosans he talked to, but perhaps that was natural at this stage. There were no soldiers on the streets and no curfew; no evidence to support the pessimistic reports that had come from the State Department. . . .

MacArthur feels that we have not improved our position by kicking Chiang around, and hoped that the President would do something to relieve the strain that existed between the State Department and the Generalissimo. He suggested the President might reiterate his previous statements by threatening the Chinese Communists that he would withdraw the inhibition to attack the airfields on the mainland if the Chinese continued to do this work, or to build up their positions. I told him that if he wanted to make that recommendation to the President it was up to him, but I assured him that I would strongly recommended to the President against his doing so. I emphasized the overpowering importance of UN unity and that this would only give further trouble and give the Russians a chance to develop an entering wedge.

MacArthur strongly supports the development of strong forces in Europe, and further believes we should be more vigorous in strengthening the military forces to resist Communism in the East. He believes the Chinese Communists will not move their own troops south, but will train Indochinese and Burmese, equip them, and attempt to create by infiltration and support by well-equipped local Communist troops dissension, with the eventual hope of taking over these areas. Nehru, he believes, is concerned over the threat of communism, but is acting wrongly in thinking he will get anywhere by appeasement. "We should fight the communists every place—fight them like hell!" He considers the Truman Doctrine "great." It should be carried out more vigorously. We should organize economic assistance in the East as we have been doing in the Marshall Plan in Europe. Large sums are not required. This assistance should be capably directed. We should see that it gets to the people and corruption is avoided.

When he saw me off at the airport, he said loudly so that all could hear, "the only fault of your trip was that it was too short."

Attached to Harriman's personal report was a memorandum of the military discussion as prepared by General Ridgway. This was a summary of a two-and-a-half-hour presentation in which General MacArthur had stated his need for additional combat ground forces, both American and Allied.

I had asked Harriman to visit MacArthur so that the general might be given a firsthand account of the political planning in Washington. There had been several of our top military leaders who had visited Tokyo and had discussed the strategy of the Far Eastern situation with

MacArthur, but Harriman, who, of all my advisers, had the best knowledge of the economic recovery program, was particularly qualified to pass to MacArthur the views I held with regard to our over-all foreign policy.

General MacArthur's visit to Formosa on July 31 had raised much speculation in the world press. Chiang Kai-shek's aides let it be known that the Far East commander was in fullest agreement with their chief on the course of action to be taken. The implication was—and quite a few of our newspapers said so—that MacArthur rejected my policy of neutralizing Formosa and that he favored a more aggressive method.

After Harriman explained the administration's policy to MacArthur, he had said that he would accept it as a good soldier. I was reassured. I told the press that the general and I saw eye to eye on Formosa policy.

To make doubly sure, on August 14 the Joint Chiefs of Staff informed General MacArthur, with my approval, that the intent of the directive to him to defend Formosa was to limit United States action there to such support operations as would be practicable without committing any forces to the island itself. No commitments were to be made to the National Government for the basing of fighter squadrons on Formosa, and no United States forces of any kind were to be based ashore on Formosa except with the specific approval of the Joint Chiefs of Staff.

I assumed that this would be the last of it and that General MacArthur would accept the Formosa policy laid down by his Commander in Chief. But I was mistaken. Before the month ended—on August 26—the White House Press Room brought me a copy of a statement which General MacArthur had sent to the commander in chief of the Veterans of Foreign Wars. This document was not to be read until August 28, but MacArthur's public relations office in Tokyo had handed it to the papers several days in advance, and when I first heard about it, on the morning of August 26, a weekly magazine was already in the mails with the full text.

The substance of the long message was that, "in view of misconceptions being voiced concerning the relationship of Formosa to our strategic potential in the Pacific," the general thought it desirable to put forth his own views on the subject. He argued that the oriental psychology required "aggressive, resolute and dynamic leadership," and "nothing could be more fallacious than the threadbare argument by those who advocate appeasement and defeatism in the Pacific that if we defend Formosa we alienate continental Asia." In other words, he called for a military policy of aggression, based on Formosa's position. The whole tenor of the message was critical of the very policy which he had so recently told Harriman he would support. There was no doubt in my mind that the world would read it that way and that it must have been intended that way.

It was my opinion that this statement could only serve to confuse the world as to just what our Formosa policy was, for it was at odds with my announcement of June 27, and it also contradicted what I had told the Congress. Furthermore, our policy had been reaffirmed only the day before in a letter which, on my instructions, Ambassador Austin had addressed to the Secretary General of the United Nations, Trygve Lie.

The subject of Formosa had been placed before the Security Council by the Russian delegation, which charged us with acts of aggression in our aid to Chiang Kai-shek, and I had approved a State Department proposal that we counter this charge with a declaration that we were entirely willing to have the United Nations investigate the Formosa situation. Mr. Malik, the Russian delegate, was trying to persuade the Security Council that our action in placing the Seventh Fleet in the Formosa Strait amounted to the incorporation of Formosa within the American orbit. Austin's letter to Trygve Lie had made it plain that we had only one intention: to reduce the area of conflict in the Far East. General MacArthur's message—which the world might mistake as an expression of American policy—contradicted this.

Of course, I would never deny General MacArthur or anyone else the right to differ with me in opinions. The official position of the United States, however, is defined by decisions and declarations of the President. There can be only one voice in stating the position of this country in the field of foreign relations. This is of fundamental constitutional significance. General MacArthur, in addition to being an important American commander, was also the United Nations commander in Korea. He was, in fact, acting for and on behalf of the United Nations. That body was then debating the question of Formosa, and its members —even those outside the Soviet bloc—differed sharply in their views regarding Formosa. It was hardly proper for the U.N.'s agent to argue a case then under discussion by that body.

I realized that the damage had been done and that the MacArthur message was in the hands of the press.

I gave serious thought to relieving General MacArthur as our military field commander in the Far East and replacing him with General Bradley. I could keep MacArthur in command of the Japanese occupation, taking Korea and Formosa out of his hands. But after weighing it carefully I decided against such a step. It would have been difficult to avoid the appearance of a demotion, and I had no desire to hurt General MacArthur personally. My only concern was to let the world know that his statement was not official policy.

I had a meeting scheduled for that Saturday morning, August 26, with Dean Acheson, Louis Johnson, John Snyder, Averell Harriman, and the Joint Chiefs of Staff. I read this group the MacArthur statement and asked each of them if he had had any advance knowledge of it. It was a surprise and a shock to all. I then instructed Secretary Johnson to send a personal message to MacArthur telling him that I wanted him to withdraw the statement. This, I knew, would not prevent its distribution, but it would make clear that it had no official standing and that it had been taken back by the man who had written it.

On August 26, 1950, Secretary Johnson sent the following message to MacArthur:

"The President of the United States directs that you withdraw your message for National Encampment of Veterans of Foreign Wars, because various features with respect to Formosa are in conflict with the policy of the United States and its position in the United Nations."

General MacArthur complied with this directive at once, but I felt that I ought to supplement Secretary Johnson's telegram with a more detailed exposition of our policy. A clear summary of our Formosa position was contained in the letter which Ambassador Austin had written to Trygve Lie, and I decided to call this letter to MacArthur's attention. I knew that a copy had been sent to his headquarters, but it might well have been misplaced among the many papers reaching there from Washington. A personal letter from me would make certain that it would be read, I thought. This is the letter I wrote General MacArthur:

I am sending you for your information the text of a letter which I sent to Ambassador Austin dated August 27. I am sure that when you examine this letter, and the letter which Ambassador Austin addressed to Trygve Lie on August 25 (a copy of which I am told was sent your headquarters that night), you will understand why my action of the 26th in directing the withdrawal of your message to the Veterans of Foreign Wars was necessary.

General Collins and Admiral Sherman have given me a comprehensive report of their conversation with you and of their visit to the United Nations forces now fighting under your command in Korea. Their reports are most satisfactory and highly gratifying to me.

The text of the letter to Ambassador Austin referred to above follows:

"As I told you on the telephone this morning, I want to congratulate you on your able presentation of the views of the United States Government in the Security Council of the United Nations from the first onset of the aggression against the Republic of Korea. Throughout the entire course of the proceedings you have represented this Government with great effectiveness and in full accordance with my directions.

"The letter which you addressed to the Secretary General of the United Nations on August 25 on the subject of Formosa admirably sums up the fundamental position of this Government as it had been stated by me on June 27 and in my Message to the Congress on July 19. You have clearly set forth in that letter the heart and essence of the problem. You have faithfully set down my views as they were then and as they are now.

"To the end that there be no misunderstanding concerning the position of the Government of the United States with respect to Formosa, it may be useful to repeat here the seven fundamental points which you so clearly stated in your letter to Mr. Lie.

"1. The United States has not encroached on the territory of China, nor has the United States taken aggressive action against China.

"2. The action of the United States in regard to Formosa was taken at a time when that island was the scene of conflict with the mainland. More serious conflict was threatened by the public declaration of the Chinese Communist authorities. Such conflict would have threatened the security of the United Nations forces operating in Korea under the mandate of the Security Council to repel the aggression of the Republic of Korea. They threatened to extend the conflict through the Pacific area.

"3. The action of the United States was an impartial neutralizing action addressed both to the forces on Formosa and to those on the mainland. It was an action designed to keep the peace and was, therefore, in full accord with the spirit of the Charter of the United Nations. As President Truman has solidly declared, we have no designs on Formosa, and our action was not inspired by any desire to acquire a special position for the United States.

"4. The action of the United States was expressly stated to be without prejudice to the future political settlement of the status of the island. The actual status of the island that it is territory taken from Japan by the victory of the Allied forces in the Pacific. Like other such territories, its legal status cannot be fixed until there is international action to determine its future. The Chinese Government was asked by the Allies to take the surrender of the Japanese forces on the island. That is the reason the Chinese are there now.

"5. The United States has a record through history of friendship for the Chinese people. We still feel the friendship and know that millions of Chinese reciprocate it. We took the lead with others in the last United Nations General Assembly to secure approval of a resolution on the integrity of China. Only the Union of Soviet Socialist Republics and its satellites did not approve that resolution.

"6. The United States would welcome United Nations consideration of the case of Formosa. We would approve full United Nations investigation, here or on the spot. We believe that United Nations consideration would contribute to a peaceful, rather than a forceable solution of that problem.

"7. We do not believe that the Security Council need be, or will be, diverted from its consideration of the aggression against the Republic of Korea. There was a breach of the peace in Korea. The aggressor attacked, has been condemned, and the combined forces of the United Nations are now in battle to repel the aggression.

"Formosa is now at peace and will remain so unless someone resorts to force.

"If the Security Council wishes to study the question of Formosa, we shall support and assist that study. Meanwhile, the president of the Security Council should discharge the duties of his office and get on with the item on the agenda, which is the complaint of aggression against the Republic of Korea, and, specifically, the recognition of the right of the Korean Ambassador to take his seat and the vote on the United States resolution for the localization of the Korean conflict.

"These seven points accurately record the position of the United States.

"In the forthcoming discussion of the problem in the Security Council you will continue to have my complete support.

"Sincerely yours,
"Harry S. Truman"

The visit to Japan and Korea by General Collins and Admiral Sherman, to which I referred in my letter to MacArthur, marked an important phase in our effort in Korea. By early August our forces there had been built up to a ground strength of sixty-five thousand men, sufficient to hold the Pusan beachhead and enough to give encouragement to offensive planning, and on August 10 the Secretary of Defense informed me that it was planned to send nearly two more divisions to Korea before September 25. Naval and air forces had been similarly increased and further build-ups were in preparation.

To provide the forces General MacArthur had called for, we had drawn on troop units in the continental United States, in Puerto Rico, in Hawaii, and had even brought some marines back from duty with the fleet units in the Mediterranean.

General Collins and Admiral Sherman had left for Tokyo on August 19 for their detailed conference on General MacArthur's plans for an offensive, and on their return they placed these plans before me for my information and advised me that the Joint Chiefs had approved the plans. It was a daring strategic conception. I had the greatest confidence that it would succeed.

My confidence was expressed in a broadcast I made to the nation on September 1. "Two months ago," I said, "Communist imperialism turned from the familiar tactics of infiltration and subversion to brutal attack on the small Republic of Korea. The friendly nations of the world faced two possible courses: To limit their action to diplomatic protests while the Communist aggressors swallowed up their victim; or to meet military aggression with armed forces. The second course is the one which the free world chose. Thus, for the first time in all history, men of many nations are fighting under a single banner to uphold the rule of law in the world. This is an inspiring fact."

I declared that our aims and intentions could be put down in eight points: "1. We believe in the United Nations and pledge ourselves to seek peace and security through that organization. 2. We believe that

Koreans have a right to be free, independent, and united. 3. We do not want the fighting in Korea to spread into a general war; it will not spread unless Communist imperialism draws other armies and governments into the fight of the aggressors against the United Nations. 4. We hope in particular that the people of China will not be misled or forced into fighting against the United Nations and against the American people who have always been and still are their friends. 5. We do not want Formosa or any part of Asia for ourselves. 6. We believe in freedom for all of the nations of the Far East. 7. We do not believe in aggression or in preventive war. 8. Our men are fighting for peace today in Korea; we are working constantly for peace in the United Nations and in all the capitals of the world."

The decision to take the offensive in Korea made it necessary to consider on a high policy level what our subsequent course of action should be. This was done in National Security Council discussions which finally resulted in a policy statement that I approved on September 11, 1950.

The National Security Council recommended that our course of action would be influenced by three factors: action by the Soviet Union and the Chinese Communists, consultation with friendly members of the United Nations, and the risk of general war.

General MacArthur was to conduct the necessary military operations either to force the North Koreans behind the 38th parallel or to destroy their forces. If there was no indication or threat of entry of Soviet or Chinese Communist elements in force, the National Security Council recommended that General MacArthur was to extend his operations north of the parallel and to make plans for the occupation of North Korea. However, no ground operations were to take place north of the 38th parallel in the event of Soviet or Chinese Communist entry.

A Joint Chiefs' directive based on this recommendation, which I approved, was sent to General MacArthur on September 15.

September 15 was D-Day at Inchon. The 1st Marine Division and the Army's 7th Infantry Division went ashore there and established a bridgehead. Then these two units, comprising the X Corps commanded by Major General Almond, moved toward Seoul in order to free the Korean capital of the enemy. Resistance was fanatical, but on September 28 the liberation of the city was complete, and on September 29 Syngman Rhee moved his government back. Earlier, on September 26, a juncture had been effected between elements of the 1st Cavalry Division of the Eighth Army, which had broken out of the Pusan perimeter, and 7th Infantry Division troops from the Inchon area. The enemy was disorganized and badly shaken.

I sent a message of congratulations to General MacArthur:

"I know that I speak for the entire American people when I send you my warmest congratulations on the victory which has been achieved under your leadership in Korea. Few operations in military history can match either the delaying action where you traded space for time in which to build up your forces, or the brilliant maneuver which has now resulted in the liberation of Seoul. I am particularly impressed by the splendid cooperation of our Army, Navy and Air Force, and I wish you would extend my thanks and congratulations to the commanders of those services—Lieutenant General Walton H. Walker, Vice Admiral Charles T. Joy and Lieutenant General George E. Stratemeyer. The unification of our arms established by you and by them has set a shining example. My thanks and the thanks of the people of all the free nations go out to your gallant forces—soldiers, sailors, marines and airmen— from the United States and the other countries fighting for freedom under the United Nations banner. I salute you all, and say to all of you from all of us at home, 'Well and nobly done.' "

I had already given approval to new instructions which the Joint Chiefs of Staff had transmitted to MacArthur on September 27, in which he was told that his military objective was "the destruction of the North Korean Armed Forces." In attaining this objective he was authorized to conduct military operations north of the 38th parallel in Korea, provided that at the time of such operation there had been no entry into North Korea by major Soviet or Chinese Communist forces, no announcement of an intended entry, and no threat by Russian or Chinese Communists to counter our operations militarily in North Korea. He was also instructed that under no circumstances were any of his forces to cross the Manchuria or U.S.S.R. borders of Korea, and, as a matter of policy, no non-Korean ground forces were to be used in the provinces bordering on the Soviet Union or in the area along the Manchurian border. Similarly, support of his operations north or south of the 38th parallel by air or naval action against Manchuria or against U.S.S.R. territory was specifically ruled out.

The directive further instructed the Far East commander the action he should take in the event of Soviet entry into the conflict or entry by the Chinese Communists. It read:

"In the event of the open or covert employment of major Chinese Communist units south of the 38th parallel, you should continue the action as long as action by your forces offers a reasonable chance of successful resistance."

In compliance with this directive, General MacArthur submitted his plan for operations north of the 38th parallel, the substance of which was an attack north along the western coastal corridor by the Eighth Army and an amphibious landing by the X Corps at Wonsan on the east coast of North Korea. The Joint Chiefs approved this plan on September 29.

On September 30 I went aboard the *Williamsburg* for a week's cruise and work on the Potomac. I had learned that one of the hardest things for the President to do is to find time to take stock. I have always believed that the President's office ought to be open to as many citizens as he can find time to talk to; that is part of the job, to be available to the people, to listen to their troubles, to let them share the rich tradition of the White House. But it raises havoc with one's day, and even though I always got up early, usually was at work ahead of the staff, and would take papers home with me at night to read, there always seemed to be more than I could do.

I do not know of any easy way to be President. It is more than a full-time job, and the relaxations are few. I used the presidential yacht, as well as the Little White House at Key West, less for holiday uses than as hideaways, and they were very useful when I wanted to catch up on my work and needed an opportunity to consult with my staff without interruptions.

Even so, the daily press of paper work did not let up during such trips. If I went out on the *Williamsburg,* for instance, a plane would bring mail and newspapers every morning, usually around nine or nine-thirty. Powerful radio equipment aboard enabled me to talk to anybody at the White House or through the White House switchboard to anyone who could be reached by telephone.

So when I went aboard the *Williamsburg* on September 30, I was in constant contact with what was going on. I was advised that on October 1 MacArthur had informed the Joint Chiefs of Staff that he wanted to issue a dramatic announcement on the occasion of the crossing of the 38th parallel but that the Chiefs had stopped him. They pointed out that such a statement would be unwise and instructed him to let operations proceed without calling special attention to the fact that his forces had entered North Korea.

On October 2 MacArthur reported that Republic of Korea Army units were operating north of the 38th parallel, that progress was rapid, and that there seemed little enemy resistance. On October 3 the State Department received a number of messages which all reported the same thing: The Chinese Communists were threatening to enter the Korean conflict. Chou En-lai, now the Foreign Minister of the Chinese Communist regime, had called in the Indian Ambassador to Peiping, K. M. Panikkar, and had told him that if United Nations forces crossed the 38th parallel China would send in troops to help the North Koreans. However, this action would not be taken if only South Koreans crossed the 38th parallel.

This message was at once transmitted to General MacArthur.

Similar reports had been received from Moscow, Stockholm, and New Delhi. However, the problem that arose in connection with these reports was that Mr. Panikkar had in the past played the game of the Chinese Communists fairly regularly, so that his statement could not be taken as that of an impartial observer. It might very well be no more than a relay of Communist propaganda. There was also then pending in the Political and Security Committee of the General Assembly of the United Nations a resolution recommending that all appropriate steps be taken to insure stability throughout all of Korea. This resolution, if adopted, would be a clear authorization for the United Nations commander to operate in North Korea. The key vote on the resolution was due the following day, and it appeared quitely likely that Chou En-lai's "message" was a bald attempt to blackmail the United Nations by threats of intervention in Korea.

The possibility of Chinese intervention in Korea, however, could not be discounted, and I therefore instructed the Joint Chiefs of Staff to prepare a directive to General MacArthur to cover such an eventuality. The Joint Chiefs submitted their recommendation to me through the Secretary of Defense, George C. Marshall, who had succeeded Louis Johnson on September 21, and I approved the following message to General MacArthur:

"In light of the possible intervention of Chinese Communist forces in North Korea the following amplification of our directive [of September 25] is forwarded for your guidance:

" 'Hereafter in the event of the open or covert employment anywhere in Korea of major Chinese Communist units, without prior announcement, you should continue the action as long as, in your judgment, action by forces now under your control offers a reasonable chance of success. In any case you will obtain authorization from Washington prior to taking any military action against objectives in Chinese territory.' "

This directive was sent to General MacArthur on October 9. In the meantime, however, I had reached another decision. I wanted to have a personal talk with the general.

The first and the simplest reason why I wanted to meet with General MacArthur was that we had never had any personal contacts at all, and I thought that he ought to know his Commander in Chief and that I ought to know the senior field commander in the Far East. I have always regretted that General MacArthur declined the invitations that were extended to him to return to the United States, even if only for a short visit, during his years in Japan. He should have come back to familiarize himself with the situation at home. This is something I have always advocated for our foreign service personnel—that they should spend one year in every four in their own country. Then they would understand what the home folks were thinking.

Events since June had shown me that MacArthur had lost some of his contacts with the country and its people in the many years of his absence. He had been in the Orient for nearly fourteen years then, and all his thoughts were wrapped up in the East. I had made efforts through Harriman and others to let him see the world-wide picture as we saw it in Washington, but I felt that we had had little success. I thought he might adjust more easily if he heard it from me directly.

The Peiping reports of threatened intervention in Korea by the Chinese Communists were another reason for my desire to confer with General MacArthur. I wanted to get the benefit of his firsthand information and judgment.

For a short time I thought of flying to Korea to pay our troops there a brief visit. I realized that MacArthur would feel that his place in those perilous days was near his forces and that he would hesitate to make the long trip across the ocean for what might be only a few hours' talk. I suggested, therefore, that we meet somewhere in the Pacific, and Wake Island was agreed on as a good location.

I announced that I was going to meet General MacArthur over the weekend of October 13–17. The reason I chose this weekend was that I had agreed to speak on October 17 in San Francisco, where a little over five years earlier I had spoken at the signing of the United Nations Charter. Then, on October 24, I was scheduled to address the U. N. General Assembly in New York. Naturally I wanted to be able to include in these speeches a firsthand account from the United Nations commander, and, in this sense, the journey I had in mind would be taken on behalf of the United Nations as well.

I left Washington aboard the presidential plane Independence on the afternoon of October 11 on the first leg of the trip, which took us only as far as St. Louis. After an overnight stop there the flight was resumed at two-thirty in the afternoon of the twelfth, and six and three quarters hours later we landed at Fairfield-Suisun Air Force Base in California.

The first portion of our long flight across the ocean began shortly after midnight that night, but I had gone aboard the plane about an hour earlier and was asleep before the take-off. I woke up around five o'clock in the morning—or at least my watch gave that time. I discovered when I went forward to the pilots' section, however, that by local time it was only three. I had breakfast and then went forward again and sat in the second pilot's seat as we approached the Hawaiian Islands. It was still dark, but at regular intervals the lights of ships could be seen below. These were the destroyers the Navy had stationed along my route —just in case a mishap occurred to the plane. Colonel Williams, the pilot, said that visibility was exceptionally fine that morning; in any case, I had a breath-taking view of the entire chain of islands rising slowly out of the western sky, tiny little dark points in a vastness of blue that I would not have believed if I had not seen it myself. Then slowly the specks of land took shape and were distinct islands. At last the plane passed Diamond Head, circled low over Pearl Harbor, and came in for a landing at Hickam Air Force Base.

I was welcomed by an official party headed by Governor Stainback, Admiral Radford, commander of the Pacific fleet, and other high officials, both military and civilian.

Later that morning Admiral Radford escorted me on a boat trip about Pearl Harbor. He showed me the remnants and reminders of the tragic day in 1941, and he also showed me the fine facilities that served as the base for our great Pacific fleet today. I had lunch at the Officers' Club at Pearl Harbor and made a brief speech to the guests. In the afternoon I visited Tripler General Hospital and talked to some of the wounded who were there from Korea. Between Pearl Harbor and the hospital I seemed to have passed from one epoch of history into another, and yet 1941 was less than ten years ago.

The Independence left Hickam Field a few minutes after midnight on Saturday, October 14. Again I had retired before the plane was airborne and slept most of the way. I was asleep when we passed the international dateline, and I did not know that favorable wind conditions had gotten us ahead of schedule so that the pilot had to cut speed in order not to get to Wake Island before the prearranged arrival time.

I got up an hour before landing time, had breakfast with some of the members of my party, and at six-thirty the plane rolled to a halt on the Wake Island landing field. It was dawn. By local time it was Sunday, October 15.

General MacArthur was at the ramp of the plane as I came down. His shirt was unbuttoned, and he was wearing a cap that had evidently seen a good deal of use.

We greeted each other cordially, and after the photographers had finished their usual picture orgy we got into an old two-door sedan and drove to the office of the airline manager on the island.

We talked for more than an hour alone.

We discussed the Japanese and the Korean situations.

The general assured me that the victory was won in Korea. He also informed me that the Chinese Communists would not attack and that Japan was ready for a peace treaty.

Then he brought up the subject of his statement about Formosa to the Veterans of Foreign Wars. He said that he was sorry if he had caused any embarrassment. I told him that I considered the incident closed. He said he wanted me to understand that he was not in politics in any way—that he had allowed the politicians to make a "chump" (his word) of him in 1948 and that it would not happen again.

I told him something of our plans for the strengthening of Europe, and he said he understood and that he was sure it would be possible to send one division from Korea to Europe in January 1951. He repeated that the Korean conflict was won and that there was little possibility of the Chinese Communists coming in.

The general seemed genuinely pleased at this opportunity to talk with me, and I found him a most stimulating and interesting person. Our conversation was very friendly—I might say much more so than I had expected.

A little after seven-thirty we went to another small building, where other members of our parties had gathered. The others at this meeting, besides General MacArthur and myself, were Admiral Radford, Ambassador Muccio, Secretary of the Army Pace, General Bradley, Philip Jessup and Dean Rusk from the State Department, Averell Harriman, and Colonel Hamblen of Bradley's staff.

It was not until much later that I learned that Miss Vernice Anderson, the secretary to Ambassador Jessup, was next door and, without instructions from anyone, took down stenographic notes. This fact later became known during the hearings following General MacArthur's recall, and there was a good deal of noise about it. I can say that neither I nor Mr. Jessup nor anyone else had given Miss Anderson instructions to take notes; as a matter of fact, she was not brought along to take notes but merely to have a secretary available for the drafting of the communiqué that would have to be issued at the end of the meeting.

In any case, Miss Anderson's note-taking became known later on, and the record of what was said in this larger meeting at Wake Island has been printed in the newspapers and in some books as well. I will therefore relate here only the high points of the discussion—those things that so impressed me at the time that I remember them even without notes.

General MacArthur stated his firm belief that all resistance would end, in both North and South Korea, by Thanksgiving. This, he said, would enable him to withdraw the Eighth Army to Japan by Christmas. He would leave two divisions and the detachments of the other United Nations in Korea until elections had been held there. He thought this might be done as early as January and that it would then be possible to take all non-Korean troops out of the country.

Quite a bit of discussion followed about the aid Korea would need for rehabilitation once the conflict had been concluded, and both General MacArthur and Ambassador Muccio answered questions which were put to them by me and other members of my party. When Secretary Pace asked General MacArthur what the Army or ECA could do to help him, the general said, without any hesitation, that he did not know of any commander in the history of war who had ever had more complete and adequate support than he had received from all agencies in Washington.

I remember that we talked about the prisoners our forces had taken, and the general said that they were the happiest Koreans in all Korea. They were well fed and clean, and though they had been captured as North Korean "Communists," they were really no different from other Koreans.

Then I gave MacArthur an opportunity to repeat to the larger group some of the things he had said to me in our private meeting.

"What are the chances," I asked, "for Chinese or Soviet interference?"

The general's answer was really in two parts. First he talked about the Chinese. He thought, he said, that there was very little chance that they would come in. At the most they might be able to get fifty or sixty thousand men into Korea, but, since they had no air force, "if the Chinese tried to get down to Pyongyang, there would be the greatest slaughter."

Then he referred to the possibilities of Russian intervention. He referred to the Russian air strength, but he was certain that their planes and pilots were inferior to ours. He saw no way for the Russians to bring in any sizable number of ground troops before the onset of winter. This would leave the possibility of combined Chinese-Russian intervention, he observed, with Russian planes supporting Chinese ground units. This, he thought, would be no danger. "It just wouldn't work," he added, "with Chinese Communist ground and Russian air."

Most of the later discussion was given over to the subject of Japan. MacArthur expressed himself strongly in favor of a Japanese peace treaty and approved especially of the State Department draft. He also said, in reply to a question from me, that he thought a Pacific pact would be a good idea but that it would mean very little because the Asian nations had no military strength and therefore any agreement like that would be a one-way street, with the United States giving the Pacific nations a guarantee without getting much of anything in return. He thought a presidential statement would accomplish just as much as a pact in that area.

This formal conference ended at a little after nine o'clock. General MacArthur then had further discussions on technical matters with Secretary Pace and General Bradley, while Ambassador Muccio talked with the State Department officials in the party.

General MacArthur was anxious to return to Tokyo, and we decided, therefore, to leave Wake Island before lunch. The time differential between Wake Island and Tokyo would have thrown the general's return into the night hours if we had stayed and had lunch together, as I had planned.

I awarded General MacArthur a fourth Oak Leaf Cluster to his Distinguished Service Medal and also made an award to Ambassador Muccio. Then the general and I looked over the communiqué which General Bradley and Ambassador Jessup had drawn up, and MacArthur initialed it to indicate that it expressed his views.

As we returned to our planes I told MacArthur that I thought we had had a most satisfactory conference and that I hoped our next meeting would not be too long delayed. We shook hands, and he wished me "Happy landings" as I went aboard the Independence.

The return trip took us back across the international dateline on our way to Hawaii. It had been Sunday, October 15, when I left Wake Island, but it was Saturday, October 14, once again when I disembarked from the plane at Hickam Air Force Base. In this manner, although I had just spent Sunday on Wake Island, it was Sunday again the next day.

Most of the day was given over to work on the speech I would deliver in San Francisco. We had a lunch at a beach reservation and a drive to some of the scenic spots of the islands in the afternoon. The trip from Hawaii to San Francisco was made on Monday, October 16.

It was the following evening when I spoke in the San Francisco Opera House. I reported to the American people on the Wake Island meeting, and talked about Korea as a symbol of United Nations action.

"I have just returned from Wake Island," I said, "where I had a very satisfactory conference with General Douglas MacArthur.

"I understand that there has been speculation about why I made this trip. There is really no mystery about it. I went because I wanted to see and talk to General MacArthur. The best way to see him and talk to him is to meet him somewhere and talk to him.

"There is no substitute for personal conversation with the commander in the field who knows the problems there from first-hand experience. He has information at his fingertips which can be of help to all of us in deciding upon the right policies in these critical times.

"I went out to Wake Island to see General MacArthur because I did not want to take him far away from Korea, where he is conducting very important operations with great success. Events are moving swiftly over there now, and I did not feel that he should be away from his post too long.

"At the same time I believed my trip to Wake Island would give emphasis to the historic action taken by the United Nations on Korea. For Korea has become the symbol of the resistance of a united humanity against aggression.

"I also felt that there was pressing need to make it perfectly clear— by my talk with General MacArthur—that there is complete unity in the aims and conduct of our foreign policy.

"I have come back from this conference with increased confidence in our long-range ability to maintain world peace.

"At Wake Island we talked over the Far Eastern situation and its relationship to the problem of world peace. I asked General MacArthur for his ideas on the ways in which the United States can most effectively assist the United Nations in promoting and maintaining peace and security throughout the Pacific area.

"We discussed Japan and the need for an early Japanese peace treaty. Both of us look forward with confidence to a new Japan which will be peaceful and prosperous.

"General MacArthur told me about the fighting in Korea. He described the magnificent achievements of all the United Nations forces serving under his command. Along with the soldiers of the Republic of Korea these forces have now turned back the tide of aggression. More fighting men are coming from free nations all over the world. I am confident that these forces will soon restore peace to the whole of Korea.

"We here at home in America naturally take special pride in the superb achievements of our own soldiers, sailors, marines and airmen. They have written a glorious new page in military history. We can all be proud of them.

"It is also a source of pride to us that our country was asked to furnish the first commander of United Nations' troops. It is fortunate for the world that we had the right man for this purpose—a man who is a very great soldier—General Douglas MacArthur.

"Now I want Wake Island to be a symbol of our unity of purpose for world peace. I want to see world peace from Wake Island west all the way around and back again. I want to see world peace from Wake Island all the way east and back again—and we are going to get it!

"The United Nations action in Korea is of supreme importance for all the peoples of the world.

"For the first time in history the nations who want peace have taken up arms under the banner of an international organization to put down aggression. Under that banner, the banner of the United Nations, they are succeeding. This is a tremendous step forward in the age-old struggle to establish the rule of law in the world. . . .

"Today as a result of the Korean struggle the United Nations is stronger than it has ever been. We know now that the United Nations can create a system of international order with the authority to maintain peace.

"When I met with General MacArthur we discussed plans for completing the task of bringing peace to Korea. We talked about the plans for establishing a 'unified, independent, and democratic' government in that country in accordance with the resolution of the General Assembly of the United Nations.

"It has been our policy ever since World War I to achieve these results for Korea.

"Our sole purpose in Korea is to establish peace and independence. Our troops will stay there only so long as they are needed by the United Nations for that purpose. We seek no territory or special privilege in Korea or anywhere else. We have no aggressive designs in Korea or in any other place in the Far East or elsewhere. And I want that to be perfectly clear to the whole world.

"No country in the world which really wants peace has any reason to fear the United States of America.

"The only victory we seek is the victory of peace.

"The United Nations forces in Korea are making spectacular progress. But the fighting there is not yet over. The North Korean communists still refuse to acknowledge the authority of the United Nations. They continue to put up stubborn, but futile, resistance.

"The United Nations forces are growing in strength and are now far superior to the forces which will oppose them. The power of the Korean communists to resist effectively will soon come to an end. . . .

"Here, in San Francisco, five years ago, we hoped that the Soviet Union would cooperate in this effort to build a lasting peace.

"But communist imperialism would not have it so. Instead of working with other governments in mutual respect and cooperation, the Soviet Union attempted to extend its control over other peoples. It embarked on a new colonialism—Soviet style. This new colonialism has already brought under its complete control and exploitation many countries which used to be free countries. Moreover, the Soviet Union has refused to cooperate and has not allowed its satellites to cooperate with those nations it could not control.

"In the United Nations, the Soviet Union has persisted in obstruction. It has refused to share in activities devoted to the great economic, social, and spiritual causes recognized in the United Nations Charter. For months on end, it even boycotted the Security Council. . . .

"The Soviet Union and its colonial satellites are maintaining armed forces of great size and strength. In both Europe and Asia, their vast armies pose a constant threat to world peace. So long as they persist in maintaining these forces and in using them to intimidate other countries, the free men of the world have but one choice if they are to remain free. They must oppose strength with strength.

"This is not a task for the United States alone. It is a task for the free nations to undertake together. And the free nations are undertaking it together.

"In the United Nations, Secretary of State Dean Acheson has proposed a plan for 'Uniting For Peace,' to make it possible for the General Assembly to act quickly and effectively in case of any further outbreak of aggression. . . .

"Now, the Soviet Union can change this situation. It has only to give concrete and positive proof of its intention to work for peace. If the Soviet Union really wants peace, it must prove it—not by glittering promises and false propaganda, but by living up to the principles of the United Nations Charter.

"If the Soviet Union really wants peace, it can prove it—and could have proved it on any day since last June 25—by joining the rest of the United Nations in calling upon the North Koreans to lay down their arms at once.

"If the Soviet Union really wants peace, it can prove it by lifting the Iron Curtain and permitting the free exchange of information and ideas. If the Soviet Union really wants peace, it can prove it by joining in the efforts of the United Nations to establish a workable system of collective security—a system which will permit the elimination of the atomic bomb and the drastic reduction and regulation of all other arms and armed forces.

"But until the Soviet Union does these things, until it gives real proof of peaceful intentions, we are determined to build up the common defensive strength of the free world. This is the choice we have made. We have made it firmly and resolutely. But it is not a choice we have made gladly. We are not a militaristic nation. We have no desire for conquest or military glory. . . ."

CHAPTER 24

Throughout October the campaign in Korea made excellent progress. Pyongyang, the North Korean capital, was taken on October 19, and day after day MacArthur's forces were on the march.

These forces under his command had by now begun to take on a more and more international character. By mid-October there were in Korea, besides United States and Republic of Korea troops, ground units of Australia, Great Britain, and the Philippines. A Swedish hospital field unit was in action. Infantry from Thailand and Turkey were being disembarked at Korean ports, ready to join in the action. Naval assistance had come from Australia, Colombia, France, Great Britain, the Netherlands, New Zealand, and Norway. Furthermore, Belgium, Colombia, Canada, Ethiopia, France, and Greece were preparing ground units for movement to Korea. With every passing day the "unified command" became more and more a United Nations army. All in all, considering monetary and supply contributions, forty-two nations had by then offered their aid to the United Nations.

I realized that such a multi-national army created new and added problems for its commander. General MacArthur and his successors in command, General Ridgway and General Clark, deserve the highest credit for proving that it is possible to take fighting men from many nations and forge them into a successful army.

Among the many national elements, the Koreans themselves presented a problem. The Korean Army was green and inexperienced when the attack came. Its officers knew little of modern military techniques, and its top leaders lacked training and qualifications. General Mac-

Arthur did not have great confidence in the Korean Army at that time. The Joint Chiefs of Staff had instructed MacArthur that in his advance north he should not place non-Korean elements near the Manchurian and Soviet borders. But in his order to his commanders the general provided for the drive to the north to be spearheaded by American units. After the border was reached, South Koreans were to take their places "where feasible." The Joint Chiefs, expressing concern, asked MacArthur the reasons for this change.

In his answer General MacArthur said that the ROK forces were not of sufficient strength to accomplish the initial security of North Korea and that he considered it essential to use more seasoned and experienced commanders. MacArthur said he saw no conflict in his orders and the directive given him which stated: "We want you to feel unhampered tactically and strategically to proceed north of the 38th parallel." MacArthur added, "I am fully cognizant of the basic purpose and intent of your directive, and every possible precaution is being taken in the premises. The very reverse, however, would be fostered and tactical hazards might even result from other action than that which I have directed. This entire subject was covered in my conference at Wake Island."

While MacArthur's forces were moving north without too much opposition, there was considerable speculation about the likelihood of the Chinese Communists taking some action in North Korea. On October 20 the CIA delivered a memorandum to me which said that they had reports that the Chinese Communists would move in far enough to safeguard the Suiho electric plant and other installations along the Yalu River which provided them with power. The State Department's reaction to this report was to suggest that General MacArthur issue a statement to the United Nations that he did not intend to interfere with the operations of the Suiho and other power plants. The Joint Chiefs said that such an announcement would be undesirable from a military point of view. When the situation was placed before me, I instructed the Joint Chiefs to communicate the State Department's suggestion to MacArthur, asking if he had any objection to the issuing of such a statement. General MacArthur felt, however, that he did not wish his hands tied in such a manner, and the statement was therefore not issued.

It is very doubtful that it would have made any difference anyhow. As we were later to learn, the Chinese Communists had already started their move into North Korea, although it was not until October 31 that we gained evidence that they were in the battle area and actually fighting against the United Nations forces.

The first report came from the headquarters of the X Corps in the Wonsan sector of North Korea. Prisoners captured on October 26 and later days had been identified as Chinese and, on interrogation, proved to be members of organized Chinese units. The prisoners stated that their units had crossed the Yalu River on October 16, only one day after General MacArthur had assured me on Wake Island that if any Chinese were to enter Korea they would face certain disaster but that he did not expect them to try anything that foolish. I asked the Joint Chiefs of Staff to obtain an up-to-date estimate of the situation from General MacArthur. This was MacArthur's answer, received on November 4:

"It is impossible at this time to authoritatively appraise the actualities of Chinese Communist intervention in North Korea. Various possibilities exist based upon the battle intelligence coming in from the front:

"First, that the Chinese Communist Government proposes to intervene with its full potential military forces, openly proclaiming such course at what it might determine as an appropriate time; second, that it will covertly render military assistance, but will, so far as possible, conceal the fact for diplomatic reasons; third, that it is permitting and abetting a flow of more or less voluntary personnel across the border to strengthen and assist the North Korean remnants in their struggle to retain a nominal foothold in Korea; fourth, that such intervention, as exists, has been in the belief that no UN forces would be committed in the extreme northern reaches of Korea except those of South Korea. A realization that such forces were insufficient for the purpose may well have furnished the concept of salvaging something from the wreckage.

"The first contingency would represent a momentous decision of the gravest international importance. While it is a distinct possibility, and many foreign experts predict such action, there are many fundamental logical reasons against it and sufficient evidence has not yet come to hand to warrant its immediate acceptance.

"The last three contingencies, or a combination thereof, seem to be most likely condition at the present moment.

"I recommend against hasty conclusions which might be premature and believe that a final appraisement should await a more complete accumulation of military facts."

Thus General MacArthur warned against any hasty action and specifically discounted the possibility that the intervention of the Chinese Communists was a "new war." It came as something of a shock, therefore, when within two days he began to sound the alarm.

I was in Kansas City on November 6; it was the day before election, and as usual I planned to cast my ballot in Independence. That morning I received an urgent call from Dean Acheson. The Secretary of State was calling from a conference in Washington with the Under Secretary of Defense, Robert Lovett, and the matter before them was of such importance that they felt an immediate decision was necessary.

This was the situation and developments as Acheson reported to me over the telephone. Under Secretary of Defense Lovett had come to his office, Acheson said, at ten o'clock to tell him that a message had just been received from the Air Force commander in the Far East, Lieutenant General Stratemeyer. MacArthur had ordered a bombing mission to take out the bridge across the Yalu River from Sinuiju (Korea) to Antung (Manchuria). Ninety B-29's were scheduled to take off at one o'clock Washington time to take part in this mission. Lovett had told Acheson that from an operational standpoint he doubted whether the results to be achieved would be important enough to outweigh the danger of bombing Antung or other points on the Manchurian side of the river.

Assistant Secretary of State Dean Rusk pointed out that we had a commitment with the British not to take action which might involve attacks on the Manchurian side of the river without consultation with them. He also told Mr. Lovett that the State Department had presented MacArthur's report on Chinese Communist intervention to the United Nations and that an urgent meeting of the Security Council had been requested. At this meeting we would try to get a resolution adopted calling on the Chinese Communists to cease their activities in Korea; this was necessary in order to maintain U.N. support for any further action to be taken. Mr. Rusk also mentioned the danger of involving the Soviets, especially in the light of the mutual-assistance treaty between Moscow and Peiping.

Acheson went on to say that Lovett and he had agreed that this air action ought to be postponed until we had more facts about the situation there. Lovett then called Marshall, who agreed that the attack was unwise unless there was some mass movement across the river which threatened the security of our troops. Then Lovett called the Air Force Secretary, Mr. Finletter, and instructed him to tell the Joint Chiefs what Mr. Rusk had set forth and to tell them that he (Lovett) and Acheson both felt that this action should be postponed until they were able to get a decision from me.

I told Acheson that I would approve this bombing mission only if there was an immediate and serious threat to the security of our troops. Acheson said that nothing had been heard from MacArthur since his last report, and that report had contained no statement of any further movements across the river but had spoken only of reserves on the Chinese side. I told Acheson that we would have to find out why Mac-Arthur suddenly found this action necessary and told him to have Lovett issue instructions accordingly.

The Joint Chiefs of Staff carried out my instructions in a message that went out at eleven-forty Washington time, only an hour and twenty minutes before the planes were to take off from their Japanese bases. In the message that was sent, MacArthur was advised that consideration was urgently being given to the Korean situation at the governmental level. He was informed that there was a commitment not to take action affecting Manchuria without consultation with the British, and that until further orders all bombing of targets within five miles of the Manchurian border should be postponed. Meanwhile, he should forward his estimate of the situation and his reasons for ordering the bombing of the Yalu River bridges.

This was MacArthur's reply:

6 November 50

Men and material in large force are pouring across all bridges over the Yalu from Manchuria. This movement not only jeopardizes but threatens the ultimate destruction of the forces under my command. The actual movement across the river can be accomplished under cover of darkness and the distance between the river and our lines is so short that the forces can be deployed against our troops without being seriously subjected to air interdiction. The only way to stop this reinforcement of the enemy is the destruction of these bridges and the subjection of all installations in the north area supporting the enemy advance to the maximum of our air destruction. Every hour that this is postponed will be paid for dearly in American and other United Nations blood. The main crossing at Sinuiju was to be hit within the next few hours and the mission is actually being mounted. Under the gravest protest that I can make, I am suspending this strike and carrying out your instructions. What I had ordered is entirely within the scope of the rules of war and the resolutions and directions which I have received from the United Nations and constitutes no slightest act of belligerency against Chinese territory, in spite of the outrageous international lawlessness emanating therefrom. I cannot overemphasize the disastrous effect, both physical and psychological, that will result from the restrictions which you are imposing. I trust that the matter be immediately brought to the attention of the President as I believe your instructions may well result in a calamity of major proportion for which I cannot accept the responsibility without his personal and direct understanding of the situation. Time is so essential that I request immediate reconsideration of your decision pending which complete compliance will of course be given to your order.

General Bradley read this message to me over the phone. There were grave dangers involved in a mass bombing attack on a target so close to Manchuria and to Soviet soil. An overly eager pilot might easily bring about retaliatory moves; damaged planes might be forced to land in territory beyond our control. But since General MacArthur was on the scene and felt so strongly that this was of unusual urgency, I told Bradley to give him the "go-ahead."

This was the message sent MacArthur by the Joint Chiefs:

"The situation depicted in your message (of November 6) is considerably changed from that reported in last sentence your message (of November 4) which was our last report from you. We agree that the destruction of the Yalu bridges would contribute materially to the security of the forces under your command unless this action resulted in increased Chinese Communist effort and even Soviet contribution in response to what they might well construe as an attack on Manchuria. Such a result would not only endanger your forces but would enlarge the area of conflict and U.S. involvement to a most dangerous degree.

"However in view of first sentence your message (of November 6) you are authorized to go ahead with your planned bombing in Korea near the frontier including targets at Sinuiju and Korean end of Yalu bridges provided that at time of receipt of this message you still find such action essential to safety of your forces. The above does not authorize the bombing of any dams or power plants on the Yalu River.

"Because of necessity for maintaining optimum position with United Nations policy and directives and because it is vital in the national interests of the U.S. to localize the fighting in Korea it is important that extreme care be taken to avoid violation Manchurian territory and airspace and to report promptly hostile action from Manchuria.

"It is essential that we be kept informed of important changes in situation as they occur and that your estimate as requested in our [message of November 6] be submitted as soon as possible."

On this day, November 6, General MacArthur issued a communiqué in Tokyo in which he announced that his forces were now faced by a new and fresh army backed up by large reserves and adequate supplies within easy reach of the enemy but beyond the limits of the present sphere of military action.

The Central Intelligence Agency also now supplied me with an estimate of the situation based on their sources of information. It reported that there might be as many as two hundred thousand Chinese Communist troops in Manchuria and that their entry into Korea might stop the United Nations advance and actually force the United Nations forces to withdraw to defensive positions farther south. The estimate concluded by pointing to one inescapable fact: With their entry into Korea, the Chinese Communists had staked not only some of their forces but also their prestige in Asia. It had to be taken into account that they knew what risks they were taking; in other words, that they were ready for general war.

General MacArthur's estimate of the situation arrived in two messages on November 7. In the first of these messages MacArthur referred back to his initial appraisal (of November 4) of the Chinese intervention and concluded that he had been confirmed in his belief that this was not a full-scale intervention by the Chinese Communists. He conceded the possibility that the intervening forces might be reinforced to "a point rendering our resumption of advance impossible and even forcing a movement in retrograde." He was planning, he said, again to assume the initiative in order to take "accurate measure . . . of enemy strength." And he went on to say: "I deem it essential to execute the bombing of the targets under discussion as the only resource left to me to prevent a potential buildup of enemy strength to a point threatening the safety of the command. This interdiction of enemy lines of advance within Korea is so plainly defensive that it is hard to conceive that it would cause an increase in the volume of local intervention or, of itself, provoke a general war.

"The inviolability of Manchuria and Siberia has been a cardinal obligation of this headquarters from the beginning of hostilities and all verified hostile action therefrom is promptly reported. The destruction of hydroelectric installation has never been contemplated. Complete daily situation reports will continue to be furnished you as heretofore."

The second message from MacArthur read:

7 November 50

Hostile planes are operating from bases west of the Yalu River against our forces in North Korea. These planes are appearing in increasing numbers. The distance from the Yalu to the main line of contact is so short that it is almost impossible to deal effectively with the hit and run tactics now being employed. The present restrictions imposed on my area of operation provide a complete sanctuary for hostile air immediately upon their crossing the Manchuria-North Korean border. The effect of this abnormal condition upon the morale and combat efficiency of both air and ground troops is major.

Unless corrective measures are promptly taken this factor can assume decisive proportions. Request instructions for dealing with this new and threatening development.

Every military commander and every civilian official in the government is, of course, entitled to his views. Indeed, we would have a poor government if we expected all our public servants to be of one mind and one mind alone. I valued the expression of MacArthur's opinions, and so did the Joint Chiefs. There was never any question about my high regard for MacArthur's military judgment. But as President I had to listen to more than military judgments, and my decisions had to be made on the basis of not just one theater of operations but of a much more comprehensive picture of our nation's place in the world.

We were in Korea in the name and on behalf of the United Nations. The "unified command" which I had entrusted to Douglas MacArthur was a United Nations command, and neither he nor I would have been justified if we had gone beyond the mission that the United Nations General Assembly had given us.

There was no doubt in my mind that we should not allow the action in Korea to extend into a general war. All-out military action against China had to be avoided, if for no other reason than because it was a gigantic booby trap.

The Central Intelligence Agency's estimate of the situation was that the Russians were not themselves willing to go to war but that they wanted to involve us as heavily as possible in Asia so that they might gain a free hand in Europe.

I asked the Joint Chiefs of Staff to give their views on the military significance of the Chinese Communists' intervention in Korea. This is what they recommended:

"1. Every effort should be expended as a matter of urgency to settle the problem of Chinese Communist intervention in Korea by political means, preferably through the United Nations, to include reassurances to the Chinese Communists with respect to our intent, direct negotiations through our Allies and the Interim Committee with the Chinese Communist Government, and by any other available means.

"2. Pending further clarification as to the military objectives of the Chinese Communists and the extent of their intended commitments, the missions assigned to the Commander in Chief, United Nations Command, should be kept under review, but should not be changed.

"3. The United States should develop its plans and make its preparations on the basis that the risk of global war is increased."

General Marshall, as Secretary of Defense, concurred in these conclusions.

At a meeting on November 9 the National Security Council held a full discussion of these views of the Joint Chiefs and of the general problems created by the Chinese intervention. I was unable to attend this meeting but was given a report of the proceedings afterward.

General Bradley stated at this meeting that there were three possible intentions of the Chinese Communists with which we would have to reckon. First, it was possible that the Chinese desired only to set up a buffer area that would protect their interests in the power facilities along the Yalu River. If this were the case, then negotiations might be fruitful. Second, the Chinese Communists might wish to force us into a war of attrition that would commit our forces to the point where we might be in danger of losing if the Soviets decided to start a global war. Third, we had to consider in our planning that the Chinese might have it as their aim to drive us completely off the Korean peninsula. This last possibility, so the Joint Chiefs of Staff thought, would mean World War III, because the Chinese Communists would be unable to do it alone, and Soviet entry would inevitably extend the fighting to every point of contact between East and West.

General Bradley said that in his opinion we should be able to hold in the general area of our present positions but that there would be an increasing question of how much pressure we could stand without attacking Manchurian bases. The Joint Chiefs of Staff, however, were of the opinion that such an attack should be a United Nations decision, since it exceeded the terms of the resolution under which the U.N. forces were operating.

General Bradley noted that General MacArthur seemed to think that the bombing of the bridges across the Yalu would stop the flow of Chinese Communist troops into Korea. Bradley himself, however, thought that this was rather optimistic.

Secretary of Defense Marshall pointed out at this meeting of the National Security Council that our eastern front in Korea was widely dispersed and thinly spread and that this represented an added risk. General Bradley replied that of course General MacArthur had done this in order to carry out his directive that he was to occupy the whole country and hold elections.

General Bedell Smith of Central Intelligence said that the Yalu River would be frozen over in about fifteen to thirty days and would be passable, with or without the bridges.

Secretary Acheson asked General Bradley if there was any line that was better from a military point of view than the present one, and Bradley replied that from a purely military point of view the farther back the line was the easier it would be to maintain. He added, however, that he realized that any backward movement of our forces would lose us support and might lose us the South Koreans' will to fight.

Secretary Acheson expressed himself as feeling that the Russians were especially interested in the idea of defense in depth. He suggested, therefore, that a buffer area in Northeast Korea be established under a U.N. commission, with a constabulary but no U.N. armed forces. The Chinese, Acheson said, had two interests: The first was to keep us involved, while the lesser interest was in the border and the power plants. He thought that we ought to explore privately the possibility of a twenty-mile demilitarized zone, ten miles on each side of the Yalu. He went on to say that the trouble with any such proposal, of course, would be that the Communists would insist on all foreign troops leaving Korea, and thus abandon Korea to the Communists.

When Secretary Acheson summarized this discussion, he pointed out that it was agreed that General MacArthur's directive should not now be changed and that he should be free to do what he could in a military way, but without bombing Manchuria. At the same time, the State Department would seek ways to find out whether negotiations with the Chinese Communists were possible, although one problem was that we lacked any direct contacts with the Peiping regime through diplomatic channels.

The situation in Korea, it should be pointed out, was not the only instance of a new aggressiveness on the part of Communist China. There was evidence that the Communist rebel forces in Indo-China were receiving increasing aid and advice from Peiping. Also, in the last days of October, Communist China had moved against the ancient theocracy of Tibet.

We were seeing a pattern in Indo-China and Tibet timed to coincide with the attack in Korea as a challenge to the Western world. It was a challenge by the Communists alone, aimed at intensifying the smoldering anti-foreign feeling among most Asian peoples.

Our British allies and many statesmen of Europe saw in the Chinese moves a ruse to bring to a halt American aid in the rebuilding of Europe. They knew that nothing had hurt world Communism worse than the policy of the United States: aid to Greece and Turkey, the Marshall Plan, the decision to hold fast in Berlin, the North Atlantic Treaty Organization. The Kremlin could never communize Europe as long as that policy was followed and the United States stood ready to back it. The first commandment of Soviet foreign policy has always been to divide the enemies of the Soviet Union, and the unity that United States leadership had created in Europe was the most important target for world Communism's attack.

I had no intention of allowing our attention to be diverted from the unchanging aims and designs of Soviet policy. I knew that in our age, Europe, with its millions of skilled workmen, with its factories and transportation network, is still the key to world peace.

There have been, and there are, men in the United States, some well-meaning, some misguided, some malicious, who would have us believe that we must impose our way of life on the people of Asia even at the cost of letting Europe go. I cannot agree. But partisans of this point of view are vocal, and they have the means to make themselves heard. The Senate is a great sounding board. The speeches of the Asia-first advocates in the Senate and elsewhere receive wide publicity and never fail to arouse fear in the minds of our friends abroad. During my presidency our policy was never dictated by any other nation, however friendly to us. We maintained a deep devotion to the ideal of peace—peace through the United Nations, peace by working with others who had shared our aims and our attitudes.

The month of November 1950 saw us, therefore, occupied in three moves, so far as Korea was concerned. One was to reassure our allies in Europe, especially the British and the French, that we had no intention of widening the conflict or of abandoning our commitments in Europe for new entanglements in Asia. The second was in the United Nations, where we sought the maximum support for our resistance against the Chinese intervention in Korea, without, however, pushing the U.N. toward military sanctions against Peiping—which would have meant war. The third effort was directed toward ascertaining the strength and the direction and aim of the Chinese Communist effort.

General MacArthur started his Eighth Army on a major attack on November 24. He announced that it was a "general offensive . . . to end the war . . ." and he told one of his commanders to tell the troops that they would be home by Christmas! Previously, on November 6 and 7, he had sounded an alarm in his messages to Washington that seemed to portend impending disaster. But now, apparently, the grave danger did not exist, since he announced victory even before the first men started marching.

Yet on the same day a national intelligence summary of the CIA had been made available to General MacArthur which stated that the Chinese Communists would "at a minimum" increase their operations in Korea, seek to immobilize our forces, subject them to prolonged attrition, and maintain the semblance of a North Korean state in being. It also stated that the Chinese possessed sufficient strength to force the U.N. elements to withdraw to defensive positions.

The intelligence summary proved correct. By November 28 it was clear that the Eighth Army had run up against vastly larger forces and that the X Corps, on the east coast, was in what the communiqué writers like to call a "fluid situation"—which is a public relation man's way of saying that he can't figure out what's going on!

Now, no one is blaming General MacArthur, and certainly I never did, for the failure of the November offensive. He is no more to be blamed for the fact that he was outnumbered than General Eisenhower could be charged with the heavy losses of the Battle of the Bulge. But—and herein lies the difference between the Eisenhower of 1944 and the

MacArthur of 1950—I do blame General MacArthur for the manner in which he tried to excuse his failure. In the first place, there was no need for him to proclaim this as an "end-the-war" offensive. If he knew that the forces opposing him were not so strong that they could stop him, then certainly his earlier message to the Chiefs of Staff had been wrong. But if he had been right earlier in November, then he could hardly have expected to score an easy victory now.

Perhaps these inconsistencies were to be expected, MacArthur had many times in World War II announced victory while his troops still faced the stiffest part of the battle. But there was no excuse for the statements he began to make to certain people as soon as the offensive had failed. Within a matter of four days he found time to publicize in four different ways his view that the only reason for his troubles was the order from Washington to limit the hostilities to Korea. He talked about "extraordinary inhibitions . . . without precedent in military history" and made it quite plain that no blame whatsoever attached to him or his staff.

The record shows, however, that General MacArthur himself reported to the Joint Chiefs of Staff, on November 6 and 7, that the Chinese had intervened in Korea in strength. He had himself furnished us the information that there were sizable reserves across the Yalu River. He had requested—and been given—permission to bomb the bridges across which these reserves might flow into Korea.

Of course he had been denied authority to bomb bases in Manchuria and to engage in "hot pursuit" of enemy planes fleeing from Korea into Manchuria. The State Department and the Joint Chiefs of Staff were in agreement that it would be desirable to have U.N. approval for such a policy and therefore, with my approval, inquiries were made of all United Nations countries that had forces in Korea. Without exception, they indicated strong opposition. Indeed, they also stressed their wish that no non-Korean units should be placed in the area immediately adjacent to the Yalu River if our offensive should carry us that far.

There was no doubt that we had reached a point where grave decisions had to be made. If we chose to extend the war to China, we had to expect retaliation. Peiping and Moscow were allies, ideologically as well as by treaty. If we began to attack Communist China, we had to anticipate Russian intervention. Of course we wanted no war on any scale. But neither did we or the world want Communist slavery. And the question now was whether we had actually reached the point where this slavery so threatened us that we had to move to the destruction of cities and the killing of women and children.

I can only assume that General MacArthur thought so and that those who wanted his plans carried out thought so too. It was not improbable that Communist China would have moved into full-scale war after we bombed Manchurian bases. I believed Russia would have so moved also.

Yet repeated statements by MacArthur led many people abroad to believe that our government would change its policy. We could not permit such confusion to continue. On December 5, therefore, I issued an order to all government agencies that "until further written notice from me . . . no speech, press release, or other public statement concerning foreign policy should be released until it has received clearance from the Department of State." A second notice admonished "officials overseas, including military commanders and diplomatic representatives . . . to exercise extreme caution in public statements, to clear all but routine statements with their departments, and to refrain from direct communication on military or foreign policy with newspapers, magazines, or other publicity media in the United States."

A few months earlier there had been one incident of a high official talking out of turn about foreign policy. That was when Secretary of the Navy Francis Matthews made a speech on August 25. Mr. Matthews, speaking in Boston, said that we ought to fight a "preventive war." I have always been opposed even to the thought of such a war. There is nothing more foolish than to think that war can be stopped by war. You don't "prevent" anything by war except peace.

Mr. Matthews, of course, was surrounded by admirals and other high Navy people, and he had not had much experience in dealing with men in that category. He told me he had heard so many of them talk "preventive war" that he had repeated the phrase without realizing just how far it took him away from my policy. He was very contrite and full of regrets when I talked to him and explained why I could not have members of my administration going around the country advocating a view that was so completely opposed to the official policy of the government.

General MacArthur was a more serious offender with his press interviews and communiqués in which he sometimes hinted and sometimes said that if only his advice had been followed all would have been well in Korea.

In the first place, of course, he was wrong. If his advice had been taken, then or later, and if we had gone ahead and bombed the Manchurian bases, we would have been openly at war with Red China and, not improbably, with Russia. World War III might very well have been on.

In the second place, General MacArthur himself had been the one who had said there was no danger of Chinese intervention. At Wake Island he had told me categorically that he had no evidence that a massed intervention was threatening. More important still, he had told me that he could easily cope with the Chinese Communists if they actually came in. He had said that if the Communists from China tried to retake Pyongyang they would be inviting slaughter.

Even before he started his ill-fated offensive of November 24, he still talked as if he had the answer to all the questions. But when it turned out that it was not so, he let all the world know that he would have won except for the fact that we would not let him have his way.

This was simply not true. General MacArthur had been given fullest information on the reasons for our policy. He had told numerous visitors to his Tokyo office, including Harriman, and he had told me at Wake Island that he understood these reasons although he did not believe in them. Of course every second lieutenant knows best what his platoon ought to be given to do, and he always thinks that the higher-ups are just blind when they don't see his way. But General MacArthur—and rightly, too—would have court-martialed any second lieutenant who gave press interviews to express his disagreement.

I should have relieved General MacArthur then and there. The reason I did not was that I did not wish to have it appear as if he were being relieved because the offensive failed. I have never believed in going back on people when luck is against them, and I did not intend to do it now. Nor did I want to reprimand the general, but he had to be told that the kinds of public statements which he had been making were out of order.

This was the background for the order of December 5.

By that time a new point of disagreement had come up between General MacArthur and the defense chiefs. On November 28 General MacArthur had reported that he was changing his plans from the offensive to the defensive as provided for in the directives which he had been given. In his message on this subject he made the statement that "we face an entirely new war. . . ." His message said, "The resulting situation presents an entire new picture which broadens the potentialities to world embracing consideration beyond the sphere of decision by the theatre commander. This command has done everything humanly possible within its capabilities but is now faced with conditions beyond its control and its strength."

On the following day General MacArthur submitted a recommendation that we go back and take up the offer made seven months earlier by Chiang Kai-shek of thirty-three thousand Chinese Nationalist troops for Korea. At that time he himself had advised against using these troops. His recommendation now was, of course, in line with his view that the Korean action had become a war with Communist China. I instructed the Joint Chiefs of Staff, after a lengthy conference in which State Department and Defense Department took part, to call MacArthur's attention to the international implication of his recommendation, and the following message was sent on November 29 by the Joint Chiefs of Staff:

"Your proposal is being considered. It involves world-wide consequences. We shall have to consider the possibility that it would disrupt the united position of the nations associated with us in the United Nations, and have us isolated. It may be wholly unacceptable to the commonwealth countries to have their forces employed with Nationalist Chinese. It might extend hostilities to Formosa and other areas. Incidentally, our position of leadership in the Far East is being most seriously compromised in the United Nations. The utmost care will be necessary to avoid the disruption of the essential Allied line-up in that organization."

Of course the situation in Korea was the subject of many long and anxious discussions in my office. The future of our policy, not only in Asia, but in Europe as well, was at stake, and we spent a good deal more time searching for the answers to the tremendous problems before us than merely worrying over General MacArthur's lack of discretion.

On November 28, when the bad news from Korea had changed from rumors of resistance into certainty of defeat, I called a special meeting of the National Security Council. My own first knowledge of the extent of damage that the Chinese were inflicting on our troops had come at six-fifteen that morning, when General Bradley had telephoned me a cable report from General MacArthur. General Bradley and the Chiefs of Staff had been in session all the day before, examining the situation, and they felt that while it was serious they were doubtful that it was as much a catastrophe as our newspapers were leading us to believe.

General Bradley, however, stressed the danger that might arise if the Communists decided to use their air potential. It was our information that there were at least three hundred bombers on fields in nearby Manchuria. These bombers could hurt us badly, both by attacks on the airlift and by surprise raids on our closely jammed planes on Korean fields. Despite these facts, General Bradley said that the Joint Chiefs of Staff did not believe that General MacArthur should be authorized to bomb airfields in Manchuria.

I asked if there was any way to lessen the damage we might suffer from a sudden air attack by the Chinese Communists, and General Vandenberg said there was none, short of moving our planes back to

Japan. This, of course, would mean a considerable slowing up of our own military operations.

I asked Secretary of Defense Marshall for his comments on the situation, and he reported that the civilian heads of the services, too, had been in conference all day as a result of the developments in Korea. They had talked over what new requirements this would place on the procurement and supply of both men and matériel. A second military supplemental budget estimate was ready, and it was Marshall's opinion, as he had made clear to me earlier that day, that it ought to be sent over to Congress at once. I was therefore able to inform the meeting that the Budget Director had already been instructed by me on this point.

General Marshall then talked about the diplomatic aspects of the situation, saying he thought it essential for the United States to go along with the United Nations approach to the Korean question, even if going along with the United Nations meant some difficult problems for us. He said that he felt it essential for us to keep a unanimity of approach in the U.N. He was emphatic on one point, on which he said the three service Secretaries agreed as the most important: that we should not get ourselves involved either individually or with the United Nations in a general war with China. Marshall said he did not think it was likely that the U.N. would get us "in such a fix," but he thought we should recognize that there were some people at home who seemed to want all-out action against China.

Bradley said this reflected the Joint Chiefs' thinking too. If we allowed ourselves to be pulled into a general war with China, it would be impossible to continue the build-up of forces in Europe. Secretary Pace added that it was important that everyone in the room understand that we had only the 82nd Airborne Division available at home and that the National Guard units that had been called into federal service would not be ready for combat until the middle of March.

At this point Vice-President Barkley broke in. The Vice-President did not often speak in these NSC meetings, and this was an indication of the worry and concern felt by the members of the Senate with whom he associated daily. What Barkley wanted to know was whether it was true that General MacArthur had made the statement that "the boys will be home by Christmas," adding that this seemed incredible. Did MacArthur know what was going on, he asked, and how could a man in his position be guilty of such an indiscretion?

Secretary Lovett and Secretary Pace explained that MacArthur had "officially" denied the statement but that there was no doubt that he had made it. Secretary Pace had heard him make a similar statement at Wake Island and so had General Bradley, and Lovett said there was a stenographic transcript available. General MacArthur had said that he had been "misinterpreted," and General Bradley came to Mac-Arthur's defense by saying that he thought the statement was designed for the consumption of the Chinese Communists to show them that we had no permanent designs on Korea and no intention of continuing the war.

Barkley was still upset. "This is an incredible hoax," he exclaimed. I told him that, whatever we might think of the statement, we would have to be very careful not to pull the rug out from under the general. We simply could not afford to damage MacArthur's prestige. But Barkley still felt deeply perturbed.

There was discussion then of the number of replacements MacArthur would need and what we might be able to send him. General Collins said he thought that a line could be held in Korea. The X Corps in the east was in a precarious position but probably could be pulled back to safety.

I asked Dean Acheson then to comment on the situation from his point of view, and the Secretary of State began with the statement that the events of the last few hours had moved us very much closer to the danger of general war. There had always been evidence of some Chinese participation in Korea, of course, but now we had an open, powerful, offensive attack. He said that we needed to bear in mind that the Soviet Union was behind every one of the Chinese and North Korean moves and that we had to think of all that happened in Korea as world matters. We should never lose sight of the fact that we were facing the Soviet Union all around the world.

Of course, Acheson continued, if we openly accused the Soviet Union of aggression, the United Nations would be demolished. If we came out and pointed a finger at the Soviet Union, it would serve no purpose, because we could do nothing about it. To make the accusation, however, and then to do nothing about it would only weaken our world position. If we proposed action against the Kremlin, on the other hand, we might find ourselves alone, without allies.

As for the Chinese Communists, Acheson went on, we ought to draw a line and not try to walk both sides of the street. There was no use denying that they were fighting us, so we had better stir up trouble for them. There were a number of ways in which that could be done besides playing with Chiang.

As for the conflict in Korea, the Secretary of State was of the opinion that we should find some way to end it. If we went into Manchuria and bombed the airfields there with any degree of success, "Russia would cheerfully get in it." We had banked our entire foreign policy on the idea of keeping Russia contained, and we had succeeded in repulsing her attempts to break out. If we allowed the Russians now to trap us inside their perimeter, however, we would run the risk of being sucked into a bottomless pit. There would be no end to it, and it would bleed us dry. The Russians had tried to lure us into traps time and again. This one differed only in being bigger than the earlier ones.

Averell Harriman, who took part in the meeting, said that we ought to give careful attention to the mood of the free world. We had to maintain our leadership, and the immediate appointment of a supreme commander for the NATO powers would prove that. The free nations would stick with us if they felt sure that we were going to stick with them.

I said that it would be easier to convince the free world if some of our press were not so anxious to prove the contrary. Three of our biggest publishers, I think, were dividing our people and leading the world to believe that the American people had no confidence in their government. The campaign of vilification and lies and distortion of facts in so many of our papers was the greatest asset the Soviets had.

I told the National Security Council that I had thought at first that I ought to go before Congress and address a special session but that I did not now think this would be right. Korea was a United Nations matter, and our country should not make an individual approach to it.

The Cabinet met shortly after this meeting adjourned, and again Korea was discussed. The members of the Cabinet were briefed by General Bradley and by Dean Acheson on the most recent developments, and again we talked over the damage that had been done to the nation's international position by the reckless charges and the rumor-mongering of the recent political campaign.

A lot of hard work was put in during the next few days to re-evaluate our plans and programs and to prepare for the next steps that would have to be taken. Most of my occasional callers had to give way to a steady stream of the top officials of the government. At the press conference on Thursday, November 30, I made a statement for publication that was intended to reflect our concern and also our determination.

"Recent developments in Korea," the prepared copies of this statement read, "confront the world with a serious crisis. The Chinese Communist leaders have sent their troops from Manchuria to launch a strong and well-organized attack against the United Nations forces in North Korea. This has been done despite prolonged and earnest efforts to bring home to the Communist leaders of China the plain fact that neither the United Nations nor the United States has any aggressive intentions toward China. Because of the historic friendship between the people of the United States and China, it is particularly shocking to us to think that Chinese are being forced into battle against our troops in the United Nations command.

"The Chinese attack was made in great force, and it still continues. It has resulted in the forced withdrawal of large parts of the United Nations command. The battlefield situation is uncertain at this time. We may suffer reverses as we have suffered them before. But the forces of the United Nations have no intention of abandoning their mission in Korea.

"The forces of the United Nations are in Korea to put down an aggression that threatens not only the whole fabric of the United Nations, but all human hopes of peace and justice. If the United Nations yields to the forces of aggression, no nation will be safe or secure. If aggression is successful in Korea, we can expect it to spread throughout Asia and Europe to this hemisphere. We are fighting in Korea for our own national security and survival.

"We have committed ourselves to the cause of a just and peaceful world order through the United Nations. We stand by that commitment.

"We shall meet the new situation in three ways. We shall continue to work in the United Nations for concerted action to halt this aggression in Korea. We shall intensify our efforts to help other free nations strengthen their defenses in order to meet the threat of aggression elsewhere. We shall rapidly increase our own military strength.

"In the United Nations, the first step is action by the Security Council to halt this aggression. Ambassador Warren Austin is pressing for such action. We shall exert every effort to help bring the full influence of the United Nations to bear on the situation in Korea.

"Some had hoped that the normal peaceful process of discussion and negotiation, which is provided through the United Nations, could be successfully entered into with the present Chinese Communist delegation at Lake Success. There is, however, no indication that the representatives of Communist China are willing to engage in this process. Instead of discussing the real issues, they have been making violent and wholly false statements of the type which have often been used by the Soviet representatives in an effort to prevent the Security Council from acting.

"We hope that the Chinese people will not continue to be forced or deceived into serving the ends of Russian colonial policy in Asia. I am certain that, if the Chinese people now under the control of the Communists were free to speak for themselves, they would denounce this aggression against the United Nations.

"Because the new act of aggression in Korea is only a part of a world-wide pattern of danger to all the free nations of the world, it is more necessary than ever before for us to increase at a very rapid rate the combined military strength of the free nations. It is more necessary than ever that integrated forces in Europe under a Supreme Command be established at once.

"With respect to our own defense, I shall submit a supplemental request for appropriations needed immediately to increase the size and effectiveness of our armed forces. The request will include a substantial amount for the Atomic Energy Commission in addition to large amounts for the Army, the Navy, and the Air Force.

"I expect to confer tomorrow with Congressional leaders and ask them to give urgent consideration to these new appropriations.

"This is a time for all our citizens to lay aside differences and unite in firmness and mutual determination to do what is best for our country and the cause of freedom throughout the world. This country is the keystone of the hope of mankind for peace and justice. We must show that we are guided by a common purpose and a common faith."

The congressional leaders met with me in the Cabinet Room at eleven o'clock the next day, December 1. Present from the Senate, besides the Vice-President, were McKellar, Connally, Lucas, Tydings, Russell, Thomas of Utah, Wherry, Bridges, Gurney, and Wiley; from the House, the Speaker and Representatives McCormack, Vinson, Richards, Cannon, Mahon, Taber, Easton, Short, Halleck, and Arends. With me were Acheson, Marshall, Lovett, Bradley, Harriman, Lawton of the Bureau of the Budget, Bedell Smith, Admiral Souers, and James Lay of the National Security Council.

General Bradley gave the congressmen a full description of the current military situation in Korea, and I invited them to address questions to the general. Senators Connally, Gurney, Wiley, and Bridges took the lead in the questions that followed: How many planes were there? What was the distance from here to there? and so forth. Then Senator Wherry wanted to know why our intelligence had not seen this attack coming, and he would not be satisfied with any explanation that Bradley would give. He was antagonistic and abrupt in his manner.

General Smith then set up a huge chart that showed the Soviet Union, its satellites and its neighboring areas. He showed how the events in Korea tied in with events in Europe. The Russians had just completed large-scale maneuvers, with over half a million men taking part. They had concentrated on river crossing and airborne operations. The Russians had also recently consolidated their Siberian forces under a single, unified command. This was unusual for them and deserved watching.

The Central Intelligence chief then gave some figures on the state of Russian and satellite manpower and the training and equipment of these forces. The congressmen were visibly impressed, with the exception of Wherry. The senator from Nebraska, with doubt and disbelief written all over his face, wanted to know how Smith had gotten his facts. Had he used all sources? What were those sources? Smith side-stepped these questions very smoothly, but when he began to take up Korea and China, Wherry again wanted chapter and verse for everything mentioned.

Time went quickly in this exchange of questions and information, and I had to ask General Smith to conclude his presentation so that I could speak to the group. I pointed out that we had been hard at work since June on our defenses. Much had already been done to bring the armed forces up to strength; there had been one supplemental military appropriation and I would send up another now. This represented estimates that were arrived at before the Chinese intervention, and undoubtedly we had to step up our timetable as a result of the Korean events.

I then read to the group extracts from the message I intended to send to Congress and gave them the figures of the supplemental appropriation request, adding that I would be available to answer any questions that anyone might have about this request, and so would the members of my staff and administration. But I wanted to stress that speed was essential if these new funds were to be of any use to us in the present critical international situation.

I said that our entire effort had been bent in the direction of preventing this affair in Korea from becoming a major Asiatic war. We were not in a position to assume the burdens of a major war, but most of all, I did not wish to have any part in the killing of millions of innocents as would surely happen if the fighting was allowed to spread.

Meanwhile, the picture in Korea was not getting any brighter. On December 3 MacArthur reported as follows:

3 Dec 50

FROM: MacArthur
TO: Joint Chiefs of Staff

The X Corps is being withdrawn into the Hamhung area as rapidly as possible. The situation with the Eighth Army becomes increasingly critical. General Walker reports, and I agree with his estimate, that he cannot hold the Pyongyang area and under enemy pressure, when exerted, will unquestionably be forced to withdraw to the Seoul area. There is no practicability, nor would any benefit accrue thereby, to attempt to unite the forces of the Eighth Army and the X Corps. Both forces are completely outnumbered and their junction would, therefore, not only not produce added strength, but actually jeopardize the free flow of movement that arises from the two separate logistical lines of naval supply and maneuver.

As I previously reported, the development of a defense line across the waist of Korea is not feasible because of the numerical weakness of our forces as considered in connection with the distances involved: by the necessity of supplying the two parts of the line from ports within each area; and by the division of the area into two compartments by the rugged mountainous terrain running north and south. Such a line is one of approximately 120 air miles with a road distance of approximately 150 miles. If the entire United States Force of seven divisions at my disposal were placed along this defensive line it would mean that a division would be forced to protect a front of approximately 20 miles against greatly superior numbers of an enemy whose greater strength is a potential for night infiltration through rugged terrain. Such a line with no depth would have little strength, and as a defensive concept would invite penetration with resultant envelopment and piecemeal destruction. Such a concept against the relatively weaker North Korean Forces would have been practicable, but against the full forces of the Chinese Army is impossible.

I do not believe that full comprehension exists of the basic changes which have been wrought by the undisguised entrance by the Chinese Army into the combat. Already Chinese troops to the estimated strength of approximately 26 divisions are in line of battle with an additional minimum of 200,000 to the enemy rear and remnants of the North Korean Army are being reorganized in the rear and there stands, of course, behind all the entire military potential of Communist China.

The terrain is of a nature to diminish the effectiveness of our air support in channelizing and interrupting the enemy supply system; it serves to aid the enemy in his dispersion tactics. This, together with the present limitation of international boundary, reduces enormously the normal benefit that would accrue to our superior air force.

With the enemy concentration inland, the Navy potential is greatly diminished in effectiveness; amphibious maneuver is no longer feasible and effective use of naval gunfire support is limited.

The potentials, therefore, of our combined strength are greatly reduced and the comparison more and more becomes one of relative combat effectiveness of ground forces.

It is clearly evident, therefore, that unless ground reinforcements of the greatest magnitude are promptly supplied, this Command will be either forced into successive withdrawals with diminished powers of resistance after each such move, or will be forced to take up beachhead bastion positions which, while insuring a degree of prolonged resistance, would afford little hope of anything beyond defense.

This small command actually under present conditions is facing the entire Chinese nation in an undeclared war and unless some positive and immediate action is taken, hope for success cannot be justified and steady attrition leading to final destruction can reasonably be contemplated.

Although the command up to the present time has exhibited good morale and marked efficiency, it has been in almost unending combat for five months and is mentally fatigued and physically battered. The combat effectiveness of the Republic of Korea Forces now at our disposal is negligible; for police and constabulary uses they would have some effectiveness. The other foreign army contingents, whatever their combat efficiency may be, are in such small strength as to exercise little influence. Each United States division at my disposal other than the First Marine Division is now approximately 5,000 men under strength and at no time have they achieved their full authorized numerical complement. The Chinese troops are fresh, completely organized, splendidly trained and equipped and apparently in peak condition for actual operations. The general evaluation of the situation here must be viewed on the basis of an entirely new war against an entirely new power of great military strength and under entirely new conditions.

The directives under which I am operating based upon the North Korean Forces as an enemy are completely outmoded by events. The fact must be clearly understood that our relatively small force now faces the full offensive power of the Chinese Communist nation augmented by extensive supply of Soviet matériel. The strategic concept suitable for operations against the North Korean Army which was so successful is not susceptible to continued application against such power. This calls for political decisions and strategic plans in implementation thereof, adequate fully to meet the realities involved. In this, time is of the essence as every hour sees the enemy power increase and ours decline.

I approved an immediate reply by the Joint Chiefs of Staff to MacArthur. I took the position that we must not sacrifice men. Until the United Nations decided to support a major move, it seemed best to concentrate our strength in beachheads that we might be able to hold.

3 Dec 50

We consider that the preservation of your forces is now the primary consideration. Consolidation of forces into beachheads is concurred in.

At the same time, I directed General Collins to fly to Tokyo at once and to find out both there and in Korea what the latest facts were. On November 30 I received a message from British Prime Minister Clement Attlee asking if he might come to Washington and discuss, on a person-to-person basis, what meaning we should give to the Korean events and where we might go from there.

CHAPTER 25

The first among the United Nations to join us for action in Korea were the United Kingdom and other Commonwealth countries. They did this in spite of the fact that Communist activity in Malaya put a heavy drain on British manpower. The British, however, had shown much concern over the danger that the conflict might enlarge and draw in the Soviet Union.

There had been some indication of this concern when our Air Force bombed the North Korean port of Rashin early in August. This city was a proper military target because of the important chemical and munitions plants there, but it was only seventeen miles from the Soviet border, and there was some fear abroad and in our State Department, too, that the Russians might take this as an attack aimed at them.

After the first signs of Chinese intervention, and following MacArthur's request for authority to retaliate against air attacks on his forces from Manchurian bases, the State Department had consulted the British and all other governments with forces in Korea to obtain their reaction. All of them, and not merely the British, were strongly opposed.

The anxiety of our allies became even more pronounced after a highly secret report was received from Peiping on November 15, stating that a top Russian diplomat there had said that if Manchurian airfields were bombed by United Nations planes the Soviet Air Force would strike back in force.

The massive counterblow by which the Chinese halted MacArthur's offensive was perhaps even more of a shock abroad than it was for us at home. Foreign newspapers speculated openly about the American reaction, quoting some of our more saber-rattling senators and talking about MacArthur's ill-concealed disapproval of the American government's policies. There actually were open predictions that we would disregard the United Nations and plunge straight on into war with China and with anyone else who might be on China's side.

The possibility of general war, of course, was much more frightening to the inhabitants of Paris and London—barely recovered as they were from the ravages of the last war—than to a great many Americans who had not been subjected to the destruction of their cities. Europeans generally assumed that a new war would be a battle of atomic weapons, and the slightest mention of atomic bombs was enough to make them jittery. Of course it should never be forgotten that America had yet to prove to Europeans that the defense of Europe was something we would take seriously. Since newspapers sometimes seem to prefer to report bad news, most Europeans had heard only that there was opposition to NATO and to the sending of troops to Europe and to almost anything else that they thought might help them if they were to be subjected to attack.

Just how sensitive and on edge the world had become was demonstrated when the words "atomic bomb" were mentioned at my press conference on November 30.

At that conference I made the remark that "we will take whatever steps are necessary to meet the military situation, just as we always have."

"Will that include the atomic bomb?" one of the reporters asked.

"That includes every weapon that we have," I replied.

"Mr. President," the questioner shot back, "you said 'every weapon that we have.' Does that mean that there is active consideration of the use of the atomic bomb?"

"There has always been active consideration of its use," I told him. "I don't want to see it used. It is a terrible weapon, and it should not be used on innocent men, women and children who have nothing whatever to do with this military aggression. That happens when it is used."

To make quite sure that no one would misunderstand my words, I authorized Charles Ross, my press secretary, to issue a separate clarifying statement after the press conference.

"The President wants to make it certain," this read, "that there is no misinterpretation of his answers to questions at his press conference today about the use of the atom bomb. Naturally, there has been consideration of this subject since the outbreak of the hostilities in Korea, just as there is consideration of the use of all military weapons whenever our forces are in combat.

"Consideration of the use of any weapon is always implicit in the very possession of that weapon.

"However, it should be emphasized, that, by law, only the President can authorize the use of the atom bomb, and no such authorization has been given. If and when such authorization should be given, the military commander in the field would have charge of the tactical delivery of the weapon.

"In brief, the replies to the questions at today's press conference do not represent any change in this situation."

In spite of this assurance that the use of the atomic bomb was still subject to my approval and that I had not given such approval, news reports persisted that I had threatened to use the A-bomb in Korea. In London, one hundred Labor MP's signed a letter to Prime Minister Attlee to protest the possibility of the use of the atomic bomb. During a debate which our embassy described as "the most serious, anxious, and responsible debate on foreign affairs conducted by the House of Commons since the Labor Party came to power in 1945," not only the followers of Mr. Aneurin Bevan but also Churchill, Eden, and Butler talked about "disquiet" and generally indicated that they wanted to be assured that events in Korea would not propel the world into a major war. Typical, perhaps, was the comment of the Conservative leader Butler, who said that "the British people as a whole wished to be assured before their fate was decided [by the extension of the war to China] that they were helping to decide their own fate."

Attlee announced at the end of this debate in the House of Commons that he was planning to fly over for conferences with me, and so greatly was the tension relieved by his statement that it brought cheers from both sides of the House. No one who read the accounts of this debate could possibly escape the fact that the British were seriously worried.

Clement Attlee arrived in Washington on December 4, and we had our first formal talks from four to five thirty-five that afternoon.

I opened the conference with a few words of welcome and then asked General Bradley to summarize the military situation in Korea. Attlee inquired about the control of the air over Korea, and Bradley assured him that there was no trouble so far; that we were operating from five carriers and seven good airfields in Korea.

Secretary of Defense Marshall pointed out that it was important to realize that the enemy was using manpower without regard to losses and also that, owing to the manner of their operations—without trucks or mechanized equipment—it was much easier for them to conceal their movements than for us.

I said that we were faced with very grave military decisions but that the political decisions were no less difficult. I expressed the hope, however, that we could have a free and frank discussion. We had obligations in the East and in the West, I stated, and did not intend to run out on any of them even though it might prove difficult to meet all our obligations. I expressed the belief, however, that we should first discuss the problem of the Chinese Communist intervention and asked for Attlee's comments.

Attlee began by saying that it was important to maintain the prestige and authority of the United Nations. He pointed out that the United States had been the principal instrument for supporting the United Nations and that the United Kingdom was giving what help it could. But the United Kingdom would not be able to get any additional strength into Korea for several months and, from General Bradley's report, Attlee said he understood that the crisis might come much sooner.

The Prime Minister said that opinion in the United Nations and in the countries of Europe, Asia, and America had to be considered. He had been in close touch through all this time with the Asian members of the Commonwealth and suggested that we ought to look also at the point of view of the Chinese Communists. They were feeling flushed with success and would not want to settle for some principle announced by the United Nations, to which they did not belong. They would want to feel their own strength and independence. Thus, even if the Russians might think of a settlement, that might not necessarily convince Mao Tse-tung.

What, Attlee asked, were the Communists likely to demand as the price for a cease-fire? There was danger that if we showed a spirit of accommodation the price would go up. But he thought we ought to discuss just how far we were prepared to go, what kinds of things we wanted to negotiate, and where we should stand firm. Whatever decision we reached, he said, was apt to be distasteful, but we had to bear in mind that the West could not be given up, that it was still the vital point in our line against Communism.

I asked Secretary Acheson to express our position in the matters touched on by the Prime Minister, and the Secretary pointed out that, first of all, it had to be remembered that the central enemy was not China but the Soviet Union. All the inspiration for the Korean action came from Moscow. No doubt there had been some arrangement between the Chinese and the Russians to make the Chinese think they had strong Russian support. While their attack was going well, there seemed little limit to what they might try to do and, if they could drive us out of Korea, they would do so. And no one could tell how much farther they might be inclined to go.

Regarding the question of all-out war against China—meaning land, sea, and air action—Acheson assured the British conferees that there were "not many of the President's advisers who would urge him to follow that course." He added, however, that he could not be optimistic about prospects of negotiations with the Chinese Communists. We did not have an alternative of either negotiating or becoming involved in war. We were actually involved at the moment.

Acheson analyzed the problem of negotiations. From a military point of view, he observed, there seemed to be an advantage to us from a cease-fire as soon as possible. But the fact that it would be advantageous to our side naturally meant that it would be disadvantageous to the Chinese, and therefore they would not be likely to accept it. From a political standpoint, there might be some advantage in suggesting a cease-fire as far as world opinion was concerned; but if negotiations resulted, the question would arise as to what price would be asked. It seemed predictable that the Chinese Communists would ask for recognition of their government, for a seat in the United Nations Security Council, and for concessions on Formosa. They might even insist that any Japanese peace settlement had to have their assent.

We had to remember, the Secretary continued, that this intervention in Korea was not a spontaneous maneuver. It had design. If we became preoccupied in Asia, Russia would gain a free hand in Europe. But if we settled with the Communists—for instance, at the price of Formosa— this fact would be used against us in the most devastating manner throughout Asia. He could not believe, he said, that the Chinese action was just a burst of Chinese military fervor or that they would become calm and peaceful if we gave them Formosa and made other concessions. On the contrary, if we gave concessions, they would only become more aggressive. If we yielded to the Chinese Communists the effect on the Japanese and the Filipinos might be serious. And if we did not negotiate and did not make a settlement, we might be able to fight on in Korea, giving the Chinese as much punishment as possible, and our position would be no worse. We should, he thought, make it a policy not to recognize the enemy's gains.

Prime Minister Attlee asked at this point how long the beachheads could be held as an annoyance to the Chinese Communists without too much loss. General Bradley and Secretary Marshall both spoke in reply, declaring that the eastern-sector beachhead could probably not be held but that the western sector, based on Inchon and Pusan, could probably hold for some time, especially if it should become possible to reinforce that area with troops evacuated from the eastern sector.

The Prime Minister inquired what the reaction of the American public would be if we continued to hold the beachheads with continuing losses. Would there not be a demand for all-out war against China?

I replied that such demands could be heard now. We were making great sacrifices, and vast sums of money had been appropriated. It was my hope that we could hold the line in Korea until the situation improved the chances for negotiations. I admitted that all my military advisers had told me that there was no chance to hold the line. But that, I still wanted to try.

Attlee observed that opinions differed on the extent to which the Chinese Communists were Kremlin satellites.

I said that in my opinion the Chinese Communists were Russian satellites. The problem we were facing was part of a pattern. After Korea, it would be Indo-China, then Hong Kong, then Malaya. I said that I did not want war with China or any nation but that the situation looked very dark to me. The Chinese Communists, in my belief, had made up their minds what they wanted to get, including a U.N. seat and Formosa—or war.

Acheson remarked that it really didn't matter too much whether the Chinese Communists were satellites or not. They would probably act in much the same way, regardless of the answer to that question. But he thought it would be a mistake to count on their good will. He said there was a saying among State Department officials that with communistic regimes you could not bank good will; they balanced their books every night.

General Marshall recalled the several meetings he had had with Mao Tse-tung and with Chou En-lai during his mission to China. He said that Chou on one occasion had with great emphasis told Mrs. Marshall at the dinner table that there was no doubt they were Marxist Communists and that he resented people referring to them as merely agrarian reformers. Marshall said there had been not the slightest attempt to conceal their Moscow affiliations. They regarded the Russians as co-religionists, and this feeling was thoroughly indoctrinated in their troops.

I told Attlee that I relied on General Marshall's judgment, especially since he had spent a year in closest contact with these people. And I also wanted to add emphasis to what Acheson had said about our desire to avoid war with China. I therefore recounted what had transpired on Wake Island between MacArthur and myself, especially pointing out that I had told MacArthur to avoid giving any provocation to the Chinese in Manchuria and the Russians in Vladivostok, and adding that we had no desire to act in this matter except as members of the United Nations.

Then I read to the Prime Minister the following memorandum that had been agreed on by the State and Defense Departments and to which I had given my approval.

"1. It would be militarily advantageous in the immediate situation if a cease-fire order could be arranged provided that considerations offered were not so great as to be unacceptable. This might insure full support of the United Nations. Arrangements for a cease-fire must not impose conditions which would jeopardize the safety of United Nations forces nor be conditioned on agreement on other issues, such as Formosa, and the Chinese seat in the United Nations.

"2. If a cease-fire should be effected which permits a stabilization of the situation, United Nations should proceed with the political, military and economic stabilization of the Republic of Korea while continuing efforts to seek an independent and unified Korea by political means.

"3. If the Chinese Communists reject a cease-fire and move major forces south of the 38th parallel, the United Nations forces may face a forced evacuation of Korea. The consequences of a voluntary abandonment of our Korean allies would be such that any United Nations evacuation must be clearly the result of military necessity only."

At this point I paused in the reading of the memorandum and emphatically repeated that it was out of the question that we should get out voluntarily. All the Koreans left behind who had been loyal to the United Nations would face death. The Communists cared nothing about human life. With this made clear, I continued with the memorandum:

"4. If the situation in the preceding paragraph develops, the United Nations must take immediate action to declare Communist China an aggressor and must mobilize such political and economic measures as are available to bring pressure upon Peiping and to affirm the determination of the United Nations not to accept an aggression. Also, there is the possibility of some military action which would harass the Chinese Communists and of efforts which could be made to stimulate anticommunist resistance within China itself, including the exploitation of Nationalist capabilities.

"In addition to the measures indicated above, the United States and United Kingdom should consult immediately about other steps which might be taken to strengthen non-communist Asia. These steps might include:

"(a) Restoration of considerable self-government to Japan, the acceleration of efforts to obtain a Japanese peace settlement, the strengthening of Japanese capacity for self-defense, the greater utilization of productive capacity to strengthen the capabilities of the free world, and the prompt admission of Japan into international organizations. United Kingdom reluctance to move on these three points should be discarded in light of the new critical situation.

"(b) Appropriate military arrangements between nations in southeast Asia capable of effective mutual support.

"(c) Special efforts to convince non-communist Asia of the nature of the threat which confronts it and to urge upon the governments concerned the need for concerted Asian action to resist communist aggression in that area.

"(d) Intensification of economic and military assistance to encourage the organization of resistance to communist encroachment.

"(e) Intensification of psychological and cover activity against communist regimes and activity in Asia."

Commenting on the last two items, I said that I had been thinking about some kind of Marshall Plan for Southeast Asia. ECA had done a lot of good work there. A special plan was under way for the Philippines to stabilize their situation, and I expressed my hope that it would receive speedy approval in Congress. Plans of this kind, I said, deserved consideration and discussion.

Sir Oliver Franks, the British Ambassador in Washington, then skillfully summarized the discussion we had had and, after agreeing to a brief statement for the reporters, the meeting was adjourned.

Our next session was aboard the presidential yacht *Williamsburg* the following day, December 5, 1950. After a luncheon at which some congressional leaders were present, the same group that had conferred the previous afternoon met again. Charlie Ross, my long-time friend and press secretary, was also present. It was to be almost his last official function. That evening, while he was still at his desk, Charlie suffered a heart attack and died. We had been friends since high school days, and his loss grieved me very much. It struck me like a loss in my immediate family.

The earlier part of our December 5 meeting aboard the *Williamsburg* was taken up largely with a discussion of the text of the resolution to be introduced in the General Assembly of the United Nations. When the minor differences on this matter had been ironed out, however, I spoke about my deep concern and extreme preoccupation with the military situation in Korea.

I said again that I was determined that we would not back out—that if we got out, someone would have to force us out. We certainly could do no less for the South Koreans who had been loyal to us. I said that I realized that we were exposing our fleet and air arm to the danger of a surprise attack from Manchuria. "We did not get into this fight," I said, "with the idea of getting licked. We will fight to the finish to stop this aggression. I don't intend to take over military command of the situation in Korea—I leave that up to the generals—but I want to make it perfectly plain that we cannot desert our friends when the going gets rough."

I got a little warm as I talked, but Clement Attlee was no less sincere when he answered: "We are in it with you. We'll support you. We'll stand together on those bridgeheads. How long we can hold on is a matter of opinion."

I said again that, whatever we did, it could never be a voluntary withdrawal from Korea. "I don't want to get out," I insisted, "if there is any chance that we can stay."

"You can take it from me," Attlee repeated, "that we stand with you. Our whole purpose is to stand with you."

I thanked him for his attitude and for his words. Loyalty to principles and friends and also to treaty commitments is a British attitude, and it is ours too.

Attlee then returned to the discussion that we had had the day before, stating first what he thought we had agreed on. It seemed to him that there was agreement not to get bogged down in a major war with China and that we had ruled out bombing industrial centers in China. Then he restated the proposal Acheson had made; namely, that we should remain in Korea until forced out and not get into any negotiations. The Prime Minister's reaction to this was that, in the first place, it would be difficult to get U.N. action on any move that might appear directed against Peiping or likely to result in retaliations. He did not think, in the second place, that we would be able to hurt China much, while the Chinese might do us a good deal of harm. It seemed to him, he said, that we would wind up either in a shooting war or in negotiations.

Attlee then proceeded to give us the point of view of his government. In his opinion the Chinese Communists were potentially ripe for "Titoism." He could not consider that China was completely in the hands of Russia, and therefore the aim ought to be to divide the Russians and the Chinese—who are natural rivals in the Far East.

"I think," he said, "that all of us should try to keep the Chinese from thinking that Russia is their only friend. I want the Chinese to part company with Russia. I want them to become a counterpoise to Russia in the Far East. If we don't accept this theory, if we just treat the Chinese as Soviet satellites, we are playing the Russian game."

Secretary Acheson answered the Prime Minister with a rhetorical question. What, he asked, did the American people think of as a long-range view? He said he did not see how it was possible for any administration to offer to the American people a foreign policy which, on one ocean, had a policy of isolationism, while at the same time it was advocating a very vigorous foreign policy, the opposite of isolationism, over the other ocean. We could not possibly be isolationists in the Pacific, ignoring there what the Communists in China had been doing, while at the same time we were taking a strong anti-isolationist stand against the threats of the Communists in Europe.

Acheson then made another telling point: Our country had gone on to do something quite vigorous in the case of a minor aggression in Korea. Now we were faced with a bigger aggression, the aggression of Communist China—we had even suffered a setback at the hands of this aggressor. If we accepted this larger aggression, it could not fail to affect our entire thinking about aggression—and not only in Asia but also in Europe. It would be a very confusing thing to try to get the American people to accept aggression in the Far East and not accept it in Europe.

The Secretary of State also called the attention of our British guests to the fact that Chiang Kai-shek was another complicating factor, for Chiang, rightly or wrongly, had become something of a symbol.

I gave Attlee a short summary of the kind of trouble that Chiang presented for us. I pointed out that his friends, especially in the Senate, kept up a running clamor on his behalf. Yet all of Chiang's actions suggested that he was not interested in improving the conditions of the territory he controlled but rather that he hoped to get us involved on China's mainland. And to this Acheson added that, entirely apart from Chiang Kai-shek, Formosa could not be allowed to fall into Communist hands. If, while we were so heavily engaged in Korea, he said, we permitted Formosa to be attacked and fall, we would raise the gravest dangers in Japan and the Philippines which were the bases from which our operations were being conducted and upon which our whole Pacific position rested.

We could not buy the friendship of the Chinese Communists, Acheson insisted, and we ought not try to prove that we were more friendly to them than the Russians. After what they had done to us, it seemed to him that the Chinese would have to prove that they were *our* friends. Our position now, Acheson went on, was that we ought to get the military power and the strength to stop this sort of thing from happening in the future. We had to have a policy that would keep going on the basis of strength.

I expressed my full agreement with the presentation the Secretary had made and added that it was important to realize that the United States could do nothing abroad without solid backing at home. We could not back out of the Far East. The American people would not stand for it. It was impossible.

Attlee said he understood that our foreign policy was dependent upon keeping the American people together. But it was also essential, he added, to keep the United Nations together. Furthermore, we had to keep Asian opinion together—nothing would be more dangerous than for the Asians to split away from us. Acheson broke in. "Weakening the United States," he said, "would be definitely more dangerous."

Attlee continued to argue the case for a policy that would consider the adherence of the Asian nations to the West as the primary aim. He turned to me, saying that he knew that I would have to consider public opinion about Chiang Kai-shek and Formosa but that he hoped I would also remember that whatever we did would have to be done through the U.N., and it could not be done there by the efforts and votes of just the United States and the United Kingdom, "important as we are."

Sir Oliver Franks proved himself again a fine diplomat as he stepped in and summarized the points that we appeared agreed upon. This brought the discussion back to specific points and first to the question of whether the seating of the Chinese Communists at the U.N. should be considered as a subject that might be included in negotiations with them.

Acheson took the position that we should not even consider it. If we did, we would in effect be saying to the Communists that they had won the game and could now collect the stakes; it would be like offering a reward for aggression. For that reason, if for no other, Acheson preferred that there be no negotiations at all, even if the Communists won and forced us out of Korea.

I asked General Marshall to speak to the same point, and the General said that he had very strong feelings in the matter from a military point of view. Supported by General Bradley, he stated the reasons why we could not afford to have our chain of island outposts split by a Formosa in hostile possession.

The British then advanced the idea that perhaps Chiang could be left in control on Formosa while at the same time we might recognize that China (proper) was under the Peiping regime. General Marshall made the comment that the biggest problem connected with Chiang was the fact that there was no replacement for him—that it had long been "brutally evident" that, despite the strong opposition to Chiang, there was nobody who could succeed him.

The meeting adjourned at 4:50 P.M.

Two meetings were held on December 6, the morning meeting being given over almost entirely to economic matters. The British had come to Washington with a list of the raw materials they needed in order to get their defense program stepped up properly. Their problem was simply that they could not import without exporting but that they had to import to rearm. The postwar "austerity" had forced the British economy to cut back to bare essentials, especially those required for the physical rebuilding of the country, and, as Attlee put it that morning, "we can't cut back much more; we don't have any fat left to sweat off."

There were some commodities which the British needed at once, such as zinc, sulphur, and cotton. Attlee asked that we consider these needs but that we also discuss with them the feasibility of setting up combined machinery to handle such economic problems, similar to the setup we had had during World War II.

I assured the Prime Minister that my associates and I appreciated the nature of the problem, which we had discussed at a Cabinet meeting the day before. I told him also that the staff and the Cabinet members had been instructed to talk to the members of the British group and that it would be agreeable to me if they held full-dress discussions of all problems connected with raw-material shortages—that I hoped they would come up with something that could be approved before our Washington talks came to an end. I announced that I had asked Stuart Symington, chairman of our National Security Resources Board, to be chairman of the U.S. group of conferees and that their talks could start that same afternoon.

Shortly before we went into that morning meeting, Under Secretary Lovett called from the Pentagon, reporting that the radar screens of some air defense installations in the Far North were reporting large formations of unidentified planes approaching. Fighter planes were sent up to reconnoiter and alerts were flashed to air centers in New England and beyond. But about an hour later—while I was meeting with Attlee— Lovett notified me that the report had been in error. Some unusual disturbance in the Arctic atmosphere had thrown the radar off.

Our afternoon was devoted to discussion of the European situation, especially the matter of getting the countries of NATO to agree on an integrated military setup. The British were anxious to see such an arrangement come into being soon and renewed their arguments that American troops in Europe—even if they were green and had to be trained there—would serve better than anything else to stimulate European efforts. We agreed on the text of a letter to the French to persuade them to speed up their action on the proposal for the integration of European defense forces.

Our meeting on December 7 brought us back to the Far Eastern situation. Attlee pointed out that it had been agreed that we would try to avoid a general war with China but that we would hold on in Korea as long as we could. He was of the opinion that this would still force us to come to a Far Eastern settlement sooner or later, and he wanted to develop his thoughts on that subject.

First, his government thought that China (meaning Communist China) ought to be seated in the U.N. The Prime Minister admitted that this was one point on which his people differed from us. But he thought that somewhere, somehow, we would find ourselves dealing with the Chinese Communists. The British, he said, had found out that it did not pay to pretend that the "nasty fellow" on the other side was not there.

Attlee also had doubts about a limited war in Korea. He said he saw the reason behind it and certainly considered it, rationally, the thing to do. But he foresaw trouble because, he believed, we would find people clamoring for total victory—and that meant unlimited war.

"I think," said the Prime Minister, "if China were in the United Nations, there would be a possibility of discussion. That, I know, is distasteful to you. But I think if there is to be a settlement, it is better to have it come through the United Nations. I'm inclined to think myself that if the present Chinese government were in the United Nations, we would get less loss of face than if we were dealing with someone outside."

Once the Chinese Communists were in the United Nations, Attlee concluded, it would be possible to use the arguments of the principles of the United Nations in dealing with them. It was not possible to do this so long as they stayed outside.

Dean Acheson answered the Prime Minister's argument on the matter of limited action. Acheson admitted that there was not very much that we could do to Communist China unless we wished to engage in all-out war. But, the Secretary of State said, our attitude toward Communist China would mean a lot in the Far East. It would help us to build up Japan and the Philippines and other Asian states. Our policy in the Far East should be controlled, he thought, not by formal logic but by the results of our acts.

The Secretary of State noted that we were under Soviet pressure in many parts of the world. All around the globe the Kremlin seemed to be stepping up its campaign against America. We would have to answer our Far East question in the light of the one overriding consideration, "How near is war?" If we assumed that the Communists were indeed moving with great speed toward war, then it would be a grievous mistake to try to buy off the aggressor just before he broke loose. It would only weaken us. It might tempt the aggressor more. "My own guess is that it wouldn't work," the Secretary continued. "All we might get would be time, but never enough time to do any good. Just enough time to divide our people bitterly. Just enough time to lose our moral strength."

Attlee seemed a little taken aback. Acheson, he said, was assuming that negotiations would mean retreat all along the line. He was assuming that Formosa would go Communist, but perhaps it would not. Perhaps we could limit our negotiations to the question of keeping the Communists on the 38th parallel in Korea.

Acheson replied that his point was that we should not get into negotiations until we knew where we were going. If we had a cease-fire now, we would be negotiating from weakness. If we could hold on and perhaps improve our position, we could approach a cease-fire quite differently. Of course if we got thrown out of Korea there would be no negotiations, but we would have made our point.

I added that we would face terrible divisions among our people here at home if the Chinese Communists were admitted to the United Nations, and I could not see what we could gain that would offset this loss in public morale. If we admitted the Chinese Reds to the U.N., would they be any different from the Russians? I said I expected them to behave just like the other satellites.

I talked, as strongly as I knew how, about the language the Chinese Reds were using about us at Lake Success and the falsehoods they were spreading. I said their handling of our missionaries and of our consuls was a blot on humanity. There was nothing in getting them admitted to the U.N. until they changed their ways.

Sir Roger Makins, British Deputy Under Secretary of State, noted that any policy that our governments followed ought to be a United Nations policy. I quite agreed. Sir Roger continued to say that it followed that any policy we had would have to be one that could command a majority in the General Assembly. As he saw it, there was a very strong sentiment in the United Nations for a negotiated settlement. That feeling, he thought, was so strong that if we had not been so careful in the past to negotiate everything pertaining to Korea through the United Nations we would now be having real trouble trying to keep other nations with us. He thought that perhaps we ought to let the United Nations find the way to some settlement.

Dean Rusk, our Assistant Secretary of State in charge of Far Eastern affairs, agreed with Sir Roger that we ought, by all means, keep the other countries with us. But he said that he could see no reason why we should have to prove our good will by agreeing to the seating of the

Chinese Reds in the U.N. in order to get a settlement. We had taken the initiative a number of times in the U.N. to demonstrate clearly our peaceful intentions and had always run into the Russian veto. If we agreed to admit the Chinese Communists now just so we could talk with them, we would have made a major concession. We had over and over again shown our willingness to talk and should not be asked now to make concessions before we were allowed to talk.

General Marshall said he knew that we were all agreed on staying out of a general war with China. We were agreed on that, he said, primarily because we were faced with the threat of a global war. Since that threat was real, and since we knew that we were dealing with people with whom it was almost impossible to negotiate, it would be very dangerous to go into negotiations at a time and in a way that would only reveal our weakness.

We could not afford to let Formosa go, Marshall said. It was of no particular strategic importance in our hands, but it would be of disastrous importance if it were held by an enemy. He said he had no immediate answer to the problem except to maintain our position and use the time to gather strength on all fronts.

At this point I sketched in some of the history of the Cairo Declaration with regard to Formosa—a declaration framed at a time when Japan was the overwhelming enemy in the Pacific. Our objective then had been to establish a power in the Pacific that would be friendly to the United States and to the United Kingdom and, anticipating a bit, to the United Nations. It was also our objective to upset the enemy by announcing our aims.

But now, I continued, the situation was reversed. The nation we had hoped to establish—China—had not only fallen into unfriendly hands but also was now "viciously hostile" to the United States.

Our position in Korea, I went on, had been brought about by my decision to give the fullest support to the United Nations resolution against aggression, and I was glad that the British were with us. The purpose of our action was to protect a little country from the result of aggression, and we had been on the verge of succeeding when a "viciously hostile" country intervened.

"We can't open our whole flank now by giving up Formosa to that country," I said. "We just can't agree with that. I think in the long run the Chinese will realize that their real friends are not in Moscow and Siberia; they are in London and in Washington."

"You won't bring them to that realization," the Prime Minister said without smiling, "if you keep fighting them."

"No," I said, "but I won't back out of Korea. . . ."

"I am with you there," said Attlee.

There was a pause. We had made our points and knew where we differed.

Lord Tedder and General Marshall now began to discuss what a continued policy of limited hostility to Communist China might mean, and Field Marshal Slim and General Bradley joined in. After the discussion had gone in this direction for a while, Averell Harriman asked to speak. He thought, he said, that it was vitally important for everyone to realize that we were basically concerned with the morale of the free world. If we gave in to Communism, morale would slip badly. We would do nothing but harm in Europe if we were to surrender in the Far East. The only way out of the crisis was to adopt a most vigorous program of strengthening the free world. This meant any number of things, but most of all it meant NATO. There simply was no hope for vigorous action on North Atlantic Treaty matters unless the United States and the United Kingdom could be together on the Far East.

I expressed my agreement with the views of Harriman. Sir Oliver Franks, as he had done at the previous meetings, proceeded to pull the threads of the conversation together. He stressed the fact that the British had not come to Washington to insist on some specific set of conditions but only to ask us to consider their views and to share our thoughts with them. He said that there was obviously no doubt on the basic issues; namely, the avoidance of general war and the determination to remain in Korea. He thought that General Marshall's remark about waiting for time to go by was very relevant, and said that the British had not come with any fixed ideas of what concessions should be made or that any concessions had to be made. As he saw it, there was, as a result of the talks, a much more real understanding of what the other government's views were and that this would be very useful and very helpful in the future. The differences had been in emphasis rather than in approach.

Dean Acheson said he concurred.

I asked Attlee if he thought we could adjourn the meeting until eleven o'clock the next day, when we might review the work of our various expert groups and agree on a communiqué to be issued. The Prime Minister said that was agreeable to him.

I found occasion to talk with Attlee more informally at a small stag dinner at the British Embassy that evening, and spoke to him about the problem of the men composing the Senate opposition who seemed to be violently determined to disrupt the nation's foreign policy. Only that day twenty-four senators, all Republicans, had joined in a resolution offered by Senator Kem—from my own state of Missouri—with the "1000 per cent support" of Senator Wherry, demanding to be informed about the "secret commitments" I had made to Attlee. These were the men who saw nothing wrong in plunging headlong into an Asian war but would raise no finger for the defense of Europe; who thought a British Prime Minister was never to be trusted but Chiang Kai-shek could do no wrong.

Attlee, in turn, spoke of the opposition from some of his own Labor Party leaders, especially Aneurin Bevan and his group, and the trouble they gave him. We talked as only two men can talk who have spent a lifetime in politics—we probably understood much better what the sources of many of our problems were than we could have stated in a public communiqué.

The Friday meeting had been intended as just a formality to give us an opportunity to approve the communiqué of the conference. But in the meantime General Collins had returned from his trip to Japan and Korea, and I asked him to come in and give his report on the battle situation to the combined British-American group. Collins gave us a detailed account with the aid of large-scale maps. He showed us, division by division and almost battalion by battalion, where the U.N. forces were. He reported that the Eighth Army commander, General Walker, was convinced that he could hold southern Korea, provided he was not required to make a defense of Seoul. Collins said that MacArthur shared this confidence and, after his own inspection, Collins did too. General Walker was also reported to be confident that he could hold a sizable part of Korea for an indefinite time, basing his supply lines on the port of Pusan. The situation of the X Corps in the east was still serious, but Collins had no doubt that it would be possible to get practically all of it out by sea, adding that, from a military point of view, the situation in Korea was serious but no longer critical.

The meeting then proceeded to the reports of the experts and the drafting of the communiqué. This latter job was turned over to some of the diplomatic experts present, and our remarks were informal while we waited for them to return.

During this interval Attlee raised the subject of the atom bomb. He and I were sitting alone, and he asked me if my recent press-conference statement had been intended to be a hint of some sort that perhaps we were giving more active thought to using the bomb. I assured him that nothing of the sort was intended and told him in detail how the statement came to be made. We agreed then to insert a short passage in the communiqué to give new emphasis to the true facts with respect to the bomb.

Again, as in our earlier sessions, Sir Oliver Franks was helpful. The British Ambassador was a tall, slim man with a keen mind and a friendly approach to the questions before us. When the Prime Minister and I were stalled on certain sentences in the communiqué, he knelt down between us and suggested words and sentences which were often adopted. I asked him what the Prime Minister's constituents and his government would do if they could see a picture of the British Ambassador on his knees to the President of the United States. He was as tall kneeling as Attlee and I were sitting. It was just a convenient posture from which to work across the writing arm of my desk, with the Prime Minister on one side and me on the other.

The final communiqué related that we had reviewed together the outstanding problems facing our two countries in international affairs. It reaffirmed that the objectives of our two nations in foreign policy were the same; namely, to maintain world peace and respect for the rights and interests of all peoples, to promote strength and confidence among the freedom-loving countries of the world, to eliminate the causes of fear, want, and discontent, and to advance the democratic way of life.

The communiqué also noted that the discussions had been keynoted by this unity of objectives of our two countries and made it clear that there was no difference between us as to the nature of the threat our countries faced or the basic policies which had to be pursued to overcome it. We announced that we had carefully reviewed the situation in Korea, which was one of great gravity and far-reaching consequences, and added that we were in complete agreement that there could be no thought of appeasement or of rewarding aggression, whether in the Far East or elsewhere. Lasting peace and the future of the United Nations as an instrument for world peace depended upon strong support for resistance against aggression.

"For our part," we stated, "we are ready, as we have always been, to seek an end to the hostilities by means of negotiation. The same principles of international conduct should be applied in this situation as are applied, in accordance with our obligations under the Charter of the United Nations, to any threat to world peace. Every effort must be made to achieve the purposes of the United Nations in Korea by peaceful means and to find a solution of the Korean problem on the basis of a free and independent Korea. We are confident that the great majority of the United Nations takes the same view. If the Chinese on their side display any evidence of a similar attitude, we are hopeful that the cause of peace can be upheld. If they do not, then it will be for the peoples of the world, acting through the United Nations, to decide how the principles of the Charter can best be maintained. For our part, we declare in advance our firm resolve to uphold them."

We did not omit from the communiqué that the two governments differed on the question of the Chinese seat in the United Nations. In fact, we noted that we had discussed our difference on this point and were determined that it would not interfere with our united effort in support of our common objectives.

Finally, the communiqué dealt with free world security. We noted that the urgency of building up the strength of the whole free world had only been increased by the events in Korea and that adequate defense forces were essential if war was to be prevented.

We announced the following conclusions:

"1. The military capabilities of the United States and of the United Kingdom should be increased as rapidly as possible.

"2. The two countries should expand the production of arms which can be used by the forces of all the free nations that are joined together in common defense. Together with those other nations the United States and the United Kingdom should continue to work out mutual arrangements by which all will contribute appropriately to the common defense.

"We agreed that as soon as the plan now nearing completion in the North Atlantic Treaty Organization for an effective integrated force for the defense of Europe is approved, a Supreme Commander should be appointed. It is our joint desire that this appointment shall be made soon.

"In addition to these decisions on increasing our military strength, we have agreed that the maintenance of healthy civilian economies is of vital importance to the success of our defense efforts. We agreed that, while defense production must be given the highest practicable priority in the case of raw materials whose supply is inadequate, the essential civilian requirements of the free countries must be met so far as practicable. In order to obtain the necessary materials and to devote them as rapidly as possible to these priority purposes, we have agreed to work closely together for the purpose of increasing supplies of raw materials. We have recognized the necessity of international action to assure that basic raw materials are distributed equitably in accordance with defense and essential civilian needs. We discussed certain immediate problems of raw materials shortages and consideration of these specific matters will continue. We are fully conscious of the increasing necessity of preventing materials and items of strategic importance from flowing into the hands of those who might use them against the free world.

"In the circumstances which confront us throughout the world our nations have no other choice but to devote themselves with all vigor to the building up of our defense forces. We shall do this purely as a defensive measure. We believe that the communist leaders of the Soviet Union and China could, if they chose, modify their conduct in such a way as to make these defense preparations unnecessary. We shall do everything we can, through whatever channels are open to us, to impress this view upon them and to seek a peaceful solution of existing issues.

"The President stated that it was his hope that world conditions would never call for the use of the atomic bomb. The President told the Prime Minister that it was also his desire to keep the Prime Minister at all times informed of developments which might bring about a change in the situation.

"In this critical period, it is a source of satisfaction to us that the views of our governments on basic problems are so similar. We believe that this identity of aims will enable our governments to carry out their determination to work together to strengthen the unity which has already been achieved among free nations and to defend those values which are of fundamental importance to the people we represent."

CHAPTER 26

The first two weeks of December 1950 were a time of crisis. The military news from Korea was bad.

It is unfortunate that some people forget so quickly. People who had for years blocked a sound military policy for our country and would have cut back on everything to satisfy a balance sheet were now the ones who shouted loudest. They wanted to know why we did not have divisions ready to rush to MacArthur's aid. There were some who wanted to pull all our troops out of Korea, turn our backs on Europe, and build up a "Fortress America." Then there were those who wanted to give up on Korea and concentrate on Europe alone, while others thought we should fight a full-scale war in China and abandon our position in Europe. There were even a few who thought we ought to provoke war on a world-wide basis right then and there, and some actually said that I had brought on a foreign policy crisis on purpose so that I might gain more power for myself.

It is characteristic of any system where free expression of opinion prevails that the critics and the malcontents will be heard more often than those who support the established policy. In the first place, people who are satisfied with a policy have no reason to be noisy about it; in the second place, our means of communicating and consolidating public opinion—the press and the radio—emphasize the differences of opinion rather than agreements. A President must not be influenced by this distortion of opinion. He must be able to distinguish between propaganda and the true opinion of the people. The task is not easy, and in December 1950 it seemed especially tough.

I had just received the views of the British Cabinet through Clement

Attlee. General Collins, whom I had sent to Japan and Korea for a firsthand look at the situation, had brought back a summary of the views of General MacArthur.

The Far East commander had told the Chief of Staff of the Army that he saw three possible courses for action.

The first of these was to continue action against the Chinese in Korea only. This would mean that our forces would remain under the same restrictions that they were under then; namely, no air attacks on bases in Manchuria, no naval blockade against the China mainland, no use of Nationalist Chinese troops, no large-scale reinforcements of the U.N. troops in Korea. In General MacArthur's opinion, to take this alternative was the same as surrendering. He was certain that sooner or later, if we followed this course, we would be compelled to withdraw from Korea. The best we could hope for might be a good delaying action.

General MacArthur favored the second course. This provided for a blockade by the United Nations of the coast of China and called for the bombing of the Chinese mainland. MacArthur also specified that the maximum use be made of Chinese Nationalist forces in Korea, and at the same time troops of Chiang Kai-shek would be "introduced" into South China, possibly through Hong Kong. "Subsequent operations in Korea, or withdrawal therefrom, should be dependent upon Chinese reactions."

There was a third possible course, according to MacArthur, and that was that the Chinese Communists would voluntarily agree to remain north of the 38th parallel. An armistice on that basis, MacArthur told Collins, should be accepted by the U.N. In his opinion, unless the United Nations was willing to accept the second alternative as suggested by him, an armistice under the supervision of a U.N. commission would be the most desirable solution.

General MacArthur had given his views to Collins in private, and the Chief of Staff had observed the proper secrecy in reporting them. But enough was known of MacArthur's views among the press representations in Tokyo and enough became known through his various statements and interviews to give the American public the impression that he had offered the only sure way to victory in Korea. But a fearful difficulty lay in the fact that the course advocated by MacArthur might well mean all-out, general world war—atomic weapons and all.

I have never been able to make myself believe that MacArthur, seasoned soldier that he was, did not realize that the "introduction of Chinese Nationalist forces into South China" would be an act of war; or that he, who had had a front-row seat at world events for thirty-five years, did not realize that the Chinese people would react to the bombing of their cities in exactly the same manner as the people of the United States reacted to the bombing of Pearl Harbor; or that, with his knowledge of the East, he could have overlooked the fact that after he had bombed the cities of China there would still be vast flows of materials from Russia so that, if he wanted to be consistent, his next step would have to be the bombardment of Vladivostok and the Trans-Siberian Railroad! But because I was sure that MacArthur could not possibly have overlooked these considerations, I was left with just one simple conclusion: General MacArthur was ready to risk general war. I was not.

I was disturbed to find General MacArthur's views and mine so far apart. But of course it was always proper and appropriate for him to advance his opinion to his Commander in Chief. If he had gone no farther than that, I would never have felt compelled to relieve him.

I believe that one of the problems of top military leaders is that too many of them come to rely on "briefing." They get most of their facts and their opinions from their staffs, in condensed form. Now any top official must operate that way; the President of the United States has to depend on briefing. But there is one important difference: The President has as his staff people of many different ideas, people who move in and out of his official family; they each have skills and professions of their own; their futures do not depend on their efficiency reports. In the military, however, and especially among the professionals, strong convictions and a critical mind may spell the end of a career. While I was a colonel in the field artillery reserve I read all the Army manuals on how a staff officer ought to function—and I know what the book says; but I also know that a President has to work to keep himself from being encircled by yes-men, while a military leader has far less reason to make that effort. But if he does not, his picture of the situation can gradually become more and more slanted. Because of the practice of rotation of assignments this does not usually happen, but MacArthur had not followed this practice: He had been surrounded by virtually the same group of friends and ardent admirers for years. No wonder he could not understand why the former non-coms were not flocking to return to the colors or what the United Nations had come to mean in the life of the Western nations; and no wonder he believed that America was willing to plunge into an Asiatic war! He had lost contact with his own people.

Around the President of the United States a staff performs a very different function. Like a military staff, it carries out the President's decisions (or at least some of them), but of much more importance, the staff must provide him at all times with the fullest possible range of arguments that might affect his decisions. A yes-man on the White House staff or in the Cabinet is worthless!

I always took care to get the fullest possible discussion of every problem before I reached a decision. I read countless background papers and made sure that my advisers included different points of view. Of course, when a decision had been made, I expected my staff to support me, but until the decision was reached, I wanted them to argue. I am convinced that this is sound and worth while. It has only one weakness: Many times, outsiders hear about these arguments and think that a fight is on, and then the headlines and the gossip columnists have a field day. And we had to do a good deal of arguing that December.

Not only was there the question of military policy, but also there were many others. In the United Nations, thirteen Asian-Arab nations had sponsored a resolution looking toward a cease-fire in Korea. Some of our people thought it was a futile gesture because the Chinese Communists would undoubtedly refuse to talk unless they first got a price—which we could not pay. But world opinion seemed to be strongly in favor of trying to get a cease-fire. The General Assembly adopted the resolution on December 14. It called for a three-man group to determine the basis on which a cease-fire might be reached in Korea and to make recommendations to put it into effect. On January 2 the three men—Entezam of Iran, Pearson of Canada, and Rau of India—reported to the U.N. that their effort had failed. The Chinese Communists were unwilling to consider truce talks except on their own terms.

In the meantime, steps had been taken to speed up our military program and provide it with sound economic supports. I had already decided, as soon as the first bad news arrived from Korea, that I ought to proclaim a national emergency. We discussed this to some extent in the Cabinet meeting on December 8, just before the conclusions of the talks with the British. I authorized General Marshall then to inform the appropriations committees on the Hill that a proclamation of national emergency was planned for the near future.

Of course I did not want to announce that an emergency was at hand without suggesting what we ought to do about it. The next days were therefore full of conferences.

On December 11 I met with the National Security Council to discuss the question of the cease-fire resolution in the United Nations. In the talks with Attlee it had been agreed that neither we nor the British would seek a cease-fire. However, the resolution of the thirteen Asiatic countries in the U.N. made it necessary for us to decide whether we would go along with any effort to secure a cease-fire at this time.

I reminded the members of the Council that in the talks with Attlee there had been a clear understanding that we would not surrender; that if we left Korea, we would have to be pushed out. General Bradley pointed out that it would be difficult to agree to a cease-fire unless it included free inspection of both sides, perhaps by a U.N. commission. I agreed that there should be free access to all of Korea, since we could not sit still and let the enemy build up.

Secretary Marshall observed that a cease-fire would stop all air reconnaissance and might push our Navy back. The Communists could then have a large build-up, and if we objected, they would say that we had not lived up to the cease-fire. On the other hand, if we opposed a cease-fire, our friends would think that we were objecting a peaceful solution.

Dean Acheson asked the military members what danger there was that we might get thrown back even farther by a new Communist advance before a cease-fire could be reached. General Bradley said that he thought this was not likely because the Chinese were beginning to have supply troubles.

Admiral Davis from the JCS staff observed that from a purely military point of view it was preferable not to have a cease-fire at this time, but if there had to be one, we ought to state our conditions clearly, and they should include reinforcements, movement to a suitable line of demarcation, and other points. We should, of course, insist on completing the removal of the X Corps from the northeast sector.

I said that I had never thought that we should agree to a cease-fire without first arriving at terms.

General Marshall pointed out that the first item, reinforcement, would prove difficult because of basic differences in concepts. For example, General MacArthur would have to be able to replace men who were sent home, but for the Chinese this might be an excuse for a further build-up.

Vice-President Barkley was of the opinion that we should not be maneuvered into a position where we might be accused of opposing a cease-fire. General Bradley wanted to know if orders should go out to MacArthur to pull back to the 38th parallel. I replied at once that we should hold our present positions as tenaciously as possible while the X Corps was being taken out of the northeast and until there actually was a cease-fire. Marshall said that the plans now called for a careful retirement and wanted to know if I would be opposed to such plans. I said, "No," but that I did not want to engage in a hurried withdrawal. I did not want to make a political decision to pull back but thought the rate of withdrawal should be directed by military considerations. The present directive to MacArthur was still adequate and effective.

I spoke next about my discussions with Attlee and noted that, with the exception of the matter of seating the Chinese Communists in the U.N., the meeting had shown remarkable agreement between the two governments. I stressed the importance of working closely with the British, for it was only in co-operation with them that the power of the United States could make itself felt fully, both in the Pacific and in the Atlantic. I observed, however, that both governments were agreed that it would be disastrous to get tied down in a general war with the Chinese Communists.

General Marshall reported that it appeared fairly certain now that we would be able to hold a line in Korea and that the evacuation of the X Corps would succeed. But the general situation, he thought, was just as dangerous as ever. One problem, the Defense Secretary said, was that Congress seemed to be talking about war and warlike measures like full mobilization when we were not militarily in a position to back up this kind of talk. But in order to have the necessary powers available to the President to improve that position he thought it was essential that the existence of a national emergency be declared.

General Bedell Smith commented on probable Soviet reactions to full-scale mobilization in the United States. The first point of this estimate was that we had to assume that the Russians expected us to increase military preparations in the United States as a result of their activities. But since the Russians probably operated on a fairly flexible timetable, it had to be assumed that our mobilization would cause them to do no more than adjust that timetable. They would probably not rush into a general war at once but would simply make sure that they did not give us an opportunity to outdistance them in military strength.

What had to be expected, then, would be that the U.S.S.R. would seek to weaken the Western alliance further by playing on the war fears of the western Europeans, by peace overtures and diplomatic peace feelers, by offering to discuss disarmament, by sabotage acts, and by local acts of aggression in widely scattered areas. If this did not materially hinder the American program for mobilization, then it would probably be to the Soviets' advantage to seize the initiative by launching an immediate attack against the West.

General Marshall pointed out that we were just on the verge of launching the NATO armed forces and that our entire international position depended on strengthening western Europe. We could not rush into measures for Korea and the Pacific that would cause such Russian reactions that our European allies would be scared away.

I asked Secretary Snyder's opinion on the question of declaring a national emergency, and he said that it was necessary in order to convince the Congress. He observed that one side of Congress was pushing very hard, perhaps even too hard, for military measures, while another side was refusing to vote taxes, saying that we had plenty of time.

I announced then that I would hold a meeting with congressional leaders on Wednesday to outline a program of action and inform them of my decision regarding the declaration of a national emergency. I would then make a national broadcast to explain the situation and call for support of our program.

The meeting with the congressional leaders took place at 10 A.M., Wednesday, December 13. It was a completely bi-partisan group, with the senior Democratic and Republican members of the Committees on Foreign Relations, Armed Services, and Appropriations. In addition to the members of Congress, there were present: Acheson, Marshall, Snyder, Symington, John Foster Dulles, Harriman.

I told the congressional leaders that we were faced with the necessity for a sharp step-up in our mobilization. In order to help this situation along I was considering issuing a proclamation of national emergency. So that the members of Congress might understand the situation facing us, I read them a summary of an intelligence report on the probable Soviet moves in connection with the present situation.

According to evidence from authoritative Russian sources, the report said the four principal ends which Russia hoped to achieve were: first, the withdrawal of United Nations forces from Korea and of the United States Seventh Fleet from Formosan waters; second, the establishment of Communist China as the dominant power in the Far East, including the seating of Peiping in the United Nations; third, the reduction of Western control over Japan as a step toward eventual elimination of all Western influence in that country; and, fourth, the prevention of West German rearmament.

The intelligence report stated that it was expected that the Russians would continue to offer to meet with the Western powers in order to maintain their pose as champions of "peaceful settlement," but there was nothing to suggest that the Russians would yield or even relax their pressure on any of these points. Calls for conferences would be for the purpose of creating confusion in the United States and western Europe. The Kremlin itself continued to regard conferences as places to consolidate gains already won, or being won, by force. Their attitude never changes; only their approach may be different so as to meet pending conditions.

Soviet pressure on Korea could be expected to continue, but Soviet military preparations and the nature of Soviet propaganda indicated that moves in other areas were possible. The points that appeared most critical were Berlin, Western Germany, Indo-China, Yugoslavia, and Iran. In each of these areas a minor incident could easily be created which would give the Russians an excuse for open intervention. Even without that, pressure could be increased at a rate that might seriously endanger the Western position.

Finally, while Russia had been using talk of a new world war mostly to frighten the West and to reduce the will to resist Russian pressures, we had to be realistic and include in our plans the possibility that the Kremlin might not be bluffing and might have decided that the time was in fact ripe for a general war with the United States.

Acheson stated that he was in complete agreement with this appraisal of the situation by our intelligence agencies and that it was clear that since June the Soviet Union had been engaged in an all-out attack on the leadership of the United States. It was also clear that the Soviet leaders recognized that their policy might bring on a general war and that they were prepared to run that risk. He also pointed out that the key to the Russian game was a "trap play"—to see how much of our strength they could make us dissipate while their main strength remained free for future use.

Their main effort at the moment, Acheson said, was to divide us from our allies, and this effort was meeting with some success.

Acheson said that we had only one choice open to us, and that was the greatest possible build-up of our own military strength and that of our allies. This meant preserving our strength and not overcommitting it while the build-up was under way. He could see no other way to stop the Soviet drive for world domination.

I now called on Secretary of Defense Marshall, who described the military picture. The Secretary of Defense opened his remarks with a summary of our ground strength in being. There was only one United States Army division in the United States; it would be spring before any other divisions would be trained and ready for action. He then turned to Korea and gave a brief summary of our position there, saying that our forces would soon be in reasonably strong defensive positions and that they should then be able to hold with some firmness for some time to come.

He turned from this subject to Japan and said that we had no combat troops there at all and that security was being maintained by seventy-five thousand Japanese police. This, Marshall said, was a matter of deep concern to the Defense Department since we could not know what the Russians might do next. They had many strong military bases, especially air bases, within easy striking distance of Japan.

Meanwhile, Marshall continued, things were coming to a head in Europe. While we were completing arrangements for an integrated European defense force and a supreme commander, the Russians were stepping up their propaganda and agitation. They had several times warned that they would not "tolerate" any arming of West Germans and might be ready to back this threat with force.

General Marshall then reviewed the question of appropriations and said that, under the speed-up plan, we were trying to procure by 1952 what had been planned for procurement by 1954. This speed-up process would, of course, create strains, especially in the matter of equipment. The Army was already finding it difficult to negotiate contracts because no legal authority existed to give military contracts priority over civilian requirements, and industry was not overly eager to convert from civilian goods to wartime production. This was really the crucial point of the whole program, how to accelerate the matériel procurement for the men of the enlarged services.

I pointed out that this would be one of the areas where the declaration of national emergency would help, though it would also be useful in other ways. It would give the Chief Executive some authority and powers which he needed and would generally enable us to approach our aim: "Proper and orderly mobilization as quickly as it can be done, while we stabilize the economic situation at the same time so contractors can fulfill their contracts and obligations to deliver military equipment on schedule."

In connection with economic stabilization plans, I announced a meeting with members of Congress and others the next day to discuss price controls, wage stabilization measures, priorities, allocations, and other things. I named those to be asked to this meeting and explained that the proclamation of national emergency would care for some of these problems but not all. It would be necessary to come to Congress for further authority.

Recalling the extremely dangerous world situation that had been brought about by the intervention of the Chinese in Korea, I assured them that we could meet this great danger, but quick and determined action was essential.

Senator Taft at once wanted to know whether the plans for expansion of the services which Marshall had discussed meant full mobilization or just an intermediate stage on the road to full mobilization. I replied that this was not full mobilization and that there would be no full mobilization unless we should find ourselves in a general war.

Senator Taft did not seem satisfied with this answer but wanted to know what percentage of full mobilization was proposed. I answered, whatever mobilization was necessary to meet the situation as it developed, and General Marshall added that we were not now concerned with full mobilization but rather with the preparation of the base for full mobilization if that should become necessary.

Senator Wherry said that it seemed to him that the President was asking for the authority for full mobilization but was asking for it in the hope that he would not need to exercise all the powers. I agreed that there was no intention of using authority beyond the point where needed.

Senator Taft reminded the meeting (though it was plain that he meant to remind me) that any action I might take would be subject to the provision of funds by the Congress, and I agreed, adding that those actions were a matter of concern to the entire Congress, not just the appropriations committees. That was the reason so many of the congressional leaders had been invited to the White House this morning to talk these matters over.

Congressman Vinson asked whether the decision to issue a proclamation of national emergency had already been taken. I said yes, unless this group showed me sound reasons to the contrary. John McCormack noted that in a few respects emergency declarations issued by Franklin D. Roosevelt in 1939 and 1941 were still in effect but that the situation was quite different and that it seemed appropriate to declare a new emergency based on the new situation.

Congressman Vinson remarked that if an emergency were proclaimed there would be no further need for congressional action in the fields of contract negotiations, priorities, or allocations. This authority existed under emergency conditions, according to a law enacted in September of this year.

Senator Taft, however, saw no reason for a declaration of national emergency. He thought everything authorized by the September law could be done without a proclamation, but Charles Murphy, counsel to the President, explained that there were a number of other acts which gave the President powers contingent upon the existence of an emergency.

Congressman Martin wanted to know what, besides contract negotiations, would be made easier by such a proclamation. In reply I handed him a list of legislative provisions compiled by the Department of Justice, all of which would become effective in the event a national emergency was proclaimed by the President.

Congressman Martin inquired if there was any other legislation needed at this session of Congress. I thought not but hoped Congress would attend to the key items in our mobilization and defense effort: the military appropriations, aid to Yugoslavia, the tax bill, and civilian defense legislation.

Martin then said he wanted to ask a question that might be out of order, but he wondered whether we were doing anything to get additional support from other countries. I replied that that had been one of the reasons Attlee had come to Washington. Martin, however, said that he was thinking more in terms of immediate assistance in Korea. Were we making any effort in India and Japan and among the "Chinese who are friendly" to get "fighting bodies"?

General Marshall said there was a question of practicability here. We could hardly use any Japanese because the Russo-Chinese pact was aimed specifically at the possibility that one of these two countries might be fighting the Japanese, in which case the other was obligated to come in. He did not think there was much hope of getting help from India, which, he said, was trying to perform the rope trick.

Sam Rayburn then asked if I did not want to get the sentiment of all members of Congress present on the specific question of declaring a national emergency. I replied that I was anxious for each of them to speak and asked each man, in turn, to state his view.

Barkley said that we would be remiss in our duties to the people if we failed to take all steps necessary to protect the nation. For our own sake, and to strengthen our friends in the world, he thought I should go ahead and proclaim the emergency.

Speaker Rayburn was still uncertain and wanted to hear the reaction of some of the other gentlemen first. Joe Martin was also undecided but seemed to question the need for a declaration.

Senator Taft doubted that the legal reasons for issuing a proclamation were pressing and was generally opposed to the idea of declaring an emergency "without knowing the details of what is involved"—such as the draft and taxes.

Congressman McCormack said that the most imperative need at the moment was to make America strong. We had to recognize that democracies are complacent and that it takes strong words and strong action to awaken them and to make them do what is needed to defend themselves. Whereupon Taft broke in to say that he did not want to be misunderstood: he was all in favor of building up the armed forces; that was not the point on which he was dissenting. McCormack then went on to say that in his opinion a declaration of a national emergency was a frank, definite, affirmative act of leadership. It should be done.

Senator Wherry spoke in a very different vein. He would go along, he said, with the program to strengthen the nation, but as to the proclamation he thought he needed more facts. Also, he was doubtful about a number of our commitments abroad, though he did not say which ones, and he wondered why the additional authorities the President wished to obtain under the proclamation of emergency could not be asked for, one by one, from the Congress. He turned to me and asked me point-blank why, if I wanted more power, I did not ask Congress for it. I replied that many of the powers needed would have to be discretionary if I were to act as promptly as emergency situations might require. Wherry asked why I could not ask for just some of the powers rather than for powers sufficient for a full mobilization. I explained that time was of the essence and that it would not be practicable to request authorization for the expansion of our forces in piecemeal fashion. Wherry shot back that of course I should know; I was the only one who had the facts. I replied that the facts were available to Wherry and to everybody else in the room. They had been given as thorough a briefing as any civil official had ever been given and they were to ask more questions if they wanted to.

I was still smarting under Wherry's attack. I said I thought everyone knew that I was not interested in greater powers. Members of Congress would surely recall that I had from time to time voluntarily given up powers and had even asked Congress to repeal some of the powers given to me as President. But that was all in the past. The situation we were facing was very critical. I was asking for powers now, not because I wanted them, but because it was essential that I have them.

Senator Connally thought a declaration of national emergency ought to be issued because it would prove abroad that we had determination. But the American people would have to be told just what such a declaration involved and implied.

I said that I expected to go on the air on a four-network hookup and that I would state exactly why this declaration of national emergency was necessary and what steps would be taken. Connally commented that developments in Korea had made everybody jittery, and therefore a presidential speech would be a good way to let the American people understand what they were up against.

Congressman Vinson also approved an immediate proclamation of a national emergency, saying that this should be followed at once by the impositions of allocation systems and price controls on all commodities vital to the national defense. Senator McKellar said he feared some people might read a declaration of national emergency as a declaration of war but that he was sure an emergency existed and should be proclaimed. Senator George had some doubts about issuing a proclamation while there seemed to be evidences of divided opinion in the Congress, but he hoped that these differences of opinion could be overcome and said that then the proclamation should be issued. He also thought that economic controls should follow at once, as well as a new program of taxation to keep pace with the new demands on the budget. Senator Millikin thought the proclamation involved a question of timing. If it was issued at the wrong time, it might be misconstrued by the people. There ought to be some preparation for such a drastic step. He then repeated a point Taft had made, that an emergency proclamation would be a headline for one day and might needlessly alarm the people. He thought the most important thing would be to make it clear to the public that our best recourse would be to build up our military strength and keep it up at all times.

Congressman Richards, the acting chairman of the House Foreign Affairs Committee, said that prices and wages were intermixed with the entire defense program and that in the speech I might make the people would want to hear about prices and wages as well as about defense plans. Congressman Eaton thought an emergency ought to be declared and a sharp build-up of our forces started, not because it might scare the Russians—in his opinion it would not—but because it would make it clear to the rest of the world that we were determined to stop the Russians. Senator Lucas said that it would be a fatal blow to our position in the world if those present at this meeting were to go out and trumpet their disagreements to the press. He himself agreed with those who wanted a full exposition of our program to go out at the same time as the proclamation of the national emergency, but he thought that it would be most harmful if Senators Taft and Wherry and Congressman Martin were to leave the White House after this conference and tell the press that there was no need at all for a declaration of national emergency.

Mr. Taber, whom I next asked to speak, said that he thought the people were confused and upset. But he was satisfied that they would go along if they were given a definite policy and a definite program, and in his opinion the build-up of military strength had to be that program. Dewey Short stated his conviction that Congress should be very reluctant to delegate powers. But in this instance, he said, it had to be done. He thought that Congress should back the President and he hoped that there would be unanimity in any action the President might take.

Since by this time every member of Congress present had had an opportunity to speak, I expressed my appreciation for their coming and for the frankness of their opinions and adjourned the meeting.

I held another meeting, this time with the emphasis on the economic problems of allocations and wage and price controls, with a different group of congressmen the following day. I met with my staff and members of the Cabinet in several sessions on this and the following day as well. In these meetings the details of the program were worked out and the speech to announce it had its first drafting.

The National Security Council met the afternoon of December 14 to discuss the implications, political, military, and economic, of the proposed program. I was anxious to make sure that our military production requirements would be met, but I also realized that the civilian population had to support such a program and that rationing and similar strict controls would not be popular.

The situation was further complicated, of course, by the noisy demands of some of our newspapers and politicians who wanted a "crash program" of armament—a dramatic mobilization of the entire nation such as we would have in time of war. I opposed this clamor for full mobilization. We were fighting in Korea, but we intended to limit the fighting to that country and not plunge into a world-wide war. Furthermore, there was danger that we might arm so rapidly now that at some extremely critical moment we might be at a military disadvantage because our equipment had become obsolete. What we needed was to speed our original plan, so as to reach the 1954 goals in 1952, and then level off production and preparation to attain not merely a base, but a base that could be kept up to date, for the rapid expansion if general war should come.

As we talked this over in the NSC meeting, comparisons with the increase of forces at the beginning of World War II readily came to mind. Mr. Lovett, for instance, remarked that on December 31, 1941, after two years of mobilization, our armed forces had numbered only 1,688,271, and Vice-President Barkley commented that it took us only a very little time after that to build up a force ten times that size. Several times during the meeting I pointed out that this was the position we had to work for: to get our machinery, military and industrial, in such condition that the maximum expansion could set in on the shortest possible notice.

On Friday evening, December 15, at ten-thirty Washington time, I went on the air to tell my fellow countrymen what we faced and what we would have to do.

"First," I said, "we will continue to uphold, and if necessary, to defend with arms, the principles of the United Nations—the principles of freedom and justice.

"Second, we will continue to work with the other free nations to strengthen our combined defenses.

"Third, we will build up our own Army, Navy and Air Force, and make more weapons for ourselves and our allies.

"Fourth, we will expand our economy and keep it on an even keel."

I went on to discuss each of these points in detail, and at the end announced the issuance of a proclamation the following morning declaring that a national emergency existed. "This," I said, "will call upon every citizen to put aside his personal interests for the good of the country. All our energies must be devoted to the task ahead of us.

"No nation has ever had a greater responsibility than ours at this moment. We must remember that we are the leaders of the free world. We must understand that we cannot achieve peace by ourselves, but only by cooperating with other free nations and with the men and women who love freedom everywhere.

"We must remember that our goal is not war but peace. Throughout the world our name stands for international justice and for a world based on the principles of law and order. We must keep it that way. We are willing to negotiate differences, but we will not yield to aggression. Appeasement of evil is not the road to peace.

"The American people have always met danger with courage and determination. I am confident we will do that now, and, with God's help, we shall keep our freedom."

The mail, telephone and telegraph messages that poured into the White House after this radio speech indicated overwhelming approval. Only a small percentage were in dissent. But I was greatly annoyed that there should arise at this time a noisy clamor of complaints by some senators that I should prove my desire to promote the national interest by, of all things, firing Dean Acheson!

The Secretary of State had long been under attack from certain elements of the press and of the Congress. This most recent attack on him aroused me to such anger that I issued a statement. I am sure that Acheson would not have consented, either to the statement or to its tone, if he had been in Washington at the time. However, I had once told a press conference that I would "bust loose" one of these days— and this was it!

"There have been new attacks," I said, "within the past week against Secretary of State Acheson. I have been asked to remove him from office. The authors of this suggestion claim that this would be good for the country.

"How our position in the world would be improved by the retirement of Dean Acheson from public life is beyond me. Mr. Acheson has helped shape and carry out our policy of resistance to communist imperialism. From the time of our sharing of arms with Greece and Turkey nearly four years ago, and coming down to the recent moment when he advised me to resist the Communist invasion of South Korea, no official in our government has been more alive to Communism's threat to freedom or more forceful in resisting it.

"At this moment, he is in Brussels representing the United States in setting up mutual defenses against aggression. This has made it possible for me to designate General Eisenhower as Supreme Allied Commander in Europe.

"If Communism were to prevail in the world today—as it shall not prevail—Dean Acheson would be one of the first, if not the first, to be shot by the enemies of liberty and Christianity.

"These recent attacks on Mr. Acheson are old in the sense that they are the same false charges that have been made time and time again over a period of months. They have no basis in fact whatever.

"It is the same sort of thing that happened to Seward. President Lincoln was asked by a group of Republicans to dismiss Secretary of State Seward. He refused. So do I refuse to dismiss Secretary Acheson.

"If I did anything else, it would weaken the firm and vigorous position this country has taken against communist aggression.

"If those groups attacking our foreign policy and Mr. Acheson have any alternative policies to offer, they should disclose them. They owe it to their country. This is a time for hard facts and close thinking. It is not a time for vague charges and pious generalities.

"There are some Republicans who recognize the facts and the true reasons for these attacks on Secretary of State Acheson and who do not agree with their colleagues.

"This nation needs the wisdom of all its people. This is a time of great peril. It is a time for unity, for real bi-partisanship. It is a time for making use of the great talents of men like Dean Acheson.

"Communism—not our own country—would be served by losing him."

History, I am sure, will list Dean Acheson among the truly great Secretaries of State our nation has had. I had four Secretaries of State in a little less than eight years: Edward R. Stettinius, Jr., was in office when President Roosevelt's death placed me in the White House; James F. Byrnes served for about eighteen months, the final months of the war and the beginnings of the postwar period; General George C. Marshall was Secretary of State for two years, the years of aid to Greece and Turkey, of the Marshall Plan, and of the Berlin blockade; Dean Acheson held the office for four years, and he had been Assistant Secretary and Under Secretary before that. There were few men who came to the secretaryship as fully prepared for the job and as eminently qualified as Acheson was. His keen mind, cool temper, and broad vision served him well for handling the day-by-day business of the great issues of policy as well as the Department of State.

Acheson had been subjected to closest questioning by the Senate Committee on Foreign Relations at the time of his confirmation. But now the attacks had become vitriolic—especially since our action in Korea. Most of the criticism came from those members of the Senate who have sometimes been called the "China First" block. These men kept repeating the completely baseless charge that somehow Acheson had brought about the Communist victory in China, and they now charged that it was Acheson who was depriving General MacArthur of the means of gaining victory.

With his Formosa statement to the Veterans of Foreign Wars and with his more recent public utterances, General MacArthur had given these Acheson-haters an argument behind which they could gather their forces for the attack. In other words, they wanted Acheson's scalp because he stood for *my* policy. There was never a day during the four years of Dean Acheson's secretaryship that anyone could have said that he and I differed on policy. He was meticulous in keeping me posted on every development within the wide area of his responsibility. He had a deep understanding of the President's position in our constitutional scheme and realized to the fullest that, while I leaned on him for constant advice, the policy had to be mine—it was.

The men who struck out against Acheson were thus in reality striking out at me. Unfortunately, the long years during which the Republican party had been in a minority position had brought about the rise of a faction within that party that seemed to know no approach to government except to belittle, to denounce, and to negate. It was distressing that even in a period of crisis these men could not see that a two-party system, in order to succeed, needs a *responsible* opposition as much as a working majority.

I could certainly have done no more to stress just how serious a crisis we were in than what I had done at my several meetings with the leaders of Congress; namely, to make available to them the same kind of top-secret briefing that my advisers and I had access to. This is one of the problems of our system: The President cannot possibly give all the secret information that comes to him to every member of Congress— there are so many of them that secrets would be certain to leak out— and yet he must have their support and co-operation for policies based on this kind of information. Bi-partisanship in foreign policy means simply that the President can repose confidence in the members of the other party and that in turn the leaders of that party have confidence in the President's conduct of foreign affairs.

The way the American party system functions, leadership in a party depends as much on the accidents of seniority as it does on individual merits and achievement. This means that mutual confidence and bi-partisanship depend to large degree on who the leaders of the other party are. When Arthur Vandenberg spoke for the Republican senators, there was never a doubt in my mind that his judgment and his discretion warranted discussion with him of the most sensitive diplomatic problems. He understood and appreciated, when Marshall and Lovett sought him out in private to talk over their headaches with him, that he was placed in a position of highest trust and gravest responsibility. There were occasions when Senator Vandenberg disagreed with my policies, but he never attempted to sabotage them.

Senator Wherry and a few others I could name, however, seemed to have a very different attitude toward bi-partisanship. To them, it was a one-way street. A bi-partisanship approach to foreign policy seemed to them to mean that the President took no move whatsoever that was not first cleared with them. In turn, they would be under no responsibility whatsoever to support the President.

Some other people apparently think that bi-partisanship in foreign policy is something that can be had by setting up a mechanism for consultation or that you can get, by including individuals who are listed as members of the other party in some more or less important positions in the foreign policy field. That does not always mean that they are really representative of that party. But none of this will make any difference unless there is a spirit of trust and confidence. This working relationship is not possible unless the members of Congress approach foreign policy in a responsible, positive way. It cannot work unless the President can rely confidently on the judgment and the discretion of the members of the opposition when he talks to them about matters which, if they were prematurely revealed, would affect the security of the nation.

Unfortunately, the men who so loudly demanded Acheson's dismissal had given ample proof that they would use any information that might be given them as partisan campaign material—and they never stopped their partisan campaigning.

CHAPTER 27

While public attention was concentrated on Korea, our military and intelligence experts were more and more concerned about the possibility that Russia might strike against Japan while that country was without military protection. Our needs in Korea had left the American occupation authorities without any combat troops in Japan, and though MacArthur had begun to encourage the Japanese to build up a national police force that might be able to put up at least a passing defense, it would take time for this to be accomplished. Accordingly, on December 19, General MacArthur asked the Joint Chiefs for reinforcements for Japan.

The Joint Chiefs of Staff and General Marshall held a series of meetings with State Department officials, trying to find some way to meet the problem. Reinforcements were simply not available. We could not send the 82nd Airborne Division. It was the only troop unit in the United States ready to go, and we had to keep a minimum reserve at home. The National Guard divisions would not be ready for shipment overseas before March. The military chiefs thought that we might consider ways to withdraw from Korea "with honor" in order to protect Japan. The State Department took the position, however, that we could not retreat from Korea unless we were forced out. Anything less would be an abandonment of the principle that caused us to go in in the first place.

One of the means by which some relief could be given to the Far Eastern situation was to increase the size of the army of the Republic of Korea. President Rhee had repeatedly asked that he be given more arms, but we had been unable to do much more for him because our own needs were hardly filled. On January 3, 1951, however, the Joint Chiefs asked for MacArthur's opinion, informing him of the types and quantities of arms and ammunition that could be made available.

Based on these figures, the Joint Chiefs estimated that the ROK forces could be increased by from 200,000 to 300,000 men, armed with rifles, auto rifles, carbines, and submachine guns, and they asked MacArthur to make recommendations.

The general replied on January 6, reporting that arms had been made available not only to the South Korean Army but also to Youth Corps and similar groups, but that enemy guerrillas continued to operate effectively in many widely scattered regions of South Korea. Guerrilla forces friendly to us, however, had accomplished little in Communist rear areas —primarily owing to lack of strong-willed leadership—and ROK Army units had consistently failed to perform adequately. The general was convinced that our weapons and munitions would be put to better use if they were not given to the South Koreans but were made available, instead, to the newly established National Police Reserve of Japan.

By this time the situation in Korea had begun to improve. The evacuation of the X Corps from the Hungnam area had been successfully completed, and the elements of that corps had joined and been placed under the command of the Eighth Army, which, following the death of General Walker in a jeep accident, had been given a new commander in the person of Lieutenant General Matthew B. Ridgway.

General MacArthur repeatedly advised the Joint Chiefs that in his opinion the war should be expanded by attacks on airfields in Manchuria, by a blockade of the China coast, and by the utilization of the Formosa Chinese. In a message on December 29, for instance, after restating his views, he said that he knew that this course of action had been rejected because of fears that it might provoke China into all-out war with us. In his opinion, however, this was not pertinent, for he thought that nothing could aggravate the situation vis-à-vis China. What the Russians might do, nobody could tell. If he received the four additional divisions he asked for for Japan, however, he would be able to slow the Chinese up if they attempted to attack there.

It was also his opinion that if we did not intend to expand the war the only other chcice would be to contract our position in Korea gradually until we were reduced to the Pusan beachhead and then evacuate, despite the fact that this would have a poor effect on Asian morale.

This withdrawal movement, it should be pointed out, appeared already to be forced upon us when the Communists staged a major attack on the Eighth Army on January 1, forcing us to abandon the city of Seoul.

On January 9 the Joint Chiefs of Staff informed General MacArthur, with my approval, that the retaliatory measures which he had suggested were being given consideration in Washington. He was further assured that I appreciated fully the extent to which Chinese Communist entry into Korea and now into South Korea had changed the situation. However, he was advised that there were other considerations which required us to maintain our present policy in Korea, and he was therefore directed to defend successive positions, inflicting as much damage on the enemy as possible. Primary consideration, however, should be given to the safety of his troops and to his basic mission of protecting Japan. If it should become evident, in his judgment, that evacuation was essential to avoid severe losses of men and matériel, then he was to withdraw to Japan.

General MacArthur responded to this directive the following day with a request for clarification. He stated that his command was of insufficient strength to hold a position in Korea and simultaneously to protect Japan against external assault. He further asserted that, if he had to continue to operate under the limitations and with the strength that he had been given, the military position of his command in Korea would eventually become untenable. He pointed out that the United Nations troops were tired as a result of a long and difficult campaign, that they were, he asserted, embittered by unwarranted criticism, and that their morale was sinking rapidly. In his opinion, unless there were overriding considerations, his command should be withdrawn from the Korean peninsula just as rapidly as was tactically feasible.

On the other hand, he said, if political[1] reasons demanded that we hold a position in Korea, then we ought to accept the military consequences, which he predicted would be heavy casualties and a grave hazard to the security of Japan.

When General Marshall brought me this message from MacArthur, I was deeply disturbed. The Far East commander was, in effect, reporting that the course of action decided upon by the National Security Council and by the Joint Chiefs of Staff and approved by me was not feasible. He was saying that we would be driven off the peninsula or, at the very least, suffer terrible losses. Events were to prove that he was wrong, but it was the proper procedure for him to voice his doubts and to ask for reconsideration of the Washington decision. I asked the National Security Council to meet in a special session on January 12 to discuss the MacArthur message and what should be done about it.

At this meeting I expressed the view that it was important to keep MacArthur fully informed on political as well as military matters. We

---

[1] "Political," in its use in these discussions, refers to world affairs and not to the home front.

had done that all along. He had received copies of many important papers even though few, apparently, had really found their way to his desk. I would therefore send a personal message to General MacArthur bringing him up to date on our foreign policy. This was my message to MacArthur:

January 13, 1951

I want you to know that the situation in Korea is receiving the utmost attention here and that our efforts are concentrated upon finding the right decisions on this matter of the gravest importance to the future of America and to the survival of free peoples everywhere.

I wish in this telegram to let you have my views as to our basic national and international purposes in continuing the resistance to aggression in Korea. We need your judgment as to the maximum effort which could reasonably be expected from the United Nations forces under your command to support the resistance to aggression which we are trying rapidly to organize on a world-wide basis. This present telegram is not to be taken in any sense as a directive. Its purpose is to give you something of what is in our minds regarding the political factors.

1. A successful resistance in Korea would serve the following important purposes:

(a) To demonstrate that aggression will not be accepted by us or by the United Nations and to provide a rallying point around which the spirits and energies of the free world can be mobilized to meet the world-wide threat which the Soviet Union now poses.

(b) To deflate the dangerously exaggerated political and military prestige of Communist China which now threatens to undermine the resistance of non-Communist Asia and to consolidate the hold of Communism on China itself.

(c) To afford more time for and to give direct assistance to the organization of non-Communist resistance in Asia, both outside and inside China.

(d) To carry out our commitments of honor to the South Koreans and to demonstrate to the world that the friendship of the United States is of inestimable value in time of adversity.

(e) To make possible a far more satisfactory peace settlement for Japan and to contribute greatly to the post-treaty security position of Japan in relation to the continent.

(f) To lend resolution to many countries not only in Asia but also in Europe and the Middle East who are now living within the shadow of Communist power and to let them know that they need not now rush to come to terms with Communism on whatever terms they can get, meaning complete submission.

(g) To inspire those who may be called upon to fight against great odds if subjected to a sudden onslaught by the Soviet Union or by Communist China.

(h) To lend point and urgency to the rapid build-up of the defenses of the western world.

(i) To bring the United Nations through its first great effort on collective security and to produce a free-world coalition of incalculable value to the national security interests of the United States.

(j) To alert the peoples behind the Iron Curtain that their masters are bent upon wars of aggression and that this crime will be resisted by the free world.

2. Our course of action at this time should be such as to consolidate the great majority of the United Nations. This majority is not merely part of the organization but is also the nations whom we would desperately need to count on as allies in the event the Soviet Union moves against us. Further, pending the build-up of our national strength, we must act with great prudence in so far as extending the area of hostilities is concerned. Steps which might in themselves be fully justified and which might lend some assistance to the campaign in Korea would not be beneficial if they thereby involved Japan or Western Europe in large-scale hostilities.

3. We recognize, of course, that continued resistance might not be militarily possible with the limited forces with which you are being called upon to meet large Chinese armies. Further, in the present world situation, your forces must be preserved as an effective instrument for the defense of Japan and elsewhere. However, some of the important purposes mentioned above might be supported, if you should think it practicable, and advisable, by continued resistance from off-shore islands of Korea, particularly from Cheju-do, if it becomes impracticable to hold an important portion of Korea itself. In the worst case, it would be important that, if we must withdraw from Korea, it be clear to the world that that course is forced upon us by military necessity and that we shall not accept the result politically or militarily until the aggression has been rectified.

4. In reaching a final decision about Korea, I shall have to give constant thought to the main threat from the Soviet Union and to the need for a rapid expansion of our armed forces to meet this great danger.

5. I am encouraged to believe that the free world is getting a much clearer and realistic picture of the dangers before us and that the necessary courage and energy will be forthcoming. Recent proceedings in the United Nations have disclosed a certain amount of confusion and wishful thinking, but I believe that most members have been actuated by a desire to be absolutely sure that all possible avenues to peaceful settlement have been fully explored. I believe that the great majority is now rapidly consolidating and that the result will be an encouraging and formidable combination in defense of freedom.

6. The entire nation is grateful for your splendid leadership in the difficult struggle in Korea and for the superb performance of your forces under the most difficult circumstances.

[s] Harry S. Truman

General MacArthur had, as he had in previous wars, displayed splendid leadership. But I wanted him to accept, as a soldier should, the political decisions which the civil authorities of the government had determined upon.

Our forces stemmed the tide in Korea in January 1951. The enemy was stopped and in some sectors of the front pushed back. When General Collins visited the Eighth Army, he reported on January 17 that the army was in good shape and improving daily. The Chinese had apparently reached a point where their supply lines were getting too long for effective operations.

Another result of the visit of Generals Collins and Vandenberg to the Far East was that they were able to report that General MacArthur said that unless Russia actively intervened it now appeared feasible to continue operations in Korea for as long as it was to our over-all national interest to do so without seriously endangering the Eighth Army.

When General Collins and General Vandenberg returned, they reported to me and told me of their observations in Korea and their conversations with MacArthur. I was reassured by their report, but the situation was still far from giving any feeling of relief. On January 18 intelligence reports had indicated a possible regrouping of the enemy in Korea that might mean a new offensive. The same report spoke of increasing Communist attention to Japan. There were military activities in South China that could be signs of an impending attack on Hong Kong. All this could mean that Peiping was ready for major thrusts in all directions.

From the very beginning of the Korean action I had always looked at it as a Russian maneuver, as part of the Kremlin's plan to destroy the unity of the free world. NATO, the Russians knew, would succeed only if the United States took part in the defense of Europe. The easiest way to keep us from doing our share in NATO was to draw us into military conflict in Asia. We could not deny military aid to a victim of Communist aggression in Asia unless we wanted other small nations to swing into the Soviet camp for fear of aggression which, alone, they could not resist. At the same time, it served to weaken us on a global plane and that, of course, was Russia's aim.

Our policy was to maintain our position in Asia, promote the defense and unity of Europe, and prepare America. As I saw it then, and as I see it now, these three purposes depended upon each other, and one could not be attained without all three parts of our policy being vigorously pursued.

I had occasion to make my position clear when the French Prime Minister, M. René Pleven, visited Washington at the end of January. He and I had three sessions together, the first of which was devoted to Asian problems.

After Pleven had given me the situation in Indo-China, where the French had been fighting Communist rebels since 1946, I told him that I saw no way for us to recognize the Communist regime in Peiping, that I was convinced that the Communists had moved on South Korea because they had come to fear the progress the Western powers had been making in the Far East. There had been very real progress in Japan. There had been good progress in the Republic of Korea. The French themselves had been making progress in Indo-China. By the attack on South Korea, the Soviets were trying to offset all the gains that had been made in the Far East and, of more importance, they were trying to wreck the whole program. I assured M. Pleven that the policy of the United States was based upon the proposition that the peace of the world, which we had fought to attain, could not be divided and that *only collective security* could bring about world peace. We would negotiate with the Chinese to restore peace in Korea, but not at the price of collective security and national self-respect.

There is, of course, a difference between broad policy aims such as the President establishes and detailed applications of policy that have to be worked out on a day-by-day basis. On these details of application there normally are differences of opinion and discussions. Sometimes the details grow into proportions where the President must make the decision, but normally there are a great many conversations, conferences, study papers, etc., before a matter is placed before the President. Throughout the early months of 1951, Defense and State Department officials met repeatedly to plan possible courses of action in Korea and in Asia generally.

In March, as the tide of battle in Korea began to turn in our favor, both groups favored a new approach to a negotiated cease-fire. The reasoning was that, in the first place, since we had been able to inflict heavy casualties on the Chinese and were pushing them back to and beyond the 38th parallel, it would now be in their interest at least as much as ours to halt the fighting, and secondly, the invaders stood substantially ejected from the territory of the Republic of Korea.

The Department of State drew up a statement which they proposed I should issue. On March 19 Secretary Acheson, General Marshall, and the Joint Chiefs of Staff held a meeting at which they discussed this draft. They also agreed to inform General MacArthur that there was going to be a presidential announcement and to ask him to offer his recommendations.

I was just ending a brief vacation at the Little White House at Key West, Florida, where I kept in constant touch with Acheson and Marshall, when on March 20 the Joint Chiefs of Staff, carrying out the agreement of the preceding day, sent this message to General MacArthur:

"State Department planning a Presidential announcement shortly that, with clearing of bulk of South Korea of aggressors, United Nations now preparing to discuss conditions of settlement in Korea. United Nations feeling exists that further diplomatic efforts toward settlement should be made before any advance with major forces north of 38th parallel. Time will be required to determine diplomatic reactions and permit new negotiations that may develop. Recognizing that parallel has no military significance, State has asked Joint Chiefs of Staff what authority you should have to permit sufficient freedom of action for next few weeks to provide security for United Nations forces and maintain contact with enemy. Your recommendation desired."

In his reply the following day General MacArthur recommended that no additional restrictions be imposed on his command. He pointed out that, with the forces at his command and operating under the limitations which had been placed on him, it was not practicable for him to attempt to clear North Korea of the enemy and that he felt for that reason his current directive covered the situation quite well.

Following the receipt of MacArthur's reply, the Joint Chiefs of Staff again met with the Secretary of Defense and the State Department, and further details of the proposed presidential announcement were worked out. Furthermore, State Department officials met with the Washington representatives of the other nations that had troops in Korea in order to obtain their approval to the proposed draft.

This was the draft:

"I make the following statement as Chief Executive of the Government requested by the United Nations to exercise the Unified Command in Korea, and after full consultation with United Nations Governments contributing combat forces in support of the United Nations in Korea.

"United Nations forces in Korea are engaged in repelling the aggressions committed against the Republic of Korea and against the United Nations.

"The aggressors have been driven back with heavy losses to the general vicinity from which the unlawful attack was first launched last June.

"There remains the problem of restoring international peace and security in the area in accordance with the terms of the Security Council resolution of June 27, 1950. The spirit and principles of the United Nations Charter require that every effort be made to prevent the spread of hostilities and to avoid the prolongation of the misery and the loss of life.

"There is a basis for restoring peace and security in the area which should be acceptable to all nations which sincerely desire peace.

"The Unified Command is prepared to enter into arrangements which would conclude the fighting and ensure against its resumption. Such arrangements would open the way for a broader settlement for Korea, including the withdrawal of foreign forces from Korea.

"The United Nations has declared the policy of the world community that the people of Korea be permitted to establish a unified, independent and democratic state.

"The Korean people are entitled to peace. They are entitled to determine their political and other institutions by their own choice and in response to their own needs.

"The Korean people are entitled to the assistance of the world community in repairing the ravages of war—assistance which the United Nations is ready to give and for which it has established the necessary machinery. Its member nations have already made generous offers of help. What is needed is peace, in which the United Nations can use its resources in the creative tasks of reconstruction.

"It is regrettable that those who are opposing the United Nations in Korea have made so little response to the many opportunities which have been and continue to be afforded for a settlement in Korea.

"A prompt settlement of the Korean problem would greatly reduce international tension in the Far East and would open the way for the consideration of other problems in that area by the processes of peaceful settlement envisaged in the Charter of the United Nations.

"Until satisfactory arrangements for concluding the fighting have been reached, United Nations military action must be continued."

The thought behind this was that a suggestion of our willingness to settle, without any threats or recriminations, might get a favorable reply.

Unfortunately, the careful preparations were all in vain. The many hours spent to secure the approval of the other governments, the detailed discussions among diplomats and defense leaders became useless when on March 24 General MacArthur released a statement that was so entirely at cross-purposes with the one I was to have delivered that it would only have confused the world if my carefully prepared statement had been made.

What General MacArthur said was this:

"Operations continue according to schedule and plan. We have now substantially cleared South Korea of organized Communist forces. It is becoming increasingly evident that the heavy destruction along the enemy's lines of supply, caused by our round-the-clock massive air and naval bombardment, has left his troops in the forward battle area deficient in requirements to sustain his operations. This weakness is being brilliantly exploited by our ground forces. The enemy's human wave tactics have definitely failed him as our own forces have become seasoned to this form of warfare; his tactics of infiltration are but contributing to his piecemeal losses, and he is showing less stamina than our own troops under the rigors of climate, terrain and battle.

"Of even greater significance than our tactical successes has been the clear revelation that this new enemy, Red China, of such exaggerated and vaunted military power, lacks the industrial capacity to provide adequately many critical items necessary to the conduct of modern war.

He lacks the manufacturing base and those raw materials needed to produce, maintain and operate even moderate air and naval power, and he cannot provide the essentials for successful ground operations, such as tanks, heavy artillery and other refinements science has introduced into the conduct of military campaigns. Formerly his great numerical potential might well have filled this gap but with the development of existing methods of mass destruction, numbers alone do not offset the vulnerability inherent in such deficiencies. Control of the seas and the air, which in turn means control over supplies, communications, and transportation, are no less essential and decisive now than in the past. When this control exists as in our case, and is coupled with an inferiority of ground fire power as in the enemy's case, the resulting disparity is such that it cannot be overcome by bravery, however fanatical, or the most gross indifference to human loss.

"These military weaknesses have been clearly and definitely revealed since Red China entered upon its undeclared war in Korea. Even under the inhibitions which now restrict the activity of the United Nations forces and the corresponding military advantages which accrue to Red China, it has been shown its complete inability to accomplish by force of arms the conquest of Korea. The enemy, therefore, must by now be painfully aware that a decision of the United Nations to depart from its tolerant effort to contain the war to the area of Korea, through an expansion of our military operations to its coastal areas and interior bases, would doom Red China to the risk of imminent military collapse. These basic facts being established, there should be no insuperable difficulty in arriving at decisions on the Korean problem if the issues are resolved on their own merits, without being burdened by extraneous matters not directly related to Korea, such as Formosa or China's seat in the United Nations.

"The Korean nation and people, which have been so cruelly ravaged, must not be sacrificed. This is a paramount concern. Apart from the military area of the problem where issues are resolved in the course of combat, the fundamental questions continue to be political in nature and must find their answer in the diplomatic sphere. Within the area of my authority as the military commander, however, it would be needless to say that I stand ready at any time to confer in the field with the commander-in-chief of the enemy forces in the earnest effort to find any military means whereby realization of the political objectives of the United Nations in Korea, to which no nation may justly take exceptions, might be accomplished without further bloodshed."

This was a most extraordinary statement for a military commander of the United Nations to issue on his own responsibility. It was an act totally disregarding all directives to abstain from any declarations on foreign policy. It was in open defiance of my orders as President and as Commander in Chief. This was a challenge to the authority of the President under the Constitution. It also flouted the policy of the United Nations.

By this act MacArthur left me no choice—I could no longer tolerate his insubordination.

In effect, what MacArthur was doing was to threaten the enemy with an ultimatum—intimating that the full preponderance of Allied power might be brought to bear against Red China. To be sure, he said that this would be a political decision, but considering his high office, the world would assume that he had advance knowledge that such a decision would be made.

This was certainly the immediate effect among our allies. From capitals all over the world came rush inquiries: What does this mean? Is there about to be a shift in American policy?

There was more involved than the fate of a prepared statement that the President of the United States had intended to make, or even than the diplomatic furor created by this "pronunciamento," as the Norwegian Ambassador called it when he inquired at the State Department what it meant. What was much more important was that once again General MacArthur had openly defied the policy of his Commander in Chief, the President of the United States.

I held a conference with Dean Acheson, Robert Lovett, and Dean Rusk at noon that day, Saturday, and reviewed the order which had been sent to MacArthur on December 6, requiring that all public statements be cleared with the department concerned. I asked the others if there could be any doubt as to the meaning of this order, and they all agreed that it was a very clear directive.

I instructed Lovett to have a priority message sent to General Mac-Arthur that would remind him of his duty under this order, for the main thing to do now was to prevent further statements by the general.

I was aware of the fact that in an earlier statement the same month General MacArthur had already issued a challenge to the policy of the President. On March 7 he had dictated a statement to reporters to the effect that unless I accepted his policy there would be "savage slaughter." However, he had then at least admitted that it was not his to make the decision. But now, by his statement, he had in a very real sense influenced the course of policy, and further statements like this could only do untold harm.

This message was therefore sent to him:

24 Mar 51

FROM JCS PERSONAL FOR MAC ARTHUR

The President has directed that your attention be called to his order as transmitted 6 December 1950. In view of the information given you 20 March 1951 any further statements by you must be coordinated as prescribed in the order of 6 December.

The President has also directed that in the event Communist military leaders request an armistice in the field, you immediately report that fact to the JCS for instructions.

BRADLEY

I can only say that on that day I was deeply shocked. I had never underestimated my difficulties with MacArthur, but after the Wake Island meeting I had hoped that he would respect the authority of the President. I tried to place myself in his position, however, and tried to figure out why he was challenging the traditional civilian supremacy in our government.

Certainly his arguments and his proposals had always received full consideration by me and by the Joint Chiefs of Staff. If anything, they—and I—had leaned over backward in our respect for the man's military reputation. But all his statements since November—ever since the Chinese entry into Korea—had the earmarks of a man who performs for the galleries. It was difficult to explain this latest development unless it is assumed that it was of importance to the general to prevent any appearance that the credit for ending the fighting should go elsewhere.

I reflected on the similarities in the situation that had faced Abraham Lincoln in his efforts to deal with General McClellan. Carl Sandburg tells a story about Lincoln's relationship with McClellan: The general occasionally made political statements on matters outside the military field, and someone asked Lincoln what he would reply to McClellan. Lincoln's answer, so the story goes, was this: "Nothing—but it made me think of the man whose horse kicked up and stuck his foot through the stirrup. He said to the horse: 'If you are going to get on, I will get off.' "

Lincoln had had great and continuous trouble with McClellan, though the policy differences in those days were the opposite of mine: Lincoln wanted McClellan to attack, and McClellan would not budge. The general had his own ideas on how the war, and even the country, should be run. The President would issue direct orders to McClellan, and the general would ignore them. Half the country knew that McClellan had political ambitions, which men in opposition to Lincoln sought to use. Lincoln was patient, for that was his nature, but at long last he was compelled to relieve the Union Army's principal commander. And though I gave this difficulty with MacArthur much wearisome thought, I realized that I would have no other choice myself than to relieve the nation's top field commander.

If there is one basic element in our Constitution, it is civilian control of the military. Policies are to be made by the elected political officials, not by generals or admirals. Yet time and again General MacArthur had shown that he was unwilling to accept the policies of the administration. By his repeated public statements he was not only confusing our allies as to the true course of our policies but, in fact, was also setting his policy against the President's.

I have always had, and I have to this day, the greatest respect for General MacArthur, the soldier. Nothing I could do, I knew, could change his stature as one of the outstanding military figures of our time— and I had no desire to diminish his stature. I had hoped, and I had tried to convince him, that the policy he was asked to follow was right. He had disagreed. He had been openly critical. Now, at last, his actions had frustrated a political course decided upon, in conjunction with its allies, by the government he was sworn to serve. If I allowed him to defy the civil authorities in this manner, I myself would be violating my oath to uphold and defend the Constitution.

I have always believed that civilian control of the military is one of the strongest foundations of our system of free government. Many of our people are descended from men and women who fled their native countries to escape the oppression of militarism. We in America have sometimes failed to give the soldier and the sailor their due, and it has hurt us. But we have always jealously guarded the constitutional provision that prevents the military from taking over the government from the authorities, elected by the people, in whom the power resides.

It has often been pointed out that the American people have a tendency to choose military heroes for the highest office in the land, but I think the statement is misleading. True, we have chosen men like George Washington and Andrew Jackson, and even Ulysses S. Grant, as our Chief Executives. But only Grant among these three had been raised to be a professional soldier, and he had abandoned that career and been brought back into service, like thousands of other civilians, when war broke out. We have chosen men who, in time of war, had made their mark, but until 1952 we had never elevated to the White House any man whose entire life had been dedicated to the military.

One reason that we have been so careful to keep the military within its own preserve is that the very nature of the service hierarchy gives military commanders little if any opportunity to learn the humility that is needed for good public service. The elected official will never forget— unless he is a fool—that others as well or better qualified might have been chosen and that millions remained unconvinced that the last choice made was the best one possible. Any man who has come up through the process of political selection, as it functions in our country, knows that success is a mixture of principles steadfastly maintained and adjustments made at the proper time and place—adjustments to conditions, not adjustment of principles.

These are things a military officer is not likely to learn in the course of his profession. The words that dominate his thinking are "command" and "obedience," and the military definitions of these words are not definitions for use in a republic.

That is why our Constitution embodies the principle of civilian control of the military. This was the principle that General MacArthur threatened. I do not believe that he purposefully decided to challenge civilian control of the military, but the result of his behavior was that this fundamental principle of free government was in danger.

It was my duty to act.

I wrestled with the problem for several days, but my mind was made up before April 5, when the next incident occurred.

On that day Representative Joseph W. Martin, the minority leader in the House, read a letter in the House which General MacArthur had addressed to him. Martin, an isolationist with a long record of opposition to forward-looking foreign policies, had written to MacArthur early in March and, among other things, had said that it was sheer folly not to use Chinese Nationalist troops in Korea. Then he had asked if this view paralleled the general's.

General MacArthur's reply, written on March 20, read as follows:

"I am most grateful for your note of the eighth forwarding me a copy of your address of February 12. The latter I have read with much interest, and find that with the passage of years you have certainly lost none of your old time punch.

"My views and recommendations with respect to the situation created by Red China's entry into war against us in Korea have been submitted to Washington in most complete detail. Generally these views are well known and generally understood, as they follow the conventional pattern of meeting force with maximum counterforce as we have never failed to do in the past. Your view with respect to the utilization of the Chinese forces on Formosa is in conflict with neither logic nor this tradition.

"It seems strangely difficult for some to realize that here in Asia is where the Communist conspirators have elected to make their play for global conquest, and that we have joined the issue thus raised on the battlefield; that here we fight Europe's war with arms while the diplomats there still fight it with words; that if we lose this war to Communism in Asia the fall of Europe is inevitable, win it and Europe most probably would avoid war and yet preserve freedom. As you point out, we must win. There is no substitute for victory."

The second paragraph of this letter was in itself enough of a challenge to existing national policy. MacArthur had been fully informed as to the reason why the employment of Chinese Nationalist forces was ruled out. He himself, only eight months earlier, had endorsed the merit of this decision. Later, when he had changed his position and reopened the subject, he had again been advised that this was part of the over-all policy on which the President had decided. So, in praising Mr. Martin's logic and traditional attitude, he was in effect saying that my policy was without logic and violated tradition.

Now, the tradition of which he wrote—that of meeting force with maximum counterforce—is in itself not one that exists outside military textbooks. To be sure, it is a good rule for the employment of troops, but it has no bearing on the relations between governments or between peoples. The American people have accomplished much and attained greatness not by the use of force but by industry, ingenuity, and generosity.

Of course the third paragraph of MacArthur's letter was the real "clincher." I do not know through what channels of information the general learned that the Communists had chosen to concentrate their efforts on Asia—and more specifically on his command. Perhaps he did not know just how much effort and how much sacrifice had been required to stem the Communist tide in Iran—in Greece—at Berlin. Perhaps he did not know how strenuously the Kremlin wished to block the emergence of a united front in western Europe. Actually, of course, my letter of January 13 had made it clear that Communism was capable of attacking not only in Asia but also in Europe and that this was one reason why we could not afford to extend the conflict in Korea. But then MacArthur added a belittling comment about our diplomatic efforts and reached his climax with the pronouncement that "there is no substitute for victory."

But there is a right kind and a wrong kind of victory, just as there are wars for the right thing and wars that are wrong from every standpoint.

As General Bradley later said: "To have extended the fighting to the mainland of Asia would have been the wrong war, at the wrong time and in the wrong place."

The kind of victory MacArthur had in mind—victory by the bombing of Chinese cities, victory by expanding the conflict to all of China— would have been the wrong kind of victory.

To some professional military men, victory—success on the battlefield alone—becomes something of an end in itself. Napoleon, during his ill-fated Moscow campaign, said, "I beat them in every battle, but it does not get me anywhere."

The time had come to draw the line. MacArthur's letter to Congressman Martin showed that the general was not only in disagreement with the policy of the government but was challenging this policy in open insubordination to his Commander in Chief.

I asked Acheson, Marshall, Bradley, and Harriman to meet with me on Friday morning, April 6, to discuss MacArthur's action. I put the matter squarely before them. What should be done about General MacArthur? We discussed the question for an hour. Everyone thought that the government faced a serious situation.

Averell Harriman was of the opinion that I should have fired MacArthur two years ago. In the spring of 1949, as in 1948, MacArthur had pleaded that he could not come home because of the press of business in Tokyo, and it had been necessary for the Secretary of the Army, Kenneth Royall, to intervene urgently from Washington in order to get MacArthur to withhold his approval from a bill of the Japanese Diet which was completely contrary to the economic policy for the occupation as prescribed by the governmental authorities in Washington.

Secretary of Defense Marshall advised caution, saying he wished to reflect further. He observed that if I relieved MacArthur it might be difficult to get the military appropriations through Congress.

General Bradley approached the question entirely from the point of view of military discipline. As he saw it, there was a clear case of insubordination and the general deserved to be relieved of command. He did wish, however, to consult with the Chiefs of Staff before making a final recommendation.

Acheson said that he believed that General MacArthur should be relieved, but he thought it essential to have the unanimous advice of the Joint Chiefs of Staff before I acted. He counseled that the most careful consideration be given to this matter since it was of the utmost seriousness. He added, "If you relieve MacArthur, you will have the biggest fight of your administration."

We then joined the Cabinet for the regularly scheduled meeting. There was comment all around the table, of course, about the letter to Martin, but there was no discussion of the problem of what to do with MacArthur. After the Cabinet meeting, Acheson, Marshall, Bradley, and Harriman returned with me to my office, and we continued our discussion.

I was careful not to disclose that I had already reached a decision. Before the meeting adjourned, I suggested to Marshall that he go over all the messages in the Pentagon files that had been exchanged with General MacArthur in the past two years. Then I asked all four to return the following day at 9 A.M.

The next morning, Saturday, April 7, we met again in my office. This meeting was short. General Marshall stated that he had read the messages and that he had now concluded that MacArthur should have been fired two years ago. I asked General Bradley to make a final recommendation to me of the Joint Chiefs of Staff on Monday.

On Sunday, the eighth of April, I sent for Acheson to come to Blair House, and I discussed the situation further with him. I informed him that I had already that morning consulted with Snyder. I then told Acheson that I would be prepared to act on Monday when General Bradley made his report on the recommendations of the Joint Chiefs of Staff.

At nine o'clock Monday morning I again met with Marshall, Bradley, Acheson, and Harriman. General Bradley reported that the Joint Chiefs of Staff had met with him on Sunday, and it was his and their unanimous judgment that General MacArthur should be relieved.

General Marshall reaffirmed that this was also his conclusion. Harriman restated his opinion of Friday. Acheson said he agreed entirely to the removal of MacArthur.

It was only now that I answered that I had already made up my mind that General MacArthur had to go when he made his statement of March 24.

I then directed General Bradley to prepare the orders that would relieve General MacArthur of his several commands and replace him with Lieutenant General Matthew Ridgway, the commanding general of the Eighth Army in Korea. I instructed him to confer with Secretary of State Acheson, since the office of Supreme Commander, Allied Powers, was also involved.

The same group reported to me at the White House at three-fifteen on Monday afternoon with the drafted orders, which I signed.

It was decided that the notification of these orders should be given to General MacArthur through Secretary of the Army Pace, who was then in Korea. We understood that he was at Eighth Army Headquarters. I asked Acheson to transmit the orders to Pace through Ambassador Muccio and that Pace was to go to Tokyo and personally hand the orders to General MacArthur.

But our message was delayed in reaching Pace, first because of mechanical difficulties in transmission, and second because Pace was at the front with General Ridgway.

I requested Secretary Acheson to inform congressional leaders and to advise John Foster Dulles of our action regarding MacArthur, and to ask Dulles to go to Japan and assure the Yoshida government that the change in commander would not in any way affect our policy of pushing the Japanese peace treaty to a speedy conclusion. This Dulles agreed to do.

A change in plans became necessary, however, when late on the evening of April 10 General Bradley came rushing over to Blair House. He had heard, he said, that the story had leaked out and that a Chicago newspaper was going to print it the next morning. That was when I decided that we could not afford the courtesy of Secretary Pace's personal delivery of the order but that the message would have to go to General MacArthur in the same manner that relieving orders were sent to other officers in the service.

Under these new circumstances I felt compelled to have Joseph Short, my press secretary, call a special news conference for 1 A.M., April 11, which was as quickly as it was possible to have the orders, in their slightly changed form, reproduced.

The reporters were handed a series of papers, the first being my announcement of General MacArthur's relief.

"With deep regret," this announcement read, "I have concluded that General of the Army Douglas MacArthur is unable to give his whole-hearted support to the policies of the United States Government and of the United Nations in matters pertaining to his official duties. In view of the specific responsibilities imposed upon me by the Constitution of the United States and the added responsibility which has been entrusted to me by the United Nations, I have decided that I must make a change of command in the Far East. I have, therefore, relieved General MacArthur of his commands and have designated Lieutenant General Matthew B. Ridgway as his successor.

"Full and vigorous debate on matters of national policy is a vital element in the constitutional system of our free democracy. It is fundamental, however, that military commanders must be governed by the policies and directives issued to them in the manner provided by our laws and Constitution. In time of crisis, the consideration is particularly compelling.

"General MacArthur's place in history as one of our greatest commanders is fully established. The Nation owes him a debt of gratitude for the distinguished and exceptional service which he has rendered his country in posts of great responsibility. For that reason I repeat my regret at the necessity for the action I feel compelled to take in his case."

The second document was the actual order of relief. It notified General MacArthur that he was relieved of his several commands and instructed him to turn over his authority to General Ridgway. There was a further document instructing General Ridgway to assume the functions formerly held by General MacArthur and informing him that Lieutenant General Van Fleet was on his way to Korea to take Ridgway's post as Eighth Army commander.

A number of background documents were also released. These included my order of December 6 concerning the clearance of public statements, the notification to MacArthur of the proposed presidential statement, his own counterpronouncement, the reminder that followed it of the clearance-of-statements requirements, the letter to Congressman Martin, the message of the JCS to MacArthur on January 4 asking for his advice on the arming of additional ROK Army units, and his reply of January 6.

The last two papers were included because of a new statement of MacArthur's that had just come to light. A periodical that had always been critical of administration policy had sent a series of questions to MacArthur. One of them had been aimed at the arming of South Koreans. The magazine said it had heard that South Koreans were eager to defend themselves but that "Washington" had refused them arms.

The principal reason, of course, that the Republic of Korea's request for additional arms had been denied was that General MacArthur had recommended against it in his message of January 6. But he had told this periodical that the matter was one that involved issues beyond his authority—implying that if it had been up to him the ROK's would have received the additional arms!

As far as I was concerned, these papers stated the case. The American people were still faced with Communist aggression in Korea; the Communist conspiracy was still threatening the West in Europe and in Asia. I went on the air on the evening of April 11 to restate the government's policy to the American people. I explained why we were in Korea and why we could not allow the Korean affair to become a general all-out war. I proclaimed our desire to arrive at a settlement along the lines of the statement that had been drafted in March and then not used. I explained why it had become necessary to relieve General MacArthur.

"The free nations," I told the radio audience, "have united their strength in an effort to prevent a third world war.

"That war can come if the Communist leaders want it to come. But this nation and its allies will not be responsible for its coming."

CHAPTER 28

The return of General MacArthur to the United States set off a wave of emotion and a great deal of oratory. I had expected this, and it did not upset me. In fact, I let it be known that I thought it only proper that the general should be invited to address the Congress and that his achievements as a great soldier should be acclaimed.

I felt quite differently, however, about the hearings that followed before the combined Senate Committees on Armed Services and Foreign Relations. In these so-called MacArthur hearings nothing was turned up to give much encouragement to the domestic critics of the administration policy. On the contrary, the combined committees concluded, as they had to conclude if the Constitution was to maintain its meaning, that the Commander in Chief was entirely within his rights if he thought it necessary to remove a military commander.

But the people who must have gotten a great deal of satisfaction out of the hearings were the Soviet leaders. The committee Republicans (with few exceptions) made this an occasion to spread on the record almost every detail of our strategic planning. To be sure, arrangements had been made to delete from the published record such passages as might be objectionable on security grounds. But, with as large a committee as they had and all other senators invited to attend, the newspapers were generally able to find out what had been deleted from the record.

This matter concerned me so much that I asked the National Security Council to give some thought to the problem of preventing security leaks through congressional channels. We spent some time discussing the matter in the meeting of the NSC on May 25, but neither then nor at any time later could we arrive at a practical solution.

The problem, of course, is that members of Congress, and the newspapers too, consider, and rightly, that the government's business is the public's business and therefore everybody's business. "Everybody," of course, includes everybody who can read the Congressional Record, the hearings and reports of committees, and not just the newspapers. We worry a lot about the chance that some employee of the government might give away secrets, and we fire and humiliate people because of the mere suspicion that they might perhaps someday be indiscreet. Yet for the price of a good clipping service an enemy of the United States can acquire untold items of information about our plans and intentions and even about our installations and our equipment. This is made public because "the people are entitled to know."

Since no two people are likely to agree where the security needs end and the public intrest begins, all an enemy of the United States has to do is to stir up a good fuss that will lead to a congressional probe. Then he will probably receive at no extra charge all the information he wants.

During the MacArthur hearings this was evident almost daily.

Another matter that came up during these hearings was the character of the relationship between the President and his advisers. General Bradley, bearing up under unfriendly questioning by most of the Republicans on the committee, declined politely to tell the senators what had gone on at a conference he had with me. He told the senators that if he were to testify and quote his conversation with his Commander in Chief he would be destroying his usefulness as an adviser to the President.

I backed General Bradley completely in this matter, for it involved far more than just Harry Truman talking to Omar Bradley. It was a basic question of the meaning of the separation of powers in our government.

The men who wrote our Constitution knew what they were doing when they provided for three clearly separate branches of the government. They were mostly men trained in the law, and they were all well informed on the history of government from Babylon to Britain. They were convinced that the government of the new nation should be one that would protect individual freedom and allow it to flourish. They knew that arbitrary and even tyrannical government had come about where the powers of government were united in the hands of one man. The system they set up was designed to prevent a demagogue or "a man on horseback" from taking over the powers of government.

As a young man, I had read Montesquieu's *Spirit of the Laws* and the *Federalist Papers,* that collection of essays by Hamilton, Madison, and Jay that explains so much of what the Constitution was intended to mean. Later, during my evening studies of the law, I had read some of Blackstone and Coke and the *Commentaries* of Judge Story. This reading and the study of history and of our government have been the foundation of my thinking about the Constitution. It is a document of remarkable qualities, and every American owes it to his country to absorb not only its words but also the great ideas for which it stands.

The greatest of these, in my opinion, is the idea of a fair trial. We inherited from the British this idea that no man shall be considered guilty until a fair, judicial process shall have found him so.

Next to this, the most important thought expressed in our Constitution is that the power of government shall always remain limited, through the separation of powers. This means that each of the three branches of the government—the legislative, the judicial, and the executive—must jealously guard its position. This jealous concern is a good thing. When I was a senator, I was always anxious to see the rights and the prerogatives of the Congress preserved. If I had ever held judicial office, I would have considered it my duty to keep alert to any possible interferences with the independence of the judiciary. As President, it was my duty to safeguard the constitutional position of the office I held —the presidency of the United States.

There is no office quite like the presidency anywhere else in the world. It has great powers. But these powers must be safeguarded against inroads, just as Congress must look after its powers and prerogatives.

Now the running of government is, of course, a highly practical matter. You do not operate somewhere in a theoretical heaven, but with a tough set of tough situations that have to be met—and met without hesitation. It takes practical men to run a government. But they should be practical men with a deep sense of appreciation for the higher values that the government should serve.

As a practical proposition, the executive branch of the government can no more operate by itself than can the Congress. There have always been a few congressmen who act as if they would like to control everything on the executive side, but they find out differently when the responsibility of administration is on their shoulders. But no President has ever attempted to govern alone. Every President knows and must know that the congressional control of the purse has to be reckoned with. And so Presidents, as a practical proposition, have usually leaned over backward in providing the Congress with information about the operations of the executive departments.

There is a point, however, when the Executive must decline to supply Congress with information, and that is when he feels the Congress encroaches upon the Executive prerogatives. Congress, of course, is anxious to obtain as many facts as it can; most of the time this is for legitimate reasons of legislation, but sometimes it is for the sole purpose of embarrassing and hamstringing the President—in other words, for partisan political reasons. When that happens, it is the President's solemn duty to resist the demands for fishing expeditions into his private files. Not even the so-called weak Presidents would stand for it.

I always tried to take care of and preserve the position of the high office I held. The President cannot function without advisers or without advice, written or oral. But just as soon as he is required to show what kind of advice he has had, who said what to him, or what kind of records he has, the advice he receives will become worthless. Advisers, to be of value, must feel that what they say or write will be held in confidence, that the man or the office they advise will appreciate the fact that they are expressing opinions, and that probably they are not the only ones asked for opinions and advice. The minute an effort is made to challenge that decision after it has been made and to determine whether the opinions or the advice on which it was made was "right" (with retribution and criticism for those who were not "right"), independent thought, which alone produces sound decisions, will be stymied or killed.

While some of the senators were busy trying to prove that I had kept General MacArthur from scoring major successes on the battlefield, his successor in Korea was doing a fine job of carrying out the administration's policy. General Ridgway did not always agree with policy or with the Joint Chiefs of Staff, but he was meticulous in carrying out directives. He took firm and effective hold in Japan. There had been some people who had predicted trouble in Japan because of the great admiration the Japanese people had come to hold for General MacArthur. But General Ridgway's calm and efficient manner assured the continued success of the occupation. The change-over proved to the Japanese people that in a democracy the civilian authorities are above the military, that generals are not, like their own wartime leaders, a law unto themselves, and that they must carry out what the elected officials of the government tell them to do.

Another early test for General Ridgway came in the relations with the Republic of Korea and President Syngman Rhee. The ROK government had consistently urged that it be given weapons for its various youth groups. I had indicated to the Joint Chiefs of Staff that I would not agree to our arming what amounted to political units, but I had told them to study the long-range possibilities of building a more effective army for the Republic of Korea.

President Rhee had asked for arms with which to equip ten additional divisions of his ROK troops, but Ridgway advised against this. His own experience as Eighth Army commander had taught him that the ROK's first need was to improve the leadership before equipment and supplies were increased. In reporting this to the Joint Chiefs of Staff, he quoted a message he had received from General Van Fleet on April 28.

"The basic problems with ROK Army," this message read, "are leadership and training; not manpower or equipment. Lack of leadership extends throughout except in rare instances. If excess trained officers and non-commissioned officers are available they are needed in units presently constituted. Until such time as above deficiencies are corrected it would be a waste of vitally needed equipment and supplies to permit organization and supply of additional units. It is estimated that since the begining of the Korean campaign equipment losses in ROK Army have exceeded that necessary to equip 10 divisions; this without inflicting commensurate losses on the enemy and in some cases without the semblance of a battle. . . ."

General Ridgway recorded his agreement with this estimate by Van Fleet. Both generals made it their business to convince President Rhee that this lack of leadership could be cured only by Korea's civil government. They told him that the long-range solution required the creation of a high-principled, loyal, professionally competent officer corps, which did not exist, and that they were planning measures to produce this result. They added, however, that until satisfactory leadership could be developed, all further talk of expanding the ROK military forces and providing further equipment for such forces would have to be postponed. Rhee was not happy, but out of this very frank exchange there soon grew a training program that helped build an ROK army of considerable competence.

The most important development in Korea, however, was the beginning of the truce negotiations.

The Chinese Communists' "spring offensive" had been thrown back late in May, and United Nations forces held a line generally near the 38th parallel. There were further advances beyond the parallel in June, including the temporary capture of the North Korean capital city of Pyongyang, but generally fighting was light.

On June 1 Trygve Lie, the Secretary General of the United Nations, stated that a cease-fire "approximately along" the 38th parallel would fulfill the purpose of the United Nations; namely, to repulse the aggression against the Republic of Korea. On June 7 Secretary of State Dean

Acheson made a similar statement, which was in line with the recommendation of the National Security Council which I had approved. We had first discussed a formulation of our objectives in Asia at a meeting of the NSC on May 2, and the discussion was continued and concluded on May 16. Regarding Korea, we distinguished between the political aim—a unified, independent, democratic Korea—and the military aim of repelling the aggression and terminating the hostilities under an armistice agreement. With the fighting ended, the purpose would be to establish the authority of the Republic of Korea over all of Korea south of a northern boundary line suitable for defense and administration and not substantially below the 38th parallel, to provide for the withdrawal of non-Korean armed forces from all of Korea, and to build up the ROK forces so as to deter or repel a renewed North Korean aggression.

This policy represented no change. Throughout the Korean affair it had always been my conviction that the United Nations would and should have to prove that aggressors would not be allowed to keep the fruits of their misdeeds. But I never allowed myself to forget that America's principal enemies were sitting in the Kremlin, or that we could not afford to squander our reawakening strength as long as that enemy was not committed in the field but only pulling the strings behind the scenes.

For these reasons, once the territory of the Republic of Korea was virtually cleared of aggressor troops, our readiness for negotiations toward an armistice received new emphasis. At last, on June 23, Jacob Malik, the Soviet representative to the U.N. Security Council, in a speech over the U.N. radio, indicated that the Russian government believed discussions should be started between the belligerents in Korea. Two days later the Peiping newspaper, *People's Daily,* said that the Chinese people endorsed Malik's peace proposals.

I was in Tennessee at the time, dedicating an aviation engineering development center at Tullahoma, and I used this occasion to give expression to some of my thoughts on the position of the United States in the world and on our foreign policy. Here are some of the things I said that afternoon:

"Since World War II we have done our best to build an international organization to keep the peace of the world. We have done that in the interest of the United States, because the only sure way to keep our own country safe and secure is to have world peace. . . .

"Never before has an aggressor been confronted with such a series of positive measures to keep the peace. Never before in history have there been such deterrents to the outbreak of a world war.

"Of course, we cannot promise that there will not be a world war. The Kremlin has it in its power to bring about such a war if it desires. It has a powerful military machine, and its rulers are absolute tyrants.

"We cannot be sure what the Soviet rulers will do.

"But we can put ourselves in a position to say to them: Attack—and you will have the united resources of the free nations thrown against you. Attack—and you will be confronted by a war you cannot possibly win. . . .

"The Kremlin is still trying to divide the free nations. The thing that the Kremlin fears most is the unity of the free world.

"The rulers of the Soviet Union have been trying to split up the nations of the North Atlantic Treaty. They have been trying to sow distrust between us and the other free countries. Their great objective is to strip us of our allies and to force us to 'go it alone.'

"If they could do that, they could go ahead with their plan of taking over the world, nation by nation.

"Unfortunately, it isn't only the Kremlin that has been trying to separate us from our allies. There are some people in this country, too, who have been trying to get us to 'go it alone.' . . .

"Partisan efforts to label our foreign policy as 'appeasement'—to tag it as a policy of 'fear' or 'timidity'—point to only one thing. They point to our 'going it alone,' down the road to World War III.

"Is it a policy of fear to bring the free nations of the world together in a great unified movement to maintain peace? Is it a policy of appeasement to fight armed aggression and hurl it back in Korea?

"Of course it is not. Everybody with any common sense knows it is not.

"And look at the alternatives these critics have to present. Here is what they say. Take a chance on spreading the conflict in Asia. Take a chance on losing our allies in Europe. Take a chance the Soviet Union won't fight in the Far East. Take a chance we won't have a third world war.

"They want us to play Russian roulette with the foreign policy of the United States—with all the chambers of the pistols loaded. . . .

"In Korea and in the rest of the world we must be ready to take any steps which truly advance toward world peace. But we must avoid like the plague rash actions which would take unnecessary risks of world war or weak actions which would reward aggression."

In this same speech I also repeated that we were ready to join in a peaceful settlement in Korea, but that it would have to be a real settlement that would restore the peace and security of the people of Korea.

The State Department had meanwhile instructed Ambassador Kirk in Moscow to check with the Soviet government on Malik's statement, and the reply showed that Malik had expressed an official viewpoint.

There were a number of conferences in the State Department and between State and Defense officials. As a result of these I received a recommendation that our next step should be a statement by General Ridgway offering to meet the Communist commander. I approved the text, and it was sent to the Far East commander on Friday, June 29, with instructions to broadcast it at 6 P.M. Washington time that day:

The President has directed that at 0800 Saturday Tokyo Daylight Saving Time you send following message by radio in clear addressed to Commander in Chief Communist Forces in Korea and simultaneously release to press:

"As Commander in Chief of the United Nations Command I have been instructed to communicate to you the following:

"I am informed that you may wish a meeting to discuss an armistice providing for the cessation of hostilities and all acts of armed force in Korea, with adequate guarantees for the maintenance of such armistice.

"Upon the receipt of word from you that such a meeting is desired I shall be prepared to name my representative. I would also at that time suggest a date at which he could meet with your representative. I propose that such a meeting could take place aboard a Danish hospital ship in Wonsan Harbor.

"(Signed) M B Ridgway, General, U. S. Army
Commander in Chief
United Nations Command"

This message was followed by further instructions to General Ridgway concerning the conduct of any negotiations that might develop. This document was again prepared in co-operation by the State and Defense Departments. General Bradley brought a draft to the *Williamsburg* late at night on June 29, and I studied it there and approved it.

It read as follows:

PERSONAL FOR GENERAL RIDGWAY FROM JCS

1. This message cancels our previous directives regarding armistice terms and contains instructions regarding such terms for your guidance in any conversations which might develop between you and the Commander in Chief of the Communist forces in Korea. It is believed that the chance for a successful conclusion of such negotiation may depend upon secrecy in at least the opening stages; it is not, therefore, intended to make these instructions public.

2. General policy.

a. Our principal military interest in this armistice lies in a cessation of hostilities in Korea, an assurance against the resumption of fighting and the protection of the security of United Nations forces. . . .

b. We lack assurance either that the Soviet Union and Communist China are serious about concluding reasonable and acceptable armistice arrangements or that they are prepared to agree to an acceptable permanent settlement of the Korean problem. In considering an armistice, therefore, it is of the utmost importance to reach arrangements which would be acceptable to us over an extended period of time, even though no progress is made in reaching agreement on political and territorial questions.

c. Discussions between you and the commander of opposing forces should be severely restricted to military questions; you should specifically not enter into discussion of a final settlement in Korea or consideration of issues unrelated to Korea, such as Formosa and the Chinese seat in the United Nations; such questions must be dealt with at governmental level.

3. You are authorized to adopt, for negotiating purposes, initial positions more favorable to us than the minimum conditions set forth in these instructions. However, great care should be used, in putting forward a negotiating position, not to allow talks to break down except in case of failure to accept our minimum terms; not to appear to overreach to an extent to cause world opinion to question our good faith; and not so to engage U.S. prestige in a negotiating position as to make retreat to our minimum terms impossible. Our minimum position is essential to us but we must recognize that it will not be easy for opponents to accept; the difficulty of your negotiation is fully appreciated here.

4. Pursuant to the above, the armistice agreements:

a. Shall be confined to Korea and strictly military matters therein, and shall not involve any political or territorial matters.

b. Shall continue in effect until superseded by other arrangements.

The Communist commander's reply to Ridgway's message was broadcast from Peiping on July 1. He agreed to meet for "talks concerning cessation of military activities and establishment of peace" and suggested that the meeting place be at Kaesong, near the 38th parallel. Liaison officers met for the first time on July 7, and on July 10 the first meeting of the delegations was held.

From the first meeting on, the Communists proved that they were intending to stall and delay until they got things their way. In the months that followed, our negotiators, headed by Admiral Joy and later by General Harrison, showed outstanding patience and perseverance at their task. As had been the case with reports from the field of battle, I daily received full accounts of the proceedings in the truce tent. No major steps were taken without specific approval of the President, even to the wording of announcements made by the Far East commander or the chief negotiator at crucial points.

Repeatedly I made it clear that if these truce talks failed it would have to be under conditions that would make it plain to the world that the failure was caused by the enemy, not by our side.

The negotiations were complicated by frequent declarations from Syngman Rhee that he would not accept less than a unified Korea, but substantial progress was made between November and January, and before this period had passed it began to look as if agreement could be reached. Then new complications arose. Some of these were connected with such small points as what word should be used for "Korea." The most stubborn issue, however, involved the repatriation of prisoners of war.

We were most anxious, of course, to bring our prisoners back home. There had been many stories and much evidence of inhuman treatment of prisoners taken by the Communists. The Communists, however, refused Red Cross inspection of prison camps, although they finally furnished our side with a list of prisoners' names. Still, this accounted for only about one sixth of the number of prisoners they themselves claimed to have captured, and, in turn, they charged that the list the United Nations Command had furnished was incomplete.

On January 1, 1952, our side proposed that all prisoners of war who wished to be returned should be exchanged. It was here that the most serious wrangling began; it was here, also, that I insisted that we could not give ground.

Communism is a system that has no regard for human dignity or human freedom, and no right-thinking government can give its consent to the forcible return to such a system of men or women who would rather remain free. Just as I had always insisted that we could not abandon the South Koreans who had stood by us and freedom, so I now refused to agree to any solution that provided for the return against their will of prisoners of war to Communist domination. A public statement I made on May 7, 1952, expressed my thoughts in official language, but there is one sentence in it that says exactly what was in my mind in words that mean what they say:

"We will not buy an armistice by turning over human beings for slaughter or slavery."

As far as I was concerned, this was not a point for bargaining!

Here is the full text of that statement:

"1. The United States fully approves and supports without qualification the proposal for reaching an armistice which General Ridgway has offered to the Communist aggressors in Korea.

"2. Last July the U.N. forces had repulsed Communist aggression in Korea, had proved to the Communists that aggression cannot pay, and had brought new hope for peace to free men around the world. The Soviet Union then indicated that Korean hostilities could be terminated by a military armistice. The U. N. Command in good faith and in a sincere desire to find a basis for a peaceful settlement began armistice talks with the Communists in Korea.

"3. After many trying months of negotiation, in which each issue has been dealt with individually, tentative agreement has been reached on all but three issues. It is now apparent that the three remaining issues cannot be resolved separately. The U. N. Command proposal offers a just and a real opportunity to resolve these three issues together and simultaneously. The three-point proposal is:

"a. That there shall not be a forced repatriation of prisoners of war —as the Communists have insisted. To agree to forced repatriation would be unthinkable. It would be repugnant to the fundamental moral and humanitarian principles which underlie our action in Korea. To return these prisoners of war in our hands by force would result in misery and bloodshed to the eternal dishonor of the United States and of the U.N.

"We will not buy an armistice by turning over human beings for slaughter or slavery. The U. N. Command has observed the most extreme care in separating those prisoners who have said they would forcibly oppose return to Communist control. We have offered to submit to an impartial re-screening—after an armistice—of those persons we would hold in our custody. Nothing could be fairer. For the Communists to insist upon the forcible return to them of persons who wish to remain out of their control, is an amazing disclosure before the whole world of the operation of their system.

"b. That the U. N. Command will not insist on prohibiting reconstruction or rehabilitation of airfields.

"c. That the neutral nations supervisory commission should comprise representatives of our countries: Poland and Czechoslovakia, chosen by the Communists; Sweden and Switzerland, chosen by the U. N. Command.

"4. The three parts of General Ridgway's proposal are all parts of a whole. They must be considered as an entity—not piecemeal. Our agreement is contingent upon acceptance of the whole proposal. This is our position. The Communists thus far have indicated only a willingness to withdraw their proposal that the U.S.S.R. be a member of the neutral inspection commission. This spurious issue was raised by them late in negotiations and its withdrawal is no real concession on their part.

"5. The patience and understanding shown by General Ridgway and the U. N. Command negotiators merit the highest praise. In spite of almost overwhelming provocation, they have made real progress in reaching agreement on many substantial terms for an armistice. General Ridgway's proposal offers a sound and sensible way to settle the remaining issues all at once. It will have compelling appeal to those sincerely desiring peace."

The proposal to which this message referred was a three-point plan for the adjustment of the outstanding differences at the conference, which had been shifted in the fall of 1951 from Kaesong to Panmunjom.

The Communists, however, still refused to make any concessions on the prisoner-exchange issue. They wanted to swap all the prisoners they held for all the prisoners held by our side. I had made it very clear that I would not agree to any trade of prisoners that might result in forcibly returning non-Communists to Communist control. To have agreed would have been not only inhumane and tragic but dishonorable as well, for our checks in the PW camps showed that the vast majority of the Chinese and North Koreans taken by our side preferred not to be returned under such conditions. We proposed, however, to exchange all who wanted to be exchanged.

Communist agents who had allowed themselves to be captured for the sole purpose of getting control of the prisoner stockades actually succeeded, in some instances, in establishing reigns of terror. This, however, did not change many minds among the prisoners. The riots that resulted, however, created additional problems for our commanders.

The Far East Command changed hands in May 1952, when I sent General Ridgway to Europe to take the place of General Eisenhower as Supreme Allied Commander in Europe. To replace Ridgway, the Defense Department recommended, and I approved, General Mark W. Clark, our wartime commander in Italy.

General Clark's job was not easy. Almost as soon as he assumed command he was faced with a ticklish situation at the prison camp on Koje Island, where Communist prisoners of war had managed to kidnap the American general in charge. The truce negotiations seemed completely stalled, but the Red spokesman, General Nam Il, insisted on continuing the meetings, at which he made long propaganda harangues. President Rhee, who was at odds with his National Assembly, proclaimed martial law and had a number of his political opponents arrested.

Meanwhile, Communist strength in North Korea had been building up, and General Clark was forced to raise the question of additional troops. Apparently much had been done to improve the ROK Army since the spring of 1951, for Clark urged strongly that it be expanded, and he also brought up the matter of Chinese Nationalist aid once again, urging that Chiang Kai-shek be asked to contribute two divisions.

Our own military adviser on Formosa, Major General Chase, was not in favor of sending any of Chiang's units to Korea at that time. The Joint Chiefs of Staff, however, examined the military advantages of such a move with care and advised the Secretary of Defense that it would be desirable, from their point of view, to bring Chinese Nationalist units to Korea, and Secretary Lovett held full discussions with all his advisers on the matter, informing me periodically of the progress of the talks.

The Secretary had a careful study made of the various alternatives by which some relief might be brought to the American troops who had furnished so much of the fighting strength in Korea for over two years. In the end it was found that there would be no advantages in the addition of Chinese Nationalist units that could not be gained by increasing the ROK forces. There was nothing to suggest that the two Chinese divisions that might have been sent from Formosa, partly trained as they were, would have made a significant difference in the Korean situation in 1952.

The issue with regard to our Korean policy, however, is not what might have been done but rather what had to be done.

I have gone into considerable detail in giving the facts about our action in Korea, for what we and our allies did about Korea will have a profound influence on the future peace of the world. This was the toughest decision I had to make as President. What we faced in the attack on Korea was the ominous threat of a third world war.

I prayed that there might be some way other than swift military action to meet this Communist aggression, for I knew the awful sacrifices in life and suffering it would take to resist it. But there was only one choice facing us and the free world—resistance or capitulation to Communist imperialist military aggression. It was my belief that if this aggression in Korea went unchallenged, as the aggression in Manchuria in 1931 and in Ethiopia in 1934 had gone unchallenged, the world was certain to be plunged into another world war.

This was the same kind of challenge Hitler flaunted in the face of the rest of the world when he crossed the borders of Austria and Czechoslovakia. The free world failed then to meet that challenge, and World War II was the result. This time the free nations—the United Nations— were quick to sense the new danger to world peace. The United Nations was born out of the ashes of two world wars and organized for the very purpose of preventing or dealing with aggression wherever it threatened to break out or actually occurred.

That is why the United Nations responded with such spontaneity and swiftness. This was the first time in the history of the world that there was international machinery to deal with those who would resort to war as a means of imposing their will or their systems on other people.

At the very outset we knew that the United States would have to carry the major burden. That was inevitable because of our geographic position and our strength. Our allies were still rebuilding their shattered nations and binding the slowly healing wounds of their civilian populations. Most of them, too, faced possible aggression by the Communists on their own frontiers.

The Communist aggressors had on several earlier occasions sought to probe what we would do if they moved to conquer and expand. They learned in Iran and Greece and Turkey and in Berlin that we would not be intimidated or bluffed. But up until Korea they had confined their action to subversion, indirect aggression, intimidation, and revolution.

In Korea, however, the world faced a new and bold Communist challenge. Here for the first time since the end of World War II the Communists openly and defiantly embarked upon military force and invasion.

The Communists moved without warning and without excuse. They crossed the 38th parallel of Korea with tanks and planes in open warfare.

We could not stand idly by and allow the Communist imperialists to assume that they were free to go into Korea or elsewhere. This challenge had to be met—and it was met. It had to be met without plunging the world into general war. This was done.

We have learned bitterly and tragically from two calamitous world wars that any other course would lead to yet another world war.

CHAPTER 29

On November 1, 1951, the United Steelworkers of America announced that when their contracts with the steel manufacturers expired early in 1952, they would want improvements of some working conditions and a substantial wage increase. This was the beginning of a series of events that eventually made it necessary for the government to seize the nation's steel plants.

The demands of the steelworkers did not seem out of line to me. Korea and the needs of the defense program had greatly increased the volume of business being done by the steel mills, and the steel companies' profits were rising. For the three years preceding the Korean emergency the average profit in the steel industry had been $6.59 per ton. For 1951, however, the first full year of Korean war requirements, the profit, after taxes, was $7.07 per ton. Furthermore, in the light of the huge orders the Defense Department had placed with them on the authorization of Congress as requested by the Executive, 1952 promised to be at least as good for the steel manufacturers, if not better.

We had this economic situation on our hands: The industry was making more money, while the workers in the plants found that the increases in the cost of living had cut down the purchasing power of their pay. The cost of food and clothing and similar basic items had gone up.

Wages, however, were only one of the issues which the union wanted to negotiate. There had been a general worsening of relations between the union and some of the companies, especially United States Steel. The difficulty had arisen over company efforts to introduce an incentive-pay wage system. The workers charged, rightly or wrongly, that this system would treat them as if they were machines, and they resented it.

I believe many well-meaning citizens fail to realize that for the workingman the union is far more than a means of securing higher wages. In this age of the machine, the individual worker does not get much of a chance to feel that what he is doing is important. The union worker, like anyone else, wants to feel that he is achieving something, and through his unions he gets the sense of human dignity and of joining with others in doing something worth while. That is why he resists any tampering with unions.

There is such a long history of union suppression by employers, and the employer opposition to unions, that it should not be surprising that workers tend to think that most employers are out to kill the unions and that anything employers want by way of a change is intended to be the first nail in the union's coffin. One reason why unions object to incentive pay is that they see it as a means to deny them the right to act as bargaining agents for wages. To deprive them of this right would curtail or even destroy one of the most important functions of the unions.

Some of our more enlightened industries have understood this and have developed labor-management relations resulting in greater efficiency. Relations between management and labor on this basis bring about harmony and understanding profitable to both the workers and the company. But in some industries unionism has never been fully accepted.

In 1951 the steel industry said that it did not wish to discuss the union's demands for increased wages and changes in working conditions, and the union announced that the workers would strike on December 31. I had no way of knowing why the companies refused to negotiate with the union. Perhaps they thought this was an opportune time to get tough. Perhaps they believed that the urgent needs of the defense program would bring the government into the dispute and force continued production at unchanged contract conditions. Whatever the reasons, the officials of the Defense Department and of the defense production agencies viewed the impending strike with the gravest alarm. Secretary of Defense Robert A. Lovett had for months been pointing out to me that the national defense program would be endangered if a strike was allowed to halt production. All the members of the Cabinet agreed with Lovett that it would be harmful to the country and injurious to our campaign in Korea if our steel mills were allowed to close down. We were then not only trying to keep our forces in Korea, as well as elsewhere, fully equipped, but we had allies to whom we had promised arms and munitions and whose determination to resist Communism might depend on our ability to supply them the weapons they so badly needed.

It was obvious that the best interests of the nation would be seriously affected if a strike in the steel industry took place.

On December 22, I referred the dispute between the United Steelworkers and the steel companies to the Wage Stabilization Board for solution. The unions immediately responded to this action by agreeing to postpone the strike so that production would not be interrupted.

To put off the strike in the hope of negotiating a solution, I had a choice of two alternatives as provided by the Congress. The first was the Taft-Hartley Act, which had a provision for an eighty-day injunction. Contrary to the claims of some uninformed people, this is not a mandatory provision. On the contrary, it provides in cases of strikes endangering national health and safety that the President *may* appoint a board of inquiry to determine the facts and to report to him. Upon receiving that report, the President *may* instruct the Department of Justice to ask for a court order to enjoin the strike for eighty days. During this period the board of inquiry attempts to bring about a settlement. At the end of eighty days, unless a solution is reached, the strike may legally proceed and the President must then report the facts to the Congress along with his recommendations.

There was the other alternative in the Defense Production Act of 1950 which declared that it was "the intent of Congress, in order to provide for effective price and wage stabilization . . . and to maintain uninterrupted production, that there be effective procedures for the settlement of labor disputes affecting national defense." This authorized the President to provide for procedures similar to those that had existed in World War II with the War Labor Board.

Acting under a directive from Congress, I had set up a Wage Stabilization Board and had assigned to it the function of settling labor disputes affecting national defense. In 1951 Congress had received a full report on the record of how this Board operated as an alternative to the procedure laid down in the Taft-Hartley Act. A move had been attempted in the House of Representatives to deprive the WSB of the right to handle labor disputes. This move was defeated, however, and Congress extended the Defense Production Act with full knowledge that it included an alternative method for the handling of labor disputes.

In deciding on a choice, then, between the two alternatives, I first considered the Taft-Hartley Act. But the Taft-Hartley Act had been designed primarily for peacetime labor problems. The Wage Stabilization Board, however, had been established especially for defense labor disputes and had been reaffirmed by the Congress in this function within the year. The kind of situation we were facing caused me to turn to the Wage Stabilization Board.

From January 10 through February 26, 1952, the Wage Stabilization Board held extensive hearings and discussions with the parties, and on March 20, it submitted its report to me. On the wage issue it recommended that the union be given an increase in three stages over an eighteen-month period, for a total increase of 26.4 cents per hour. This was less than the union asked for. On the other points, too, the Board pared down the union's requests. On some it recommended that the union's requests be rejected altogether. Weighing the result against the current and prospective earnings of the industry, the proposal seemed to me to be fair and workable.

Charles E. Wilson, Director of Defense Mobilization, reported to me on March 24 that the companies would flatly reject the recommended settlement. He said that there would be an industry refusal followed by a prolonged strike and that the only thing that would prevent a shutdown of the mills would be to grant the price increase requested by the companies.

In order to prevent a national crisis, I would not object to a reasonable price increase that would meet the cost of the higher wage scale. When we had a steel strike in 1946, I had had a calculation made by the experts to show just how much the then proposed wage hike would drive production costs up, and a price increase was based on that calculation. On the basis of the figures before me in the present case, however, I felt that the price increase the steel companies were demanding was entirely out of reason and that it had come at a bad time for the country.

The industry wanted a flat increase, to be applied to all finished steel regardless of selling price. It is, of course, a fact that the price of steel ranges widely from the cheap finish to the specialty and high-quality steels. To apply a flat dollar increase to existing prices would have the result of a proportionately greater hike in the prices for the lower grades, but it would hardly affect the price of steel produced to sell at top rates. I did not think that this was a fair method of spreading the increased cost.

The profits of the steel companies were constantly rising. The nation was drafting its men to serve on the field of battle, and I thought that the ammunition and arms manufacturers and their raw-material producers ought not to use the emergency to insist on extra profits. The attitude of the companies seemed wrong to me, since under the accelerated defense program the government was by far the biggest customer for steel and steel products. To hike the prices at this time meant charging the government more for the tools of defense.

I realized, of course, that any wage increase means adding cost to production, but I was *not* willing to commit myself to a flat figure to be applied across the board, without proof that it was made necessary by the wage increase.

Steel is of such importance in our highly mechanized economy that any rise in the price of steel is soon reflected in price increases of a large range of goods, from refrigerators and automobiles to tin cans and bobby pins. A disproportionate rise in the cost of steel would have an inflationary effect. Because of this I felt that I would be justified in agreeing to a steel-price increase only if the steel industry would carry more than its normal share of the production cost. In this case, however, the steel industry was actively seeking to get much more than its share of the profits, and at the expense of the government.

To my regret, Wilson interpreted my willingness to consider an adjustment to cover the actual added costs as a promise to meet the companies' full demands. When I corrected his interpretation and put him straight, he resigned.

It was now apparent that a settlement would be difficult to reach.

A long round of conferences and consultations began. Dr. John Steelman, my assistant, whose specialty was labor problems, held meetings in his office with groups and individuals representing labor, management, and government. The conferees reported to me on their talks and asked my opinion or decision on some point, but no progress was being made. On April 7 the unions announced that they would go out on strike against the steel companies.

I again called in all my principal advisers to decide what steps to take to meet the emergency. Secretary of Defense Lovett said emphatically that any stoppage of steel production, for even a short time, would increase the risk we had taken in the "stretch-out" of the armament program. He also pointed out that our entire combat technique in all three services depended on the fullest use of our industrial facilities. Stressing the situation in Korea, he said that "we are holding the line with ammunition, and not with the lives of our troops." Any curtailment of steel production, he warned, would endanger the lives of our fighting men.

Gordon Dean, chairman of the Atomic Energy Commission, expressed grave concern over the delay which any lack of steel would mean for the major expansion of facilities for atomic weapons production. Henry H. Fowler, Administrator of the National Production Authority, told me that in addition to military equipment and atomic energy construction, power plants, railroad construction, shipbuilding, machine-tool manufacture, and the like, all would come to a halt if the steel mills closed down. He pointed out that it would depend on the inventory situation how soon the steel shortage would make itself felt in the manufacturing plants, and in certain types of ammunition there was virtually no inventory stock on hand.

Secretary of Commerce Sawyer briefed me on the effect a shutdown would have on the several transportation programs. His figures showed that a ten-day interruption of steel production would mean the loss of ninety-six thousand feet of bridge and fifteen hundred miles of highway. He reported that in the event of a steel shutdown only twenty-one of the ninety-eight ships then under construction in American yards could be completed, and thirty-nine others would have to be abandoned entirely. He informed me that the effect on airplane production would be such that Convair and Douglas, for instance, would have to halt their assembly lines within sixty days. There was a danger that some manufacturers would not await the onset of the shortage but would close down as soon as steel production ceased.

Oscar Chapman, Secretary of the Interior, said that the maintenance and expansion of facilities in the petroleum, gas, and electric-power utility fields depended on steel materials. Coal mines and coke ovens require steel for any number of accessory, but essential, uses.

With Dean Acheson I discussed the impact which this threatening paralysis of our defense economy might have on our relations with the rest of the world. Any failure on our part to deliver what we had promised to furnish our allies under the Mutual Defense Assistance Program would seriously undermine their faith in our ability to aid them in critical moments. Russia would be cheered by such evidence of a slowdown in our rearmament. We could not overlook even the possibility that Russia would believe us so weakened by an extended strike as to invite further aggression, and there might be other "Koreas."

All of this presented a very serious picture. The Congress was debating and doing a lot of talking about the steel crisis, and I would have welcomed any practical solution from it. But discussion was not enough. I had to act to prevent the stoppage of steel production, which would imperil the nation. Unless some last-minute effort brought peace and a settlement, I could see no alternative but to order the seizure of the steel mills by the government.

The expression "government seizure" sounds forbidding. Some people believe that seizure means confiscation or expropriation of private property. But what really happens is that the government merely assumes temporary custody of the properties. The very same people responsible for the management before seizure are kept on to continue the management of the mills and plants on behalf of the government. In this way the government can make sure that there is no interruption of production.

Neither management nor labor likes government seizure. They are not supposed to like it, any more than the government likes it, and they should not like it. It is much better for everyone for labor and management to work out their own problems without government interference. But when they reach an impasse that endangers the country, as they did in this case, seizure is an effective way to help bring them to a settlement.

During my occupation of the White House I had been frequently urged by department heads to seize an industry or a plant that was strikebound or threatened with a strike. But except in a few critical instances, I refused to do it. I have always considered seizure a last resort—something the President should turn to only when there appears to be no other way to prevent injury to the national interest, or when it is necessary to protect the whole country.

It was for that reason that I waited until the afternoon of the very last day before the strike was to begin before issuing the seizure order. I spent most of that last day with Dr. Steelman and with Secretary of Commerce Sawyer, whose job it would be to supervise the seized industry. Then, just a few hours before the mills were scheduled to be struck, I issued Executive Order No. 10340 to seize the steel mills, and later in the evening of that same day I addressed the nation by radio, explaining the reason for this action.

"If steel production stops," I explained, "we will have to stop making shells and bombs that are going directly to our soldiers at the front in Korea. If steel production stops, we will have to cut down and delay the atomic energy program. If steel production stops, it won't be long before we have to stop making engines for the Air Force planes.

"Our national security and our chances for peace depend on our defense production. Our defense production depends on steel. . . .

"I have no doubt that if our defense program fails, the danger of war, the possibility of hostile attack, grow much greater.

"I would not be faithful to my responsibilities as President if I did not use every effort to keep this from happening.

"With American troops facing the enemy on the field of battle, I would not be living up to my oath of office if I failed to do whatever is required to provide them with the weapons and ammunitions they need for their survival."

I announced that I was instructing Secretary of Commerce Sawyer to take possession of the steel mills and to keep them operating, and that Dr. Steelman was directed to bring the representatives of the steel companies and of the steel workers' union to Washington in a renewed effort to get them to settle their dispute.

I reviewed for the American people the developments that had led up to the situation, stressing the fact that in normal times collective bargaining is the proper way to settle wage and working conditions but that during this period of defense build-up it was vitally important to prevent a runaway inflation. Congress had laid down a basic policy that everyone had to sacrifice some of his own interests to the national interest, and the rules that had been established in accordance with this congressional policy were fair and equitable and had been fairly and equitably applied in this case. The union had accepted them, but the companies had not. The companies, I was sorry to say, had taken the position that unless they could get the large increase they demanded in the price of steel there would be a shutdown of the industry.

I pointed out the disastrous effect on the entire price-stabilization program if a substantial steel-price increase were granted, and explained how it would raise the price of all goods using steel, from tanks to egg beaters, and how it would create a precedent for the many other industries that would like to increase their prices. "If we gave in to the steel companies on this issue," I said, "you could say goodbye to stabilization. If we knuckled under to the steel industry, the lid would be off. Prices would start jumping all around us—not just prices of things using steel, but prices of many other things we buy, including milk and groceries and meat."

I explained that Congress had given me a choice of using either the Wage Stabilization Board or the Taft-Hartley Act injunction; that I had decided to go through the Wage Stabilization Board and, as a result, that ninety-nine days' production had been gained instead of the eighty which an injunction could have given. Congress, however, chose neither to suggest to me nor empower me to use both alternatives, and we were therefore now at the point where only government seizure could prevent the threatened shutdown. I made it quite clear that I had no desire to have the government run the steel plants any longer than was absolutely necessary to prevent the shutdown, but under my sworn duties as President I considered it unavoidable to seize the mills now if there was no other way to prevent a stoppage of steel production.

On the following day I sent a message to the Congress to report the action I had taken, and I asked Congress to provide specific legislation for terms and conditions for the government operation of the mills. I said in this message that I would be glad to carry out any policy which Congress might want to write with regard to the situation, even if it wanted to cancel what I had just done, and I added that unless there was congressional action I would naturally have to take the responsibility myself.

In my opinion, the seizure was well within my constitutional powers, and I had acted accordingly. The Constitution states that "the executive power shall be vested in a President of the United States of America." These words put a tremendous responsibility on the individual who happens to be President. He holds an office of immense power. It surely is the greatest trust that can be placed in any man by the American people. It is trust with a power that appalls a thinking man. There have been men in history who have liked power and the glamour that goes with it: Alexander, Caesar, Napoleon, to name only a few. I never did. It was only the responsibility that I felt to the people who had given me this power that concerned me. I believe that the power of the President should be used in the interest of the people, and in order to do that the President must use whatever power the Constitution does not expressly deny him.

When there is danger that a vital portion of the economy will be crippled at a time that is critical to the nation's security, then, in my opinion, the President has a clear duty to take steps to protect the nation. "Must a government, of necessity," Lincoln once asked, "be too *strong* for the liberties of its people, or too *weak* to maintain its own existence?" History has recorded Lincoln's answer in his deeds.

My own answer to this question is that I am convinced that government can be *both* free *and* strong. What is more, I am sure that it takes a strong government to preserve the liberties of the people and that only a free government has the kind of strength that will assure its survival. The essence of government in a democracy is that it be responsible, and to me that means that the responsibilities of government be accepted and carried out—until the voters transfer them to the hands of someone else—whose duty it then becomes to *act* in the best interest of the nation as he sees it.

This responsibility of government, actively to promote the national interest, rests heavily on the shoulders of the President, but it also rests on the shoulders of the Congress, which cannot meet its responsibilities merely by following a course of negation. The Congress cannot perform its constitutional functions simply by paralyzing the operations of the government in an emergency.

I had hoped that the Congress would respond to my report with some positive action. I would have been more than willing to carry out faithfully whatever policy the Congress might have decided upon. However, the only action that seemed forthcoming was entirely negative: An amendment was introduced in the Senate to the Third Supplemental Appropriations Bill to restrict the use of appropriated funds for the operations of the steel mills under my seizure order. This was a purely political exercise of the power to legislate in an appropriation bill and was a kind of action I had always opposed. This action by the Senate prompted me to write a letter to Vice-President Barkley as the President of the Senate.

"I have no wish," I wrote, "to prevent action by the Congress. I do ask that the Congress, if it takes action, do so in a manner that measures up to its responsibilities in the light of the critical situation which confronts this country and the whole free world. . . .

"A shutdown in steel production for any substantial length of time whatever would immediately reduce the ability of our troops in Korea to defend themselves against attack. If the Communists stage another offensive in Korea this spring, the success or failure of that offensive may well depend on whether or not we have kept our steel mills in production. . . .

"I hope that any legislation passed by the Congress on this subject will provide a method by which the steel mills can be kept in continuous operation. . . ."

I am sorry that the Senate did not respond to this letter. Many southern senators joined with all but two of the Republicans, Morse and Langer, to write the amendment into the bill, but no positive action and no constructive suggestion for dealing with the crisis came from the Congress. Why, I will never know.

Meanwhile, Dr. Steelman continued his talks with the negotiators for management and labor. Secretary of Defense Lovett appeared before the negotiators to impress upon them the seriousness of the defense situation and to point out the dangers that would result from any stoppage of production, however brief.

The steel companies had reacted violently to the seizure, beginning with a radio and television broadcast by Clarence Randall, president of the Inland Steel Company, on the day following my address to the nation. The companies now resorted to court action.

The first phase of these proceedings, which eventually reached the Supreme Court, took place on April 29, when Judge David Pine of the United States District Court for the District of Columbia ordered Secretary of Commerce Sawyer to return the mills to the companies. On the following day, however, the Court of Appeals stayed this order so that the Supreme Court could decide on the government's right to seize the plants.

The steelworkers' union had stopped work after Judge Pine's ruling, but when the Court of Appeals issued the stay which followed, the unions immediately returned to work. The companies and the government then asked the Supreme Court to review Judge Pine's ruling, and while the high court deliberated as to whether and when it should hear the case, negotiations continued, mostly in John Steelman's office, toward a direct settlement of the dispute.

By May 3 Ben Fairless, president of U. S. Steel and the principal spokesman for the companies, and Phil Murray, president of the United Steelworkers (and also of the Congress of Industrial Organizations), had at last cleared away some of the major points of disagreement. John Steelman passed the word to me that for the first time there was a real chance that agreement might be obtained. But while the White House and the labor-management negotiators were still at work, the news ticker flashed the report that the Supreme Court had agreed to hear the case promptly. This abruptly ended all negotiations. The steel companies that morning had been willing to make significant concessions, but they now withdrew from all talks. If the Court had not made the announcement for perhaps twenty-four or forty-eight hours, there is a strong likelihood that agreement would have been obtained.

The government's case was presented in the Supreme Court by the Solicitor General, Philip B. Perlman, an outstanding lawyer and dedicated public servant. He presented the government's case ably and forcefully.

The steel companies were represented by John W. Davis, the 1924 Democratic presidential candidate, who led a contingent of high-powered corporation lawyers from New York, Philadelphia, Cleveland, Pittsburgh, and Washington.

The argument for the Government of the United States by the Solicitor General was twofold. First, that the Court should not entertain the complaint because, whatever damage the companies might suffer through the seizure, they would be able to recover. Second, that the taking of the companies' property was a valid exercise of the authority of the President of the United States.

It seems to me that there have been few instances in history where the press was more sensational or partisan than in its handling of the steel seizure. What was more disturbing was what amounted to editorial intervention by the press of America in a case pending before the Supreme Court of the United States. News stories and editorials decrying seizure and inflaming public opinion were prejudging and deciding the case at the very time the Court itself was hearing arguments for both sides. The steel companies bought full-page advertisements and ran them in newspapers throughout the country to denounce the President of the United States. Large sums of money were spent to influence public opinion against the government.

For the government, I took the position that, once the case had reached the courts, it was not proper for me to express an opinion.

I have always believed that the way our newspapers sometimes comment on matters pending in the courts is an unethical attempt to influence a judge in deciding a case. Certainly in the steel case every effort made was to spread a slanted view of the situation and to color the atmosphere. The public relations experts for the companies skillfully shifted public attention from the price demands of the industry to the supposedly abnormal and unprecedented act of the President.

A little reading of history would have shown that there was nothing unusual about this action—that strike-threatened plants had been seized before by the government, even before the nation was engaged in any shooting conflict. But these matters received no mention or, if they were mentioned, were glossed over quickly, as if they had no meaning for the present.

I would, of course, never conceal the fact that the Supreme Court's decision, announced on June 2, was a deep disappointment to me. I think Chief Justice Vinson's dissenting opinion hit the nail right on the head, and I am sure that someday his view will come to be recognized as the correct one.

The Chief Justice, in his own opinion, commented on the majority view of the Court in these words: "The diversity of views expressed in the six opinions of the majority, the lack of reference to authoritative precedent, the repeated reliance upon prior dissenting opinions, the complete disregard of the uncontroverted facts showing the gravity of the emergency and the temporary nature of the taking all serve to demonstrate how far afield one must go to affirm the order of the District Court."

I am not a lawyer, and I leave the legal arguments to others. But as a layman, as an official of the government, and as a citizen, I have always found it difficult to understand how the Court could take the affidavits of men like Lovett, Chapman, and many others, all of whom testified in great detail to the grave dangers that a steel shutdown would bring to the nation—affidavits that were neither contradicted nor even contested by the companies—and ignore them entirely.

I could not help but wonder what the decision might have been had there been on the Court a Holmes, a Hughes, a Brandeis, a Stone.

Word of the Court's decision reached me in my office in the early afternoon of June 2, and before three o'clock I had issued an order to Secretary of Commerce Sawyer to comply with the decision and return the plants to the steel industry. At four-thirty a hurriedly called meeting convened in my office. Defense Secretary Lovett was present, along with Secretary of Commerce Sawyer. The new Attorney General, James P. McGranery, was also there, together with Solicitor General Perlman,

Secretary of Labor Tobin, and several members of the White House staff. I wanted to know what course these advisers would recommend in the light of the Court's decision. Should we now resort to the Taft-Hartley Act's injunction? And, if not, what else was there to do? Going around the table, I asked each of those present to state his opinion. Only one or two thought that I should start proceedings under the Taft-Hartley Act. Most took the position that, having used the Wage Stabilization Board, this route was no longer open to me. There was also some feeling that the Supreme Court opinion had strengthened the bargaining position of the industry to such an extent that it would be even more difficult than before to mediate any sort of settlement.

On June 10 I made one further effort, by an appeal for legislation to permit me to seize the strikebound plants. But the Congress refused to grant this authority. Throughout the nation the steel mills lay idle.

The strike lasted fifty-three days and ended only when an agreement was finally reached between management and labor. This came only after an increase had been granted in the price of steel. To settle the strike, the companies were allowed to add as much as $5.65 per ton.

I approved this price increase with a reluctant heart, for I was convinced that it was wrong—as wrong as it had been in March and April when I had refused to consider approve that much. But now the Supreme Court had denied the power to bring the plants under government operation, and Congress had turned down my appeal for authority to seize. The companies therefore now held all the advantages. If we wanted steel—and we wanted it very badly—it would have to be on the industry's terms.

The strike ended on July 24. Six hundred thousand steel workers had been idle for over seven weeks. Twenty-five thousand iron-ore workers had been on a sympathy strike for a part of that time, and lack of steel had caused the layoff of three hundred thousand workers in the automobile industry. The daily loss in wages and production during this period was estimated at forty million dollars. The total loss was estimated in excess of two billion dollars! Nor does this take into consideration the higher price the nation paid after the settlement for the steel and steel products needed for the defense effort.

When General Van Fleet came back from Korea in March 1953, he complained that his troops had been short of certain types of ammunition in the summer and early fall of 1952. This was a fact that should have been no surprise to the American public. The affidavits of Secretary Lovett and National Production Administrator Fowler in the steel case had stated that a stoppage of steel production would affect our ability to ship sufficient munitions to the front in Korea!

I think that we were fortunate that nothing more serious happened in Korea as a result of the steel shutdown. The actions of the administration succeeded in keeping production going from December 31, when the strike was first set to begin, until June 2—fully five months. This was valuable time gained. But the seven weeks that were lost could never be replaced, no matter how the lawyers argue.

Whatever the six justices of the Supreme Court meant by their differing opinions about the constitutional powers of the President, he must always act in a national emergency. It is not very realistic for the justices to say that comprehensive powers shall be available to the President only when a war has been declared or when the country has been invaded. We live in an age when hostilities begin without polite exchanges of diplomatic notes. There are no longer sharp distinctions between combatants and noncombatants, between military targets and the sanctuary of civilian areas. Nor can we separate the economic facts from the problems of defense and security.

In this day and age the defense of the nation means more than building an army, navy, and air force. It is a job for the entire resources of the nation. The President, who is Commander in Chief and who represents the interest of all the people, must able to act at all times to meet any sudden threat to the nation's security. A wise President will always work with Congress, but when Congress fails to act or is unable to act in a crisis, the President, under the Constitution, must use his powers to safeguard the nation.

CHAPTER 30

Whenever the President of the United States finds it necessary to veto a major bill which has been approved by both
Houses of the Congress, he is sure to find himself in the center of a
bitter controversy involving large groups both inside and outside the
federal government. This was clearly demonstrated during my final year
as Chief Executive when I refused to approve legislation turning over
the nation's vast offshore oil resources to the coastal states. The three
states concerned with this legislation were Texas, Louisiana, and California, off whose shores the principal known oil deposits existed.

I never hesitated to veto any bill presented to me when I was convinced that it failed to serve the best interests of the majority of the
people in all parts of the country. I found it necessary to veto more
major bills than any other President, with the possible exception of
Grover Cleveland.

Chief among these were the Taft-Hartley bill of 1947, imposing harsh
restrictions on the hard-won rights of labor; the Kerr bill of 1950,
excusing independent gas producers from reasonable price-fixing supervision by the Federal Power Commission; the Internal Security bill of
the same year; the McCarran-Walter bill of 1952, which would have
established an inhumane policy toward eligible foreign persons who
wished to emigrate to America; and a number of tax bills which, in my
opinion, were unfair or unwise.

The veto power of the President is one of the most important instruments of his authority, even though the legislation he rejects may later
be passed over his veto by the Congress. In the veto message the Chief
Executive has an opportunity to set forth clearly and in detail before

the nation the policies of his administration. I always gave more studied attention to the messages which accompanied my disapproval of congressional legislation than to any other White House pronouncements.

One important lack in the presidential veto power, I believe, is authority to veto individual items in appropriations bills. The President must approve the bill in its entirety, or refuse to approve it, or let it become law without his approval. He cannot veto any separate item of which he may disapprove, for fear of killing an otherwise sound piece of legislation. As a senator I tried to discourage the practice of adding riders deliberately contrived to neutralize otherwise positive legislation, because it is a form of legislative blackmail. The honest way was to defeat legislation by voting against it rather than by adding crippling amendments to render it ineffective.

The question of ownership of submerged oil deposits off the coast of the United States has been a subject of controversy for many years. During my administration the problem became particularly acute in California, where drilling was progressing at an increasing rate after some three or four decades of limited operations. Extensive operations were also being carried on in the offshore regions of Texas, Louisiana, Florida, and Mississippi in the Gulf of Mexico.

Long before I became President, bills and joint resolutions introduced in the Seventy-fifth and Seventy-sixth Congresses sought to put the national ownership of these deposits on record. These proposals were introduced by Senators Nye and Walsh, and by Representatives Hobbs and O'Connor, but none of them was enacted into law.

The issue of state as against federal ownership came to a head during my administration.

I lost no time in trying to clarify this long-standing dispute. On September 28, 1945, I had issued two proclamations and two Executive Orders asserting the jurisdiction of the United States over the natural resources of the "continental shelf" under the high seas contiguous to the coast of the United States and its territories. The immediate purpose for these moves by me was to establish fishery conservation zones. But in a White House statement released that day I said:

"Petroleum geologists believe that portions of the continental shelf beyond the three-mile limit contain valuable oil deposits. The study of sub-surface structures associated with oil deposits which have been discovered along the Gulf Coast of Texas, for instance, indicates that corresponding deposits may underlie the off-shore or submerged land. The trend of oil-productive salt domes extends directly into the Gulf of Mexico off the Texas coast. Oil is also being taken at present from wells within the three-mile limit off the coast of California. It is quite possible, geologists say, that the oil deposits extend beyond this traditional limit of national jurisdiction.

"Valuable deposits of minerals other than oil may also be expected to be found in these submerged areas. Ore mines now extend under the sea from the coasts of England, Chile and other countries.

"While asserting jurisdiction and control of the United States over the mineral resources of the continental shelf, the proclamation in no wise abridges the right of free and unimpeded navigation of waters of the character of high seas above the shelf, nor does it extend the present limits of the territorial waters of the United States.

"The advance of technology prior to the present war had already made possible the exploitation of a limited amount of minerals from submerged lands within the three-mile limit. The rapid development of technical knowledge and equipment occasioned by the war now makes possible the determination of the resources of the submerged lands outside the three-mile limit. With the need for the discovery of additional resources of petroleum and other minerals, it became advisable for the United States to make possible orderly development of these resources. The proclamation of the President is designed to serve this purpose."

I made it clear that the federal government was not interested in the title to the tidelands of any coastal state. Tideland is that part of the land next to the sea which is covered and uncovered by the tides. Low tide is the boundary of the land mass of the United States. High tide creates tidelands. About this territory there was no dispute at all, although the term "tidelands" was repeatedly and erroneously brought into the argument by opponents of the administration simply to cloud the issue, just as "socialized medicine" was constantly used by the opposition in an attempt to confuse the provisions of the national health insurance program.

The offshore oil and mineral resources from low-water mark to the three-mile limit fall, as the Supreme Court has held, within the full "domination" and "power" of the United States Government. From the three-mile limit to the end of the continental shelf it is the policy of the United States Government, in the words of a proclamation which I signed on September 28, 1945, that they are "appertaining to the United States, subject to its jurisdiction and control." This supervision and control of the continental shelf, which is defined as submerged land contiguous to the continent and which is covered by no more than six hundred feet of water, are essential to the national security and require a navy and coast guard.

No state in the Union is a free and independent entity. Each one is a part of the United States, and the national government embodies the interests of all the states. When the Congress gives away the interests which should benefit the whole country to a few states, it violates its trust. The Congress, I felt, had no more business to give away the undersea resources than it had to give away the White House or the Capitol grounds to any state.

The conflict and confusion that would arise from any other definition of the limit of state title to coastal areas, except the low-tide mark, is obvious from the conflict of claims even among the states themselves. Texas, for instance, claims that it is entitled to territory extending three Spanish leagues—about ten and a half miles—into the sea, on the grounds that the annexation statute permitted the state to keep the public lands of the Republic of Texas, which originally were measured as the Mexicans had measured them. Other coastal states claim the traditional three-mile limit. The only right rule is that all states have a claim to land uncovered by the tides but not to any beyond the low-tide mark.

It was obvious to me that this confusion needed to be resolved by the highest court in the land. Certain coastal states were authorizing the withdrawal of oil from the newly discovered deposits of the continental shelf, which, in my opinion, was not theirs to dispose of. I therefore instructed the Attorney General in 1945 to bring suit in the United States District Court for the Southern District of California against the Pacific Western Oil Corporation in order to force a test case and thereby a settlement of the problem which now was no longer merely a matter of legal title but of oil riches of immense value.

This argument over title to an estimated fifteen billion barrels of oil was adjudicated for the first time in 1947. The United States Supreme Court held that the federal government had "dominant rights." This ruling in favor of the federal government was upheld on principle twice by the U. S. Supreme Court in 1950.

The private oil interests, seeking to exploit these oil-rich areas without federal control and supervision, now concentrated their pressure on the Congress. They hoped to have the Congress cancel out what the Supreme Court had ruled. As a result, there were pending in Congress in the spring of 1952 a Senate joint resolution and at least fourteen House resolutions with respect to the title to submerged lands under the marginal sea and inland waters. The Senate measures had been introduced by Senator McCarran, and their purpose was to confirm the title of the respective states to such lands and to convey the interest of the federal government in all such properties to the states themselves. The House resolutions were substantially similar.

The special interests probably never worked harder on any legislation than on the Senate joint resolution which reached my desk late in May of 1952. It was designed to make an outright gift of the offshore resources of the country to three states at the expense of the other forty-five. There was little question as to what action I would take on the bill, but the first public suggestion of a presidential veto was made in the following remarks in an address I delivered on May 17:

"Take the problem of off-shore oil, for example. The minerals that lie under the sea off the coasts of this country belong to the Federal government—that is, to all the people of this country. The ownership has been affirmed and re-affirmed in the Supreme Court of the United States. These rights may be worth as much as somewhere between forty billion and 100 billion dollars.

"If we back down on our determination to hold these rights for all the people, we will act to rob them of this great national asset. That is just what the oil lobby wants. They want us to turn the vast treasure over to a handful of states, where the powerful private oil interests hope to exploit it to suit themselves. . . .

"I can see how the Members of Congress from Texas and California and Louisiana might like to have all the off-shore oil for their states. But I certainly can't understand how Members of Congress from the other forty-five states can vote to give away the interest the people of their own states have in this tremendous asset. It's just over my head and beyond me how any interior Senator or Congressman could vote to give that asset away. I am still puzzled about it. As far as I am concerned, I intend to stand up and fight to protect the people's interest in this matter."

Five days later, at a White House press conference, I came near committing myself more definitely to a veto but held to my practice of withholding comment to the press on pending legislation.

The most complete condensed history of the "tidelands" issue, along with an interpretation of the significant aspects of the legislation needed to clear up the problem, is set forth in the veto message of May 29, 1952.

I said that I had concluded that I could not approve the joint resolution because it would turn over to certain states, as a free gift, very valuable lands and mineral resources now belonging to the United States as a whole—that is, to all the people of the country. I explained that I did not believe such an action would be in the national interest and did not see how any President could fail to oppose it.

I noted that the lands and mineral resources in question were under the open sea off the Pacific, the Gulf, and the Atlantic coasts of our country. Contrary to what had been asserted, this resolution would have no effect whatever on the status of the lands under navigable rivers, lakes, harbors, bays, sounds, and other navigable bodies of water that are inland waters. Neither would it have any effect on the tidelands. All such lands had long been held by the courts to belong to the states or their grantees, and this resolution would make no change in the situation.

The only lands that would be affected by this resolution were those under the open ocean for some miles seaward from the low-tide mark or from the mouths of harbors, sounds, and other inland waters. What this resolution would do would be to give those lands to the states that happen to border on the ocean.

I called attention to the fact that, whatever may have been the opinion of various people in the past, the legal controversy had resolved in the only way such legal questions can be resolved under our Constitution— that is, by the courts, and in this case by the Supreme Court.

The real question presented by this joint resolution was therefore this: Should the people of the country give an asset belonging to all of them to the states that happen to border on the ocean? The real purpose and sole effect of the resolution, I stressed, would be to give to a few states certain undersea lands and mineral resources which belonged to the entire nation.

"I cannot agree," my message continued, "that this would be a wise or proper way to dispose of these lands and mineral resources of the United States. Instead, I think the resources in these lands under the sea should be developed and used for the benefit of all the people of the country, including those who live in the coastal States.

"The Continental Shelf," I pointed out, "which extends in some areas 150 miles or more off the coast of our country, contains additional amounts of oil and other minerals of huge value. One oil well, for example, has already been drilled and is producing about 22 miles off the coast of Louisiana. . . .

"The intent of the coastal States in this regard has been made clear by actions of the State legislature of Louisiana which has enacted legislation claiming to extend the State's boundary 27 miles into the Gulf of Mexico, and of the State legislature of Texas which has enacted legislation claiming to extend that State's boundary to the outer limit of the Continental Shelf. Such an action would extend Texas' boundary as much as 130 miles into the Gulf of Mexico. . . .

"If the Congress wishes to enact legislation confirming the States in the ownership of what is already theirs—that is, the lands and resources under navigable inland waters and the tidelands—I shall, of course, be glad to approve it. But such legislation is completely unnecessary, and bears no relation whatever to the question of what should be done with lands which the States do not now own—that is, the lands under the open sea."

I wished, however, to promote constructive thinking on the issue and therefore went on to indicate the outlines of what would appear to me to be a reasonable solution.

"First," I pointed out, "it is of great importance that the exploration of the submerged lands—both in the marginal sea belt and the rest of the Continental shelf—for oil and gas fields should go ahead rapidly, and any fields discovered should be developed in an orderly fashion which will provide adequate recognition for the needs of national defense."

This, I noted, could be done by providing for federal leases to private parties for exploration and development of the oil and gas deposits in the undersea lands. As passed, the resolution would make no provision whatever for developing the resources of the Continental shelf beyond the marginal belt, and it made no provision at all for the national defense interest in the oil under the marginal sea.

The President, I contended, should have authority to withdraw from disposition any unleased lands of the continental shelf and reserve them in the interest of national security. Yet the Congress had omitted entirely this or any other similar provision, and in passing the legislation the Congress was surrendering priceless opportunities for conservation and other safeguards necessary for national security. "I regard this as unfortunate," I wrote, "and it is for this reason especially that the Department of Defense has strongly urged me to withhold approval from S. J. Res. 20.

"I urge the Congress to enact, in place of the resolution before me, legislation which will provide for renewed exploration and prudent development of the oil and gas fields under the open sea, on a basis that will adequately protect the national defense interests of the Nation."

My second point was that the Congress should provide for the disposition of the revenues obtained from oil and gas leases on the undersea lands. A resolution introduced by Senators O'Mahoney and Anderson would have granted the adjacent coastal states thirty-seven and a half per cent of the revenues from submerged lands of the marginal sea. I said I would have no objection to such a provision, which was similar to existing provisions under which the states received thirty-seven and a half per cent of the revenues from the federal government's oil-producing public lands within their borders.

I noted also that there was another suggestion, which had been offered by Senator Hill on behalf of himself and eighteen other senators. This was that the revenues from the undersea lands, other than the portion to be paid to the adjacent coastal states under the O'Mahoney-Anderson resolution, should be used to aid education throughout the nation.

"When you consider," I wrote, "how much good such a provision would do for school children throughout the nation, it gives particular emphasis to the necessity for preserving these great assets for the benefit of all the people of the country rather than giving them to a few of the states."

I concluded that the resolution before me failed to serve the best interests of the nation. It made a free gift of immensely valuable resources, which belonged to the entire nation, to the states that happened to be located nearest to them. I could find neither wisdom nor necessity in such a course, and I therefore felt compelled to return the joint resolution without my approval.

I continued to fight against the efforts of the oil interests to influence legislation which would give them the offshore wealth they hoped to get through this Senate joint resolution. Later in the year the incoming Republican administration was promising support of the states in their claim to these national resources, but I never changed my conviction that these resources were the property of all the people, and just four days before I left the White House I issued an Executive Order setting aside the submerged lands of the continental shelf as a naval petroleum reserve, to be administered by the Secretary of the Navy. The objective was to conserve and utilize the great oil and gas deposits in these lands in order to promote the national security.

The tremendous importance of oil to the government is difficult to overestimate. Statistics compiled for the year 1952 showed that the domestic consumption of petroleum products in the United States averaged about 7,300,000 barrels per day. A large part of that daily consumption was attributable to agencies of the federal government, particularly the three military departments of the Army, Navy, and Air Force.

The domestic production of petroleum during the year averaged about 6,800,000 barrels per day. It was clear, therefore, that the production of petroleum in the United States during 1952 fell far short of meeting the consumption, and this deficit was expected to grow larger year by year.

In view of the great demand for oil by the government for defense purposes, I considered it of the utmost importance that the vast oil deposits in the continental shelf be put to use for the national security. At that time there were twenty-two known oil fields in the continental shelf adjacent to the coasts of California, Louisiana, and Texas. These known fields contained estimated proven reserves aggregating approximately 492,000,000 barrels of oil. Moreover, it was estimated that the continental shelf adjacent to the coasts of these three states actually contained a grand total of about fifteen billion barrels of oil.

It was always my firm conviction that it would be the height of folly for the United States to give away the vast quantities of oil contained in the continental shelf and then buy back this same oil at stiff prices for use by the Army, Navy, and Air Force in the defense of the nation.

CHAPTER 31

My decision not to be candidate for re-election in 1952 goes back to the day of my inauguration in 1949. On this day, facing four more years of the presidency, I kept reviewing the many grave problems that confronted the nation and the world. And I found myself thinking about my own future, and how long a man ought to stay in the presidency, and a nation's need for constant renewal of leadership. I now was certain that I would not run again. But I could not share this decision with anyone. By the very nature of his office, this is one secret a President must keep to himself to the last possible moment.

More than a year later, on April 16, 1950, I wrote out my thoughts and my intentions in a memorandum which I locked away:

"I am not a candidate for nomination by the Democratic Convention.

"My first election to public office took place in November, 1922. I served two years in the armed forces in World War I, ten years in the Senate, two months and 20 days as Vice President and President of the Senate. I have been in public office well over thirty years, having been President of the United States almost two complete terms.

"Washington, Jefferson, Monroe, Madison, Andrew Jackson and Woodrow Wilson, as well as Calvin Coolidge, stood by the precedent of two terms. Only Grant, Theodore Roosevelt and F.D.R. made the attempt to break that precedent. F.D.R. succeeded.

"In my opinion eight years as President is enough and sometimes too much for any man to serve in that capacity.

"There is a lure in power. It can get into a man's blood just as gambling and lust for money have been known to do.

"This is a Republic. The greatest in the history of the world. I want this country to continue as a Republic. Cincinnatus and Washington pointed the way. When Rome forgot Cincinnatus, its downfall began. When we forget the examples of such men as Washington, Jefferson and Andrew Jackson, all of whom could have had a continuation in the office, then will we start down the road to dictatorship and ruin. I know I could be elected again and continue to break the old precedent as it was broken by F.D.R. It should not be done. That precedent should continue not by a Constitutional amendment,[1] but by custom based on the honor of the man in the office.

"Therefore, to re-establish that custom, although by a quibble I could say I've only had one term, I am not a candidate and will not accept the nomination for another term."

In March of the same year, 1951, I took the memorandum out at the Little White House in Key West and read it to my White House staff. The reaction was to be expected. The staff responded with deep emotion and expressions of protest and disappointment. They pleaded with me not to make public any such announcement. But I had no intention of doing this until the proper time.

My mind was made up irrevocably against running in 1952, and I was concerned with the problem of suggesting the right man to present to the people as the standard-bearer for the Democratic party. The most logical and qualified candidate, it appeared to me, was the Chief Justice of the United States, Fred M. Vinson.

Vinson had a rich background of experience in all three branches of our government. In this respect, there was no other person who could match his record in either party. He served many terms in Congress, where he was recognized as an expert on tax matters and other subjects. He served on the federal bench. During the war he was called by President Roosevelt to take on the job of Economic Stabilizer. He later came into the White House as assistant to the President in charge of the big job of managing the war economy and reconversion to peacetime production. Vinson had additional Cabinet experience in the post of Secretary of the Treasury in my own administration. And when the Supreme Court developed internal conflicts, I again reached out for Fred Vinson and his remarkable administrative talents and appointed him Chief Justice upon the death of Chief Justice Stone.

Vinson was gifted with a sense of personal and political loyalty seldom found among the top men in Washington. Too often loyalties are breached in Washington in the rivalries for political advantage. Not so

---

[1] The Eightieth Congress had proposed such an amendment to the Constitution (now the Twenty-second), but at the time of this memorandum it had not yet been ratified by a sufficient number of states.

with Vinson. He was a devoted and undemonstrative patriot who could also consistently practice personal and party loyalty.

I never knew Vinson intimately when I was in the Senate and he was in the House, although we often met on government business. It was after I moved to the White House that I became fully acquainted with him and developed a great respect for him. We worked very closely together. We discovered a common interest in history and had to settle many a disputed date or place by later research. Vinson had a remarkable grasp of history, modern and ancient. He constantly read important books on history and kept in touch with current publications. His liberalism was broad and deep. I recall one incident that will illustrate Vinson's loyalty and devotion to duty. When I was getting ready to go to Potsdam for meetings with Churchill and Stalin, I asked Vinson to come along to assist me there. But he declined, saying: "Mr. President, you are going out of the country, and you will be gone many weeks. I think that I had better stay on the job here at the White House and see that there is no interruption in the flow of work."

In the summer of 1950, after I had written the memorandum concerning my decision not to run again, I first approached Vinson with the suggestion that he should become the candidate to succeed me. But he declined.

In the fall of 1951 I invited Vinson to visit me at the Little White House in Key West, and there, in the complete privacy of that retreat, I resumed my talks with him about his becoming the Democratic candidate for President. I confronted Vinson with a summary of the reasons that made him the logical man to be the President of the United States. We talked about it from one end to the other, and he finally said that he would speak to Mrs. Vinson about it. He always consulted her when anything vital came up in his career. I have never come in contact with a more devoted couple.

Back in Washington, Vinson told me that after talking it over with Mrs. Vinson and after most serious consideration he still felt honestly and in his heart that he did not think he should use the Court as a steppingstone to the presidency. To this argument I replied that the Court had been used by other men I knew, that Charles Evans Hughes had used it, and that in my opinion there would be nothing wrong in his becoming a candidate. But shortly after this meeting, and after I had another talk, this time with Mrs. Vinson, the Chief Justice firmly declined on the basis of his physical condition. I think that if Vinson had become President he would have ranked high among Presidents—but it probably would have further shortened his life.

With the self-elimination of Vinson, the field was now wide open as far as I was concerned. My staff and the Democratic organization renewed their pressure on me to reconsider running in 1952. But my answer was the same, that my mind was made up and that we would have to look elsewhere for a standard-bearer.

I began to canvass the situation from one end of the country to the other. It is a most difficult task to find men qualified by temperament, outlook, and capacity to fill any top post in our government. We knew from experience that good men in government usually will rise to their duties and responsibilities even though they may have been presumed inadequate. But in the case of the presidency there are so many considerations involved that, despite the many qualified men to choose from, there was no one who stood out at this time as the "natural" choice. This search for the best all-around candidate led to my consideration of Adlai E. Stevenson, the governor of Illinois. On May 8 I wrote the following memorandum:

"I've said that no third term appeals to me. On April 16 '50 I expressed my opinion on that.

"Now if we can find a man who will take over and continue the Fair Deal, Point IV, Fair Employment, parity for farmers and a consumers protective policy, the Democratic Party can win from now on.

"It seems to me now that the Governor of Illinois has the background and what it takes. Think I'll talk to him."

I liked Stevenson's political and administrative background. I admired him personally. I liked his forthright and energetic campaign for the governorship. He proved in that contest that he possessed a knowledge and "feel" for politics, that he understood that politics at its best was the business and art of government, and that he had learned that a knowledge of politics is necessary to carry out the function of our form of free government.

I had an especially high regard for Stevenson's many contributions to the federal government as special assistant to many agency heads and Cabinet members. His work on the United Nations and in the State Department demonstrated that he had a clear grasp of the role of this country as the leader among nations and of our program to secure the peace.

Here are some notes I made after my talks with Governor Stevenson:

"Early in January 1952, I asked Adlai Stevenson, Governor of Illinois, to come to the Blair House for a talk. He came one evening about 8 P.M. We talked for an hour or more.

"I told him that I would not run for President again and that it was my opinion he was best-fitted for the place. He comes of a political family. His grandfather was Vice President with Grover Cleveland in the campaign and the election of 1892. The grandfather had been on the ticket with Winfield Scott Hancock in 1880. He had served in Congress.

"Adlai's father had been connected with the government of the State of Illinois. Adlai had served the country in the State Department and the United Nations. He had made an excellent Governor of Illinois.

"When I talked with him, I told him what I thought the Presidency is, how it has grown into the most powerful and the greatest office in the history of the world. I asked him to take it and told him that if he would agree he could be nominated. I told him that a President in the White House always controlled the National Convention. Called his attention to Jackson and Van Buren and Polk. Talked about Taft in 1912, Wilson in 1920, Coolidge and Mellon in 1928, Roosevelt in 1936, 1940, 1944. But he said: No! He apparently was flabbergasted. . . .

"On March 4 Governor Stevenson came to see me again, this time at his request, to tell me that he had made a commitment to run for re-election in Illinois and that he did not think he could go back on that commitment honorably. I appreciated his viewpoint, and I honored him for it. He said he would not want to have people believe that he was announcing for re-election in his great state just as a steppingstone to the White House."

But I felt that in Stevenson I had found the man to whom I could safely turn over the responsibilities of party leadership. Here was the kind of man the Democratic party needed and, while I would not pressure him, I felt certain that he would see it as his duty to seek the nomination.

On March 29, at the annual Jefferson-Jackson Day Dinner in the National Guard Armory in Washington, D.C., I announced that I would not run again.

About fifty-three hundred Democrats were present when I departed from my prepared speech near the end and made this statement: "I shall not be a candidate for re-election. I have served my country long, and I think efficiently and honestly. I shall not accept a renomination. I do not feel that it is my duty to spend another four years in the White House."

There was a moment of stunned silence in the hall. Then shouts of protest went up, and they were repeated when I concluded my remarks and when I left the hall.

When I arrived at the White House after the announcement, I found the ushers and doormen almost in tears, and the two maids who were taking care of my mother-in-law were weeping. I told them to calm down and stay on the job.

I had expected that some of my friends would be disappointed and even shocked at the suddenness of this public announcement. But I am sure they must have known that I had given this decision long and careful study and had put off making it public until I thought the proper time had come.

The man who occupies the high office of President is always aware that he is there only because more people wanted him than wanted the other fellow. But if he is to judge his situation by the people around him, he will hear a hundred voices telling him that he is the greatest man in the world for every one that tells him he is not. A President, if he is to have clear perspective and never get out of touch, must cut through the voices around him, know his history, and make certain of the reliability of the information he gets.

Anyway, there was no chance that I would change, and at this point I was even more certain that under the circumstances it would be better for me, the party, and for the country to have a change in leadership.

I am inclined to think that if I had announced early in 1950 or 1951 that I intended to carry the fight myself to a conclusion General Eisenhower would not have been the Republican candidate—and perhaps not the President. I hold to that opinion because I am sure that Eisenhower in 1952 thought that he would have no fight for the election and that perhaps the Democrats would nominate him also.

There were a number of other good men who were frankly candidates for the Democratic nomination. I understood well enough that historically no candidate could be certain of nomination by the party in power unless he had the support of the President in the White House. I therefore gave careful study and consideration to each of the candidates. I discussed their qualifications with members of my staff and my advisers. The more I weighed the situation, the more apparent it became that Governor Stevenson seemed best qualified on the basis of background, experience, and broad capacity.

One of the ablest and most deserving contenders for the nomination was Averell Harriman. His record of government service was long and distinguished. Harriman had served in many important posts during the critical war and postwar years. His work in the handling of Lend-Lease from London was outstanding. He served brilliantly as Ambassador to Russia and Great Britain. He was a very able Secretary of Commerce in my Cabinet and did a great job of administering the Marshall Plan in Europe. I held Harriman in the highest regard, and still do, but I felt that with his limited experience in elective politics and no experience in campaigning for an elective office he was somewhat handicapped at this particular time.

Some weeks before the convention Harriman came to see me to ask if I would be agreeable to the New York delegation's putting him in nomination. I replied to Harriman that it was all right for him to take the step but that when the time came for the convention to nominate its candidate for President I wanted him to be in line to help nominate that man, whoever he was. Some of the party leaders also approached me to ask if they could help Harriman, and I told them that of course they could. There were groups in other parts of the country who wanted to put Harriman forward. I assured Harriman that, if it came to a show-down between him and Stevenson, I was committed to Stevenson because I felt that he would be the strongest candidate the Democratic party could offer at this time. This understanding between Harriman and myself was behind some of the developments at the convention in July.

Estes Kefauver made an energetic and extensive campaign for the nomination. His record as a member of the House and his work in the Senate were in most respects highly commendable. I knew of his popularity. I approved of what he undertook to do with his investigating committee, but I did not approve of the methods he used and the way he went about it.

Robert S. Kerr from Oklahoma was another favorite-son candidate. He was an able, courageous, and effective senator. Unfortunately, Kerr had sponsored a bill which I had to veto because I did not consider it to be in the public interest. Bob Kerr had demonstrated that as governor and as senator he possessed administrative and legislative ability of high order. But his background of representing the oil and gas interests in the Senate made him ineligible in my opinion. I have always felt that any man who goes either to the Senate or the House to represent a special interest in his own state and who sponsors legislation to help that special interest forfeits any claim to national leadership in the Democratic party. Historically, the Democratic party is not a special-interest party.

Dick Russell of Georgia was a candidate to be reckoned with. He had ability, integrity, and honesty. He was one of the best-informed men in the Senate and perhaps the best-informed on the agricultural situation of the nation. As a senator Russell was always able to present any problem in a clear and straightforward manner so that everyone understood it. His skillful handling of the MacArthur committee hearing demonstrated his ability, wisdom, and judicious temperament as a chairman. But being from Georgia, where the race issue was so heated, he did not have a serious chance of being nominated. I believe that if Russell had been from Indiana or Missouri or Kentucky he may very well have been the President of the United States.

As the time for the Democratic National Convention in Chicago drew nearer, Adlai Stevenson continued to be reluctant to commit himself. He refused to allow me to support him publicly for the nomination. After several conferences with Frank McKinney, chairman of the Democratic National Committee, Governor Stevenson still held out. It therefore became necessary, with the convention close at hand, for the party to decide on some other strong candidate and unite behind him. This is where Vice-President Alben Barkley played a key and dramatic role.

Barkley was at the height of his popularity with the people, with the party, and with the Congress. But for his age he would have been a most logical candidate. The presidency being the man-killer that it is, age could not be passed over lightly. Perhaps in the case of Barkley, whose vigor and stamina defied time, this did not quite apply, but it was still a problem to reckon with.

At about this time—about two weeks before the convention—Barkley let it be known that he would like to be a candidate for the presidency. I invited him to a meeting at the White House at which Chairman McKinney and members of my staff were present. At this meeting we informed Barkley that up to that time Stevenson had refused to run and that if he (Barkley) was serious about wanting the nomination we would support him.

Barkley went to the Chicago convention on the opening day, July 21, with that commitment. But in one essential respect Barkley failed to follow our suggestions to him. In meeting with the leaders of labor to enlist their support, we told him to be sure to see the leaders one at a time. Instead, he arranged a breakfast meeting with all sixteen labor leaders at once. We knew that they would never commit themselves in a crowd, and all that came of this meeting with the labor leaders was a unanimous turndown. I am of the opinion that if Barkley had been advised by a manager skilled in dealing with labor this rejection would never have occurred and Barkley would have been the Democratic nominee.

That same afternoon, after his disastrous meeting with labor, Barkley called me in Washington. He told me he was going to withdraw as a candidate. I urged him to stay in the race, but he told me that his wife and his supporters had advised him that under the circumstances it would be best for him to withdraw, and that his reason for calling me was to tell me that he had already announced his decision to the press. I told Barkley that I understood his being hurt by the action of the labor leaders but that I thought he was acting on an impulse and that he would regret it if he went through with his decision to pull out and leave the convention so abruptly.

Shortly after my conversation with Barkley, I received a call from

Secretary of Commerce Charles Sawyer, who told me that he did not think it was right for Barkley to be allowed to leave Chicago until he had made a personal appearance before the convention. I agreed with Sawyer and telephoned Chairman McKinney to suggest that he should have Barkley presented to the convention for a farewell speech. This was arranged, and on the morning of July 23 Alben Barkley was escorted to the speaker's platform to receive one of the greatest ovations ever accorded anyone at a national political convention.

Barkley's extemporaneous address was a memorable highlight of the 1952 convention. It was acclaimed as one of the most heart-warming and moving speeches ever brought before such a gathering. It was the "Veep" at his best. I think it was the greatest and grandest exit a major withdrawing candidate could make.

But this extraordinary picture was soon to be spoiled when Barkley unexpectedly allowed three delegates from other states than his own to put his name in nomination. He told me afterward that his reason for this—even though he told me he had withdrawn—was that it was beginning to look to him as if the convention might be deadlocked and that, if that happened, it would turn in his favor after all. But I was sorry that he had permitted his nomination and thus detracted from his magnificent farewell address.

On the following day, July 24, I received a telephone call at the White House from Governor Stevenson. He said that he called to ask whether it would embarrass me if he allowed his name to be placed in nomination. I replied with a show of exasperation and some rather vigorous words and concluded by saying to Stevenson, "I have been trying since January to get you to say that. Why would it embarrass me?"

From here on, events began to move swiftly and to shape the course of the convention leading to the nomination of Stevenson.

I transmitted instructions to my alternate on the Missouri delegation, Thomas J. Gavin, to get behind the Illinois candidate.

Senator Brien McMahon from Connecticut, who was on his deathbed, had nevertheless managed somehow to keep in touch with developments at the convention. He informed McKinney and me that he would release the Connecticut delegation when the time came and left orders to be called, regardless of his physical condition. Thus Connecticut became the first state to break the deadlock and move into the Stevenson column. This started the swing to Stevenson, and my announced open support cinched his nomination.

Actually, if Barkley had not withdrawn when he did, and if he had not made it irrevocable in his call to me, I would not at this late date have been able to tell Stevenson that I would support him, and Barkley would have been the Democratic nominee.

By the fourth day of the convention the movement for Stevenson had crystallized into a draft of the man who so reluctantly, and at long last, had announced himself as a candidate for the presidential nomination.

On Friday afternoon, July 25, Mrs. Truman and I boarded the Independence and took off for Chicago. The plane commander, Colonel Williams, had installed a television set in my quarters. We watched the convention all the way and saw the results of the second ballot and the start of the third. The plane landed at the Chicago airport about 3:30 P.M. The mayor of Chicago, Mr. Martin Kennelly, and Chairman McKinney met me there, and we rode to the Blackstone Hotel.

I saw a number of my friends at the hotel and then got to work on my speech. It was about 1:45 A.M. when I arrived at the International Amphitheatre and entered the convention hall. The convention had recessed about 4 P.M., and I did not appear until after it reconvened and after Stevenson's nomination.

I walked the length of the platform with Stevenson and presented him to the convention with the promise: "I am going to take my coat off and do everything I can to help him win."

The convention recessed again after Stevenson had made his speech of acceptance. Meanwhile, Sam Rayburn, Stevenson, McKinney, and I retired to a small private room behind the stage in the hall and discussed possible candidates for Stevenson's running mate. I left before a decision was reached, but before leaving I suggested that Senator John Sparkman of Alabama would be the best asset to the ticket. He was nominated by acclamation on a voice vote without a ballot being taken, and the thirty-first Democratic National Convention was adjourned.

In his campaign for the presidency Stevenson lived up to his reputation as a man of eloquence. His eloquence was real because his words gave definition and meaning to the major issues of our time. He was particularly effective in expressing this nation's foreign policy. He made no demagogic statements. He made no extravagant promises. He was not vague with generalities but would talk to the point. While some felt he may have talked over the heads of some people, he was uncompromising in being himself. His was a great campaign and did credit to the party and the nation. He did not appeal to the weakness but to the strength of the people. He did not trade principles for votes. What he said in the South he would say in the North, and what he said in the East he would say in the West. It will be to his credit that, although given provocation by the opposition, he stayed away from personalities and accusations.

But Stevenson's attitude toward the President he hoped to succeed was a mystery to me for some time, and I believe Stevenson made several mistakes. Whether this was due to the urgings of his advisers or bad information or perhaps to the contagion other good citizens were suffering as a result of reading the anti-Democratic press, I do not know.

The first mistake he made was to fire the chairman of the Democratic National Committee and to move his campaign headquarters to Springfield, Illinois, giving the impression that he was seeking to disassociate himself from the administration in Washington, and perhaps from me. How Stevenson hoped he could persuade the American voters to maintain the Democratic party in power while seeming to disown powerful elements of it, I do not know.

Unfortunately, Stevenson, in an interview in Oregon, quoted a reporter's phrase in answering a question and said that he would clean up "the mess in Washington." I wondered if he had been taken in by the Republican fraudulent build-up of flyspecks on our Washington windows into a big blot or "mess." For several years the Republican opposition had tried to make a case against the administration, only to find that the administration was always alert in rooting out corruption or bad practices wherever they existed. As long as there are those who will pay to corrupt, there will always be some who will yield to corruption. This is as true in private business as it is in public or government business. This is true in industry and banking as well as in the federal government. It is vastly less prevalent in the government. By this inadvertence in Oregon, Stevenson provided the Republican opposition with the audacity to go ahead with the two phony issues of the Eisenhower campaign—corruption and Korea.

Another mistake in Stevenson's campaign was his failure to coordinate and give proper recognition to existing Democratic organizations in the major population centers. This came as a surprise to me. I had attributed to him realistic political judgment as governor of Illinois. I had thought some solid political instincts had filtered down to him from his very astute grandfather of the same name.

By alienating many influential Democratic political leaders at the outset Stevenson may have thought he was attaining full freedom of action. But in reality he needlessly sacrificed basic political backing and perhaps millions in votes. I say this despite the fact that he got more popular votes than any Democratic candidate for the presidency up to that time, except for F.D.R.'s overwhelming victory in 1936.

There is more to the business of party leadership and party politics than the making of speeches, even though the speeches may be brilliant. A politician soon learns that his performance on the stage depends as much on the stagehands as on his own skill. Stevenson now knows as well as anyone that politics is a highly organized effort on the part of a great many people, and amateurs soon must learn quickly or fail. I have always defined politics to mean the science of government, perhaps the most important science because it involves the art and ability of people to live together. Running for office and electioneering are only a part of politics. Holding office and administering that office for the best interests of the people are the fulfillment of politics. The difference between the two major political parties in this country, as I see it, is that whereas Republicans descend to the people at each election to court them, we Democrats are always with and among them and maintain constant contact through established political organizations. Hence a Democratic candidate for any office will usually fare better in his campaign if he does not throw away organization support without good reason.

Another mistake in the 1952 campaign was that there was little or no co-ordination between Washington and Springfield. Actually, there were two campaigns being waged by the Democrats, and this often led to overlapping and confusion. It was an unfortunate situation that could have been avoided.

When it seemed to me almost too late, Stevenson asked me to get into the campaign, which I did as soon as I could, and I gave it all I had. It seems to me that another mistake by Mr. Stevenson was to allow himself to go on the defensive in Cleveland and other cities on the question of so-called Communists in government. The most brazen lie of the century has been fabricated by reckless demagogues among the Republicans to the effect that Democrats were soft on Communists. The Republicans used the technique of fear and the big lie to confuse and frighten our people. The historic fact is that it was under a Democratic administration that those economic and military measures were taken which saved Western civilization from Communist control.

It was the Democratic administration that prosecuted the known Communist conspirators in this country and convicted them without throwing away our Bill of Rights by resorting to totalitarian methods.

What is just as important, we strengthened our economy by maintaining full employment and prosperity and thus helped defeat Communism where hunger and misery threatened free peoples.

This is a record without parallel in history. All Americans, whatever their politics, may feel justly proud of the role of this country in this great period of continuous struggle for the world's freedom.

It seems to me that Stevenson, who knew the facts, since he had taken part in the administration's fight against Communism, as had Eisenhower, should have resisted vigorously any maneuvers to put him on the defensive as an opponent of Communism. He should never have yielded to the challenge of contemptible demagogues, many of whom flinched while the administration fought Communism.

I am sure that if Stevenson had accepted in good faith the proposition I made to him on January 30, 1952, and enabled us to make the proper build-up, there would have been no contest to speak of at Chicago, and I think he would have received at least three million more votes. Perhaps this would not have produced enough more votes to elect him, but there would have been enough to rebuke Eisenhower for his demagoguery and endorsement of the Jenner-McCarthy big lie.

Having said this, I want to make clear that my admiration for Stevenson as the spokesman and the standard-bearer of the party was justified by his brilliant exposition of the main issues. His ability to put into inspiring words the principles of the Democratic party earned him fame and world-wide recognition. I hold him in the highest regard for his intellectual courage. It took courage to speak with candor and forthrightness in the face of the demagogic campaigning conducted by the Republicans. Stevenson, even in defeat, left a profound and enduring impression on the American people. The nation and the party were richer for his inspiring and high-level campaign.

Stevenson, of course, faced very formidable opposition in the great popularity of General Eisenhower, whom the Republicans had appropriated. Any Democratic nominee would have had to face the enormous psychological handicap of campaigning against a very popular military hero. Some Republican leaders believed they could not win with Senator Taft or with any other traditional Republican. The Republicans, being a minority party, knew they had to borrow strength from the Democratic and independent vote. Their only hope of gaining such strength was to find a candidate whose appeal to the voters would cut across party lines. The popularity of a war hero like that of General Eisenhower seemed to provide a rare political opportunity to a rebellious Republican clique.

In 1948 and 1952 there were even some Democrats who, fearful of defeat, also wanted to seize upon the popularity of this man. Major wars always bring to the fore certain military figures whose popularity, as much as their military skill, serves to build the morale of the people. The luster of such figures cuts easily across party lines. Many of us did not know whether Eisenhower was a Republican or a Democrat until he announced himself as a candidate on the Republican side. He had been persuaded that his popularity was such that he would have no opposition in the Republican party, and he had even been encouraged to feel that the Democrats might very well make it unanimous by also nominating him on the Democratic ticket. These advisers apparently did not speak for the entire Republican leadership and certainly not for the Democrats. There followed a bitter struggle in the Republican leadership, and Eisenhower found himself knee-deep in politics. He had to make use of the machinations of Dewey and Brownell as well as of his personal popularity to win the Republican nomination.

Those of us who knew Eisenhower through his long service in uniform under two Democratic Presidents had reason to hope that he would campaign on a high level. He had been assigned important roles and given a part in the historic struggle of the battle against the totalitarian powers and in the military rebuilding of the Western powers in the postwar period. He measured up to his assignments with distinction and the well-deserved gratitude of the Allied world. He had the opportunity to know and to understand what was happening in the world and what we were doing as a nation. He helped carry out important policies of two administrations and had the fullest opportunity to express himself on many important decisions.

We were shocked and disappointed to find that he would lend himself to the type of campaign that followed. He permitted a campaign of distortion and vilification that he could not possibly have believed was true. There were mass accusations of subversion and corruption against the Democratic administration. Yet two years of Republican rule have failed to produce any evidence to justify the vile accusations of the campaign, despite the feverish searchings of his Attorney General. Hard as it was for us to understand this side of Eisenhower now revealed to us, it was even more of a jolt to see our foreign policy used as a political football. But when our struggle in Korea was appropriated for partisan political purposes at a time when we were negotiating for armistice in the face of a most stubborn and tricky foe, I felt that we had reached a situation that was politically and morally intolerable. I could understand certain extreme isolationists using Korea as a political weapon, but I will never understand how a responsible military man, fully familiar with the extreme delicacy of our negotiations to end hostilities, could use this tragedy for political advantage. I regret that such a chapter should have been written into our political history. When General Eisenhower, in his Detroit speech, proposed that if elected he would journey to Korea in person to put an end to the fighting, he must have known that he was weakening our hand in negotiations. He must have known that he could accomplish little, if anything, by such a trip. He also must have known that by making this statement he was leading the American people to believe that the day after he became President he would bring them peace in Korea. The fighting continued for many months after the new administration took over, and peace in Korea is yet to be achieved. No man in our national life had a better reason to know or a better opportunity to find out the nature of the enemy. No man had less right to use this crisis for political purposes.

There is something else that I shall never be able to understand. During his campaign through Wisconsin, when he delivered a major speech in Milwaukee, General Eisenhower was persuaded to delete from his speech a personal tribute to his former chief, General Marshall. Eisenhower agreed to the deletion in order to make possible the presence of Senator McCarthy on the platform with him.

I would like to believe that in this instance Eisenhower permitted himself to be badly advised because of his political inexperience. It may be that Eisenhower had yielded to frantic expediency because of his discovery that he could not get the nomination or the presidency without a contest and a vigorous personal campaign. In order to win the nomination he had to go in hot pursuit of delegates, which involved a bitter attack on Taft. And then he had to wage an all-out campaign to win the election.

In the first instance he had discovered that he had to go in hot pursuit of delegates, which involved a bitter attack on Taft in order to win the nomination. And then he discovered that he had to wage an all-out campaign to win the election. He emerged as a different personality with a new cloak of the politician not too unwilling to engage in cynical partisan campaigning.

General Eisenhower won. He received the greatest number of votes cast for any presidential candidate in the history of the nation. But proportionately he did not come close to the majorities of Franklin Roosevelt in 1932 and in 1936, or that of Harding in 1920 or Herbert Hoover in 1928. But for the first time in the nation's history more than sixty million persons went to the polls, and although Stevenson came within 163,000 votes of surpassing even the total of F.D.R. in 1936, he was beaten by more than six million votes.

But it is as dramatic as it is significant that more than twenty-seven million Democrats resisted the appeal of a military hero to stand by their basic party convictions and voted for Stevenson.

This is a remarkable achievement in the face of the tremendous personal popularity of Eisenhower and the type of campaign waged, which combined to bring out millions of voters who had never previously exercised their right and duty to vote.

Were it not for these millions of one-time voters, I doubt if the Republicans would have carried either the Senate or the House of

Representatives, even by the slim margin which they were able to squeeze out.

Stevenson and the Democratic party achieved this historic fact without engaging in narrow partisan appeals and without preying upon the false hopes of a nation in a crisis.

CHAPTER 32

I voted early, before breakfast, on November 4, 1952, in the Memorial Hall at Independence, where I had been voting for more than three decades. It is a short walk from my home. But this voting was a new experience. It was one of the few times in more than thirty years that I was marking a ballot on which my name did not appear as a candidate for some office. Mrs. Truman and Margaret walked along with me to the polls, and we thought of the happy prospect of returning to the peace and quiet of our home in Independence.

Immediately after voting we boarded the presidential train for the return to Washington. I turned my attention to official business. As in all previous elections, once the campaign was over, I stopped thinking and speculating about it. I went to bed at the usual hour, when only scattered returns were reported.

But I thought we had lost the election even before I had gone to bed.

At midnight I was awakened by someone who handed me a whole stack of ticker reports, and I saw that Eisenhower was going to win the election.

I turned in then, to sleep. I did not hear Stevenson concede the election. The reports the next morning showed that Eisenhower had won by the largest popular vote in history.

I was disappointed, but I was not surprised. As I studied the returns I saw that the total popular vote in the congressional election was larger for the Democratic side, but the distribution of the vote was such that it gave the Republicans a narrow majority and control in Congress.

Throughout our history there has always been a handicap of waging political battle against a military man who was also a war hero.

Returning to Washington, I sent the following message to General Eisenhower from the train at Martinsburg, West Virginia:

Congratulations on your overwhelming victory. The 1954 budget must be presented to the Congress before January 15th. All the preliminary figures have been made up. You should have a representative meet with the Director of the Bureau of the Budget immediately. The Independence will be at your disposal if you still desire to go to Korea.

Harry S. Truman

At 2:17 P.M. that afternoon, November 5, at the White House I received the following telegram:

I deeply appreciate your courteous and generous telegram. I shall try to make arrangements within next two or three days to have a personal representative to sit with the Director of the Budget. I am most appreciative of your offer of the use of the Independence but assure you that any suitable transport plane that one of the services could make available will be satisfactory for my planned trip to Korea. With your permission I shall give the Secretary of Defense the earliest possible notice of my proposed date of departure.

Dwight D. Eisenhower

Upon receiving General Eisenhower's telegram, I sent another message to him that same day inviting him to the White House to discuss an orderly transfer of the government to the new administration. This was my message:

Thank you for your prompt and courteous reply to my telegram. I know you will agree with me that there ought to be an orderly transfer of the business of the executive branch of the government to the new administration, particularly in view of the international dangers and problems that confront this country and the whole free world. I invite you, therefore, to meet with me in the White House at your early convenience to discuss the problem of this transition period, so that it may be clear to all the world that this nation is united in its struggle for freedom and peace.

Harry S. Truman

Following my messages to Eisenhower I issued a public statement on the elections, announcing at the same time that I had invited the President-elect to the White House. This was my statement:

"The people of the United States have elected General Dwight D. Eisenhower as their President. In our democracy, this is the way we decide who shall govern us. I accept the decision as representing the will of the people, and I shall give my support to the Government they have selected. I ask all my fellow citizens to do the same.

"The new Administration and the new Congress will face extremely difficult problems, particularly in the field of foreign affairs. The proper solution of those problems may determine whether we shall have a third world war—and, indeed, whether we shall survive as a free and democratic nation. Moreover, there is no quick and easy solution to these problems. They will require sacrifice and hard work on our part for years to come. We must support our Government in the measures that are necessary to protect our freedom and achieve peace in the world, even though the way be long and hard.

"I stand ready to do all that lies within my power to facilitate the orderly transfer of the business of the Executive Branch of the Government to the new Administration. I have already sent a message to General Eisenhower suggesting that he have a representative meet with the Director of the Bureau of the Budget, so that he will be fully informed as to the items in the Budget. It will be necessary for me to send the Budget to the Congress since, under the law, it must be transmitted by January 18th. Steps will be taken to cooperate with respect to other matters relating to the transition to a new Administration where General Eisenhower wishes that to be done. I am inviting the General to meet with me here in the White House at an early date to discuss these problems, in order that it may be plain to the whole world that our people are united in the struggle for freedom and peace.

"I could not conclude this statement without expressing my admiration and gratitude to Governor Stevenson for the campaign which he conducted. He lived up to the finest traditions of our democracy. It is plain that, in him, we have a great new leader who will contribute much to our national life in the years ahead.

"We shall have other elections in the future. There we can again present our views and our differences for the decision of the American people. In the meantime, it will be in the best interest of all of us to close ranks and work together for our mutual welfare as citizens of this great Republic."

After releasing the statement I issued a verbal directive to the White House staff and all members of the Cabinet and heads of agencies to start at once to prepare material for the meeting with Eisenhower. I asked for comprehensive reports and charts on the most urgent and immediate of the business confronting the White House.

I was anxious to bring about an orderly transfer of the government and do everything possible to make certain that there would be no break in the continuity of foreign policy.

In this field I felt that I had no reason for misgivings about the incoming President despite his regrettable misuse of the Korean tragedy for campaign purposes. The incoming President was, or should have been, acquainted with the world situation. After all, he had been Allied commander in Europe, Chief of Staff, had previously visited China, Korea, and Formosa and later went back to Europe to organize the NATO forces. No man had had a better opportunity to know the whole situation, especially when he had taken such an important part in it.

On the following day, November 6, I received this telegram from General Eisenhower:

Augusta, Ga., Nov 6—11:45 A.M.

THE PRESIDENT
THE WHITE HOUSE

Thank you for your telegram. I am gratified by your suggestion that we have a personal meeting in the interest of orderly transition. Because I obviously require a reasonable time for conversations and conferences leading up to the designation of important assistants I respectfully suggest that we tentatively plan the proposed meeting for the early part of the week beginning November 17. In the meantime with your permission I shall try to take immediate advantage of your suggestion concerning a budgetary representative and will additionally propose other individuals for indoctrination in several of the other departments in the federal government. In this way our own conference can achieve maximum results. I share your hope that we may present to the world an American unity in basic issues.

Respectfully
Dwight D. Eisenhower

That same day I had already sent a letter by special courier to General Eisenhower bringing to his attention some special international situations on which I had to make policy decisions. This is the letter:

November 6, 1952

Dear General:

Following up my telegram of yesterday afternoon I had a consultation with State, Treasury, Defense and Budget.

There are some really fundamental things pending before the United Nations that must be met in a positive manner. I wish you would suggest somebody, in addition to the person who is to talk to the Budget Director, to discuss these matters authoritatively with the Secretary of State, the Secretary of the Treasury, and the Secretary of Defense.

There is a resolution pending on Korea in the United Nations.

The Iran problem is an extremely delicate one and affects our relations with Great Britain.

The Tunisian problem is also in that same class and affects our relationship with France and South Africa.

There is a National Security Council problem pending regarding the allocation of resources. A preliminary report is due November 15th.

All these things are vital policy matters which can only be decided by the President of the United States, but I would prefer not to make firm decisions on these matters without your concurrence, although the decisions will have to be made. These things affect the whole American policy with regard to the free world.

If you could designate someone to act authoritatively for you, or come yourself to sit in on these meetings, it would be the proper solution to the problem.

Sincerely yours,
Harry S. Truman

Honorable Dwight D. Eisenhower
President-elect of the United States
Augusta National Golf Course
Augusta, Georgia

As a result of my own experience and the historic experience of all Presidents since Washington, I wanted to help the new President to familiarize himself with what was going on before taking over.

The pressures and the complexities of the presidency have grown to a state where they are almost too much for one man to endure. Important decisions cannot wait. A President must decide not only on the facts he has but the experience and preparation he brings to them. It is a terrible handicap for a new President to step into office and be confronted with a whole series of critical decisions without adequate briefing. I thought it was an omission in our political tradition that a retiring President did not make it his business to facilitate the transfer of the government to his successor.

This omission goes back to very early days in our history. John Adams, the second President, left the White House in the middle of the night because he did not want to meet Jefferson on the day of his inauguration. This made it difficult for Jefferson, but compared to the situation today, this was but a minor difficulty. In Jefferson's time our population was only 5,308,000 as compared to the 160,000,000 at the time I had to turn over the government to Eisenhower. We have counties now with almost as many people as the entire nation had in Jefferson's day.

In more recent history Woodrow Wilson got no turnover of government from President Taft, although Taft rode with Wilson to the inauguration. Taft did not fill Wilson in on any business of the government.

Wilson did not turn over the government to Harding, but at that time Wilson was an invalid, having had a stroke during a campaign to rescue the League of Nations.

Herbert Hoover invited President-elect Franklin D. Roosevelt to come to the White House shortly after the election in 1932 to discuss the national crisis. Roosevelt went to the White House twice—once in late November and once in December. But he declined to share the responsibility of actually making decisions and taking actions. Roosevelt gave as his reason that he had no constitutional authority as President-elect to share in the responsibility of decisions which only a President can exercise. Except for the last two weeks before the inauguration, when the outgoing and the incoming Secretaries of the Treasury worked together informally, there was no administrative turnover.

On April 12, 1945, when I became President, the turnover involved something different. President Roosevelt had died suddenly, and I had to learn as best I could. There was a world war going on, and there was a natural military approach to all problems, with everybody wanting to win the war. The one thing in everybody's mind was to win the war, and this made the business of government a going concern so that the turnover in a way was the business of carrying on. There was non-partisan continuity with a nation strongly united.

But now we faced a different situation with the nation having just gone through a most regrettably bitter campaign.

I was determined that we should have an orderly turnover of every department of the government to assist the incoming administration to keep this nation a going concern.

On November 7 I received the following reply from General Eisenhower:

Augusta, Ga.,
Nov. 7, 1952

Dear Mr. President:

Because I believe so firmly in true bi-partisan approach to our foreign problems, I am especially appreciative of your letter of November 6 suggesting that I have a representative sit in on discussions involving a number of impending decisions in this field. However, because I have had no opportunity to accumulate a staff of advisors and assistants, it will take me a little time to designate anyone who could participate profitably in this kind of conference. I shall give priority attention to the matter and I will communicate with you further no later than Monday next, November 10th.

In your letter you use the word "authoritative" by which I take it you mean that my representative be able accurately to reflect my views. This he will be able to do, but quite naturally this will likewise be the limit of his authority since I myself can have none under current conditions.

Respectfully,
Dwight D. Eisenhower

On the same day I telegraphed the President-elect:

Honorable Dwight D. Eisenhower
President-elect of the United States
Augusta National Golf Course
Augusta, Ga.

Your telegram of yesterday arrived just after my messenger had departed for Augusta. We evidently are thinking along the same lines with regard to the transfer of the Executive Branch of the government. I will be happy to see you the seventeenth if that date is entirely satisfactory to you. I will appreciate your appointing the liaison man for State and Defense at the earliest possible moment. It also will require considerable time to close up the budget and get it ready for presentation before January 18th. I hope your man can report to the Budget as promptly as possible.

Harry S. Truman

Two days later, November 9, President-elect Eisenhower telegraphed as follows:

Augusta, Ga., Nov. 9 5:10 P.M.

The President
The White House
    With further reference to your several messages I am designating Senator Henry Cabot Lodge, Jr., of Massachusetts, to serve as my personal liaison with those departments and agencies of government, other than the Bureau of the Budget, where such liaison may prove useful in facilitating the transfer of public business from the old to the new administration.
    Senator Lodge will come to Washington during the current week and will notify the Executive offices of his arrival.
    I am also designating Joseph M. Dodge, of Detroit, to act as my personal liaison for similar purposes with the Director of the Bureau of the Budget. Mr. Dodge plans to come to Washington on November 12 and will soon thereafter get in touch with the Director of the Bureau.

Dwight D. Eisenhower

I immediately wrote out an answer on the manila envelope in which the Eisenhower message was brought to me in my study in the White House, which I then dictated to the communications room. This was the message:

Nov. 9, '52

Hon. Dwight D. Eisenhower
Augusta, Ga.
    The two gentlemen you named are eminently satisfactory to me. I appreciate your promptness in naming them.

The President

Meantime, Secretary of State Acheson had expressed his concern to me about the effect of the proposed trip of Eisenhower to Korea upon the armistice negotiations and the U.N. support of those negotiations. Acheson left the following memorandum with me on November 6:
    "Yesterday we discussed an urgent problem concerning the situation in Korea and in the United Nations General Assembly.
    "As you know, the 8th session of the United Nations General Assembly, meeting in New York, now has before it, as its first and most important item of business, the question of Korea. After a long and intensive period of diplomatic preparation, prior to the opening of the General Assembly, the United States, along with twenty other sponsoring countries, has introduced a resolution supporting the conduct of the

armistice negotiations by the United Nations' Command, specifically endorsing the UNC position on non-forceable repatriation of POWs and calling upon the Communists to accept this principle which is apparently the last obstacle to an agreement on an armistice.

"There has been a very high degree of support for principles embodied in the United States resolution and it was our hope and expectation that it would shortly be passed by an overwhelming majority, thus bringing the maximum pressure of the General Assembly and world opinion upon the Communists to accept an armistice upon the basis of the proposals of the UNC. However, in view of General Eisenhower's imminent trip to Korea and uncertainty in their minds as to whether he will support the position thus far taken by the United States in the armistice negotiations, many of the delegations appear reluctant to proceed with the resolution. The Soviets and the 'neutralist' delegations will be quick to exploit this situation to increase confusion and doubts in the Assembly to the disadvantage of the United States.

"There is also considerable speculation among the delegates regarding possible results of General Eisenhower's trip. Some delegates seem to think that the trip may affect the position taken by the UNC at Panmunjom, possibly changing the views thus far held by the UNC negotiators. Others speculate that it may result in important military decisions of grave concern to them.

"If General Eisenhower feels that it were possible for him to do so, a statement by him setting forth the purposes of his trip to Korea and his support for the efforts now being made by the U. S. Government in the General Assembly, would be of the greatest assistance in meeting this critical situation. . . ."

I told Acheson that I wanted to take the matter up with the general on his forthcoming visit to the White House.

I wanted to make sure that our international leadership was not lost. The international leadership involved the peace of the world and the lives of millions of people.

Ever since I had announced that I was not a candidate in 1952, I had given considerable thought to the problem of an orderly turnover of the government to my successor. Even before the Democratic and Republican conventions in Chicago had nominated their candidates, I had made up my mind to keep both candidates informed about the important developments of our foreign policy. I had a double purpose in mind. First, I wanted to keep foreign policy out of partisan politics. Second, I wanted to make sure that because of our responsibility of world leadership whoever was elected would be fully informed and prepared to conduct foreign affairs.

For this reason, on August 13, even as the election campaigns got under way, I sent the following telegram to General Eisenhower:

The White House
August 13, 1952

Honorable Dwight D. Eisenhower
Brown Palace Hotel
Denver, Colo.

I would be most happy if you would attend a Cabinet luncheon next Tuesday the nineteenth. If you want to bring your press secretary and any other member of your staff I'd be glad to have them. If you can arrive at about twelve fifteen, I'll have General Smith and the Central Intelligence Agency give you a briefing on the foreign situation. Then we will have luncheon with the Cabinet and after that if you like I'll have my entire staff report to you on the situation in the White House and in that way you will be entirely briefed on what takes place. I've made arrangements with the Central Intelligence Agency to furnish you once a week with the world situation as I also have for Governor Stevenson.

Harry S. Truman

The following day Eisenhower declined my invitation, replying as follows:

Dear Mr. President:

Thank you for your offer to have me briefed by certain agencies of the government on the foreign situation. On the personal side I am also grateful for your luncheon invitation.

In my current position as standard bearer of the Republican Party and of other Americans who want to bring about a change in the National Government, it is my duty to remain free to analyze publicly the policies and acts of the present administration whenever it appears to me to be proper and in the country's interests.

During the present period the people are deciding our country's leadership for the next four years. The decision rests between the Republican nominee and the candidate you and your Cabinet are supporting and with whom you conferred before sending your message. In such circumstances and in such a period I believe our communications should be only those which are known to all the American people. Consequently I think it would be unwise and result in confusion in the public mind if I were to attend the meeting in the White House to which you have invited me.

As you know, the problems which you suggest for discussion are those with which I have lived for many years. In spite of this I would instantly change this decision in the event there should arise a grave emergency. There is nothing in your message to indicate that this is presently the case.

With respect to the weekly reports from the Central Intelligence Agency that you kindly offered to send me, I will welcome these reports. In line with my view, however, that the American people are entitled to all the facts in the international situation, save only in those cases where the security of the United States is involved, I would want it understood that the possession of these reports will in no other way limit my freedom to discuss or analyze foreign programs as my judgment dictates.

Very respectfully,
Dwight D. Eisenhower

Eisenhower's telegram angered me. It was apparent that the politicians had already begun to mishandle him. On August 16 I wrote in longhand this personal letter to Eisenhower:

Dear Ike:

I am sorry if I caused you any embarrassment.

What I've always had in mind was and is a continuing foreign policy. You know that is a fact because you had a part in outlining it.

Partisan politics should stop at the boundaries of the United States. I'm extremely sorry that you have allowed a bunch of screwballs to come between us.

You have made a bad mistake, and I'm hoping that it won't injure this great Republic.

There has never been one like it and I want to see it continue regardless of the man who occupies the most important position in the history of the world.

May God guide you and give you light.

From a man who has always been your friend and who always intended to be!

Sincerely,
Harry S. Truman

Three days later, on August 19, General Eisenhower sent me a personal reply, also written in longhand. In his letter he expressed sincere thanks for the courtesy of my note of the sixteenth. He said he wished to assure me that my invitation caused him no personal embarrassment. His feeling, he said, was that, having entered this political campaign, he would become involved in the necessity of making laborious explanations to the public if he had met with me and the Cabinet. He went on to say that since there was no hint of national emergency in my telegram of invitation and he no longer belonged to any of the public services, he thought it wiser to decline.

General Eisenhower said he wished to repeat that he was grateful for the invitation and for the offer to send him the CIA weekly reports. He said he would keep in touch with the foreign situation through these reports. He closed his letter by assuring me of his support of real bipartisanship in foreign problems.

On the morning of November 18 Secretary of State Acheson, Secretary of the Treasury Snyder, Secretary of Defense Lovett, and Assistant to the President Averell Harriman conferred with me on the various items of business to be taken up with Eisenhower that afternoon. The meeting was scheduled for 2 P.M.

General Eisenhower arrived at the White House executive offices at one fifty-five and was immediately escorted to my office. He was accompanied by Senator Lodge and Mr. Dodge, but I invited the President-elect to meet with me privately before we held a general session with our aides.

Eisenhower was unsmiling. I thought he looked tense. I wanted him to be at his ease. Before getting to the purpose of the conference, I talked to him about some of the paintings hanging in my office, and I pointed to the large and magnificent globe he had used in World War II. Eisenhower had given me this globe at Frankfurt, where I saw him during the Potsdam conference. I offered to leave this globe for him in the White House. He accepted. He remained unsmiling. I then got down to business.

I told him I thought it was necessary to have this meeting in the best interests of the country and that I had two important reasons in mind.

We needed to reassure other countries that there was some stability about our foreign policy and allay uneasiness during this period of transition.

And I said I wanted to make it plain that my offer to co-operate in an orderly transfer of government to his administration was a genuine offer to do what was best for the country. I had no purpose or intention of setting any political trap or trying to shift any responsibility that was mine as President.

I told him that the Constitution leaves the powers and duties of the presidential office on the outgoing President until the inauguration of his successor. The responsibility would be mine until January 20, and I expected to exercise it.

I said I understood that any President-elect was naturally and properly reluctant to take on any of the political responsibilities of the office before taking on the legal powers as well.

I stated that my administration did not expect the new administration to take on responsibility prematurely. There might be some foreign policy issues where we could not succeed unless other nations had assurance of the continuity of our policy under the new administration.

This would be something beyond the power of the present administration to determine.

I said, "We will tell you about these issues and would welcome concurrence if you want to give it.

"But we will not press for it. This is a matter on which you will have to make up your own mind on the basis of what is best for America."

I suggested that we talk about some of these international problems when we joined the others in the Cabinet Room.

But before going to the Cabinet Room conference I wanted to tell President-elect Eisenhower a few things about atomic energy which I thought it important for him to know.

I outlined the atomic energy matters which required the President's decision and how the President worked with the Special Committee of the National Security Council. I called his attention to problems in the atomic field as they concerned our relations with the United Kingdom and Canada.

I offered to arrange to have the chairman of the Atomic Energy Commission, Gordon Dean, bring him up to date on the atomic energy program.

Our meeting lasted twenty minutes, and I then escorted the general into the Cabinet Room.

We were joined in the Cabinet Room by Secretary Acheson, Secretary Lovett, Secretary Snyder, Harriman, Senator Henry Cabot Lodge, and Joseph M. Dodge.

I opened the meeting with the following statement:

"I have invited you gentlemen to meet with me here to establish the framework for full understanding of our problems and our purposes in the interim until January 20th.

"So far as our relations with other countries are concerned, I think it is important during this period to avoid needless difference between this administration and its successor for several reasons.

"First—it will show the world national unity in foreign policy as far as politically possible.

"Second—it will help to maintain respect abroad for the power and influence of the United States, and to sustain the confidence of our allies and friends in our foreign policy.

"Third—it will help to check the Kremlin's efforts to divide the United States from its allies and friends, and it may help to keep the Kremlin from creating a crisis in the mistaken notion that we are divided or wavering in our purposes to preserve the unity of the free world.

"It is also my purpose to do what can be done by this administration to facilitate the orderly transfer of our duties to our successors. I think that is in the best interest of the country.

"I want to make available to General Eisenhower and his associates the information that will be helpful to them in taking over the operation of the Government.

"It is not my purpose to try to shift responsibility for actions taken by the government between now and January 20th. I am going to follow the policies I believe to be right up until that time and I will take full responsibility for them.

"There are certain questions on which it might be very important to our foreign policy for General Eisenhower to express his views. But it is up to him to decide whether or not he will do so.

"I welcome General Eisenhower's selection of Senator Lodge and Mr. Dodge to establish liaison with this administration. We will give them our full cooperation.

"If General Eisenhower wishes to designate additional representatives from time to time, we will be glad to work with them also.

"We want to do all we can to help the incoming administration by filling in the background of current problems and by making available in advance information concerning the problems you will have to deal with.

"It is not our purpose or intention to attempt to commit or bind the incoming administration.

"All we are doing is trying to make a common-sense approach to the situation."

I then informed the others that I had just had a private conversation with General Eisenhower. At this point the President-elect asked me whether I would give him a memorandum of our conversation. I assured the general I would be glad to do so.

I then handed him a two-page memorandum prepared by the Secretary of the Treasury, John Snyder, outlining certain problems which would have to be dealt with by the incoming administration. This memorandum, intended for information and consideration by Eisenhower and his advisers, touched on the financing of the federal government and the international position of the United States.

The President-elect's financial advisers were invited to call at the Treasury at any time, where they would receive full briefings from the Treasury's experts.

I then asked Secretary of State Dean Acheson to outline certain matters which required either immediate attention or which General Eisenhower should have actively in mind.

Before Acheson spoke, General Eisenhower asked whether he should take notes or whether he would be given a memorandum on the points to be raised. Acheson agreed to give General Eisenhower a memorandum covering these matters.

Acheson then said he would cover a number of pressing matters where action was called for daily and which would have important influence in the weeks and months following the taking over of the government by the new administration on January 20, 1953.

To conserve time, Acheson dealt with only the most important problems. He told General Eisenhower that he felt it was advisable for him to broaden his liaison with the State Department so that as many as possible of the men on whom General Eisenhower would depend would become familiar with the subjects which would have to be dealt with after January 20.

Acheson then dealt with the United Nations discussions over Korea, particularly as they related to the prisoners-of-war issue.

He explained the threatened break in the solidarity of the majority of the United Nations resulting from the compromise proposal put forth by India a few days before.

The British, Canadian, and French representatives had indicated a readiness to work out some modification of the Indian proposal which would give a better public appearance, but these would be, in fact, a surrender of the principle on which we had stood; namely, a free choice on the part of the prisoners of war.

Acheson said that a most serious situation was developing in New York. The debate with Vishinsky had ended in a very general acceptance of the idea that force should not be used to make prisoners return. Even Vishinsky was not willing to espouse the opposite principle. The course taken by the neutralist nations—India and Indonesia, etc.—was to circumvent this principle. In this they were strongly supported by the Canadians and British, and now had the support of the French and some others. The method of circumvention was very simple. The prisoners were to be turned over to a Commission. The Commission was not to use force on the prisoners, but the Commission was to repatriate the prisoners, and these men were to remain prisoners until repatriated. If the prisoners were not repatriated in three months, they were to be turned over to a political conference which would undoubtedly continue the same process.

"The attempt here," the Secretary of State continued, "was to accept the words of the principle and still keep the results desired by the Communists—that is, the repatriation of the prisoners. The prisoners had no exit from captivity under the Commission except to be repatriated.

"Certain clear results would flow from such a proposal if it were adopted. In the first place, we would obviously in the view of the entire world have repudiated our own principle. The circumvention was clear and obvious to all. In the second place, we would undoubtedly be called upon to use force against the prisoners to turn them over to a Commission, which, although it did not use force, would keep them in captivity until they returned home.

"In the third place, we would have a most precarious armistice, with the possibility of grave trouble arising in the prison camps.

"The Army would be deprived of all observations over enemy lines, and it would be unable properly to deploy the forces in the Command.

"The Communists would be free to rehabilitate air fields in North Korea. At any moment we might be charged with violating the armistice because the proposal regarding the prisoners was unclear and unworkable and almost certain to lead to misunderstandings.

"Therefore the situation in New York called for the most energetic action on the part of the United States to defeat or alter this attempted circumvention of the principle. This involved keeping aligned with us the British, French and others. There was obviously a show-down coming. The attitude of President Truman and his Cabinet advisers was clear. Therefore, if there was to be yielding, it could only be by those who were attempting to put through this new idea.

"The debate would begin tomorrow, Wednesday. Voting on proposals might come as early as Saturday, but more probably next week.

"Any statement on this matter, supporting the view held by this government, by General Eisenhower would be of the greatest possible assistance. I have prepared the sort of a statement which might provide this assistance and I am handing it to Senator Lodge.

"I have informed the British, Canadians and French that any division between them and us on this essential matter would have the gravest consequence here in the United States, through disillusionment regarding collective security. The consequences would not be confined to Korea, but would also have implications in NATO and other arrangements of the same sort."

This is the statement that we suggested that Eisenhower make:

PROPOSED STATEMENT ON KOREA

The American people earnestly want peace in Korea. They insist, however, on an honorable armistice. The armistice should be a clean and clear armistice which settles all the military problems and leaves nothing to chance or misconstruction.

Our prisoners of war in Communist hands must be promptly returned. Communist prisoners of war in our hands should be allowed to go home. But it is clear to me that those who violently resist return to the Communists cannot be driven back. They cannot be held in indefinite captivity. They must be released as free men.

I hope that the General Assembly of the United Nations will take a firm stand on these matters.

No immediate response from General Eisenhower was asked on this proposed statement. But General Eisenhower said that he was seeing

British Foreign Secretary Eden on Thursday and would discuss the question of Korea with him.

Acheson then dealt with the situation in Iran, which had developed to a critical point. This was the dispute between Iran and the United Kingdom over oil. Secretary Acheson suggested that the new administration should be closely in touch with this situation because considerable difficulties were likely to arise from it. He thought that some American initiative and unilateral action might stimulate both parties toward a common solution.

Acheson told of some of the latent complications between France and Germany in connection with NATO, which, of course, was familiar ground to General Eisenhower.

Reviewing the situation in Southeast Asia, Acheson reported:

"We had been concerned for a long time about the course of action in Indo-China. There was a strong body of opinion in France which regarded this as a lost cause that was bleeding France both financially and by undermining the possibility of French-German equality in European defense.

"There had been a noticeable lack of French aggressive attitude from a military point of view in Indo-China. The central problem in Indo-China was the fence-sitting by the Population. They would never come down on one side or another until they had a reasonable assurance of who would be the victor and that their interests would be served by the victor.

"We are helping France to the extent of carrying between one-third and one-half of the financial burden of the Indo-Chinese war. We have had military discussions between the five powers—the United States, the United Kingdom, France, Australia and New Zealand—which had not been effective in devising agreed military solutions against the contingency of overt Chinese intervention in Indo-China. The French now sought political discussions to carry the matter forward.

"This is an urgent matter upon which the new administration must be prepared to act."

Acheson pointed out that all these foreign problems were covered in a survey which I had ordered made regarding the use of our resources in foreign aid.

Mr. Dodge (who worked on this survey for me) said that he was familiar with it. Mr. Acheson added that it involved a study of the proper assignment of resources to foreign aid as against domestic rearmament, of allocation between military and economic assistance, of allocations between areas.

When Acheson concluded his presentation, General Eisenhower said that he would like a memorandum of what the Secretary of State had said. He would give it careful study, as well as the suggested statement on Korea.

General Eisenhower said that he recognized the seriousness and critical nature of the matters discussed. He then said that he was preparing immediately on the conclusion of this meeting to go with Secretary Lovett to meet the Joint Chiefs of Staff for a military briefing.

I had asked General Omar Bradley, chairman of the Chiefs of Staff, to stand by at the Pentagon to give General Eisenhower a special briefing on Korea.

General Eisenhower and I then went over a draft of a joint statement which I had had prepared at the White House. It was adopted after two changes requested by the general. The conference ended at 3:15 P.M., and the following joint statement was then issued from the White House:

"President Truman and General Eisenhower met today at the White House. After conferring together by themselves, they met with the Secretaries of State, Defense and Treasury, the Director of Mutual Security, and General Eisenhower's associates, Senator Lodge and Mr. Dodge.

"At the end of the talks, the President and General Eisenhower issued the following statement:

" 'We have discussed some of the most important problems affecting our country in the sphere of international relations. Information with respect to these problems has been made available to General Eisenhower.

" 'Under our Constitution the President must exercise his functions until he leaves office, and his successor cannot be asked to share or assume the responsibilities of the Presidency until he takes office.

" 'We have worked out a framework for liaison and exchange of information between the present Administration and the incoming Administration, but we have made no arrangements which are inconsistent with the full spirit of our Constitution. General Eisenhower has not been asked to assume any of the responsibilities of the Presidency until he takes the oath of office.

" 'We believe, however, that the arrangements we have made for cooperation will be of great value to the stability of our country and to the favorable progress of international affairs.

" 'We are confident that this meeting and that the arrangements we have made today for liaison and cooperation between the present Administration and the new Administration furnish additional proof of the ability of the people of this country to manage their affairs with a sense of continuity and with responsibility.' "

When the general and his aides left, I was troubled. I had the feeling that, up to this meeting in the White House, General Eisenhower had not grasped the immense job ahead of him. There was something about his attitude during the meeting that I did not understand. It may have been that this meeting made him realize for the first time what the presidency and the responsibilities of the President were. He may have been awe-struck by the long array of problems and decisions the President has to face. If that is so, then I can almost understand his frozen grimness throughout the meeting. But it may have been something else. He may have failed to grasp the true picture of what the administration had been doing because in the heat of partisan politics he had gotten a badly distorted version of the true facts. Whatever it was, I kept thinking about it.

INDEX

INDEX

A

AAA. *See* Agricultural Adjustment Administration
A-bomb. *See* Atomic bomb
Abbott, Rev. Jacob, *119*
Abdul Ilah, Prince, 148
Acheson, Dean, 117, 130, 428–31; and atomic energy, *526*, 6, 302–4, 308–9; and Byrnes resignation, *548–49, 551;* and China-Korea-Formosa policy, 64, 67, 75, 332–38, 340–43, 346, 374–75, 379–80, 387–88, 390, 402–6, 409, 418, 420, 438–39, 455–56, 510–11; on Soviet pressures, 97–101, 103–5, 370, 387, 406–7, 421; on Marshall, 112–13; on Marshall Plan, 113; and Berlin blockade, 130; on Palestine, 146–47, 149; and NATO, 240–57; and MacArthur, 356, 442, 447–48; at Attlee-H.S.T. meetings, 397–409; on steel crisis, 470; at Eisenhower-H.S.T. conferences, 513–20
Acheson-Lilienthal Report, 6, 8–10, 15
Act for International Development (1950), 234–45. *See also* Point IV

Adams, John, *196–97,* 192, 508
Adams, John Quincy, *58,* 172, 193
Adenauer, Dr. Konrad, 255
Adriatic, *200, 243, 249, 407*
Advisory Council for Japan, *540*
Africa, *374,* 233–38. *See also* North Africa
Agricultural Adjustment Act (1938), *155*
Agricultural Adjustment Administration (AAA), *152, 494,* 262
Agriculture: H.S.T. knowledge of problems, 262; New Deal program, 262–63; H.S.T. policies, 174–75, 263–67; in Point Four, 237. *See also* Food; Price supports; *and below*
Agriculture, Department of, *181, 309, 325–26, 465, 468–73, 488,* 75, 117, 211
Agudas Israel of America, 146
Aid to other nations. *See* Lend-Lease; Marshall Plan; Point Four; *and under name of country*
Air Force: procurement, *181–83, 184,* 53; budgets, *230,* 34; band, *334;* proposals for separate department, 49–50;

S